ENGENDERING THE STATE

Family, Work, and Welfare in Canada

In the early part of this century the mother was the educator and moral centre of the Canadian household. Between the onset of the First World War and the development of the modern social security state in the 1940s, however, an ideological shift took place. While Canada endured the effects of two world wars, industrialization, and economic and political crises, welfare entitlements based on family reproduction were replaced by state policies that promoted paid labour in the workplace. To a nation gripped with new and great anxieties, the mother no longer appeared capable of functioning as its vitally adhesive force.

The necessity of stabilizing the paternal position of the father as breadwinner in order to sustain the family and support economic progress became the progressively dominant view. Although this thinking effectively helped a portion of the population achieve economic autonomy, its damaging effects were wide reaching. Women, unskilled labourers, and the chronically indigent had been left resourceless.

The author's explanation of gender's role in the conception of modern Canadian welfare policy takes current scholarship into novel territory. Her analyses of the perspectives of maternal feminists, clergymen, organized labour, businessmen, university social scientists, welfare administrators, social workers, and government policy makers are fascinating to read and contribute greatly to our understanding of the current debates in welfare policy making.

NANCY CHRISTIE is an independent scholar in Toronto and co-author with Michael Gauvreau of the Innis prize-winning *A Full-Orbed Christianity: The Protestant Churches and Social Welfare in Canada*.

NANCY CHRISTIE

Engendering the State

Family, Work, and Welfare in Canada

UNIVERSITY OF TORONTO PRESS
Toronto Buffalo London

© University of Toronto Press Incorporated 2000
Toronto Buffalo London

Printed in Canada

ISBN 0-8020-4768-8 (cloth)
ISBN 0-8020-8321-8 (paper)

Printed on acid-free paper

Canadian Cataloguing in Publication Data

Christie, Nancy, 1958–
    Engendering the state : family, work, and welfare in Canada

    Includes bibliographical references and index.
    ISBN 0-8020-4768-8 (bound)   ISBN 0-8020-8321-8 (pbk.)

    1. Family policy – Canada – History – 20th century.   2. Social security –
    Canada – History – 20th century.   3. Public welfare – Canada – History –
    20th century.   4. Welfare state – Canada.   I. Title.

    HV108.C474 2000   361.6'1'097109041   C99-932628-7

Frontispiece: *Allan Gardens, Toronto, Ontario* (1957), by Michel Lambeth.
Courtesy Canadian Museum of Contemporary Photography, 65-3023.

University of Toronto Press acknowledges the financial assistance to its
publishing program of the Canada Council for the Arts and the Ontario Arts
Council.

This book has been published with the help of a grant from the Humanities
and Social Sciences Federation of Canada, using funds provided by the
Social Sciences and Humanities Research Council of Canada.

University of Toronto Press acknowledges the financial support for its
publishing activities of the Government of Canada through the Book
Publishing Industry Development Program (BPIDP).

This Book Is Dedicated to

Nancy Sutton

1908–1998

I am a widow with three children, two over 16. I get $35. I am very thankful for it. We are sure of a roof over our heads. But only widows and orphans know what worries, sorrows and heartbreak go on under that roof.

The Mothers' Allowance Act was a very noble idea of someone for a mother to keep the home and children together ... Every cheque day is a heartache, but Dec. 22 is the worst, as we have to make our own Christmas. Last winter was the only winter I received coal from the mothers' allowance. Rent and fuel are our nightmare.

A Mother. Toronto Star, 18 September 1937

The original idea back of the allowance being granted was only to assist the mothers and was never intended to supply fully the necessary funds to maintain the home ... There are two objections to entirely maintain these homes: First, you take away their independence and initiative to help themselves; secondly, the cost is too great.

Member of County Board. Toronto Star, 16 September 1937

One soldier's widow applied to the Soldier's Aid Commission for aid to supply clothing for three school aged children, but was turned down because she was in receipt of the allowance, though within a day or two the said commission granted aid to the child of a man who had never gone overseas to help him to take a business course. Evidently the education of a relief recipient was much more important than clothing for the orphans of a veteran.

14th Batt. Veteran's Widow. Toronto Star, 9 September 1937

Contents

Preface

/

On the frontispiece of this book, we encounter a man carrying his wife's purse, standing prominently in the foreground, while his wife recedes further from the camera's eye. The photographer, in capturing this moment in Allan Gardens in 1957, is clearly attempting to make an ironic statement about gender relationships and the breadwinner ideal. Though it was not the intent of the photographer, this image perfectly encapsulates the central questions posed by *Engendering the State*: What relationship between the genders did the state endorse within the family? Who – married men or married women – were to have conferred on them the right to welfare entitlements? This book explores the gendered complexion of state welfare policies as they unfolded between 1900 and 1945. Just as is happening in the photograph, in which the woman is gradually disappearing from the public gaze, welfare initiatives as the twentieth century progressed shifted their focus from family reproduction to a conception of welfare citizenship that stressed the rights of the paid labour of male workers – a process that reached its fruition when a national program of family allowances was implemented in 1944. *Engendering the State* is first and foremost a historical investigation of how the breadwinner ideal became increasingly embedded in Canadian welfare strategies.

The sheer bulk and striking presence of the married man in the photograph symbolizes the growing preoccupation of state officialdom with defending the rights of male workers both in the workplace and in the domestic sphere. But it also exemplifies the curious dynamic that came to prevail between working-class Canadians and the State. Michel Lambeth, who took the photograph, is typical of many of the welfare recipients whose lives are recorded in this study. Born Tommy

Lambeth in 1923, his parents were recently arrived British immigrants. He grew up on DeGrassi street in the heart of working-class east Toronto. His mother, Maisie (Smith), whose father was a journeyman carpenter, had been 'ophaned' in North Croydon, England when her mother died following the birth of her fourth child, Nancy Smith. Maisie's life may have been somewhat easier than that of her sister Nancy, who had twice been sent for 'adoption' by Canadian families (and who was twice sent back to her natural family). Maisie and her other siblings were taken in by her grandparents, for whom they worked until the adolescent daughters immigrated to Canada after the First World War. There, Maisie met and married a fellow worker at the fashionable King Edward Hotel, Thomas Lambeth, who later worked as a stationary engineer for Continental Can. The Lambeth family got by because the breadwinner survived; Maisie's sister Nancy was not so fortunate. After marrying John Jones, a deliveryman for the *Toronto Telegram*, in 1927, the nineteen-year-old Nancy, while pregnant with her second child, was suddenly widowed when her young husband died in St Joseph's Hospital as the result of an untreated burst appendix. As so often happened before the modern welfare system was founded, the Lambeths took Nancy and her daughter Norma into their already crowded home, for only after her second child, John, was born was Nancy Jones eligible to apply to the Ontario Mothers' Allowances Commission. The welfare visitors were persistently intrusive, and at one point she was separated from her children by an enforced stay at the tuberculosis sanitorium at Gravenhurst. Despite all this, her meagre allowance – which she often had to supplement by taking low-paying work as a charwoman – enabled her to keep her family together, until the more buoyant wartime economy allowed her to find employment at sufficient wages that she was able to go out some evenings and, it followed, meet her second husband. In the end, it seems, only the reacquisition of a working male breadwinner provided Nancy Sutton's family with the moderate prosperity necessary to ensure that her children would be educated and thus able to seek some measure of upward social mobility. War, as *Engendering the State* argues, often benefited families that otherwise could not have made ends meet.

Tommy Lambeth, as the son of a semiskilled worker, had his hopes dashed by the limited horizons of working-class Toronto, which prescribed for him a technical and commercial rather than an academic education. But the Second World War enabled him to pursue the education of his choice. Having signed up with a tank battalion, Tommy

Lambeth was able to accrue sufficient veterans' educational benefits that he was able to study at the London School of Arts and Crafts and at the Studio of the sculptor Ossip Zadkine in Paris. Living in near-poverty, Lambeth became a convert to anarchism in Paris. Even though he achieved a modicum of success after exhibiting his drawings at the Galerie du Dragon, Lambeth was repatriated in 1948, having finally run out of his share of the Canadian government's military benefits. Back in Canada this talented photographer, painter, and writer was deemed by the Canadian state to be a failure because he did not conform to the breadwinner ideal as it had become enshrined in 1950s Canada. Not only did Lambeth fail to hold on to a steady job as a photographer for the *Toronto Star*, but he broke with convention by marrying an older woman, who often supported him. The photograph on the frontispiece of this book thus takes on a more disturbing quality, for in it he is being bitingly critical of the stultifying orthodoxy of the day, which firmly relegated women to the shadowy margins of both the family and the workplace, and which lifted to pre-eminence the male breadwinner, who is portrayed here in all his grossness and anthropoid repugnancy, having appropriated the purse, which (we assume) properly belongs to his wife.

I have many people to thank. First, my editor, Gerry Hallowell, for supporting this project and for guiding the book so carefully toward publication. Also, his editorial assistant, Jill McConkey, who happily fielded my many queries. In particular, I wish to commend Frances Mundy for her commitment and assiduity, which in no small way contributed to the smoothness of the production process. As always, I owe my greatest thanks to Professor John Kendle, who offered constant encouragement and has also, as on so many occasions, faithfully read the entire manuscript and made numerous suggestions for its improvement. Thank you, John. I would also like to thank Craig Brown for reading and offering his expert advice for the chapter on the Canadian Patriotic Fund, and James Struthers for his suggestions regarding government relief policies during the 1930s. I wish also to acknowledge Joan and Paul Emory, who provided crucial memories of the life of Michel Lambeth. Anyone reading this book will also recognize that I owe a great intellectual debt to Donna Andrew's work on charity in Britain, Susan Pedersen's work on the welfare systems in Britain and France, and Linda Gordon's path-breaking theoretical perspectives, which focus on the relationship between the welfare state and its clients.

Numerous librarians and archivists lent me their specialized knowledge, which as any researcher knows is absolutely critical when it comes to rooting out obscure and underused manuscript collections. I wish to offer deepest thanks to archivists at the Ontario Archives; the University of Toronto Archives; the McCord Museum; the Provincial Archives of Manitoba; Queen's University Archives; McGill University Archives; the Rare Book Library, McGill University; Thomas Fisher Rare Book Library, University of Toronto; University of British Columbia Library, Department of Special Collections; and the Metro Toronto Central Reference Library, Baldwin Room. Most of all, I owe a great burden of debt to the archivists at the National Archives of Canada and to the librarians in the microfilm room of the Robarts Library, University of Toronto, who valiantly offered me their assistance after my computer and four months of research were stolen from our house by a homeless person. On hearing of this setback, the archivists gave of their valuable time to help me retrace my steps. I cannot thank them enough.

The government policymakers whom I study would applaud my approach to research and writing, for in the absence of access to government assistance, I have relied on the self-sufficient family unit to sustain my efforts. Most importantly, I owe greatest thanks to my own male breadwinner, Michael Gauvreau, not only for finding work and ably supporting his dependants, but for all his unpaid labour – most notably the time he has expended in reading this rather lengthy manuscript and in helping with the tedious job of creating a healthy index. But most of all, as my primary academic colleague, he has offered tremendous support and encouragement throughout the often isolating process of research and writing. Like many women before me I have relied on the support of my extended family, especially that of my mother, Norma Christie, who volunteered to proofread the entire manuscript, a parental duty she may well later have regretted. Finally, I dedicate this book to my grandmother, Nancy Sutton. Only on her death last year did we discover, among her personal papers, documents attesting that she had received an Ontario Mother's Allowance – a fact that she had obliterated from her memory. Paradoxically, her only memory of the invasive investigations of welfare visitors was confused with the hectoring visits of her own mother-in-law – a mistaken identity so evocative of her working-class sensibility, which emphasized so strongly the public ideal of the self-sufficient family.

ENGENDERING THE STATE

Family, Work, and Welfare in Canada

Introduction: The Cultural Context of the Canadian Welfare State

I began writing this book with the aim of exploring the origins of the Canadian welfare state between 1900 and the end of the Second World War. I intended to focus on events between the implementation of various pieces of provincial mother's allowance legislation during the era of the First World War and the passage in 1944 of the federal Family Allowance Act. The central questions that soon presented themselves to me were these: Why did the maternalist ideology which manifested itself in the national movement for mothers' allowances and which was the first acknowledgment by government of the importance to the nation of the reproductive work of women, not become the template for our modern social security system, as happened in many European societies?[1] And why, after a system of children's allowances had been in force during the First World War for soldiers' families, were these allowances not followed up with a popular feminist campaign for family allowances? And when family allowances were finally legislated at the federal level in 1944, why were they embedded in a public discourse of full employment for men rather than either that of the economic independence of women or the relief of working-class family poverty?

In *Engendering the State* I examine the trajectory of Canadian welfare and family policy between 1900 and 1945. This investigation has three broad fronts: social and cultural movements; state legislation; and the meaning of welfare provision as it was reinterpreted by its largely female beneficiaries. In short, this is as much a history of the ideology and social structures that gave rise to various welfare entitlements as it is a study of government legislation and administration.

The welfare state in Canada was not directly formed, as in other countries, as a response to the growing political power of organized labour;[2] nor was it constructed to forestall the growth of socialism; nor was it fashioned by the imperatives of big business.[3] The passage of welfare legislation in Canada was driven mainly by the fear of family breakdown; this is what animated both the child welfare movement of the first decades of the twentieth century and the modern social security state of the 1940s. Because reformers and government policymakers focused overwhelmingly on the question of family stability, no one can study Canadian social policy without addressing adequately the issue of gender. The fundamental goal of all welfare legislation – be it military family benefits, mother's allowance legislation, unemployment insurance, or modern social security measures such as the family allowance – was the fostering of self-sufficient and independent families in which the male was the breadwinner. The entire superstructure of this small, non-interventionist liberal state rested on this one crucial orthodoxy. In other words, the evolution of the Canadian state reflected gender rather than class imperatives; its base was the male breadwinner and its superstructure was the liberal notion of government as both umpire and night watchman.[4]

In this book I will argue that the notion that welfare was primarily a private and family responsibility continued to animate the discourse on welfare even during the Second World War, when the modern social-security state was being created. On this issue there was little dissent between 'right' and 'left' or between middle-class reformers and organized labour. All welfare legislation prior to the Second World War, whether it was needs- or rights-based, means-tested or universal, had as its goal the promotion of the work ethic. Those who formulated the public ideologies were overwhelmingly preoccupied with using welfare provision to stimulate work – a subtle but also coercive means for compelling men to support their dependants. In this way the State not only regulated women but also, in myriad ways, dictated gender roles for men. During the nineteenth century, public debate had focused on women entering public space;[5] the reverse was true in the twentieth century, when the discourse of welfare entitlement revolved almost entirely around the increasing problem of the absent, truculent, or delinquent male breadwinner. Indeed, public awareness of the growing problem of disorderly men was the engine that drove twentieth-century welfare legislation.

Male gender norms have rarely been decoded by historians simply because they have come to be regarded as normative. In particular, the relationship between gender and the work ethic has been neglected in previous scholarly accounts of the Canadian welfare state. Because they have concentrated on welfare entitlements that have been derived from paid work for men, these earlier accounts have been blind to the fact that they have themselves imbibed the very gender categories that were consciously imposed by welfare experts and legislators. For example: the concept of unemployment insurance was constructed on the notion that only men had a right to work – and to the citizenship rights conferred by work. Because these culturally constructed male citizenship rights were in turn predicated on a conception of masculinity which stated that a man's primary duty was to work in order to sufficiently maintain his wife and children, they effectively barred women – especially married women – from independent access to welfare entitlements.

Richard Titmuss, the great historian of the British welfare state, mused in a 1957 lecture at the University of Toronto that a recent study of the Peek Frean plant in Bermondsey, England, continued to debate about women while 'man's place tends to be taken for granted.' It is a great irony that he was thus lapsing into the very gender fallacy on which he was commenting. He observed that 'his thesis was that understanding of processes of change in society as a *whole* and their effect on *human beings* is essential to interpretation of current attitudes to work and patterns of family life.'[6] Thus he failed to recognize that his assumption that men – and by association male work – constituted the 'whole' of society was an attitude constructed by the very welfare legislation he was studying. Many others since him have made the same error. Historians of family policies must learn to pick apart the cultural assumptions, idealizations, and norms that have long implanted a gender bias in studies of the relationship between work and welfare. In this book, I investigate in detail how the breadwinner ideal transformed itself slowly through time with changes in cultural preoccupations, social circumstances, and the economic environment. By disentangling the changing social context that fed the rhetoric of gender norms, I hope to circumvent this aforementioned tendency to imbibe the very gender conventions this book analyses.

The first chapter looks at the decades during which the ideal of the mother-centred home was first promoted as a definitive *public* ideology. This ideal was articulated by evangelical clergymen anxiously defending the spiritual sanctity of the home to ensure future converts; by middle-class feminists working to expand the social parameters of female endeavour without transgressing the 'natural' functions of motherhood; and by child welfare reformers, who played on popular fears of social decay and family instability in order to promote the new field of child rescue. The breadwinner ideal was first articulated during the First World War; but it moved from the purview of the churches and into the public sphere of government activity not as a result of middle-class opinion but rather through the agitation of working-class soldier-recruits. In fact, the regulations assigning military pay were the achievement of soldiers' wives who lobbied for legislation to reinforce the responsibility of absent husbands to support thier families. This relationship between working-class agitation and government promotion of the breadwinner ideal arose again during the Second World War.

By the end of the First World War, the imperative to reassert the breadwinner ideal (i.e., a man's duty to seek work) actually *curtailed* the growth of new state welfare legislation, namely, unemployment insurance. The need to uphold the breadwinner ideal indirectly helped create welfare entitlements for women in the form of mothers' allowances. This form of assistance was not believed to infringe on gender norms, because the breadwinner had been removed through death or incapacity. The Great Depression, however, marked a decisive watershed in Canadian welfare history. Because of the overwhelming threat posed to male work, and hence to social stability, the concept of welfare entitlements was reformulated so that the focus shifted away from female reproduction and toward an exclusive emphasis on paid male labour outside the home. This preoccupation with the personality of the male, within both the home and the workplace, nullified the principle of separate spheres by 'banishing' women from the calculus of public policy. Indeed, as I argue, it was this legacy of the Great Depression, which gave priority to male work, that during the Second World War informed discussion of the family allowance – a policy that had more to do with fiscal management and full employment than with women's economic rights within the home. In sum, the breadwinner ideal affected welfare entitlements in a great variety of ways, but there was also one constant: 'personal responsibility'[7] of the male breadwinner to support his dependants and thus preserve family stability and independence.

In elaborating this argument, I have pursued a deliberately cultural approach that focuses on the broadly held economic and social preoccupations of not only legislators but also social workers, reform activists, clergymen, women, organized labour, the military, the business community, and social scientists. I have attempted to trace the changing power relationships and alliances between and among these various producers of public ideologies. Because this book emphasizes the shifting ideological contours of the Canadian welfare state, it is not simply a standard narrative of evolving government policy; rather, it can also be read as a set of parallel narratives relating to each of the above listed political, social, and economic constituencies. This book draws from personal papers, government records, institutional papers, and popular magazines – all of which tend to reflect middle-class concerns and values. But it also uses a wide range of case files (and correspondence) about (and by) the beneficiaries of the welfare state, and thus provides an important entrée into the attitudes, perceptions, and values of the Canadian working class – in particular working-class women. *Engendering the State* thus brings together two seemingly disparate approaches. In doing so it deconstructs the ideology of dominant groups and the experiences of working-class women in the home and the workplace.[8]

On one level, the State is defined by government activity. But further than that, it is significantly moulded, from above and below, by popular agitation for legislation – a feature of the Canadian welfare state that has continued unabated into the modern era. I do not wish to argue that working-class women consistently or directly determined the specifics of welfare policies; but I do wish to emphasize that especially during the two world wars, when morale in the military was an important consideration of government policymakers, working-class wives wielded considerable power. At other times, however, working-class values have done much to reaffirm certain status quo tendencies, if only indirectly. For example, by the end of the 1920s many beneficiaries of mother's allowance began to balk at their older children having to work to help support the family. Thus it might well be argued that the concept of working-class family members providing direct economic support for one another, which has been so well delineated by Bettina Bradbury,[9] began to break down just before the Great Depression, at the direct instigation of working-class women and men – a process that saw its final fruition during the Second World War, when military authorities and a new cadre of social workers rejected the traditional notion which prescribed that children in families receiving government assistance must by convention support their mothers and younger siblings.

The insistence of working-class mothers on rejecting work in favour of education for their children coincided with the development of a school of thought among organized labour, middle-class reformers, and social scientists during the Great Depression that the absence of paid work for men would irrefutably erode well-established gender boundaries between home and work. As one consequence, these groups reformulated the family and the workplace as singularly male preserves. This new emphasis on the male right to work and maintain his dependants eviscerated once and for all the expectation that either one's children or one's wife would seek to supplement the family income. Into this newly created gap between the male wage and family need flowed the cultural demand for family allowances, which provided a more modern solution to the problem of the family economy. All of this suggests how a cultural approach can unearth a complex of social practices, cultural beliefs, and traditions from various income and interest groups, which in turn intersect and thus explain in a holistic fashion the emergence of particular policies at specific historical junctures. From this perspective, the State is moulded in the penumbra between language, experience, and administrative application.

This approach, however, does not suggest that the State is one hegemonic entity. In this book I argue that no one interest group has ever dictated government policies, which arise out of cross-class and cross-gender alliances. I also question whether one unified middle class exists at all. Although 'hegemony' has become a buzzword in contemporary historical scholarship, hegemonic theories, when placed under the microscope of historical evidence, are exposed as decidedly deficient and as not reflecting the complexities of the past. As recent scholarship in Britain has well demonstrated, the ideal of *a* middle class was itself a constructed ideology that was decisive to the formation of a culture that saw itself pitted against the dominance of the aristocracy.[10] In Canada the diversities within the middle- and working-class cultures have barely been investigated. And when older, economic conceptualizations of class are finally studied, they will be refuted.

Engendering the State provides a window into the links between classes as they emerged and changed during the first four decades of the twentieth century. I show not only how shifting cross-class and cross-gender alliances existed – for example, reformers, feminists, and trade unionists all lobbied vociferously for mothers' allowances – but also how such alliances were extremely porous and constantly being reformed. Whenever a loose consensus of opinion formed around a particular legislative measure, it was soon found to have been built upon a quicksand of shifting motives and expectations. For example, feminists and clergymen elaborated a new, gendered definition of pauperization that largely exonerated women from the workhouse test; and progressive businessmen and reformers were preoccupied with finding means for producing larger numbers of technically trained workers, whose numbers had been depleted by war but who were considered the indispensable engine of industrial growth and hence national economic efficiency; while organized labour endorsed government assistance to widowed women to keep them out of the workforce and from lowering the standard male wage. If a 'hegemonic' ideology did in fact exist to sustain the movement for mothers' allowances, it revolved around the status of the male-as-breadwinner and the goal of maintaining traditional gender preserves – which is not to say that the ideal did not transcend class identities. As I argue, the notion that 'paternal' government aid should replace the breadwinner's wage after he died was adamantly adhered to by working-class widows. When provincial administrations compelled these women to work for welfare, they protested virulently and loudly against what they perceived to be a middle-class transgression of working-class gender norms.

In *Engendering the State* I argue that state welfare policy does not merely reflect class interests, nor does it impose 'middle class' values on recalcitrant families. The picture is more complex than this, and indicates that various middle-class groups were in conflict over the meaning and interpretation of particular welfare policies. More often, the ideological fissures occurred along gender lines or, in the case of the two world wars, between military and civilian families. Indeed, the breadwinner ideal, with its embedded notion of family self-sufficiency, was a cultural goal shared by both middle- and working-class Canadians. Moreover, the attitudes of working-class women did not automatically or consistently conflict with state officialdom, as the 'moral regulation' school of thought would contend.[11]

As I demonstrate throughout this book, often the fiercest advocates of the interventionist state were working-class women, who were in the greatest pecuniary need and who had the most to fear from family instability and breakdown. The story of a Winnipeg woman whose working-class husband deserted her during the First World War (a common story) stirringly reminds us that social control was not simply the function of government. This working-class wife not only demanded more generous welfare assistance for women, on the basis that it was the duty of the State to fulfil the prerogatives of the male breadwinner when he was absent, but also lobbied constantly for laws that would help eradicate prostitution, to which many unsupported women (like her sister) had fallen prey. In this instance, and many similar, impoverished women with children preferred the 'paternalism' of the State to domination either by male relatives or neighbours. The moral regulation of women was sought not just by middle-class reformers, but often also by hapless deserted wives like Mrs I., who was drawn, as she had always feared, into a life of prostitution and dependence on the male criminal underworld of Winnipeg, when the Deserted Wives' Fund finally ended in the early 1930s.[12] What this case and many others make clear is that the social control theory of state building must be adapted to historical evidence; and that a model that centres on conflict must be replaced by one that takes into account the complex process of negotiation that female beneficiaries undertake when they consent to accept government welfare aid.

The development of the Canadian welfare state must be perceived as an evolving, multilayered process involving fluctuating and competing public ideologies. However, welfare legislation is the practical manifestation of broader social goals, and is the creation of particular individuals. For this reason, actual government policies must be examined in detail. That being said, government policymaking cannot be studied in isolation from broader social movements. Historians who focus only on those government policies that were codified in law can be led imperceptibly into a whiggish celebration of success. Moreover, not only does society create those policies, but we cannot adequately understand the disjunctures between the aims of government administrators and the wider culture unless we study the two in tandem. As an illustration of the imperative need to study policymaking as a process firmly imbedded in the wider society, the introduction of federally funded family allowances in 1944 cannot be understood apart from popular ideology, even though these allowances were brought into being in an era when policy was formulated by a small coterie of social scientists. Indeed, it might well be argued that family allowances legislation emerged in an era when mass culture was beginning to emerge and when Canada was fighting a war of ideologies, so it is even more important that historians study the underlying cultural ideals that propelled this government expansion. If we do not take this approach, we will not be able to discern clearly the fundamental goals of this legislation or disentangle the rhetoric and the political posturing from their real ideological firmament. After the immensely provocative and persuasive Beveridge Report was tabled by the British government, a wide cross-section of Canadians began to anticipate a comprehensive social security state. Without knowing this, historians will fail to recognize that Mackenzie King implemented family allowances in 1944 as a means of obviating the further growth of the welfare state, in the belief that such a relatively limited government expenditure would create full employment and thus allow returned soldiers to once again take up their responsibilities as husbands and breadwinners. Thus, when we take a cultural approach to studying the growth of the welfare state, we are able to gauge both the continuities and the disjunctures between society and government.

I will devote considerable attention to the social outlook and recommendations of several individuals: the child reformer J.J. Kelso; Helen Reid and Herbert Ames, wartime welfare workers in Montreal; Rev. Peter Bryce and Mrs Adam Shortt, administrators for the Ontario Mothers' Allowances Commission, A.P. Paget of the Manitoba Mothers' Allowances Commission; several social workers, including F.N. Stapleford, Robert Mills, Dorothy King, Bessie Touzel, and Charlotte Whitton; labour activists such as J.S. Woodsworth, Tom Moore, and Percy Bengough; early advocates of family allowances legislation such as the French-Canadian priest Leon Lebel; social scientists such as Harry Cassidy, Leonard Marsh, and George Davidson; and government policymakers such as Bryce Stewart, R.B. Bryce, Ian Mackenzie, and Brooke Claxton. But I do no approach these individuals as the primary causal agents for particular welfare measures. I have attempted to place the ideas of thse individuals within the larger stream of culture; had I not done so, I would have been suggesting that the history of Canadian welfare resembled a morality play or a platitudinous melodrama of heroes and antiheroes. Charlotte Whitton's defence prior to the Second World War of needs-based, provincially funded welfare relief appears much less jaundiced and conservative when it is understood that her outlook was shared by a wide cross-section of Canadian reform constituencies; even her later diatribes against cash family allowances must be analyzed in terms of her professional angst over her exclusion from the inner councils of social security policymaking, and appear less antediluvian when it is noted that the Trades and Labour Congress likewise recommended payments in kind, so that an adequate living wage could be preserved for working-class families.[13]

I may not have entirely escaped such emotive historical judgments. I have, however, attempted to recover the voices of as broad a sample of Canadian popular opinion as is possible within the limitations imposed by traditional archival sources. Regrettably, I wasn't able to interview contemporary witnesses, the vast majority of whom are long dead. However, I *have* read women's and other popular magazines of the time, hundreds of contemporary pamphlets, surviving welfare case histories, and extensive government records, as well as the voluminous correspondence of important welfare institutions such as Charlotte Whitton's Canadian Council on Child Welfare, now known as the Canadian Council on Social Development. This clearing house of Canadian social work has offered me a panoramic view of the day-to-day practice of welfare administration in several provinces. No less extensive private collections such as that of Harry Cassidy have provided insights into the ideological and professional dimensions of policy creation in the 1930s and 1940s, in both the private and the public sectors.

The one obvious gap in this book relates to the development of welfare strategies in Quebec. This is partly because the history of welfare policy in that province has already been well researched by Quebec historians, most notably by Denyse Baillargeon, Dominique Marshall, and Andrée Levesque.[14] Moreover, the trajectory of welfare policy was determined in Quebec to a great extent by the relatively late development of maternal feminism, in opposition to the Roman Catholic church, whose interests at least until the 1930s lay in reasserting patriarchal power within the family (see Chapter 5). In Chapter 1 there is little discussion of maternal feminism in Quebec except as relating to Protestant and English reform networks in Montreal; this is because there was virtually no child welfare activism within Roman Catholic circles at this time in Quebec, while the interests of reform-minded women centred on gaining the vote and on lobbying for policies to protect women in the workplace.[15] *Engendering the State* is, however, punctuated with discussions of policy development in Quebec. In particular, I discuss in depth the 1931 Provincial Royal Commission on Social Insurance, and the advocacy of family allowances by Father Lebel during the late 1920s.

The cultural perspective I take in this book has allowed me to develop several subthemes. Thus, when I describe how the maternalist welfare state of the first two decades of the twentieth century was transformed during the Great Depression into a set of entitlements founded on the workplace rights of men, I also describe how perceptions of the family changed over the same decades. As I argue in the first chapter, the public articulation of a maternal-centred notion of family life was coincident with the rise of evangelicalism, as clergymen became increasingly preoccupied with converting children and with responding to the failure of men to attend to family needs other than material ones. In this way, the welfare state emerged out of Protestant ideals of the family and society. This explains in part why English and Protestant Canadians felt betrayed by the Family Allowances Act of 1944 – it was generally believed to encourage the spread of Roman Catholicism. Protestant ideology was actively promoted in the first decades of the twentieth century by clergymen, maternal feminists, and child welfare reformers. This movement did much to affirm that the family was no longer a merely 'private' institution; rather, the family unit served specific national and social ends, and as such the welfare and stability of families was a matter of public (and later, state) concern. This idealization of separate spheres may have relegated women to the home; even so, it amounted to a distinctly feminist outlook, for it acknowledged the importance of women's special reproductive qualities and destigmatized many women who relied on welfare entitlements.[16]

The 1930s witnessed a rapid breakdown in the public's commitment to complementary roles for men and women: the reification of paid labour undermined women's special claims on the State, by shifting the rights of social citizenship irrevocably toward male breadwinners. In turn, these exclusively male welfare entitlements (the workplace was now rigidly defined as a male sphere) reformulated family stability in terms of economic security and abjured the notion that the home was the sanctuary of the affections and moral values. In this book I suggest that the process of secularization began with the emergence of this masculinized and materialistic vision of family life. Secularization was thus a strongly gendered process, for in rejecting the spiritual wellsprings of the family, welfare policymakers and social scientists (such as Leonard Marsh) were also eviscerating from their concept of domesticity the centrality of the female mother figure. In many respects, the opposition to cash family allowances in 1945 – and especially to the notion that they should be paid to the father – was an attempt by feminists and old-guard social workers to reassert this now decayed maternalist paradigm.

The Great Depression marked another watershed in idealizations of the household: it was during this time of mass male unemployment that the notion that the economic security of the home must be provided exclusively by the male breadwinner became axiomatic. This ideal of the family wage became a core social assumption and was confirmed in welfare policies such as the Unemployment Insurance Act of 1940, which established the principle that a man's benefits – which were in lieu of his wage – must entirely support his family, without extra supplements specifically designed for dependants. As a result of this decisive cultural shift of the 1930s, children in families receiving military allowances during the Second World War were no longer expected to contribute their earnings to the mother in the absence of the male breadwinner. By 1945 the notion of family economic interdependence, whereby either children or the wife traditionally supplemented the head of the family's wage, was a thing of the past as far as governments were concerned, and even administrators of various provincial mothers' allowances programs, who had earlier employed welfare entitlements as a means to uphold family interdependence, no longer exhorted widows or older children to work in exchange for state assistance.

Another key theme in this book is the interpenetration of private and public welfare that so characterized the Canadian welfare state. Like *A Full-Orbed Christianity,*[17] this book traces the changes in how public policy was formulated. In this sense it is a history of the emergence and shifting influence of significant vested interests. In the early twentieth century, welfare policy was generated by an alliance of clergymen, maternal feminists, social workers, and child welfare advocates – groups that coalesced in 1920 to form the Canadian Council on Child Welfare, headed by Charlotte Whitton. These groups constituted the mainstream of social policymaking well into the 1930s, when for a brief time the largely female-led private family welfare organizations experienced a resurgence in power.[18] For a short period during the Great Depression, the issue of female dependency was again central in the debate over welfare policy. But by the end of the Depression the old social reform and social work network was in tatters, and a new cadre of social scientists, most importantly Leonard Marsh and Harry Cassidy, had taken centre stage. The rise to power of these economic technocrats symbolized the transition away from spiritual and maternal interests, toward a preoccupation with the problem of male employment. The older, child welfare alliance died when Charlotte Whitton was removed from the directorship of the Canadian Council on Social Development. This important national research institute for welfare policy was now usurped by a modern bureaucrat, George Davidson, who became one of the most important propagandists for King's Liberals and their family allowance legislation. The passage of the Family Allowances Act in 1944 reflected the dominance of the 'experts' in government (though King was reluctant to consult them). This legislation was largely the creation of the Economic Advisory Council, the haven of the new breed of young Keynesians, which was instrumental in transforming social security from a comprehensive program for protecting individuals from social risk, into a limited fiscal policy intended to stimulate consumer spending and generate jobs for men.

Because welfare history is so intimately connected to the gendered notion of work, this book not only contributes to our understanding of feminism between the world wars, but also makes a contribution to labour history. I argue that feminism in Canada was an extremely conservative social force, as was organized labour, with which women were often closely allied through a shared goal of preventing women from transgressing traditional gendered norms by seeking paid labour outside the home. Much of *Engendering the State* focuses on delineating the pattern of women's paid labour between the First and Second World Wars, and argues that during those decades, and even at the height of the Great Depression, women did not consciously oppose the breadwinner ideal.[19] Particularly, this study reveals that married women were consistently reluctant to enter the workforce in larger numbers. Indeed, because of the generous allowances for soldiers' families in both world wars, few married women were compelled to supplement the husband's meagre wartime wage – a policy that contrasted with mothers' allowance legislation, with its miserly allowances designed to ensure that widows worked for their welfare.[20] Given the low rate of married women's active participation in the workforce until the late 1950s, the question that must be posed is this: What fuelled the excessive agitation to defend the status of male breadwinners during this period? I argue in this book that it was the *failure* of male breadwinners to fulfil their obligations to support their dependants that sustained and propelled the breadwinner ideal. Throughout this period reformers, policymakers, and social investigators were constantly exercising themselves over male inadequacies, focusing in particular on problems such as family desertion, divorce, widowhood, enforced absences during wartime, and men's inability to find gainful employment. Except that single women were persistently scrutinized,[21] the weight of state policing and regulation through welfare entitlements thus fell overwhelmingly on men.

Engendering the State is not a narrowly conceived study of government welfare legislation; rather, it is a study of gender relations, family ideology, work, the process of policymaking, the encounter between working-class women and the State, and the impact of war on society. It is thus a composition of intertwining narrative themes which in concert explore the changing social philosophies and national goals that undergirded family welfare policies, and the evolving cultural ideals that created and infused the gendered definitions of citizenship rights and welfare entitlements.

1

The Evangelical Morphology of the State and the Redefinition of the Patriarchal Family

The King is there in state, and constitutes authority, that is the father; and the parliament is there in which there is great deliberation, for the mother represents the parliament and the members of parliament; and there is also the judge and jury, represented by the mother, and the army and navy behind the government, that is the father ... It is the mother that makes the home, the personality of the mother that lives in the home, not the father.

This early twentieth-century injunction by the Protestant clergyman Rev. J. Nicol was a direct refutation of the traditionally patriarchal vision of family relations. Writing in 1911 in the *Canadian Home Monthly*, Nicol asserted dramatically that 'useful' citizens were only truly made within families dominated by the mother. Just as the King had become a mere figurehead in relation to Parliament, the father's authority within the family depended almost entirely on democratic discussion in which the true locus of power was the mother. Nicol's theme, 'The Influence of the Home on the Nation,' was hardly new — the metaphor of family had been deployed regularly since the eighteenth century in discussions about the functions of the State.[1] However, it stood in marked contrast to nineteenth-century admonitions that proper governance, within both families and society, could be ensured only by the moral authority and leadership of fathers.[2]

Throughout the nineteenth century the Protestant churches had played a prominent role in defining 'domesticity' in Canadian culture.[3] Similarly, in the early decades of the twentieth century, evangelicalism continued to view the family as an essential locus of activity if Protestantism was to maintain its vitality and strengthen its cultural authority. Yet Protestantism was not the defender of an immutable patriarchal formulation of family relations, as some historians have contended.[4] Hannah Lane has argued persuasively, that the prescribed roles of men and women within Protestantism, and within the family itself, were not remarkably different.[5] From the 1880s onwards, women through their clear numerical dominance in evangelical church congregations, and their active membership, were responsible for the tremendous growth in Protestant churchgoing; in no small way they thus contributed to the self-confident zeal and optimism encountered in mainstream Protestant churches.[6] The importance of women as seekers of converts and as the organizational backbone of new extradenominational Protestant institutions such as the YWCA and the WCTU was recognized by male clergymen, who as a result were highly sensitive to the rising aspirations of women. As a consequence of forging alliances with women's organizations, Protestant church leaders were at the forefront of the movement to subvert traditional patriarchal family relations and reformulate them in favour of women's authority.

An ideology of domesticity emerged in Canada only at the turn of the last century. American and British historians have argued that the concomitant ideals of 'separate spheres' for men and women and the 'cult of domesticity' arose out of the convergence of three broad historical phenomena: the growth of evangelicalism, the development of specifically middle-class values, and the development of 'commercial society,' in which work was increasingly separated from the home.[7] In Canada these sweeping cultural, social, and economic changes were delayed. Until the late nineteenth century, evangelicalism was a muted voice in the public culture of Protestantism. Only after 1870, when Protestant institutions began growing dramatically, did middle-class evangelicals begin assertively challenging the dominance enjoyed by the established Anglican and Presbyterian élites in politics, philanthropy, and education. John Webster Grant has characterized the late nineteenth century as an era of feverish church building during which the growth of evangelicalism was magnificently demonstrated in every city and town in Ontario.[8] More specifically, as Lynne Marks has demonstrated, the 1880s was the decade during which the middle class embraced the values of evangelical Protestantism. Indeed, evangelical notions of morality, respectability, and family relations had become so 'normal' among the middle class that their increasingly aggressive assertion led to an equally self-conscious response from 'unchurched' members of society, many of whom belonged to the semiskilled and unskilled working class.[9]

The ascension to power of Oliver Mowat in 1872 represented a sea change in the fortunes of evangelicals, for his was the first government in the Protestant heartland of Ontario to promote and defend a host of policies dear to the hearts of evangelicals: economy and retrenchment in government; support and recognition for church colleges at provincial universities; temperance; children's and women's labour protection; and child welfare. The intent of all these policies was to protect the sanctity of the home and the unity of the family.[10] Most significantly, in 1893 Mowat's government passed the Child Protection Act, the clear intent of which was to convert or 'save' wayward children — a concept at the very heart of the evangelical creed of conversion. This 'social Protestantism' reached its apogee at the beginning of the twentieth century, by which time it had pressed its creeds forcefully into the public domain. The Protestant churches had thrust the tenets of social Christianity to the forefront of the social reform movement, and in doing so had transformed discussions of family life and domesticity so that they were no longer private and religious in nature but rather intersected with larger questions of citizenship and state policy.[11]

Changes in economic relations paralleled this slow emergence of middle-class, evangelical culture in Canada. As Marjorie Cohen and Craig Heron have both argued, industrialization and urbanization did not happen evenly across Canada, and partly for that reason the concomitant split between the private and public spheres, between the family and the market, developed more slowly than in the United States.[12] Largely because of Canada's predominantly rural economy, the transition of women's work within the home 'from household production to socialization of children'[13] appeared later here. As late as the first decade of the twentieth century, the belief that women made important economic contributions to household production was still strongly held among the rural Ontario Women's Institutes.[14]

As Cecilia Morgan has demonstrated, during most of the nineteenth century the prescriptive literature on domesticity was encountered almost solely in the religious press.[15] And such sermons as could be found about the relationship between husbands and wives focused mainly around one fairly specific concern: family worship. One of the first suggestions that men and women belonged to separate spheres appeared in March 1881, in a sermon by the Reverend Robert Wallace, a Presbyterian. In it he systematically developed the notion that the wife's 'proper department' was with her 'household duties' and that the home was 'her throne of influence and power,' while the prescribed role of the 'divinely appointed head of the home,' the husband, was to acquire 'manly character' by making his family 'independent' in the marketplace, thus preserving them from becoming 'dependent on the cold charities of the world.'[16] Yet even this peroration to domesticity restricted itself narrowly to the ambit of the church, and similar divisions of the 'proper sphere' of men and women between public and private spaces were not often encountered until the turn of the twentieth century. After 1900, following the lead of the WCTU – the first important women's organization to offer a sustained critique of male behaviour within the family – the Protestant clergy and laity, both male and female, began asserting a maternalist ethos that became through their efforts part of an ongoing public discourse that soon was filling secular newspapers, journals, and reform debate with particular ferocity.

The intensity of discussion that developed after 1890 concerning the importance of the family arose in part out of middle-class anxiety over the increasing threat of social unrest brought about by industrial and urban growth.[17] Child welfare reformers such as J.J. Kelso often cited 'parental affection' as the most important prophylactic against increased criminal behaviour among orphaned children, and considered the 'elevation of home life' as a necessary 'safeguard of society.'[18] While it must be recognized that a concern for social order pervaded the language of reform in this period, such fears had also been cited by education reformers of the early nineteenth century, who made it their quest to replace parental responsibility with the parental authority of the State. However, by the early twentieth century the central pivot of debate was not over the goal of reform, which was generally agreed to be social order. Rather, the debate revolved around the best means for achieving 'good citizenship and national well-being.'[19] In this vein, fierce arguments erupted within the middle class over whether institutions such as schools, orphanages, and reformatories were better vehicles than the family for properly developing that most important moral attribute – individual spiritual responsibility, upon which modern society was thought to depend for its smooth development. By the beginning of the twentieth century a new consensus had emerged among reform constituencies that institutional life produced a citizenry of faceless automatons. Institutional life, by stressing the importance of the group over the individual, led to the erosion of individual moral choice and self-discipline, and for that reason was destructive of 'natural laws' of biological and ethical evolution. Thus most social commentators would have agreed with the assertion of G.A. Macdonald, editor of the *Renfrew Journal*, that 'no matter how humble the home may be if moral and sanitary requirements are met, boys and girls so raised are better fitted to make their way in life than those brought up in "bunches" in institutional care.'[20]

The concerted attack upon institutional life orchestrated by the new middle-class reformers, who included in their ranks clergymen, child welfare advocates, public health professionals, and even educators, owed less to industrialization than to vast changes that had taken place in how social cohesion and government stability were defined. In the early nineteenth century, advocates of educational reform – most notably Egerton Ryerson – had justified the expansion of state authority on the basis that institutions must usurp the role of parents. This contention was founded on a conception of polity that saw social mores as the outcome of the 'machinery of civil government.' In Ryerson's view, if legislation and laws were fundamental to the formation of men's character and morals, the family must necessarily be subordinate to educational institutions as responsible receptacles of national character and political citizenship.[21] Ryerson was a Methodist evangelical who naturally insisted on the importance of individual piety and moral responsibility. However, Ryerson's evangelical emphasis on inner spiritual qualities as the wellsprings of public behaviour was tempered by his Liberal–Tory political leanings. In the context of colonial politics, Ryerson associated the Reformers with excessive partyism and unstatesmanlike political selfishness. He perceived these attributes as associated with the excesses of liberties within the 'reform household' or family, within which sexual licence led this 'hermaphrodite spawn' to produce that 'monstrous bastard,' party despotism.[22] In Ryerson's interpretation of ideal citizenship, individualism was socially disruptive (rather than the leaven of social virtue, as later evangelicals would have it); it was also the precursor to greater excesses of liberty (which he explicitly defined as female). These vices needed to be tamed by the 'political machine' of the constitution, what he termed male statesmanship.[23]

By the late nineteenth century, such hierarchical, mechanistic visions of society, with their emphasis on political institutions as the chief vehicles of moral virtue, had given way to a less politically defined conception of society, one that was animated more directly by evangelical precepts of individual free will and moral individualism. Although an evangelical like Ryerson, the Presbyterian layman J.J. Kelso rejected older, Tory visions of the place of evangelicalism in favour of an evangelicalism flavoured by the tenets of late-nineteenth-century liberalism, in which human character was thought to be moulded not by outside influences but rather by the inner spark of spiritual conversion. 'It is the awakening of the soul,' wrote Kelso in 1916, 'the planting of some good impulse within, that leads to all lasting improvement.'[24] According to this liberal conception of the modern polity, outlined by John Millar in 1901, civil order did not flow from correct laws and political institutions; rather, democratic political institutions were themselves the product of social cohesion and class unity founded upon the collective character of individual morality.[25] The strong belief that so many evangelical reformers held in the relationship between careful religious training and individual self-reliance,[26] led them to extol the domestic realm, as well as the privileging of parental control over teachers and educational institutions. Millar, like Kelso and James L. Hughes, criticized the schools for teaching a sterile intellectualism and a flaccid moralism and for failing to admonish students in those truly spiritual qualities that alone formed the well-springs of social progress. In his view the only agency that could achieve the evangelicals' end by attending to the 'fundamental work of character development' was the family. According to James L. Hughes, the family was the most 'comprehensive influence.' It was also a natural adjunct to the work of the church and Sunday School, for it alone could develop the spiritual culture as well as precepts of individuality, which together formed the basis of social stability and progress within a liberal–democratic state.[27]

Ryerson's view was that the State must extend its power to usurp parental control, with the goal of ensuring that individuality would remain subordinate to the civil order.[28] In direct contrast, late-nineteenth-century reformers, like the child welfare advocate J.J. Kelso, championed state intervention as the principal means by which to *reinforce* parental responsibility and promote the economic self-reliance of families. Kelso defended his child welfare legislation against the popular perception that it was encroaching on parental rights and destroying that crucial sense of self-reliance, on the basis that it only policed families whose 'moral sense is dead.' As Kelso explained in his 1896 paper 'Revival of the Curfew Law,' he was not advocating the extension of state policing to families on any 'socialistic presumption'; rather, he condoned state incursion into family life only as a buttress for those broadly interconnecting Christian values of individual salvation, independent manhood, and economic self-reliance. In other words, child protection agents could infringe on individual liberty only when the parents failed to fulfil their duties to the State, for it was only then that parents forfeited their own 'natural' moral rights.[29] The view that the State should educate the masses rather than relieve them of their responsibility for securing the welfare of their own families was not simply a middle-class point of view. In Canada, ideals of familial independence and self-reliance were also enshrined in the policies of organized labour, which championed state incursions in the area of family and child welfare only if they underscored 'economic independence' and left the individual workingman with the freedom 'to map out his own destiny.'[30]

Although Kelso and other reformers saw home, church, and school working harmoniously for the upward progress of society, their vision of limited state responsibility had its provenance in a peculiarly evangelical perspective that gave pre-eminent place to the home – the traditional locus for childhood conversion. In one of his frequent homilies on the importance of family life to both the church and society, Rev. Joseph Krauskopf declared that 'there never will be, a better schoolroom or a better church than a mother's heart ... The soul which a mother taught to believe continues to believe.'[31] Indeed, by the beginning of the twentieth century, middle-class conceptions of the family and of the relationship between the individual and the State were conceived within an overtly religious conception of Christian responsibility. For parents were primarily responsible for training their offspring to become self-reliant Christian citizens, but at the same time it was the duty of the State to protect and preserve the family in order that Christian values and the Protestant churches might endure in the broader community. Out of this reciprocal relationship founded on Christian tenets, Kelso delineated the boundaries of the modern state – by which Kelso meant 'all members of the body politic'[32] rather than simply government institutions – which he believed should intervene only to ensure that 'good influence should be focused on the home' so that 'parental responsibility' might be developed and 'church connections' preserved.'[33]

The impetus behind those social reforms which increased the intervention of the State grew out of changes within the mainstream Protestant churches. After 1900 a new group of reform-minded young clergyman became leaders within their churches, and the mainstream Protestant denominations began devoting themselves explicitly to this new 'social evangelism' with the goal of ensuring that Christianity interacted dynamically with the changes in modern society. These progressive clergymen explicitly eschewed the older theological exclusivity of Protestantism in favour of the tenets of social service, with the result that the Protestant churches were able to stay in the forefront of the reform movements of the day; that being said, this new social Christianity was firmly underpinned by a traditional emphasis on the divinity of Christ and the existence of human sin.[34] Indeed, J.J. Kelso, one of the foremost advocates for government intervention in the private realm of the family, sought to rescue children from poor home environments for the purpose of winning them back to Christianity. His chief aim was not to combat poverty; rather, he saw the normalizing of family life as an essentially Christian endeavour and thus saw the spiritual comforts of religion as more important than the material comforts of charitable giving. As he said, 'Christianity should never be content to hand over to the world its sacred obligation to minister to the poor in the spirit of the Master.'[35] Like those clergymen who promoted the new social evangelism, Kelso interpreted all social problems in terms of how they affected the state of Christian belief and the power of Protestantism in Canadian society. 'Social welfare,' wrote Kelso, 'is essentially an expression of Christianity,' and 'reformers are the advance agents of the irresistible will of Almighty God.'[36]

This new movement within the mainstream Protestant churches toward social Christianity was not a radical departure from Methodist and Presbyterian traditions; rather, it involved a search for new methods for ensuring the permanence of the evangelical missionary impulse to convert new members to the will of the Almighty. The interest of clergymen, and of laymen like Kelso – himself a Presbyterian active in Sunday School teaching – in reforming families arose directly out of their concern for ensuring that the mainstream Protestant denominations would, through a steady stream of personal conversions, continue to grow in numbers and influence. 'In mission work as in church work,' stated Rev. T.E. Shore, 'the best results are reached among the children: and if the family is the unit of society, then the nearer we can get to the cradle in our mission work, the sooner we can save the home and save society.'[37] The Methodist and Presbyterian churches were the driving force behind government legislation to protect mothers and children.[38] Not only that, but many of the agents of the local children's aid societies were either clergymen or Protestant laymen who aggressively sought childhood conversion in Sunday School.[39] Indeed, Kelso achieved his child welfare reforms largely through his widespread connections with local clergymen, and the momentum behind child welfare legislation was sustained by the expanding authority of the mainline Protestant churches.[40] It is not insignificant that both Kelso and Ontario's first Deputy Minister of Public Welfare, B.M. Heise, began as Sunday School teachers and saw child saving literally as an extension of the institutional church, with the State as but one of the many means by which Protestantism was able to proselytize.[41] What historians have traditionally interpreted as the expansion of the secular state was in fact the interpenetration of Protestant missionary goals into new state bureaucratic structures.

As Marguerite Van Die and Neil Semple have argued, throughout the nineteenth century evangelicals placed increasing emphasis on childhood conversion. The emphasis on childhood as a crucial linchpin in perpetuating revivalism reached its zenith in the first decades of the twentieth century, as theological debates raged over whether children were sinful and therefore needed to repent, or whether childhood was a state of innocence during which Christian belief must thus be contin- uously nurtured.[42] Kelso's own views on childhood spirituality reflected this broader emphasis within evangelicalism. 'Christianity,' wrote Kelso, 'makes childhood an object of care and affection, it sets it in the centre of the world's thoughts and endeavours to make it a type of the Kingdom of Heaven on earth.'[43] However, child-centred social reform did not emerge out of the nurture model, as Neil Semple has argued; Kelso adhered much more firmly to an older, conversionist model that Marguerite Van Die has identified with the outlook of Nathanael Burwash. While administering the Ontario government's Child Protection Act, Kelso spoke of 'saving' children. But by this he did not mean merely rescuing them from the streets or from poor envi- ronments; rather he defined 'saving' children as bringing them to rec- ognize their sinful natures and the need for personal conversion. Clearly, Kelso envisioned his welfare work in terms of home mission- ary endeavours; to that end, he exhorted Christian men and women to 'see in each homeless child the blessed Master pleading with them.'[44] His discursive writings on child welfare often described instances of children 'bursting into the full sunshine of God'[45] as they underwent a conversion experience. Moreover, he described his personal influence on wayward boys as 'an instantaneous awakening of the soul,'[46] and claimed that his approach was more effective than an evangelical sermon from the pulpit in converting children to Christianity. In a similar vein, W.K. Richardson referred to his work with girls at the Victoria Industrial School as a 'prophet's life' wherein he fought against evil. In 1915 Richardson joyfully described his work with one lad in particular as a success, even though the boy later drowned while washing sheep, because the boy not only had learned the value of work but had sensed the importance of atonement.[47] Thus, while child welfare reformers paid lip service to placing orphans with foster homes as a means of making them into responsible workers and hence useful citizens, their primary motive for interfering with parental control was to win young souls to Christ.[48]

The child welfare bureaucracy that began to emerge in the 1890s established a web of machinery that utilized the official public apparatus of laws and state-supported charitable organizations, like the children's aid societies, to reinvigorate the older, evangelical practice of family worship. The new, progressive church leaders in the Methodist and Presbyterian churches set out on a great project of expanding church institutions, such as Sunday Schools, young people's leagues, and YMCAs and YWCAs, with the goal of reviving the evangelistic spirit within these denominations. But many remained sceptical that the pulpit and these church agencies could to any degree replace the all-enveloping influence of family piety as a stimulus to evangelical fervour. As early as 1883, Elizabeth Shortt – later one of the architects of Ontario's mothers' allowance legislation, which had as one of its principle aims the ongoing maternal instruction of children at home – agreed with her future husband, Adam Shortt, that the pulpit was a failure in terms of Christian teaching and that 'the greatest good is to be brought about through the mother's training of the children.'[49] Despite the attention that church leaders lavished on mass revivals in the early decades of the twentieth century, there was an enduring and even heightened emphasis on the efficacy of family worship. Reminiscences by prominent church leaders such as Nathanael Burwash (the Chancellor of Victoria College), the missionary W.A. Mackay, and the Hon. Dr H.J. Cody, Minister of Education and later President of the University of Toronto, flourished during this period.[50] They each emphasized that daily sessions of family prayer during childhood were the central catalyst for their own conversion experiences and for the longevity of their Christian commitment. Most important, however, they recalled the profound influence of their mother. Memories of family worship from the nineteenth century tended to emphasize the authority of fathers as leaders of family worship, but by the turn of the twentieth century there was a new emphasis on mother-love. This elevation of mothers to the centre of the evangelical experience within the home paralleled developments within evangelical thought itself, which by this time had shifted rather decisively away from what one Methodist referred to as the 'darker' sides of sin and damnation,[51] and toward a more optimistic vision of fellowship with Christ – a vision which looked to love and the affections as the wellsprings of faith. According to Kelso, neither God's punishment nor parental chastisement could lead to perpetual Christian perfection – only 'love can unlock the heart and redeem and permanently reclaim the offender.'[52]

Since the early nineteenth century, evangelicals had celebrated the domestic sphere and the religious family unit as the fulcrums evangelical piety. But the indelible link between Protestantism and domesticity, with its emphasis on the affections and morality as the central bonds of society, reached its apex in Canada at the turn of the twentieth century. The intensity of discussion about the benefits of an enhanced role for mothers both within the family and within society was fuelled in part by the burgeoning feminist movement. Many women, like Mrs Donald Shaw, shared the ideology of the mainstream churches, and in their magazine articles referred to motherhood as a facet of the Divine – as a spiritual vocation. Other women, such as Constance Lynd, applied the concept of maternalism in a more radical manner, both as a vehicle to argue for more female control over childbirth and as a standard by which a new morality might arise. In this guise, maternal feminism was not merely a reactionary middle-class ideology but – as the author of 'The Need for a Women's Court' argued – a means to change 'the false conventional idea of morality' that women were sexual temptresses victimizing hapless men.[53] Men were likewise exponents of this new, desexualized image of womanhood. In his 1914 article 'The Ascendancy of Womanhood,' Rev. Joseph Krauskopf, a supporter of the feminist notion of companionate marriage, argued against the older, Biblical view of women as a 'primal source of evil' born of Eve's temptation; in the same vein, he condemned the contemporary double-standard regarding sexual morality for men and women.[54] By reconfiguring the natural role of women from that of wife and sexual partner to mother, male and female champions of the idea of more democratic family relations were removing women from the ambit of sexuality and thus squarely focusing the blame for prostitution, unmarried motherhood, and all sexual crimes on undisciplined male sexual impulses. As Dr Laura S. Hamilton concluded in her 1918 article for the *Canadian Home Journal*, the solutions for all social problems lay with the reformation of men. Like other maternal feminists, Dr Hamilton rejected late Victorian mores, which stressed female immorality, and held men responsible for creating 'abnormal' familial relations, which they precipitated by causing illegitimate births or by deserting their wives.[55]

However, the ideology of maternalism expanded far beyond immediately feminist concerns, and by the First World War had thoroughly grafted itself onto a wide range of social reform currents. Maternalism became part and parcel of a larger transformation within public culture – one that led away from an emphasis on the intellect and toward a conception of political economy that recognized the greater authority of the affections in harnessing disruptive modern social forces into a more peaceful unity. This emerged in Canada as the result of a convergence of several forces: the influence of broadly idealist thought upon the social sciences, the increasing influence of the institutional churches in the public realm, and the emergence of female reform organizations.[56]

After the turn of the twentieth century, the permeation of idealist conceptions of society, which placed a priority on ethics and morality as the primary bonds of social cohesion, was accelerated in Canada by the striking effect of Methodism and Presbyterianism on social debate and public policy. Discussions of the nature of poverty, class conflict, and the conundrum of social progress were overlaid with specifically Protestant animadversions against materialistic values. Writers for *Woman's Century,* such as Albert Roberts, attributed all social decline to a too-strong emphasis on the 'masculine' intelligence, which functioned on a merely material plane. Against male rationality, which he believed to be an outmoded principle of social organization, Roberts juxtaposed the 'maternal instinct.' In his view, in an increasingly interdependent modern society, social consciousness could be developed only through moral and spiritual values, and thus it lay wholly within the female purview to 'weld society into a complex organism' and combat the 'industrial juggernaut.' Only the 'mother instinct,' with its close associations with 'a sense of God,' could awaken Canadians to recognize the ravages of 'the modern industrial inferno.'[57]

At one level, the emergence of a conception of the 'social soul'[58] reflected the growing public influence of the mainstream evangelical denominations, Methodism and Presbyterianism, on Canadian cultural life. The increasing volubility of critiques offered by leading clergyman, and by lay evangelical commentators, regarding the ineffectuality of fathers within the family sphere, also underscored that specifically 'female' values were being more readily absorbed within Protestantism itself. It is not surprising that the Protestant denominations were beginning to acknowledge more often the value of women's special concerns: as Hannah Lane and Lynne Marks have demonstrated clearly, the growth and power of mainstream evangelicalism since the mid-nineteenth century was largely the result of bringing new converts – namely their children and husbands – into the fold of the various Protestant denominations.[59] In this light, the Protestant churches by recognizing family values were in effect recognizing the social values of Canadian women. And this emphasis on families was only enhanced by the new importance of social Christianity, which further solidified the connection between the churches and women's social reform aspirations.[60] Thus after 1900 the social reform programs of the mainstream denominations began more closely to reflect the family protection issues that were so central to evangelical women's groups, most notably the WCTU.[61] Male social reformers, and active evangelicals like J.J. Kelso, evoked a conception of family preservation that was remarkably similar to that of the WCTU and of other feminist organizations. Thus, Kelso disparaged fathers who 'shirk[ed] their responsibilities' by deserting their wives because of a generic male deficiency in 'natural affection.' Moreover, he blamed fathers for failing to fight for higher wages with which to support and protect their families; and he placed the blame for marital breakdown on men, specifically middle-class men, who favoured club life over the tempering and civilizing function of the home, where the 'primary instinct of the maternal soul' reigned supreme.[62]

The responsibility for infusing modern materalistic life with spiritual purpose was seen as laying wholly with women. After 1900, this perception was advanced with ever-increasing frequency by both male and female reformers. The idea of the maternal-centred family would soon become an overarching metaphor for a broader Protestant, middle-class critique of society. Indeed, the primary motivation behind J.J. Kelso's campaign for mothers' allowances was an evangelical one, and part of a broader crusade against the materialism of modern society. As he pointed out, these allowances were intended to rescue impoverished but moral mothers, whom he called 'that noble band of women the world over who put character and service far ahead of wealth.'[63] Rev. George Pidgeon forcefully drew the connections that many of his contemporaries saw between the insinuation of Protestant values throughout society, and the belief that society is largely an ethical organism, and the privileging of women's values in the reclamation of the family and society. In the 1910 Presbyterian pamphlet *Canadian Problems*, Pidgeon's conception of proper family and social relations drew from a decidedly conservative outlook that harkened back to a conception of the community as an immediate extention of family affections, whereby individual desires must be subordinated to the larger good.[64] Like many other reformers of the day, Pidgeon believed that women's morality would check the anarchic individualism of male desire, which led to family desertion and the breakdown of the family wage, and which inevitably weakened both the ethical bonds of the social fabric and the political economy of the nation. This Protestant definition of family relations reflected the continuation of a nineteenth-century tension between 'private,' female morality as against the 'public,' male domain of market forces; but it was also the harbinger of a newer outlook that would collapse the boundaries between private and public by overtly identifying the morals of the female family sphere with the 'national morality.'[65]

For the most part, maternal feminists shared the view of evangelical clergymen and laymen: that home and State were indivisible. In 1918, A.A. Perry commented favourably that the world war just ended had blurred the traditional boundaries between the private 'female' domain of the family and the 'public' male domain of the nation-state. 'Through the war,' she wrote, 'the preservation of the child has become not only the highest type of philanthropy, but the most stark racial necessity. So, Woman and Woman's work become, at last, of the first national importance, and Home and State, are seen by even the most short-sighted to be an Indivisible Whole.'[66] Scholars like Carole Pateman[67] contend that with the growth of state welfare policies, the division between private and public along gender lines remained. Historian Linda Gordon refutes this, arguing that feminists welcomed maternalist welfare policies, which allowed massive state intervention into the private realm of family life, because such legislation provided women with entitlements that counterbalanced the disadvantages of their 'privateness' within the home.[68] Canadian women were just as active as American women in their efforts to transform the relationship between the State and the family, to redefine the patriarchal family, and to foster a more democratic conception of equal rights within the family. Between 1900 and 1920 the National Council of Women sought to have their maternalist vision of the family incorporated into law and government policy. As early as 1900, Canadian feminists were lobbying provincial governments to revise the various child welfare acts so as to provide equal guardianship rights, which at that time were still denied to women.[69] In an attempt to appeal more strongly to the more conservative male interests in the government, rather than campaigning for women's rights based solely on the individual rights of mothers, maternal feminists stressed the importance of children. Thus in 1920 Dr Augusta Stowe-Gullen, in a submission to the Ontario cabinet requesting equal guardianship rights for women, defended the feminist cause by referring skilfully to the importance of children both to the nation and to women.[70] This strategy would pervade all subsequent campaigns for maternalist-centred state welfare policies.

The final obstacle in the long struggle of women for equal rights within the family was to reverse the legislation stating that the religion of children was dictated by the religion of the father.[71] At this crucial juncture, the limitations of the maternalist redefinition of the family became evident. The very ideology of maternalism became contested terrain as it became incorporated into state welfare policies, for here it soon came into conflict with other imperatives of the State as envisioned by evangelical child welfare reformers – namely, the State's function as an important proselytizing arm of the mainstream Protestant denominations. Nowhere was the decidedly Protestant tenor of state welfare policies more clearly evident than in the implementation of the Child Protection Act. This legislation was unashamedly employed, both within government ranks and within the local children's aid societies, as a coercive tool for channelling recalcitrant Roman Catholic children into Protestant foster homes and thereby ensuring their rapid conversion. Thus, while J.J. Kelso and other evangelicals defended the equal right of women to care for and train their children as part of their ideal of a maternal-centred domestic sphere,[72] they did so only to the extent that 'God's law'[73] of female piety did not undermine the power and authority of the Protestant churches. After the turn of the twentieth century, the Roman Catholic community became more self-confident. In response, to forestall what they saw as the aggrandizement of Roman Catholicism, the Protestant state flexed its muscles and vociferously championed the traditional legal right of fathers to determine the religion of their children. In 1914, Kelso issued his circular underscoring the rights of fathers in matters of family religion; from then on, Protestants and Catholics found themselves locked in a fierce struggle over how the religious complexion of welfare state policies would be determined. And whenever the maternalist ideal of the family conflicted with the missionary imperatives of the Protestant churches, the former was severely circumscribed. Although maternal feminists lobbied strenuously for reform of the law pertaining to paternal rights over the religious training of children, practical reform of this last vestige of male authority within the family was the result of activities of the Roman Catholic Church, which vociferously defended the rights of mothers, though not from a feminist perspective but rather because maternalism was deemed to be the critical vehicle for defending the religious rights of Roman Catholic families.

The reinterpretation of the patriarchal family thus owed less to maternal feminism than historians have assumed. The demands of women to have guardianship legislation reformed reached fruition, in 1920, only after the ideological context of the debate had been transformed by decades of effort by Roman Catholic activists such W.L. Scott, the lawyer who headed the Ottawa Children's Aid Society. Indeed, in Canada the axis of parental authority within the family shifted toward the mother during the first decades of the twentieth century largely because the moral economy of the family had become tangled in a web of religious controversy and because the rights of mothers had come to be perceived by male church and state welfare leaders as integral to the broader imperatives of Protestant–Catholic relations. Religion was the dominant factor determining the contours of Canadan family welfare policy prior to 1920; gender was not a fixed standard but rather was constantly mediated and influenced by religious concerns. This is all clearly revealed by how the Child Protection Act was implemented in Ontario. Under the terms of this act, the religion of the father took priority except in cases where the mother was unmarried, in which case her religion determined that of her children.[74] In order to conform to the law, it was incumbent on the children's aid societies (CASs), the private organizations that worked in harmony with the provincial secretary's office to enforce child protection in Ontario, that they 'should not show any bias one way or another on the question of religion.'[75] For the most part, the local CASs held to the terms of the law and dutifully sent Roman Catholic children to Roman Catholic foster homes and Protestant children to those of their fellow Protestants. But the animating principles undergirding the juvenile court system and the CAS itself were clearly Protestant, as most of the judges and officials were prominent Methodist laity and clergy. For example, one of Toronto's leading juvenile court judges and an active member of the CAS was Rev. J.E. Starr, a leading Methodist and pastor of Berkeley Street Church; the Rev. Dr William Hincks was a special children's judge in Toronto and a leader of the Methodist Ministerial Association; and Inspector Stark of the Toronto Police Department was a prominent supporter of the Sunday School movement as well as a vocal champion of both church attendance and the need to instil the 'veneration of religion' among children. Most decisively of all, Protestant expansion with its equation of 'the Child, the Home, the Parent, the State,' was rigorously promoted as the official outlook of Ontario by the provincial secretary, W.D. McPherson, who was the Grand Master of the British American Orange Order.[76] As one result, Roman Catholics outside of Toronto took very little interest in the work of the CASs, because they perceived them to be 'a Protestant society' whose active officials were all militantly anti-Catholic. The Protestant hierarchy very much wanted to blame the Catholics themselves for violating their own religious rights through their lack of involvement in the child welfare movement. Yet it is clear that the daily press openly defended the Protestant character of the State, in part by retailing lurid, largely fictional tales of Catholics wrongfully abducting Protestant orphans. In one typical article of this genre, it was claimed that one Bertha Wilson, an innocent Protestant orphan, had been forced into a life of crime after she had been compelled to run away from the Catholic Sunnyside Orphanage for asserting her Protestant convictions. The article concluded with Wilson proclaiming in juvenile court that she was not a Catholic 'so I ran away. I am a Protestant and I'm going to stick to my religion.'[77]

By the second decade of the twentieth century, militant Protestants such as Kelso, Superintendent of Neglected and Dependent Children, and Provincial Secretary W.D. McPherson[78] were becoming increasingly restive about the implications of these subclauses of the Child Protection Act, as the number of mixed marriages between Protestants and Roman Catholics increased dramatically. The systematic increase in interfaith marriage was the result of greater upward mobility among Irish Roman Catholics. The historian Mark McGowan has estimated that upwards of 14 per cent of all Catholic marriages were mixed by 1910, and that by 1920 one marriage in three was interfaith.[79] With palpable anxiety, Kelso recounted how the marriage of a sixteen-year-old Protestant girl to a Catholic man had been all too easily facilitated by a reckless city clerk in Chatham. As Kelso told McPherson's successor, H.C. Nixon, 'they were married by a coloured man, the garbage collector of the town named J.C. Browning. It appears that this man is a local preacher and claims authority to perform a marriage ceremony.'[80] The newly self-confident Catholic hierarchy, which was keenly aware of the aggressiveness of Protestant missionary activity among the Irish and recently arrived Roman Catholic immigrants, further aggravated Protestant–Catholic relations by attempting to bypass Protestant strictures concerning the religion of children. One method was to enforce with greater vigilance the church's right to have Protestant males sign marriage contracts in which they agreed to forego their common law rights and have their children raised in the religion of their wives.[81]

Just prior to the First World War McPherson and his underling Kelso began using the power of the State to counteract the growing self-confidence of the Roman Catholic Church. To this end, Kelso interceded with increasing boldness in questionable cases with the goal of placing Catholic children in Protestant foster homes. Often he merely enforced the law as it stood, such as in the case of Reginald Badgerow, the child of a widow, born out of wedlock. The mother, a Protestant, wished to adopt him out to a Roman Catholic family. In this instance Kelso worked within the powers accorded him as Superintendent of Neglected and Dependent Children, and decided that the adoptive parents were not suitable. Interestingly, they were not turned down because the prospective father was a working-class man who worked for the Toronto Transit Commission as a trackman, or because their home was located in an extremely dubious neighbourhood called the Devil's Elbow, a haven for Toronto's young criminal class (these would have been conventional rationalizations for rejecting adoptive parents). Rather, the couple's application was denied because the man was a Catholic. Here religion took precedence over class considerations, for as Kelso argued, the fact that the man was now unemployed and worked only occasionally held little weight against the more baneful consideration of the 'religious question.'[82]

Kelso often preyed on helpless victims of poverty, such as one widowed mother who, although she herself was a Protestant, was forced by poverty to send her children to the St Joseph's Catholic Orphanage, where 'she could get them taken care of cheaper.' Predictably, Kelso interceded and sent the children to a Presbyterian orphan's home. The mother only regained control of the religious upbringing of her children when she remarried a few years later.[83] Nor did the authority of fathers prevent Kelso from deploying the power of the State in the service of Protestant goals, though here he was more circumspect. There was one extraordinary case in which a Roman Catholic father converted to Protestantism *after* his daughter had been rightly placed with a Roman Catholic foster mother by the authorities. In this situation, Kelso made it appear that the CAS and the Ontario government were the champions of the rights of natural parents; he held up the father's recent declaration that he was a Protestant to show that 'there is not at the present time any doubt as to her being a Protestant,' even though this totally negated the religious principles of the child. In full knowledge that he was interfering with an earlier decision of the local police magistrate of Arthur, Ontario, to have the child given a Catholic upbringing, Kelso deftly used the supposed moral deficiences of the Catholic foster mother to legitimize his hasty removal of the girl from her home.[84]

In other situations, Kelso clearly bent the law. In one case, an illegitimate child was born to the daughter of a prosperous merchant, and Kelso personally intervened in a legal adoption in order to prevent the child being sent to a respectable Catholic family.[85] The increasingly common pattern of family desertion presented new difficulties for Kelso, who believed the state machinery should protect the needs of the Protestant churches. In many situations where the father had deserted, the mother schooled her children according to her own religious beliefs. In one such case, Kelso deliberately bypassed the law, which stated that the religion of the father must be followed even if he had deserted. Although this particular boy had been raised a Protestant by his mother, the law stated that because his father was Catholic he must be sent to the Roman Catholic Industrial School. Kelso had often disparaged the arguments of his foe, W.L. Scott, that one should respect the child's religion, but in this case he adamantly defended the pleas of the Protestant boy, whom he claimed had 'wept bitterly' at the prospect of becoming a Catholic.[86] When Mr Jones, a widower, made a legitimate demand that his two girls be sent to a Catholic foster home because he had signed up to fight in the war, the local agent of the CAS vociferously opposed the father's request, at first by attempting to undermine the father's character by claiming he was a thief and a drinker, and later by stating that the father was in fact an Anglican and was making up his Catholic affiliation so that his children might be placed with his common law wife.[87]

In the hands of militant Protestants like Kelso and McPherson, gender was a very pliant category that could be moulded to suit any religious need. Thus when the juvenile courts followed the letter of the law and placed two orphaned children with the St Vincent de Paul Orphanage, Kelso directly refuted Judge Boyd's decision and placed the demands of family members – in this case the protests of an Anglican grandmother – above the laws of the State, all because the father was both an Italian and a Catholic. In those numerous cases in which a mother could no longer financially support her children, Kelso deployed effectively all the legal power proferred by the CASs to intervene into family relations; but in situations where the mother happened to be Protestant and the father Catholic, Kelso happily overturned CAS convention and acceded to the wishes of the family to have children sent to a Protestant orphan's home.[88]

Perhaps the best example of the duplicitous means Kelso used to implement his proselytizing ends was the case of Jewel Folkard, an illegitimate child born to a working-class woman, Hazel Folkard. Both the natural mother and the prospective adoptive parents were Roman Catholics, and although they knew it was illegal to adopt a Catholic child into a Protestant home, Kelso played on the fact that the foster mother was a 'poor working man's wife' unable to pay the lawyer's fees, as well as on the natural mother's fears that her child would not be adopted. He finally bamboozled the unwitting Catholic woman into circumventing normal legal procedures, claiming that if she went to the St Vincent de Paul Society he would 'make it nasty for you' but if she did it his way 'no one will know about it' and the 'Catholics will [not] make a row.'[89] This Protestant raiding of Catholic children had become so commonplace by 1917 that it precipitated an investigation by the inspector for the Roman Catholic Children's Aid Society, William O'Connor, who related many instances of Catholic children being placed in Protestant homes, but no cases of the reverse.[90] O'Connor's protests to the Orangeman W.D. McPherson fell on deaf ears.

By 1919 it had become so obvious that Ontario's policies were de facto Protestant policies, that the provincial secretary defended his illegal purloining of Catholic orphans by baldly asserting that it was less objectionable to place Catholic children with Protestant families because their religion would be less interfered with there. 'Catholics,' stated McPherson, 'were so much more particular about their religion and about going to church.'[91] McPherson's 'piece of sophistry' – as W.L. Scott called it – demonstrated the extent to which Protestant religious and family values had permeated state welfare policy; the provincial secretary no longer identified his activities in terms of Protestant missionary activity. Rather, he took for granted the Protestant agenda that undergirded child welfare principles and thus juxtaposed these supposedly 'secular' government views of family reconstitution against the initiatives of Roman Catholic Children's Aid Society workers, whom he portrayed as having distinctly religious priorities. Like other Protestant leaders of the day, McPherson and Kelso accepted the notion that while the continuation of the Protestant revival in its broadest cultural sense must be protected through a range of institutions beyond the pulpit, Roman Catholic religious belief remained a signally 'private' concern that therefore must remain constrained within the immediate realm of the parish church.

The problem of Catholic aggrandizement, as perceived by militant Protestant laymen within the Ontario child welfare hierarchy, was exacerbated by the dramatic increase in eastern European immigration in the first decades of the twentieth century. Unlike the threat posed by intermarriages between Protestants and Catholics, which could be circumvented by finagling the existing child welfare laws, immigrant families presented a more intractable difficulty, for here, marriages had taken place almost invariably between two Catholic parents. As Kelso informed the provincial secretary in 1914, the arrival of large numbers of immigrants demanded that 'the clear lines of demarcation' be drawn between 'Roman Catholicism and Protestantism, with its many branches.' Roman Catholicism also had many branches, as was illustrated by the nationalist rifts between Eastern Orthodox Catholics who rejected the authority of the Holy See, and the Greek Catholics, the majority of Ruthenians or Ukrainians, who though not calling themselves Roman Catholics still observed papal authority. However, Kelso and his Protestant colleagues were unwilling to recognize the subtleties of what they regarded as a heathen faith. Accordingly, in the summer of 1914 Kelso issued a controversial circular to all the local children's aid societies in Ontario, which stated that in future under the terms of the Act for the Protection and Reformation of Neglected Children, all Eastern or Greek Catholics, irrespective of their theological relationship with the Pope, must be considered Protestants: 'Will you please make a note of the fact that in future where children are brought before the courts professing to be Greek Catholics they should be classed as Protestant, except where there is direct evidence to the contrary.'[92]

Lay advocates of the Catholic Church, such as W.L. Scott, Bishop Scollard from Sault Ste Marie, and the Right Rev. Nicetas Budka, Bishop of the Ruthenian Catholics, reiterated time and again that all Eastern Catholics – almost 80 per cent of Ruthenian immigrants – recognized papal authority, and that only a small number of eastern European immigrants considered themselves members of the Greek Orthodox Church.[93] But their injunctions and protests made little impression on a government that saw the religious clauses of the various child protection acts as a powerful means for proselytizing newly arrived Catholics. Against the constant volleys of Catholic leaders demanding that the offending circular be rescinded, Kelso and the provincial secretary collected written statements from Greek Orthodox Catholics and various Protestant CAS agents claiming that all Greek Catholics wanted their children to be placed in Protestant homes. On top of all this, the not unbiased opinion of Professor Wrong, from the Department of History, University of Toronto, was solicited to lend a scholarly tincture to the Protestant cause.[94] Kelso constantly hedged and dodged the cogent arguments presented by Catholics, who were of course outraged by this new attempt to make the CAS and the child welfare bureaucracy into a 'sort of proselytizing Agency.'[95] When W.L. Scott stated that he intended to ensure that the provisions of the welfare acts would be carried out with regard to the rights of Catholic families by having the circular overturned, 'so long as there is any step open to me to obtain redress,' Kelso retorted disingenuously that this could not be done because it would establish 'a general rule which will interfere with individual wishes.'[96] He directed Catholics to resort to the courts, where their rights would be established on a case-by-case basis[97] and so not disturb the Protestant bulwarks he was so skilfully erecting around family policy.

The real sticking point of Kelso's circular was the codicil that all Greek Catholics were to be considered Protestant unless they could prove otherwise. In the Protestant government arsenal, this was a particularly powerful weapon. Because of the extreme shortage of Ruthenian churches in Ontario, the majority of Eastern or Greek Catholics were forced to attend either Eastern Orthodox churches, which did not recognize the Holy See in Rome, or even Anglican churches. More often, eastern European children attended no churches at all, which made them vulnerable to Protestant arguments that because they did not regularly attend church they were not practising Catholics. When Bishop Scollard and various Catholic CAS agents from Northern Ontario pointed out that using church attendance as the basis for determining a person's religion was prejudicial because eastern European immigrants were prevented from practising their Catholic faith because they could not speak English, Kelso merely replied that this was simply more evidence that it was difficult to ascertain 'the precise religious belief of these foreigners,' and all the more reason to place them in Protestant families. In frustration over the lack of respect shown for Catholic religious convictions, Bishop Scollard hotly replied: 'We do not want a single child that does not belong to us – but we do want and in fact we are bound in conscience to take care of the souls of our own subjects. Withdraw and amend that instruction. Why should there be any hesitation and delay about doing it?'[98] Such was the impasse between Protestants and Catholics, in the already heated political climate occasioned by the issuing of Regulation 17, which limited the rights of French-Canadian Catholics in Ontario schools, that Protestants like the Rev. J.A. Klesnikoff of the Baptist Evangelical Mission Among Foreigners saw this defence of the right of Catholic parents to determine the religious upbringing of their children as yet another ploy to wrest innocent Protestants from the evangelical fold.[99] The juvenile judge, E.W. Boyd, expressed the true cause of alarm among child welfare reformers – that if these immigrant children were raised as 'pure Roman Catholics' they would not learn 'Western ideas of morality,' they would keep having large families, and their children would continue to be wards of the State, not having been taught the Protestant values of work and family independence.[100]

The intention of the Protestant child welfare organizations and the Ontario government was to pit family members against one another or, failing that, to override parental responsibility altogether, in order to gain ascendance for Protestant values in Canadian society. In practice, they did not entirely succeed. Catholic parents were equally adept at using the Catholic parish to exert their rights concerning the religious education of their natural children. Working-class Catholic families did not accede meekly to the State's authority when its goals flew in the face of their own ethnic and religious identity.[101] Roman Catholic parents understood clearly that religion was central to their sense of family and community; despite their poverty, they adamantly sought redress through the courts to retain control over the religious upbringing of their children. Poor Greek-Catholic parents, many of whom had lost many of their rights while in jail, nevertheless proceeded to protest in court against having their children sent to Protestant foster homes.[102] They won their cases, as did Mr Jones, a father who had volunteered for the war in 1915. With the help of his local parish priest, Rev. A. O'Malley, and a sympathetic Oshawa juvenile court judge, Jones argued successfully that the CAS, by neglecting to ask about his religion, had not followed due process. In the end, the courts forced the CAS to protect the religious rights of this widower.[103] Parents like Jones were not particularly antistate – in many cases they had called on the CAS and child welfare authorities to protect the children they could no longer support. Thus, while many Catholic parents invited the state to intervene to protect the welfare of their children, they were at the same time extremely protective of the religious sanctity of the home. Like Protestants, they considered moral education a vital part of proper parenting, and piety a central wellspring of both family and community relations. Thus, the parents of May Olive Wing took the intiative in placing her in an orphanage, but at the same time they fought fiercely against the proselytizing designs of J.J. Kelso so that their child could be raised in the St Patrick's Orphanage.[104]

The degree to which working-class Catholics considered religion pivotal to parental control is well illustrated in the case of the Bigras children. This celebrated case demonstrates how the Catholic Church used the 'private' realm of the courts to defend family responsibility and the rights of individual parents against the Protestant incursions of the state welfare edifice. At another level it shows the various ways in which family members used the existing welfare machinery to serve their own personal ends, and how agents of the State preyed on such family conflicts. Adolph Bigras of the village of Rockland, near Ottawa, on becoming widowed, approached the local CAS to find care for his young children. At this stage he was desperate because the local Catholic orphanage had turned him away because he was not a regularly practising Catholic. The local CAS agent, a Protestant clergyman named McEwan, knew that Adolph Bigras and his wife Alexina had consistently raised their children in the Catholic faith, but was determined that these children should be raised 'in the tenets of the Protestant faith' – a determination reinforced by the demands of the grandfather, who had recently converted to Protestantism. A fervent Baptist, the grandfather provided McEwen with the necessary details – that Adolph had already been turned down by the Catholic orphanage for help, that he was a poor and illiterate labourer, and that he did not understand English. This allowed them to trick the young widower into relinquishing his children to the Protestant authorities, by having him sign his mark on a transfer order he was unable to read.[105]

Catholic welfare crusaders had come to view the courts as a crucial venue for defending parental rights against the aggressive Protestant incursions of government welfare managers like Kelso; and after 1917, Catholic Church authorities had brought increasing pressure to bear against state authorities over the issue of the Greek Catholics. Under McPherson's leadership, the Orange Order responded by placing many of the juvenile courts under the effective control of Protestants.[106] Kelso was confident that the government had gained supremacy over the juvenile courts, which would faithfully defend the Protestant faith, and forced the Bigras case before the bench. In 1923, at great expense to the local Catholic community, which had to take up a local collection on behalf of Adolph Bigras, W.L. Scott took up the case. Kelso chose to view the case simply as a 'family quarrel' – as a conflict between a Protestant grandfather and his Catholic son. Likewise, Adolph Bigras saw it as a personal crusade, as a way to defend the fact that, despite his lack of regular church attendance, he was a Catholic all the same. The *Catholic Record*, however, appreciated the symbolic importance of the case, declaring that it amounted to a conflict between the 'Protestant parties' and the Catholic community. The courts interpreted the case in the context of the rights of the state versus those of individuals. The judge stated that his decision turned on the religion clauses of the Child Protection Act. In finding for Adolph Bigras, he emphasized those clauses which prohibited the State and its agents – in this case the head of the Children's Aid Society of Prescott-Russell – from using their 'public' offices to 'proselytize' Catholic individuals. The significance of this notorious case was perhaps best explained in *Le Droit*, whose editor castigated the Children's Aid Society for having 'superseded its power by tearing away children from Catholic families to place them in Protestant families' and for using the mendacious pretext of 'benevolence' to 'make themselves agents of Protestantism.'[107]

In the *Bigras* case Scott had resorted to legal means to defend the right of fathers to determine the faith of their children. But this case was somewhat unusual, in that it involved an intrafamilial religious dispute. The more common pattern involved a Catholic woman married to a Protestant man, and Scott set out to defend marriage agreements that established the mother's right to determine the religious education of the children. Another typical case that came before Scott was that of a young woman who had left her foundling at a Catholic convent. Because it was not an orphanage, the Catholic sisters asked the local police to intercede and place the baby in a proper Catholic orphanage. The policemen, perhaps because they were tired and Protestant, were reluctant to travel across Ottawa to the Catholic Orphanage, and so they left the foundling at the Salvation Army Maternity Hospital, right across the street from the convent. (Cases similar to this were very common, and Scott would defend the legal right of the child to be brought up in the religion of the mother, should she be unmarried.) As Scott politely informed Kelso, when the mother left her baby at the convent, this had to be interpreted as 'a clear indication of the intention of the mother' that her child be raised as a Catholic. As he so often did, Kelso prevaricated, and the case ended up in court. Cases of desertion, unmarried motherhood, and widowhood involving the intermarriage of Protestants and Catholics came before the courts quite frequently, and as a result most of Scott's legal defences were on behalf of Catholic women. One can conclude from all this that while the emphasis on motherhood and maternalism was just as prevalent within Catholicism as in the Protestant faith, because of the emphasis on the Virgin Mary and because of the power of female-centred parish organizations,[108] Catholic laypeople were instrumental in heightening the maternalist tenor of family welfare policies in Ontario, largely as a result of the decisions they won in court. Largely to defend the Catholic faith, Scott campaigned to have clause 28 of the Child Protection Act amended in favour of maternal religious rights. Scott also worked hard to counteract the impression among Catholic 'labouring people' that the children's aid societies were merely 'Child Snatchers,'[109] and to restore their faith in the state welfare machinery to protect Catholic children. In 1917, Scott proposed that the Ontario child welfare bureaucracy recognize marriage agreements 'which state that the child will be brought up in the faith of the mother.'[110]

From the perspective of Catholics, the principle of paternal rights clearly favoured Protestantism. In a letter to Premier Drury's Catholic representative in the cabinet, Manning Doherty, Scott underscored this connection between the male-centred family and Protestantism: 'If a child is being brought up a Catholic but has a Protestant father there is never any hesitation in placing the child before the Court and having it committed to the Society as a Protestant child, but if a child is being brought up Protestant but owing to the fact that the father was a Catholic it would have to be committed as a Catholic child if committed to the Society means are taken of dealing with it without its being brought before the Courts at all and in that way it is heads I win tails you lose.'[111]

As the cornerstone of his campaign to end the Protestant state's persistent manipulation of fathers' rights, Scott set out to entirely disenfranchise fathers in terms of religious rights within the family. If the rights of Catholics were to be upheld, the authority of fathers would have to be completely eroded, because even when the mother was unmarried, and according to the law the illegitimate children were automatically assigned the religion of the mother, Protestants like juvenile court judge Boyd often went to great lengths to dredge up the natural father, not for the purpose of making him financially liable to support the family, but to transform his progeny into Protestants. In 1918, Boyd flagrantly transgressed the law by giving the child of a Greek Catholic mother to Protestant authorities, on the spurious grounds that she had been made pregnant by an Eastern Orthodox man. This case more than any other confirmed the need to amend the clause relating to the religious authority of fathers over their children. For as T. Louis Monahan informed Scott, this case had provoked so much animosity toward the Protestant-dominated court system that it inspired the Catholic hierarchy to begin vigorously defending the religious rights of both mothers and children.[112]

To further bolster the rights of mothers – especially those who had been deserted or widowed, or who had illegitimate offspring – Scott stressed that the religious convictions of the children must not be interfered with. The view of the Catholic Church was that children's rights were synonymous with maternal family authority. By 1917, Catholic laymen like Scott, who was at the forefront of child welfare activities and thus well placed to witness the effects of state legislation on interfaith marriages, were becoming increasingly anxious about how the Catholic Church was losing its power to ensure the religious dominance of women in Catholic families through the use of marriage contracts. This problem was rendered more acute in those abnormal situations in which the male breadwinner had either died or deserted; for in such cases the rights of women were entirely expunged. Scott well knew that militant Protestants had for decades held up patriarchal authority as the central bastion of a distinctly Protestant conception of the family order, and that they would resist any overt

championing of mother's rights by the Catholic Church.[113] So he skilfully compromised, extolling the rights of children to determine their
own religious identification. Scott recognized that this ideal of children's religious independence was only a piece of sophistry whose real
intent was to uphold the pre-eminent religious role of women, especially in Catholic families. For as he stated in his 31 October 1917 memorandum, 'where one parent is dead or deserted, and where it is not
shown that such child's wishes should prevail, the surviving and sustaining parent should be consulted.'[114]

In the first decades of the twentieth century, the ideology of maternalism was forged in the crucible of religious controversy. Faced with the
ongoing task of expanding the authority of the church, Protestant
reformers under the impetus of social Christianity actively transformed gender relations within the family. This redefinition of the
paternal family was largely a Protestant endeavour. The blurring of the
boundaries between the public and the private, which was brought
about by the State's increasing intervention into family relationships,
was an immediate consequence of the Protestant missionary zeal to
proselytize and make new converts. After 1890 the family came to be
seen as the symbolic junction between the public interest and private
welfare. Hence, in 1896 *The Report upon the Sweating System in Canada*
concluded: 'Whatever objections may be properly urged against interference of this nature in the case of families working in their own
homes, none can, I think, be validly advanced on the ground of the
improper sanctity of the home, against subjecting to inspection and
regulation ... the privacy which makes the home sacred has been sur-
rendered.' Parents no longer had an 'indisputable right' over their offspring now that the family had become so 'sacred to society' and so
crucial to the moral and material progress of the nation.[115]

   In the same vein, the response to state incursions into the family
took shape within a religious idiom. Militant Protestants tend to force
their values on family welfare policies. In reaction, ordinary Catholic
parents and their religious leaders resorted to the courts to defend the
right of parents to control religion within the 'private' family. Catholics
were successful in asserting traditional parental authority against the
modernizing initiatives of state welfare reformers. They also significantly reworked the contours of public discourse about the family, and
shifted the axis of gender relations within the domestic sphere away
from legalistic patriarchal authority and toward the moral dominance

of mothers. The intertwined concepts of the mother-centred family and state maternalism soon extended their reach far beyond the immediate purview of religious institutions. After the First World War they became interwoven with the broader, nationalist concerns of industrial efficiency and social citizenship. However much maternalism informed these more secular ends, government welfare policies in the decades leading up to the Second World War continued to be animated by explicitly Protestant attitudes toward both gender and the family.

2

'While the Breadwinners Are at War': Gender and Social Policy, 1914–1918

Before enlisting he was assured that his mother and little sister of twelve would be attended to and protected by the Government for whose country he has gone to fight and die for if needs be ... His mother is sacrificing her boy, her comfort, her support ... Her boy is living up to his bargain ... am I to think this lad will be discouraged by learning the news that his country did not live up to the agreement ... they made with him.

J.J. Kerr on Pte W.C. Croft, Canadian Reserve Cyclists, 27 March 1917[1]

The First World War was one of the pivotal events of modern history. It destroyed the aristocratic monarchies of Europe, dramatically shifted alignments within the world economy, unleashed new, more radical political ideologies, and for five years severely dislocated traditional social patterns in the participating nations. Although far from the front lines in geographic terms, Canadian society was profoundly shaken by the war, and nowhere was this more true than within families. As one commentator observed, the 'household' was the focal point of all the social dislocation arising from the war.[2] Especially disruptive of the social order was the enlistment of soldiers: the departure of so many men from the domestic sphere destroyed vast networks of social relationships. These men, 'the humus and root-holds of countless family groups,'[3] were torn loose from their communities as the war began. Large numbers of workers moved to the cities to avail themselves of the larger pay packets offered by the munitions factories; and with only 30 per cent of the first contingent of soldiers made up of Canadian-born recruits, countless soldiers' wives returned to England

and Scotland to rejoin their blood relations. Moreover, thousands of women experienced severe dislocation as they followed their husbands to their training camps; they also faced social and economic deprivation as the high wages of skilled workers were replaced by the paltry wages of the active soldier. On top of all that, migration from the countryside was accelerated by the war as higher rates of welfare support drew hundreds of dislocated soldier families into the cities and larger towns.[4]

As Paul Kellogg concluded, the war represented a vast landscape of social upheaval and cultural dissolution, in which the lack of moral restraint and loss of identity experienced by the solitary soldier on the military front was paralleled by the 'unravelling fabric of family life at home.' That being so, the redemption of both national and family unity lay with the social policies of the Canadian Patriotic Fund (CPF), which was established to minister to the economic and social needs of the wives and children of the soldiers of the Canadian Expeditionary Force.[5] This chapter examines how the war dissolved traditional family relationships, and how both government and private social welfare organizations attempted to stabilize the family. More particularly, it focuses on a historical topic that has barely been researched – how working-class families experienced the war.

For all the enormity of the human tragedy on the battlefield, and even though a majority of Canadian working-class wives and mothers suffered great economic and psychological hardships arising from the loss of the male breadwinner, gender relations within both the family and the workplace remained remarkably undisturbed by the national experience of going to war. However, the war did have a decisive impact on social policy. The magnitude of the conflict demanded the creation, for the first time in Canada, of a national strategy of family welfare. Yet governments were only reluctantly drawn into the problem of family welfare; indeed, the military authorities did little to intercede in order to reinforce the status of the male breadwinner. Rather, the agitation for military policies that would maintain soldiers' families – either through a system of compulsory assignment of pay to the soldiers' wives or through the creation of supplementary assistance through semiprivate organizations such as the CPF – came from the Canadian working class. The reluctance of working-class men to enlist, unless they had assurances from the Canadian military that their families would be provided for in their absence, was the main impetus for government intervention in the private domestic sphere.

The Dominion government finally bowed to working-class wives' demands for compulsory assigned pay; but the program it finally instituted was consciously designed so as not to infringe on the sanctity of prewar wage contracts, and as such was meant to maintain only the male breadwinner and one dependant, usually the wife.[6] In other words, the standard living wage, from the point of view of government authorities, was not intended to fully address families' needs. The way the government shored up the ability of breadwinners to maintain their families had the effect of restraining wages and thus complemented the wartime policy of the dilution of labour. At one level, the policy of compulsory assignment of pay helped stabilize working-class family life, which was the central purpose of wartime social policy; at another level, this policy severley hobbled the labour movement. The Dominion's half-hearted defence of the male breadwinner norm may have succeeded in its aim of upholding soldier morale, but it also left in abeyance the problem of family poverty.

It was the growing recognition among social reformers like Herbert Ames and Helen Reid in Montreal, that the exigencies of war would destroy the viability of the Canadian family, that propelled the involvement of the CPF. The leaders of this organization were animated largely by the maternalist-centred ideal of the family, which held that the wellspring of society was the spiritual and affectional qualities imparted by the mother within the domestic sphere. This concern with child rearing would increase throughout the war as fears grew that Canada's population would be decimated – a fear based in large part on imperial and national economic interests, and that focused attention sharply on reproduction within the family. These looming questions about domestic stability generated an alternative strategy for maintaining the breadwinner norm that served to reinforce government policies regarding assignment of pay. In essence, by paying women for their mothering skills, and for their national service in keeping the family inviolate during a time of national crisis, the CPF established the principle of family allowances, which provided assistance on the basis of the number of children.

During the Second World War, soldier's wives would be paid not for mothering but rather on the basis of their marital relationship.[7] In contrast, during the First World War unmarried mothers and common law wives with children were granted liberal assistance from the CPF, although admittedly they had to demonstrate need. In sum, during the First World War it was motherhood rather than the rights of the male citizenry that was held to be the pre-eminent qualification for welfare entitlement. This is illustrated by the fact that married women without children were discriminated against, and paid a benefit substantially less than that of their mothering sisters; and that a woman who married after her husband had enlisted was summarily disqualified from any public aid unless she had children.[8] Childless wives were compelled to seek paid employment in the workplace in order to supplement the male wage. These two welfare strategies – the government policy of compulsory assigned pay and the CPF's recognition of rights derived through motherhood – formed the twin poles between which the debate over public welfare would evolve from the First World War to the end of the Second World War.

For the duration of the war, this dual system of government and private assistance remained intact. But when the war ended and the soldiers returned, government welfare assistance ended abruptly, as did private philanthropic endeavours, because of the deeply held cultural convention that family security and self-sufficiency was still first and foremost the reponsibility of the male breadwinner. The resurgence of the breadwinner norm, which emphasized the personal responsibility of the male wage-earner to seek work and support his dependants, dictated the temporary and contingent nature of government welfare policy, and decidedly militated against the embryonic movement among organized labour and social reformers for a national system of unemployment insurance for men. Ironically, the war thus created an environment in which the desideratum of working-class culture – for the male to head the household – was reinforced, with the state becoming the surrogate for absent husbands and sons by caring for their dependants. From the perspective of government policymakers, the aim of welfare policy during the war was the temporary one of stimulating the recruitment of working-class volunteers, who out of concern for the welfare of their families were reluctant to enlist. In other words, these wartime policies began as reflections of and responses to working-class male attitudes to domesticity. By war's end, the alternative system of family allowances offered by the CPF and its maternalist ideology was in retreat. That the principle of children's allowances was only tenable in the absence of male breadwinners explains why a system of mothers' allowances for widows rather than family allowances became the linchpin of postwar government welfare strategy.

The problem raised by the mass exodus of male breadwinners brought the economic and gender relations of the Canadian family into sharp relief, and led, in 1918, to the first public policy attempts to make 'official' the family model of the male breadwinner with his dependent wife and children. Working-class mothers expected state assistance in return for consenting to allow their sons to perform their patriotic duty. However, Helen Reid, who supervised the female volunteer relief workers for the Montreal branch of the CPF, observed that the creation of a wartime family policy pointed out a conjunction of working-class and middle-class sensibilities regarding family life. The ideal of the male breadwinner cut across class lines and was rigorously upheld both by working-class husbands, wives, and mothers, and by middle-class social reformers. Wrote Reid in 1917: 'When a man goes to the front, we take it that he leaves his wife and family with us in trust. Anything we can do to assist the family to lead a normal life, anything we can contribute towards their physical, intellectual or moral welfare, in addition to granting them financial aid, we regard as activity within our legitimate field of service. Our efforts to help the soldier's wife are limited only by the extent of her willingness to accept our aid.'[9]

'Keep the Home Fires Burning'[10]

The CPF originated during the Boer War as a private organization to help the wives and children of volunteer recruits.[11] It was not until the First World War that it expanded into a large-scale national relief organization with semi-official status. Sir William Mulock, the former Postmaster General, was the chairman of its executive. Its non-partisan board included members of Parliament, such as Conservatives R.B. Bennett and C.A. Magrath, the prominent Ontario Conservative MPP W.F. Nickle, and prominent individuals such as William Lyon Mackenzie King and the Montreal financier William Dobell.[12] The observation by an American social worker, Paul Kellogg, that this was 'a revolutionary conception of family help'[13] was no mere truism. Its concept of encouraging national war service among both skilled and unskilled working people distinguished it from prewar systems of relief, which were viewed as mere charity to the idle and improvident. Spokesmen for the fund downplayed the relief aspects of its program, out of concern not to offend working-class ideals of independence and respectability; but they also frequently cautioned that the assistance the fund provided must not be perceived as a pension, or as a universal right given by the State. Indeed, they emphasized repeatedly both the temporary nature of the fund and the needs-based as opposed to rights-based character of aid it provided: 'It deals with a limited group of beneficiaries through a limited time, but with greater freedom to make its help fit the family than any existing government department.'[14]

Administrators of the fund regularly reminded respectable working-class wives that their system of relief was not a dole; nevertheless, it kept many families who had once existed on a skilled worker's wages at the level of bare subsistence – barely above the standard of living of unskilled labourers. The wife was allotted her own maintenance of $10.00 per month; her first child was allocated $7.50, the second $4.50, and all remaining children $3.00 per head. These rates were merely guidelines and varied greatly not only between cities but within smaller municipalities and rural townships. Because of the higher cost of living, western Canadian families were allowed up to $40.00 of family support per month, while Eastern Canadian cities faced a cap of $30.00.[15] In practice, however, most families received far less. In Prince Edward Island, even large families might only receive the munificent sum of $10.00 a month; in Nova Scotia they were offered on average $12.50; in Montreal and Toronto families were granted $16.00; and where the cost of living was higher, such as in Northern Ontario mining communities, Manitoba, and British Columbia, grants rose to $18.00 per month. Grants were the highest in Saskatchewan and Alberta, where both recruitments and CPF subscriptions were proportionately greater than in the rest of Canada.[16] In determining the degree of material aid to be dispensed to a soldier's dependants, the fund often took into account his prewar income level and class circumstances.[17] This only reinforced class demarcations. In other ways, however, the impact of the war transcended class boundaries. The income of working-class families was significantly disrupted by the war; but the Montreal Branch was also supporting nearly 500 officers' families by the end of 1916[18] – striking testimony that middle-class families were also seeing their standard of living drastically reduced. Class distinctions permeated the attitudes of the fund, and officers' families were granted on average almost double the benefits of working-class soldiers' families ($26.57).[19] By 1918 the living standards of the dependants of *all* soldiers, irrespective of rank or class, had fallen appreciably behind the escalating cost of living, and many women who had never considered working had been forced into the formidable public world of wage earning.

The CPF was regarded by Prime Minister Borden's government to be a indispensable component of the war effort, and was rapidly incorporated by Parliament. On the fifth day of the war session, a centralized national fund was established.[20] Because a vast number of the first contingent was made up of previously unemployed workers, thousands of families with limited savings were immediately thrown into penury either because husbands refused to assign an adequate proportion of their pay to their wives or because the military authorities were dilatory in allocating government assistance to families suddenly thrown into economic dependency. However, a more endemic problem faced even those families in which the breadwinner had been employed before the war; as a result of the meagre military pay of one dollar per day, the standard of living of thousands of skilled-working-class families fell to that of unskilled workers. It was the growing recognition of this threat to family stability that caused the fund's growth to mushroom soon after it was incorporated. By 6 November 1914, in Montreal alone there were 1,327 applicant families from the first contingent.[21] By 1915 this number had more than doubled; and while recruiting remained buoyant that year, the Montreal branch of the CPF was receiving up to four hundred calls a day from needy wives. By 1917, 10,301 families had applied in Montreal, divided almost equally between English- and French-speaking families; while Toronto regularly had triple the caseload of Montreal. In Montreal alone, many women would have shared the experience of Mrs Rickaby and her three young children, who until the fund interceded had been left with no food and only 'a little wood in the house,' because her husband had been out of work for six weeks prior to enlisting with the Victoria Rifles; or Mrs Livesay, whose husband's former employer, Gourock Ropeworks of Montreal, was locked in a dispute with the fund over who should support the family. As a result, Mrs Livesay was without any financial assistance for some months.[22] It was largely as a result of working-class soldiers' wives protesting that military funds were going to their husbands rather than to themselves, and lobbying vocally through their organization, the Soldiers Wives' League, that an expansion occurred in the responsibilities of both the government and the CPF.[23]

The First World War was also decisive in stimulating the growth of social work networks. By war's end, in Montreal alone there was a phalanx of no less than seven hundred volunteer women, both French and English, divided into twenty-five districts, who attended to the economic, legal, and spiritual needs of newly impoverished soldiers' families.[24] The exigencies of war also compelled thousands of middle-class women to leave the private domestic sphere to participate in the public realm of homefront patriotic service, as hundreds of suffrage associations and other women's groups rallied to the cause. The war forged a new relationship between the State and the Canadian working class as thousands of working-class wives were made beneficiaries of state/private assistance. More significantly, these women took a leading role in shaping wartime family policies, by founding a national organization of Soldiers' Wives Leagues, which lobbied the federal government to recognize the role of wives in meeting in the economic responsibilities of their male-breadwinner recruits.[25]

In August 1914 the CPF was a multipurpose organization. Prior to Borden's anouncement in October 1915 that henceforth the government would fully control and finance the military prosecution of the war,[26] it helped purchase machine guns and other military hardware; in several urban centres it also functioned as a general relief organization. In September 1914, Clarence Smith, the head of the Relief Committee of the Montreal branch, announced that his organization had already aided 500 families whose poverty was entirely unconnected with the war. Such double-purpose funds persisted for a few months and assisted families in which 'the bread-winner has not gone to the front, but who is out of work and in need through the indirect effects of war.'[27] This relief of the 'locally unemployed'[28] soon halted. In response to exhortations from potential working-class enlistees, middle-class recruiting agencies such as the Speaker's Patriotic League accepted that the scope of the fund must be drastically altered so as to be less of a dole-giving concern and more of a non-stigmatizing compensator for the performance of patriotic military service.[29] This change in policy came about when it became all too apparent that working-class recruits were reluctant to sign up out of fears for their families' economic well-being. The poignant appeal of Pte M.C. Lewis to Prime Minister Borden in 1916 captured well the fears that skilled workers had for the dependants they were leaving unattended while they fought in Britain or France. In exchange for war service, Lewis asked the government to preserve his prewar class status as well as his role as head of a family: 'I was on the G.T. Rly. and made good wages. My wife and children had all the comforts that could be given them and we both worked hard to get our home together. I am no beggar sir and all I ask for, is that my wife and children are looked after while I am away and my house and bit of land protected.'[30]

Working-class attitudes toward the family, characterized by the ideal of a male breadwinner and dependent wife and children, directly shaped this transformation of the goals of the CPF. Sir Herbert Ames, the fund's honorary secretary, observed on 12 August 1914 that at all the armouries men were 'wobbling between the call of duty and the closer ties of family relationships.' In order to keep enlistment levels flowing, the CPF's decision makers decided to declare publicly that their organization would meet the demands being made by working-class heads of families: 'They need have no fear for their families.' The fund, they insisted, would act as a surrogate for the absent soldiers, fathers, and sons by attending to the financial, psychological, and legal needs of their dependants.[31]

The transformation of the CPF in the early months of the war into an organization whose primary purpose was to stimulate recruitment was largely a response to the sensibilities of working-class breadwinners. Having noted the overwhelming concern that working-class recruits had for the welfare of their wives, children, and mothers, middle-class propagandists honed in on the working-class family as the key metaphor of recruitment. What began as largely a working-class male concern – namely, the preservation during wartime service of their status as 'the father and head of family'[32] was soon transformed into a middle-class tool of war. To palliate the fears of breadwinners, recruiters engineered public spectacles at which soldiers on furlough thanked the fund for temporarily assuming their role as head of family while they were doing their patriotic duty. On one skilfully dramatized occasion, a soldier with half of his face shot off announced to the gathered crowd: 'All I've come for is to thank the ladies for the fine way they treated my wife and children when I was away at the front. I wouldn't have missed the fighting for all the world, and it was certainly fine to come home and find the family had been so well cared for.'[33]

The CPF was not established out of any inherent concern among middle-class military leaders to regularize traditional gender relations within the Canadian family; the military concerned itself with social policies only insofar as these coincided with its overriding goal, which was to maximize enlistment. After 1915 the efforts of the fund were firmly wedded to military exigencies, largely because recruitment had become uneven, and because there was no centralized control and registration of manpower.[34] From that time on, all policy changes within the CPF were motivated less by concern for soldiers' families than for the needs of the military. For example, no dependants were allowed access to the fund for reasons of mere unemployment; when a bread-winner was simply on home duty or was in training before actually seeing service on the front, his family was denied access to the fund. In the situation where a man had deserted during training and then re-enlisted, his family received aid only after he had arrived at the front. This rule was reversed only in 1917, when policymakers wanted to encourage men previously declared medically unfit to re-enlist. A woman who married her husband after he enlisted was denied access to benefits – a policy overturned in 1918, after recruitment slumped severely. Assistance was granted to wives wishing to return to England only if their husbands were in combatant roles. For similar reasons, dependants of those recruited for the Forestry and Engineering corps were exempt from the fund.[35]

Although it was not the main concern of the CPF and the Militia Department to preserve traditional domestic relations during wartime, their relief policies had an enormous impact on Canadian families. Susan Pedersen has argued that the wartime policies followed in Brit-ain did little to challenge traditional family structure, and that welfare practices established there between 1914 and 1918 were peculiarly gender-based. This was especially so with regard to how the State implemented its military separation allowances; this universal, rights-based program was intended to replace the male wage directly on behalf of the dependent wife. Pedersen has identified this policy as central to the creation of the administrative logic that from that time on would profoundly affect British welfare policies.[36] Observations such as those of Paul Kellogg, the American social worker and charity reformer, reveal a similar conception of the family as upheld by British social policy. As he noted in his 1917 pamphlet *The Patriotic Fund of Canada*: 'In all cases the theory of the fund has been neither to see women bearing the double responsibilities of mother and father, forced to go out and earn a living while the man fights overseas; nor on the other hand to see the grant to go as a surplus to women who, from choice or fortune, gain an ample income elsewhere.'[37]

Kellogg here makes it clear how the policy after 1918 was strongly influenced by marital relationships. But he is also obscuring the true 'family' logic that animated earlier fund activities. A more accurate account of the logic underlying fund policies was given by Sir Herbert Ames, who in his 1917 article '"Fight or Pay": Canada's Solution,' wrote that the fund was intended 'to bridge the gap between bare subsistence and decent living. It takes over the family when the soldier enlists and cares for it until he returns.'[38] By *family*, Ames was referring not simply to husbands and their immediate dependants, namely, their wives; rather, the CPF included in its conception of 'dependant' all manner of relations, such as children, mothers, and sisters; it even offered entitlements to male relations of soldiers, namely, fathers if they were elderly and incapacitated.[39] Admittedly, there was a pecking order of rights, insofar as mothers of soldiers and unmarried wives had to document their financial reliance on the enlisted man.[40] Moreover, decisions about grants to deserted wives were at the discretion of local committees.[41] As a further incentive to enlistment, the fund also provided welfare benefits to common law wives, deserted mothers, and separated wives, if they had a court order.[42] In this regard, Canadian wartime family policy bore a greater resemblance to the French model of family welfare, which, as Pedersen has also shown, included all family members. Again as with the French example, Canadian welfare strategies greatly emphasized the care of children and so – if we follow Pedersen's logic – were much less gender driven than those of Britain. For example, in Canada, when the regulations of the fund denied assistance to those wives whom it regarded as 'immoral,' or in situations where the wife had been deserted and was otherwise ineligible to claim fund support, administrators were often more than willing to thwart official guidelines in order to support the children,[43] with what they often referred to as 'family allowances.'[44] The CPF interpreted care for families to mean care for the *children*, as was made clear in its 1915 report, which stated that those who stayed at home 'must work for the welfare of the families of the brave men who have placed their bodies between us and the German bullets! (We must work for the welfare of their children who will be our future citizens and soldiers!).'[45]

In September 1914, following the lead of the British government, the Canadian government instituted a separation allowance, at a flat rate of $20.00 per soldier's family, to be paid directly to the wife each month.[46] This was seen as a replacement for the male breadwinner's lost wages, as evident in the fear expressed by Sir Herbert Ames that such government intercession into both the marketplace and the family would all too easily release absent husbands from 'the moral and legal obligation'[47] to support their dependants. In another context, Philip Morris, the national administrator of the CPF, specifically related the level of assistance of both the fund and separation allowances to the soldier's wage, and viewed them as monetary replacements when the soldier was on active service and was removed from his 'customary field of work.'[48] Although the separation allowance was paid directly to the wife, it was clear that it represented the government's recognition of the soldier's right to a family wage. Thus, when the fund insisted that its primary function was to assume the 'responsibilities'[49] of the men at the front, this was interpreted as meaning that separation allowances were a direct replacement for lost wages and were intended to preserve the status of skilled workers: 'If we are to ask the Canadian-born artisan, in receipt of good wages, to enlist, we cannot expect him to leave his wife with only above subsistence for herself and children.'[50]

The introduction of separation allowances was not without controversy. In Britain a broad-ranging system of government-administered social welfare programs had existed since 1911; in contrast, Canadian government leaders were reluctant to introduce any measures that would permanently expand the scope and bureaucracy of the federal state. Administrators deftly attempted to preserve the limited contours of the 'Victorian' state[51] and to shift the burden of responsibility in all areas beyond the immediate purview of military operations into the hands of local governments or private bodies. When the separation allowances were introduced in September 1914, the government instructed that the $20.00 be deducted from the amount that employers were continuing to pay their absent male employees; by thus having the state directly replace these wages, it hoped to induce private businessmen to continue paying those employees who had enlisted in the belief that prewar wage controls would be honoured. It soon became apparent that businesses were continually delinquent in sending out pay lists of these men; and as a result the whole strategy of the federal government to preserve private initiative in wartime failed. In fact, so effectively did government separation allowances, in combination with the CPF's initiatives, replace the wages of absent male breadwinners, that businesses withdrew their portion of wages from soldiers' families. Government officials (and those of the CPF) were in constant conflict over who was primarily responsible for upholding the standard of living of Canadian skilled workers – the federal government, business, or the family itself. Such conflicts arose repeatedly during the first years of the war; private business interests consistently withdrew, forcing the federal government and its philanthropic partners to step into the breach.[52]

As the war dragged on, the economic position of working-class families of soldiers grew worse, especially after 1917, when inflation began to rise rapidly. Now organized labour began pressing the government to extend separation allowances, so that they might be granted not only to husbands to support their wives, but also to mothers of soldiers and to the families of munitions workers in Britain; these people, they argued, were serving the Empire with as much vigour as the common soldier at the front.[53] The federal government agreed to make the separation allowances available to dependants besides the wife, but this hardly detracted from its commitment to the ideal of the breadwinning husband with a dependent wife. The rights of mothers continued to be severely circumscribed. Unlike those of soldiers' wives, their claims were not deemed a universal right but were adjudicated according to need.[54]

Separation allowances did not ineluctably define family and gender relations in Canada between 1914 and 1918. This must be understood in the context of how the boundaries between private and public welfare shifted during the war. In Britain, organized labour had a direct voice in formulating government war policies; and Labour members of Parliament and cabinet ministers, who bridled at any hint of charity, successfully campaigned to have the government bureaucracy take over the administration of all family welfare.[55] In contrast, Canada's wartime welfare policies remained under the control of private agencies. Separation allowances and assigned pay were managed by the CPF, and were administered according to the needs-based ideology of this private organization, and thus were not defined as a universal right. It was the policies of the fund, not those of the State, that left their mark on Canadian social policy after the war.

As the war progressed, private citizens, labour unions, and local governments increased their pressure on the federal government to assume direct control of such a massive national welfare system. Sir Herbert Ames and other leaders of the fund fended off such government appropriation of their organization, believing while they did that their network of 'visitors' and their principles of economic assistance better served the needs of individual families. The CPF's rhetoric often underscored that its pledge was with the male breadwinner; but their ideology of the family was at odds with the narrow emphasis that state separation allowances placed on the citizenship rights of the individual male soldier. In fact, the fund's policymakers, including Sir Herbert Ames, were the original advocates of a family allowance–type system, insofar as they recognized that the male wage – albeit during wartime in the form of assigned pay and separation allowances – was inadequate to support numerous offspring. As Ames explained: 'Since pay and separation allowance depended solely on rank, the condition and needs of the home were, from a military point of view, a matter of secondary importance.'[56]

The fund's emphasis on family need might be interpreted as merely a continuation of earlier attitudes toward charity for the poor; even so, it formed the kernel of a much more radical conception of redistributing national income on the basis of family size. Although fund workers – most of whom were female – made much of the fact that separation allowances were paid directly to the wife, they nevertheless were the severest critics of the allowances. Having witnessed in their daily investigations of soldiers' families the severe distress experienced by large families, they became the strongest advocates for new strategies for shoring up and supplementing the traditional male family wage. In fact, it was the CPF that formulated new conceptions of wage earning by distinguishing between the rights of single and married wage earners. The progressive nature of the fund's work was emphasized by Paul Kellogg, who denigrated separation allowances as old-fashioned because they failed to distinguish between single and married men, and also signally ignored the fact that married men were making a greater 'patriotic' contribution to Canada by raising large families. As more and more men died at the front, this pronatalist rhetoric on the homefront became increasingly voluble till it formed the ideological underpinning of family allowances. As Kellogg stated in his popular 1917 pamphlet: '[The Patriotic Fund] must break away from the cast iron army regulations which treated the childless wife of a young recruit on the same footing as the family next door with half a dozen children to clothe and house, to feed and send to school.'[57] It was this emphasis on child-rearing and large families, and not the emphasis on the individual male breadwinner represented by the policy of separation allowances, that became one of the animating principles behind the postwar military conception of family welfare rights.[58]

Leaders of the CPF eschewed state incursions for another reason: in their view, community solidarity was best enhanced through spontaneous voluntary effort.[59] The fund encouraged voluntary subscriptions through rallies, propaganda in the form of leaflets, and a monthly bulletin. The purpose of all of these was to persuade ordinary Canadians that the war was a classless crusade and that patriotism was the cement of social unity. Headlines such as 'Morgan Gives Twenty Thousand; and Scrub Woman One Day's Pay'[60] were meant to demonstrate how the war drew together the richest and poorest in Canadian society. In addition, the fund sent out countless lists of contributors, which included large industries such as the Canada Cement Company, the Canadian Pacific, Canadian National, and Canadian Grand Trunk Railways, the Christie-Brown Company, and Sun Life Insurance, as well as ordinary Canadians such as the girls from Young's Business College, the stenographers from the Royal Bank, individual boy scouts, various Doukhobors and Mennonites, bridge-playing Montreal lady fundraisers, and patriotic hockey players from Winnipeg. Especially poignant was the contribution which came from a lone Inuit from Herschel Island in the Northwest Territories, and another from a munificent Cree Indian from File Hills Agency, Saskatchewan, who gave $300.[61]

Such propaganda belied the fact that during wartime, state and private machinery grew much more coercive. For example, the deputy minister of Indian Affairs, Duncan Campbell Scott, purloined part of the treaty money for the fund; many municipalities and later provincial governments taxed residents as voluntary subscriptions fell behind after 1916; and hundreds of businesses literally garnisheed the wages of workers.[62] The fund claimed that piece workers in Vancouver had given up 5 per cent of their earnings for the families of soldiers; it did not mention that most of the workers did not do so as a matter of choice. Certainly in some factories, like Canada Express, workers voluntarily created their own machinery for raising contributions, out of their own commitment to helping families 'during the absence of their breadwinners.' And in some factories, in Hamilton and Brantford for example, the workers established their own patriotic organizations, through which male workers volunteered to help the wives of their comrades.[63]

After the first few years of the war it became commonplace in most industries to deduct one day's pay a month from the wages of workers. In due course this produced extreme resentment among Canadian workers and a backlash against the CPF. In The Pas, Manitoba, lumber workers threatened to go on strike to protest such 'patriotic' pay deductions,[64] and in British Columbia, where such deductions were most common, labour unions campaigned hard to have the federal government raise funds for family welfare through general taxation. As one private and confidential memorandum from the fund observed in 1917: 'The situation is rendered more difficult by the attitude of organized labour throughout British Columbia which has taken the position that stoppages of pay shall not hereafter be allowed.'[65]

After 1916, mass meetings of organized labour were held with ever greater frequency in major centres such as Edmonton and Toronto.[66] Animosity against the private management of working-class family needs became widespread among the public, as farmers, businessmen, mayors of small municipalities, and even provincial government leaders – including Premier Lomer Gouin of Quebec – pressured the federal government to intervene in a policy issue that they saw as central to the prosecution of the war. In practical terms, many labour organizations objected to voluntary subscriptions on the grounds that they placed far too great a burden on the working classes. However, the loud calls for the state to assume greater responsibilities also represented a broad ideological transformation – one brought about specifically by the war,[67] and especially by conscription. As one working-class activist observed: 'The services of every man in time of War belong to the State.'[68] If it was the duty of the State to compel men to fight, then, it was popularly reasoned, it was in turn 'the duty of the State to make full and ample provision for the widows, orphans and dependents' of the soldier, rather than making them 'dependent on charity.'[69]

When this popularly held belief in the reciprocity between the duties of the Canadian people and the obligations of the State was thought to be traduced, there were irate denunciations. Thus, W.A. Janes slandered Borden as a 'Prussian Pimp' for deploying the coercive power of government by passing conscription, without recognizing his government's 'sacred Duty' to the dependants of those same soldiers as a right of citizenship.[70] Ordinary Canadians were willing to accept the voluntary nature of the CPF as long as enlistment was also considered a voluntary matter. Rankled by the scrutiny into working-class family life that accompanied the needs-based ideology of the fund, with its vestigial stigma of charity, working-class men and women campaigned vociferously to have wartime welfare policies made a matter of universal right. F.M. Kidd informed Borden in 1916 that however much fund representatives insisted that their financial aid was a payment for patriotic effort or a substitute for male wages, 'the recipient of a share of that fund will, upon opening the package, no matter how splendid the covering, Charity inside every time.'[71]

Despite the protests of organized labour and calls by a broad spectrum of Canadians for greater state intervention into the private lives of soldiers' dependants, the federal government did not accede to their demands. Certainly in practical terms the exigencies of modern warfare necessitated greater federal government activity; nevertheless, the

First World War did little to change the ideological outlook of government officials, who throughout the conflict firmly adhered to prewar conceptions of limited state growth. At the same time, it was directly out of this concern for curtailing the growth of government that the military authorities and Dominion politicians responded positively to the urgings of working-class soldiers' wives that the state pass a law compelling their often recalcitrant husbands to assign a portion of their pay; after all, this effectively shifted responsibility for family welfare back onto the shoulders of the male breadwinner, and thus back into the private sphere. Many working-class males were reluctant to enlist because of their concern for the welfare of the wives and children. But there was another side to this particular coin: throughout the war, the same complaint was heard over and over – namely, that soldiers were persistently delinquent in sending a portion of their $1.10-a-day pay to their wives. An observation made by T.W. Crothers, the minister of labour, regarding Canadian munitions workers in Britain reflected a problem that was widespread among men serving in all branches of the war effort: 'There have been a good many cases where the men have substantially abandoned their families here, sending no money for their support whatever. There appears to have been considerable very poor stuff amongst the men who went over.'[72] This problem was particularly rampant in the forestry and technical units, where enlistees had been gathered from poor stuff indeed, the majority being re-enlisted deserters.[73]

By 1917, government officials were becoming increasingly concerned about the seemingly exponential growth in the relief obligations of the CPF and the real possibility that after the war unemployment, disability, and thus family poverty might be so extensive as to require a permanent state bureaucracy. In this climate, male policymakers such as Crothers suddenly became sensitive to the tribulations of working-class soldiers' wives. However, even after constant complaints and pressure from the Soldiers' Wives Leagues (the mutual protection leagues founded by working-class women),[74] the male-dominated leadership of both the CPF and the military did everything to avoid interfering in what they considered at the time a mere private conflict between husband and wife. Except when there were war considerations, government and welfare officials had no intrinsic interest in ensuring that a male breadwinner supported his family. Working-class women, however, believed that within the contract of marriage, the primary responsibility of the male head of the family was to provide economic support. While many women might endure physical abuse without considering ending their marriages, women such as Mrs Eva Murray of Clarendon, Ontario, believed that her husband's failure to support her and her six children economically was certainly grounds for divorce.[75]

Both middle-class female visitors and working-class women well understood the caustic comment of Helen Reid, the convener of visitors for the Montreal branch of the CPF, that many men would rather fight Germans or re-enlist than 'face the struggle of supporting his family; many a man would rather face the German fire than the great responsibility of his family's welfare under the abnormal conditions existing.'[76] At every meeting in Ottawa of the fund's executive, the issue of assigned pay and the need for government intervention in this area was raised; and at every meeting, politicians backed away from interfering with soldiers' working pay. As early as 14 August 1914, some committee members were suggesting that the government ought to make a uniform ruling regarding assigned pay, with the goal of ensuring that the wife would receive a monthly cheque. But by 24 August of that year, only half the committee members were in agreement on this, and most of those objected to the wife handling her husband's pay packet, and voted merely to have it placed in trust. At a meeting of the Montreal branch, Clarence Smith, the director of relief, expressed his belief that wives could not act responsibly with either governments or their husbands, so 'it was suggested by Mr. Reford that our Committee withdraw assistance from the Patriot Fund unless the family agrees to allow an officer of the Fund to act as Trustee.'[77] When Sir John Gibson again proposed on 13 October 1914 that 50 per cent of each soldier's pay be sent directly to the wife, discussion was deferred; on 11 November, A.E. Kemp, a cabinet minister, and T.C. Casgrain, an MP from Quebec, squelched discussion and refused to offer an opinion from the government; and as late as December 1914, government members would only agree to 'urge' reluctant breadwinners to assign their pay to their dependants, with the caution that this must be done on a voluntary basis, 'if they so desire.' So fearful were government officials about interfering with the prerogatives of male breadwinners to distribute their own wages as they saw fit, that a full year later committee members were still unmoved by the pleas of soldiers' wives, and were still seeking legal loopholes by referring to the Minister of Justice the issue of 'compel[ling] soldiers to assign pay.'[78]

By the beginning of 1916, official sanction had been granted for the principle of compulsion with respect to assigned pay. This commitment clearly emanated from the desire of the government to deliver more funds into the hands of wives, who miraculously were now deemed responsible administrators of family finances. From 1916 onwards, the government's social policy was dictated by postwar concerns. It was expected that soldiers' wives would be able to put aside sufficient savings to offset the need for government assistance during the immediate period of demobilization, when high unemployment among returned soldiers was expected.

At the very moment when the government was sanctioning the principle of compulsory assigned pay, a decisive shift took place in government policy. The government, by making assigned pay uniform within the military, seemed to be becoming more interventionist with regard to gender issues in Canadian families. In actual fact, this period marked the *limit* of state expansion. Henceforth, policies that promoted savings among soldiers' families and that compelled older children and other competent dependants to undertake waged work, together with the new willingness of the CPF to contribute to the life insurance plans of soldiers, all conspired to preserve the well-circumscribed limits of the prewar Canadian state. After May 1915, once assigned pay was made compulsory, every local committee of the fund was instructed to educate women on the value of thrift and on how to open savings accounts, so that following the temporary and aberrant upheaval of war 'a soldier's family may be independent.'[79] Interestingly, the pamphlet 'Open a Bank Account,' issued to women on 1 April 1915 as 'moral suasion,' placed the onus for the welfare of the returned soldier's family squarely on the wife, who was expected to set aside, from her meagre allowances, funds that to all intents and purposes were meant to serve as a form of unemployment insurance. If there was going to be an active role for governments in postwar social policy, it was not going to focus directly on dependants; rather, it was going to merely indirectly sustain the family, by focusing on returning soldiers and their search for work.[80]

'If they used the wives a little better'[81]

As 'Before You Go,' a pamphlet distributed to every soldier explaining how to apply for family allowances and assign his pay, made demonstrably clear, a serviceman's application for separation allowance and assistance from the CPF entailed 'a species of contractual understanding' between the male head of the family and the State.[82] Philip Morris, the head of the CPF, pointed out that if there also existed a contract with the soldier's wife, her claim to assistance depended entirely on her husband's capacity as a serving soldier. In this way, male citizenship rights were privileged; even so, the immediate impact of such wartime family welfare strategies was felt by women – the wives, the mothers, and less frequently, the sisters of soldiers – and it was they who forged a new relationship with the state and with semipublic bodies such as the CPF. Although working-class women fully endorsed the concept of welfare aid based upon the husband's or son's service, they also believed that they were contributing to the allied victory by sacrificing their men to the war effort and were advancing national progress by raising their children and preserving family life. As a consequence, by war's end working-class women believed that as patriotic women they had a separate but equal claim on the state. While continuing to protest against the niggardliness of wartime family assistance, they also became outright champions for the direct entitlement of women to government aid and protection. Such an attitude among working-class women had the potential to powerfully reshape welfare policies, as was recognized by the CPF's leaders, who constantly warned local branches against giving way to women's demands for 'an unnecessary measure of generosity.' Their fear was that female dependants might be too quick to perceive that the 'act of enlistment' on the part of male breadwinners engendered 'automatically a claim on the Fund.'[83] This would amount to a separate vested right for women.

A central historical problem for scholars of the First World War has revolved around the extent to which the war affected both working-class standards of living and its role in either reinforcing or reordering class relations. While these issues have preoccupied historians in Britain, there have been few similar inquiries in the Canadian historiography of military conflict.[84] In Britain, the historian Arthur Marwick has argued that the war eroded class barriers; however, Bernard Waites has challenged this view, claiming that the enforced contact between the classes brought about by government welfare policies, together with spiralling inflation, actually sharpened social tensions and class dichotomy.[85] By war's end, middle-class observers in Canada believed that the patriotic effort had been a great social leveller and that the war 'as nothing else in human history has broken down the wall of partition between the classes.'[86] But such optimistic assessments of the war belied the fact that wartime social policy had the preservation of class boundaries as its very basis. If, as fund officers themselves conceded, public assistance was often parsimonious, their attitude did not flow from any concern with lesser eligibility – the fear that recipients would be made unwilling to work, for during the war the claims made on the State bore no relation to male unemployment. Rather, the philosophy of policymakers was unashamedly class-based: 'There is no desire to treat soldiers' families niggardly. On the other hand, it is most important, from every point of view, that their incomes should not be unreasonably in excess of their needs, or more than their men will be able to earn for them when they return.'[87]

The few CPF family case files that have survived from Frontenac County, Ontario, provide a small window for answering the question of whether working-class families experienced an improvement in their social circumstances as a result of the war. Because its mission was to aid impoverished families, the fund was one of the first large-scale organizations to study unemployment patterns in Canada. Judging from the statistics from the Montreal branch, it is clear that a substantial number of families would have benefited immediately as their male breadwinners enlisted. In the first contingent of 5,014 who signed up, a striking 1,874 – 37 per cent of all volunteers – had been unemployed. The following year, as a result of the severe economic dislocations caused by the transformation to a war economy, unemployment had risen among the second contingent: 1,425 out of 3,445, or 41 per cent, had neither a job nor adequate savings with which to support their familial dependants.[88] And even those soldiers who did have work would, like thousands of Canadian male workers, have experienced income instability as a result of high levels of seasonal unemployment. In addition, as Bettina Bradbury has demonstrated, many skilled workers who worked year round were never paid regularly by their employers. For a great number of working-class families, the war meant a regular pay envelope for the first time. This reinforces the observation of one working-class wife that 'now I get money reg'lar, you see, and don't 'ave 'im.'[89] In a study of a large number of Montreal families, Helen Reid reported the astounding finding that the vast majority of women did not know what their husbands earned.[90] For this reason alone, the wives of soldiers welcomed a paycheque from the government and preferred the military system of compulsory assigned pay, because it meant that for the first time in their lives, they would have exclusive control over the family economy. Many working-class wives may well have accepted the war with equanimity, and perhaps considered the absence of the male breadwinner as an opportunity to better feed the children and herself.

For those soldiers who did have steady employment, like John Wesley Carey from Omemee, Ontario, a trainman for the CPR, who earned $70.00 a month, enlistment did indeed entail 'great personal sacrifice.'[91] That wartime could cause a rapid and decisive reduction in a wife's economic and social status was illustrated by the trials of the unfortunate Mrs Louisa Laferme. After her husband signed up in Winnipeg, she and her two young children followed him to Port Arthur. Because of her reduced circumstances she relocated once again to Parham, Ontario, in the expectation that in the townships surrounding Kingston she would receive higher rates of CPF assistance. Her hopes were dashed, for there she received a mere $5.00 for herself and $12.00 for her children, and out of this meagre public wage she had to pay rent of $50.00. Her attempts to keep up her husband's life insurance policy compelled her to sell all their furniture. Mrs Laferme had been accustomed to a much higher standard of living, since her husband had earned very high wages as a skilled machinist in Winnipeg's munitions factories. Like many working- and middle-class French women, Mrs Laferme had attempted to augment her husband's wages by buying her own sewing machine, but even this became an additional economic burden during wartime, for she still owed $14.00 on it – a debt which the fund refused to discharge.[92]

The disjuncture between prewar and wartime economic levels was most acute among families of skilled workers, who made up approximately 44 per cent of enlistees. One of the most drastic instances of downward mobility among wives of skilled workers was that of Ida Copp, whose husband Clarence earned $100.00 a month as a CPR agent at Harrowsmith. Since she was childless, Ida Copp received only $5.00 a month from the CPF. After this was added to his assigned pay of $17.00 and her automatic separation allowance, she was forced to live on $40.00 a month. The fund strategically gave childless wives a meagre $5.00 a month as incentive for them to search out paid work. In a small village like Harrowsmith this would have been almost impossible, especially when we consider that during the war one of the principal strategies whereby women could earn money within the home – namely, the taking in of lodgers – was no longer viable due to the shortage of single men.[93] The catastrophic fall in Mrs Copp's standard of living was somewhat exceptional; the experience of Cecilia Doyle, the wife of a chauffeur from Toronto who earned $68.00 a month, was closer to the norm for families of skilled workers. During the war Mrs Doyle's disposable income was $51.00 – a drop of appromately 20 per cent from prewar levels.[94]

If the husband was willing to assign pay slightly over and above the requisite rate of $15.00 per month, and if the number of children was sufficient to enable a wife to qualify for the CPF assistance, many families were just able to maintain their prewar living standards. Those who did best as a result of the wartime welfare economy were the families of unskilled workers, who made up almost 19 per cent of volunteer enlistees.[95] Ellen Gillings would have welcomed the war, largely because it meant that for four years she lived as a single person on $40.00 a month paid directly to her. This was $10.00 higher than her husband, a 'decorator' in Moose Jaw, had made. Further, this increase was enhanced by the fact that she no longer had to feed and clothe him.[96] It is not surprising that the women who most often commented that 'never before [had they] been in receipt of a regular income' were the wives and mothers of unskilled workers. Thus, Almeda Cassell may well have rejoiced that her son by becoming a soldier had enabled her at the very least to provide basic sustenance for her six other children. The First World War provided her with an entitlement – albeit through her son – that she otherwise would not have had, since her incapacitated husband had no similar claim for regular relief.[97]

These wartime family case files make clear that the crucial factor in determining the level of family welfare and sustenance was the number of children a woman had. Today, we have government family allowances, so we take for granted that welfare is dispensed on the basis of the number of mouths one must feed; but this form of entitlement has not always formed the basis of welfare policy. The Old Poor Law or Speenhamland system in England topped up a family's earnings according to the number of children; however, this approach to poverty was emphatically rejected in the 1830s, when Malthusian political economists castigated it as encouraging overpopulation and thus improvidence – a concern that continued to suffuse twentieth-century debates on family allowances. As historians have pointed out, the Speenhamland system of wage supplements was more effective at relieving family poverty, and this approach to welfare policy slowly gained ascendancy once again in the early twentieth century, when pronatalist arguments, which were in turn connected to considerations of national economic progress, became the core of economic thought.[98]

However, the Victorian perception that children's allowances naturally led to idleness was never fully expunged from social policy discussions, and did much to undermine the nascent wartime movement for a system of government family allowances.

In the view of the CPF, children enhanced women's claims for financial support. This is why women such as Elizabeth Cox, who had six children, received an income well above that provided by her husband George, an unskilled labourer who prior to the war had only worked sporadically. Now contrast the experience of Mrs Cox with that of Grace Hawke, the wife of a tenant farmer, who had only one child – Beula, aged seven – and so made only half of what her husband earned before the war.[99] So decisive was the impact of CPF children's allowances on working-class domestic budgets that the wives of even skilled workers, who otherwise would have suffered a decline in income, actually fared better if they had more children. For example, Vallinia Davey from Cobourg, Ontario, amassed a family wage slightly higher than what her blacksmith husband earned prior to the war; while the wife of a guard at the Kingston Penitentiary, Margaret Jane Courtenay, would have suffered little financial sacrifice by allowing her husband to sign up.[100]

The welfare efforts of the CPF among working-class families clearly revealed very high rates of poverty and a general inability to save, even among skilled workers' families – a fact that shocked welfare workers, who previously associated poverty with the supposed idleness and lack of moral discipline of the unskilled worker. More tellingly, the war testified clearly that the traditional wage economy, whereby wages were paid to individual male workers and not on the basis of family size, was glaringly inadequate. The discovery that the male wage was inadequate, and the obvious need for new conceptions of the family wage, was one of the important legacies bequeathed by the First World War to the ongoing public debate regarding the relationship between employment, poverty, and family dependency in Canada.

The unwritten assumption that emerged as the war continued – that only the mothering of children created a legitimate claim for welfare rights – is best illustrated by how those who designed welfare policy treated soldiers' mothers, who were past their child-rearing years. A clear indication that these were 'second-class' mothers is the following statistic from the Montreal branch: of the claimants it assisted in 1916 (3,514), only 27 per cent (966) were considered eligible for welfare.[101] As a group, soldiers' mothers fared decidedly worse than soldiers' wives. According to the case files, these mothers often sent off more than one son to fight in the war, and many of them were still raising young children. Yet even though, like the wives of soldiers, they often had large families to support, policymakers arbitrarily categorized them as 'childless,' on the false assumption that all their offspring were fully matured. CPF relief workers strongly emphasized the rearing of children, and the lengthening casualty lists from the battlefields only reinforced their prejudice that the mothers of serving soldiers were not true dependants because they should be supported either by their grown offspring or, if not yet widowed, by their husbands.

Even the usually sensitive Helen Reid, the convener of Montreal's relief workers, castigated those mothers who protested the meagre grants on which they were expected to exist ($5.00, the same rate as was given childless wives). One irate mother of a soldier publicly scorned the work of the fund by attaching posters to Montreal store windows with the slogan 'Who Gets the Patriotic Pay? Not the widowed mothers who have sent their sons away and done their bit.' Reid had the audacity to retort that this woman had seen 'improvement financially' because she no longer had to feed her grown boy, and claimed that she was now making more than her son had when he was supporting her, namely, $70.00 a month. In fact, the CPR had recently stopped paying her son's wages, and she was living on precisely the same amount as before the war. What apparently galled Reid was that this working-class woman had the impertinence to desire a standard of living above that of unskilled wage earners without working for wages herself: 'The regular Government allowance places the family in better circumstances than they were when the wage-earner was at home.' This demonstrates forcefully that class and gender assumptions had been incorporated, consciously or not, in wartime definitions of welfare rights.[102] As the headline of the newspaper report recording this widow's protest – 'Patriotic Fund Kindness Shown by a Complaint' – made all too clear, any grants made to widows were viewed as charity, as a 'kindness' rather than a universal entitlement.

The military propaganda paid constant homage to mothers;[103] but as the natalist imperative for plentiful new offspring grew stronger throughout the war, the obligations to mothers of soldiers faded accordingly. Within months of the war's outbreak, mothers of soldiers (who had benefited well during the Boer War) were effectively disenfranchised by a new requirement to prove that their sons had been their sole support. This led to much more continuous and invasive investigation of these women, as the case of Mrs Cecilia Mitchell makes clear: her sons Zeb and Henry had scraped out a living hunting and fishing in the bush and so never received actual wages. In addition, such bureaucratic rules were inimical to the reality of many working-class family's lives. Although Mrs Mitchell's case may have been somewhat exceptional, thousands of mothers had difficulty proving their sons had been their sole support,[104] especially after 1915, when Philip Morris of the CPF passed the constrictive regulation that sons had to have given at least $12.00 a month to their mothers, and that mothers in turn should be supported only up to 'that deficit.'[105] Such new regulations created hardship for women who were 'not entitled,' like Mrs Robson, a soldier's mother, who believed she had a right to a grant from the fund because her husband was an unemployed carpenter.[106] 'Absence of employment'[107] was not a basis for a rightful claim; the permanent disability of the husband *was* such a basis, although these claims were often disputed by local committees. 'Regarding the application for Separation Allowance on account of the soldier marginally noted,' wrote A.C. Bradley in 1918, 'the Separation Allowance board have directed me to state that they find it difficult to accept the fact that Mrs McDonald's husband is totally incapacitated, in view of the fact that his family grew so rapidly from year to year.'[108]

In applying for assistance, the mother of a soldier stood a much better chance if she lived in a small, rural community where personal relationships counted heavily. In Frontenac County, for example, there was a very high rate of funding for mothers, largely because local reeves, clergymen, and county clerks, including J.W. Bradshaw, had personal knowledge of and sympathy for the straitened circumstances of these mothers. More cynically, these local officials were often anxious to fully exploit the various legal loopholes by which women could claim welfare, so that the local relief rolls could be kept pared down. Whatever the motivation, Bradshaw often wrote on behalf of women like Emma Clark, whose impecunious husband gathered rags and bones, reducing her to a 'poor ill-fed and clothed looking woman'; and Mrs James Campbell, who had two sons overseas and seven other children to raise, whom Bradshaw maintained had 'a really just claim and is worthy of every consideration at your hands'; and the dedicated mother of the 'shiftless' Pte Bert Charlton, who 'has always worked, done washing and housework around the village all her life, is now an old woman, and can not work as hard as before.'[109] Even the prime minister occasionally lent a supporting hand if a woman had several sons at the front.[110] But most women lacked sympathetic sponsors. The widow Isabella Black had charred and taken in lodgers in order to raise her son, a skilled machinist at the Bertram Foundry in Dundas, Ontario. Now she was suddenly forced, by the enlistment of her son, into several more years of unexpected wage labour. Many elderly women faced the same scenario. The plaintive story of Mrs Jones summarizes the frustration these older women felt, and points out that public bodies felt no obligation to compensate them for the sacrifices they were making on behalf of the nation and the Empire. In a letter written in 1920, Mrs Jones informed Premier E.C. Drury that she had picked berries for ten years only to send all her sons to their death in France. Now she was old and unable to work, and was surviving on a meagre pension that was no recompense for the catastrophic losses she had suffered. She ruefully commented: 'so this is what the army had done for me.'[111]

In exchange for public financial assistance during the war, working-class women had to endure increasing and often punitive levels of state supervision. The paternal role ascribed to the CPF, with its ideal of taking 'the place of the soldier who has gone to the front,' was not limited to financial assistance; it also involved a broad regimen of moral regulation, legal advice, financial instruction, and lecturing on what middle-class reformers deemed proper mothering techniques. These activities were not precisely specified and for that reason had limitless potential for intruding into working-class lives. The influence of the fund's relief committees soon spread like mustard gas in the trenches and craters of the western front, into the hidden intersticies of the families of soldiers. Declared the *Montreal Star*:

> The families visited should also bear in mind that 'the father away' means much more than 'the wage earner gone.' The wife no longer has him to advise or share her responsibilities, and if this visiting is carried out properly the intercourse cannot fail to be of benefit to both sides, and surely none of us want to miss the mutual sympathy and better understanding we are learning from this shoulder to shoulder fighting for the best things in life.[112]

The fund interpreted the notion of filling 'the father's place in the family'[113] to mean admonishing women to pay their debts, open savings accounts, clean the house, send their children to school, attend church regularly, and avoid unsavoury acquaintances and dubious recreations, such as drinking in pubs and frequenting dance halls and movie theatres.[114] As the relief officer for the Montreal branch stated, both financial aid and advice was to be accepted by women in a subservient manner 'as both a congratulation and a warning.'[115] More distressing still, the authorities manipulated working-class wives into conforming to prescribed codes of behaviour and accepting their lot without protest by subjecting them to films which graphically depicted the stark contrast between the relative peace of the Canadian homefront and the horrors of trench life in Belgium and France.[116]

Here, on a vast scale, was what Mariana Valverde has termed 'the moral regulation of women.'[117] Wartime created an extensive system for family visits for the simple reason that social investigation was considered one of the most resplendent patriotic duties that could be undertaken by middle-class women, who would otherwise be idle.[118] In wartime narrative, the chaos created by female immorality was frequently equated with the intangible social upheaval of the war and newspaper articles with such titles as 'Finds Deterioration in Characters of Soldiers' Wives' abounded.[119] There was an awareness that the 'respectable' wives of skilled workers had to be treated with some degree of circumspection – visitors were warned frequently not to 'tamper with folk' or 'offend the sensibilities of the wife' – but this did little to prevent the female visitors from intervening if the wife of a soldier was not caring for her children properly, or was failing to keep up her husband's life insurance policy, or was wasting her allowance on unnecessary 'luxuries.'[120] It should not be denied that the fund's visitors did at times help by offering needed sympathy, interceding with landlords, and dispensing helpful instruction on where to secure medical treatment. That being said, many visitors were high-handed in their actions. Some purloined large portions of assistance to be placed in trust until her husband's return (a policy of the Saskatchewan Patriotic Fund); others constantly offered unwelcome advice about child rearing, cooking, gardening, and dairying. Such advice was rarely accepted by working-class wives as the equivalent of advice 'that she would otherwise expect from her husband.'[121]

At one level, wartime welfare policies were instrumental in reordering the traditional working-class economic strategies of families. By stipulating that the earnings of children be deducted from CPF assistance, public officials shifted the responsibility for the working-class family economy onto the shoulders of the parents, in this case the mother.[122] But at another level, prewar family norms were actively policed. For example, the fund adamantly disagreed with the recruitment policy of the federal government that gave equal rights to common law and legal marriages, and with the government's view that 'when a man enlists to go overseas it is not the time to interfere forcibly with his domestic life.' Because the fund administered government allowances, it was often able to override military regulations and assert its more conservative conception of domestic norms. Administrators regularly disenfranchised unmarried wives even though technically, government regulations considered them entitled to welfare support.[123] Every woman receiving CPF assistance had to reveal at regular intervals her financial situation.[124] Not only that, but all manner of 'abnormal' conduct was rooted out. Thus, Mrs E. Morris of LeBreton Street in Ottawa was severely chastised for losing her position as a government charwoman, which compelled her to make a claim for fund assistance; and Mrs Daisy Justice had her funds suspended because she supposedly neglected her children by leaving them unattended during the day. There were many public accounts of improprieties, such as a soldier's wife and her mother who spent the family sustenance on drink, which they imbibed in an evening of revelry with several men. Another woman was mercilessly tracked down by the local milkman, who reported that she was living with another man. And in 1916 every movement of Gertrude Pringle was traced when it was discovered not that she, but that her mother, lived with another man.[125]

At the very inception of the CPF in August 1914, a separate legal aid department was organized, ostensibly to represent women against duplicitous landlords, but in reality to prosecute cases of fraud in which women were accused of lying about their marital status, the level of support they were receiving, and the number of children they had, or – in the case of Mrs J.J. Lowes – of collecting funds from two municipalities concurrently.[126] The claims of female dependants were firmly grounded on the rights of their soldier husbands, yet the punitive aspects of state intervention implicit in this social contract fell wholly upon wives and mothers. The unjust nature of wartime social policy, with its gender bias, was no more clearly revealed than when the government decreed by regulation that if a soldier deserted the army, the wife was to be held accountable by the state and all assistance was to be summarily terminated.[127] The prevailing view among the military hierarchy was that wartime exigencies made the ransoming of women and children acceptable, and that 'the innocent must sometimes suffer through no fault of their own.'[128]

Modern feminist historians have made much of the fact that state welfare entitlements during the First World War, though more generous and 'rights-based,' ultimately established an administrative logic in social policy according to which dependent wives had a claim on the State only 'in relation to particular deserving classes of men.'[129] In its broadest sense, this interpretation of the emerging welfare state is correct. However, it neglects the attitudes of working-class women at the time and their role in determining the boundaries of state management of the family. It also ignores how wives and mothers of the soldiers of the Canadian Expeditionary Force utilized the rhetoric of national service that underscored wartime welfare rights, to forge a parallel vision of direct female entitlement based on their own service to the State, which took the form of sacrificing their male relatives to the Empire and mothering future citizens. For the most part, working-class female dependants were sanguine about the fact that their right to welfare assistance hinged on the responsibilities of their soldiering men. Thus Mrs Sidney Charlton believed that she had a right to share directly in her son's citizenship rights by virtue of having released him for war service. Indeed, merely by writing to the clerk of Frontenac County she was implicitly establishing her own direct relationship with the public authorities. In the third month of the war, in a series of letters, Mrs Charlton reminded J.W. Bradshaw that since she had sacrificed her son, the State had a reciprocal obligation to support her:

> I now sat down to drop you a few lines to see if yout got my other letter or not or if they are going to help me or not I havent got nothing and all my help is gone he was my main stay and guide and I owe house rent and havant got no wood or nothing so plees try and get me help for I need it very much plees answer it and let me know right if you pleas I would very much like to [work] but I am an old woman 52 years of age we miss Bert very much so pleas answ.[130]

Working-class women actually furthered state intervention into the private realm of the family during wartime, in the sense that they quickly recognized that they could use the extensive wartime powers of the state, with its intricate web of military regulations, as a means of protecting their families against delinquent husbands. The CPF case files reveal the extent to which the war functioned as the most effective available defence of the marriage contract. Many separated women had their lives greatly enhanced by the official policy of the fund and the Department of the Militia, which stated that during wartime court judgments for alimony would be enforced by the federal government.[131] Prior to the war, women like Mrs Helen Rea had no legal apparatus available to them by which to ensure that the local police magistrate's family support orders would be enforced. Wartime conditions decisively benefited Mrs Rea, who exploited with great agility every possible financial claim she had on her husband, Allen Rea. Between 1914 and 1919, Mrs Rea used the government to redirect his assigned pay, his separation allowance, his CPF grant, and even his post-discharge gratuity to her. Working in her favour was the fact that she had two children to support, so her right to state aid was derived less from her status as a wife, than from her role as mother. When peacetime brought an abrupt end to her claims on the State, Mrs Rea, faced with the prospect of waged work, reconciled with her husband. In September 1919 she informed the Frontenac County Clerk, J.W. Bradshaw, that 'we have decided to forget the past and I am leaving to join him [her husband] in Hamilton this week.'[132]

If women were 'morally regulated' during wartime, so likewise were men. The husband of Sarah Jane Kish failed to contact her. When she heard, from a returned soldier, that he was about to marry an English girl, she called on the legal machinery of the Department of Militia to enforce her marriage contract. Skilfully trading on her own good conduct – the fact that she paid her husband's debts, and kept her aged mother, who cared for her children while she supported them all by 'work[ing] out' – Sarah Kish was able to persuade government officials to intervene so that her husband's pay would be sent directly to her.[133] In the same way that Sarah Kish used her good 'wifely' conduct as the foundation of her claim, the beleaguered Prudence Hancock of 303 Seaton Street, Toronto, established her entitlement through her role as the mother of three children, two of whom were the issue of Thomas Hancock's first marriage. Prudence had left her husband in Northern Ontario because of cruelty. She became the housekeeper of the recently widowed Hancock. Just before he enlisted in the first contingent in August 1914, she found herself pregnant. As he left for France, Hancock wholly abdicated his obligations to his family; not only did he deny that the newborn belonged to him, but he saddled Prudence with the fees for maintaining his other two children at the Kingston

Orphans' Home. CPF officials treated this 'unmarried wife' with all too obvious moral opprobrium. Even so, they felt compelled to intercede forcefully on her behalf because of her status as a mother, and they were instrumental in securing for her the highest rate of funding. With unusual candor they admitted that this token $46.00 a month was 'not any too much to look after the needs of four persons and keep up a home.'[134] In a similar case, Pte Christopher Armstrong enlisted as a single man even though he was married and had one child. The mother of his wife requested state intercession, which resulted in the unmasking of the husband's fraud. The novelty of women having an actual 'relationship' with the State was revealed by the mother's apprehension that such state enforcement might make their private lives the subject of public discussion in their small community.[135]

State authorities, in conjunction with the CPF, often lobbied on behalf of wives whose husbands had sent separation allowances to former wives. They also enabled foster women to claim their rights as mothers, and required male members of the Forestry Battalions to send home their bonus pay from their technical work, for they had 'as a rule large families.'[136] Official declarations that welfare assistance was a male right were often ambiguously interpreted at the local level; in practice, women were identified as more 'deserving,' as illustrated by the case of Mrs Emma Madigan. Her husband had deserted her eleven years earlier to take up with a woman living on the prairies. For all the years since, she had 'worked out' in order to raise her son, who despite his mother's sacrifices had wrongfully assigned his pay and separation allowance to his long-absent father. In her efforts to seek her proper entitlement, she was defended by outraged middle-class men who believed that she was fully entitled to be named the rightful 'dependant' and to receive her son's pay.[137]

Working-class wives and mothers of soldiers rarely disputed that their welfare rights derived from their relationship with their husbands and sons, although, as we have seen, they also often argued that as child-rearing mothers they had a separate but equal claim on the State. What female dependants did contend regularly was that the rights of their male breadwinners were not being honoured by the Dominion government. Hundreds of women wrote to the prime minister or to local CPF officials demanding, as did Mrs Mildred Brewer, 'the money I am entitled to.' When Mrs W.H. Turnham of Harrowsmith, Ontario, stated that 'I am entitled to every cent when times are so hard,' she, like Mrs Bertha Kirk, was proudly reminding the government that she was a dependant of her deserving soldier husband: 'The least you could have done was send me my Patriotic money as promised my Husband when He enlisted.'[138]

If working-class wives and mothers accepted the State as a surrogate for their husbands, they also objected to the 'uncontrolled discretion' of government officials. When working-class women believed that the unwritten contract between their husbands and the government had been violated – for instance, when their private lives were scrutinized too often or too closely – they registered their discontent by refusing to recognize the authority of female visitors.[139] What compelled thousands of women to seek legal redress was the question as to whether the wartime application by husbands for assigned pay, separation allowances, and the CPF established a public contract that took priority over the pre-existing, private marriage contract between husband and wife.

At the root of Mrs Wineas Zwingel's legal battle with the Borden government was a dispute over whether 'her husband's assigned pay is her absolute property & the Department [of the Militia] has no control over it.' This dispute arose in 1917, when her CPF grant was stopped. Soon after, because the Department of the Militia left the administration of government family policies in the hands of the fund, Mrs Zwingel also lost her husband's assigned pay and separation allowances – items that she believed were her universal right as a soldier's wife. In order to stave off the frequent visits of this irate woman to the fund offices, officials of the Montreal branch accused her of breaching a civic by-law by 'keeping a blind pig.' Worse still, they offered to reinstate Mrs Zwingel's entitlement to CPF assistance only on the condition that she sell the candy-and-tobacco store that her soldiering husband had left in her care and that she had agreed to maintain for him. At first she refused, and the blind pig issue was raised once again as 'a piece of persecution.' As her lawyer stated, 'This woman accuses the Patriotic Fund of having abused her, of having persecuted her, of having slandered her & of having starved her.' From the perspective of the outraged Mrs Zwingel, the CPF in stating that 'when we think you need money we will send you some' was not only acting in a high-handed manner but also wildly overstepping its role as her husband's surrogate; in doing so, it was seriously encroaching on working-class attitudes toward the marriage contract between husband and wife.[140]

Thousands of similar cases arose between 1914 and 1918. So ominous was this form of women's protest, which threatened by legal means to transform what the government perceived as a temporary wartime expedient for the recruitment of male soldiers into a permanent civil vested right, that in October 1915 the federal government passed a law denying Canadians the right to challenge through the courts its wartime family welfare policies. In doing so, the government was upholding the position of the CPF as a direct arm of the state, with 'absolute and uncontrolled discretion in the matter of distributing the funds subscribed for the purpose of assisting the dependants of those who have volunteered for active service.'[141] By focusing on the 'dependants' of soldiers, the federal government was squelching the right of women to protest; more subtly, it was also attempting to prevent working-class women from claiming further rights.

Here the federal government was reacting less to overt legal challenges than to a more intangible problem – namely, the growing belief among working-class wives and mothers that what the government saw as a temporary extension of charity, was in fact a universal right. This conviction, which the government was anxious to quash, grew as the war continued, especially after 1916. Working-class women were now consistently referring to both government and CPF assistance as a 'right.'[142] The wives of soldiers believed fervently that their willingness to cooperate in the war effort by releasing their male breadwinners to fight was a form of war service equal to that of their husbands; and that the reduction they experienced in their standard of living constituted a real sacrifice; and that their efforts to raise their children as future citizens established a legitimate claim for state assistance; and that women's experience of war should be recognized as the basis of a universal right rather than as the needs-based offerings of charity. Nowhere is this belief stated more eloquently than in a poignant but assertive letter written in 1917 by Mrs J.W. Cary of Sharbot Lake, Ontario:

Why should my allowance be suspended on account of me receiving C.P.R. wages? They think I should not be in need of any money but expect I can live and keep three children on $45 a month. I might say it is next to impossible for me to live on it. That amount is less than 1/2 what my husband earned while in civilian life. I knew I would be making a sacrifice in the money part by allowing my husband to go still I let him go hoping and keeping heart until the day he should return, thinking I would be able to get along on sixty dollars.

How do the officials of [the] Patriotic Fund know whether I can live on $45 or not? Is it any business of theirs if I could save a few dollars of C.P.R. wages? No it is not. This Fund is not a charity. At least, if it is such mine can be stopped for all time as I have never yet had to accept charity. Of course we all know this is only what a great majority of soldiers wives have had to stand, waiting until the day our husbands will return to take up these mean and dirty acts against us.

If some of the officials of this Fund would get out and fight and let their wives live on $45, they would be more willing to give us every cent we could get ... They want the men to go and fight but do not want them to get their just dues. It is too bad our men are compelled to fight for such men as have the distributing of other people's money. Is it any wonder there are no recruits? If they used the wives a little better, the men would enlist but there is no use going away to fight and leave their wives at the mercy of such small-souled men ... If I was not entitled to it I would let it drop.[143]

'To undertake men's work'[144]

The year 1916 marked a watershed in wartime social policy. Until that time the more broadly inclusive, family-oriented strategy of public welfare had gone largely unchallenged. But in that year the Imperial Munitions Board (IMB) launched an aggressive campaign to 'dilute' labour by recruiting women into munitions factories. Organized labour responded decisively and with determination. As well, the policy of Sir Joseph Flavelle and Mark Irish at the IMB to employ large numbers of both single and married women was viewed by women's organizations, the Great War Veterans' Association, the CPF, and working women themselves, and finally by Sir Robert Borden's government, as an offence to cherished cultural norms of family life and to gendered relations in the workplace. More significantly still, at this pivotal juncture of the war the death tolls were mounting and the idea of wage labour for women was perceived as trangressing the well-entrenched belief in the sanctity of motherhood. This is because as never before, population growth was considered the very wellspring of national regeneration. In the later years of the war this strong gender imperative, which emphasized the right of male soldiers to employment, did much to reconfigure the more child-centred family policy that had emerged under the impress of the CPF. Social policy now focused almost exclusively on the individual male worker.

In June 1916 an article in *The Weekly Tattler* titled 'The Feminine Side of the War' concluded: 'The emancipation of women has been accomplished with the least possible effort.'[145] Modern historians in Canada have embraced this line of argument, viewing the war as an important milestone in the transformation of the terrain of women's work.[146] By relying on the statistics of Flavelle – who himself admitted that munitions factories had failed to keep accurate statistics, and who had a vested interest in inflating such numbers – these scholars have exaggerated the degree to which women were entering the labour force for the first time. Flavelle's sweeping statement that 'tens of thousands'[147] of women who had never hitherto worked had entered the munitions factories, is belied by the statistics of Women's War Registry. The middle-class leaders of this organization were in fact crestfallen when they discovered that very few working-class women desired work; and that of those who applied, most were experienced factory workers, a large number of whom were single. Of those who were the first to register with them in July of 1916, 66 per cent had previous factory experience, and only 22 per cent were wives or mothers of soldiers.

The Women's War Registry was founded in 1916 ostensibly to encourage 'women representing all classes' of society to take patriotic work in the munitions factories; in this regard this organization was a signal failure, for most of the applicants were middle-class single young women in their early twenties who wanted clerical work. In one particular month, only one woman desired employment in an armaments factory,[148] and by the end of 1916 in Montreal only 150 women had volunteered to register.[149] James Brierley, the vice-president of the Citizens' Recruiting Association, was among many who were confounded by the statistics, which clearly demonstrated that women found wage work unattractive. A mere 5,000 to 8,000 women not previously employed had entered the Canadian workforce by 1916.[150] Even propaganda articles such as 'Many Women Make Munitions in the Toronto Plants' could not hide the fact that only a total of 200 women were working in those plants in the summer of 1916.[151] As James Naylor has pointed out, women presented no real challenge to male workplace strongholds, as they were working in only a handful of munitions factories, which were concentrated in a few large centres.[152] If the goal of the Women's War Registry was to organize 'the unemployed women,'[153] it was a distinct failure. As M. Chase Goring informed Miss Ethel Hurlbatt: 'Of the women registered only some three or four were W.W.R. in the strict sense. The others were regular working women who had not been working since their marriage or for other reasons but are now anxious to get back to work on account of high wages being paid in the munitions plants.'[154]

During the war, large numbers of women – even in the absence of a male breadwinner – eschewed paid labour. This can be explained by the activities of the CPF, which heavily influenced the structure of female employment. Working-class women who were eligible for a regular and directly provided state wage almost always preferred to stay home to raise their children. And when wages rose appreciably in 1916, women generally responded by choosing to work shorter hours; clearly, they did not want their paid work to interfere with their maternal duties.[155] Somewhat disingenuously, the leaders of the CPF denied they were playing havoc with the IMB's policy of encouraging female labour; whatever their disavowals, it was evident from several sources that the fund did function to preserve traditional gender roles. A.O. Dawson, the president of Canadian Cottons Limited, welcomed female workers at his mills largely because the textile industry had long been an acceptable female sphere of work. He explained to Miss Hurlbatt: 'Many married women, who are accustomed to working in the Cotton Mills, and whose husbands have recently gone to the front, have been dealt with so generously by the Patriotic Fund, that they refuse to work any longer.'[156] The CPF worked hand in hand with local businesses to ensure that women who worked were effectively denied assistance from the fund. This effectively drove women back *into* the home – so much so that day nurseries in Montreal, which depended on the daily dues from working women, accused the fund of 'robbing them of their charges.'[157]

At the beginning of the war the CPF had no clear policy of excluding working women from benefits. However, after protests from skilled workmen, a policy was instituted whereby the regular earnings of women were deducted from the fund, and married women were allowed only casual earnings from two or three days' work per week. At the same time, the fund, by offering childless wives $5.00 per week, encouraged their participation in the workforce; and as a national public body it was instrumental in constructing new distinctions between the work of single and married women. In addition, the fund policed class boundaries very effectively; for example, in order to palliate the constant protests from middle-class matrons over the severe shortage of domestic servants, fund leaders passed the punitive regulation that all remuneration of domestic servants would be summarily deducted from fund payments to these workers.[158]

Flavelle attempted to make the IMB's policy of diluting labour a patriotic issue – part 'of the duty of the State,'[159] in order to convince businessmen to hire women; however, even such incentives made little headway. In part, because of organized labour's antagonism to the 'unnecessary dilution of labor,'[160] and in part because of the widely accepted norm of the breadwinning husband with his dependent wife and children, businessmen preferred to rely either on old men, or on much maligned 'alien' or unskilled Chinese labourers. Some even advocated the importation of Austrian and German prisoners of war. In their view, women posed a threat to paid labour as an exclusively male preserve.[161] Even though the war had caused enormous upheaval within families and had transformed thousands of women into heads of families, both the business community and organized labour clung to the belief that women had no dependants and, if they were hired, would directly undermine the ideal of a family wage. This attitude helped preserve into the second decade of the twentieth century what Craig Heron has termed 'paternalism' in industrial relations.[162] For example, the official policy of the Midland Engine Works was to hire 'married [men] as much as possible.' In Moose Jaw a munitions factory employed 200 workers, all of whom were 'married men.' The munitions factories in Winnipeg, where unemployment among men remained high throughout the war, followed the same policy. This preference for married men was castigated by Mark Irish, who accused Winnipeg employers of a lack of 'war spirit' because they did not hire women.[163]

This cultural view of gendered work was all-encompassing. It had been shown conclusively in both Britain and Canada that women were often more adept than men in making certain types of munitions;[164] that because much munitions work was piecework, dilution of labour meant that women could be paid much less than their male counterparts; and that increasing shortages of male labour necessitated some degree of substitution. Despite all this, businessmen refused to hire large numbers of women. In part, this was because they feared that while the prices for munitions remained low, the efficiency of their plants would be compromised. In part it was because labour laws demanded that special housing be built for female employees, and even the larger firms balked at such extra expenditures in wartime, especially since munitions manufacturing was almost certainly a temporary measure.[165] Even Mark Irish, the chief promoter of female labour, had to admit that the necessity of building housing, health, and recreational facilities for female munitions workers was a serious obstacle to his plan.[166] Like most other Canadian businessmen, Irish accepted that women could perform only certain types of labour, and was leery of sending women into explosives plants, on the basis that some kinds of work were 'masculine.'[167] Similarly, the executives of steel companies and other heavy industries continued to define work in overtly gendered terms – referring to it as 'work for rough men' – as a strategy for buttressing the position of skilled labour so that an adequate pool of trained labour would remain intact for the postwar economy.[168] Broad cultural attitudes regarding the proper spheres of work for men and women permeated the language of wartime discussion, and underscored that the substitution of women for men was only temporary. Strongly evocative of the way that work remained consistently gendered throughout the war was an IMB circular that stated: 'If you are a woman doing woman's work, or a man doing man's work in making shells, you are helping to Win the War.'[169] Even working-class women themselves accepted the traditional parameters of work. As Mrs Marjorie Dapp observed of her job at the Canada Cement Company: 'It was a man's position in pre-war days.'[170]

The policy of the IMB was intended to aid recruitment.[171] Even so, the federal government not only refused to shore up the IMB's initiative, but also supported the conservative ideologies of both business and organized labour regarding the replacement of skilled workers with untrained women. For Flavelle and Irish, the federal government's policy was a constant source of exasperation. They were attempting to extend the boundaries of female work and, by defining a new category of 'unemployed' women, to overturn the prevailing assumption that women did not work. Meanwhile, the federal government was staying the course of prewar work patterns. In 1916 T.W. Crothers, the federal Minister of Labour, advocated the easing of immigration restrictions and even the calling back of skilled soldiers, as had already been done in Britain, so that women's labour would be used only as a last resort.[172] As of October 1916, the only company that had embraced Irish's initiative was The Packard Fuse Company of St Catharines, Ontario, which, remarkably, had committed itself to hiring a whole factory of women.[173] Yet that very same month, R.B. Bennett, the new Director of National Service, was explicitly and all too publicly thwarting the IMB's dilution policies. Long before introducing his own scheme of unemployment insurance, which was intended to reinforce the individual male's right to work and the notion of a 'family wage,' Bennett firmly enunciated this traditional cultural imperative in a salvo directed at Mark Irish. He stated that he was 'extremely emphatic that the employment of women will create a female industrial army doing the work of men at a lower wage, which, when the Overseas Forces return, will be opposed by a male army of unemployed.' He conceived that 'the women once engaged in factory work will never give it up.' In yet another public broadside, Bennett attacked both the IMB and the newly formed Women's War Registry, which he detested for its policy of introducing middle-class women into the ranks of labour. He announced that there was no need for women's work in munitions plants, not even by temporary 'patriotic' women. Bennett criticized those feminists who saw an intrinsic value in the work of women, when he stated that only 'deserving and dependent women' with 'dependants,' should obtain work, and that he preferred to defend the 'redistribution of wealth to the poor and needy' undertaken by the CPF. Fully two decades before passing his own program of state welfare relief, Bennett was formulating a two-tiered, gendered conception of social policy: employment for men and welfare support for 'dependent' women. It is not surprising that Flavelle described Bennett as a 'dangerous man' and enthusiastically embraced the idea of conscription.[174]

In Britain, organized labour had Labour Party ministers strategically placed in Cabinet, and so had a direct influence on the Lloyd George government. For this reason, during the war labour was able to control the pace and extent of dilution of labour by women; and most importantly, it was able to dictate the implementation of statutes that officially declared that such female labour would persist only for the duration of the conflict.[175] In Canada the influence of organized labour increased only after 1916, when trade unions became more unified around the issue of dilution of labour in the face of the IMB's aggressive promotion of that policy. Mark Workman, the president of Dominion Steel Corporation in Sydney, Nova Scotia, observed caustically that the war 'has resulted solely in labor realizing its power.'[176] This was not simply the usual conservative business complaint against labour campaigns for higher wages and an eight-hour day. While somewhat overstated, Workman's remark had a rational basis: by 1916 various Conservative MPs, including H.H. Stevens, were pressuring Borden to accede to labour's demands for representation on government boards and commissions. This effort bore fruit in 1918 when Borden invited the leaders of organized labour to a war conference. 'The chief point I wish to impress on you,' wrote Stevens, 'is the imperative necessity of securing the confidence of the labour men of Canada by recognition and consultation.'[177] Stevens's exhortation to the prime minister was an obvious reaction to the stern request made by the powerful Vancouver Trades and Labour Council on 22 December 1916 that the federal government intervene to halt the IMB's policy of 'beat[ing] down the wages of the skilled mechanic by introducing female labor to perform the same work at a lower wage.'[178]

The battle to preserve the family wage of skilled workers was fought not only on the public front but also in the private realm, as is revealed by the following letter, from the wife of a mechanic-soldier to the Women's War Registry. One can assume that Mrs R.W. Peardon of Montreal was reflecting the sentiments of other soldiers' wives: 'Since registering my name, I have received a letter from my husband, stating that he does not approve of my going to business, if I could possibly manage without. So under the circumstances, I feel my duty at present is to remain at home.'[179]

Labour organizations protested against piecework and deskilling in munitions factories, and advocated equal pay for equal work for women. This was not simply a reaction to the IMB's more overt policies of dilution; rather, attacks on dilution were part of a larger struggle against the endemic erosion of fair wage clauses by the contracting out of munitions work.[180] By war's end, the escalation in labour protest was conditioned not simply by the widening gap between wages and inflation, but was specifically incited by the inflammatory pronouncement by Mark Irish that for the purposes of continued business efficiency female workers should be encouraged to seek re-employment after the war ended.[181] This galvanized another powerful defender of male perogatives – the Great War Veterans' Association, a group that would do much to promote the Winnipeg General Strike, and that in 1918 deployed a procession of 4,000 returned soldiers to protest the labour policies of the IMB.[182] The issue of a decent wage – read a 'family wage' – which so consistently informed labour's demands during the wave of strikes that rolled across Canada in 1918–19, was rooted in a deeper cultural anxiety among Canadian workers, expressed succinctly in 'Women in Industry,' published in *The Journal of Commerce* in 1916:

The difficulty is that once women have been admitted into walks of life, hitherto unopened to them, they cannot be ejected in a body at the conclusion of the piece. If they enter industrial life on the principle of equal pay with men for equal work, [they] will become part of the foundation of the social structure of this country. If they enter on a lower scale of wages they must make up their minds to accept the results of such a policy as a permanency.[183]

Organized labour's condemnation of the waged work of women during wartime had a broad impact; as a result of it, the Women's War Registry quickly adjusted its mandate. What began as an organization for making an inventory of both middle- and working-class women who might undertake work 'outside their sphere'[184] and for assisting the aims of the IMB,[185] metamorphosed into an organization that closely followed the dictates of the trade unions.[186] In the face of union protests and the attitudes of working-class soldiers, the chief recruiting officer of Montreal directed all women's organizations in that city to ensure 'that women doing the *men's* work not get a lower wage,'[187] which might further erode the prewar status of male skilled workers. Many working-class women who desired to serve their country were dismayed to discover that the Women's War Registry only wanted middle-class women to volunteer, because obviously, they wouldn't remain in the workforce to compete with returned soldiers. As one anonymous working women rightly observed: 'I fully understood this registry was for every woman, not for a certain class of women.'[188] The head of the Montreal Women's War Registry, Miss Ethel Hurlbatt, pointedly ignored the pleas for work from her working-class sisters and favoured the animadversions of the Trades and Labour Council (TLC). Hurlbatt's organization directed its appeals only to *leisured* women, the aim of this being to placate union leadership: 'I might add that I do not suppose that it will ever happen that an individual woman will be called on to replace an individual man, but as more men enlist labour will shift to fill the gap they leave and in time the reserve of women ... will fill up the vacancies thus left.'[189] By the fall of 1916 almost all patriotic organizations were fully aware of the objections being raised by the TLC to female munitions work and were tailoring their appeals for recruitment accordingly. In deference to organized labour, Dr A.H. Abbott of the University of Toronto, founder of the Toronto Patriotic Speaker's League, announced that 'women who offer themselves for positions ordinarily occupied by men, cannot be looked on in any way invading the territory belonging to male labour. They are simply offering their services for which no men can be obtained.'[190] As Abbott and Hurlbatt both emphasized, female patriotic *service* was no real substitute for male *work*.

When the Women's War Registry was founded in 1916, the CPF's female leaders, most notably Helen Reid in Montreal, were willing to compromise some of their principles regarding the welfare of women and children within the home, in acknowledgment of growing shortages of male labour. Responding to the requests of the Women's War Registry, Reid urged that 'women with small children be offered half time work only as they would then be able to give proper attention to their duties and to their young families. If they take up whole time work we shall of course be obliged to know what arrangements they have made in the interests of their families while they are at work.' In order to 'safeguard the homes of the soldiers in their absence,' the CPF obtained lists of all female applicants to the Women's War Registry, complete with addresses, marital status, and number of children, and decided on a case-by-case basis whether a woman could work.[191] Escalating wartime inflation, together with increasing pressures on the revenues of the fund, which kept benefits at a subsistence level, forced the CPF to soften its policy regarding women's work. This allowed married women to work outside the home two to three days a week.

Because the CPF had barely augmented its benefits, by 1917 more soldiers' wives were compelled to seek paid employment.[192] Yet even this small increase in the total number of married women working outside the home generated immediate concern among those middle-class constituencies most preoccupied with the protection of motherhood.[193] Newspaper articles began to proliferate outlining the dangers of factory work for women and the insidious ways that poor industrial health standards, long hours, and the harassment of women were interfering with the training of young working-class women to be 'good mothers and good housewives.'[194] For somewhat less disinterested reasons, organized labour railed against women in industry on the basis that it might 'jeopardize the sacred duties of motherhood.'[195] By 1917, the interests of organized labour and middle-class reformers had coalesced on the issue of the protection of motherhood and (it followed) the defence of the male family wage; this is clear from the fact that in 1917 the CPF *Bulletin* republished a speech made in Toronto by Samuel Gompers, the head of the American Federation of Labour. In it, he appealed to working-class mothers' own desire to protect their families and pointed out their misplaced belief that by working they were helping their children's welfare, when in reality women's work imperilled family welfare by 'endangering the wage scale and upsetting the standards of the [male] workers.'[196] By the war's end, the CPF dovetailed its home protection policies with the wage protection policies of organized labour. 'The policy of the fund will be to encourage the mother, who goes out to work, to stay at home where she is needed for domestic duties and the care of her children,' recorded the *Montreal Herald* in 1917. 'In doing so, it was felt that this was her duty to her husband at the front, and was also in the best interests of the country, not only for the present, but most especially for the future.'[197] It was these twin pillars – the protection of motherhood and defence of the male right to a family wage and employment – that would inform public policy once the war ended.

'I want to be a man again as I was before and make my own living'[198]

At war's end the principles that had guided the family welfare policies of the Canadian Patriotic Fund were irrevocably altered when the powerful male-dominated trade unions and the Great War Veterans' Association combined their strength to pressure for government protection for unemployed returned soldiers.[199] Throughout the war the CPF had considered the family as a unit and placed particular emphasis on the needs of children. However, once the Borden government intervened to establish the Federal Emergency Appropriation Fund – again under the auspices of the CPF – the concept of 'dependency' was redefined largely in terms of men and, most significantly of all, in terms of re-establishing *individual* soldiers.[200] As a result of their wartime observation of the special plight of large families, many CPF branches had recognized that the traditional wage structure must be supplemented with some sort of allowance for dependant children; and in this spirit of support for the family as a whole, they recommended that the CPF become a formal arm of the federal government. Thus their concept of the privileges of women and children would be incorporated into official policymaking. The Alberta Returned Soldiers Commission suggested that the CPF be amended, but not in favour of the unemployed returned breadwinner; rather, it recommended a system of supplementary payments that would go directly to women and children. Wrote the fund secretary:

> I think you will agree that it is not the intention of the Federal Government that the dependants of men who died for the Empire, should have

to accept charity at the hands of the public, and such will be the necessity if immediate action is not taken to place the dependants on the Patriotic, or some other Federal Government Fund, and to increase their pensions, through the medium through the medium of that Fund, to an adequate amount, which will make it possible for them to decently maintain themselves and their families.[201]

Even the Montreal director of the emergency fund for returned soldiers, Major L. Gauvreau, defended the rights of large families and the continuation and extension of children's allowances by the CPF.[202] In attempting to protect motherhood, the Soldiers Wives' Leagues and the female leaders of the CPF emphasized the high mortality rates among children; clearly, they preferred a system of state benefits that would supplement the often inadequate male wage rather than compelling women to become 'the mother who supplements her husband's wages by going out to work.'[203] Even the Minister of the Interior, the Hon. W.J. Roche, recognized that the male breadwinner's wage was often not sufficient to support dependants.[204]

Once federal government policies were in place to encourage employment for returned soldiers, the advocates of what was in essence a form of family allowances had to fight a rearguard action. Major L. Gauvreau and other defenders of the rights of skilled workers highlighted the privileges of the married man and denigrated the footloose and irresponsible single unemployed soldiers – a paradigm that would animate discussions of unemployment for the next two decades. Meanwhile, the regulations of the FEAF were framed with the deliberate intention of reducing state welfare expenditures through employment policies that once again shifted the responsibility for family welfare onto the shoulders of the individual male breadwinner. As Gauvreau observed: 'Surely, the logical thing to do ... would be to give preference to the married man, thereby saving the country money and helping a reliable citizen to establish himself in a home conducted in such way as would benefit this country by bringing up his family under the conditions to which they are entitled.'[205] In the future, women's and children's entitlements were to be derived from the largesse of the male head of the family and were thus to be a function of his individual employment status.

W.A. Riddell, the Deputy Minister of Labour for Ontario, fully endorsed the FEAF's policy of discriminating against single unemployed men and recommended rigorous investigation of their claims to public assistance. This was not because he championed the ideal of small public-welfare expenditures, but rather because he feared that high levels of fraud might undermine public confidence in the idea of unemployment insurance, which in his view was enshrined in the policies of the federal fund for returned soldiers.[206] Likewise, Premier Hearst's Minister of Labour believed that such a fund was an obvious precursor to a general federal scheme of unemployment insurance; and with this end in view advocated that one year of unemployment insurance (on the British model) be incorporated into demobilization procedures.[207] However, Prime Minister Borden skilfully circumvented the demands by organized labour and the Great War Veterans' Association that the emergency program of relief for soldiers become a permanent system of unemployment insurance. By placing its administration in the hands of a private body, the CPF, Borden ensured that this scheme of unemployment relief, which upheld the exclusive right of men to employment, would remain a temporary measure that would cease once demobilization was complete, and would not augment the federal bureaucracy.[208] In Britain, male breadwinners' rights endured in civilian government policy because they were easily grafted onto prewar schemes of unemployment insurance in which the principle of male state entitlements was already established;[209] in Canada, emergency funds for returning soldiers were sharply dissociated from situations where the breadwinner failed to secure work. A breadwinner's claim to relief funds was thus deemed to derive from his military service, not his employment status. Administrators of the fund stressed that this form of relief was not 'a right' and, further, bluntly asserted that 'unemployment of husband does not in itself constitute a claim for assistance to his family provided he is in a condition to work.'[210]

This broadly conceived and unspecific notion of service to the State undergirded the immediate postwar concept of social citizenship. Its elastic nature provided a ripe opportunity for 'the soldier women of Canada'[211] to reconfigure wartime state entitlements for women and children into a set of social rights for soldiers' widows. After 1918, as a corollary to the elevation of the rights of married men, the widows of soldiers were deemed much more deserving than the mothers of soldiers, solely because of their status as wives. Thus, widows of soldiers received their pension 'as a right, wholly without reference to her financial position'; this contrasted starkly with the lack of rights of mothers of soldiers, who had to prove 'substantial dependency.' As part of this general defence of the position of skilled workers, agitation spread throughout Canada to raise the pension rates for widows above the family wage of an unskilled worker.[212] This campaign was spearheaded by Mrs Janet Kemp, the president of the Vancouver War Widows' Association, who argued for improved state benefits for widows and their children on the principle that women were 'performing national service' by raising the next generation of citizens and soldiers. 'Must not Canada,' wrote Mrs Kemp to Sir Robert Borden, 'admit that her permanency and very special duty is to the weak – to the widow, the fatherless, the orphan, the dependent widowed mother, – made so by War? Women and children first!'[213]

What began as a campaign that might have developed into a more fundamental critique of the standard male wage structure, insofar as it stressed the benefits of children's allowances within government pensions for widows, was soon transformed into a less radical defence of 'the living wage.' This happened mainly through the efforts of labour leaders like R.A. Rigg, secretary of the Winnipeg Trades and Labour Council, and the Great War Veterans' Association. These groups drew a direct connection between the entitlement of widows and the pension rights of those male soldiers who had made the ultimate sacrifice.[214] Women unwittingly reinforced the tendency that had been emerging since 1916 to interpret a woman's welfare rights in terms of her function as the wife of a deserving male husband, when they insisted that their citizenship rights be conflated with those of their husband, in much the same way as their right to vote during the war was conceived as a 'surrogate'·right in the absence of the male breadwinner.[215]

Even those reformers like Helen Reid, who had done so much to champion the rights of large families and the policy of supplementing the male wage through children's allowances, succumbed to the ideal that male breadwinners had the right to a decent 'family wage' when they recommended a postwar program of mother's allowances to ensure that poorly supported widows would remain forever out of the paid labour force. This had the effect of removing what was then considered one of the most intractable obstacles to the winning of higher wage rates in the peacetime economy.[216] From the preoccupation with natalism and 'conserving potential motherhood'[217] that suffused the ideology of women's groups, organized labour, and the federal government, there might have emerged by war's end a new and creative strategy designed to bridge the gap – which had become tellingly obvious as a result of the war – between the male wage and the number of children in the family unit. Instead, the government heightened its commitment to the male breadwinner model, which reasserted male citizenship rights, while women had to content themselves with needs-based allowances for widowed mothers.

As a result of this unquestioning adherence in the postwar years to traditional gender norms within both the family and the workplace, the concept of family allowances endured only for as long as the 'breadwinners were away,' and failed to become an intrinsic element of postwar social policy. The CPF's policy of mothers' and children's allowances did not become enshrined in federal statutes; but neither did the male right to protection against unemployment become incorporated into a legislative policy of unemployment insurance. Thus in Canada (in contrast to both France and Britain), even though the emphasis shifted back to the male wage and the married male breadwinner after 1916, these ideals of gendered relations within the family remained untethered to specific social policy legislation. Indeed, the Great War bequeathed a much more ambiguous legacy regarding gendered entitlements to public welfare assistance. As of the war's end, there existed in Canadian culture three streams of welfare strategies that continued to inform public debate until the next war began: a defence of the 'family wage,' mothers' allowances, and family allowances. The provenance of all three lay in the experience of the First World War. In the immediate postwar decade, the idea that entitlements were derived from one's service to the State was expanded by women into a broad conception of social citizenship that in turn would inform maternalist state policies – most notably allowances for motherhood.

3

'A Peaceful Evolution of Industrial Citizenship': Maternalism, National Efficiency, and the Movement for Mothers' Allowances

Such a policy may be characterized as paternalism by old-fashioned doctrines, but it is a measure of social justice, in harmony with the increasing tendency to humanize a social system which bears heavily on many individuals through no fault of their own.

Rev. Peter Bryce, 'Pensions for Widowed Mothers'

As long as mothers' pensions do not form part and parcel of the social administration of a State, it is utterly unavoidable that a considerable number of mothers whose husbands are either dead or disabled or who have deserted their families or are otherwise incompetent, have to enter the ranks as breadwinners.

W.A. Riddell, 'Memorandum on Mothers' Pensions,' 15 February 1917[1]

The policies of the Canadian Patriotic Fund, by focusing attention on the redistribution of income to families with children during the First World War, offered an oblique but nonetheless substantive criticism of the traditional Canadian wage structure. This chapter has two themes: why the ideology of children's or family allowances neither emerged after the war as a focal point of public debate nor was embedded in the logic of state welfare policies (as happened in Britain); and why the recognition during the war of the profound inadequacies of family living standards was instead transfigured into a widespread movement for mothers' allowances.

In considering why Canadian reformers and policymakers followed the American model rather than the British example of state family allowances, it is tempting to focus on differences in how constituencies and interest groups mobilized opinion. For example, it might be argued that the debate in Canada was strongly affected by the *absence* of a powerful female figure like Eleanor Rathbone, who campaigned for the endowment of motherhood in England as part of a feminist critique of the breadwinner norm. Similarly, some scholars have maintained that Canadian social reformers and feminists gravitated to mothers' allowances because of their strong connections with their American counterparts. The analysis of shifting networks of various interest groups offers a compelling and useful account of how welfare systems develop in different political cultures or nations,[2] but it fails to explain how certain specific policies become widely acceptable within the broader society. In the Canadian context, as James Struthers has made so clear,[3] the influence of mobilized women's organizations in Ontario immediately following the war was indispensable to the enactment of mothers' allowance legislation in that province. However, this does not explain why policymakers, who did not share some of the more radical critiques of poverty and visions of a positive state offered by a range of reform constituencies (but especially women's groups), became so well disposed toward what at the time amounted to a sharp disjuncture in provincial government policy. By enacting mothers' allowances, conservative governments like Ontario's were committing themselves to breaking long-standing traditions of private charitable relief – traditions on which their adamantine commitment to the minimalist state was based. It follows that policymaking and the forces impelling the State to expand its responsibilities – and its administrative capacities – must be understood as part of changing cultural patterns and national goals.

In Britain and Canada, both family and mothers' allowances were in large part a response to endemic social inequalities that had been starkly highlighted by the war experience – namely, the precarious nature of the family economy of the skilled worker, who supposedly was the bulwark of the country's national wealth and hence its social advancement. However, each welfare strategy held very different implications for the wage structure. The movement to endow motherhood through a system of family allowances was, as Susan Pedersen has argued, less successful in Britain and was refashioned into a policy of contributory widows' pensions;[4] but in Canada, groups outside immediate feminist or social maternalist circles deemed mothers' allowances highly desirable, for several reasons. First, such allowances appealed to the natalist public health agenda, which was at the height of its influence immediately after the war, when there was intense sensitivity to concerns over unfitness, the physical deterioration of the nation, and the obvious need for population growth. Second, the feminist campaign for social rights fed heartily on the public's recognition of the contribution of motherhood to the nation. Finally, such allowances were perceived by those who were concerned about economic efficiency, and who saw in home education a vital adjunct to technical education, to be an effective, indirect method for training a new generation of skilled workers. Most importantly, however, mothers' pensions appealed to a broad spectrum of opinion, ranging from businessmen to labour leaders to feminist activists, because it was believed they would uphold that broad network of interlocking reform measures, including protective labour laws for women and children and minimum wage legislation, which aimed at sustaining higher levels of wages for male breadwinners. Thus, even though they arose directly out of a postwar preoccupation with social inequality and labour disruption, mothers' allowances served broad economic imperatives. And in turn, mothers' allowances, because they upheld the status of the ideal male breadwinner – who by responsibly maintaining his wife and children supported a unified family economic unit, the anchor upon which all social equilibrium and national progress depended – appealed to more conservative members of society (especially government leaders), who believed that such legislation, by fostering family responsibility, was the most economical means by which to protect the minimalist state.

A central question facing historians of welfare policies is this: To what extent did the policy at hand constitute a radical break with traditions of charity, by offering a non-stigmatizing benefit for motherhood? Or did it in fact reinforce conservative social norms? An examination of the campaign for mothers' allowances in its broadly cultural context demonstrates the drawbacks to considering the concept of 'social justice' adumbrated in the first epigraph by the Rev. Peter Bryce in isolation from the conservative business and labour ideology of W.A. Riddell, who linked national efficiency to the enshrinement of the breadwinner ideal. Rather, one should consider the contemporary problems of social inequality as being on a continuum with national efficiency. Having done so, one can make sense of this apparent paradox. Canadian women were at the forefront in calling for a redefinition of the role of the State, for the movement of the family from private institution to public policy, for the endowment of motherhood as a nationally recognized goal, and for a redefinition of 'the deserving poor'; yet at the same time they sought out ideological alliances with organized labour by endorsing a panoply of progressive labour legislation that had as its goal the bolstering of the male family wage. From the perspective of contemporary maternal feminists, there was no conflict between on the one hand championing mothers' allowances as a means for redistributing national income to help impoverished widows, and on the other hand championing those allowances as a conservative economic instrument.

In a revealing letter to J.J. Kelso in 1918, Howard Falk, the director of the Winnipeg Council of Social Agencies, outlined his conception of the political economy of mothers' allowances. Falk emphasized how 'social justice' meshed imperceptibly with national economic goals by showing how relieving the poverty of widowed mothers was directly related to the shoring up of the standard of living of the 'independent self-supporting worker.' It made 'good business' to pay a 'salary' to mothers in their homes at an 'adequate' level, he stated. He reasoned that doing so would ensure that women did not compete with men in the workplace, and would also, because women would be educating their children both at home and at school, 'increase the earning capacity' of the next generation of industrial workers and thereby protect future governments from even greater demands by more radical advocates of welfare growth, by ridding society of the residuum, by making 'families wholly independent.'[5] Similarly, Helen Reid, who had done so much in Montreal during the war to make women's poverty a focus of public debate, was able to identify the loss of 'the breadwinning father,' with its implications for the family and for the national standard of living, as a worse fate than the loss of the moral mother – a concern of prewar Christian reformers. Thus, she was able to seamlessly advocate mothers' allowances and old age, unemployment, and health insurance, since all of these sustained the wages of male workers and functioned as prophylactics against the problem of the 'sub-standard man.'[6]

Notwithstanding the ideology of endowment of motherhood, and of the social citizenship of women, mothers' allowances came about largely as a result of a broader consensus regarding the norms of the male political economy, which was based on the ideal of masculine family independence. The movement for mothers' allowances was undergirded by a wide and seamless ideological spectrum that encompassed both maternal social citizenship, with its insistence on public endowment in exchange for women's reproductive service to the State, and a concept of economic national efficiency based on male work and wages, with its corporatist overtones. This was best illustrated by Helen Reid, who in 1920 quoted Herbert Hoover's prescription for social regeneration: 'If we could grapple with the whole child situation for one generation, our public health, our economic efficiency, the moral character, sanity and stability of our people would advance three generations in one.'[7]

'Every citizen a wage-earner'[8]

One of the first social reformers to advocate a province-wide system of outdoor relief or aid to dependent mothers with young children was J.J. Kelso. As Kelso himself made clear in his article 'Aiding Destitute Mothers,' he envisioned his campaign for mother's pensions as yet another avenue of attack against the placement of children in public institutions, privately owned orphanages, and creches. He pressed for 'some financial assistance' for destitute mothers 'so that they may not be compelled to neglect them [children] by going out working, or put them in public institutions where they would be deprived of the mothering and normal training to which they have a just claim.'[9] Administrators of orphans' homes, most of whom were women, quickly discerned Kelso's motives; during the first provincial government study of mothers' pensions, the Superintendent of the Girls' Home exclaimed: 'Are you going to close up all our homes?'[10]

Kelso's concern for mothers' pensions was firmly wedded to his conception of Christian motherhood and of the home as the locus for teaching Christian values, 'in the fear and admonition of the Lord' (see Chapter 1).[11] Kelso rightly pointed out that providing economic support for deserving mothers in their own homes marked a distinct break with 'old methods of poor relief' by making a 'more dignified provision' for widows and deserted mothers.[12] But his linking of mothers' allowances to public fears regarding delinquency and criminality among children – fully 40 per cent of all delinquents, he contended, came from households where the mother, because there was no male breadwinner, undertook paid work outside the home[13] – placed him firmly within the traditional late-nineteenth-century framework of the children's aid societies (CASs). Indeed, Kelso, who fretted constantly about the lack of public and government recognition for his child-saving campaign, conceived of a government program of outdoor relief for mothers as a means for extending the power of the children's aid societies. In his 1896 report as Superintendent of Neglected and Dependent Children, he maintained that women could be helped in their homes by either municipal or church organizations.[14] But as the CAS movement remained otiose into the early twentieth century, he came to recommend a program of mothers' allowances that would build on the existing network of children's shelters, whereby juvenile court judges would recommend which mothers were deserving of aid.[15] In an effort to protect the provincial power of the CASs, Kelso refused to endorse the proposal of the National Council of Women, which in 1915 lobbied Prime Minister Borden on the issue of establishing a national scheme of mothers' pensions, to be strongly linked with a military system of widows' pensions, which were more demonstrably rights-based.[16]

Kelso's claim that granting such wide additional powers to the CASs would obviate the need for 'any extensive additional machinery' made little impact even on the fiscally prudent government of Premier W.H. Hearst. By 1918 the child-saving movement, with its strong connections to the juvenile court system, had been shunted aside by other reform interests. Between 1917 and 1920 the rhetoric of juvenile delinquency persisted in government discussions of mothers' allowances, but it occupied a comparatively minor place. The child-saving network became marginalized while government policies for outdoor aid for widows were being developed, as shown by the fact that the Ontario Provincial Secretary, W.D. McPherson, chastised Kelso for trying to force the hand of the Hearst government. Also, Kelso was summarily omitted from any further engagement with the mothers' allowances campaign. That the CASs had been wholly circumvented is evident in an acerbic letter from Hugh Ferguson, a local CAS agent, to W.L. Scott, the head of its Ottawa branch: 'We hear that Rev. Peter Bryce, who is one of the leading men of the Social Service Council along with Mr. Agar, had a scheme on a while ago to get the Children's Aid work all under his thumb, and have Mr. Kelso pensioned or something else.'[17]

The problem of juvenile deliquency did not remain the guiding imperative behind the campaign for mothers' allowances. This was not simply because of changing machinations among reform lobbyists, as

Hugh Ferguson claimed. Rather, the jettisoning of CAS influence beto-kened a profound change in conceptions of poverty, social distress, and family disruption. Most important of all, it indicated an altered relationship between the individual and the community. This shift in emphasis away from the moral fibre of family life toward economic determinants of family disunity and thus social decay was occasioned largely by the experience of the First World War. It is best symbolized by the fact that the Canadian Conference of Charities and Corrections changed its name to the Canadian Conference on Public Welfare. As Frank N. Stapleford, general secretary of the Toronto Neighbourhood Workers' Association, made clear, with this change in nomenclature, delinquency and poverty were no longer perceived as symptoms of a lack of individual moral discipline and probity; the conference now embraced an 'attitude which looks upon crime and poverty as patho-logical conditions which may be largely removed by a readjustment of social forces. The first attitude sees the individual dependent as a dis-tinct and separate problem. The other sees him in relation to his whole social environment.'[18] Social workers like Stapleford now deemed the strong tincture of immorality that hung around older, more individual-istic views of civil well-being to be somewhat irrelevant to the new the-ories, which focused on political obligation and social responsibility and which gave clear priority to macro-economic interpretations of the common good, whereby the needs of the State took precedence over individual self-interest. Thus, in the years immediately following the First World War, social reformers spoke of citizenship less in terms of individual Christian morality and more in terms of 'economy, efficiency, sacrifice, service, and cooperation'[19] – characteristics that stressed the common good rather than individual rights and virtues.

Even stalwart champions of individual morality like W.L. Scott, the head of the Ottawa CAS, increasingly placed juvenile delinquency in the context of the general health and population growth of the entire nation.[20] In the same vein, another reform activist declared that the duty of all social workers was to train their clients to 'experience the joy of sinking the individual desire, for the good of the group' and pro-moted mothers' allowances for similar ends – namely for their function in furthering the 'interests of economy and good citizenship.'[21] In the wake of this new reification of the common good and this subordina-tion of individual ends to those of the 'State' – which symbolically began to be capitalized after the war – many of those who promoted mothers' allowances wished to have unmarried and deserted mothers benefit from this form of state aid, because they no longer deemed immorality in and of itself to be the root cause of social retrogression. Likewise, the home was no longer the private haven for instilling merely Christian moral precepts, for – as the war had so well demonstrated – family life and maternalism had become part and parcel of public policy. Because the family was the ideological and economic anchor of patriotism and national defence, it was the logical beneficiary of State protection.[22] As its advocates so often declared, mothers' allowances were intended not for individual ends, but rather to further national economic efficiency and as 'an investment in potential citizenship.'[23] As Stapleford attested, mothers' allowances were intended not just for reforming individual mothers and children, but 'for the future well-being of the State.'[24]

This dramatic shift in attitudes did not centre on the traditional liberal verities of individual rights and private self-control; rather, it conceived of citizenship in terms of the common good and collective identity – what Sir Robert Borden referred to as the individual's realization of 'his duty of service to the State.'[25] Individual rights, noted Borden in his 1914 address 'The War and Its Causes and Its Messages,' were no longer natural or automatic, which is how they had been defined by nineteenth-century liberal theorists; rather, they were wholly dependent on the degree to which individuals performed their duty to the State. The war thus engendered new definitions of public and private. Borden characterized the Empire as a family, with the parent state of Britain encircled by her dependencies or offspring, and likewise declared that the 'manhood' of the nation were responsible to their dependants or offspring, who in turn must be taught their own duties to contribute both economically and militarily to the defence of their family and to the Canadian nation.[26] The First World War directly challenged the nineteenth-century concept of the individual's autonomy from the State, and was decisive in transforming the traditional Victorian state's primary role. Before, the State had protected the rights and property of the individual; now it was the essential force defining national identity.[27] As Stapleford argued, the war had sounded the death knell for those *laissez-faire* doctrines long embedded in traditional liberalism; for it had demonstrated how the State's ability to finance and organize massive collective efforts was an enriching and positive influence on national life. According to Stapleford, the sanctity of private contract was a recipe for anarchy, while State controls were symbols of 'co-operation and mutual help'[28] and evocative of Christian virtues of 'service and sacrifice.'[29] 'Internal organization, wider social control, and a positive State programme.' Stapleford concluded, 'are the conditions of success for a nation under modern conditions.'[30]

What confirmed child welfare as a national issue was the crisis of depopulation and falling birthrates following the war. The care and protection of children was perceived to be a profoundly important issue – one far broader than the problem of delinquency, for it also encompassed national health and population growth, upon which depended industrial expansion and national wealth. During the 1920s, child welfare became the centrepiece of public discussion, because in the minds of reformers, businessmen, clergyman, and labour leaders, conservation of child life was directly linked to material prosperity. It became a frequent observation in wartime that 'the standard of prosperity is not to be found in the development of what is ordinarily defined as our natural resources, but in the number of prosperous homes, and happy well-trained children.'[31] Increasingly reformers and business commentators saw the 'entire fabric of national business' as intertwined with the family economy. Not only did this raise the thrifty housewife to a key position in national economic performance, but increasingly, it also drew a correlation between economic standards in the home and national economic efficiency. This in turn brought to the forefront the question of how to imbue workers with proper economic values. Especially, it emphasized the home training of the male child.[32]

After 1918, articles abounded redolent with fears regarding Canada's lack of readiness to compete with the new standards of industrial performance set by the modernized, research-driven cultures of Germany and the United States. Some advocated new structures and institutions such as a National Advisory Council for Scientific and Industrial Research[33]; others believed that the solution for avoiding the boom-and-bust cycles of prewar days was to create a more skilled, efficient, and fit workforce. It was from this latter perspective that children were deemed to be the key to solving the problem of a 'wasted prosperity.'[34] In a postwar economy characterized by rising inflation and falling wages – which in turn precipitated widespread strikes and social conflict – fears increasingly centred on the number male loafers and idlers that seemed to be proliferating in Canadian industrial cities as returned servicemen awaited either jobs or relief. In this social climate, themes of national wealth became ever more strongly linked with the problem of the family economy, which was where the fundamental values of the responsible worker were thought to reside. 'The family that works as a unit is usually a prosperous family. So with the country,' wrote Mrs Wilson.' 'By co-operation we can accrue wealth, efficiency, influence and power to strike out and establish ourselves in the midst of the best nations of the world.'[35]

This preoccupation with industrial wealth, and with the contribution that families, and most notably women, could make to training an ambitious, thrifty, and hard-working class of skilled workers, was critical in persuading traditionalists in provincial governments to greatly expand the sphere of state activity into areas once deemed decisively the realm of private family initiative. Just prior to the war, the dictates of political economy had overwhelmed older arguments that women's primary role was within the domestic circle, as the guardians and exemplars of Christian morality. This is indicated by the shift in how J.J. Kelso argued on behalf of mothers' pensions. At first he had stressed the moral education of children as the cure for juvenile delinquency in his advocacy of mothers' allowances; yet by 1912 he was emphasizing economic considerations. If women were paid to raise their children, Kelso contended, 'the children would grow up in a normal way to become useful and industrious citizens, adding by their labour to the wealth of the community, rather than becoming an expensive addition to the dependent classes.'[36] By war's end such reasoning was more fully appreciated in government, business, and labour circles. In 1915 the Ontario Commission on Unemployment had observed that, in the words of Gilbert Jackson, the University of Toronto political economist, 'the small, shiftless pauper class in Toronto graduated into that class through the ranks of casual labour.'[37] After the war, this seemed to have become social reality. The unchecked proliferation of unskilled and transient workers was seen by commentators at both ends of the political spectrum as undermining national efficiency, and was thought to be an early sign of everincreasing economic retrogression and social degeneracy. The vast numbers of incapacitated soldiers who might never again work to support their families, and the lack of either lengthy apprenticeships or technical education among young demobilized men, and the deskilling of labour during the war as a result of the employment of women and aliens, and the advance of technology, all profoundly disturbed both business and labour. These groups feared for the status of the skilled worker and for the wages of the Canadian male workforce, and were profoundly worried that the war had so depleted the skilled workforce that future industrial expansion would be impossible. Mothers' allowances were thus seen as but another means by which governments might accomplish their traditional task of fostering economic growth and protecting the interests of business. More important, aid to mothers would provide an indirect means of managing and educating the future labour force, without appearing to breach the code of government noninterference in relations between labour and capital.

When observers of the Canadian social condition commented that 'it is the quality of our citizenship that counts in the upbuilding of a nation,' they were referring not so much to personal moral character – although this element had not been entirely expunged from postwar definitions of good citizenship – as to the creation of an 'honest and industrious' citizenry of skilled workers.[38] From 1900 onwards there was a general recognition among both reformers and policymakers that the working man was the bulwark and strength of the nation,[39] largely because he was the engine of industrial progress. During the 1907 debate in the Senate on the question of old age pensions, G.W. Ross proclaimed that the working man was the cornerstone of Canada's prosperity; and informed his colleagues that workman's compensation and old age annuities were practical emblems of the new public recognition that the wage earner was a key factor in political economy, and so must be integrated into the broader social citizenship.[40] Like other progressive liberals, Ross straddled two worlds, old and new: the former called for state grants in old age, with the goal of preventing the scourge of dependency from interfering with the free market economy and prosperity; the latter called for state-funded social entitlements for workers, a conception that decisively broke with older, more punitive notions of poor relief and the workhouse.[41] Herbert Ames, the Montreal reform businessman, would have agreed with Kelso's contention that 'the widespread recognition of the rights of the working classes is indeed one of the most hopeful signs of the times.'[42] Ames himself advocated a more inclusive notion of citizenship rights; in an 1894 address to the Montreal YMCA, he revised older political notions of nation building, arguing that it was work – and especially the work of skilled workmen – that must form the essence of a progressive Canadian state.[43]

This early twentieth-century preoccupation with integrating the social classes into a larger conception of the common good, with its overtones of social democracy, was transfigured after the war so that it reflected more conservative business imperatives. The earlier emphasis on the rights of labour was softened in light of the requirements of national efficiency, which demanded that individual workers embrace specific duties and responsibilities. This transition from rights to duties was outlined by C.V. Corless, who in an address to the Royal Canadian Institute in 1919 spoke of a new postwar society in which the traditional underpinning of social democracy, the securing of 'the greatest benefit to all,' would serve a rather different end – the ensuring of 'social control.' By social control, Corless meant social *harmony*, a condition that in 'our present, highly organized, industrial, democratic society' could only be achieved by creating a large body of workmen who understood their economic and social place. Furthermore, the mental state of these workers would have to be so reformed through education, both in the home and in school, that a highly regimented working class was thereby created, one that thoroughly embraced the values of economic service. On the one hand, Corless seemed to be advocating progressive labour legislation such as Whitley councils, industrial democracy, and a living wage; on the other, his conception of industrial and social democracy was rooted in a highly conservative ethos whereby labour's primary responsibility was to employers and to the principle of national efficiency.[44]

This postwar discourse, which wedded industrial democracy with national efficiency, makes sense of J.J. Kelso's dicta that 'there is no higher patriotic duty than to inculcate the nobility of labour'[45] and that the 'child becomes the mediator between the social classes.'[46] The bonds of industrial and social peace were to be secured not by new institutional structures or by legal enactments, but rather by the education of children by mothers in the home. Only this would instil in children proper notions of ambition, productivity, responsibility, and loyalty to one's employer. Those children would then grow up to be skilled labourers, paid wages high enough to support a family, and thus become the critical social linchpin. By their example, these skilled workers would hold together disparate classes and interests within an overarching conception of the common good founded upon a combination of one's responsibility to family and to the State. In language redolent of neo-Lamarckian notions of recapitulation, E.A. Bott, a University of Toronto psychologist, in 'Studies in Industrial Psychology,' concluded that the transmission of work habits was a singularly biological process, whereby 'progressive stages of an organic growth in the individual' mirrored the conditions of home, school, and work. From this, it followed that the home training of children by mothers was the primary 'pre-industrial' force moulding the attitudes of future workmen. The shift in attention from educating children at school to maternal training within the home had begun at the turn of the century, and was accelerated after the First World War by new ideas of political economy, and by concerns over national efficiency and industrial growth, which were now believed to hinge as never before on early childhood training. From this perspective, family relationships were important because they taught cooperation and interdependence – characteristics crucial in instilling in young male workers proper attitudes toward work. Thus, children should be trained by mothers to be ambitious and to seek skilled and consistent work. Most importantly, male offspring were supposed to learn the all-important values of service and duty, both to one's employer and one's dependants. 'The worker-in-his-work,' stated Bott in 1920, 'characterizes the child discharging his duties and responsibilities in the family circle quite as much as it does his career through school and later in industry.'[47]

In earlier times, clergymen and reformers had stressed that the home was the centre for instilling narrowly Christian virtues and sentiments; by war's end, the family circle had been reconceived almost entirely in economic terms. Moral training was never perceived as conflicting with the development of the work ethic; that being said, the physical well-being and technical training of children was heavily emphasized during the decade that engendered the movement for mothers' allowances.[48] The spirit of the time called for the development not of industrial machines but of 'technical workmen,' whose skills and wages would support the entire edifice of industrial expansion and social uplift. In such a climate it was possible to define the child as a 'primary national asset'[49] and thus to consider mothers' allowances as a much less radical piece of legislation. As Rev. Peter Bryce, the chairman of the Ontario Mothers' Allowances Commission, attested, the benefits paid out by this legislation would 'ultimately be saved in a better type of citizen, in a higher productive capacity on the part of our citizens.'[50] When promoters of mothers' allowances identified poverty as an integral concern of the State, this was based on fears that if the children of 'desolate widowhood' were denied a broad field of opportunities,[51] the majority of workers in the next generation would remain confined to the ranks of the unskilled. In the certain absence of adequate wages, there would be neither breadwinners nor homemakers, because of the 'incapacity of the breadwinner to provide adequately for his family and widowhood.'[52] Those wishing to highlight the social benefits of mothers' allowances for government officials in Ontario, approvingly quoted from a grateful widowed beneficiary of state aid, who recounted that in the absence of such funds 'my older children had to leave school and go to work as soon as they were able and now they are unskilled workers. Now that I have a regular allowance coming in, my little ones shall have the chance denied the older ones.'[53] And in its 1926 annual report, the Ontario Mothers' Allowances Commission favourably reported that it had concrete evidence that the children of beneficiaries were entering the industrial world at wages substantially higher than those of their parents.[54] From this perspective, a proper system of mothers' allowances was indeed a combination of justice and 'self-interest on the part of the State.'[55] Those who sponsored the legislation believed that having inculcated in future male breadwinners attitudes of service to one's employer and responsibility to one's family, the state might wither away as family dependency was eliminated. Mothers' allowances were but a means of maximizing social efficiency, and would obviate the need for state charity.[56] Fundamentally, mothers' allowances were a temporary public investment to shore up the ideal of family independence through private means.

Indeed, themes of family responsibility permeated most social reform discourse in this period. The *Report of the Committee on Child Labor* for Ontario emphasized that child labour laws should not be too restrictive, and argued against a binding rule that no child could work before the age of fourteen. The reasoning here was that sending male children to work at as early an age as possible would 'make it imperative that he should contribute to the support of himself and others.'[57] Anxieties over whether the ideal of the family economy could be sustained, whereby male heads of the family would be naturally imbued with enough of what Rev. S.D. Chown called 'the spirit of manliness,'[58] which would lead them to economically support their wives and children reached a fever pitch as the war ended in 1918. Falling wages and rising unemployment were forcing thousands of returned men to leave home in search of work – a development that exacerbated the wartime trend of men abandoning the care of their dependants. After the First World War, family desertion came to be seen not simply as the reflection of moral failure, but as a social problem of enormous proportions[59] – what the director of the Montreal Family Welfare Association termed 'an infection ... in the social system.'[60] Social workers marshalled daunting statistics showing how widespread the phenomenon of family disintegration had become. In one survey of 136 Winnipeg family case histories, 109 cases of poverty (84 per cent) were attributed to desertion by the father. The Montreal Society for the Protection of Women and Children reported a startling increase in desertion, with 885 cases of non-support and desertion, and by 1929 concluded that desertion was the single largest cause of family distress. More disturbing still, reformers began to recognize that there was no effective legal means by which to enforce sanctions against this form of 'delinquency.'[61] As George H. Corbett, head of the Montreal Society for the Protection of Women and Children, confided to Helen Reid, existing legal structures were entirely inadequate, and the lack of responsibility among male breadwinners was one of the largest contributors to the problem of dependency in Canada. Observed Corbett of a delinquent father who deserted his pregnant wife and child: 'If this man like so many of the others, knows the law, or its lack, and refuses to recognize his responsibility; his wife and children and the coming child will have to depend upon public charity – no matter how willing we might be to use our influence and persuasion to bring him to time.'[62]

Although moral opprobrium remained at the core of discussions of desertion, condemnation was less frequently meted out to women. Some did believe that most often it was the actions of wives that forced husbands to flee their responsibilities, or that deserted women were the first to fall into 'immoral habits'[63]; but generally speaking, the postwar discourse on desertion took the form of a forceful critique of the 'recalcitrant husband.'[64] Typical cases recorded by social work agencies focused on the moral degeneracy of the irresponsible husband, who had either entered into a bigamous marriage during the war, or deserted his wife after an adulterous liaison. A man named Price came to Canada during the war and married a woman in Montreal at the Welsh Mission. Seven years later he deserted her and returned to his other wife in Scotland. The injured party was described as 'a very respectable type' who only 'deteriorated very considerably in every way' as a result of this 'awful injustice.' As a result, this woman and her three children barely subsisted on the charitable relief dispensed by the Ladies' Benevolent Institution. The Canadian government spent $3,000 attempting to compel the 'delinquent' Price to maintain his Canadian dependants. Another man had married in England and left his family dependent on Poor Law relief. After immigrating to Montreal he earned $100 a month as an elevator attendant, but he adamantly refused to recognize his wife's legitimate claim, and even worse, seemed not to care for his children, preferring the company of a saleswoman from one of the Montreal department stores. Even when men were located, they refused to fulfil their 'civil responsibility' by providing economic sustenance for their dependants.[65] In W.A. Riddell's 1917 'Memorandum on Mothers' Pensions,' a document prepared for the Ontario government, several juvenile court cases were described in detail, ostensibly to show how mothers who entered the workforce damaged family life. Yet in most of the cases offered, the father (if still living) was described as a moral failure: drunken, unemployed or working as a casual labourer, and lacking in affection for his family[66]; while the mother was portrayed as a long-suffering and hardworking victim of male shiftlessness.

Discussions of desertion thus remained both moral and gendered,[67] but the animus had now shifted toward men. Walter Rollo, the head of the Hamilton branch of the Trades and Labor Congress and later Minister of Labour for Ontario, insisted that the weight of condemnation must fall upon the male head of the family, concluding that the State must help these helpless women because they had become impoverished 'through no fault of their own.'[68] Since desertion was no longer generally perceived as a moral failure on the part of the wife, many labour leaders, public health officials, and female superintendents of orphanages, and various representatives of women's organizations, all of whom testified at the hearings of the Ontario investigation into mothers' allowances, argued forcefully that deserted women should be included as beneficiaries of the new legislation. This widespread public recognition of the problem of male family desertion also injected new energy into an older perspective that saw desertion as occupying a private domain insofar as it related to relations between husband and wife. Those who did not wish the state to interfere with the marriage bond sought merely to reinforce various provincial statutes so that wives would be able to compel husbands to support them, and to have family desertion embedded in the Criminal Code.[69] For similar reasons, unmarried mothers were encouraged to utilize the legal machinery of the Unmarried Parents' Act. The majority of social workers considered unmarried mothers the victims of unrestrained male lust, and their marital status the result of male irresponsibility; nevertheless, they rejected the notion that the State should pay these mothers to raise their children on the same basis as widows, fearing that such state paternity would undermine the institution of marriage.[70] In order to explain why most social reformers and government officials preferred the private avenue of the courts, as opposed to direct state aid in the form of mothers' allowances, as the remedy for 'the wholesale breaking up of families,'[71] one must examine the prevailing attitudes toward family responsibility that provided the justification for mothers' allowances.

Many social workers recognized that legislation had failed to compel husbands to support their families. (As Mrs Crerar rightly observed, 'We cannot always make men moral by law.'[72]) Even so, government representatives such as W.A. Riddell were unwilling to fund deserted women and their children out of public coffers. They maintained that state funding might encourage men to desert and abandon all familial responsibility, and that it might therefore appear that the State was sanctioning family breakdown. 'In the unsettled circumstances following the war,' Riddell informed Premier Hearst, 'men should not be led to believe that if they shift their family responsibilities the state will take them up.'[73] All agreed that the goal of both private charity and state relief measures must be to reinforce family responsibility among male breadwinners, but by the 1920s a debate had emerged over the best means to protect the modern family. As a 1919 article in the *Toronto Mail* attested, no one disputed the usefulness of the State in giving help to widows and 'those left destitute by the desertion of husbands.' The incubus that threatened to shatter the reform consensus was the problem of not wanting to 'encourage shiftlessness and lack of responsibility of relatives.'[74]

The central issue in the debate over including deserted women as beneficiaries of mothers' allowances, was this: Was it more profitable to the State in the long run to prevent the break-up of families by supporting, in the short run, deserted women who were compelled by poverty to give up their children to the children's aid societies? Or was the more enduring method to 'strengthen and ennoble family ties' to teach male children, the future male breadwinners, how to become 'useful, respectable men'?[75] Some, like W.H. Lovering, a former local officer of the CPF, championed those women who had been deserted 'through no fault of their own,' claiming that direct economic aid in the form of outdoor relief had been a 'moral lever'[76] to these women, whose homes had shown such great improvement, and who had become such models of family unity that 'some of these neglectful husbands are going back to take up their domestic obligations.' Notwithstanding his advocacy on behalf of deserted women, Lovering cast his proposals firmly within the overarching ideology of the natural rights of the male breadwinner. Thus, he defused objections from exponents of the model of the self-sustaining family headed by a male breadwinner by stating that the CPF succeeded by virtue of the fact that it paid benefits 'in recognition of the husband.'[77] The idea that the solution for the apparent breakdown of family responsibility during the war lay in making the State 'the foster parent of these children,'[78] and that such a strategy would be favoured by government because it could only serve to increase 'the wealth of the trained human asset,'[79] could not in the final analysis compete with the pre-eminence that makers of social policy placed on the shibboleth of family independence, whereby ideally a well-trained, skilled wage earner wholly supported his wife and children, or, in his absence, the wages of his children combined with contributions from other relatives sustained the integrity of home life. Indeed, the only provincial jurisdiction to provide state assistance for deserted women was Manitoba, which until the 1930s continued to make grants to those dependant women who had been deserted by their soldier husbands after the conclusion of the First World War.[80] True to the principles of the Charity Organization Society, the drafters of mothers' allowances programs adhered to the nineteenth-century belief that there was no better form of social insurance for the family than personal obligation.[81]

Although in many ways mothers' pensions broke with the perspectives of private charity by offering a nonstigmatizing payment to widows for their children, long-standing fears that poverty was an inheritable trait permeated the debate over mothers' allowances in the years following the war.[82] Those who believed that men could only achieve 'the full stature of manhood' by becoming 'self-maintaining wage earners'[83] came to dominate this debate in the provinces. And because the mothers' allowance movement succeeded mainly by enshrining the ideal that the father had a moral obligation to provide economically for his wife and children,[84] deserted, divorced, and unmarried mothers were ultimately disenfranchised from any entitlements to state economic aid.[85] Despite the public consensus that these women were not at fault in routing the male breadwinner from the home, even the plight of their impoverished offspring (who were often institutionalized) was insufficient to combat the stalwart dedication of government policymakers to the deeply imbedded social norm of family independence. The equation between the family and the state posited by progressive reformers, in which the family was seen as the foundation of the nation and the home the basis of all social ideals, was instrumental both in reconceiving the family as a public institution and in reconfiguring the boundaries of state action. In this sense, mothers' allowances paradoxically became a force that *circumscribed* government growth. Mothers' allowances seemed to *enlarge* the scope of state authority; however, because these social entitlements remained firmly and enduringly attached to the ideal of the self-sustaining family economy, they were able to elicit considerable support from conservative business, labour, and government constituencies. Thus, the defence of the status of the skilled male breadwinner was instrumental in preserving the minimalist state.

'The Cradle and the Nation'[86]

The experience of war ushered in a new dispensation for women and marked the beginning of a new role for motherhood and family life in the sphere of public policy. All of this was clearly enunciated in the November 1918 issue of *Woman's Century* in the very month in which the cessation of hostilities was declared. 'Through war,' observed Anne Anderson Perry, 'the preservation of the child has become not only the highest type of philanthropy, but the most stark racial necessity. So, Woman and Woman's work become, at last, of the first national importance, and Home and State, are seen by even the most short-sighted, to be an Indivisible Whole.'[87] In earlier articles such as 'Woman, Where Are You Going?' this writer had expressed fears that if the 'cradle is to be nationalized,' women would be ineluctably harnessed to a regime of State polygamy, a form of 'nationalized slavery,' in which they would become the hapless victims of uncontrollable male sexual appetite, licensed by state-driven imperatives that aimed at replacing future soldier-citizens after the slaughter of war. 'No sane woman,' wrote Perry, 'will ever regard the cradle as she is advised to do, as the replenisher of trenches, the producer of food for cannon; and above all, no sane woman will ever consent to being regarded either by herself or the males as merely the female animal of the species who must multiply at the demands of men and military, in the interests of a Deified State.'[88] By war's end, however, she no longer saw in state motherhood the disregard of the family as a sacred unit or the erosion of female rights; for the ravages of war, with total losses of allied men at six million, had further diminished the potential for increasing the birthrate.[89] Perry vouchsafed a natalist program that would at last publicly affirm women's contribution to the nation.

Like most of feminists, Perry saw in motherhood the means by which to further women's freedom and women's rights, especially regarding state entitlements for women's care. While rhetoric about eugenics and population growth was mouthed by male doctors and other public health officials, feminists deftly played on widespread fears of postwar depopulation by championing motherhood as a national cause. In this way, they made it the chief vehicle for promoting women's issues. Utilizing the language of race and fitness that so characterized male eugenic advice to women, Marjorie MacMurchy stated that if a woman wished to be considered 'a true nation builder,' she should help replenish the pool of fit children.[90] Women did not dissent from male public-health perspectives; rather, in order to solidify women's influence, they allied themselves with such constituencies by stressing that motherhood was a 'sacred national duty.'[91] 'If we are to be a great nation,' declared Helen Reid, 'we must begin at the bases, the health of the nation, and see that we have healthy boys and girls born to be our future citizens.'[92] In the new, postwar calculus of the responsibilities of the individual and of the State, women used their role as mothers and their indispensable service to repopulating the nation as a platform from which to demand reciprocal government payment. As the National Council of Women argued, if women were to be the seed for the most 'valuable asset' of the nation – that is, fit citizens – then the state should pay for this female burden of developing Canada's future citizens by funding well-baby clinics, free milk stations, and education for scientific motherhood, as well as a national scheme of mothers' pensions.[93]

Canadian social feminists utilized the postwar preoccupation with population growth and its associated exaltation of motherhood to argue that biological reproduction and moulding the character of children constituted services to the State equivalent to the sacrifices of soldier-citizens. In so doing, they established a new definition of social citizenship on which to base female entitlements to state assisance. More than any other group in Canada, women were instrumental in transforming traditional male-centred definitions of political citizenship founded on suffrage, into a new conception of social citizenship – a 'civic charter of freedom'[94] – that stressed one's contribution to 'the social economy and public service'[95] as the basis of community rights and obligations. Excising the primacy of the franchise from her definition of citizenship, Agnes Maule Machar wrote in 1916:

One of the first duties of the citizen, is consideration for the interests and well being of others. No functions are more important from this point of view than those of the 'mother.' For, it is undeniable that the mothers' self-sacrificing devotion to the infancy and development of the future citizen lies at the very foundation of the commonweal, – second, in no small degree to the material prosperity and outward security gained by the strong arms of its manhood.[96]

The notion that the State's obligations to its citizenry were founded on one's service to others dovetailed with the tenets of social Christianity, and in no small way explained why the mainstream Protestant denominations so strongly supported the postwar reform agenda of Canadian feminists – especially their espousal of a system of mothers' allowances.[97]

In positing that nationalism was a collective identity formed out of a common conception of ethics and character, which were believed to be essentially the product of maternal care in the home, women such as Adelaide Hoodless were consciously rejecting the older, male-dominated vision of constitutional patriotism in favour of one that saw women overtly 'as a national factor.'[98] Women reversed the traditional perception that morals and hence loyalty flowed imperceptibly out of one's identity with civil government.[99] Unlike earlier commentators such as Egerton Ryerson and Goldwin Smith, who conceived of patriotism as entirely coterminous with constitutional rights, modern interpreters of Canadian nationalism such as George M. Grant and George Wrong conceived of national life as the product of common moral sentiments and traditions, which they believed flowed biologically from generation to generation. The ideological dispute between Smith and Grant did not entail simply a conflict between views of American continentalism or loyalty to Britain; rather, George Grant, who was committed to the possibility of an independent Canadian nationalism, rejected Goldwin Smith's argument that, because patriotism was simply a reflection of political identity, ethnic identities in Canada, represented by Englishmen, Irishmen, and Scotchmen, could never coalesce into a wider, organic Canadian nationalism.[100] In conceiving of nationalism largely in social–biological terms, and of community identity in terms of 'unbroken traditions' passed down through the ages through the 'unity of the family,'[101] those like George Grant and George Wrong represented a more modern view of the relationship between the individual and the State, which was now bound by the independent variable of character.[102]

This transmutation in nationalist interpretations toward the concepts of 'biology' and 'family' provided social feminists with an important ideological wedge, with which they were able to elaborate a new equation between individual motherhood and the State, and between social relationships and political rights. Indeed, Canadian social feminists were at the forefront of new definitions of political economy, in which the 'sense of community' was formed out of a 'sense of duty,' and the State was no longer considered an abstraction separate from its citizens. Concepts of loyalty and political economy were now linked by the concept of family relations, so that the general public welfare of the people was deemed to constitute the fabric of the State. As Mrs Warwick Chipman of the Montreal Council of Women stated, the new individualism was defined by one's 'cordial service toward the state that is administered with closest attention to public welfare, as to make loyalty the distinctive characteristic of that people.'[103]

By incorporating changing notions of nationalism and political economy into their arguments for female social rights, women were constructing a new entity called the 'social,' which connected what hitherto had been the discrete categories of the economic and political, and using this to advance the idea that governments should automatically protect family life and the welfare of its citizens. Through effective public activism, maternal feminists propelled the issue of motherhood and family welfare to the centre of public discussion,[104] and were instrumental in determining new legislative agendas for governments. Hence, in a 1919 article 'The Big Legislative Issues,' a prominent social reformer observed that the State was now recognizing all issues which affected individuals in their social relations, such as public health, children, and other dependants. These were now considered part of the polity. 'Governments,' he wrote, 'are organized to protect and promote human welfare. States prosper and progress just in proportion to the care which they give to the development of the intelligence, morality, health and happiness of their people.'[105] However much women were the dominant force in reconceptualizing, for male reformers and policymakers, the powers of the state in the years following the First World War, they nevertheless saw this reconceived relationship between the individual and government as essentially a contract between mothers and the State – what one reformer referred to as 'The Mother State and her Weaker Children.'[106] The female author of 'What Twelve Canadian Women Hope to See as the Outcome of the War' pointed out the extent to which the new political economy of the State was determined by the social service of motherhood and thus fulfilled an essentially female reinterpretation of citizenship: 'From the new pure and passionate patriotism upspringing in their souls, women will cry: "We have given our sons to our country! They are gone, but teach us, oh, Lord! – teach us mothers of the race, to save the coming generation ... Let the tendrils of affection of each boy and girl reach out from the family to the state, from the state to the nation, from the nation to the world."'[107]

By establishing motherhood, reproduction, and the moulding of character as the wellspring of national identity and social cohesion, Canadian feminists were able to marshal powerful arguments concerning their social rights, which later informed important pieces of state welfare legislation for protecting women and children – most significantly, mothers' allowances. An important ideological corollary to these new gendered notions of state rights was a revised view, offered by maternal feminists and male reformers concerned about the welfare of women and their offspring, regarding who constituted the deserving and undeserving poor. This new perspective mainly exonerated women from the punitive and stigmatizing aspects of traditional poor relief and was a crucial factor in persuading cautious governments to embrace the notion that poverty was the product of social forces rather than of individual moral failings. The severing of the causal link between moral weakness and pauperization that underlay this sharp reversal informed much of the public debate regarding mothers' allowances. Although this feminist critique of poor law ideology, including its gendered notion of deservedness, was integrated into state welfare policies, a considerable gap continued to exist between the intentions of reformers and actual government policies. This is best illustrated by the fact that despite feminists' insistences that deserted and unmarried mothers should receive state welfare entitlements equal to those of disadvantaged widows because all women were now relieved of the taint of personal responsibility for their indigence, these classes of women were not recognized in the various provincial mothers' allowances acts.

Prior to 1900, poverty was considered in all quarters as exclusively the outcome of flaws in individual moral character. This attitude formed the basis of the punitive facets of poor-law regimes with their workhouse tests, rooted in the concept of lesser eligibility.[108] Concepts of poverty, however, have always been gendered, insofar as the general prejudice against outdoor relief – that breeding ground of pauperization and idleness – was often abrogated in practice in favour of widows and children, largely because public sentiment frowned on women being forced to work for wages.[109] Here, the intransigence of the breadwinner ideal, which so permeated contemporary readings of political and moral economy, served to benefit women. Yet in Canada, despite the absence of a legal panoply of poor laws (except in New Brunswick and Nova Scotia), the undergirding principles of that ideal remained enshrined in social policy. By the late nineteenth century they were given renewed impetus by the establishment in various urban centres of Charity Organization Societies (COSs). However, just as these organizations were gaining a firm toehold within the networks of private charity, newer ideas about poverty were emerging.

One of the first and most consistent defences of a non-stigmatizing system of outdoor relief was enunciated in 1897 by Agnes Maule Machar, a dominant force in relief administration in Kingston, and a particular champion of the rights of widows and orphans. Building on nineteenth-century gendered notions of the deserving poor, Machar declared that 'aside from the consideration that the most "undeserving" often have young and helpless families, whom we cannot leave to perish, they would have to be very undeserving to be worthy of capital punishment by starvation.' What was particularly novel about Machar's examination of social distress was that she considered the problem of poverty not in moral terms but rather as 'the waste product of modern social forces.' It was this emphasis on the social dimension of poverty that made Machar's treatise so path-breaking. Machar rejected the notion that there was a moral aspect to pauperization, and that poverty was causally linked to idleness, improvidence, and intemperance – largely considered male attributes by Machar – and concluded: 'Shall we dare to stigmatize these degenerates as unworthy, when they are simply what heredity, environment and our social sytem has made them.'[110] Machar's plea had little immediate impact on how charity was dispensed. However, the germs of this new conceptualization of poverty had taken root by the first decades of the twentieth century, even though the advocates of this new approach to reform had to wage a running battle with the well-entrenched COSs. While the Canadian Conference of Charities condemned outdoor relief at its 1899 conference, this was the high-water mark for traditional notions of poverty and poor relief.[111] By the end of the First World War, a sea change had occurred in the approach reformers were taking to evaluating the contributory causes of family poverty. In a headlining article in the *Christian Guardian*, 'Causes of Poverty,' Frank Stapleford of the Toronto Neighbourhood Workers' Association refuted older notions which held that poverty was the outcome of defects of character: 'The victims of poverty,' he admonished, 'are the casualties of the social order.' Stapleford never entirely severed the link between morality and impoverishment; but at the same time, like many of his reform colleagues, he accepted that poverty – the product of illness, unemployment, and death of the breadwinner – was a condition far beyond the control of the individual and that its remedy therefore lay beyond the realm of personal mores. From this new reform perspective, if moral issues were related to poverty, they were both subsidiary to and a consequence of inadequacies within the 'industrial system.' The moral component of social distress would never be fully expunged from contemporary discussions of poverty, largely because the large majority of reform leaders were clergyman who, because they insisted that social distress had a spiritual dimension, were able to sustain a central role for the imperatives both of social Christianity and of the mainstream Protestant denominations.[112]

Like older poor relief policies, the early twentieth-century progressive emphasis on social diagnosis was likewise gendered, in that it continued to make an issue out of male profligacy. But in the crucible of war, the ideology of motherhood as the key to national regeneration acquired such unassailable moral armour that the age-old Christian dictum, often used by poor law advocates, that 'the poor, ye have always with you' lost much of its cultural authority – especially as it applied to women. Proclaiming the rights of procreative mothers as superior to those of destructive male soldiers, Constance Lynd argued that the State must take up the duty of 'mothering' all children. In an unusual declaration she called for both mothers' pensions and a system of general family allowances: 'Give us mothers' pensions. Give us children's pensions. Free the mother and child from poverty.'[113]

In contrast, the Federal Emergency Appropriation Fund administered by the CPF to relieve unemployed demobilized soldiers – what many saw as the precursor to government unemployment insurance schemes – came under consistent attack. Advocates of mothers' allowances condemned soldiers so maintained as 'wards of the State,'[114] and moral condemnation remained rife throughout discussions of male unemployment. In one particularly pungent memorandum to Premier Drury of Ontario, an anonymous writer castigated the work of the Soldiers' Aid Commission, informing him that it was a common observation that if 'a returned soldier drinker wished the price of a crock, he should interview the Secretary of the Soldiers' Aid Commission.'[115] The traditional poor law outlook, with its injunctions against moral deficiency, remained a fixture of discussions of postwar male unemployment. In his 1918 article for *Woman's Century*, 'Mothers' Pensions in America,' Otto McFeely decried 'the idea that children should be kept in poverty because their father is a drunkard, a criminal or incompetent, is unhuman, wasteful and bad policy from every point of view.'[116] J.J. Kelso agreed that women should not be forced to suffer 'the disgrace of poverty,'[117] for he believed that female poverty was due to uncontrollable social factors 'through no fault of their own.' However, he described male poverty as a 'social disease,' to be combatted 'through moral stimulation,' which might engender a 'new vision of manhood,'[118] rather than through government grants. In arguing on behalf of state aid for mothers, Kelso observed: 'The idle men should be compelled by law to work and a man who will remain at home and allow his wife to work and support his family should not be allowed to live.'[119] Ironically, it was this enduring gendered assumption regarding the origins of poverty, combined with the breadwinner ideal, that slowed the creation of state welfare rights for men (i.e., a system of unemployment or social insurance) and that resulted in mothers' allowances being the first government legislation to break with traditional means of female relief, namely, private charity, municipal relief, and the House of Industry.[120]

Because women comprised the vast majority of relief visitors who worked for the CPF, and also formed the largest constituency benefiting from this semigovernmental system of assistance, it is not surprising that women's networks became the driving force behind the broad cultural transformation in public attitudes to poverty following the First World War. By 1920 the belief that women were poor 'through conditions over which they have no control'[121] was largely uncontested in the forum of women's magazines. As the article 'Mothers' Pensions in Ontario' in the *Ottawa Journal* in 1920 explained: 'The idea was gaining headway that people suffering for causes seemingly beyond their control should not be dependent upon uncertain sources for assistance.'[122] Canadian women were at the forefront in disengaging concepts of poverty from immorality. Their campaign on behalf of respectable motherhood gained particular force after demobilization, in the wake of the slaughter on the battlefields, when it was tragically demonstrated how widowhood and desertion ignored class boundaries. Thousands of wives of skilled wage earners and salaried workers experienced the impact that the permanent absence of the male breadwinner had on both their standard of living and their class status. As the problem of poverty began to reach the 'average family,' the notion that immorality and poverty were linked lost much of its sway: 'It seems obviously a sound principle that no child should be separated from the care of a good mother because the latter has the misfortune to be poor and yet such separations are taking place everyday merely on the grounds of poverty alone.'[123]

However, the idea that a woman was immoral by virtue of her poverty remained deeply rooted in the administration of child welfare, and continued to be a basic tenet of the children's aid societies. This was poignantly illustrated by the plight of Mrs C. who fled her alcoholic husband, a prestigious local professional man. On leaving her husband, Mrs C. was compelled to take up paid labour as an apprentice in the garment industry. Her class status thus immediately declined, as did perceptions of her respectability and ability to be a good mother. The Ontario Provincial Secretary maintained that her ability to mother was disqualified by her poverty; as the most important consideration in the assignment of custody of her children, he cited 'the means you have of maintaining and supporting them properly.' Mrs C., however, believed that her function as a mother gave her an automatic claim to respectability and morality and overrode any disadvantages arising from her straitened circumstances: 'I appeal to you as a parent to see that I get a mother's chance. I am working in the hope of having my children. If I am not to get them ... all my motherly hopes would be forever destroyed.' That her morality was unconnected with her economic status was confirmed by the Rev. R.P. Bowles, Principal of Victoria College and Mrs C.'s girlhood pastor, who placed the burden of moral condemnation on the head of the wastrel, abusive, drunken husband.[124]

The theme that women victimized by the untimely loss of the male breadwinner were forced both to enter the workforce and to give up their children against their will, suffused discussions of state payments to widows and deserted mothers. Stories of young mothers with large numbers of children whose husbands' unions paid no sickness benefits, who were forced to accept insubstantial private charity, or who had to rely on meagre handouts from the CASs, proliferated following the war. One woman was deserted by her husband, who had claimed to be going on a business trip. Although helped out by municipal relief and by the Hebrew Benevolent Fund, she was forced to sell all her furniture. She had six children under sixteen, and one can only guess that she – like thousands of other women – was ultimately forced to break up her family and send her children to foster care.[125] Such piteous tales served their rhetorical aims; the idea that they were poor 'through no fault of their own' stimulated the 'humanitarian principles' of 'the State,'[126] and thereby became an underlying principle of Ontario's mothers' allowances scheme.

State recognition of the plight of widows was, however, not solely the achievement of organized social feminism. Because the critique offered by women of traditional relief measures converged with wider fears concerning the integrity of the family, maternal feminists were able to forge alliances with more conservative interests.[127] In the end, the sanctity of the home and the privileges of the male breadwinner were enshrined by mothers' allowance legislation because Canadian feminists were less radical than their British counterparts; and because they were less committed to the idea that endowment for motherhood was a means to economic independence for women, than they were to the aim of keeping women out of the workforce in order to sustain the buoyancy of male wages. The views of the chairman of the Ontario Mothers' Allowances Commission, the WCTU, the National Council of Women, the CASs, and the Trades and Labour Council of Canada coalesced around the national economic imperative of protecting the wages of skilled workers. The feminist movement to free women from the moral stigma of poverty was instrumental in achieving state welfare entitlements for women, but these benefits were in the final analysis a solution to the problem of male work, which remained the pivot around which the discussion of mothers' allowances revolved. As J.J. Kelso explained to the women's club of Montreal in 1909: 'One of the greatest crimes that could be committed was to take a poor mother who for some cause had been deprived of the breadwinner of the family and compel her to go out and work in order to support her children, and to do menial work for which she was not fitted while the children ran in the streets. It was punishing her because of conditions for which she was not in any way responsible.'[128] Perorations about the plight of impoverished women were not merely sentimentalism, nor were they a means to highlight the right of women to economic independence.

Rather, stories of how hapless widows were being corralled into menial jobs were oblique references to how married women's work posed a threat to the male wage. The portrayal of mothers' pensions as an act of social justice was thus inextricably wedded to traditional conceptions of the domestic ideal of the male breadwinner and his family of dependants. Writing in 1917, the year in which the Imperial Munitions Board began its national campaign to recruit female factory workers, W.A. Riddell, the Superintendent of Trades and Labour for Ontario, commented that 'as long as mothers' pensions do not form part and parcel of the social administration of a State, it is utterly unavoidable that a considerable number of mothers whose husbands are either dead or disabled or who have deserted their families or are otherwise incompetent, have to enter the ranks as breadwinners.'[129]

By directly situating both a general cultural defence of motherhood and arguments for its support by government within the context of population growth and national economic efficiency, maternal feminists were demonstrating that political economy was no longer just a male domain; in this area of policymaking, women played an important role. All policies connected with the 'protection of the home' were now identified with the goal of creating national wealth, and by virtue of that were part of the basis on which women argued for 'a place equal to man in all departments of life.'[130] Few Canadian feminists used the phrase of Eleanor Rathbone, the British labour feminist, 'the endowment of motherhood';[131] and even those who did, like 'Aunt Adelaide,' a regular columnist for The Statesman, a journal of progressive liberal thought, did not refer to endowment in terms of the individual rights of women, or in terms of women's economic self-sufficiency. Rather, like the vast majority of feminists in Canada, Aunt Adelaide's outlook was much more conservative in its assumptions; in her view, the goals to be furthered by state policies, such as protective factory legislation for women and children, minimum wages, and mothers' allowances, were national economic goals and linked to a defence of the wages of skilled male workers.

In Canada there was a decided absence of public support for expanding individual rights.[132] The concept of the individual was always cast within the framework of one's duties, which in turn implied that one's behaviour and actions were valid only insofar as they served the larger interests of the community. This missing strand of individual rights – the mainstay of nineteenth-century liberal thought – confirms an observation made both by political scientists and by historians: Canada's political culture was grounded in a particularly conservative, organic, community-driven variant of liberalism.[133] As a result, advocates of both mothers' allowances and a minimum wage for women and children defended these causes largely on the basis of how they affected the future motherhood of the nation. Thus, while Alison Craig, one of the foremost promoters of a minimum wage for women in Winnipeg, articulated a conception of a living wage for women, she more often insisted that 'deeper than all considerations of industrial equity, important as these are, must be remembered that the girl workers of today are the mothers of the next generation. Not only must they be guarded from exploitation for their own sakes, but for the sake also of the trust they hold for the nation.'[134] Likewise, J.W. Macmillan, a Presbyterian minister who later chaired the Ontario Minimum Wage Board, promoted policies to protect women in terms of their contribution to the wider community. According to Macmillan, mothers' allowances, together with a minimum wage for single women, were mere variants of Macdonald's National Policy of tariffs, in that they contributed to national efficiency and economic progress by helping protect the rights of the wage earner. In Macmillan's view, mothers' allowances were not a radical measure; rather, they fell within a long-established tradition of liberal thought which held that governments intervene as little as possible in economic life and only for the sake of creating an environment of equal opportunity for all. As he stated: 'In former days the government of the country used to subsidize railways, companies, factories, and business houses for the general uplift and progress of the community. These subsidies may have been unfairly taken advantage of, but the general principle of the State assisting industry – and through industry its people – was still good, although it was being done in another form.'[135]

In the estimation of Canadian social feminists, there was no inherent conflict between the protection of motherhood, with its goal of 'training [children] to be useful citizens,' and the ideal of social democracy through economic growth; for mothers' allowances, in conjunction with a minimum wage and shorter working hours for women, prevented male wages from falling and thus afforded both present and future wage earners 'the chance to express their manhood' through their ability to support their dependants. A woman's contribution to the nation no longer revolved merely around her ability to protect the morals of the family; in the new, postwar matrix of political and domestic economy, women had a direct physical and economic contribution to make to national policies, by reproducing 'the race' and by protecting 'higher wages for fathers.'[136] Feminists drew a direct connection between the defence of motherhood and the defence of the 'living wage' for men.[137] Thus, important social reformers and feminists like Margaret McWilliams could, during the Winnipeg General Strike, speak in tandem about protecting the wages of working girls *and* shoring up of the male family wage[138]; while the women who participated in the Women's War Conference, hosted by the Borden government in March 1918, could advocate a set of interlocking legislative recommendations that included a minimum wage, mothers' allowances, equal pay for women, and shorter working hours for women and children. These policies were all intended to sustain the wage levels of male workers, which had come under pressure from rising inflation and the dilution-of-labour policies pursued by the IMB.[139] Significantly, this conference came on the heels of the Labour Conference held just weeks before; and its relationship to the aspirations of organized skilled workers was explicitly recognized by Alison Craig, who commented in her column in the *Winnipeg Free Press*, 'Over the Tea Cups,' that 'we need not more but less division between men and women. Their interests are not really separate but are human interests, the interests of the nation.'[140]

The agitation by Canadian women for a minimum wage for single working girls was directly related to their immediate preoccupation after the war with maintaining a living wage. Feminist critiques of the family wage scale such as one offered in an editorial in *Woman's Century* in 1915, which decried the practice of determining wage scales based on the ideal male breadwinner, because it encouraged the public to forget that many unmarried women had dependants, were palatable only while the breadwinners were at war.[141] By 1919 women's periodicals were overwhelmingly preoccupied with the inability of skilled workingmen to properly maintain their families. Indeed, they viewed the question of the family wage as the central issue of social reconstruction. As Mary Power of the Ontario Child Welfare Bureau declared at the 1920 Social Welfare Congress: '*The whole question was one of a living wage.*'[142] The campaign for mothers' allowances focused heavily on the need to sustain the wage levels of skilled wage earners by keeping widows and deserted women out of the workforce. Mr Axford of the Brantford Children's Aid Society, made a point of mentioning this when he testified at a hearing on mothers' allowances, held by the Ontario

Labour Department, that 'the matter of wages today is practically pro-
hibitive for a laboring man to keep up his home.'[143]

Postwar progressives considered the legislative protection of women
and children as complementary to organized labour's platform for furthering the rights of trade unions. There is no greater illustration of this
than a publication of Premier E.C. Drury's Farmer–Labor government,
*Report of the Accomplishments of the Department of Labor and Health and
Outline of Legislation to Advance the Rights of Wage-Earners and to Protect
the Interests of Women and Children Enacted Under the U.F.O-Labor
Government*.[144] Along the same lines, Bryce Stewart, one of Canada's
foremost exponents of social insurance, spoke at the 1920 Social
Welfare Congress of Montreal on the problem of unemployment; while
his wife, who was later to become chair of the Ottawa Mothers' Allowances Board, gave an address on limiting the labour of women and
children in industry.[145] Mothers' allowances were the outcome of the
combined interests of maternal feminists and labour, as shown in
Ontario by the fact that the two female members of the Mothers'
Allowances Commission, Mrs Adam Shortt and Minnie Singer, represented these two constituencies.[146] Moreover, the campaign for mothers' allowances in Manitoba was instigated by the Trades and Labor
Congress[147]; and in Ontario in 1919 the deputation to the premier on
behalf of this legislation was headed by the Rev. Peter Bryce, and
included the Rev. Gilbert Agar of the Social Service Council of Ontario,
Mrs Heustis of the Local Council of Women, and Mr J. Gunn of the
Trades and Labor Council (TLC). Thus, it was the issue of how to protect the family wage and the status of the male breadwinner as the
head of the family (which was believed to have been eroded during
wartime), more than any other, that brought maternal feminists
together in a loose alliance with organized labour. It is noteworthy that
the Canadian Council on Child Welfare, founded in 1920 and headed
by Charlotte Whitton, often functioned as a podium for the Trades and
Labor Congress. The policies of Whitton's organization on child
labour, mothers' pensions, and the minimum wage dovetailed with
those of Tom Moore, President of the TLC.[148]

Women had not been hired in vast numbers to replace male workers
during the First World War; even so, organized labour feared that they
might enter the paid workforce in ever larger numbers at insufficient
wages, which would have depressed both the status and the standard of
living of male workers and their families. By war's end, so crucial had
gendered perceptions of work become to the self-perception of the

Canadian labour movement, that even the smallest fillip in work by married women was interpreted as a strike at the heart of labour rights – namely, access to a family wage. It is not wholly insignificant that on the morning the Winnipeg General Strike began, the *Winnipeg Free Press* reported the arrival of 100 widowed munitions workers from Britain.[149] William Ivens, one of the central figures in the 1919 strike, had long campaigned for a 'living wage' for workers; a year earlier he had been a central figure in the agitation for a broader system of mothers' allowances in Manitoba that would have included benefits for widowed, deserted, divorced, and unmarried women, who might otherwise compete with returned soldiers in the industrial workplace.[150]

After the war ended, this preoccupation with protecting the status and earnings of male heads of families propelled women's groups, organized labour, and government departments of labour to orchestrate a campaign exhorting women to leave paid labour and reoccupy their customary sphere within the home. During the war, the Union Government Publicity Bureau had viewed women as a national asset because of their patriotic work, both paid and unpaid; but by war's end, women's contributions to the economy were being reconstituted in terms of the old dichotomy whereby men were the producers and women were the consumers, savers, and reproducers.[151] Organized labour, together with progressive businessmen, asserted their own version of citizenship rights, which complemented the notion of social citizenship elaborated by social feminism, in which it was stated that it is 'our inalienable right as citizens of the Dominion' to be able to rear families and build homes.[152] Playing on wartime themes of patriotism and national duty, the Ontario Department of Labor issued a circular to all female munitions workers which, though both manipulative in tone and patronizing in its message, reflected a policy that was generally accepted among female and male reformers:

To women workers: Are You Working for Love or Money? Are you holding a job you do not need? ... You took a job during the war to help meet the shortage of labour. You have 'made good' and you want to go on working. But the war is over and conditions have changed. There is no longer a shortage of labour. On the contrary Ontario is faced by a serious situation due to the number of men unemployed. This number is being increased daily by returning Soldiers. They must have work. Do you feel justified in holding a job which could be filled by a man who has not only himself to support, but a wife and family as well? Think it over.[153]

This excessive concern for the position of the male breadwinner did not rest upon the actual work patterns of women – especially married women. Both organized labour and women's groups constantly deployed the potential *threat* of women's work and its ability to shock normative sensibilities about gender roles, as a strategy for coalescing public interest around the talismanic issue of protecting both the home and the family wage. As early as 1892, even after confirming with statistics that very few married women worked outside the home in factories, Jean Thomson Scott concluded her treatise *The Conditions of Female Labour in Ontario* with a jeremiad against breaching the traditional conventions of gender in the home and the workplace:

> Another result of the indiscriminate and extensive employment of women is increasing danger to the life of the home. It is generally conceded that the family is the great safe-guard of a nation's prosperity, and anything that would endanger it cannot but be looked upon with disfavour and even alarm. What does the displacing of men by the competition of women at lower wages mean if not that the former often find employment more difficult to obtain or less profitable than formerly, and are less able to provide means of maintenance for a family? Man was intended by nature to be the bread-winner of the family; and if family life is to be maintained such he must remain; so that the persistent usurpation of his place by unfair competition must mean eventually a danger to the continuance of the home.[154]

Clearly, women as well as men were instrumental in fashioning the breadwinner ideal, both for public consumption and as a problem for legislative solutions.

In its efforts to enlist public support for higher wages for skilled workers, organized labour constantly raised the spectre of family disintegration. By supporting legislative enactments that protected women and children, organized labour was seeking to protect the wage packets of skilled labourers. From the point of view of trade union leaders, mothers' allowances allowed a modicum of government intervention that would bolster male wages, and do so without establishing a precedent of direct government interference in the contractual determination of wage scales, which was the cornerstone of the modern labour movement. Thus, mothers' allowances and a minimum wage for women were the essential corollaries of labour's campaign for collective bargaining insofar as they protected the wages of skilled workers.

Principal J.H. Riddell of Wesley College in Winnipeg thus saw the achievement of a minimum wage for women as a fulcrum for lifting the family wage: 'Every wage earner,' reported the *Winnipeg Free Press*, 'is entitled to a fair living wage; not a wage that will just serve to keep body and soul together, but a wage that will enable the honest, industrious worker to live in comfort, enjoy a few of the luxuries of life and provide against the time when it will be no longer possible to earn the daily bread.'[155] Labour reformers likewise saw mothers' allowances as a natural corollary of industrial democracy. Thus, defenders of post-war schemes of Whitley Councils (which were meant to enhance dialogue between labour and management), like Robert MacIver, head of the Department of Political Economy at the University of Toronto, advocated a liberal scheme of mothers' pensions with benefits sufficient to ensure the complete 'economic independence' of women.[156] MacIver's concept of 'economic independence' was not related solely to the rights of women; it was also aimed at enhancing the bargaining position of male workers on the shop floor by solving the problem of female competition in the workplace. Leaders of the TLC, including Tom Moore, cast their support of government-funded mothers' allowances in language that resonated with the concerns of women's groups, public health advocates, educators, and juvenile court judges, by stressing issues such as the rights of mothers, national physical deterioration, and the repression of delinquency. However, this was a convenient rhetorical disguise that hid the real reason why they supported policies that sanctioned unprecedented government intervention in working-class family life. The TLC's real goals were to maintain a high wage structure and uphold the rights of unionized labour to free contract. While Moore, like most progressive reformers, accepted that modern civilization had grown so complex that government regulation of some traditionally private spheres was warranted, he saw this expansion of public authority as the least intrusive means for preserving the general self-sufficiency of working-class families, which was ultimately based on the responsibility of the individual male breadwinner to support his dependants.[157]

The leaders of organized labour perceived that minimum wage legislation would ensure the buoyancy of the wages of skilled male workers by limiting the diminution of the wages of single working girls; they also saw mothers' allowances as the best means for compelling those married women who were bereft of their male breadwinners to remain within the purview of the home. Male labour unions had long condoned home work for women, reasoning that supporting 'sweated' trades for widows was preferable to competing with them in factories. For example, the 1896 parliamentary commission to examine the sweating system raised the hobgoblin of unprotected children as its rationale for relegating widows to piecework outside the industrial workplace, which did not threaten men's wage contracts.[158] Also, the interest of social feminists in mothers' allowances as a means to protect motherhood intersected with a more self-interested motive among the middle class – the need for a ready pool of unskilled domestic labour. In this way, the aims of Canadian feminists and the goals of organized labour came together over the issue of keeping women out of the industrial workplace. However, organized labour and maternal feminists came into conflict over the issue of how much in benefits the state should pay to keep mothers at home raising their children. Labour fought for generous benefits that would offer no incentive for women to seek paid labour. In contrast, many middle-class feminists supported less generous benefits under mothers' allowances, in the hope that this would force widows to seek part-time work, such as charring and domestic service. Indeed, certain middle-class feminists had been highly critical of the CPF because, they contended, its lavish payments created a shortage of domestics.[159] By the end of the First World War, the shortage of female domestics had become so acute that women's organizations agitated successfuly for the creation (in 1919) of a Canadian Council on Women Immigration for Household Service within the federal Department of Immigration. As a consequence, female domestics were now one of the few 'preferred' categories under the newly restrictive postwar immigration policy.[160] Significantly, Mrs Adam Shortt, who was to become a member of Ontario's Mothers' Allowances Commission, was also president of the Women's Immigration Hostel, which housed, trained, and recruited domestics for Canadian middle-class homes.[161] The TLC supported the creation of the Canadian Council for the Immigration of Women for Household Service, with the rider that it be represented on its executive. The TLC wanted to be able to monitor imported domestics so as to ensure that they did not flee their employment and swell the ranks of female factory workers.[162]

Thus organized labour, feminists, and government policymakers agreed on the general principle of mothers' allowances. However, labour had less impact on the final shape of the legislation in Ontario, Manitoba, and British Columbia, because the idea of liberal benefits conflicted with broadly accepted cultural assumptions, which emulated the work ethic. All reform interests converged around the goal of upholding the position of the male breadwinner, but diverged widely over the means to achieve that goal. One network of reformers argued for generous state benefits; organized labour did so out of its concern for protecting male wages; child welfare advocates sought to preserve the bonds between parent and child within the home; and the more progressive wing of maternal feminism, by equating motherhood with citizenship, sought broad social entitlements as a right for women, whom they believed were, by virtue of their contribution to the nation, exonerated from the moral stigma of poverty. Pitted against this more liberal coalition were government policymakers, business interests, and conservative social feminists such as Mrs Adam Shortt. These people accorded a pre-eminent place to the doctrine of family independence, which privileged the ethic of work and economic cooperation within the family sphere – an ideal that in their view transcended the boundaries of gender. The first group of reformers, though more radical in their views regarding political economy and the social diagnosis of poverty, were, ironically, strict adherents to traditional notions of separate spheres for men and women; while conservative policymakers ruptured the conventional division between unpaid domestic work for women and waged work for men outside the home, by so reducing the level of allowances paid to widows that they were compelled to seek waged work and thus fulfil the traditional role of the male breadwinner. These overlapping but also competing visions of welfare entitlements established the parameters of the campaign for mothers' allowances. It was the touchstone of family independence that solidified the consensus and that was responsible for moving policymaking toward a more conservative pole between 1916 and 1920, when Saskatchewan, Alberta, Manitoba, British Columbia, and Ontario enacted mothers' allowance legislation.

4

Mothers' Allowances and the Regulation of the Family Economy

If the amount allow[ed] is insufficient, the mother does not stay at home. She works as before, and the children are on the street, and have no better home than before the Act came into force ... the discontinuance of the present policy would undermine the whole principle upon which the legislation is based.

A.P. Paget, Director, Manitoba Mothers' Allowances Commission

If the individual members within a family in need of social aid have a right to look to the whole community for provision of that social aid, then surely there must be an obligation upon those who are insisted in turn to take their part in improving the condition of those dependent upon them ... If the right of the individual to live his or her own life, regardless of obligations upon them, is to be carried out, then it has to operate all along the line, and that individual has no right, in my judgement, to ask the community to sacrifice for him when he is not willing to sacrifice any measure himself.

Charlotte Whitton to Ernest Blois, 27 February 1936

Feminists, clergymen, and social reformers had promoted mothers' allowances as a special, non-stigmatizing form of public assistance, one that exempted women from the old, poor law strictures; even so, government administrators began in the early 1920s to undermine the child protection tenets of this legislation, the purpose of which had been to preserve family life by keeping the significant mother-figure in the home. Thus, an alternative approach to solving the problem of the 'pauperizing tendency'[1] began to emerge, when administrators of the various provincial acts began to enforce regulations designed to encourage 'the spirit of self-help.'[2] Mothers were now being compelled to enter the workforce as female substitutes for the male breadwinner; government assistance was now perceived as merely supplemental to the family wage and as not destructive of the male breadwinner's responsibility both to his family and to the State. As Charlotte Whitton observed, the primary intent behind state welfare had to be to preserve the equation between community obligations and individual rights. Accompanying this retooling of mothers' allowances into a form of workfare, older children were now exhorted to contribute their wages to the family economy, the intent being to preserve the ideal of the family as an economically (rather than mainly spiritually) interdependent unit. Administrators abhorred moral lapses among their female beneficiaries; even so, it was the penalties for violating the breadwinner norm by *failing to work and to instil the work ethic in their children* that were enforced most rigorously; it was these transgressions, and not immoral sexual behaviour, that were most likely to result in disqualification. More importantly, the issue of work was now the central locus of class conflict as well as the primary source of tension between middle-class welfare officials and working-class beneficiaries, who had interpreted mothers' allowances to mean that the State would entirely replace the lost breadwinner by offering dependent women a substantive 'family' wage. By the 1920s, as postwar fears regarding population questions and the problem of juvenile delinquency receded, the child welfare network of feminists and clergymen lost ground to the advocates of national economic efficiency and to the defenders of an older ideal of the work ethic, upon which the limited state so depended for its longevity.

From Mothers' Pensions to Mothers' Allowances

In 1917, when state aid to mothers was first mooted in Ontario, the perception was that such government legislation was more akin to pensions for soldiers' service than an extension of private charity. Because in wartime child and family welfare was seen as 'not charity but patriotism,'[3] this early movement for mothers' pensions was debated in the language of rights-based entitlements and in terms of social insurance policy. It was thus severed from its earlier attachment to the work of the children's aid societies, which were preoccupied with juvenile delinquency.[4] At this time, only a minority of social reformers were critical of the two-tier system of military versus civilian family relief. These groups criticized the existing system of assistance to mothers and their children because it framed such benefits as a supplement to soldiers' pensions and referred to them as 'Widows' Pensions,' and offered women state protection only in terms of their status as wives of citizen soldiers.[5] Because in 1917 mothers' pensions were perceived as part of the war effort – and especially as a method for garnering voluntary enlistments – it was considered vital to dissociate them from charity and from the taint of pauperization. Writing before the introduction of conscription, W.A. Riddell, the Ontario superintendent of Trades and Labour, observed in an official memorandum to Premier Hearst that 'no one will but admit that a deserving mother in a home suddenly deprived of the breadwinner ought to be placed in a position where she can continue to care for her children and her home without being subjected to the stigma that always attaches to charitable relief.'[6]

Between 1919 and 1920, before public opinion turned decidedly against the relief of returned soldiers, mothers' pensions were viewed as a precursor to a broader program of social insurance that would eventually include male unemployment and sickness insurance. Riddell, in his 1917 outline and impending legislation for mothers, buttressed his arguments by quoting from esteemed New Liberal and Progressive thinkers such as L.T. Hobhouse and John Dewey. In this vein, he stated that a scheme of mothers' pensions was more important than old age and other forms of social insurance. By concentrating on the interests of the child, and seeing the mother as 'of secondary importance,' Riddell was able to articulate a generous, rights-based scheme which marked a decisive and radical break with the philosophy of needs-based private charity and public municipal relief the intent of which was to include all categories of single motherhood: widows and deserted and unmarried mothers. Riddell used Colorado's Mothers' Compensation Law, which resembled workman's compensation, as the model for his 1917 proposal for an Ontario Mothers' Pensions Act:

It is a recognition by the state that aid is rendered not as a charity but as a right – as justice due mothers whose work in rearing their children is a work for the state as that of the soldier who is paid by the state for his services on the battle-field; it is a recognition for the first time by society that the state is responsible in a measure for the plight of the mother and acknowledges its responsibility by sharing the burden of her poverty that is created largely by the conditions that the State permits to exist.[7]

At war's end, many of the more liberal aspects of this legislation were still before the public, largely because feminist organizations were at the height of their influence in 1918. In 1914 the Local Council of Women of Toronto, under the guidance of Mrs Heustis, had established a privately funded experiment in mothers' aid that saw as its principal aim the relieving of all womanhood from the burden of poverty.[8] Their intimate acquaintance with the social distress of impoverished motherhood informed their demands to Premier Drury in 1920: 'We would have you give some consideration, also, to the deserted wife and the unmarried wife, remembering that the child is the primary object.'[9] Between 1918 and 1920, women's periodicals were filled with solicitations on behalf of deserted and unmarried mothers; these publications became the chief locus of agitation to make the machinery for administering mothers' allowances as flexible and discretionary as possible.[10] It was only by 1929 that CAS activists, together with mental hygiene experts, began to conceive of unmarried motherhood as a social rather than a moral question[11]; a decade before that, social feminists had been championing the rights of these 'defective' women, and had been instrumental in transforming what had been viewed as a problem of private rights between a woman and the responsible father (which belonged in the courts) into a matter of public responsibility.

Middle-class women urged that the state become, in the words of magistrate Emily Murphy, 'the ultimate parent of all children, but ... always be the parent of the illegitimate.'[12] Feminists agitated for a system of mothers' allowances, because this system of protection against the lack of 'sex-control' was preferable to the alternative – the legitimizing of illegitimate children, which would mean that properly married women would have to endure a system of legalized 'polygamy.'[13] Others, like the Rev. J.R. Mutchmor of Winnipeg, campaigned to have mothers' allowances extended to unwed mothers, largely as an attempt to limit the influence of the CAS on government policymaking[14]; meanwhile, female superintendents of orphans' homes were urging governments to include unmarried and deserted women as beneficiaries so that the large burden of children in their institutions, occasioned by the war, might be relieved.[15] Despite the weight of public opinion in favour of state rights for unmarried and deserted mothers, many government officials continued to inveigh against the blurring of the lines between public and individual responsibility that such entitlements would encourage; they remained wedded to the notion that such familial abnormalities were moral rather than social in their derivation. Thus the often expansive vision of a system of 'childrens' allowances' (such as that proposed by the Toronto Committee on Mothers' Allowances, led by the Rev. Peter Bryce[16]) became, when translated into formal government statutes, restrictive and punitive. A case of 'real hardship' involving a deserving woman with five children between 2 and 11, deserted two years previously by her husband, was laid before Premier Ferguson. His bureaucratic response was that 'I do not think it would be wise to open the door any wider in regard to desertion.'[17] The case of Mrs Wilson from Sarnia, Ontario, a mother who had lost her marriage certificate, was even more revealing of the official mentality. A local businessman pleaded that 'surely the letter of the Law should yield to common humanity, and a technical point not rob this widow of the help the Mothers allowance would be in being able to take care of her family and give them the care they should have, as is, I believe the end to which the law was made.' Yet so inviolable was the marriage contract perceived to be that the Rev. Peter Bryce, now an administrator of the act, retorted: 'To grant allowances where there is no evidence of marriage would be to establish an undesirable precedent.' More tellingly still as testimony of the deeper goals underlying state funding for mothers, Bryce concluded that surely among her seven children there were potential wage earners who could privately support the Wilson household.[18]

By 1919 the wartime movement for mothers' pensions had been reworked into a government scheme for mothers' allowances, which were strictly limited to widows and women with incapacitated husbands.[19] Despite the urgings of the Rev. Peter Bryce and the Minister of Labour, Walter Rollo, that the benefits be made generous enough to allow a widow to stay at home full time to raise her children,[20] the principles enshrined in the Mothers' Allowances Act owed much more to the perspective of Mrs Adam Shortt, who had a preponderant influence on the final articles of the legislation. Shortt represented the continuation of older, poor-relief assumption that poverty was a moral condition and that only 'respectable' widows were entitled to assistance. She adamantly opposed the 'sentimentalists' who pictured children 'being daily torn from kindly women's arms to be placed in cruel institutions.' She even adhered to a conception of child-saving that predated even the campaigns of J.J. Kelso in the 1890s on behalf of foster homes. At the same time, like the supporters of the CASs, Shortt believed that children should be wrenched from the care of mothers for reasons of illness, improper guardianship, and mental deficiency – a perspective that became firmly embedded in government legislation and that confirmed the need, of which Shortt was a great exponent, for close supervision and rehabilitation of beneficiaries.[21] By focusing on the moral attributes of motherhood, Shortt was directly refuting the more progressive social calculus of poverty offered by less conservative feminists and social reformers; she held to the belief that all unmarried women should be defined as 'feeble-minded' and that deserted women should seek redress only through the private means of the courts.[22] At a time when most social analysis was beginning to emphasize the social and economic environment, Shortt continued to stress the moral dimensions of social distress. Unlike other women, who placed a greater priority on the direct physical and economic contributions that the family and motherhood made in service to the nation, she maintained that mothers' allowances should make children healthy in 'mind, body, and *morals*,'[23] and downplayed the ideology of social citizenship and national efficiency.

Despite her preoccupation with delinquency, which she maintained was caused by women working all day outside the home,[24] Shortt was less sanguine than either Rollo or Bryce about the need to pay a substantial grant to female beneficiaries of the State. Indeed, it was Shortt's domineering presence and her close ties with the Conservative Party[25] that enabled her to redirect the mothers' allowance movement so that it no longer focused on protecting the home and the family wage – explicit goals of both feminists and organized labour. Shortt rejected the gendered notions of work and pauperization insisted on by these two groups. In her view, allowances should be as niggardly as possible in order that the mother not be entirely relieved of the need to work – preferably as a domestic. She saw work as ennobling for both sexes and likewise viewed pauperization through idleness as a moral excrescence of women as well as men: 'Physical, mental and moral strength are only acquired by doing and struggling not by sitting down and being paid for it.'[26] She argued that if men could replace women in the home, women could likewise become wage earners – a vision of gender equality and economic independence for women[27] that many lauded as a radical feminist perspective. This resulted in thousands of women being denied adequate benefits and thus being forced to seek work outside the home. Shortt insisted that women work for their relief (the old poor-law philosophy applied through outdoor relief rather than the House of Industry), in large part because she believed that motherhood alone did not constitute a set of social entitlements for women. In her view, paid labour formed the primary claim for state benefits. Although Shortt adhered to a less gendered view of work, which tended to break down the ideology of separate spheres, it was a perspective that affronted the sensibilities of both middle- and working-class women, who maintained that women should not be compelled to work when their central function pertained to the raising of children and the care of the home. Ostensibly, Shortt's feminism advocated equality between the sexes; in practice, it coerced women to work against their will, and did not benefit women who wanted the rights of mothers to be enshrined in government welfare policies, whereby the State would wholly replace the breadwinner role of their dead or incapacitated husbands.

Unlike other reformers, Shortt sought more direct means than mothers' allowances for maintaining a future skilled workforce earning high wages: she advocated more work for men, better vocational training for children, and a system of social insurance whereby social benefits would be based solely on the activity of work. Clearly, she saw service to the state through motherhood as subordinate to male citizenship. Shortt's reconceptualizing of rights-based mothers' pensions into a needs-based system of mothers' allowances – which reflected the views of the other provincial commissioners – and the consequent whittling away of women's citizenship entitlements, must be understood in terms of her preference for German and British models of social insurance, which placed a clear priority on the citizenship rights of male workers. 'If a good workman breaks down and dies,' asked Shortt, 'having by his labour contributed to the country's development; why should his family be neglected by the country?'[28] In the end, Shortt believed that women's access to the State should be dependent on their status as wives – that is why she limited benefits to widows – and saw the program of mothers' allowances not as the precursor to an expanding welfare system, but rather as a continuation of traditional public charity, and thus separate from and inferior to a self-help system of unemployment and sickness insurance based on male wages and contributions.

In relabelling their approach 'mothers' allowances' (instead of 'mothers' *pensions*), policymakers were converting the idea of service into a notion of women's obligations to the State. This severely eroded the integrity of the notion of social citizenship advanced by Canadian feminists. In this new equation between motherhood and the State, women performed 'a piece of work in co-operation with the State' as employees of government, and the focus was no longer on the independent contribution of the citizen but rather on the State. This formulation, with its 'insistence upon the mother's responsibility to the State in the bringing up of its citizens,'[29] became the State's rationale for intervening in working-class family life by investigating and rehabilitating families. In an effort to assuage conservative middle-class elements in the community who might try to block this new legislation by complaining about the misuse of their taxes, the formulators of the Mothers' Allowances Act stressed that the new policy was widely accepted. 'It was distinctly evident to those of us present throughout,' stated W.A. Riddell, 'that this idea of the State employing the mother of its future citizens to rear her children according to approved standards and subsidizing the home for this purpose, where need exists, has taken hold of a very large element in the community and is being given expression in no uncertain voice.'[30]

When policymakers pointed out that mothers' allowances were divorced from any taint of charity, they did not mean they were not based on need, or that they fell beyond the scope of investigation. Rather, such allowances were defined as non-stigmatizing because women received them through the mail, and were not (as was the case with municipal relief) forced to publicly display their need and destitution. This constituted an important strategy in reclaiming 'family pride' and ensuring that personal responsibility would continue to be part of the ideal of family self-sufficiency.[31] Most importantly, mothers' allowances were perceived to be a radical break from the practice of charity where material aid was granted as a philanthropic offering or gift that demanded nothing of the recipient. In contrast, mothers' allowances were deemed not to be charity because in exchange for assistance, women were obligated to perform the service of raising their children. From this perspective, investigation was not a relic of old-style charity; rather, it was part of a new vision of the State – one based on a reciprocal system of duties and obligations. Although repugnant to modern sensibilities, the belief that the goal of all publicly funded social programs was to educate recipients for social responsibility, and that it was proper for the State to demand respectable conduct in return, was embedded in a wide variety of early-twentieth-century political perspectives. The ideal of the community as built upon a network of obligations was the ideological firmament that joined Fabian socialists like Beatrice Webb, social democrats like W.A. Riddell, and conservatives like Mrs Shortt.[32] All the major architects of the modern welfare state, including British advocates of social insurance such as William Beveridge and Sidney Webb,[33] and their Canadian counterparts such as Harry Cassidy, remained committed to various degrees of state compulsion and were not averse to recommending policies that would compel male wage earners to work in exchange for benefits. Thus the invasive nature of state welfare was not a function of gender. Moreover, if the numerous snitching letters from neighbours demanding equal access to state aid are any indication, the notion of an intrusive government that enforced sexual propriety, budgetary responsibility, and personal accountability in return for state aid was an ideal that transcended class boundaries. Woman invited the State to assume responsibility for their children so that they might have 'proper training'; while women who transgressed sexual norms often found themselves being regulated by the State when complained about by working-class neighbours (and in one case after the protests of an angry husband).[34]

However much working-class families were willing to participate in the community scrutiny that determined which mothers were deserving of state benefits, such investigation remained decidedly intrusive. Also, the visitors employed by various provincial mothers' allowance commissions had cultural expectations that often ran counter to the needs and realities of working-class widows. The vast majority of social investigators were Anglo-Saxon, middle-class, and female, and their cultural biases showed in their attempts to examine and reform impoverished women and their families. As the case files of European immigrant women investigated by the Manitoba Mothers' Allowance Commission make clear, however, nationality was never made a criterion for eligibility. Mrs G., a Jewish immigrant from Romania, the widow of a tinsmith with the CPR, was assigned a Jewish female visitor to interpret her needs. Although the records regarding her case often labelled her as 'hysterical' because she spoke loudly and demanded her rights in a foreign tongue, the basis of her conflict with the Manitoba government revolved not around her cultural traits, but over the issue of whether her children would attend high school rather than work. Mrs G., an educated woman, was adamant that her children be upwardly mobile and economically independent.[35]

It is not entirely surprising that female investigators would perceive women whose husbands were skilled and responsible wage earners as more deserving of state assistance and characterize them as, for example, 'a refined woman and good homemaker.' One beneficiary was described by a female visitor as an 'exceptionally fine woman and very well educated' and was quickly granted an allowance because her husband had been a bank manager.[36] Moreover, criminality among the children of applicants, refusal to send children to school, and the obvious traducing of marriage bonds were not countenanced by the commission. For example, the Brant County Board rejected Mrs Matilda Main's application on the grounds that having lived with and borne the illegitimate child of a Mr Linnington, 'the moral conditions surrounding the home are not conductive to the proper training of the children'; and Mrs Georgina Larochelle's allowance was not reinstated because the criminal records of her two older children cancelled out the good behaviour of two younger children who were cared for in a convent in Ottawa and one other who lived with an aunt in Espanola, whose conduct was beyond reproach.[37] The starkest example at hand of the disdain and opprobrium that middle-class women felt toward those not of their class or ethnic background was a visitor's report on the widow of a truck driver, whose daily job as a charwoman prevented her from caring for her own housekeeping:

> Beneficiary is sub-normal and cannot see the advantage of education and I have called on Rev. Mr. Miller who is going to see her and have a serious talk with her about E. and even G. six years should be at school. Severe measures will have to be taken to make her keep these two boys at school ... Place was fearfully untidy when I called and Beneficiary said she was away working. I told her there was no excuse and made her sweep while I was there and in fifteen minutes, she had it looking different. She and he are slack and will always be. Place is an old shack and old floor and dirty wall paper. Woman's clothes are fairly tidy children raggy and think they seldom see a bath. Has promised to do better and Rev. Mr Miller is going to do his best to make her improve if it is at all possible.[38]

While such disquisitions were often entered into the case files of these clients of the State, problems of cleanliness were rarely the sole basis for disqualifying widows from state assistance. More often than not, such tirades over a woman's ability to clean her house and properly bathe her children belied deeper frustrations. In the above case, the investigator's raging against the mother's uncleanliness was in large part a mere venting of the spleen, a result of years of frustration during which the beneficiary had seemingly ignored her cardinal duty, which was to inculcate proper work habits in her children and advise them on the necessity to contribute their wages to the family economy.[39]

There were, of course, extreme cases, such as that of Mrs A from Winnipeg. Although unable to prove that she was married, after the death of her husband from double-pneumonia 'aggravated by attempted suicide,' she was nevertheless granted an allowance from the Manitoba Mothers' Allowances Commission; however, this was temporarily rescinded a few years later when she gave birth to an illegitimate daughter, having become entangled with the delivery man from the Wet Wash Laundry service. However, despite such moral irregularity, after agreeing to no longer consort with Mr J., this young widow was once again placed on full government benefits. However, child welfare workers once again revoked her allowance after Mrs A. demonstrated extreme negligence by regularly leaving her children unattended at home when she visited her neighbour to while away her evenings listening to the gramophone. On one of these nights, unfortunately, her house accidentally burned down, resulting in the death of her baby twins. The State subsequently intervened and removed her older children from her care. The injured widow protested vehemently against this invasion of her privacy, writing in 1925 to A.P. Paget, the director of the Manitoba Mothers' Allowances Commission, that 'you carnt see what you have done but you have torn a womens children from her & thrown her on the streets it perhaps does not seam like that to you.' As she accused government authorities, 'you let [another woman] keep my children would you like someone to take yours from you I tried to get work the first four Months but you never intended to help me.' While this woman was accused of gross child neglect, immorality and mental incompetence, she nevertheless was reinstated again on government support because she was 'fond of the children and anxious to have them with her.' She was only definitively removed from the allowance rolls in 1929 – not for having male visitors but because she and her family were deemed 'self-supporting' when her daughters began to work.[40]

The emphasis that historians have placed on this discourse as evidence of moral regulation or social control of the working classes by a 'middle-class' state[41] suggests the existence of a large, bureaucratic government. While a value-laden discourse among investigators and policymakers did exist, it is not at all clear how carefully its prescriptions were implemented. Even the experienced Ernest Blois – the only investigator for all of mothers' allowances and old age pensions in Nova Scotia – admitted that the process of investigating often reluctant applicants was a precarious and often unsuccessful exercise: 'To go as stranger into the various communities visited, and secure in a short time, full and accurate information regarding prospective applicants in respect to such matters as character, competency, education, occupation, relations, family traditions, ambitions, ideals, possessions, etc., was in the very nature of the case, a somewhat delicate piece of work, and one requiring great tact, patience, and perserverence.'[42] The State's ability to demand conformity to its standards of child rearing was greatly circumscribed by the high ratio of clients to investigators. In Manitoba most applicants were never investigated before being granted an allowance because there were only six visitors for the entire province; in Ontario there was only one investigator per 300 cases.[43] As mothers' allowance programs grew, this ratio became even more imbalanced. Thus, by 1942 in Saskatchewan there was only one investigator for every 1,700 allowance cases.[44]

Adherents of the social control thesis, who stress the one-directional, top-down hegemony of the State, ignore the fact that the dynamic between beneficiaries and government can be viewed as one of negotiation, even when power relations are not equally distributed.[45] Mrs H. Huntley, who had had to wait before applying for a mothers' allowance because of the dilatoriness of the federal Pension Board, and who in the interim was forced to part with her children, was more than willing to conform to the middle-class norms established by the commission, stating in a letter to Premier Ferguson, 'i am strait woman and respectible and keep my children nice and home all so clean.'[46] Many widows agreed to expel their single male boarders when it meant gaining access to a non-stigmatizing mothers' allowance that would enable them to avoid municipal relief, private charity, and the aid of relatives and neighbours. Mrs Annie McKie poignantly expressed her circumstances to Premier Ferguson: 'Understand, that Mothers' Allowance is the only thing between health and me.'[47] This widow was complaining not about the strictures that government officials were placing on her behaviour, but about the parsimony of her benefits. Indeed, in a later letter to the premier, this savvy widow from Paris, Ontario, admonished the premier that if other women with only one child were getting an allowance – namely widows in British Columbia – she should be entitled to the same consideration.[48]

In most communities in Canada, there was little work available for widows that paid well enough for them to keep home and children together. The vast majority of widows were forced, like Mrs McKie, onto municipal relief. Because they had to demonstrate destitution before being granted relief, widows were often forced to sell many of their household goods; worse still, when widows of skilled workers and salaried men, who had once occupied a respectable position in the community, were forced into these situations, their precipitous decline in income and status became public knowledge. The desperation of widows to avoid the stigma of municipal assistance explains the large number of begging letters in which helpless widows described their plight in lurid detail to provincial premiers and, in the depths of the Great Depression, to R.B. Bennett, the prime minister. Local reeves and mayors often sponsored the widows in their communities, not simply out of humanitarian concern, but because they wished to lighten their relief rolls. As a result of these efforts to shift the burden of welfare assistance to the provincial level, conflicts often arose between local boards and the Toronto office of the Mothers' Allowances Commission. Municipal élites tended to defend the rights of widows; at the same time, in order to ensure that widows remained the financial responsibility of the Mothers' Allowances Commission, they were also more stringent in forcing deliquent widows to conform to conventional mores. 'I do not know what the unsatisfactory conditions are that have caused this suspension,' complained the mayor of Huntsville to the commission, 'but I must say that someone has to take care of this woman, and she is left now to be taken care of by Relief or charity, and I do not think that she should be thrown on our hands without giving the muncipality an opportunity to clear up whatever conditions might prevail.'[49]

Widows often preferred to be investigated by strangers when the alternative was to suffer the scrutiny and judgment of relatives. One applicant, who lost her husband to the influenza epidemic, was forced along with her six children to move to her married sister's farm, where she was compelled to take up the drudgery of milking cows.[50] Some mothers' allowance beneficiaries simply withstood the stream of urgent advice offered by female visitors, the majority of whom were educators and public health nurses.[51] Others may well have appreciated practical advice for improving their health and that of their children. To the modern eye such advice on 'scientific motherhood' may seem unduly paternalistic, and indeed, some of this advice may have been impossible for women to follow, given the shortage of indoor plumbing, hot water, and other modern amenities. However, in an era when many working-class widows lacked the resources to seek professional medical attention, the advice from investigators and the pamphlets they distributed on maternal and neonatal health did not go unwelcomed. As Helen Reid conveyed to Charlotte Whitton in 1925, thousands of Canadian women desperately sought information: 'married women reporting need of advice to prevent miscarriages, death of babies after birth due to accidents "which the doctor said he couldn't prevent," deaths of premature babies (wife 35 years, 10 babies – 5 dead at 8 & 6 mos etc.); asking also for help with health of their children. Instructions re. breasts, *intercourse*! venereal disease etc. asked for by pregnant women & the unmarried mother who want to do right by her coming child.'[52]

Many women were willing to endure a certain amount of intrusion into their lives (albeit many tried to avoid such monitoring by being conveniently absent when the investigator called) in exchange for a regular monthly cheque in the mail, which provided a measure of financial security and a great deal of peace of mind. After all, this system of benefits allowed them to raise their children in their own home.[53] On the whole, working-class widows were quite willing to accept help from visitors – such as the sending of extra milk for hungry children – and to tolerate criticisms of their housekeeping and personal cleanliness, and to conform to rules against keeping male boarders. At the same time, however, they adamantly defended their right to control their family budgets and fought against any exercise of state authority over this particular aspect of their lives. One angry beneficiary told an especially prurient investigator that 'the money was hers to do with as she wished and they couldn't tell her what to do with it.'[54] As so many case files demonstrate, working-class women were willing to accept injunctions against male visitors, as well as endless investigations by prying female social workers, but they balked at having the government instruct them on how to manage the family economy. Mrs C, an Austrian-born widow who had lost her husband, a homesteader in Manitoba, accepted years of government intrusion into her life. But when the Manitoba government ordered her to hand over her savings to the government's own bank, she decided to finally seek work rather than accept state assistance.[55]

More often, however, women protested more fiercely when they were denied benefits. Like most other married women of her generation, Mrs Hannah Campbell of Burritt's Rapids, Grenville County, did not take up paid work following her marriage. Adhering to the male breadwinner ideal, she believed that the government should provide for her when her incapacitated husband could not:

> I would like to know if you intin to send that money to me at all if you dont do as you say I wile have you pulled for not doing as you say and I want the marriage certificates at once therefore all right the ones that you got first your a smart lady to promise a thing and not do it now send me what I tould you to do and 29 doolars for my trouble of runing to the office and the chair man said that just as soon as the papers was sent he would send me the check soget to work or you will loose your position I want it at once for my husband is not able to cut any wood for me and the lock master had to supley me with some wood they took up a cection for it and eatubeels to so send it at once and dont be so stiff so if you have plenty share up with poor people if they keep such ones in position they are smart folks to have the likes of you in such a place that cant acsts as they aught.[56]

As Bettina Bradbury has argued, in industrializing Montreal during the nineteenth century the vast majority of working-class women did not work for pay outside the home, and only 5 per cent of women with husbands living worked for wages.[57] These contours of married women's work are borne out by evidence from Winnipeg. A surviving set of 1918–19 application forms from 124 Winnipeg widows affirms Bradbury's conclusions. Of this group, of whom 8 were Canadian born, 54 were British immigrants, and the remaining 62 were Eastern European immigrants, only 1 woman worked after she was married. Although British women were more likely to have worked before marriage than European women (61 versus 44 per cent), in both immigrant communities women were compelled to seek work after the breadwinner died even though none had been 'expected to work' while married. Fully 76 per cent of British widows worked after their husbands died, while 55 per cent of European immigrant women worked. Either the latter could not find suitable employment or, as the evidence suggests, there were stronger kinship and ethnic support groups available to them to soften the economic loss of the husband. What is particularly striking, however, is that even widows who did find work usually suffered a drastically reduced standard of living, relative to that provided by the husband (who was likely to have worked in the burgeoning skilled trades attached to the Winnipeg railyards) and even relative to what they earned themselves before marriage. One Scottish widow, a trained nurse prior to her marriage to a bank clerk, was forced to take up the first available work – namely sewing, washing, making paper flowers, and, finally, taking in lodgers. Women who worked as domestics for a mere $10 to $12 a month prior to marriage could not obtain even these meagre wages once they were widowed, because they were encumbered by young children. While overall, Eastern European men did not earn as much as their British counterparts, their widows faced similar deprived existences. Most of them were forced to work for the first time in their lives, and many worked very sporadically before applying for a mothers' allowance, and relied heavily on church and ethnic benevolent societies. The precarious existence of these immigrant widows is exemplified by the experience of one Ruthenian woman who, on failing to find even suitable housework because of her many children, was threatened with deportation if she applied for local relief again. What is significant about this profile of 124 Winnipeg widows is that only 3 of them reported that their children worked. What this remarkable statistic reveals is that the conventional pattern of working-class life that families encouraged their children to work was beginning to unravel following the First World War. Despite the proclivities of welfare officials, this process accelerated once working-class women were offered the alternative of government assistance.[58] What is also evident from these 124 applications is that all of these women preferred government aid to outside work that compelled them to leave their children unattended.

Everywhere in Canada, married women were reluctant to enter the paid workforce. Women's importance as home managers precluded them from taking formal, full-time paid work outside the home; this is borne out by the fact that in the first decades of the twentieth century, the vast majority (89 per cent) of beneficiaries applying for mothers' allowance in Ontario reported that they had had no employment outside the domestic sphere.[59] As Marjorie Cohen has noted, by 1921 only 2 per cent of married women worked, and 20 per cent of working women were widows. However, few of these would have been factory workers, as they would have preferred domestic service.[60] For example, most women in Nova Scotia took in sewing or laundry, or hooked mats, or kept post offices, or took in boarders. Mothers' allowance legislation did not seriously disrupt these established patterns. However, to some extent the range of women's work options was in the long term limited by mothers' allowances. For example, the strong prohibition against taking in male boarders would have created real duress for many women who had depended on this slightly more lucrative form of home work.[61]

Mothers' allowances were not necessarily detrimental to the economic standing of the family. Just as with the Canadian Patriotic Fund, the standard of living of widows of skilled workers would have distinctly fallen, but women whose husbands had been unskilled or seasonal labourers would have seen their incomes rise. That being said, the main point to remember is that the income a widow could earn on her own was invariably far less than the wages of her husband. Mothers' allowances permitted a widow to avoid the double-burden of paid and unpaid work, and allowed her to devote her entire attention to the raising of her children. It is in the context of *women's* wages, not the wages of the male breadwinner, that the economic contribution of mothers' allowances must be assessed. On the death of the male breadwinner, widows (many of whom had never worked) would have been compelled either to become domestics, which paid at most $25 per month, or to enter factory work as unskilled labour, earning apprentice's wages of only $11 to $12 per month.[62] In the biscuit and confectionery trade an experienced female worker earned $50 per month, and in the needle trades upwards of $44 per month, while a salesgirl could make between $20 and $50 a month.[63] Such wages, however, depended on a full-time job – an undertaking either impracticable or undesirable for a widow with young children.

Because most widows had never worked for wages, their lack of skills would have relegated them to the bottom rungs of the industrial workforce. Thus, the only real option for widows would have been domestic service (in urban areas) or municipal relief (in smaller towns and rural areas). It is within this context of long hours and low wages for women that one must place the favourable response of working-class women to the mothers' allowance legislation. For the many women whose husbands had been skilled workers or salaried men, the act of having to take up work in a factory was an all too obvious symbol of their downward change of class status. Mrs Mina White of Winnipeg had been warned that the allowance was only meant to support her until her 'girlie' could go out to work; nevertheless, she wrote to Charlotte Whitton, 'to thank you for the interest you have taken in my case. There is a relief off my mind to think I am going to get a mothers' allowance and I do hope and trust there will not be a hitch anywhere.'[64] Similarly, Mrs Eva Carriere wrote to the Rev. Peter Bryce, chairman of the Ontario Mothers' Allowances Commission, 'to tell you what a blessing your pension is. Now we poor widows and orphans can live like other people and have some pleasure. Before we had this pension our poor kids were certainly to be pitied but now they can pass with the others and be safe from hardships.'[65]

While widows often agitated for higher allowances,[66] it cannot be disputed that the vast majority of deserving widows believed their primary role in life was to raise their children, and that they preferred accepting state welfare to working outside the home. Because work was an enforced necessity, it was not seen as an expression of self-worth and economic independence when it conflicted with responsibilities in the home. Public assistance offered low benefits and its officials tended to be interfering, but widows still preferred it because it spared them from having to combine paid work with house work. When Charlotte Whitton sent questionnaires to Manitoba widows who had been on the mothers' allowance scheme, one of the respondents emphasized that she viewed state allowances as the preferred route to economic independence, and contrasted those benefits forcefully with the long years of unexpected and unwelcome work dipping chocolates at a Winnipeg candy factory. This meagre wage still compelled her and her daughter to live under paternal control in the household of her parents. As Mary Axworthy angrily conveyed to the Canadian Council on Child Welfare, when asked what she did when her allowance was refused on the grounds that she only had one child – who like her mother was consigned to working in the candy factory, although she had aspirations for college – 'therefore you can please yourself what you do about this answer has I have had to work 22 years to keep myself and daughter.'[67]

One should be cautious about accepting at face value the statement by Elizabeth Shortt that the Mothers' Allowances Commission was 'not concerned too much about whether a woman is respectable,' given that it was a response to criticisms that the government gleaned too much of its information regarding beneficiaries from neighbours.[68] Her statement does, however, elucidate that the system of state welfare that mothers' allowances established was based not so much on moral regulation (of sexual behaviour, character, and homemaking skills), as on the reinforcement of family economic interdependence.[69] The paramount goal of policymakers was to foster in mothers and their children positive economic values such as 'ambition, thrift and independence.'[70] With this in mind, they abjured the recommendations of reformers and organized labour and actively encouraged paid work for beneficiaries and their offspring. The monthly alllowances for widows, which ranged from between $30 and $40 for rural women and between $40 and $55 for those in urban areas,[71] were deliberately set at levels that would compel women to take paid work. A widow was now expected to replace the former male breadwinner as a role model and thus demonstrate to her children the value of responsibly supporting one's family.

The Annual Reports of the Ontario Mothers' Allowances Commission were laced with accounts of how government assistance had instilled in recipients the virtues of self-help. One woman began by taking in infants, and now operated a children's wear business out of her home. Another began by picking potatoes, and now had a thriving market garden.[72] In their efforts to champion the work ethic, even among women, policymakers turned a blind eye to 'baby farming' as long as it served to induce the spirit of family self-support. The widow of a superintendent at the Piggott Lumber Company who boarded other families' babies was lauded for her intiative and ambition – character traits she apparently passed along to her young son, who organized a paper route for himself.[73] Administrators of mothers' allowances celebrated those families who had 'been adjusted to the industrial world.'[74] The policy of mothers' allowances was that 'even a small allowance [is] a stimulus to families who are discouraged';[75] it insisted that both men and women work as a buffer against idleness and pauperization. In this way it rejected the notion, long argued by maternal feminists, that poverty and gender were linked, and placed greater weight on the need for government welfare strategies that would reinforce private family welfare and self-support in the future. As a result of these economic policies, many widows were compelled to move from job to job in search of some modicum of financial security. In one not unusual case, a woman was deserted by her husband, a skilled machinist earning $75 a month.[76] Although the mother's allowance provided her with sufficient economic independence that she was able to leave her parents' home, the granting of state assistance marked the beginning of years of scrutiny and manipulation by investigators, who cajoled her into leaving a factory job, ordered her to rid herself of her male cousin who boarded with her, and instructed her to take in sewing. During the Depression, when sewing failed to support her family, she was forced to move several times in search of good wages and good working conditions.[77]

Children and mothers were thus coerced into contributing to their household sustenance as a replacement for the male breadwinner. This amounted to a forced reordering of deeply held working-class ideals of domesticity. The vast majority of mothers who applied for state aid listed themselves as homemakers – a demonstration of the degree to which working-class wives held, as firmly as their middle-class supervisors, to the belief that the pre-eminent and natural function of women was the rearing of children and the management of the home. Working-class wives, especially those of skilled workers, likewise perceived that their respectability and economic independence flowed from their role as dependants of responsible, wage-earning husbands. This arrangement of the home and workplace was not always practicable for working-class wives; but their economic stratagems always had this ideal as the goal.[78] Mothers' allowance policies were tailored to coerce women into the paid workforce, and as such they were a fundamental challenge to the culture of working-class family life; moreover, they forced on these women the unwelcome double burden of both outside paid work and child care. Mothers' allowance legislation attempted to impose cultural values on working-class families. In the same vein, a segment of middle-class feminist opinion (represented by Elizabeth Shortt) held that work was an axiom of female emancipation, and it was this opinion that was embraced by non-feminist male policymakers, who wanted widows to enter the workforce on the grounds that it maintained the values of family self-sufficiency. Working-class widows, however, preferred paternalistic policies whereby the State acted as the economic replacement for their lost husbands, because it enabled them to preserve their function as non-wage-earning mothers, on which their notion of respectablity and independence hinged.

With the goal of protecting the domestic ideal of the male breadwinner maintaining his dependants, middle-class government officials mounted what was in effect an attack on working-class women's notions of work. Welfare policymakers were willing to countenance the temporary breakdown of the breadwinner ideal that their encouragement of women's work represented, in order to achieve their higher goal of reforming delinquent families so that young male children would learn the social value of working for higher wages in order to responsibly support their dependants. The ideal toward which state welfare hoped to work was described by G.B. Clarke in 1928: 'It was with great interest that the Friendly Visitor of the first family to be granted an allowance by the Winnipeg Committee, that this mother was no longer living in Manitoba and that her children were all in good positions, were happy and successful and supporting their mother as a matter of course.'[79] A fictitious 'specimen record' of a case history of a widow in Winnipeg demonstrated the correct economic configuration of families on welfare. It recorded the life of a widow whose Swedish husband had been employed as a brakeman on the CPR. Before her marriage she had worked as a domestic, but she refrained from working after marriage. When her husband's workman's compensation and union insurance ran out, the widow once again worked as a part-time office cleaner; her son, an office boy for a printing company, and the State, through mothers' assistance, supplemented the income of the temporary female head of the family.[80] This model of family interdependence was reinforced in all provincial mothers' allowance jurisdictions. As Dr Jamieson, the chairman of the Ontario Mothers' Allowances Commission, had this bland reply to the demands of Mrs Isabella Curtiss for a level of assistance commensurate with the wages of her husband: 'I am quite aware the amount granted under the Mothers' Allowance Act is not sufficient to maintain a family entirely, the intention being to assist a mother in the maintenance of her children.'[81] The onus was on the widow to become the main breadwinner and head of the family; state allowances were to be the wife's 'pin money' – supplements to the main family income. Women were thus encouraged to do 'a man's work' as a means for encouraging cooperative family effort. One woman was urged by investigators to remain on the family farm in Ontario (the commission was studiously aware that the allowance system could be used to help arrest the rapid depopulation of rural Ontario), to be helped by her blind sister and disabled husband.[82]

In their efforts not to diminish independence and initiative within the home, investigators encouraged the reversal of traditional gender norms by encouraging disabled husbands to supervise the children while their wives became 'the wage earner.'[83] Many widows were granted an allowance as a sop to induce them to work – along lines deemed appropriate by investigators. One husband was incapacitated and living on the family farm. His wife was granted an allowance on the condition that she leave her factory employment in Toronto and work the land until her children were old enough to manage it independently and support their parents.[84] That these breaches of the male breadwinner ideal were seen as merely temporary exigencies, and that family independence remained the lodestar of state welfare policies, is illustrated by cases in which the breadwinner was only temporarily absent. One woman had an abusive husband who had been confined in an insane asylum. On his release from the hospital, the Ontario Mothers' Allowances Commission argued that he was fit to take up remunerative work. To force the issue, the commission revoked his wife's allowance. The desperate municipal authorities of the village of Arthur petitioned on the wife's behalf against the return of this violent, abusive, unfit parent to both his home and his community; yet the government adamantly upheld the sanctity of the marriage contract, even though relations between husband and wife had broken down twelve years earlier after another woman gave birth to the husband's child and, after years of abuse, the wife on several occasions prevented the husband's return. Public officials maintained that the return of the natural breadwinner obviated the need for further government assistance to the family. 'The question of the responsibility of the care of the family,' wrote the chief investigator in 1928, 'has thus been removed from the Mothers' Allowance Commission and is one that must be decided between Mrs A and her husband. I have no doubt that Mrs A could get in touch with her husband if she so desires and find out from him directly whether or not he is able to work and support his family.'[85] A few months later, the husband conveniently died of an anemic condition. After the widow was able to demonstrate her willingness to work as a caretaker in the local Presbyterian church and had ensured that all her children over sixteen contributed to the family, her allowance was reinstated.[86]

Even though the National Council of Women and various labour unions had campaigned hard for the abolition of child labour, the overseers of mothers' allowance policies awarded benefits more readily to families in which the mother encouraged her older children to contribute their wages to the family economy.[87] In the case referred to earlier, of the mother in Grenville County who was rebuked by an investigator for keeping an unclean household and who was forced to clean it on the spot, the conflict over the issue of cleanliness amounted to a rhetorical veneer for a more important issue – the parents' lack of control over their adolescent children. The investigators evinced much more sympathy for this family – in which the father was an incapacitated eighty-three-year-old, and in which there were nine children under fourteen and two over eighteen – when the 'frail and worn' wife worked as a domestic and when the two older children contributed to the family's income. In 1927, the female case worker still held out hopes of reforming this family and impressing on them the ideal of self-sufficiency, and she praised the husband for staying at home to care for the children while his wife worked, and she described the house as 'always neat and house looked better than usual.' That cleanliness was being used in this situation as a metaphor for the work ethic became obvious when the investigator then stated: 'She [the mother] is always ready to work when she can get it, and everyone agrees that she is a hard working woman and people are glad she is getting the allowance.' But by 1933 cracks had begun to appear in the investigator's perceptions of this family's worthiness; she reported that although the mother remained 'energetic, tidy, simple, kindly, working hard,' she had however, lost control of her progeny, who 'as they become wage earners are shiftless and take no responsibility with the home or parents.' Seemingly oblivious to the fact that this was 1933, the worst year of the Great Depression, the female case worker now began to describe the father as 'careless and untidy' and sought tighter control over the family economy by having their government assistance managed by a trustee. The overall goal of the mothers' allowance system – to enforce family cooperation – was finally achieved when the father became a janitor at the local public school, the mother charred for $12.00 a week, the older son worked for $2.00 a day as a casual labourer, and the eldest daughter contributed $10.00 a month to support her younger siblings. The family's total income was now approximately $90.00 per month, which meant that the government benefit of $30.00 per month was now serving its purpose, which was to compel this family to construct a parallel system of private welfare.[88]

During the 1920s and 1930s the monitoring by the State of the economic contributions of older children became more intense. In part, this was because the paradigm of the economic interdependence of the working-class family – so well described by Bettina Bradbury – seemed to be breaking down: offspring were beginning to perceive their work in increasingly individualistic terms and were becoming reluctant to contribute their earnings to their widowed mothers and younger siblings. That the domestic ideal in which all family members contributed voluntarily to the family economy was no longer integral to working-class life was alluded to by one beneficiary of mothers' allowances. Having been deserted in 1927, this woman believed that either her husband or the State should support her. She asserted a more modern and individualized conception of the meaning of work when she told the Ontario Mothers' Allowances Commission that 'it is not right that I should be dependent on them [my children] when there is a government who looks after other matters.' Welfare investigators were noticing more and more that parents were losing control of their adolescent offspring. This may have reflected a social reality, rather than merely frustration with families who seemed to be evading their responsibilities. Many male children appeared to be balking at working-class traditions that set family duty above individual ambition. As the deserted mother described above went on to state: 'And my son that has been keeping us for the last seven years has left home to earn a little money for himself he is twenty three years old and thinks I should have help from somewhere else he says as long as he stays home and keeps us no one else will help us so I had to ask for relief the 10th of February as he had not worked all winter and nothing doing around here he got a chance on a boat and took it there are five of us left and they are cutting us 10.00 on May 1st.'[89] This change in cultural mores concerning the family economy was, of course, exacerbated by the onset of the Depression, which further eroded the intergenerational nature of the family economy by precluding potential wage-earning adolescent children from working.

As the ideal of family responsibility extolled by the Mothers' Allowances Commission became increasingly impossible for families to approach, conflicts between female beneficiaries and their middle-class overseers sharpened. The perceptions of female investigators of their clients became more pejorative, and the behaviour of the State more punitive toward these supposedly delinquent and 'pauperized' families. A mother from Muskoka applied in 1925 for a mothers' allowance for her and her six children aged three to eleven. Her husband had been first jailed and then committed to the Mimico hospital for the insane after physically abusing her and their children. She was characterized by visiting investigators as a responsible and thrifty mother and was permitted to handle her government benefits without supervision. Later, however, she refused to allow her husband back into the family circle, and then she failed to compel her grown sons to work. At this point she became the object of intense government scrutiny and was accused by investigators of hiding information and attempting to mislead them. A yawning gap had appeared between working-class and middle-class perceptions of idleness and work. In 1934 the case worker reported:

The two elder boys got jobs in a camp on the highway work but after being there for about a week came home again as the condition of the camp was such they could not stand it. Mrs. H. said to Mr. Smith and myself that there was so much drinking in the place that the boys could not put up with it.

As we both told her it was simply that neither E. or the boys wanted to work so long as they could loaf about with her to support them and provide them with food. It was a case of absolute laziness, and I do not see why the Commission should provide her with money to keep them.[90]

State regulation of working-class family life revolved not around the mothers' moral deficiencies, but rather around their economic behaviour and that of their offspring. As the statistics gathered by the Ontario Mothers' Allowances Commission demonstrate, only 21.6 per cent of women lost their benefits because of poor home conditions. When widows had their allowances rescinded, it was usually because their children were old enough to work, because they had remarried, or because it was believed they could be self-supporting.[91] The granting of mothers' allowance depended on family members being able to demonstrate a sustained work ethic. A French-Canadian woman from Timmins, Ontario, had her application turned down because her oldest male child – a labourer – worked but contributed nothing to the household. The investigator's criticism of his immoral pastime of smoking was in fact rhetorical window dressing for the more substantive invective directed against his failure to support his dependent mother and younger siblings. This woman was forced to go on municipal relief. She was granted the less stigmatizing mother's allowance eight years later, only after she ensured that her two oldest children, a domestic and a labourer, together contributed substantially more than the $25.00 of government assistance.[92] Likewise, a widow from Scarborough was described as a 'good mother' when her girls began working at a hosiery factory and her son became a farm labourer nearby.[93]

Many women who hoped that their children would rise higher than themselves measured the State's intrusiveness by the degree to which it sought to interfere with the economic relations of the family. They did not welcome those investigators who exposed the emerging tensions between the older and younger generations over whether work was for collective or individual benefit. As the *Second Annual Report* of the Ontario Mothers' Allowances Commission remarked concerning the case of a woman who fought to keep her three oldest children at home: 'The mother at first resented the suggestion that she was at all to blame for her older children's desertion of the home, but finally accepted the advice and this winter the home has had less friction and is much happier.'[94] Just as working-class youths were attempting to free themselves from the constraints of older working-class family economic strategies, in which children were expected to contribute their wages to the maintenance of the household, governments began seeking through their welfare policies to coerce already socially distressed families into adhering to these older practices of family interdependence – this, even though as the Depression took root, these practices were becoming untenable. Working-class widows wanted the State to wholly assume the responsibilities of the male breadwinner. The government would thus be protecting them against the encroachments of paid labour, and thereby helping maintain their respectability. Working-class women believed they were being paid by the State for the work of mothering their children, and they accepted the assertions of policymakers that mothers' allowances were not a form of charity because women were being paid 'a wage for public service.' Thus, they were resentful when middle-class male policymakers began to make paid work a precondition for entitlements. For all their rhetoric about the home being 'the heart of the nation,' those who administered mothers' allowances did not define women's access to state welfare solely in terms of motherhood. By asserting that women as well as men had to work in order to avoid the social disease of pauperization, government policymakers were flouting time-honoured poor law conventions that women with children should earn the right to outdoor relief without working; by breaching such gendered conceptions of work, they were also temporarily setting aside cherished norms of domesticity.

As *The Fourth Annual Report* of the Ontario Mothers' Allowances Commission attested, it did not allow 'full maintenance of the family,' but urged the mother to save and work. Her role was precisely that of the male breadwinner: 'Were the allowance made to cover the full maintenance it would create wastefulness and probably laziness ... The encouragement thus given to the mother to be industrious and endeavour to get along has a good deal to do in making her family likewise.'[95] The 'patriarchal' state, then, was not usurping the role of the deceased *father*; rather, by offering mere 'assistance' by augmenting the main family income, it was functioning in the role that the *wife* or *children* had traditionally occupied. Thus, mothers' allowances did not simply blur the lines between needs-based charity and rights-based social entitlements; because they imposed the double-duty of motherhood and paid labour, they left in dispute the question of whether a woman's entitlements derived principally from her role as mother or from her function as a wage earner. Were mothers' allowances to be, as many women and labour reformers were to argue in the following decades, the precursor of a broader 'maternalist' State? Or were they to be, as Mrs Shortt had envisioned, the stepping stone to a program of social insurance founded on the principle of male work?

The emphasis on maintaining economic cooperation within the family, and the emphasis on the responsibilities of the male breadwinner, would soon emerge as the twin pillars of welfare legislation. It was these principles that became enshrined in welfare policymaking, rather than the feminist principles of economic independence for women, a gendered vision of poverty, and a conception of social citizenship founded on the national service of motherhood. This held long-term implications for the development of the Canadian welfare state. In many respects, gendered views of work and poverty and the ideal of separate spheres greatly worked in women's favour insofar as these social norms helped confirm motherhood as a basis of state entitlement. Mothers' allowances were decisive in creating an early maternalist bias within state welfare formation, because they created a niche of female-specific entitlements. However, these rights for women remained enmeshed within the larger social imperatives (shared both by feminists and male policymakers alike) of national efficiency, the enhancement of male wages, and the reinforcement of family solidarity and self-sufficiency. All of these economic arguments were crucial in marshalling public support for mothers' allowances; however, this largely 'maternalist' agenda served, in fact, to buttress the position of skilled male workers. The creation of an ostensibly 'maternalist' state based on new conceptions of social citizenship was tethered ineluctably to a decisively male-centred set of economic imperatives. Canadian feminists, unlike the more radical of their British counterparts, were not willing fundamentally to critique the sanctity of the male wage contract; they were less interested in promoting the individual rights of women than they were in seeking public means for affirming community and familial duties and obligations. Consequently, mothers' allowances were seen not as a means to women's economic independence, but rather as a means for the State to buttress the more conservative imperative of family self-sufficiency. Mothers' allowances were in this sense paid not to the mother, but to the children and to the family as a whole.

Most middle-class feminists saw in the exaltation of motherhood a means for advancing the rights of women. For that reason they employed traditional concepts of gender roles to adumbrate a new notion of social citizenship, from which flowed state entitlements for women who had lost, through no fault of their own, the male breadwinner. The more conservative tenets of Canadian maternal feminism reinforced male-centred business and labour interests, and so did not lead to any radical questioning of the pre-eminent role of the male breadwinner. That being said, working-class women accepted the notion of separate spheres and believed that their economic independence, the elevation of motherhood, and their social rights were founded on the fact that they were dependants of a responsible, earning husband. Fiercely holding to traditional norms of domesticity, working-class widows demanded that the State substitute entirely for the deceased breadwinner; they wanted state benefits to entirely replace the lost wage, so as to enable them to remain at home to raise their children. The fundamental issue that split reform constituencies, and that divided working-class widows and middle-class government officials, was not whether the system of mothers' allowances was needs-based or rights-based. Rather, it was whether social entitlements were to be grounded on motherhood or waged labour; whether state intervention would uphold gendered visions of work in the short-term; or whether the ideal of separate spheres would be temporarily abrogated in order to protect the breadwinner ideal (and its corollory of family independence) in the future.

Despite rhetoric that insisted on the primacy of motherhood, government policymakers in practice willingly transgressed traditional gender roles by forcing women to seek paid work outside the home, because of their overweening concern for reinforcing the work ethic and the ideal of family economic cooperation within working-class homes – an ideal they perceived as threatened by postwar unemployment, the dilution of skill among workers, the problem of desertion, and changes in how young people viewed their family responsibilities. All dimensions of government policymaking were permeated by the traditional concern with pauperization and by the broadly held fear of fostering dependency. This calculus, and its attachment to poor law traditions, was instrumental in shifting the basis of modern welfare entitlements away from motherhood toward waged labour. It was economic regulation, which eventually coerced women to work – and not the regulation of sexual morality and cleanliness – that was the primary goal of mothers' allowances. It was this dimension of mothers' allowances that transgressed against the well-entrenched values of domesticity that characterized working-class life.

During the 1920s, the question as to whether one's right to state assistance was based on the service of motherhood or on the act of working for wages hung in the balance. It appeared that the movement for unemployment insurance had been stymied by the movement for mothers' allowances, which had, because of postwar concerns over depopulation and national economic efficiency, effectively identified motherhood as the primary basis of state welfare entitlements. But because this system of maternalist welfare rights was sustained by a consensus that the position of the male breadwinner had to be defended, the notion of work-based entitlements was not extinguished; rather, it was preserved, and actually affirmed in the way that mothers' allowance legislation was actually applied. Once the cultural legacy of the First World War receded and fears about population growth were replaced by the overwhelming issue of unemployment, the emergence of a new system of welfare entitlements centring on unemployment insurance very quickly led to the disenfranchisement of women's social welfare rights, as paid work entirely eviscerated motherhood as the basis for state entitlements.

5

Dismantling the Maternalist State: Labour, Social Work, and Social Catholicism Debate Family Policy, 1926–1930

We have never used the word 'Pension' in our legislation or administration as the term had appeared to us to encourage in our applicants an undue sense of their rights in claiming or demanding an allowance.

A.P. Paget, Mothers' Allowances Commission, Manitoba to Agnes McNab, Mothers' Pension Board, B.C., 12 March 1927

It is quite clear that a community which does not contain families of four or more children would be doomed to extinction ... So that the service rendered to a country by the heads of large families is obvious. It is therefore in the interest of society that these fathers should be placed in a position of security so far as the needs of their families are concerned.

Leon Lebel, *Family Allowances*, 1929

In almost every province where a system of mothers' allowances had been introduced, government benefits had been restricted to a limited category of deserving mothers – namely, widows with more than two children and women with incapacitated husbands. Despite the strictures placed on this path-breaking form of social legislation by financially austere governments, the broader social movement, which demanded more liberal welfare programs, did not disappear from the Canadian cultural landscape. Between 1926 and 1928 there arose two related (albeit dissimilar) campaigns that aimed at further extending the maternalist welfare state, which had recognized the services that family reproduction and the unpaid work of child rearing contributed to the common weal. The first, initiated by J.L. Cohen, the noted labour lawyer, and William Ivens, the Winnipeg labour activist, demanded that mothers' allowance benefits be extended to deserted, divorced, and unmarried women. The second, led by J.S. Woodsworth, the Independent Labour Party (ILP) member for Winnipeg, and Father Leon Lebel, the social Catholic commentator from Quebec, called for the introduction of a national system of family allowances.

What both of these campaigns shared was an acknowledgment that the State had a role in ensuring the 'economic stability of family life.' What disturbed Charlotte Whitton, and other adherents of the traditional boundaries between the private and public spheres, was that such legislation conceived of kinship relations almost entirely in economic rather than spiritual terms. Moreover, she objected to a national family allowance system, viewing it as a precursor to broader forms of social insurance. This new incarnation of mothers' allowances advocated by William Ivens, in combination with the family allowances championed by the ILP, would, according to conservatives, commit governments to extensive new powers. Whitton perceived these labour initiatives as radical challenges to the privileged position of the responsible male breadwinning husband and as a threat to personal initiative, the work ethic, and family economic self-sufficiency.

In the end, this two-pronged movement to bolster family-based welfare entitlements failed when it confronted Whitton, who as an ideological opponent was both politically astute and ruthlessly single-minded. During the ensuing discussions, the fate of mothers' and family allowances took unpredictable twists and turns that resulted in vastly different outcomes than any of the major protagonists intended. In order to raise a credible counterattack against what she perceived were well-orchestrated assaults by organized labour on the Canadian family, Whitton was forced to concede the viability of their argument – namely, that family security was mostly about economics rather than morality. In practical terms, Whitton succeeded in blocking further government incursions into family life, in that she was able to hold the line on mothers' allowances benefits and to defeat Woodsworth's proposals for a state-funded system of family allowances.

This ideological contest between Whitton and the ILP resulted in a decisive transformation in how the Canadian family was conceptualized.[1] The underlying principles animating family policies were transformed to such a degree that they no longer upheld the ideals of the mother-centred family: by 1930, mothers' allowances could no longer be differentiated from municipal relief and thus had lost their redemptive qualities; while family allowances (first mooted in Britain as a feminist and redistributive measure in recognition of the national importance of child rearing and of women's unpaid labour) had been reconstituted as a corollary to other state insurance proposals that aimed at reinforcing the right of male workers to a 'living wage.' In ways never intended by reformist exponents of new family welfare policies, the period between 1926 and 1928 witnessed a decisive restructuring of the ideological contours and national goals on which social welfare entitlements were based. By the end, the family and its unpaid work of reproduction and child rearing had lost precedence to the workplace and the wage-earning male breadwinner.

'"Not a statutory right" but a "social aid"'[2]

Legislative enactments only partly explain how mothers' allowances evolved, and governments of the time were vulnerable to popular social pressures. Nowhere are these points better illustrated than in the observations of Charlotte Whitton, the director of the Canadian Council on Child Welfare, and Ernest Blois, the director of child welfare for Nova Scotia. Blois believed that the Nova Scotia government had erected ironclad defences against popular protest by removing the administration of mothers' allowances from the immediate purview of government ministers and the legislative process. He was therefore outraged to discover that hundreds of 'unworthy' mothers, such as the unmarried and deserted, were receiving allowances because of 'the growing tendency in some quarters to consider all children of widowed mothers entitled to an allowance irrespective of the mother's qualifications to maintain her home and bring up her children in a proper manner.'[3]

However much provincial laws may have defined mothers' allowances as a limited form of needs-based social relief, during the 1920s public opinion gradually came to perceive allowances as a 'statutory right.' Whitton, who closely monitored shifting practices in the administration of mothers' allowances in all the provinces, concluded that she and other child welfare professionals had erred in disassociating 'the system from any aspect of charity.' They had thereby failed to suppress the 'constant agitation' from various 'other groups' who wished to detach mothers' allowances from traditional notions of pauperization and lesser eligibility and anchor them once again to the concept of rights-based pensions. Whitton looked on nervously as various labour and women's organizations launched massive campaigns which built on the perception, popular among working-class mothers, that the allowance was in fact a 'pension or compensation payment to which the applicant is entitled simply because she is a widow and not even particularly because she is in need.'[4] It became clear to welfare traditionalists that government statutes were not immutable. Whitton was especially critical of the system in British Columbia, where from their inception mothers' allowances had been seen as a pension. Whitton had hoped to reinforce the power of the local CASs by keeping mothers' allowances firmly enmeshed with other forms of local relief; however, organized labour in alliance with other reform groups was successfully lobbying to have mothers' pensions administered through the distinctly rights-based Workman's Compensation Board. Furthermore, the British Columbian Deserted Wives Maintenance Act had defined a woman as a deserving 'deserted wife' if she was by reason of her husband's cruelty or adultery unable to cohabit with him; this made many separated wives eligible for a pension. Thus, divorced wives were informally granted state benefits; not only that, but there was nothing to prevent growing numbers of unmarried mothers from applying, even though the legislation made no provision for this class of women.[5] According to Whitton, in Saskatchewan the municipalities – the level of government most vulnerable to pressures from local women's institutes – were completely indifferent to the number or classes of women recommended. In effect, public sentiment was given full reign in that province.[6]

Other provincial jurisdictions likewise succumbed to popular opinion. Nowhere was this more evident than in Manitoba, where labour agitation after the failed Winnipeg General Strike was targeting other areas for reform. By 1927 labour had succeeded in having mothers' allowances made into a 'reasonably adequate allowance.' In Whitton's view, this level of benefits dangerously eroded the principle of lesser eligibility – the foundation stone of all welfare assistance – because it surpassed the wage levels of the unskilled and seasonal labourer.[7] But labour organizations in Manitoba were not entirely happy with how the government had bowed to their demands: in order to extend to widows a level of maintenance commensurate with what the 'breadwinner' had provided, A.P. Paget, the director of child welfare in Manitoba, had held fast on extending assistance to other 'classes' of women. This made Manitoba an anomaly among provinces, and led William Ivens to launch a vigorous campaign in February 1928 calling for a provincial Royal Commission to inquire into the administration of mothers' allowances. His hope was that this would compel provincial politicians to extend benefits to deserted, divorced, and unmarried mothers.[8]

In part, Ivens was prompted to take action on behalf of unmarried and deserted women because of cases like that of Fred and Ethel Schindler. Ethel Schindler ran off with the young 'Bohemian' immigrant, who later served with the Strathcona Light Horse during the war. Because 'unmarried wives' who cohabited with soldiers were fully entitled both to their pay and to military separation allowances, Ethel never felt it necessary to marry Fred. This meant that in official terms, their two children had been 'born out of wedlock.' In 1927 she finally married Fred. However, she soon left him after he physically abused her. Technically, Mrs Schindler was ineligible for a mothers' allowance because she was a separated wife and because, in a narrow legal sense, she was an unmarried mother, as her children had been conceived prior to her marriage. It was humanitarian concern for women like Mrs Schindler that inspired Ivens and fellow clergymen to fight for changes in Manitoba's mothers' allowance legislation.[9] As Paget, the beleaguered director of the child welfare division, informed Whitton: 'Ivens is on the warpath pressing hard for an increase in our schedule and the extension of the scope of the Act to include Desertion, Penal Cases, One Child, those b.o.o.w. [born out of wedlock] in fact a regular broadside. Did you see Cohen's book on M.A. legislation? It appears under Labour auspices and Ivens uses the material to slam the Manitoba policy, minister, administration, director et al. ... The part that impresses the government most seems to be the % we take of Mothers' earnings.'[10]

From this perspective, the problem of mothers' earnings went to the heart of the issue. As demonstrated in the previous chapter, mothers' allowance legislation was ostensibly written to prevent women from having to enter into paid work outside the home, and it was on this basis that organized labour supported it. But in practice, women and children were increasingly being compelled to work for ever larger portions of their upkeep, and this threatened once again both wage levels and jobs for the 'more deserving' male breadwinner. This subtle but important shift in how mothers' allowances were distributed occurred in all provinces; but in Manitoba, where the allowances were intended to rise and fall with the cost of living, they were being used quite deliberately to bolster a widow's incentive to work. What disturbed labour leaders was not that public welfare administrators were encouraging the earning of pin money, but that by making deductions proportionally less after the recipient earned $10, women were being manipulated into working longer hours, especially after their children were in school.[11]

These work policies for widows were very effective: in 1917 only 56 per cent of Manitoba beneficiaries earned supplementary wages, but by 1926–27 fully 80 per cent of women on government assistance sought work outside the home.[12] Thus it was not a coincidence that J.L. Cohen published his digest of *Mother's Allowance Legislation in Canada* in 1927. In it he argued that because needy widows and their children were being forced to work for wages, and because deserted, divorced, and unmarried women as well as those with husbands in prison were excluded, both the wage standard and trade union solidarity were threatened. The State, he contended, was establishing a dangerous precedent by using social policy as a economic lever; by conceiving of mothers' allowances in terms of a 'business undertaking,' the State had become a 'competitive factor' in industry.[13] In an effort to end this government practice of utilizing family policies as an economic weapon with which to interfere with the independence of labour, Cohen presented his case in terms barely distinguishable from those of Charlotte Whitton. Like Whitton and other traditionalists, he interpreted mothers' allowances not in terms of women's rights, but as founded on the principle of 'assistance to dependent children.'[14] His intentions differed from hers insofar as he wanted mothers' allowances to become a rights-based entitlement that could be upheld in the courts, as well as a means of establishing a more comprehensive national system of social insurance. Nevertheless, he underscored that endowment for motherhood was not just a remedy for economic want – its chief goal was to protect the home, the primary 'unity of the social fabric,' by correcting 'ethical and social maladjustment' within the family.[15] However, he emphasized – as had reformers during the earliest campaigns for mothers' allowances – that if the stability of family life was the central preoccupation of government social policy, then *all* children no matter the character or marital status of the mother, should be protected through a system of 'special relief' at rates that would ensure a standard of living above a subsistence level and that would preclude the need for a supplementary income.

The battle between social work professionals and public opinion (through grass roots organizations of women and labour) over who would dictate family welfare policy dates from the Cohen and Ivens salvo of 1928. In 1929, Whitton rallied her social work troops and mounted a counterattack, having established herself as a one-woman Royal Commission to study the administration of mothers' allowances in Manitoba. Her social work ranks fanned out across the province interviewing working-class families, with the goal of bringing Manitoba's system of allowances in line with the wages of the 'breadwinner group.' Needless to say, Whitton's phalanx of social workers received little help from local labour leaders, who objected to their interrogations of working-class families about their income and household budgets.[16] Likewise, Whitton canvassed 500 former beneficiaries in order to demonstrate the need for a more centralized system of government control and to argue for greater participation in family reform by private agencies such as the CASs. She skilfully deployed the life histories of these women to reorient the system of mothers' allowances back to its original principles – that is, as a policy not just of economic relief but also of family reform. To shore up the character-building aspects of this system of state guardianship, Whitton firmly declared that 'greater effort should be made to require the head of the family [the widow] to enforce contribution from earning children,' and that mothers should fulfil their breadwinner role by working out as a means of 'encouraging ambition, thrift and independence'[17] among the next generation of wage earners.

The labour campaign built on the growing popular perception that mothers' allowances ought to be claimable as a legal right by all women who had lost the economic support of a male breadwinner. This labour initiative was, however, firmly squelched in Manitoba. In early 1929 the government tabled Whitton's report. As E.W. Montgomery, the Minister of Health and Public Welfare, reported the situation to Whitton, Ivens and a delegation from the TLC received the report 'to say the least ungraciously.' This is not surprising, for in it Whitton made insidious use of the testimony of hundreds of working-class beneficiaries to thwart all of labour's claims for reforming mothers' allowances. Ivens had never approved of a one-woman Royal Commission, especially when that woman was Charlotte Whitton, and was apoplectic when he discovered that the report was 'more generous to the government than it is to the widows'[18] and that it had significantly forestalled any further expansion in government responsibility in the sphere of family welfare by shifting the power base for the administration of widows' allowances back to the voluntary charity and philanthropic organizations. Thereafter, the CASs of Manitoba had much more influence over policy; from that point on, investigations would be more rigorous and would be made in accordance with a specific concept of what constituted a 'fit and proper mother.'[19] Whitton was also well aware of the depth of popular feeling regarding making unmarried mothers beneficiaries of mothers' allowances; so she strategically placed all casework for unmarried mothers firmly in the hands of the CASs, thereby isolating it from any association with mothers' allowances.

Dr E.W. Montgomery, the provincial Minister of Health and Public Welfare, remained in close consultation with Whitton at the Canadian Council on Child Welfare throughout the ensuing weeks as her report was debated in the legislature. In February 1929 he warned her that the political situation in Manitoba was 'very tense.' Fearing that her report would be ignored by the legislature, Whitton retorted fiercely that she hoped that 'there is so much material in the Report that Mr Ivens' speech thereon will be so lengthy that it will empty the House and you will therefore be able to get your estimate through an empty House with no discussion.'[20] As the new recommendations wended their way through the legislative process, the political will to oppose the minister, who was armed with Whitton's voluminous technical data, was clearly absent. Labour opposition was split when F.W. Tipping, the labour representative on the Mothers' Allowances Board, was co-opted by supporters of the legislation. When the legislative committee convened to discuss the report, only a weak tail of opposition remained; only Ivens and a Mrs Edith Rogers appeared on behalf of organized labour and women's groups.[21]

Whitton had won her first battle against those who argued that it was the responsibility of all governments to materially assist all families deprived of adequate economic security. But as Harry Bentley, the chief investigator for the Ontario Mothers' Allowances Commission, remarked: 'The war is still on and keeps us pretty busy all the time.'[22] Indeed, Whitton's conservative social work juggernaut continued to sweep across Canada, from provincial government to provincial government, relentlessly suppressing popular forces working to expand government welfare programs. Since 1920, when she established the Canadian Council on Child Welfare, Whitton had been able to transform her organization into the leading centre for collecting social statistics in an era when universities and philanthropic agencies were too small and underfunded to undertake specialized social welfare research. Because the Canadian Council on Child Welfare was a clearing house for numerous local voluntary family welfare organizations, Whitton was able to assiduously collect and analyse the newest information regarding welfare legislation and social data. Thus, she was able to establish herself as the foremost expert on Canadian welfare policy. Moreover, when in 1933 Helen MacMurchy retired from her position as head of the Child Welfare Division of the federal Department of Pensions and Health, Whitton and her organization usurped her role. This conferred even greater powers on Whitton, who became in effect an inner governmental adviser to the minister.[23] Along with her large storehouse of technical information, Whitton had, as Harold Putman put it, 'masculine logic, feminine charm and energy the despair of all'[24] – not to mention a large amount of political combativeness and an unquestioning faith in the moral rightness of her position. All of this enabled Whitton to become the policy adviser for a number of provincial governments as well as the federal government between the two world wars, and enabled her to put her imprimatur on government legislation in these formative decades of family welfare policy-making.

After her successes in Manitoba, in 1930 the financially strapped government of British Columbia called on Whitton to streamline its mothers' allowance bureaucracy. As Whitton confided to Mrs D.G. McPhail, a member of the Mothers' Pension Board, the management of mothers' allowances in that province was in a 'deplorable state.' The government was spending a million dollars a year, she remarked, but there was virtually no casework to monitor mothering skills and there were only six visitors, all of them ineffectual and untrained.[25] To her amazement and chagrin, Whitton discovered that it was regular practice among investigators to explain to potential beneficiaries the strategies they might use to baulk the system. One investigator told a woman who was living with a man that if she wanted to keep her government assistance she must either leave him or marry him; she then went on to show her how to get her assessments down low enough that she would be able to keep her allowance. Another friendly visitor often advised deserted women to apply for a mother's pension once they were divorced. It was to curb such practices, which were subtly expanding the boundaries of the original government legislation, that Whitton set about making the welfare regulations 'watertight.'[26]

British Columbia was at the time heavily pruning its civil service, so Whitton was unable to establish a broader base of professional social work investigation in British Columbia.[27] Even so, the obvious need for downsizing in the midst of the Depression meant that she could easily exact large cuts to mothers' benefits; at the same time she could aggressively weed out those mothers who were so hopeless, feeble-minded, or immoral that no degree of material aid or social investigation would be able to restore their families to 'social stability and independence.'[28] The provincial government cooperated fully with Whitton's plans to draw strict boundaries between mothers' allowances and general relief, having grown tired of municipalities dumping more and more of their relief cases on the Mothers' Allowances Commission, which was provincially funded.[29] Also Whitton's desire to rid the government of families that could become self-sufficient through work meshed with the labour minister's personal interest in having widows fill the growing demand among middle-class families for domestic servants.[30] British Columbia had long had the most liberal system of mothers' pensions in the country and had regularly granted generous benefits to widows as well as to deserted, divorced, and unmarried women. Whitton's arguments about the vital need to limit government intervention in the realm of family welfare would not have been persuasive under normal economic conditions; but this was the Depression and her recommendations for retrenching welfare benefits and for restricting the range of beneficiaries were both compelling and practicable. As a result, she was given free rein to radically restructure child and family policies in British Columbia. Endowment for mothers traditionally had been defined as a rights-based 'pension' in that province; following Whitton's assault, it was reinvented and placed on a much more voluntaristic, charity-based course. Later it would be debased even further and become a scheme of general welfare assistance.[31]

Not all provinces incorporated Whitton's proposals into their child welfare legislation. Despite representations from Whitton, the Ontario government extended mothers' allowance benefits to widows and 'other women on Indian reserves' and in 1934 was succumbing to outside pressure to allow widows with one child to apply for assistance.[32] One might have assumed that Whitton's perorations against government-funded welfare programs would have found a ready hearing in Quebec, where church-based charitable institutions were well entrenched. But even though Whitton was one of the main 'expert' witnesses to testify at the 1931 Quebec Commission on Social Insurance,[33] her recommendations and those of Mlle Cécile Joncas, who had established an experimental scheme of mothers' allowances in Quebec City with funds from the Department of Health, went largely unheeded. When a government program of allowances for needy mothers was established by the Duplessis regime in 1938, it was administered by the Department of Labour 'as a pension' to be paid automatically 'irrespective of the character of the home.'[34]

In 1930, in a missive directed to all provincial welfare officials from the Canadian Council on Child Welfare, Whitton reasserted the guiding principle of mothers' allowances, which she believed had been diluted by lack of bureaucratic attention and by external public pressure. Whitton wrote that because they were a form of 'public' assistance, mothers' allowances, 'cannot be considered as entirely the granting of financial aid to which the mother is unquestionably entitled ... It is rather a measure of social investment, on the part of the State, whereby mothers, of whose fitness for these responsibilities, the state assures itself, are indirectly subsidized by public grant, in exact proportion to their actual needs, to enable them to perform their parents' responsibilities towards their children, with the hope that these children should become desirable citizens, and social assets to the community.'[35]

It was in Nova Scotia that Whitton's conviction that policies for home protection must focus on the moral character rather than simply the economic security of the family had the most profound influence. In that province, with the strong support of Ernest Blois, the Director of Child Welfare, she was able to impress in its entirety her vision of welfare policy, in the shape of the 1930 Mother's Allowance Act. This vision was outlined in one of her famous memoranda: mothers' allowances must be funded by both the municipalities and the provinces, to proscribe against financial irresponsibility; no grants were to be made to wives of incarcerated men, as it was a grave social injustice to support dependants of crime; unmarried and deserted women must seek redress through the court system; women with one child must be excluded, as it was more morally efficacious if they be kept busy and earning a wage rather than having too much 'leisure' time; and benefits must be kept below the lowest wages of casual labourers and farmers. Above all, this 'investment of the State' must be repaid through attentive family casework.[36] As Nova Scotia's Parliament considered the legislation during the spring of 1930, Blois concurred in all that

Whitton advised through her extensive correspondence with him. Like Whitton, Blois believed that the allowance was only a 'grant-in-aid,' comparable with payments issued by the provincial Workmen's Compensation Board, and not a pension. Accordingly, he took steps to ensure that all older children contributed to the family income.[37] Blois was able to fend off popular agitation that interpreted mothers' allowances as a measure for women's rights; he also squelched any future campaigns to extend maternalist state provisions by reaffirming that the legislation was distinctly a child welfare provision. Luckily for Blois, the anticipated protests surrounding his bill were superseded by the public's reaction to a liquor control bill. Nevertheless, in order to quell any movements to amend the bill, Blois strategically framed the legislation so that '*no mother* will have any right to an allowance, in fact *no allowance will be paid to any mother*, in all cases the allowances are paid towards the maintenance of children.'[38]

The Nova Scotia Bill was, as Blois himself attested, 'a very conservative scheme for allowances.'[39] However, after 1932, as the Depression wore on in a province where mothers' allowances was the only real form of government-funded outdoor relief, the pressure to extend benefits to deserted women and to wives with incapacitated husbands became particularly acute.[40] Moreover, many of the strict provisions incorporated into the act were unenforceable. For example, as even casual, unskilled work dried up during the 1930s, welfare officials were unable to fully implement their policy that older children of mothers' allowance beneficiaries be compelled to work. Indeed, the Depression itself was the event most responsible for altering the underlying principles of mothers' allowances – despite the constant, conservative hectoring of Charlotte Whitton – and for shifting those allowances inexorably in the direction of unspecialized, general relief. Even Ernest Blois, a rigorous defender of morality-based family welfare policies, began to back away from distinguishing between worthy and unworthy mothers,[41] as the overwhelming need for simple economic relief rendered untenable his earlier preoccupation with the spiritual and affectional bonds of family life. In the end, the foundation on which mothers' allowances had been built (i.e., that they were a means to reform the character and child-rearing practices of working-class families) was eroded away by the Depression, as the gravity of the problem of unemployment swept aside maternalist definitions of deservedness and established new notions of an individual's worthiness to receive government assistance. By the end of the decade, moth-

ers' allowances no longer enjoyed special status. Thereafter, women
were granted this form of assistance not because they had fulfilled a
specific national goal by raising the next generation of citizens, but
because they were deemed to be 'unemployable' and so eligible only
for local outdoor relief. By 1940 mothers' allowances were seen as simply another form of general welfare. In order to understand how this
came about, we must first examine how the boundaries between
mothers' allowances and relief subtly shifted between 1930 and 1940,
and how prevailing notions of welfare entitlement changed so that
they emphasized economic security rather than the more sentimental
aspects of family life.

Arguably the most important force eroding the special status of
mothers' allowances was the introduction of relief on a massive scale
during the Depression. The introduction of government relief policies
resulted in an immediate lowering of mothers' allowance benefits all
across the country. 'The widespread development of direct relief,'
reported Whitton in 1933, 'by force of circumstances on a minimum
scale, has thrown into comparison the higher standards of aid generally available under mother's allowances, and is causing a steady
pressure towards the lowering of the latter to correspond with the
former.'[42] As a longtime advocate of reducing benefit rates in order to
force widows and their children into the workforce, Whitton supported this trend in family welfare policy. In the depths of the Depression, her view that all relief should be set below the minimum wage
level of the unskilled worker in order to sustain work incentives
among the general population gained widespread acceptance. Accordingly, in the early 1930s almost every provincial jurisdiction began to
reduce benefits paid to widows. Manitoba had always adjusted its levels of assistance to track the cost of living, but it reduced benefits
another 10 per cent in 1932, as did Alberta. But the widows who suffered most from this were those in Saskatchewan. There, mothers'
allowances had always been restrictively defined as a mere 'grant-in-
aid'; but as the number of applicants mushroomed during the Depression, rising 56.7 per cent in 1932 (the highest in North America), welfare officials slashed the already meagre flat rate payments, thereby
forcing thousands of single women with children onto direct relief.[43]
And to further erase the boundaries between mothers' allowances and
relief, many municipalities began using the mothers' allowance system
to shift the financial burdens of welfare onto the provinces. Thus, in the
city of Brandon, Manitoba, only twenty-four married and four single

men were on actual relief, while thirty-five relief families were assisted through mothers' allowances. A similar trend was emerging in Nova Scotia, where the mothers' allowance was becoming the obvious dumping ground for relief cases – especially for unemployed youths who continued to live in the parental home.[44]

Cash relief erased any remaining differences in standard of living between families on relief and those supported by a low-wage earner.[45] It also extinguished any remaining ideological demarcations between unemployment relief and the mothers' allowance (which was ostensibly 'a salary paid to the mother'[46] for her services to the nation). By merging mothers' allowances with general relief, the Depression removed those gender distinctions that favoured women – distinctions that had long been consciously embedded in family policy. As the Depression wore on, the glaring discrepancies in benefit levels between the mothers' allowance and direct relief created a popular backlash against welfare programs that privileged certain groups, such as widows. In no small way, this situation helped undermine the special status that maternalist welfare policies had by then achieved.

Whitton valiantly attempted to preserve older family case work norms, which insisted that material relief be granted not just on the basis of economic need but according to the character of the family and its potential to be ideologically and morally reformed. However, Whitton's ability to control the parameters of welfare policy was greatly inhibited by the levelling effects of unemployment. Not only men but also women and children were unable to find work, and this directly challenged one of the central tenets of mothers' allowance legislation – the need to preserve the work ethic. More disturbing, the growing tendency among widows on government assistance to include older 'unemployed' children within their family budget was extremely corrosive of the child protection aspects of mothers' allowance legislation. Whitton watched with growing apprehension as even professional social workers became more and more willing to blur the boundaries between unemployment relief and state payments for motherhood, by permitting single-parent families whose older children were unemployed to become beneficiaries of the mothers' allowance system. Faced with pressures from municipalities to take over the devastating burden of relief, and with the need to solve the growing problem of single men and women on relief, Manitoba welfare officials allowed older children on relief to remain at home with their families; in this way they were informally lifting the sanctions, introduced into mothers' allowance statutes, against idle children. Gertrude Childs, the head of the Mothers' Allowances Board of Manitoba's Department of Health and Public Welfare, explained how the overwhelming problem of unemployment was subtly changing how welfare entitlements for widows were defined:

> While many applications have been received where the family could be self-supporting if the children of earning age could find employment, the Child Welfare Board has taken the attitude that the Act provides for bereaved and dependent children only where such children cannot be provided for from the resources of the family, and that therefore it should not be used as a relief against unemployment. Many families under allowance where the children have been contributing are in difficulties, due to the children having only part-time employment, and in a few cases it has been necessary to make an adjustment for loss of earnings.[47]

Gertrude Childs was attempting to balance welfare theory with practice; Ernest Blois was less sanguine about Whitton's tenacious defence of traditional family reform practices. Indeed, as the Depression lingered on, social workers in Canada found themselves divided over a very basic question: Should the line be held against diluting mothers' allowances and child protection policies, or should unemployment relief become the determining principle in all family welfare policies? This was only partly a question of social work ideals;[48] mainly, it was a debate about the theory and practice of social work. As Blois noted, by 1932 there were two clearly defined camps: One group studiously maintained that mothers' allowances must protect children and establish 'Canadian standards of living' – a concern raised most often in the prairie provinces, with their large immigrant communities. The other group acknowledged that the widespread distribution of relief had radically altered the terms of debate within welfare policymaking, and recommended that provision for widows be placed under 'general relief.'[49]

Blois himself belonged to the latter group, and on several occasions during the Depression he chided Whitton for her lack of knowledge of practical welfare administration, pointing out that however much one might wish to uphold the privileged status of mothers' allowances as part of long-term national goals, prevailing economic conditions were dictating otherwise. As he informed her in 1934, too many widows were claiming access to state benefits on the basis of economic dependency alone, and because they were widows with several children, they could not – according to the letter of the mothers' allowance statutes – be deemed 'unworthy.' If, as Blois argued, widows were entitled to assistance on strictly economic grounds, what differentiated them from other relief recipients – namely, unemployed married men – who were forced to accept much lower levels of family subsistence? 'It is said, and with considerable truth,' wrote Blois in 1932, 'that probably our widows drawing Mother's Allowance and Workman's Compensation are by far the best off people in the country. This hardly seems fair or likely to create the proper spirit.'[50]

Blois was arguing that because relief had now become largely a problem affecting unemployed married men, the mothers' allowance was a discriminatory piece of welfare legislation. In the past, it had been believed that the stability of the family (and society) rested almost entirely on the spiritual and disciplinary guidance of the mother. But family policy now revolved almost exclusively around the problem of economic security and the pre-eminence of the male breadwinner. The 'moral economy' embedded in the administration of mothers' allowances was often invasive and coercive; even so, it established a set of distinctively maternalist state entitlements that recognized the difficult existence of 'abnormal' female-headed families. Depression-era welfare policies, however, had become totally preoccupied with the problem of the unemployed breadwinner, in that sense were seeking to resurrect the 'normal' family. The Canadian family was now conceived in strongly patriarchal terms; ideally, the father provided economic support for his dependants; but now he was also to usurp the spiritual and educational roles traditionally reserved for women.[51] It is from this perspective that we can make sense of the ideological about-face that Blois was making when he castigated the system of mothers' allowances as a piece of 'class legislation of a decidedly bad type.' Mothers' allowances no longer sufficiently rehabilitated families because in practice it now functioned merely as a form of material relief; not only that, but they established higher standards of living for female-headed families than for 'normal,' male-headed families on relief. It was by this logic that Blois critically assessed mothers' allowances: in his view they discriminated against deserving men, and thus fostered, in his words, 'considerable unrest.'[52]

As late as 1935, when it became palpably clear that there was no work available for children of mothers' allowance beneficiaries, Whitton adamantly maintained that both mothers' allowances and workmen's compensation must remain separate and distinct from 'emergency unemployment relief.'[53] Her protests against submerging mothers' allowances in general unemployment relief did not arise out of fears that family stability would be threatened. Rather, she feared that making mothers' allowances 'relief under another name' would obviate the need for investigation and thus establish such state provision as a legal right. As she argued, once one removed the 'proper guardianship' clauses from mothers' allowances, there was no longer a criterion by which to decide whether a mother was 'deserving' other than the fact that she was unemployed.[54] Thus, even while Whitton was defending the original conception of mother's allowances, she was obliged to concede that the practice, widespread among single women, of applying for an allowance as a form of 'direct relief' had already transformed welfare entitlements from a claim founded on motherhood to one defined exclusively by an individual's employment status.

It is indeed ironic that although Whitton desperately wished to shore up the investigative aspects of mothers' allowances during the 1930s, her equally strong commitment to upholding the work ethic by reducing all welfare benefits, together with her goal of cutting government expenditures, tended to dissolve the very boundaries she wished to preserve between mothers' allowances and general relief. Like Blois and other welfare policymakers of the 1930s, Whitton believed that the frontline of defence for the integrity of family life was first and foremost the protection of the livelihood of the male breadwinner. Whitton spent much of her time during the Depression ensuring that relief policies were correctly implemented according to her own world view. Because of her overarching concern for maintaining the principles of lesser eligibility in all welfare provision, she unwittingly contributed to the unravelling of the very principles that had long been the hallmark of Canada's various mothers' allowances systems.

Throughout the Depression, Whitton reinforced the practice – already followed in many provinces – of administering mothers' allowances as if they were another form of relief.[55] In several provinces, many widows – especially those with one child – were assisted through local relief. Indeed, Saskatchewan led the way in erasing in practice the lines that divided mothers' allowances from unemployment relief. Benefits were so inadequate that almost all beneficiaries of mothers' allowances were forced to accept either city relief or charity.[56] Similarly, in Ontario, in 1938 municipalities were instructed by the provincial relief officer to distribute fuel to mothers' allowance cases, thus placing them in the category of accepting 'partial relief.'[57] Widows with one child were particularly vulnerable to this process of achieving welfare parity by reducing all welfare benefits to relief levels. In British Columbia, all 'one child' mothers' allowance cases were transformed into direct relief cases. As if to underscore the degree to which the system of mothers' allowances had been demoted, its administration was shifted from the Workmen's Compensation Board to the Department of Welfare. More significantly, the new Director of Public Welfare, Harry Cassidy, began to refer to mothers' pensions as 'mother's relief.'[58]

Mothers' allowances were also a casualty of unemployment insurance, which created a distinctly two-tiered welfare system comprising contributory and non-contributory state benefits. The concept of maternalism vanished for good from Canadian welfare policy in 1940, when a national system of unemployment insurance was introduced, which amounted to formal acknowledgment that henceforth, state welfare benefits would be founded on the principle of waged labour. Moreover, advocates of unemployment insurance insisted from the start on a strict division between rights-based contributory insurance and needs-based relief. By doing so, they further dislodged mothers' allowances from their original privileged position in the welfare edifice. By the end of the Depression, welfare programs had been completely transformed. Widows were no longer accorded special treatment by virtue of their status as mothers of future citizens; rather, they were flung into the undifferentiated, stigmatized category of 'social assistance,'[59] which traditionally had been occupied by the residuum of the idle, incompetent, undeserving poor. Although many continued to expound the original principles that had animated maternalist state entitlements, it was clear by 1940 that the trends in social policy were toward eradicating the last vestiges of maternal citizenship. The constitutional discussions revolving around the publication of the Rowell–Sirois Report (1940) resulted in clear hierarchies being established between federally funded, contributory, self-help insurance schemes and provincially and municipally funded general assistance. This in effect gave legal ratification to what had previously been a set of loose administrative assumptions and thereby institutionalized the ideological segregation between contributory and non-contributory welfare programs.[60] In the wake of the 1940 report, many welfare officials, including J.H. Creighton in British Columbia, recommended either the total eradication of mothers' allowances or at the very least their dissolution into the clearly stigmatizing American-inspired formulation of Aid to Dependent Children.[61] From that time on, widows and deserted and divorced women, along with unmarried mothers, found themselves classed as 'unemployables,' a concept for which the sole reference point was male work. Even former soldiers on War Veteran's Allowance were granted a more favourable position than women. Although veterans were paid according to need, their benefits were deemed rights-based simply because they were seen as legitimate citizens, not only because they had defended the Canadian nation-state during the First World War, but also (and more important) because they were able to demonstrate evidence of partial employability.[62] The gendered bias of state welfare benefits had thus shifted away from women and reproduction toward men and the workplace. This ideological transformation would be accelerated by the concurrent debate over a national system of family allowances, initiated by the Independent Labour Party between 1926 and 1928.

The Failure of Family Allowances

In Quebec, Father Léon Lebel, a priest and teacher of philosophy at Immaculate Conception College in Montreal, had long recommended a system of family allowances as a measure that, by raising the standard of living for French-Canadian working-class and agricultural families, would help stem the flow of out-migration to the United States.[63] However, it was J.S. Woodsworth, the ILP member from Winnipeg, who first introduced the idea of family allowances in the House of Commons. In his speech of 14 December 1926, Woodsworth, like Lebel, conceived of family allowances as a redistributive class measure that would directly relieve poverty among working-class families. Woodsworth quoted from Paul Douglas, who the year before had published his landmark critique of the traditional wage structure in the United States, *Wages and the Family*, and who, like Woodsworth, used wage statistics to demonstrate the enormous gap in standards of living that existed between single workers and married breadwinners burdened with growing family responsibilities. Woodsworth was not the first to bring to public attention the growing problem of working-class poverty. In the latter half of the 1920s, the Montreal Council of Social Agencies carried out a series of surveys of working-class households and demonstrated that after years of strong economic growth, the wages even of skilled construction workers could not ensure a *'barely decent standard of living'* owing to seasonal interruptions in employment. Similar family budget studies were undertaken by the Catholic Guilds of Montreal, and by Miss Margaret Gould in Toronto; all of these confirmed that the wages of the father alone were rarely sufficient to meet family needs, even when the mother managed her household carefully.[64]

The leading champions of family allowances in the United States and Britain, Paul Douglas and Eleanor Rathbone, had offered systematic critiques of the theory of the living wage, pointing to the gap between the husband's wage and the needs of large families. In contrast, Canadian commentators placed their campaign for family allowances firmly within the debate over the living wage and conceived of them as a government measure for shoring up, rather than supplanting, the male wage earner's economic function as the breadwinning head of the family. For example, social workers in Montreal lobbied for governments to contribute to the male 'family wage,' believing that this would help women and children escape being forced into the workplace by poverty and the inadequacy of the male pay packet.[65] In the same vein, Georges Pelletier argued that the payment of a *'sursalaire'* for *'des chefs de famille'* by means of family allowances was a corollary for labour's arguments for a family wage, in that it would keep women from working outside the home. Pelletier, writing from a Catholic perspective on the family, believed that returning women and children to their natural domain, the home, would help secure the rights of the male wage earner by protecting his role as the exclusive and independent breadwinner.[66] These advocates of family allowances believed that by thus providing large working-class families with economic security, both traditional gender relations and the integrity of family life would be preserved.

The foremost exponent of family allowances in Britain, the feminist Eleanor Rathbone, had urged a government program of family wage supplements as a means of addressing the problem of women's economic independence. In the United States, Paul Douglas had recommended that these allowances be paid to the mother, even though his goal was less overtly feminist than that of Rathbone. In Canada, the campaign for family allowances was decidedly antifeminist in its overtones, and was entirely unrelated to the problem of acknowledging women's unpaid work in the home. Lebel and Woodsworth championed this novel approach to family policy with a view to helping organized labour achieve its goal of a 'living wage' for the male bread-winner and to thereby fulfil its ideal of worker independence, which was founded on the notion of family self-sufficiency. It is not insignificant that Woodsworth turned to the idea of family allowances only after the 1925 parliamentary committee to consider a 'minimum living wage' for male workers had failed. As Woodsworth explained to the House of Commons the following year, he believed 'that all workers, including common labourers, shall be entitled to a wage ample to enable them with thrift to maintain themselves and families in decency and comfort, and to make reasonable provision for old age.'[67] Far from being a feminist measure, Woodsworth's recommendation for family allowances was conceived as an attack on single female workers, who, protected by the existing minimum wage legislation, seemingly benefited at the expense of married men with family responsibilities who, without a wage floor, were compelled to eke out a living on wages barely higher than those of women without 'the responsibility of the family.'[68] In many respects the idea of family allowances was a radical measure insofar as it was intended to redistribute income from single to married workers; and from a socialist perspective it often was used to criticize the prevailing profit motive in industry.[69] However, in Canada family allowances carried conservative implications for gender relations, for they were consciously introduced by the ILP as a system of family security. Their intent was thus to reinforce the breadwinner ideal, the concept of a family wage, and the rights of labour to organize.

Although the idea of family or children's allowances had been incorporated into the Canadian Patriotic Fund's assistance policies during the First World War, it was still a novel idea in Canada during the 1920s. After the war, the more radical concept of family allowances had been diluted and diverted into provincial movements for mothers' allowances or pensions. Woodsworth's campaign between 1926 and 1928 was not the result of a popular movement within social work, or among feminists, or even within organized labour; it arose Athena-like, dictated largely by events taking place within the British ILP. There, in 1924, Eleanor Rathbone had published *The Disinherited Family*, in which she marshalled a massive amount of compelling statistical evidence on national income, wages, and population to demonstrate persuasively that the redistribution of national income by means of family allowances would address a very real and widespread social problem. Although Rathbone was concerned mainly about women's economic independence,[70] in the more conservative cultural climate of the 1920s, during which the women's movement was fragmenting, she insisted on placing the debate on family policy within a broader context of social and economic progress.

By broadening the cause of family allowances to encompass wider economic and social issues, the movement in Britain became decidedly more influential, and began to appeal to groups with clearly differing social and economic objectives: organized labour, businessmen, and eugenicists. For example, economists like William Beveridge were converted to the concept of family allowances because they viewed such wage supplements as a means for redistributing national income to large families without disturbing the efficiency of British manufacturing or hampering work incentives, which were so crucial to the common weal.[71] Beveridge also became an enthusiastic promoter of family allowances because he believed that such measures, when rightly utilized, could become a powerful eugenic force – one that would preserve the quality of Britain's falling population. It was with this end in view that he introduced the concept to the London School of Economics when he became its director.[72]

Family allowances also became an important weapon in the ILP's arsenal to fight for economic recovery and thus relieve widespread working-class poverty. William Beveridge won the favour of business interests, but alienated many constituencies within organized labour, by insisting that lowering wages was the best means for stimulating employment. In this regard, conservative forces saw family allowances as a useful tool, because they would solve the problem of how breadwinners were to maintain their dependants, and thereby cost the ILP one of its most effective arguments for better wage standards. Even though many trade unionists opposed family allowances, seeing them as encroaching on traditional rights of collective bargaining, the ILP enthusiastically took up the cause of family allowances, arguing that by increasing consumption levels in Britain they would act as a catalyst for general economic renewal. The consequent economic boom would in turn create jobs for working-class men and enable them to raise the standard of living of their families. Rathbone's contention that 'the family as an economic unit' must be valued for its contribution to the nation, and that working-class families deserved a larger share of the national wealth, appealed greatly to the ILP.[73] The broader economic implications of relieving working-class poverty, which Rathbone had underscored in *The Disinherited Family*, were critical in inducing the ILP to make family allowances the cornerstone of its 1926 platform, and did much to transform a mainly feminist concern into a logical defence of male rights in the workplace.

Rathbone had argued that by removing the question of maintaining dependants from the process of calculating the standard wage, family allowances would ensure equal pay for women in the workplace. In contrast, the ILP took up the cause of family allowances in April 1926 largely because it believed they would address its concerns about unemployment and solve the question of a living wage. Indeed, the ILP's belief that family allowances would resuscitate the flagging domestic market by placing supplementary funds directly in the hands of household consumers – namely working-class mothers – was first mooted during the party's Living Wage Commission, which sat in 1925 and 1926. This novel priority on consumption as the key to economic growth and employment was derived from the theories of the economist J.A. Hobson, one of the members of the commission. As the commission argued, if economic recovery could be achieved through higher national consumption, wages would in turn be stabilized, and the working-class family held intact.[74] The ILP's claim that family allowances would have no ill effects on the family wage, but would reaffirm the duty of men to support their families, was enunciated in its publication *The Living Wage*, a document that had a direct influence on Woodsworth's own interpretation of family allowances as a measure naturally beneficial to working-class families, and one that would solidify the economic and social pre-eminence of the male breadwinner.

In Britain, the ILP's campaign to make family allowances the linchpin of its policy remained mired in disputes within the labour movement. Many trade unions did not share the optimism of the ILP that with the introduction of a system of family allowances, wage levels would be either preserved or elevated. They were wary of any programs that might interfere with their ability to bargain collectively, and it was difficult not to interpret such allowances as wage supplements aimed at checking wage increases. Both in France and in New South Wales it had been demonstrated clearly that a system of supplementary allowances could be used as efficaciously by conservative business interests as by the left. In New South Wales the implementation of state-level children's allowances in 1926 resulted in an immediate paring back of the basic wage; this, even though A.B. Piddington had lobbied for such a family policy on the basis that it would help defend the rights of male workers.[75] British trade unionists were also cognizant of events in France, where family allowances were organized and funded through a syndicate of businesses and thus overtly calculated to defeat organized labour. Since they were only paid to men who worked consistently, they undermined the strike weapon; in addition, they controlled the mobility of labour; and most damaging of all, they were directly deployed to depress wages. Although they had at first been widely supported because of their pronatalist overtones, family allowances in France became convenient tools of business interests, who used them to drastically reorder the wage system and to destroy any leverage labour might have had in determining wage levels.[76]

Unlike the ILP in Britain, Woodsworth was able to arouse the interest of government in family allowances by skilfully arguing for them in the context of the living-wage debate (as had A.B. Piddington in Australia). Moreover, by positing that family allowances were a form of insurance; thus, he was able to place this radical critique of the wage system on the federal government agenda, where it was discussed by the Select Standing Committee on Industrial and International Relations between 1928 and 1929. As in Britain, however, this first attempt to establish a national system of family allowances foundered on conflicting notions of how best to preserve the wage structure and defend the independence of the male worker and his dependants.

Father Léon Lebel, a long-time exponent of family allowances, was Woodsworth's key witness. Lebel was an outspoken champion of the French-Canadian working classes, largely because he believed that the root cause of the tremendous out-migration to the United States was the large gap that existed between the husband's wage packet and his expanding family needs. With his traditionalist views regarding gender relations and the family, Lebel (like Woodsworth) saw in this system of wage supplements the optimum means for defending the rights of male wage earners. Lebel was offering a radical reinterpretation of the wage structure, insofar as he believed that wages should not be determined merely by the individual's productivity, but must, in the name of humanitarianism and social peace, be determined primarily by the needs of the family:

> All sound economists and legislators agree that the family is the fundamental unit of society. From families society draws its substance and without them it could not subsist, so that the strength of any nation and the degree of its true civilization depend in great part on the vitality of its

fundamental unit just as the strength of a living body depends on the health and vigour of the cells which compose it. Hence, a state which pretends to progressive organization should attend, in its legislation, to the means of facilitating the existence and the well-being of the family; and supposing that a change in social conditions renders the economic organization unfavorable to it, it is an essential duty of the state to modify economics in order to readapt them to the family needs.[77]

Lebel's argument began with the family, as did that of Paul Douglas and Eleanor Rathbone. That being said, his conceptualization of the relationship between the family and society was a direct function of his social Catholicism, and followed closely the Christian reformist ideals of the late Pope Leo XIII, whose numerous encyclicals called for a thorough revision of the profit motive in capitalism. From this perspective, the worker was valued not only for his contributions to industry, but also for his larger social and cultural importance to the nation. The more socialistic implications of the Pope's encyclicals were, however, tempered in Lebel's thought by an adherence to liberal principles. Like many other Catholic thinkers in Quebec, Lebel clearly saw limits to state intervention, warning as late as the 1940s against the government usurping the role of the paterfamilias. 'Society is not made up of individual atoms directly subject to the State,' he wrote in the Jesuit publication *Relations* in 1944. 'It is an organic being made up of cells which are the families. Children do not belong to the State and are not under the care or charge of the State. They belong to the parents under whose care they are. The role of the State, in case of necessity, is to help the parents acquit themselves of their responsibility towards their children.'[78]

In Lebel's social thought there was a constant tension between his reform liberalism, which was influenced by the economics of J.A. Hobson in Britain, and his more right-wing social Catholicism, with its distinct strain of corporatist ideas.[79] As a result, Lebel's recommendations wavered continually between a system of family allowances managed by a conglomerate of businessmen (on the French model), and a state-run system (of the sort that organized labour had long favoured). As much as Lebel saw family allowances as a form of class legislation, and as much as he desired to alleviate poverty – which he believed had become 'the usual condition of a section of a population' – his outlook was much less socialistic than Woodsworth's. Lebel believed in strictly limiting the boundaries of the State, and concluded that it should never directly manage the affairs of the family, which must remain private. In his view the family was sacrosanct, and as the fundamental cell of society it had to be forever shielded from the reach of government bureaucracies. Lebel viewed family allowances as akin to 'family insurance,' but he did not envision them as a forerunner for a more comprehensive state system of social insurance, as did Woodsworth.[80] Rather, he invoked the tenets of nineteenth-century liberalism, asserting that governments must only 'furnish the general means of prosperity and to encourage private initiative.'[81]

In language reminiscent of the natalist arguments of those who promoted motherhood endowment, Lebel stressed that family reproduction was as important to the social and economic advancement of the nation as productive labour in the workplace. However, his conception of the family was starkly different from the Protestant, maternal-centred ideal that so animated the movement for mothers' allowances. Lebel was greatly influenced by the natalist sentiments of French exponents of family allowances, and thus strongly emphasized the ability of family allowances to stimulate population growth.[82] Lebel's ready advice that women should shoulder extra burdens of reproduction, together with his general disregard for the rights of women even within the family domain, greatly antagonized both maternal feminists like Whitton (who objected to the fact that family allowances would make women reproductive slaves of the State) and champions of women's rights in the workplace like Agnes Macphail (who strongly promoted the widening of women's opportunities in the job market).[83] Family allowances in Canada were promoted as a bulwark of the husband within both the family and the workplace, and in that regard bore little relation to their British incarnation. In Britain, even after Eleanor Rathbone's feminist campaign was transmuted into a class initiative of the ILP, exponents of family allowances recommended that they be paid to the mother. Thus in Britain family allowances did acknowledge, however obliquely, that the mother contributed to the family by raising the children and by husbanding the weekly pay packet. In contrast, Lebel's campaign for family allowances was studiously antifeminist in its implications; by his conception, both the family and the workplace were rightly dominated by the male breadwinner. Not only were family allowances intended as a 'sur-wage' for the male worker, but they were also deemed to be financial recognition of the fact that the children belonged to the father. 'The allowance in question,' stated Lebel, 'is made to the head of a family, not because he is a worker, but because of the services he is rendering the community and the employers in furnishing producers and consumers.[84]

By elevating male rights both within the workplace *and* within the domestic sphere, Lebel was transgressing the principal articles of maternal feminism and at the same time rejecting the canons of progressive reform. By demanding that the allowance be paid to the father, Lebel also alienated Woodsworth, who, while he promoted the natural right of the male wage earner to maintain his dependants, also adhered to the vision of separate spheres that so undergirded contemporary social policy, which gave a clear place of honour to the mother in promoting the moral sanctity of family life. Given that Lebel wished to erase female influence within the family, it is not surprising that in 1928 Whitton and Macphail aggressively opposed a system of family allowances. In their view, Lebel's emphasis on population growth and large families was a recipe for relegating women to reproductive slavery.[85] Although Whitton agreed with Lebel that the State must be kept out of family life, she refused to countenance his singularly economic vision of the family. In Whitton's view, Lebel's policies would have injected market-driven (and thus male-oriented) variables into family life, at the expense of traditional ties of affection and religion, which were clearly demarcated as the women's sphere. Whitton castigated family allowances because she saw them as rendering women into mere handmaids of business profits, the suppliers of future generations of labourers. Because they make children into mere economic assets within the family, Whitton saw in family allowances a disturbing reversal of all she had fought for in her campaigns for child protection legislation.

In many respects, Whitton was being disingenuous. She deliberately misread the implications of Lebel's advocacy of family allowances in order to dismember Woodsworth's campaign to introduce a system of wage supplements, which she believed would lead to an uncontrolled expansion of the State. Whitton was well aware that many other social Catholics in Quebec, such as Georges Pelletier,[86] had promoted family allowances within the context of defending the traditional family; their view was that if a sufficient standard of living within working-class families was ensured, women and children would be relieved of the necessity to work for wages. The fact remains that by using Lebel, a conservative Catholic, as his chief parliamentary witness, Woodsworth had doomed his campaign for government-funded family allowances.

By upholding the rights of the male breadwinner not only in the work-place but also in the home, Lebel's arguments rode roughshod over Protestant cultural values. Moreover, Lebel's conceptualization of the family as mainly an economic entity was perceived as undermining the very core of the maternal feminist social outlook – namely, the defence of the small, mother-centred, spiritual family. In Britain, the case for family allowances was ruined by conflicts within organized labour over the meaning of the living wage; in Canada, the failure of the same case owed as much to its religious and cultural context as to the economic implications of family allowances for the working classes.

While it is true that Lebel, like many other social Catholics, gave priority to the citizenship rights of the male head of the family, he did so in part in order to counteract the potential opposition of organized labour. Lebel, like Woodsworth, adhered to the ILP's arguments for family allowances, stressing that they would act as a boon to consumerism, which in turn would boost home manufacturing and thus contribute to higher wage standards. Discounting the traditional panacea of the protective tariff, so popular among businessmen, Woodsworth told the House of Commons in 1926 that home trade could never be improved 'unless we increase the buying power of the masses of the people.'[87] Here Woodsworth was drawing from the path-breaking underconsumptionist theories of J.A. Hobson, upon which the ILP based its 1926 platform. Lebel reached similar conclusions by harkening back to older treatises of political economy (i.e., the thought of Jean Bodin and Adam Smith) to postulate that a high birthrate and the sheer quantity of available labour furnished the best engine for national prosperity.[88] Though their political perspectives were very different, both Lebel and Woodsworth were trying to convince organized labour that family allowances were not wage supplements and would not alter the wage system or interfere with the rights of labour to bargain collectively. By insisting that family allowances were being paid for the father's role in contributing to population growth and domestic economic consumption, rather than for his productivity in the workplace, Lebel was attempting to defuse labour opposition to family allowances, which in France had been used by capitalists to depress wages. In Lebel's estimation, family allowances were merely a payment for family reproduction and could be paid to ill, incapacitated, or unemployed male workers as well as to widows. As he argued, family allowances were not intended to alter the wage system, for a man 'may have a right to the supplementary allowance without having a right to any wage, and conversely, a man may have a right to wages without having any right to the allowance.'[89]

Lebel's pamphlet on family allowances was explicitly written to defuse labour opposition. He appealed directly to labour's agitation for a family wage, quoting from Justice Powers, the president of the Australian Commonwealth Arbitration Court, who observed that by allowing wage-earning fathers to properly clothe and feed their children, industrial discontent and misery would be removed. He also appealed to the independence of the skilled worker by claiming that with family allowances his wife need not work, and by postulating that family allowances were a step toward social democracy because they redistributed national income. Lastly, Lebel recommended that such supplements be paid only after the third child so that they would not interfere with organized labour's arguments for a family wage based nominally on a breadwinner, his wife, and one child.[90]

Despite all of this, both Lebel and Woodsworth had difficulty persuading organized labour that family allowances would reduce the cost of living to a degree sufficient to offset their admittedly limited impact in raising wages. However, the campaign for family allowances in Canada collapsed in 1928 not because it failed to rally the support of organized labour, which had no representatives on the parliamentary committee, but rather because it had no appeal to conservative social workers and businessmen, who adhered to a more laissez-faire vision of the Canadian economy. Underconsumptionist arguments had found some favour in Britain, where the economy was dictated less by foreign trade, but they made little headway in Canada, where businessmen continued to see economic expansion solely in terms of a protective tariff. As the Select Committee on Industrial and International Relations was informed, the Canadian Manufacturers Association endorsed the protective tariff and as a result had little interest in family allowances.[91]

In the flourishing economy of the 1920s, Lebel's emphasis on population growth to increase the supply of labour found no welcome among business interests. Those same interests rejected family allowances because of their implications for government growth, especially after they were publicized by the left as an indirect means for committing the State to the principle of social insurance.[92] Moreover, the consumptionist argument made by both Woodsworth and Lebel found little favour because it was an untried theoretical postulate. Also, it was enormously difficult to court popular business support for family allowances on the claim that they would ensure economic prosperity, because they had come to be associated with sluggish and uncompetitive economies. In Britain, even the keenest opponents of family allowances had reluctantly admitted their usefulness in the wake of the Royal Commission on the Coal Industry, which had revealed grossly low wages and endemic poverty in that declining industry.[93] Even though William Beveridge had endorsed them, family allowances had come to be seen as a last-ditch measure of social salvaging, to be implemented as an emergency response when wages had reached drastically low levels. It was their unfortunate association with depressed industries that prompted Charlotte Whitton to remark that Canada had no need of such economic palliatives because we were 'a young, strong, virile people, with a standard of living unsurpassed in any nation ... Her people are provident, thrifty, wholesome and ambitious. They are not the weary and sophisticated population of old and jaded nations.'[94]

A traditionalist when it came to social and economic policies, and a strident defender of Victorian notions of limited government intervention, Whitton naturally insisted that a 'decent living wage' could be achieved only if economic forces were allowed to find their own levels, undisturbed by government strictures. This *laissez-faire* attitude prevailed among federal politicians, even though Gerald Brown, the Deputy Minister of Labour, had marshalled ample and convincing statistical evidence to show that wage levels among broad sections of Canada's working people were consistently failing to meet even minimum family budgets. Whitton responded by defending higher wages, quietly skirting the point made by Woodsworth and Lebel that this would still leave an anomaly between wages and family need in large families. Her position, while conservative, was nevertheless not out of keeping with the one adhered to by organized labour throughout the world. In Britain, for example, Labour Party women likewise preferred higher wages, combined with better social services at the local level, in the belief that any supplementary allowances, either through employers or the State, would interfere with male wages.[95] Whitton's greatest fear was that government responsibilities would grow rampantly in the sphere of family self-sufficiency; but it must also be pointed out that her vociferous advocacy of higher wages mirrored the position adopted by the Trades and Labour Congress, a body affiliated with her own Council on Child Welfare. Her claim that wage levels in Canada were sufficiently buoyant was grounded on her optimistic belief that

Canada remained a 'pioneer' nation on the cusp of industrial matura-
tion – a condition which suggested that wage levels had unlimited
potential to increase. However, her reluctance to support a program
that appeared to flout the free market determination of wages was
undoubtedly derived from Tom Moore, the national president of the
TLC. Organized labour was traditionally wary of attempts by government to interfere with workers' rights to independently negotiate
wage contracts with their employers. The TLC was therefore being
ideologically consistent in opposing family allowances, which despite
Woodsworth's assurances were seen as a dangerous attempt to alter
the basis on which standard wages were founded.

The TLC's suspicions about Woodsworth and the ILP's proposals for
family allowances were further confirmed by evidence given to the
Select Committee on Industrial and International Relations. For example, Lebel vacillated constantly between endorsing a system funded by
businessmen and one financed and managed by the federal government. Whether a system of family allowances would truly benefit
organized labour's case for a living wage was further called into question by Lebel's allusions to the French model, in which allowances
were used not only to depress wages but also to suppress the freedom
of labour unions. As a consequence, it was difficult for supporters of
family allowances to erase the impression that such a program was
intended to replace the male family wage, and thus destructive of
labour's ability to agitate for a living wage in the future. This, despite
Lebel's attempts to stress that male workers were to be paid the allowance for their success in producing children for the nation. Moreover, it
remained unclear whether Woodsworth and Lebel's stress on family
allowances as a spur for increasing consumption in home markets was
a plea on behalf of working-class economic security or a sop to businessmen.

These rifts within the Canadian labour movement between those
who advocated higher wages together with a minimum wage, and
those like Woodsworth and Lebel who contended that family allowances were necessary in order to resolve the anomalies that existed
between wages and family needs, were deftly exploited by Charlotte
Whitton. In fact, she often used 'labour' arguments to promote her
own agenda. By the late 1920s the immediate postwar preoccupation
with population growth had faded, as had the demand for natalist
family policies. In order to forestall the implementation of a policy
intended to generate a higher birthrate, which she saw as destructive

both of women's rights and of the Protestant ideal of the small, affectional family, Whitton postulated that family allowances would so increase the burden of economically unproductive children that the standard of living of working-class families would be severely eroded.

More devastating to Woodsworth's position was Whitton's pointed query regarding the root cause of poverty in Canada. Was it, she asked, due to low wages, as Woodsworth contended, or was it the product of seasonal unemployment and periodic cycles of economic depression? Here, she effectively cornered Woodsworth, knowing that he could not possibly have the economic data to respond adequately. Moreover, if he agreed that wages were responsible for working-class poverty, she could easily respond by demanding higher wages; and if he chose unemployment, this would undermine his overall case for family allowances. By posing her question in this manner, Whitton had effectively avoided the real import and novelty of family allowances – namely, that they were meant to address the problem of large families. Mildred Kensit of the Children's Bureau of Montreal had quietly raised the dysgenic implications of such allowances[96] – that they would encourage the lower classes and Catholics to reproduce. As the Protestant and English-Canadian representatives on the committee, Mildred Kensit, Robert Mills, and Charlotte Whitton recognized that it would be politically explosive for them to wage open religious and cultural warfare with Father Lebel and his parliamentary champion, Henri Bourassa.[97] However, by allying herself with the ideological position on wages championed by organized labour, Whitton was able to dismantle with economic arguments a proposal she opposed largely on cultural and religious grounds.

In a similar fashion, Whitton vanquished any further claims Woodsworth might have made that family allowances were a frontline defence of the family wage and the rights of the male head of the family. This she accomplished by attaching her own *laissez-faire* notions about small government to the enduring and indisputable cultural ideal of the self-supporting, breadwinning family. 'The family allowance system,' she wrote, 'by assuming the responsibilities of the head of the family in providing maintenance for his children, and in doing so, in increasing proportion, as those obligations develop more and more beyond what he knows he can assume himself, undermines our basis of family responsibility. Because the system thus undermines the fundamental responsibilities of the head of the family for the maintenance of its members, it seems to me that it should be opposed as sub-

versive of one of the principles of the organization of society on which
western civilization has striven to insist for centuries.'[98] Here Whitton
was casting Woodsworth's proposal for a family allowance system,
which aimed at redistributing national income to working-class families, as a deliberate attack on the integrity of family life, and as an
attempt to erode the principles of independence and self-sufficiency
that Canada's male breadwinners ought to embrace as both a right and
a duty. Whitton rendered Woodsworth's arguments nugatory by char-
acterizing family allowances as a government measure calculated to
destroy the work ethic and perpetuate the miasma of pauperism that
many maintained would be spread by any expansion in government
welfare assistance to families headed by able-bodied, male breadwinners. While Whitton was prepared to countenance government
assistance to families where the breadwinner was absent, she vociferously objected to any proposals that might interfere with the male
breadwinner ideal.

Whitton's attack effectively routed Woodsworth's campaign for a
national program of family allowances. Her support of the principle of
family independence was even more insidious because it established
an argument capable of challenging any proposal for the humanitarian
redistribution of the national wealth. In 1931, in her appearance before
the Quebec Social Insurance Commission, Whitton resorted to the
same strategy to squelch proposals for new welfare legislation. Worth
noting is that the Depression was a receptive time for the arguments
she was making: any policy that might commit governments to greater
spending and might also increase the birthrate was looked on with dis-
favour. Even so, a feeble attempt to again promote family allowances
was launched, largely by social conservatives, who saw in them a
means to preserve the family amidst the growing materialism of the
modern age. Edouard Montpetit, the Chairman of the commission,
noted that in any period characterized by severe economic depression
it was difficult to argue that the wealth of the nation lay in her children. Although family allowances were endorsed in principle by the
Quebec commission, their fate was sealed when they became too
closely associated with initiatives to establish a comprehensive program of state-funded social insurance. But even with different political
and ideological arguments sustaining it, family allowances would
have made little headway during the Depression, because they could
not but be embedded in debates over the wage structure. Unfortunately for the promoters of family allowances, the issue of wages

became subordinated to that of unemployment, which by 1931 had come to be identified by politicians, economists, and social workers alike as the primary cause of poverty.[99]

By 1928 the principles animating the debate on welfare policy in Canada were radically different than in 1919. Mothers' allowances had been demoted from a popularly conceived 'right' based on motherhood's value to the nation, to a measure that was in practice indistinguishable from relief. This trend toward marginalizing women's welfare entitlements had started with Whitton's opposition to organized labour's demands that the terms of mothers' allowances be liberalized, and was accelerated in 1928 during the debate over family allowances. Although it was never Woodsworth's aim to undermine the value placed on women's work in the home, his insistence that family allowances were a class measure intended to shore up labour agitation for a 'living wage' unleashed a debate over the relationship between the family and work whose labyrinthine twists and turns would have unforeseen results.

Woodsworth and Lebel defended family allowances as a welfare measure for protecting the family by securing the livelihood of the male breadwinner; Whitton saw them very differently. Carefully ignoring the fact that when paid to the mother, family allowances tended to disaggregate the family income and to emphasize family reproduction as a valuable national asset – an argument familiar to advocates of mothers' allowances – Whitton, following Lebel and Woodsworth's lead, chose to see them as a payment to the father, and so as subversive of gender roles within both the family and the workplace. Whitton thus objected to family allowances because they encroached on traditional gendered notions of separate spheres, whereby the father was the economic provider and the mother the spiritual and cultural head of the family. Progressive thinkers like Eleanor Rathbone and Paul Douglas saw in family allowances a means for enshrining the contribution women made to the economy and for critiquing established conceptions of the male wage; Whitton saw them as a dangerous policy that would allow the economic considerations of the workplace to violate the sanctity of family and child life. While Whitton may have countenanced state 'subsidies' in the form of mothers' allowances, which were given to the family when the breadwinner was absent, she decisively opposed family allowances in the belief that they would impugn the obligation of the male breadwinnner to provide.

The first campaign for family allowances in Canada did not founder simply because it was the hobby-horse of the left, or simply because it failed to appeal sufficiently either to businessmen or to organized labour. Rather, its failure resided in the fact that family allowances provided wage supplements that helped to maintain the family, and thus were perceived by their opponents as a system of state interference that abrogated what had been the essence of reformist family policies since the early twentieth century: the responsibility of the male breadwinner to support his wife and children. What is remarkable about the debate over family allowances in 1928 is that both the left and the right agreed that welfare policies should focus on the problem of how to preserve the rights, status, and duties of the male breadwinner. The policy debates of the late 1920s therefore effectively eroded the principle of maternalist citizenship rights, by stringently limiting the scope and importance of mothers' allowances and by reformulating family allowances, so that they were no longer a distinctly feminist measure but instead one that upheld the concept of the 'family wage.'

It was the advocates of workers' rights, Woodsworth and Lebel, who established the terms of the debate over family policy by firmly embedding their proposal for a national system of family allowances in terms of their campaign for a living wage. By so doing, they unleashed a series of events that were to decisively alter the calculus of welfare policy so that it no longer emphasized family reproduction and the rearing of children as the basis for state welfare entitlements, but instead emphasized production in the workplace. As a result of this change, waged labour was now the foundation of citizenship rights. This reorientation from the family to the workplace – this reconceptualizing of the family so that it was now perceived not as a spiritual entity, a maternalist domain, but rather as an economic unit headed by the male breadwinner – was further strengthened by Charlotte Whitton when she formulated a rejoinder to the arguments laid down by Woodsworth and Lebel on behalf of family allowances. Although Whitton had long championed a maternal-centred idea of the family, her efforts to quell any further incursions by the government into the private domain of home and family led her to likewise envision the family in wholly economic terms. To forestall the appropriation of the breadwinner ideal by the ILP, Whitton took what had been merely one assumption undergirding social policy – the rights of the wage earner in the workplace – and overtly proclaimed it as the exclusive basis of social citizenship. The most important (albeit largely unforeseen) consequence of organized labour's intervention in family policy was that it affirmed the value of waged work at the expense of unpaid labour within the family. This established a new pivot around which public discussion would henceforth revolve. Furthermore, this new animating principle of welfare policymaking held long-term practical implications for the welfare rights of women. During the Depression, large-scale unemployment among men would come to be seen as the fundamental cause of poverty, and as a corollary, the relationship between family reproduction and welfare entitlements would be downplayed. Henceforth, state welfare legislation would be driven by the need to protect the work of the father, which was perceived as the family's first line of defence against dependency.

6

'Not Only a Living Wage, but a Family Wage':[1] The Great Depression and the Subversion of the Maternalist State

This individualization with which those who work outside the home receive their income has made it difficult for families to support themselves ... It is not merely necessary that the total earnings of the members of the group should be sufficient to maintain the group, but it is also necessary that they should turn a sufficient amount over to the wife or mother for her to expend for the needed collective purposes.[2]

Paul Douglas, 'The Changing Basis of Family Support and Expenditure'

Probably a larger number of females than of males 'live at home' without a recognized employment function, paid or unpaid. But a major proportion of the adult female population ... are 'home-makers' ... Nevertheless it is clear that employment in the usual sense of the word – and by the same token, unemployment – is *primarily* at least, a masculine problem.[3]

Leonard Marsh, *Employment Research*

The above epigraphs represent the two poles between which public debate over family and welfare policies developed during the decade of the Great Depression. The one, represented by Paul Douglas, the foremost exponent of family allowances in the United States, saw such supplements to the male wage as a means for preserving the older vision of a strong and interdependent family unit. According to this vision, work and consumption were shared between the sexes. This attitude preserved gender differences but also strengthened the role of women in the household. Douglas fought against the trend – increasingly prevalent by the 1930s – both in social thought and in the labour market – toward emphasizing that 'modern' wage earners (namely, men) earned their living 'purely as individuals'; he believed that this contributed, as powerfully as the exploitation of women within the factory and the store, to the increased subordination of women.

Advocates of family allowances, like Douglas in the United States and J.S. Woodsworth and Father Lebel in Canada, were seeking not only to underscore the plight of working-class families further impoverished by large numbers of children, but also to promote a conception of the workplace as a logical extension of the home, which is what it had been before industrialization began to separate those two spheres. Woodsworth and to a lesser extent Father Lebel emphasized that the raising of families was an important service to national progress, a perspective that had informed the agitation for mothers' allowances, and saw in family allowances a means to focus public attention on unpaid work in the household, which revolved around the raising of children. In their view, the wage structure needed to take into account not only the individual worker's production but also the level of *reproduction* in terms of the number of children. Because large families led to larger numbers of consumers, Woodsworth and Lebel believed that families directly fostered the expansion of homegrown manufacturing and sustained employment, and thus constituted as important a contribution to the economic efficiency of the nation as paid work itself.[4]

Pitted against this perspective, which tended to reinforce familial conceptions of work and welfare, was that of Leonard Marsh. Marsh deployed the scientific prestige of his empirical research, which generated a massive amount of statistical evidence on unemployment, to defend what was in reality a host of stridently gendered assumptions about work and welfare. Backed by his compendia of 'objective' facts on unemployment, Marsh consistently renounced the older, feminist conception of social citizenship, by reconceiving the access of citizens to state welfare benefits exclusively in terms of paid work. Marsh enjoys a high reputation among certain historians as the enlightened progenitor of Canada's system of social security – as a progressive hero of the left and our most noteworthy representative of Canadian 'Fabianism.' His research at McGill University has been seen as groundbreaking, in that it was the first such effort to have a profound impact on social welfare policy in Canada.[5]

However, Marsh appears as a darker prophet when we consider his research into unemployment during the 1930s in terms of its gender implications. Leonard Marsh at McGill University, Lothar Richter at Dalhousie, and Harry Cassidy at the University of Toronto were among a new breed of technocrats who approached Canadian social problems from a macro-economic perspective. Their brand of objective social science abjured the traditional casework studies most closely associated with the social work profession, which despite its vestigial moralism at least recognized the problem of 'abnormal' (i.e., female-headed) families. The new economists focused principally on the 'normal' family, and in their view normal families were those with a male breadwinner. The social work profession (a predominantly female profession by the 1930s) had long focused on the religious and loosely cultural aspects of family life, in which the mother occupied a central role; the new, 'factual' studies of Marsh, Cassidy, and Richter conceived of the family entirely in economic terms and thus as a singularly male preserve. Marsh's scientific welfarism eviscerated women's unpaid work from his categorization of a 'recognized employment function,' and in doing so made the concept of the breadwinner ideal the only concept on the table when the government formulated social policies, such as the unemployment insurance legislation of 1940. In sum, Marsh and his colleagues so radically reconceptualized the 'normal' family that their empirical studies totally jettisoned women from even their traditional domestic sphere.

Obsessed with the problem of unemployment and work, economists of the Depression era came to reify waged labour both as the centrepiece of national well-being and as the vital force animating individual self-consciousness. In their view, work was the wellspring of the male's perception of self, and also constituted the very core of family solidarity. At one time, religion had defined familial bonds; now, according to Marsh, family ties and affections flowed imperceptibly from the positive morale and conceptions of self-sufficiency of the gainfully employed male breadwinner. More significantly, Marsh, for all he emphasized the economic welfare of the family, failed to recognize women's indirect contribution to the economy through their purchasing power and through their unpaid work, which facilitated the 'productive' work of husbands. Advocates of family allowances believed that family considerations must inform the conceptualization of the standard wage; whereas advocates of unemployment insurance such as Marsh and Cassidy, with their male-centred notions of welfare entitlements, saw the family as an extension of the economy of the workplace and thus as an extension of the male personality.

However much campaigns for mothers' allowances and family allowances had been tangentially concerned with upholding the status of the male breadwinner, the 1930s was a decisive decade in reorienting gendered notions of welfare citizenship. As work became increasingly conceived as an exclusively male domain, women's unpaid labour – and hence their entitlement to state assistance – vanished as a topic of public debate. The issue of unemployment would define the contours of Canadian welfare policy from that time on. Once the unemployment of men, both married and single, became the exclusive focus of policymakers, and once unemployment insurance came to be seen as the primary remedy for the problem of dependency, assumptions regarding the pre-eminence of the male breadwinner that had long been implicit beneath the maternalist rhetoric, became explicit.

The introduction of a federal system of unemployment insurance affected women in several ways. First, the class implications of this legislation reinforced gender divisions. Unemployment insurance benefited skilled workers; at the same time, because it excluded unskilled work, it disenfranchised most women, more and more of whom had been compelled by the Depression to take unskilled work such as domestic service.[6] More insidious is that unemployment insurance created a two-tier hierarchy of welfare rights: contributory, rights-based insurance; and needs-based, non-contributory relief for unemployables, the majority of whom were women.[7] This served to extinguish women's state entitlements, in that women no longer had direct access to state recognition, but would receive assistance only indirectly, as the wives of entitled male citizens. But in a more fundamental way, the implementation of unemployment insurance in 1940 signalled the clear and irrevocable marginalization of women's welfare entitlements, as mothers' allowances lost their unique status and became submerged in the vast, inchoate morass of needs-driven municipal relief. Depression-era welfare initiatives implemented the ideas that had been formed during the discussions of maternal assistance and family allowances in the late 1920s, and in practice decisively reoriented both the structure and the principles of government social policy. Henceforth, female dependency was treated by law as indistinguishable from the residuum – society's unredeemable social defectives.

Conceptualizing the 'Normal' Family

Traditionally, when child welfare activists, feminists, reformers, and social workers spoke of 'Strengthening the Home,' they were alluding to the importance of moral values, piety, and the affections in maintaining the stability of kinship ties. Those concerned most with the welfare and health of women and children defined the family in cultural terms, as 'the great storehouse in which the hardly earned treasures of the past, the inheritance of spirit and character from our ancestors, are guarded and preserved from our descendants.' As family court judge R.S. Hoskins observed in 1932, the family was the primary institution of society, for through it 'each generation learns anew the lesson of citizenship that no man can live for himself alone ... It is the great shrine of religion at whose altars many of us learned our first impression of the things of the Spirit and to whose altar we turn again and again for the renewing of that faith by which we live.'[8] This emphasis on women and children, along with the conception of the family as an integrated and interdependent unit,[9] was eclipsed during the Depression; so was the power of voluntaristic welfare organizations to determine government family policy.

Whitton's influence and that of the social work perspective reached its apex before 1935. As James Struthers has demonstrated regarding the development of relief policies, and as I have shown with respect to mothers' and family allowances, Whitton and the Canadian Council on Child Welfare exerted considerable influence on both provincial and federal governments during the early years of the Depression.[10] Until that time, her close contacts with myriad local family and child welfare organizations – the vast majority of which were headed by female social workers – ensured her of a dominant position in welfare policy circles. Although the moral imperatives undergirding contemporary social work principles were often corrosive of working-class sensibilities and now appear obsolete, family casework at least focused on how individuals – especially women and children – experienced dependency. As the economic depression deepened and the potential for social unrest and political turbulence waxed, new, more scientific prescriptions were sought, ones that addressed more directly the mechanisms of capitalism and the contiguous problem of male unemployment. As a consequence, the social work perspective, with its attention to endemic poverty unrelated to the perturbations of the trade cycle, was increasingly displaced by the macro-economic, 'objective' analyses of poverty and unemployment advanced by a new cadre of self-proclaimed welfare policy experts, namely Marsh, Cassidy, and Richter. Social workers had primarily addressed the problem of dependency among 'abnormal' families, that is, those in which the male breadwinner was absent either through illness, desertion, or death. The technocrats were chiefly concerned with studying aggregates of national income, class, and occupational structure to discern the causes of unemployment; thus, they were led inextricably to a preoccupation with the 'normal' family. Even though female social workers had traditionally perceived of female dependency largely in terms of the male breadwinner, Marsh and Cassidy focused exclusively on the wage economy, and as a result women were entirely left out of the calculus of welfare policymaking during the 1930s.[11]

Charlotte Whitton's claim to being the pre-eminent authority on Canadian welfare legislation flowed directly from her exclusive command of the most recent social data. This position was directly challenged by a proliferation of university-based investigations of social and economic problems in the latter half of the 1930s, which could claim the prestige of scientific rigour and a methodology founded on systematic survey techniques. The foremost among these investigations was McGill University's Rockefeller-funded Unemployment Research Project, headed by Leonard Marsh. Marsh's central concern was to promote what he believed to be a new, more rational approach to government policymaking, one founded on a 'factual approach.' He had an unquestioning faith in the canons of scientism, which held that it was possible to empirically and precisely quantify all forms of human behaviour. He juxtaposed his more scientific endeavours, the 'study of social units by quantitative methods,' with the 'humanities,' subjects like ethics and theology, which he condemned as merely 'normative' or 'preceptual' disciplines because they had as their focus what 'ought to be.' 'The essence of scientific law,' declared Marsh in his 1935 monograph, *Employment Research*, 'is that it deals only with the latter [what is]' and that 'it is a generalization continuously open to verification by evidence.'[12]

Marsh was trained in the British tradition of social investigation at the London School of Economics, and he naturally spurned the American pattern of disciplinary specialization in the social sciences. But just as forcefully, he rejected the more philosophical approach of British social scientists such as L.T. Hobhouse, E.J. Urwick, and R.H. Tawney; he preferred the more stridently empirical approach pioneered by William Beveridge, Charles Booth, and Seebohm Rowntree in the belief that only after social scientific laws were formulated could expertise become embedded in the everyday practice of government administration.[13] But Marsh's commitment to 'objective' social science, was not removed from the purview of social reform; rather, he saw it as a means for establishing a more rationalist 'social improvement': 'The interrelation between science and society today is inescapable; it is a fact which marks off present civilization from every previous stage in the world's history.'[14] In discerning an intimate connection between academic investigation and social problems, Marsh was not simply harkening back to older social reformist traditions; he saw himself as the harbinger of a more dynamic and scientific approach to government. Indeed, he wrote his various monographs on work, unemployment, and poverty with the aim of directly appealing to an audience of politicians, welfare officials, and bureaucratic policymakers. His hope was to revolutionize and modernize the process of government policymaking. If legislative initiatives were based on rigorous scientific research of the sort that Marsh pursued, it might be possible to remove them from political considerations and at the same time establish a new echelon of élite 'experts' (like himself) at the highest levels of government.

Whatever his protestations that society must be studied as a whole, Marsh's research was very specific and focused exclusively on the problem of how 'to rationalize the labour market' – a project with distinctly 'normative' overtones: 'Whether measured merely by the number of persons they affect,' asserted Marsh in his outline for his ambitious research project, 'or by their human consequences, no problems are more vital or of wider implication than those of employment.'[15] In many respects Canadians In and Out of Work, published in 1940, was a path-breaking book insofar as it was a conscious attempt to analyze class and social structure. He was not attempting to approach Canadian social and economic development from a geographical or regional perspective, as had his McGill colleague, the sociologist C.A. Dawson, and the Saskatchewan economist George Britnell. Two University of Toronto political economists, Harold Innis and Gilbert Jackson, had conceived of the downswing in the Canadian economy during the 1930s in terms of the underdevelopment of new staples or imbalances in foreign trade, and interpreted social distress in terms of the overall decline in national income; in contrast, Marsh stressed inequalities in the distribution of wealth as they related to the problem of social stratification: 'These barriers are not the horizontal ones of geographical regions or distinctive ethnic cultures but the vertical ones of a socio-economic hierarchy.'[16]

Some historians have taken at face value Marsh's own claims to 'objectivity' and thus have accepted his statistical analysis of Canadian work patterns as an accurate assessment of the problem of unemployment.[17] Indeed, few have attempted to study closely Marsh's numerous, massively detailed volumes on unemployment. Thus, it remains unacknowledged that Marsh's 'objective' investigations of class structure and the economy of the family represent extreme examples of how the ideology of separate spheres was scientifically embedded in both economic analyses and government legislation during the Depression. The degree to which the McGill Unemployment Research Project was a glaring example of how economists use the prestige of science to lend credence to their own prescriptive goals for society has gone largely unheeded. Marsh was in fact very forthright about the conceptual framework that he established for his 'factual picture of the Canadian working force, employed and unemployed.'[18] As an economist, he was interested mainly in the law of averages; thus, he confined his study to an examination of 'the married men with normal families, "normal" being those families in which both parents are alive and living together in the same home.' Marsh, however, was not an incipient convert to family allowances at this time, though such allowances were to become the hallmark of his later recommendations for a federal social security program; he went on to write that a few of these 'normal' families 'have no children, but these are just as important as others from the viewpoint of the relation of earnings to family responsibility: the first stage of this responsibility, especially the young worker trying to take stock of the income-level of his particular class, is the ability to support a wife.'[19]

Was Marsh being disingenuous in declaring his work the first 'objective' study of class differentials in Canada? Was he unaware of the obvious conflict between his commitment to scientific empiricism and the underlying prescriptive intent of his economic research? From Marsh's perspective, there was no inherent conflict in his methodology, for wasn't the fundamental principle that men worked for wages while women provided, as 'homemakers,' unpaid 'services to the national income'[20] tantamount to a scientific law? Marsh believed that it was – or at the very least that it should be. Indeed, his work hinged on marshalling arguments for expunging from the record any evidence of women's work on the basis of which women might assert a future claim to entering the workforce. In this regard, Marsh openly declared that he had omitted women from his conceptualization of work,[21] on the basis that the vast majority – the average mean – of women were married 'housewives' and so 'without a recognized employment function.'[22] The wage-earning women who appeared infrequently in Marsh's investigation were relegated firmly to the bottom rungs of the economic ladder, and were portrayed merely as low-paid, occasional workers whose sole function was the negative one of threatening both the jobs and wages of the married male breadwinner.[23] That wage-earning women were almost entirely left out of Marsh's analysis thus spoke powerfully to the empirical righteousness of men's exclusive claims to paid employment.

Marsh made a token acknowledgment of the well-documented reality in the 1930s that many women were, as a result of their husband's unemployment, the actual breadwinners in the family. Marsh wished to circumvent this obvious challenge to the traditional male role. 'Marriage creates the principal difference in vocational evolution' for women, observed Marsh. 'Whether by choice or the force of employer preferences, customs and regulations, most women retire from the labour market if they marry. The small percentage who remain are not all white-collar workers, and do not all make substantial contributions to the family income, *as popular prejudice often supposes*.'[24] He thus concluded that the only female heads of families were those in 'broken' homes – households that were insignificant because they were aberrant and did not fall within Marsh's definition of what constituted a family. In what must have been a stunning development for social work advocates of the mother-centred family, Marsh completely discounted 'families where the chief breadwinner is a woman' on the basis that these could not rightfully be considered families at all.[25] Thus, within his established frame of reference, Marsh could rightly conclude: 'It is true, however, in more than one way that the economic status of a family is derived from that of the male head.'[26]

Marsh insisted that the husband's earnings made up at least 80 per cent of the 'normal' family income,[27] and although this left a considerable balance to be earned – first by the sons, then the daughters, and lastly by the wife – a discussion of such economic interdependence within the family was conspicuously absent from Marsh's several volumes on work and welfare. In fact, Marsh rejected the traditional organic notions of the family, adhered to by social workers and more overtly by advocates of family allowances, declaring that the family 'unit' could be 'flexibly interpreted' either as one person living alone or as a family made up of a husband and his dependent and non-contributing wife and children. Indeed, his primary interest lay with the definition of work rather than the family; where he tended to see the 'occupational unit'[28] in terms of the individual – in this case the singular male worker – so he tended to view the family. In other words, Marsh defined the family according to the occupation of one individual – the father. This had rather disastrous implications for the maternalist paradigm. According to Marsh's scientific prescriptions for the correct relations between work and home, the male breadwinner, by virtue of his economic function alone – 'his income and work experience' – wielded the decisive influence in the home, whereby he also usurped the traditional female role of morally educating his children.[29]

By defining the family as a primarily economic institution and in terms of the exclusive power of the male breadwinner, Marsh was not only routing women from the workplace, but also expelling female values from the domestic realm. Turn-of-the-century feminists, clergymen, and social reformers had contributed to the blurring of the boundaries between the private and public spheres by proposing that the values of the home and motherhood be extended into the workplace and the political arena; the economic technocrats of the 1930s completely reversed this equation, collapsing both spheres into the purview of masculine activity and authority. Thus, the family was no longer made up of separate but equal parents; rather, family relationships reflected the wider occupational structure of society. The family thus became disaggregated as the concept of work and the wage became increasingly individualized throughout the Depression. In England, feminists like Eleanor Rathbone had visualized the disaggregation of the family income as a means for elevating the separate earnings of women; in Canada, this concept was interpreted wholly in terms of the male wage. As Marsh himself concluded, his evidence showed that 'some types of dependency, those which exist within the family, may properly be called normal.'[30] Among university social scientists, therefore, the idea of a living wage was slowly being reshaped into a scientific idealization of the family wage.

Marsh's ability to translate deeply entrenched cultural assumptions into irrefutable scientific law was replicated by the new, academically trained cadre of economists. By vigorously promoting themselves as policy experts, they were able to undermine the influence of the social work paradigm and to remove the notion of the interdependence of the family economy from the purview of social scientific investigation. Lothar Richter, the head of the Institute of Public Affairs at Dalhousie University, a research centre for government policymakers, echoed

Marsh's gendered conception of the workplace. Richter appeared to value what he called the 'useful' unpaid work that married, widowed, and divorced women undertook in the home because it contributed to the economic life of the nation. However, in an unusual twist, he used the fact that they were working full-time *in the home* to argue that married women could thus be defined as 'unemployable' and, it followed, as not potential workers. In his view, the test of employability was that the person be over sixteen years, not incapacitated, and 'not a wife.'[31] Even occupations such as farming, in which the older, symbiotic relationship between the workplace and the home was perpetuated and in which the economic contribution of women was more overtly acknowledged, felt the impact of the assaults of the economic technocrats. In *Land and Labour*, G.V. Hawthorne, another contributor to Marsh's research project, utilized categories of work applicable to the urban setting to conclude that, even though 'women folk' contributed directly and considerably to the viability of the farm, by producing butter and by tending to the poultry and kitchen garden, theirs was but 'domestic' work. His account of work in the agricultural sector was thus not extended to 'housewives or other female members of the family working in the home,' as only 'those performing regular work outside the farm house are defined as gainfully occupied.'[32]

One of the few exceptions among this new breed of economists was Harry Cassidy of the University of Toronto. He was one of the few to underscore the important contributions that married women made to the family economy; moreover, throughout the 1930s he continued to conceive of the family economy in terms of the earnings of *all* its members; and in this regard, he was a strong exponent of the idea that relief should be paid according to the principle of family allowances.[33] Cassidy is a significant figure whose views reflected the massive cultural and ideological changes taking place in the 1930s. At the beginning of the decade he championed the social work perspective (i.e., that gender roles in the family were separate yet interdependent); but by the end of the decade he had moved dramatically toward the economistic model in which the family was stabilized by a male breadwinner earning a family wage. Thus, even though Cassidy's assessment of the economic problems of the 1930s was singular insofar as it persisted in relating wage scales to family size, he was severely criticized by social workers such as Margaret Gould, a strong advocate of women's right to work, for focusing on the rights and morale of the male breadwinner.[34]

Leonard Marsh and his fellow economists were not, of course, alone in promulgating a conception of work and family that expunged a female presence. As the Depression deepened, the popular sensibility that opposed married women entering the workforce and taking jobs reserved for men, especially married men, gained force. While Marsh himself was most concerned with preventing middle-class women from moving into salaried work, working-class families shared his gendered views of work. Indeed, politicians were deluged during the 1930s with angry letters from working-class women and men protesting the growing practice of married women taking paid work.[35] These letters testify to the tenaciousness with which working people defended the breadwinner ideal. Miss Lavyne Bast vociferously opposed the hiring of married women at the Scroggin Shoe Factory, believing that their husbands' wages should obviate the need for work. This highlights that although some middle-class women may have defended women's work on the basis of right rather than need, working-class wives eschewed such arguments.[36] In the same vein, Communist-inspired groups such as the London and District Unemployed Association urged working women to support their men by returning to their natural sphere, the home.[37] On occasion, these working-class protests discerned clear differences between the legitimacy of work as it applied to married and single women. Many of these irate letters were written by single women, who, interestingly, shared the fears of middle-class women that unemployment would lead to sexual immorality and prostitution. Miss Asselin of Renfrew, the oldest of a family of nine children, based her objections to married women's work on the notion of the family wage, even though her own experience – she was one of four older children who helped supplement their father's inadequate wage – demonstrated that such an ideal was, for most Depression families, wholly untenable. 'A man thats getting big wages,' she informed the Ontario Minister of Labour in 1936, 'should be able to help his wife at home and other women that are married can well afford to stay out of there and give a young girl a chance to make a clean living without going astray.'[38]

There were voices contesting such entrenched attitudes. Various business and professional women's organizations, including the Catholic Women's League, and representatives from the International Labor Office, actively lobbied against government policies excluding married women from the workplace, arguing that discrimination on the basis of sex infringed on women's political and civil rights.[39] It was, however, very difficult to counteract prevailing cultural animosities about married women's work in a time of massive unemployment.[40] With a view to keeping families intact, relief officers in some jurisdictions, such as that of greater Winnipeg, arranged that the pay of wives of men on relief not be deducted from government assistance.[41] Such work incentives for married women were, however, the exception in the 1930s; the standard practice across Canada was to fire married women, especially women in salaried jobs. For example, both the federal government and the Ontario provincial government undertook surveys of married women working in the civil service in order to expel them. To keep their jobs, separated and deserted women had to show that they were the single wage earner in the family and also had to prove that their marriage had failed through 'no fault of her own.'[42]

One of the most difficult myths to dispel during the Depression was the one which held that married women were taking jobs that legitimately belonged to men. While the pattern of women's work during the Depression remains a little understood phenomenon, the work of Denyse Baillargeon on working-class wives in Montreal suggests that very few women wished to contradict traditional gender roles by taking jobs when their husbands were unemployed. Of the thirty women she interviewed, only two became the primary breadwinner.[43] According to Susan Pedersen, a similar reluctance to traduce gender norms was evident in Britain during the 1930s.[44] The testimony of many contemporaries, however, refutes these generalizations. Writing on day nurseries in Toronto in 1933, Margaret Gould, a social worker, estimated that fully one-half of the families using those facilities were married couples; Charlotte Whitton estimated that fully one-fifth of the Canadian workforce during the Depression was made up of married women whose husbands were out of work. Interestingly, however, both Gould and Whitton stressed that these women worked to maintain the 'economic independence' of their families.[45] In other words, women worked out of need rather than as an assertion of their rights. Another survey concluded that in 13 to 14 per cent of all Canadian families, the woman was the main breadwinner, and that in fully 60 per cent, women contributed to the family budget.[46]

Notwithstanding these statistics, the fact remained that the vast majority of women who worked during the 1930s were either unmarried or widowed or deserted. Whitton estimated that by 1930, single women supporting themselves comprised one-third of the workforce;

and two-thirds of these female workers had lost their male breadwinner.[47] In Quebec alone, there were an estimated 6,000 mothers with dependent children seeking jobs or relief,[48] while in Saskatchewan, almost every widow on mothers' allowance was forced to seek either work or relief. Most took jobs as housekeepers for bachelor farmers, and were thus regularly exposed to sexual harassment.[49] Because most women seeking work were single and a large proportion of these were female heads of the family, the fact of their employment did not threaten prevailing social norms regarding gendered labour. Even so, official reports on the structure of unemployment tended to blame women's work for the increase in male dependency and tended thus to exacerbate the widespread belief that the status of the male breadwinner as the presumed economic head of the family was being rapidly eroded. In one report, the author stressed how the 'woman who has never worked outside her home is also appearing in heavier numbers ... on relief lists; as her husband finds it impossible to get work, she seeks employment in housework or at 'odd jobs' in an endeavour to earn the rent, or other income.'[50]

The reversal in work roles between men and women was brought about not so much by a mythical phalanx of women entering the workforce, as by the fact that an unprecedented percentage of the regular male labour force had been compelled, through unemployment, to depend on state charity. The distribution of relief on such a vast scale was pereived as causing a precipitous decline in working-class standards of living; it was also perceived, more devastatingly, as irreparably undermining the very essence of family stability – the preservation of proper gender relations. Family caseworkers regularly attributed the dramatic rise in family discord and desertion to the effects of unemployment on the psyche of the male breadwinner.[51] In previous decades, social workers had linked the psychological well-being of the family to the mother; now, during the Depression, social commentators conceived of familial values and attitudes in terms of the male identity. Indeed, in the public discourse of the 1930s, astonishingly little attention was paid to the anguish experienced by women and children. In contrast, much was written about the psychological devastation of men. The preoccupation of the Society for the Protection of Women and Children – an organization founded to publicly defend the rights of women within the family – with the morale of *the male breadwinner*, is very revealing of the degree to which the Depression had transformed the ideology of the family: 'The gradual loss of hope sapping the courage of the unemployed father of the family; his probable deterioration both physical and mental; his constant presence in the home, acting as a reminder of his enforced idleness and consequent powerlessness, frequently leads to nagging and recrimination and sets up very unhappy environmental influences in domestic life.'[52] One of the more disturbing consequences of the role reversal between men and women during the Depression was that, because unemployment was forcing adult males to spend more time in the home, men were defiling the sanctity of this traditionally female sphere. Social workers soon enough realized that unemployment was leading to a weakening of the authority of the male head of the family, thus encouraging moral laxity and prostitution. In a more direct manner, the sense of frustration and inadequacy felt by unemployed men was leading to an alarming increase – often alluded to by family case workers – in the rate of 'sexual aberration' within the family circle.[53]

Commentaries on the devastating effects of unemployment on the morale of men likewise abounded in economic treatises of the 1930.[54] In the view of these works, the proper intent of government welfare policy was to mirror and shore up rather than to correct social anomalies. Thus, Marsh and Cassidy argued that it was only natural for women to be dependants within the family, but they refused to acknowledge that male heads of families might suffer the humiliation of dependency by accepting government handouts. Their recommendations for government work programs along with a national system of unemployment insurance thus had a distinctly gendered goal in mind – the restoration of the male breadwinner to his rightful position as head of the family.

Prior to the Depression, society generally accepted and fostered the ideal of separate spheres.[55] But in reality the boundaries between private and public were very porous, and a great deal of cultural space existed to accept the fact that the family economy was – especially among the Canadian working classes – an interdependent system to which the husband and wife and the children all made contributions. In contrast, during the 1930s the entire social edifice was perceived as resting exclusively on the waged labour of men. Thus all social relationships, including the affectional bonds within the family, were functions of the male breadwinner's sense of self-worth and identity, which in turn was entirely derived from his employment status. That work was now synonymous with all human experience was forcefully delineated by Leonard Marsh in 1935:

For the mass of the population, success in earning a living is the basic factor on which the other aspects and interests of their lives depend. Employment – having work to do – is a primary condition of welfare and happiness in itself. Human welfare and happiness is more than a merely economic matter: it is a complex state into which physical and mental health, education, ethics, aesthetics and other factors may enter. But no one will deny its primary dependence on economic requisites.[56]

Thus, in previous decades family stability had been based on moral and spiritual values, provided in large part by the mother; but in the 1930s the vitality of family life was believed to flow directly from its economic security, to be provided by the father. Even traditionalists among social workers, who had been so prominent in elucidating the maternalist family ideal, began to champion the notion that the family wage was an individual wage identified with the male wage earner. The speakers at the Second Bilingual Conference on Child and Family Welfare, hosted by Charlotte Whitton, reflected this pressing urgency to uphold the primary claim of the male citizen when they conceded that the sanctity of family life derived principally from its economic security. 'We may immediately come to the conclusion,' wrote G.E. Tremblay, Quebec's Deputy Minister of Labour, 'that since unemployment-insurance brings material welfare to the home, it thereby removed one strong cause of its moral disintegration.' Rather than being protected by the moral spirit sustained by the mother, family unity was now deemed to be founded on material well-being, which in turn was based exclusively on male labour.[57]

It was often suggested during the Depression that the breakdown of the home was caused directly by the 'inferiority complex' of the man without work.[58] The integrity of the male personality, together with the reification of work, formed the central metaphor of the culture of the Depression; and any attenuation of masculinity was deemed to be tantamount to social disorder. In a lecture to prospective social workers at the University of Manitoba in 1934, the speaker illustrated the fear that male unemployment would unravel society's bonds when he told of a woman reduced to tears on receiving her paycheque, but who was at the same time apprehensive about accepting it 'because it would hurt her husband so badly to know that she rather than he was the wage earner.' So pervasive was the fear that such role reversals would shred the fabric of Canadian life, that even in the midst of spiralling relief expenditures, these social workers were instructed that 'it would be better to put them on direct relief instead of having the wife working.'[59]

It has become commonplace for historians to view the Great Depression as one of the most turbulent decades in terms of social and political discord. Those who have stressed the 'politics of discontent'[60] have focused largely on organized political and social protest movements and in doing so have ignored the fundamental discordance of that era – namely, the perceived disruption of relations between the sexes. Modern historians have generally ignored this gender dimension in their accounts of the politics of chaos,[61] yet contemporary witnesses of social developments returned again and again to the problem of masculine identity. Many postulated that the root cause of all economic and social conflict lay in the challenge that unemployment presented to the male breadwinner's sense of independence. Established authority in society was believed to flow from correct relations between the sexes within the home. Thus, one writer hastened to emphasize, as long as the father 'is in receipt of an allowance, or does emergency work, he continues to be the virtual head of the family' because he will continue to be seen as 'the one person on whose existence the home depends.'[62] And by thus protecting the ambitions and sense of self-sufficiency among these 'armies' of young men, those 'intangible attributes of our national life' would be preserved.[63] Leaders of opinion saw a direct connection between political peace, social cohesion, and the preservation of the masculine identity. George McCullagh, the editor of *The Globe and Mail* and founder of the ultraconservative Leadership League, argued that the problem of unemployment was a national political emergency because when men were unable to adequately maintain their dependants they were 'cut off from their rights as citizens.' The rapid 'distintegration of Canadian manhood' that flowed from this collapse of gender roles in turn was corrosive of the very 'moral fabric of the nation.'[64] The strong link in the public mind between the male identity and work was expressed in many quarters. For example, one federal MP said of the act of accepting relief for the first time: 'I've seen tears in men's eyes, as though they were signing away their manhood, their right to be a husband and sit at the head of the table and carve the roast.'[65] It was in order to correct the apparent anomalies between gender identities thrown up by the Depression that work came to be interpreted as an end in itself – as the very core of one's sense of self and the central cultural motif of an entire generation. Even leisure activities were prescribed as a substitute for paid work to the extent that they replicated the rhythms and discipline of the workplace. As the following injunction to workers at the Toronto Labour Temple makes clear, work was a metaphor for male redemption – a human function that was both instinctual and religiously ordained, and the very essence of being male. 'Idleness,' declared W.A. Case in 1936,

> is a curse to young and old alike. Man's primitive instinct is to work and the Creator has ordained that he must work to live. The hardest punishment that can be imposed on a *normal* man is to subject him to perpetual idleness. Even his leisure he only enjoys if it is calculated to fit him and if he can look forward to more work; the leisure is designed to build up his strength and stimulate a waning enthusiasm, but his great scheme in life is work. How could it be otherwise when he has probably not only himself to provide for but others? In fact when a man, an otherwise healthy man is still and will not busy himself, we suspect that he is *sick*.[66]

These sanctifications of the work ethic were, however, gender specific. Just as non-dependent working women were deemed to be abnormal, the idle, non-working male was deemed to be sick and unfit for citizenship.

At the end of the First World War, nationalism had been defined as a primarily maternal ideology, as one that rested on population growth and family reproduction; but by the midst of the Depression, the gender constituents of the nation-state had been reversed. Another article, 'Morale: The Mental Hygiene of Unemployment,' explicitly reified work as a universal panacea. Waged labour relieved men's economic insecurity as well as their sense of powerlessness and its attendant emotional problems; at the same time, it restored affectional relationships, but most important of all, it led to the 'wholesome integration of his personality.'[67] Moreover, the concept of work was seen increasingly as having more affinities with the male individual than with the family. For example, to preserve the male wage earner's sense of individual self-worth, relief policies underscored the extent to which the relief 'wage' pertained to the man alone, by directing that 20 per cent of the allowance go not to the family but to the man for his personal use.[68] The creation of work was thus seen as the reinstatement of manhood and the restoration of a 'person's independence.'[69]

Thus work became the most powerful metaphor of the 1930s; and its deeply emotive qualities spanned class, gender, and political categories. The declaration by a worker, one John Verhooven of Montreal, that 'the Dole is not what people want. Dole breeds laziness. Nor charity. Charity kills pride. What is a man without pride, or one who is lazy for that matter. *What is really needed is work,*' emerged from a political perspective far different from that of a stern government proclamation of 1932, which decreed: 'It is recommended that it should be clearly stated that no undertakings on the part of the Government shall be understood as abrogating the principle that heads of a family are responsible for supplying its needs.'[70] Both perspectives represent, however, a profound defence of the gendered division of labour and the male breadwinner norm – a credo heard with ever greater insistence throughout the 1930s.

The Depression was a crucial decade in the development of state family policies because it destroyed the delicate equipoise between family and waged work as distinct but equally important determinants of moral order and social cohesion within the nation-state. In previous decades, social relationships and individual self-realization, as well as cultural values (such as the work ethic, thrift, and loyalty to established authority), were believed to flow imperceptibly from the affectional bonds of the family. Leaders of the older, Progressive Era reform network, which was composed of social workers, clergymen, and feminists, continued to assert that moral and spiritual ties were the fundamental source of family and social stability and of economic progress; the new technocrats, who greatly influenced the government's policy-making élite, helped bring about and then and reinforce a new relationship between the family and the workplace that abjured these older categories. This new economic familial paradigm extolled by this new élite of policy experts, together with the catastrophe of the Depression itself, caused a decisive shift in cultural values and established our modern sensibility, which celebrates work as pervading all human experience.[71] By interpreting work exclusively in terms of waged labour, the public discourse of the 1930s made it a distinctly male category. And once employment came to be identified as the pre-eminent national goal, the rights of the male breadwinner became the sole basis of citizenship and hence of all state welfare entitlements. The policies formed during the Depression decade were marked by the total negation of ideas of female social citizenship, and as such they reversed the trajectory of maternalist state family policies. And in turn, while the male identity and the experience of work became increasingly individualized throughout the 1930s, the self-hood of women was slowly eradicated. The unpaid labour of women was no longer deemed a national service, and the waged labour of women was no longer regarded as legitimate in a time of grave economic emergency. As a result of all this, women, and especially wives, were no longer categorized as citizens; rather, they were defined both in public discourse and in concrete policies as mere dependants of men, with no separate identity of their own. Because policy discussions revolved around this gender-specific conceptualization of political economy, women became invisible in the public sphere of work and welfare.

Women, Work, and Relief in the Great Depression

In her 1937 article 'In Home and Office; In Factory and Shop,' Charlotte Whitton attempted to draw public attention to the plight of unemployed single women: she believed that these jobless women had, like herself, sacrificed marriage and family life as a consequence of the killing fields of the First World War. Whitton had a personal affinity for the spinster woman 'on her own' with no immediate dependants, and acknowledged in her article that there were also unemployed women, albeit relatively few compared to the vast legions of men on relief. This discrepancy between the enormity of male unemployment and female dependency, Whitton contended, had quietly effaced the problem from government attention:

> The problem of the young woman without occupation, or of the older woman on her own must not obscure this heavy problem of the woman breadwinner at the head of her own household. Otherwise, because of the comparatively small numbers involved as against the tens of thousands of male heads of families similarly placed (and particularly since her problem appears to be really one of social dependency rather than one of bona fide economic need due to lack of gainful occupation) this female head of a family in need is apt to lose out between the two stools of unemployment aid and social care.[72]

Whitton herself generally accepted the notion that female dependency was largely a problem of 'social adjustment' rather than of unemployment,[73] and in this sense she endorsed the popular prejudice that perceived women's work as illegitimate. Nevertheless she was aware that the Depression had occasioned a subtle shift in welfare entitlements away from the 'social' toward a new category of 'economic' dependency.

The difficulty during the Depression was that if a woman had no legitimate right to employment, neither could she be defined as unemployed; and as relief became increasingly weighted toward a specific type of dependency – namely, lack of work – the problem of women's poverty became stricken from the public record. Until 1931 the Unemployment Relief Committee of the city of Winnipeg did not even recognize female unemployment as a factor in its relief statistics, and when it did acknowledge the fact of unemployment among widows and deserted women with children, their independent right to welfare assistance was neatly obviated, in that they were inventoried alongside married men.[74] In the early years of the Depression, as dependency was slowly being redefined, the question of whether to categorize women as unemployed workers or as worthy recipients of government assistance based on their status as mothers was often discussed. In Ottawa, for example, a report of the Committee for Unemployed Women and Wives of Unemployed Men expressed its concern regarding this matter of eligibility, noting that it could not decide whether a single mother was worthy of relief; though technically she was unemployable because she had children to support, she nevertheless presented herself as a legitimate worker by virtue of the fact that she had walked a mile in pursuit of work and had stood in line for a sewing machine.[75] As relief administration became more bureaucratized and increasingly managed by local governments rather than by voluntary organizations, the boundaries between social and economic dependency became clearer. By 1934, city relief in Vancouver had resolved the problem by creating two relief sections: one for unemployment and one for all other forms of dependency. Only women who could demonstrate that they were the sole head of a household were to be viewed as legitimate breadwinners; and as surrogate men, they were to be included in the more prestigious unemployment relief section, where they would be supported by federal and provincial funds. The detritus of women – the elderly, unmarried mothers, and the widows on mother's pensions – were labelled 'unemployables,' along with old age pensioners and incapacitated veterans, and as such were eligible only for municipal relief or, in many circumstances, for charity from voluntary organizations.[76]

By the late 1930s, the welfare rights of women had become increasingly circumscribed. Many dependent women could not work and for that reason were prevented from obtaining relief. Traditionally, governments had repudiated any responsibility for assisting unmarried mothers on the basis that their immorality made them unworthy. By the 1930s, unmarried mothers were being denied relief because they could not demonstrate that they were employable.[77] Similarly, in Quebec in 1938, the government passed a law stating that no deserted or unmarried mothers were eligible for relief on the basis that 'women could not be regarded as breadwinners, and therefore cannot be accepted for Unemployment Relief.' By some strange logic, this government ruling also meant that these women were also ineligible for charity from local family welfare organizations, which had by this time also imbibed these new definitions of dependency. And even though the Quebec government had passed its Needy Mother's Assistance Act in 1937, it was not in place when these stringent new relief policies were enacted in the summer of 1938, and even at that, only widows were allowed this form of government aid.[78]

A few sporadic voices of opposition were raised against this narrowly conceived, male-oriented definition of the deserving poor. Limited programs existed in Quebec providing work for middle-aged women on farms, and in Ottawa the Local Council of Women and the Committee on Stabilization of Employment vociferously argued in favour of women's claims for suitable relief work under the Unemployment and Farm Relief Act.[79] The dominant trend in welfare administration was evident by the end of the decade, as Dorothy King observed in 1939. Even though it was apparent to her and to other female directors of local family welfare organizations that the Depression had 'inevitably developed an increasing burden of social dependency, apart from that caused by unemployment,' the implementation of measures to address this largely female problem had been passed down either to local government jurisdictions or to the management of voluntary charity. 'Social dependency' created by desertion, child-rearing, illness, or indigence[80] was thus pushed to the margins of welfare administration. The welfare hierarchies that emerged during the 1930s wiped out both the power of middle-class, female social workers and the claims of their working-class female beneficiaries. As a result of the redefinition of dependency, a disjunctive was established between municipal relief and unemployment relief, which led directly to women being relegated to the bottom of the government welfare hierarchy. This new paradigm was reinforced with the introduction of a national system of unemployment insurance in 1940, which insisted that work was an exclusive citizenship right of men.

The magnitude of the problem of female dependency and unemployment thus went largely unrecognized by government welfare administrators. In Ontario, the 1932 government report on direct relief, commonly known as the Campbell Report, concluded that single women's unemployment 'does not present a very serious problem in most municipalities.' They meant by this, of course, that there were fewer single women seeking employment compared with the enormous numbers of single men; they also meant that because unemployed women were not perceived to be potential converts to Communism, as were unattached men, there was less need to seek their political allegiance through government relief assistance.[81] Thus, male transiency demanded 'special and systematic provision within the municipal relief system' and various strategies for providing employment training and work experience; while those single women who had not returned to their family homes, to be cared for by their parents, were to rely on the ministrations of private philanthropy. Provincial governments were averse to funding even the most meagre of solutions to the problem of female dependency, such as the creation of hostels for homeless women; rather, they asserted that all female relief should be discharged 'through existing agencies or through arrangements with private family homes.'[82]

At the beginning of the Depression, all local relief was handled on a cooperative basis between city governments and various voluntary organizations,[83] largely because private agencies had better-established administrative and investigative networks, which helped keep government costs down. But by the early 1930s, many voluntary organizations and church-based charities were becoming restive as state relief officials became increasingly reluctant to allow private welfare agencies to continue in their leadership role.[84] In some cities, such as Halifax, which had no city relief body, the entire load of relief was carried on by local charitable organizations such as the Halifax Welfare Bureau throughout the entire decade.[85] In Montreal, relief was also largely in the hands of charitable institutions; and even after local government took over some of the burden, church-based agencies such as the St Vincent de Paul Society, the Baron de Hirsch Society, the Federation of Catholic Charities, and the Protestant Family Welfare Organization remained influential in welfare policy. These agencies, especially the Jewish ones, fought against government intrusion out of the need to defend their religious cultures; they also tended to make fewer gender distinctions, preferring to regard the family as a unit.[86] However, as the Depression wore on and governments became preoccupied primarily with unemployment relief, these private relief agencies became less influential, and at the same time the categorizing of clients became more pronounced: some agencies assisted unfranchised immigrants, some the unskilled, some the indigent, and some unsupported women. Over time, family welfare agencies came to be used more and more for investigation purposes, till by the end of the decade they had lost any power they had previously held over the financing of relief. In the words of one commentator, by the beginning of the Second World War these once powerful agencies had become no more than family counselling centres.

In 1930 private family welfare agencies had treated all 'destitute people.'[87] But as government machinery for relief became better funded and organized, voluntary institutions increasingly focused on the needs of women, who formed the largest category of 'unemployables' and whom governments defined as ineligible for state aid once unemployment relief programs were finally established. As a result, during the Depression the problem of women's dependency became almost exclusively a concern for private charity. In Montreal, aged women and women with children were assisted overnight by the Assistance Publique Hostel. Single women with no dependants faired less well and were forced to seek rest at the Meurling Refuge, which had been founded mainly to house and feed 700 homeless, single men, who were exposed to a daily regimen of stripping and delousing.[88] Women seeking work could apply to the Montreal YWCA Employment Bureau, or they could seek both work and relief at the Montreal Council of Social Agencies, which became one of the leading Protestant institutions to lobby for a better system of employment registration for women. This voluntary system had its limitations, however, in that the Emergency Unemployment Relief Committee of the Montreal Council of Social Agencies provided assistance only to British subjects.[89] Non-Protestant and non-British homeless women of the 'manual worker class' were thus forced to seek refuge at the Sheltering Home of the YWCA.[90] These two institutions did eventually cooperate in erecting two distinct employment offices for women: one for business and professional women, where in 1932, 469 women were assisted; and one for industrial and domestic workers, where there were 5,592 applicants and 1,684 placements that same year. While often criticized for providing relief and recreation to women without demanding work in return, the Montreal Council of Social Agencies insisted that 'the truth is there is no work' and became one of the foremost social service agencies to lobby for a comprehensive system of unemployment insurance, adapted to the needs of both male and female dependency.[91] By 1934, Quebec still had no government welfare department, and this organization was dispensing material assistance to some 553 unemployed women, of whom 394 were heads of families, and was creating its own voluntary system of mothers' allowances, which aided an additional 457 families.[92]

Although Ontario's state-run system of employment offices did establish its own Women's Emergency Committees, these were for the most part ineffectual in fully registering dependent women, and functioned largely to funnel all dependent women, whether single or married, whether young or old, into domestic service. These organizations were small and had little input into government policymaking.[93] As a result, in Toronto the Local Council of Women established its own emergency and relief service, which in 1931 found 900 positions for women; however, most of these were only temporary cleaning situations that appealed little to unemployed office and factory women.[94] Similar services were created across Canada. In Winnipeg, voluntary employment organizations located jobs for 86 women, but most of these were domestic service positions and were refused by the applicants, the majority of whom were 'foreign factory workers.' In Saskatoon, local women's groups helped place 364 formerly 'self-supporting women' with private farm families, where they worked for their board.[95] Sewing centres, where women were paid for making over used clothing, were located in Saint John, New Brunswick, and in Ottawa,[96] but the largest experiment of this type was established in Victoria, British Columbia. It is little realized even now that during the Depression in Canada, there was a high rate of transiency among single women, both young and old. Victoria's sewing workroom provided work for 130 of these transients, who having failed relief residency requirements had been compelled to find some means of sustenance outside regular employment or government assistance. In this workroom, displaced and indigent women were paid 80 cents a day for sewing clothing and braid rugs. Although many young women passed through its doors, the vast majority of these workroom inmates were elderly women attempting to eke out an existence until they were eligible to collect an old age pension. In an article, 'Women Befriend Women,' published in the *Victoria Daily Colonist*, this welfare way station was portrayed in glowing terms as a haven where women's faith in themselves was sustained both by 'the sympathy of their sister-women' and by the very fact of having work, which was characterized as 'the normal being's natural desire.'[97]

In reality, these privately run relief centres failed abjectly to provide adequate employment, and in most cases they contributed to the narrowing of women's work options by condemning their clients – most of whom had worked in either offices or factories – to a regimen of unskilled domestic labour. In Winnipeg, for example, the woman's hostel, which had been established to train immigrant British women as domestics, was converted in the 1930s into an employment centre for unmarried women, thus shouldering a burden that might otherwise have been carried by the provincial government.[98] In addition, the moral welfare of unemployed, idle women was closely scrutinized within these organizations headed by local women's groups. For example, the object of the Vancouver Single Unemployed Women's Aid Board was less to find suitable work for women at an adequate wage than to encourage women to make 'proper church and social contacts.'[99] Much as with the male work camps,[100] these solutions were designed as a prophylactic against moral decay – specifically, as a means to reduce the possibility of a rise in female prostitution.

The case histories of the women who applied to Vancouver's Single Unemployed Women's Aid Board reveal how the overall structure of women's work changed radically during the 1930s. This organization was led by Mrs Rex Eaton, who became prominent during the Second World War when she administered the registration of women's labour for the federal government and helped establish the vital day-nursery program. The Single Unemployed Women's Aid Board had as its aim the restoration of 'initiative and morale' among the ranks of the female unemployed. Individual middle-class women sponsored a woman on local assistance, with the object of forcing her off relief. Dorothy Farquhar, a twenty-eight-year-old woman on city relief, was a typical client. Because she was trained as a secretary, Dorothy Farquhar refused to take work outside her line for three years, and became embittered when the government threatened to cut off her relief benefits. Ministered to by a friendly, middle-class member of the Single Unemployed Women's Aid Board, Miss Farquhar was persuaded to take a job as a maid at the Anglican Indian School at Lytton; this removed her from her community and social contacts. As was reported to the Hon. George S. Pearson, the provincial Minister of Labour, the recalcitrant Miss Farquhar soon quit her job at the school and returned to Vancouver. However, having been refused city relief, 'within a fortnight through her own efforts she secured work as a domestic proving that the encouragement and interest given by the sponsor had re-established her initiative and determination.'[101] That the Depression forced a rapid deskilling of women's labour and generally resulted in a lowering of the status of women's work is likewise revealed by the case of Hilda Waite. After a long career as a schoolteacher, the well-educated Waite, having first refused housework as too demeaning, was compelled to find work reading tea cups at the Hotel Georgia in Vancouver.[102]

Prior to the Depression, the range and scope of women's work had been expanding to such a degree that many women had been able to move out of the unskilled job ghetto of cooking and cleaning and were entering office work and skilled industrial work in ever greater numbers. In British Columbia, for example, female factory workers had moved well beyond the confines of traditional female work patterns, having shifted out of textile manufacturing and into industrial work relating to brewing and food processing, and into work with urban public utilities such as the street railway and the gas, water, and light utilities.[103] However, women's claims to the right to work in tradition-ally male domains were severely delegitimated by the Depression; increasingly, the vast scale of unemployment forced them back into unskilled, low-paying jobs, most notably domestic service. Miss L.O.R. Kennedy, the superintendent of the Toronto Women's Employment Centre observed that growing numbers of married women over the age of thirty were being forced to seek employment and become 'the head of the house'[104] because their husbands were now unemployed. Yet the increasing number of female workers did not contribute to the expansion of women's opportunities in the workplace. The Depression did not restructure work patterns in Canada such that women were allowed to encroach on traditional male preserves; rather, it *circumscribed* the range of women's work. Not only were working women's wages cut, but the previous skill levels of female workers were cata-strophically eroded, as thousands of stenographers and industrial workers took up part-time household work, while qualified domestic workers remained on relief.[105]

Prior to the Depression, the minimum wage laws, though always difficult to enforce, provided at least some protection for female work-ers. During the 1930s these laws were violated on a vast scale. As a result, women's wages fell drastically, forcing many to seek relief to supplement their income. However, this regular circumvention of the minimum wage laws by employers went largely unreported because women feared for their jobs. As the Ontario Deputy Minister of Labour, A.W. Crawford, informed his minister, the Hon. J.D. Monteith, in 1933, 'there appears to be a general disposition on the part of the workers, both male and female, to accept whatever wages are offered and to leave it to the government officials concerned to discover violations of existing registration or regulations.'[106] The tendency for all workers to accept any wage helped facilitate the other tactic of tight-fisted employers, which was to replace female workers with boys or men, who were still unprotected by minimum wage legislation. This phenomenon was widespread in the 1930s, and reinforced the trend in all industries toward the deskilling of work and the rapid growth in part-time positions. But its effects were most catastrophic for unmarried women. Vast numbers of married women were entering the workforce for the first time; yet at the same time, a large proportion of the jobs held by single women were being taken away by married men desperate to maintain their family's standard of living.[107] As a result, the gender balance in the workforce remained little disturbed during the 1930s, as the in-migration of married women was counterbalanced by a decisive out-migration of younger, single women.

Although the garment workers in Toronto threatened to strike over the issue of lost wages in 1933, and although the Trades and Labour Council protested the phenomenon of replacing female workers with men, on the basis that it placed downward pressure on the male wage standard, the prevailing attitudes regarding the social imperative of upholding the rights of the male breadwinner meant that few objections were raised against the practice of firing single female wage earners.[108] Women did, however, quietly and privately protest the purposeful reduction in their skills and wages, and attempted on an individual basis to uphold their pre-Depression standards of living. That their objections to government relief and employment policies took a very different form from those of single men, who launched an organized and well-publicized protest against conditions in the work camps,[109] does not mean that women were either quiescent or passive during the 1930s. Employment statistics from that decade tell a story of strong and widespread albeit individualized protests by legions of unemployed women against attempts by women's organizations, churches, private welfare agencies, and governments to shoehorn them into low-paying, intermittent, and demeaning work as domestic day workers. Of the 4,702 women registered for work at the Protestant

Employment Bureau in Montreal, only 47 accepted work as domestics. Likewise, in Saskatoon, even untrained women entering the workforce for the first time enthusiastically registered for work until they discovered they would be forced into domestic service.[110]

Throughout the Depression the demand for domestics always far outdistanced the supply because both older women and untrained girls preferred work in offices, shops, or factories. It is small wonder. By the 1930s, most domestic work was offered on a part-time basis only, 'owing to labour-saving devices in the well-equipped, compact, modern apartment,' and also to the fact that 'many people to-day are unable to pay for the full-time services of a maid, yet require help with the children or the home.'[111] Also, working conditions were notoriously bad, as was made evident in the 'Report on Placements' written for the Ontario Department of Labour in 1933. Domestics were paid between $10.00 and $20.00 per month for full-time work, but women often had to purchase their own uniforms, and had to withstand working conditions that included unpredictable hours, elastic workloads, and conflictual social relations. Mrs Jennie Bankner, a forty-year-old widow with one child, took a position as a general housekeeper outside Toronto. She was left to sleep in the cellar and could not obtain adequate sustenance for her young daughter. She eventually left her position and applied once again for city relief. The fate of separated and deserted women was often even worse. Mrs Edith Brewer was ineligible for relief because she had separated from her husband. As a result, she was compelled to move to take a job as a domestic, which paid the grand sum of $2.50 per week. Although hired as a cook, she found she was expected to clean the entire house; more troubling still, she had to relinquish all privacy, as only the living room couch was provided as her sleeping quarters. So demeaning was this experience that she eventually returned to her husband.[112] Miss Janet Sutherland, aged twenty-seven, was willing (like many others) to take a domestic service position to preserve her economic independence from her family, even though it meant she had to relinquish her skills as a bookkeeper.[113] However, many more women followed the path of one Vancouver mother and her daughter who, though they were repelled by the thought of having to take relief, preferred it to domestic service, which they believed to be a demeaning activity for those like themselves who were of a 'respectable character.'[114]

However much middle-class women may have defended the right of unemployed women to work, their main purpose was to assist governments in their efforts to reduce the escalating relief rolls. In their view, social policies ought to mirror rather than transform the labour market; and since the ubiquitous demand was for domestic servants, female government employment officers, like Miss L.O.R. Kennedy in Toronto, were largely unsympathetic to the truculence so often demonstrated by skilled female workers, once highly paid, who refused to relinquish their status as respectable women and take domestic day jobs. Like her male counterparts, Miss Kennedy believed that unemployment was indeed a masculine problem, and that jobless women should gladly take positions that would not interfere with the family wage of those households still headed by a male breadwinner. It outraged Miss Kennedy when a woman was not content to remain at the bottom of the employment pyramid. Furiously, she informed H.C. Hudson, the general superintendent of Ontario's employment offices, that a Mrs Christie had refused to work for less than 30 cents an hour, and on top of that was refusing to accept work that did not suit her. 'Only this morning,' railed Miss Kennedy, 'an employer wanted her specially to do some ironing, and she refused, saying she liked to iron for herself and not for anyone else.'[115]

That women's claims to the right to work were clearly deemed inferior to those of men was revealed by the fact that in Ottawa–Hull, girls and women had to enter the government employment bureau through a door off a back lane, well out of sight of the men's entrance.[116] The same reluctance to acknowledge the validity of women's right to seek work was evident throughout the system of government employment offices. One woman wrote to Miss Kennedy to castigate her for cutting wages and for refusing work both to middle-aged and Canadian women. 'They order you back to wait as if you were a dog or a cat,' wrote this anonymous critic of the government's treatment of female job applicants, 'and they ring up and ask will you take a new arrival because they can get them to go out for anything she offers them ... When we had licensed employment offices we could pay our dollar and get civility and the kind of position we ask for, but under the present conditions we only get insults.' Tellingly, in light of Depression-era assumptions about the male and female spheres, this same working-class job applicant likewise believed that Miss Kennedy had no legitimate function in the workplace, and demanded that she be replaced by a *male* employment officer. The anonymous letter writer, whom Miss Kennedy later labelled 'a social misfit' because she wanted a better-paying job, concluded her outburst with the observation that 'there are plenty of returned men with families who would appreciate those positions.'[117] Miss Kennedy retorted that these charges showed evidence of 'the unbalanced mind.'[118] She got her come-uppance a few years later when she was almost fired for turning away a male applicant from her employment office. On that occasion, the 'unemployed' man turned out to be none other than the Prime Minister of Canada. As her boss, H.C. Hudson, fulminated: 'I cannot possibly conceive how any member of the Employment Service of Canada should fail to recognise the Hon. Mr. King when he visited the office.'[119]

The intractable problem of how to induce women on relief to take jobs as domestic servants was soon solved. In 1935, the Acting Secretary of Unemployment Relief for Ontario, D.B. Harkness, decreed that as of 1 August all relief to single men would be discontinued and that they were 'also advised to review the situation with respect to single women. Many complaints have been received that domestic help cannot be secured. If circumstances warrant the discontinuance of relief to single women in your municipality you are authorized to take the necessary action ... The relief lists must be purged of all employable persons for whom work is available.'[120] That same year, the government also responded to the constant demands from women's organizations by assiduously turning their attention to devising training methods by which to elevate the status of domestic service.[121] Middle-class women, long suffering from an inadequate supply of domestic labour, had been demanding since the turn of the century for such schemes to be created. The shortage of trained domestics had become particularly acute after the abrogation at the onset of the Depression of the Empire Settlement Scheme, which had been established by the Federal Department of Immigration, at the behest of both middle-class urban and especially farm women, to encourage trained British domestics to immigrate to Canada. Thus, the government was not interceding in the domestic servant problem in order to salve the needs of the unemployed, but rather to address the long-standing demands of middle-class women. Following the draconian measures of 1935, far more Canadian women entered domestic service as charwomen, housekeepers, laundresses, and cooks. Indeed, so successful was the government's pincer movement against unemployed working-class women that by the end of the decade women's work had been radically deskilled.

If the labour market of the 1930s had indeed been swelled by women 'seeking to fill the gap in the family income caused by the unemployment of the breadwinner,' it was a much more restrictive and narrow market than had existed prior to 1929. As Leonard Marsh observed, this was so because 'domestic service work is the only kind that the woman without training can secure.'[122] And as I have argued, it was also the only form of work that relatively highly skilled, experienced female workers could hope to obtain. While the majority of these women probably perceived their entry into domestic service as temporary, economists and government policymakers most definitely did not look upon such work as an aberrant job choice foisted on women by economic hardship. Rather, economists like Marsh used this restructured job market for women as objective evidence that *all* women's work was unskilled, and thus unworthy of recognition by government unemployment insurance and relief measures. Marsh compiled incontrovertible statistical evidence to demonstrate that women's work was synonymous with unskilled, temporary work. As he concluded, fully 90 per cent of all 'responsible' skilled female workers had become housekeepers by 1939.

That this condition was believed to be normative was reflected clearly in government policies. The parameters of women's work as defined by the scientific truth according to Marsh were upheld by the architects of the 1940 Unemployment Insurance Act. This federal legislation was the first explicitly rights-based system of welfare benefits in Canada, and as such it established the baseline for all future welfare legislation. This national system of state welfare benefits effectively ended the right of women to receive this élite form of state assistance – significantly not on the basis of gender, but rather by virtue of the fact that they had become categorized as unskilled and temporary workers.[123] To explain how women were cut off from this new assistance scheme, and why, even though they regularly sought to define themselves as unemployed, they continued to be seen as the victims of social dependency, we must examine closely how the exponents of a national system of unemployment insurance, in tandem with government relief officials, regarded female dependency during the latter part of the Depression.

Historians have explored extensively the organized opposition of single male workers to government relief policies.[124] Unfortunately, they have long ignored that during the Depression, feminists[125] and a wide range of welfare organizations mobilized themselves on behalf of unemployed women. In Ottawa and Regina, local women's organizations worked alongside churches and private welfare organizations to pressure governments to conduct accurate surveys of women's unemployment,[126] and in many cases they were instrumental in garnering state interest in the question. In Ontario, for example, as a result of constant lobbying by the Committee on Homeless Women and Girls,[127] the government established a central registration system for unemployed women within their employment offices. Voices of protest were also raised within government bureaucracies, and these did much to stimulate official interest in the problem of female dependency. Miss L.O.R. Kennedy, the Superintendent of the Toronto Women's Employment Office, excoriated her male colleagues over the bias inherent in government relief policies: 'In dealing with men, you have had the advantage of government schemes of assistance which have been denied us. You have placed married men on public work construction and single men on the highway road camps. We have had no such outlet. To fall back on domestic service, as I said before, has been our only course and there is a limit to this.'[128] Public protest often compelled governments to acknowledge the widespread reality of female poverty and unemployment, but was much less successful at making governments establish work programs for women. Indeed, governments often utilized newly gathered statistics on women's relief and unemployment to further segregate male and female welfare entitlements. In Ontario, for example, surveys of female joblessness were deployed to distinguish between women who were ordinary relief cases (and thus the responsibility of municipalities), and those who were legitimate workers (and thus could claim provincial assistance).[129]

In Quebec, the Montreal Council of Social Agencies, a private body, had long lobbied for the federal government to establish a special committee to study the employment problems faced by women; this organization's goal was to have women's work form an integral part of any future unemployment insurance program.[130] On behalf of the Montreal Council, Dorothy King wrote a lengthy memorandum to the National Employment Commission in which she complained that governments had grossly underestimated the severity of the problem of women's dependency by failing to keep accurate unemployment statistics. Government departments insisted on defining many women as 'unemployables' because of their family responsibilities; the Montreal Council of Social Agencies had a more progressive attitude toward women's dependency, classifying *all* women over the age of fifteen as potential wage earners. As had Cassidy in his study of relief in Ontario, King argued that relief statistics did not accurately reflect the situation faced by unemployed women. The government's relief records indicated that in 1936 there were only 14,311 women on relief; King believed that the number was five times higher.[131] Similarly, in Toronto, the Executive Secretary of the Protestant Children's Homes, Kathleen Gorrie, tabled data estimating, for example, that as of 1936 there were upwards of three million unemployed single women on relief in Canada.[132]

Unfortunately, like male social investigators, Dorothy King and her female associates had come to view women's unemployment as a problem mainly of the 'unskilled'; thus, they linked women's work opportunities with training schemes for domestic service. In this way feminists were reinforcing the attitudes of male policymakers insofar as they regarded employment programs not as a means to correct anomalies in the labour market but rather as a means to buttress the *laissez-faire* forces of supply and demand. In this vein, King concluded that it was 'an obligation to their sex' to encourage government-funded training centres for women to rectify the long-standing problem of 'a shortage of competent domestic workers.'[133] In 1936, all of these private agencies, which were organized ostensibly to address the profound reality of female destitution in the midst of the Depression, were canvassed by the Women's Advisory Committee of the National Employment Commission.[134] While the commission observed that 'unemployed women furnish a national problem,' its chairman, the rural economist Mary Sutherland, quite amazingly conceded that despite the crying need for 'constructive' work for such women, 'no single spectacular program is to be expected.'[135] While the commission brought to light the enormity of the problem of women's joblessness, particularly among older women, its recommendations were to say the least flaccid. With trying regularity, it advanced a standard program of domestic training; one of its more creative suggestions was that women could create new employment niches for themselves by growing and selling seeds.[136] Certainly, Sutherland can be criticized for seeing a rural existence as the 'key to the whole situation,'[137] and for relying largely on free market forces to stimulate work for women.[138] However, if her recommendations were unimaginative and ineffective, as indeed they were, the inadequacy of her perspective and her rural outlook were not the main reasons. The absence of creative employment strategies emerging from her committee owed much more to the widespread assumption that women's work was temporary in nature, and that female dependency demanded mainly a social rather than an economic solution.

The limited scope of the National Employment Commission's recommendations regarding women's work appear far less anomalous when we stand them beside those of the many female-dominated employment and welfare organizations. However vociferously Canadian welfare agencies and women's groups made their grievances known, they very rarely recommended novel strategies that would allow women to break out of their traditional roles in domestic service. They, like the National Employment Commission, could be condemned for forcing young women into menial labour jobs.[139] Their protests centred mainly on the availability and level of relief and on the need for adequate shelter for homeless women. Indeed, their campaigns for greater government responsibility for the problem of female dependency were driven mainly by their concern for protecting the morals of unattached women.[140] Few feminist organizations focused to any great degree on the issue of women's work or wages, and when they did, it was in the context of preserving women's morality.[141] Thus, Ruth Low, the youngest member of the Women's Committee of the National Employment Commission, a recent graduate of McGill University's School of Social Work and of Emmanuel College within the University of Toronto, and a specialist on immigrant women, contended that one of the worst effects of the Depression was that it had caused an alarming increase in female promiscuity, and worse, had made fully half of all unemployed and idle single women in the nation into homosexuals.[142] Like the male policymakers they wished to influence, these middle-class women classified women's poverty as a product of 'social' rather than 'economic' dependency. Thus they were helping reinforce rather than deconstruct the gendered divisions that were already well enmeshed in state relief policies.

Even the most radical of women, such as Miss Margaret Lade, found it difficult to free themselves from prevailing attitudes regarding the gendered division of work and welfare. Miss Lade, an Australian, had taught school in her home country, and had developed strong associations there with the radical wing of the Student Christian Movement before immigrating to Canada via Britain. Prior to leaving Australia she had done industrial work and had overseen 200 employees, but one suspects that she was also a labour organizer – a skill that she developed further when she later worked as a shopgirl at James A. Ogilvy's in Montreal and T. Eaton's in Toronto. It appears that it was her radical union principles that got her fired from these jobs so that she was forced to live on relief. In Toronto she was active in the Workers' Community League, where she led a class of folk dancing for unemployed girls. This organization had strong links to the United Church, and under its auspices Lade in 1933 recommended that the women's employment office be expanded to include a central employment registry so that a more 'scientific approach' could be used to provide more constructive help to Toronto's unemployed women.[143]

Lade succeeded in having the Ontario government recognize that the problem of women's unemployment in Toronto was far greater than it had first assumed and that its official estimate of 12,000 unemployed working women was far too low.[144] The Deputy Minister of Labour, A.W. Crawford, and Miss L.O.R. Kennedy persistently opposed Lade's proposals that the efforts of the local women's organizations on behalf of destitute women be coordinated with those of the government employment offices; in their view, the issues around women's work should fall within the purview of private, voluntary activity[145] because they had a 'social' rather than an economic basis. However, Mr Hudson, the General Superintendent of Employment Offices for Ontario, thought otherwise, holding that 'some special recognition should be given to the fact that there are unemployed women and girls in large numbers in Toronto, that everything is being done for unemployed men and that it is within the jurisdiction of the Department of Labour to make some provision for these women and girls.'[146] Miss Lade's proposals were taken as seriously as they were by the upper echelons of government because they affirmed established attitudes to women's work. Her notion that the issue of women's unemployment was at root a 'social problem,' whereby idleness led inexorably to serious moral lapses that would eventually undermine the race,[147] was consistent with the conservative values of government policymakers; so was her emphasis on the value of 'self-help.'[148] Her recommendations, such as those to establish recreation and training centres for domestics, were heeded largely because they did little to transgress gender boundaries regarding the home and workplace and because they at the same time fulfilled the demands of the labour market. Indeed, her program of rural placements for women appealed greatly to a government that was eager to shift the burden of dependency off the backs of overloaded urban jurisdictions.[149] Government officials were receptive to her ideas principally because they reaffirmed the strictures that had already been placed on women's roles. As Lade insisted, women's work was only a temporary stopgap until the male breadwinner could regain his rightful position in the family. Although Lade accepted in some measure a married woman's need to supplement her husband's earnings, an adequate family wage, supplied by the husband alone, was her ideal: 'If industrial markets, through technological changes, may not demand so many women as before, how are we going to employ our girls and our women – more especially if the family wage continues to be insufficient for wife and children, or if the single man finds economic circumstances prevent marriage?'[150] This was a far cry from those who championed women's economic independence by advocating that the wage be disaggregated and considered on the basis of the female earner as an 'individual unit.'[151]

One crucial recommendation of Lade's was deemed too radical by the Ontario government, and its rejection would effectively doom her program. This was her suggestion that because women's social dependency went hand in hand with their joblessness, the Departments of Public Welfare and Labour should coordinate their policies.[152] From the point of view of the Department of Labour, Lade's proposal to combine unemployment and ordinary relief was blasphemous in the extreme because doing so would have blurred the distinction between needs-based and rights-based entitlements on which advocates of unemployment insurance had long insisted. A.W. Crawford, the Deputy Minister of Labour for Ontario, strongly objected to any move toward amalgamating employment offices with social welfare services. His fear was that any softening of the boundaries between one's work skills and one's needs might further erode work incentives among men. Such overlapping of government jurisdictions would undermine the self-help, contributory nature of unemployment insurance, and the affinity – which he wished to underscore – between insurance and male citizenship rights.[153] As Crawford explained to the National Round Table Conference on Problems in the Social Administration of General and Unemployment Relief, convened in 1933, unemployment insurance for men was preferable to direct relief because it helped 'restore to the unemployed the desire and ability to again be self-supporting independent citizens.'[154] From the point of view of labour leaders such as R.A. Rigg, the notion of collapsing relief and unemployment measures smacked of charity. In his view, charity was only for women. He was adamant about forestalling any greater government intervention in the private sphere of women's dependency; his efforts were aimed at maintaining a strict demarcation between female relief and male social insurance.[155]

Traditional welfare agencies, such as the House of Industry in Toronto, wanted all forms of destitution to be subsumed under the general rubric of unemployment, arguing that exclusively female forms of dependency, such as desertion and widowhood, could be attributed to lack of work.[156] For their part, the self-proclaimed 'modernists' among welfare specialists, such as Cassidy and Marsh, wanted to prevent the establishment of these dangerous precedents, which in their view would undermine the status of the male breadwinner – especially the skilled worker – and his exclusive right to state entitlements. In the final report of the Montreal Council of Social Agencies, regarding the attitude to be adopted by the federal government in the matter of unemployment insurance, Marsh stressed that 'a clear distinction' must be drawn between 'unemployment and poverty,' between poor relief and unemployment relief. In his view, 'normal' public expenditures must be geared to elevating the status of the 'steadier class of workers.' He feared that the Depression was expanding the irresponsible underclass of low-skilled and underpaid workers, thus threatening the ability of families to remain independent. He also feared that it was undermining the spirit of competition in industry as well as national wage and consumption levels, the preservation of which was crucial to mitigating the effects of the Depression.[157]

Marsh's view of government intervention was that it should be limited, and that its parameters should be strictly related to programs that would reduce 'industrial instability.' He was unconcerned about those groups in society – the unskilled, women, and the elderly – who were 'unattached to industry'; these victims of 'personal destitution' he relegated to the ministrations of stigmatizing, poor relief.[158] Like Whitton, Marsh believed that welfare policies should uphold the work ethic, especially among those at the core of Canada's economic strength, the 'sturdy owner class'[159] on the land and the skilled worker. Thus, even though unskilled workers were the most vulnerable group during the Depression, Marsh did not believe that federal employment policies should be designed to serve them. As he informed Whitton, relief penalized thrift, whereas unemployment insurance would eradicate pauper attitudes because it would be based not on need but on the male breadwinner's right to state protection. Unemployment insurance, therefore, 'would not touch the casuals and the sick and the others if we could possibly avoid it, but it would win the support of those who are unemployed for no reason of their own, and those willing to work.'[160]

Far from being a Canadian Fabian, as Allan Irving and Michiel Horn have argued,[161] Marsh believed that government planning and welfare policymaking should uphold economic stratification and subtle class distinctions and should ultimately preserve the 'large section of middle class' Canadians, whose standards of living were being eroded drastically by the deflationary effects of the Depression.[162] In short, economic research should help shore up economic efficiency, while government initiatives should have as their goal the restoration of business competition in the marketplace. Marsh's attitudes toward state planning, like Cassidy's, had been drawn largely from the work of the British Political and Economic Planning group (PEP). It has become commonplace among historians to associate the concept of economic planning entirely with collectivist thought and to attribute its success to the agitation of the economic radicals, the disciples of J.M. Keynes. A British historian, Daniel Ritschel, has challenged this 'Whiggish' interpretation and argued that between the wars in Britain, policies of state regulation and the notion of economic planning itself were endorsed not only by the Left. As Ritschel has it, the technocratic faith that the scientific method could be applied to social and economic problems was never an idea disseminated by a particular political party; rather, the concept of economic planning was heavily contested terrain on which battled a wide range of political perspectives, from the far right to the far left.[163]

Indeed, as Ritschel observes, the very concept of 'economic planning' was introduced to the vocabulary of British political debate during the 1930s by Sir Oswald Mosley,[164] who in 1931, having defected from the Labour Party, established the first fascist political movement in Britain. At the same time, the Labour Party in Britain was itself deeply split over the question of the extent and permanency of government intervention in the economic sphere. While a technocratic cadre existed within it, the New Fabians never fully embraced Keynes's economic theories; in fact, they adhered to the belief that centralized economic planning was not feasible in Britain.[165] The most important advocate of state planning in Britain was the PEP, a body founded in 1931 on the explicit idea of 'planned capitalism.' Though it would later be known as one of the leaders of the Keynesian revolution in Britain because of its 1943 report 'Employment for All,' which incorporated many of the famous economist's ideas regarding the efficacy of public works in evening out the trade cycle and raising national income, the PEP derived its early recommendations largely from the thought of

Oswald Mosley.[166] In fact, the PEP held that private planning through a system of industrial self-government would preclude the need to expand the State, and its explicit goal was to forestall the socialist planning principles embedded in the platform of the Labour Party. Thus, even though the PEP might be termed technocratics because of its insistence on scientific economic planning, that group had closer political affinities with business corporatism in the United States than with contemporary collectivist thought in Britain.

It was the economic and political philosophy of the PEP, and not that of G.D.H. Cole, that provided most of the intellectual grist for Marsh's own conception of a planned economy for Canada. Indeed, a similar flexibility in the concept of planning was evident among Canadian policymakers. Calling oneself a planner did not necessarily entail a collectivist political and economic outlook, as was demonstrated by the example, not only of Marsh, but also of Harry Cassidy. While Cassidy contributed to *Social Planning for Canada* and was a member of the League for Social Reconstruction, his affiliation was fundamentally pragmatic, and was seen by him as a means for promoting his own blueprints for the welfare state. There is no better illustration of his political pragmatism than his insistence to F.R. Scott that his name not officially appear in *Social Planning for Canada*, since his association with a group that had come to underwrite the Regina Manifesto of the CCF would ruin his political career in British Columbia, where he had just taken up a post as policy adviser in the Liberal government of Premier Pattullo. Indeed, if Cassidy had any strong political affinities, they were distinctly Liberal. He told his wife Bea in 1930 on the eve of the election of Prime Minister Bennett: 'If only there was some hope for a real party of Liberalism!'[167] That Cassidy had, as James Struthers has put it, 'mildly leftist'[168] views – ones with intellectual roots both in New Liberal thought and in the more conservative corporatist thought of American businessmen – is illustrated by his career. His later affiliation with the LSR derived not so much from a particular political outlook as from his commitment to a technocratic vision of economic planning grounded in scientific research – a notion he developed while training at the Robert Brookings Graduate School of Economics and Government in Washington, D.C. Following short teaching appointments at the University of North Carolina and Rutgers, Cassidy headed up the Department of Social Service at the University of Toronto. Then, in 1934, he became the Director of Social Welfare in British Columbia. As he informed Carlton McNaught in 1943, he had become a convert to the 'mixed economy' approach of the PEP.[169] Though he feared that this kind of planning might result in economic power being concentrated in the hands of businessmen, he abjured centralized government planning. In his view, socialism had gone wrong by placing an overwhelming emphasis on government ownership and planning: 'I am not clear as to how a survival of a genuine political democracy can be guaranteed when all economic power is under the control of the state.' Thus, while Cassidy countenanced a 'general framework of economic and social control,' he nevertheless advocated government decentralization and instructed the CCF to concentrate on raising the standard of living of the sturdy, skilled labouring classes without too much 'socialization of everything.'[170] Given the limited view of government intervention expounded by Marsh and Cassidy, both of whom were to serve as policy 'experts' for Liberal governments, it is not surprising that Harold Innis would observe in 1936 that far from explicating a socialist perspective, *Social Planning for Canada* perfectly embodied the economic and political philosophy of Mackenzie King.[171]

It must be admitted that up to a point, Charlotte Whitton defended relief programs, as part of her defence of social work control of welfare policies (as James Struthers has argued[172]); but it is equally clear that her ideas about the benefits of unemployment insurance were not as different from those of the self-proclaimed modern economists as has been maintained. This is not to say that Whitton was any less conservative in her outlook than historians have argued (although I would insist that historians have often read the Whitton of the wartime era back into the 1930s); rather, it is to demonstrate that the self-styled new economists were not as radical as has been previously contended, especially when the principles undergirding their ideal of government planning are placed under close scrutiny, and approached from the perspective of how they redefined notions of dependency and in terms of how they reconstructed welfare entitlements along exclusively male-gendered lines.

The 1934 exchange between Charlotte Whitton, Tom Moore, Harry Cassidy, and Leonard Marsh demonstrates the degree to which policies emanating from different political perspectives could galvanize around a single consensual notion regarding the pre-eminence of the rights of the male worker and family breadwinner. Struthers sees the problem in terms of relief versus insurance and has postulated that the division in opinion pitted Whitton against Moore, Cassidy, and Marsh. I would argue that it was Tom Moore who was the minority voice because he protested fiercely against those policies endorsed by the others that would have restricted relief to provincial and municipal levels of government.[173] Moore and Whitton did agree, however, on the need to include unskilled and seasonal workers within the purview of unemployment insurance policies – a point of view to which Marsh and Cassidy objected strongly.[174] On the whole, Cassidy and Marsh concurred with Whitton's welfare prescriptions, although they disliked that she wished to emphasize forms of dependency outside of male unemployment.[175] Despite his reservations, Marsh declared Whitton's statement 'a constructive one'; and Cassidy remarked that he was 'in general agreement with the line of argument which you adopt.' What Marsh and Cassidy objected to most, however, was that Whitton emphasized forms of dependency beyond unemployment; if implemented, her policy might have detracted from their own campaign for unemployment insurance, which aimed at creating a new, exclusive niche of welfare rights for the fully employable, the majority of whom were able-bodied men. Marsh and Cassidy recommended a stricter division between relief and unemployment insurance; Whitton retorted with some accuracy that a system of unemployment insurance would not help the unskilled and as such would be ignoring the equally intractable problem of female dependency. As a remedy for those forms of destitution which fell outside unemployment, Whitton proposed a broader scheme of contributory social insurance for illness and widowhood.[176] In many respects, Whitton's proposals for social insurance were far broader in scope than the strongly male-oriented unemployment insurance recommendations of Marsh and Cassidy. In this one respect, Whitton's recommendations of 1934 were much more the harbinger of the 1943 social security recommendations of Leonard Marsh, than the Depression era outlook of either Marsh or Cassidy.

What Marsh, Whitton, and Cassidy did agree on was that state-managed insurance schemes, in which the worker contributed to his own welfare benefits, were an ideal form of welfare assistance because they reinforced the work ethic and sustained the notions of independence that were so cherished by the working class. Moreover, all three policy experts believed that women did not form a 'justifiable charge' on the State because their dependency did not arise primarily from joblessness.[177] Moreover, like Marsh and Cassidy, Whitton associated the positive values of economic security, integrity, individuality, self-reliance, and freedom with virility, and juxtaposed these with the female submissiveness engendered by dependency.[178] Just as Cassidy and Marsh saw unemployment insurance programs as an acknowledgment by the State of the rights of the male breadwinner, Whitton spoke of them in terms of their ability to uphold the 'the integrity of that individual who has made an effort to establish himself.'[179] While always a reluctant convert to government insurance programs, Whitton defended them from the point of view that if such policies 'developed along the line of joint protective plans in which the working citizen and the State join to provide savings or insurance,' they would sustain 'individual initiative, integrity and self-reliance' while at the same time providing the necessary 'protection of the worker of low income in the modern industrial state.'[180]

Because unemployment insurance policies were intended to keep up the 'independent character of the workingman,'[181] advocates for them pointed out that they must mirror the family wage, which was deemed to be the legitimate right of the male wage earner. Thus in his submission to the Rowell-Sirois Commission on Dominion-Provincial Relations, Leonard Marsh fiercely opposed the inclusion of graded children's allowances, which had been an important feature of R.B. Bennett's abortive 1935 legislation,[182] like all policymakers, he feared that these might raise the family's total income to such a level as to invalidate the principle of lesser eligibility.[183] More interestingly, both Marsh and Cassidy took the position that if unemployment insurance provided too generously for dependants, it might interfere with the 'modern' concept of the singular family wage. In their view, unemployment insurance was meant to help break down older concepts of the family – wherein the wife and children contributed to the household economy – by forcing all dependants to survive, with no extra allowances, on the unemployment benefits 'earned' by the male contributor alone.[184] These proposals were conservative in the sense that they did not seek to alter the balance between government intervention and free market forces. Bryce Stewart, one of Canada's foremost experts on social insurance, stated that he was anxious to 'reduce government contributions' and excessive 'government tinkering'[185] with individual initiative. Similarly, Marsh and Cassidy delineated the conservative bias inherent in Canadian welfare legislation. Both rejected the idea of incorporating family allowances into unemployment insurance benefits, maintaining that it was not the function of such a program 'to attempt to redress the inadequacy of current wages for relatively large families.' The State, far from revamping the rules of the marketplace, was to serve as the guarantor of the fundamental harmonies of supply and demand. Cassidy and Marsh confirmed that they were devotees of the older, *laissez-faire* liberal verities when they stated that unemployment insurance must ideally function as 'an extension of the *wage* system.'[186]

The widespread tendency at the beginning of the Depression to merge the private and public management of relief had been wholly transformed by the late 1930s,[187] when champions of unemployment insurance and of a system of rights-based welfare entitlements for 'employable' male workers promoted the concept of a strict demarcation between contributory insurance and relief, and between public and private welfare, and between notions of social and economic dependency. This reorientation in welfare entitlements had devastating implications for the rights of women and their access to government assistance, for it established a distinctly two-tier system of welfare benefits and thus extinguished previous concepts of maternalist social citizenship. Henceforth, citizenship rights were defined exclusively in terms of one's ability to work. As Whitton told Ernest Blois, Nova Scotia's Director of Child Welfare, in 1934, the trend in public welfare in Canada was for the federal government to assume increasing responsibility for unemployment insurance, old age pensions, and health insurance. 'I believe that this trend is unavoidable in an industrial civilization and that it can be handled in Canada only federally,' explained Whitton. 'If the Dominion power takes responsibility in these fields, I think that you will see all the detail of direct relief whether for unemployment or any other cause, of general child welfare etc., and all hospitalization and health, medical and nursing care, on the basis of relief of indigents rather than of insurance go very definitely into the hands of the provinces.'[188]

Whitton's prognostications were very accurate, with the qualifier that her promotion of contributory widows' pensions never became a feature of later comprehensive Dominion social security programs. She was correct, also, in situating the demise of female and maternal welfare entitlements in the context of the public debates over whether unemployment assistance – in fact relief given to workers who had gone beyond their unemployment insurance benefits – would become incorporated into federal contributory programs. Indeed, the question of whether unemployment relief would be considered in relation to other forms of poor relief, such as mothers' allowances, old age pensions, and medical assistance to the indigent, was one of the key issues debated by the Rowell–Sirois Commission, in that it had important implications for the future balance between federal and provincial jurisdictions.

Cassidy believed that the Depression had undermined the rights of male workers by conflating poor relief with unemployment benefits, and he actively sought to use the constitutional debates of the late 1930s to legally segregate the problem of 'periodic unemployment' from the hard core of 'impotent poor.'[189] One of the most intensely debated issues during the Rowell–Sirois Commission was whether unemployment assistance – government aid granted to workers when their insurance benefits ran out – should be a Dominion or a provincial concern. The National Employment Commission favoured federal control, as did G.F. Towers, the Governor of the Bank of Canada[190]; they saw both forms of government welfare (i.e., unemployment insurance and relief) as related to regulating the workplace and as offshoots of public works programs. Charlotte Whitton and Harry Cassidy strongly opposed this perspective; in confining unemployment assistance to lower levels of government, they hoped at the same time to carefully prescribe the limits of poor relief. Cassidy believed that the poor law principle still had integrity but that it should be restricted to the local levels of government. His reasoning was that in such a position at the 'base' of the welfare field, it could continue to encourage assistance from private charities.[191] Whitton likewise championed this view, urging that 'the relief of dependency through unemployability and from various social causes' could be more easily managed if unemployment assistance was also assigned to provincial authority.[192] Interestingly, while the foremost advocates of unemployment insurance – namely, Arthur Purvis, Cassidy, and Marsh – firmly believed in making the provinces the exclusive preserve of all old age assistance, mothers' allowances, and child welfare programs, Whitton recommended a two-tier system within mothers' allowances themselves, whereby wealthier families could pay into a contributory widows' pension scheme at the federal level.[193] Cassidy went so far as to propose that mothers' allowances and old age pensions be administered at the municipal level![194] From the point of view of Whitton, Marsh, and Cassidy, if one wished to integrate all public assistance at the provincial and local levels, it was imperative to likewise demote unemployment assistance to a needs-based category beyond the federal jurisdiction.

The national government was intended to be the preserve of all rights-based programs. Cassidy explained to Arthur Purvis, one of the architects of the Canadian Unemployment Insurance Act of 1940, that he rejected the idea of a dominion–provincial partnership in the sphere of job rehabilitation because 'when it comes to the administrative organization of the public assistance services, I am inclined to adopt the same position as the Welfare Council – that unemployment assistance can best be administered by the provinces and local authorities.' Cassidy had reached such a position because from his point of view, '"unemployment assistance" ... is closely related to other types of assistance such as general poor relief, old age assistance, and mother's pensions ... If all these services are grouped under the one governmental authority there is far greater likelihood of efficiency and economy in administration.'[195] In other words, men who did not obtain work after exhausting their unemployment insurance benefits were to be treated like other 'dependants' and to be exposed to the stigma of poor relief as further encouragement to fulfilling the work ethic.

The report of the Rowell–Sirois Commission has been seen as a significant benchmark in dominion–provincial relations because it confirmed centralizing tendencies within the federation. Yet this conclusion is not supported when the contributions of the welfare experts are examined in detail. Their recommendations were intended to reinforce 'decentralized administration,'[196] in large part to protect the exclusivity of rights-based contributory federal welfare programs. As it turned out, the debates of the Rowell–Sirois Commission foreshadowed the modern-day bifurcation between 'welfare' and 'social security,' the former term being derogatory, the latter referring to programs of higher status intended to assist those who made vital economic contribution to the nation through work. But by expanding the boundaries of needs-based poor relief at the local level, where casework investigation was more effective, Cassidy, Marsh, and Whitton were also defending the notion of limited governmental expenditure and intervention.[197]

Thus when Cassidy stated that the future of public welfare in Canada depended on the federal government assuming greater power, he meant that it should exclusively administer and fund the élite contributory insurance programs related to the problem of male unemployment.[198] Similarly, when he stated that he eschewed welfare according to need, he meant that means testing was anathema only with regard to the male wage earner.[199] As he informed the Rowell–Sirois Commission, it was important to distinguish between social insurance 'given as a right irrespective of economic need' and public assistance for the 'essentially under-privileged,' which in his view included non-contributory old age assistance, mothers' allowances, and ordinary relief.[200] Although Cassidy cast the promotion of a two-tiered national welfare system, which placed all government aid outside of unemployment relief in the hands of the provinces, in terms of defending the 'techniques of democracy,'[201] his vision of the future of public welfare in Canada was rooted in a highly gendered sense of welfare citizenship. While it may be true that he advocated provincial authority over child welfare, mothers' allowances, and relief as a means to counteract dangerous concentrations of power at the federal level, his critique of the 'socialized state' was also a means to further privilege the problem of male unemployment as against female social dependency, the plight of the 'socially abnormal.'[202]

The debate over handing the problem of female dependency over to the provincial and municipal spheres revolved around the definition of 'employables.' This question simmered beneath the surface of relief discussions throughout the Depression; it also surfaced with particular force during the hearings of the National Employment Commission. Because the provinces made no contributions for relief for unemployables, it became common practice for municipal leaders to categorize as many of the local destitute as possible as employables so as to off-load these people onto higher levels of government.[203] To argue convincingly for a national system of unemployment relief, it was crucial to show that unemployment rather than other forms of destitution constituted the largest dependency problem and thus should form the crux of political solutions. More importantly, policy experts were well aware that in Britain, the government unemployment fund became insolvent after too many classes of beneficiaries were included in it.[204] It thus became increasingly imperative to demote those types of dependency not traceable to 'industrial hazards.'[205] Leonard Marsh had defined unemployables as those who are 'neither a part of the true labour supply nor do they properly come within the scope of measures designed for the "normal" unemployed.'[206] The formidable area of dispute was not how to define the aged and incapacitated, but how to categorize unemployed women. Female dependency was thus the catalyst behind limiting federal assistance to 'employable unemployed and their dependants.'[207] As both Leonard Marsh and the members of the

National Employment Commission concluded, women could be legitimately excluded from becoming beneficiaries of federal aid simply by virtue of their gender, for women were 'by the nature of things ... dependent domestically' on someone else. They were therefore classed as 'non-worker type dependants.'[208] Thus, men were not penalized if they were not 'self-supporting,' yet unemployed women were instructed to furnish 'definite evidence' to show that they were capable of self-support. This punitive decree denied federal aid to married women with male breadwinners; it was also designed to exclude almost all women – deserted wives, unmarried mothers, separated and divorced women, and women with incapacitated husbands – from rights-based, federally funded welfare programs.[209]

Even within the restrictive terms of eligibility laid down by the federal government, the provinces and municipalities imagined incipient bases for rights-based entitlements and new means to widen government welfare commitments. 'If persons were formally declared ... to be not fully employable,' observed a perspicacious Ontario government official, 'it would be almost inevitable that all onus of finding self-supporting employment, or even partial employment, would be removed from their shoulders. Such persons would have every justification for taking the position they could not be responsible for their own support and must receive full and permanent relief assistance as a *right*.'[210] The aim of the federal government was not simply to burden the provinces with long-term dependency cases, as was suspected; in addition, it was to shift the burden of maintaining dependent women onto the family, headed by a responsible, working breadwinner.

In order to uphold the male breadwinner ideal, it was important to define all wives and mothers as 'non-worker type dependants.'[211] Harry Baldwin, the federal superintendent of relief, canvassed and compiled various perspectives on the problem, and concluded in 1936 that the majority of women on relief were unemployable 'either because of age, mental or physical handicaps, temperament etc.'[212] Many of his respondents had great difficulty circumventing the fact that one could not simply judge a woman unemployable because she was on relief, for by this logic most men would also be excluded from federal welfare programs. Many government respondents, like A.W. Barbour, the New Brunswick Deputy Minister of Public Works, invoked widely held assumptions about gendered roles in the workplace. Barbour quickly dismissed the argument of the municipalities that women on relief were in fact 'employable' because in normal economic times they could find work and be self-supporting, suggesting that this was 'a little far fetched' because in his view women were, by virtue of their sex alone, unemployable.[213] In a similar vein, the National Employment Commission argued that even though there were an estimated 15,000 families in Canada headed by women in full-time employment, they too would henceforth be ineligible for federal assistance because most of these had not been working previous to the Depression.[214] In short, women's paid work did not constitute a 'normal' part of the Canadian labour market.

Some objected to these overly rigid categories of employable and unemployable. H.A. Weir, one of the foremost advocates of youth training, opposed the federal government's interpretation of *unemployable* as those not having paid work, because this would render most of Canada's inexperienced young adults ineligible for federal relief and work training programs.[215] His criticism, however, revolved around the issue of male experience in the workplace and did not address the gender question head on. Harry Cassidy did go to the heart of the problem when he observed that the term 'employability' was 'a very relative term' and could be just as easily applied to men who, having been unemployed for some years, were no longer considered skilled or experienced workers in their chosen trade.[216] Another wrinkle was added by the Manitoba Assistant Deputy Minister of Public Works, S. McNamara, who disputed the strictures that Baldwin intended to place around women's ability to be self-supporting. As he skilfully argued, while many women, especially middle-aged women, no longer worked in the area in which they had been trained, they nevertheless had gained valid work experience in other, less skilled areas, thus making them in many cases more 'employable' than many men on relief.[217] However, despite consistent evidence that in large numbers of families women were the primary breadwinners,[218] Baldwin rendered obsolete female claims to legitimately be considered workers with full citizenship rights and with unrestrained access to either federal relief or unemployment insurance, when he stated that 'even by the laxest standard,'[219] only a few women could be considered employable.

In the wake of the National Employment Commission, the idea of an individual's 'life-long struggle for self-maintenance'[220] was peculiarly gender-specific, being ascribed exclusively to the male wage earner. Those dependent on government benefits who were not 'unemployment problems' – namely, women – were henceforth labelled 'social problems' and included as part of the great, unmoveable mass of 'chronic indigents,' which included the socially inadequate, those with personality problems, and the mentally and physically defective.[221] Exponents of maternalist welfare entitlements had based a woman's citizenship rights on her reproductive services to the nation; Depression-era policy experts such as Harry Cassidy no longer acknowledged that women rendered a contribution to the common weal. Cassidy maintained that women should be categorized with the unfit and the defective because,[222] unlike war veterans or skilled male workers, they did not receive 'state funds in return for services rendered by themselves or by their deceased breadwinners, or as a matter of contractual right.'[223] Similarly, Bryce Stewart endorsed the idea of a two-tier welfare state, one in which women and children would rank among the 'unfit'[224] who deserved only a 'residual program' of 'general assistance.'[225] Women no longer had independent access to the more meritorious forms of public welfare such as unemployment insurance; henceforth, their welfare entitlements were to be derived solely from their function as wives or dependants of male contributors. The *Interim Report of the National Employment Commission* concluded that women were among those 'not available for employment in any ordinary sense of the word' and that their economic security should ideally be provided through private means, for once the male heads of families could be placed in jobs 'the problem of their non-working dependants automatically disappears.'[226] If female dependency was thought to be 'individual' in origin, the result of 'personality defects,'[227] then its remedy likewise lay in the private realm, ideally the 'normal' family headed by a male breadwinner.

Far from functioning as the precursor of the modern social security state, unemployment insurance reinforced well-entrenched traditions of perceiving welfare policies as yet another means by which 'to enforce an adequate discharge of the responsibilities devolving upon heads of families to dependent wives and children.'[228] In keeping with this overall pattern of using welfare policies to encourage work incentives among male workers so as to ensure that families remained economically independent, by 1941 there was virtually no relief for able-bodied 'employable' men.[229] For the first time, dependency was seen as a largely female condition[230] – as the obverse of the male capacity to work.

The Depression was an era of fundamental ideological change, and nowhere was this more evident than in the sphere of welfare policy. The new conceptions of welfare entitlements that were forged during the Depression in turn transformed the gendered vision of the family. After 1940 the family was no longer seen as a primarily spiritual entity headed by an equal but separate moral mother and a breadwinning father. During the 1930s the ideal of separate spheres broke down; waged labour and male citizenship were reified, and as a result the maternalist ethos, social and moral values, and culture itself were subsumed into this economic vision. The family was no longer viewed as the foundation of society; rather, the individual and his work were seen as the only engines of national progress and social cohesion. By the end of the decade, both the family and the workplace were deemed to be the legitimate domains of the male wage earner. In this way, the Depression sowed the seeds of secularization – a process that was profoundly gendered.

Prior to the 1930s, the critical mass of dependency was defined as female; but because women were seen to be crucial to the production of national wealth (in that they reproduced and educated future citizens), reformers and governments created for them specially non-stigmatizing welfare entitlements, such as mothers' allowances, which in popular understanding were seen as a statutory right. This maternalist trajectory of welfare policymaking was arrested by the Depession. In the 1930s, unemployment became the public's overwhelming preoccupation, with the result that dependency now was seen to be a male phenomenon. Widespread unemployment was believed to be corroding the traditional right and duty of male breadwinners to maintain their dependants and establish family independence and self-sufficiency. This persistent concern with upholding the status of male breadwinners – especially skilled wage earners – led to a radical reversal of welfare entitlements; maternal contributions to the common good were consigned to a clear second place in this new welfare paradigm, which privileged paid labour as the sole foundation of welfare rights. In reaction to the perceived reordering of gender roles that policy experts believed was occurring in the labour market, the legitimacy of women's claims to paid labour was eradicated. The spectre of gender disorder was the catalyst in this process of redefining employability as a quality pertaining solely to men. The economic turmoil of the 1930s thus irrevocably destroyed the balance between the sexes, and between home and work.

This regendering of social relations and of welfare entitlements entailed also the destruction of the notion of the working class family as an interdependent unit – one in which the male breadwinner's income was always supplemented by the ancillary contributions of wives and children. This notion of sharing the work ethic within the family was enshrined in welfare schemes such as mothers' allowances; but it, too, became a casualty of the Depression after the concept of a living wage was replaced by an ideal of a family wage in which work was an individual possession of the male breadwinner alone. This individualization of work was in turn incorporated into and reinforced by welfare legislation such as unemployment insurance, which eschewed the concept of separate children's allowances in the belief that it was the responsibility of the male beneficiary to support his dependants.

The Depression amplified previous notions that the male breadwinner was the economic head of his family. All welfare initiatives were thus aimed at protecting his ability to maintain his family. During the 1930s the work ethic became identified entirely with the status of the male breadwinner; and for this reason, waged labour occupied a privileged place in the calculations of policy experts and government officials. It was primarily to protect the morale of men that clearly rights-based welfare policies were initiated. The campaign for a national program of unemployment insurance for 'legitimate' workers (i.e., skilled male labourers) led to a stratification within welfare programs, whereby work skills and gender became enmeshed. While the stated goal of unemployment insurance was to protect the steady, thrifty, skilled worker, it had distinct gender implications: since work done by women had come to be categorized as both temporary and unskilled, their claims to higher-status welfare benefits were eviscerated. Thereafter, there was a clear and irrefutable two-tier system of welfare aid: a federally funded, rights-based scheme of unemployment insurance and relief for men, and a needs-based system for women administered by the provinces and municipalities. By the early 1940s, poor relief had come to be identified almost exclusively with female dependency. Women were deemed unfit for the full benefits of welfare citizenship because they were deemed to be ineligible to work, and thus idle non-contributors to the nation's wealth. This momentous reversal in statutory welfare rights had far-reaching implications for the social security state that emerged at the end of the Second World War; even policies such as family allowances, which were not directly linked with unemployment or the labour market, were conceived wholly in terms of protecting the pre-eminence of the male breadwinner. Ideologically, the wartime incarnation of family allowances was unrelated either to women's economic independence, or to the protection of children, or to the relief of poverty among the working classes. Family allowances were seen as a key reconstruction measure because all shades of political opinion identified them as the chief spur to full employment for men and as the bulwark of the national policy of economic efficiency. The modern social security system did not represent a clear ideological departure; rather, it was the direct progeny of the Depression decade.

7

Reconstructing Families:
Family Allowances and the Politics of
Postwar Abundance

The scope of government has changed. The main function of the state used to be to hold the ring between competing interests. That was the neutral state. It has changed into the positive state, here and in Great Britain, ... and everywhere else. The state is now looked upon as a primary agency for promoting economic welfare and improving standards of living.

Brooke Claxton, 'What's Wrong with Parliament?,' Maclean's Magazine, 1 March 1943

The essential premise [is] that social security policies will have only limited success unless they are adopted as part of a programme to maintain a high level of employment and economic prosperity.

Harry Cassidy to Nora Lea, 24 February 1945

A woman's sense of not belonging in the social order, or of belonging only through citizenship gained through some male, is founded not on hypersensitivity but on plain fact.

Hope Stoddard, 'No Women Being Hired,' Canadian Forum, June 1946

The Great Depression has been perceived largely as a regressive period characterized by punitive and repressive relief measures built around a social philosophy which argued from a Christian perspective that the fear of starvation was necessary because it was what goaded individuals to seek economic salvation through work, thrift, and ambition. From this vantage point, the emergence of the comprehensive social security program embodied in Leonard Marsh's *Report on Social Security for Canada* has been viewed as the decisive watershed in Canadian welfare history – as the fulcrum of what we have come to define as the modern social security state.[1]

Alternatively, the 1930s might be viewed as fallow ground, beneath which new cultural perspectives were germinating. Michael Bliss has maintained that if Canadian history contains one dramatic cultural moment, it was the widespread rejection during wartime of the nineteenth-century notion that the work ethic – and indeed all social progress – is propelled by individual struggle and the fear of starvation. Between 1942 and 1945 it became increasingly common for politicians, social investigators, and ordinary Canadians, to stress that the *absence* of economic fears was an essential precondition for national economic and social well-being. Hope, not struggle, became the watchword for the new ideal of social security. Poverty, contended Bessie Touzel, the director of the Toronto Welfare Council, simply created individual and social paralysis.[2] Thus during the war democracy and individual liberty came to be closely identified with freedom from want, and for the first time a loose yet broad cultural consensus was forming around the idea, first enunciated by Winston Churchill, that an interventionist state, and one which provided monetary assistance, was not fundamentally in conflict with the old creed of self-reliance.[3]

In another important respect, the network of welfare entitlements established during the Depression set the parameters for wartime welfare initiatives, most particularly the introduction of family allowances in 1944. As I argued in the previous chapter, the 1930s reoriented the gender basis of welfare rights. In that bleak period of economic depression, the focus of social policies shifted away from the earlier preoccupation with family reproduction toward a singular emphasis on waged labour as the passport for welfare assistance. This male-centred system of welfare citizenship was not overthrown by the events of the Second World War, despite the popular perception that family allowances were designed to recognize the rights of non-working dependants within the family – namely, mothers and children. Certainly there were sporadic utterances, such as that of the social worker Elizabeth Wallace, that family allowances meant 'that children take their rightful place as one of the country's greatest assets.'[4] Such an outlook was in fact the swan song of the older, child welfare paradigm, which was to be obliterated by the influence of the new cadre of economic and social welfare experts, which included Leonard Marsh, Harry Cassidy, Margaret Gould, and Bessie Touzel.[5] Elizabeth Wallace, who like Charlotte Whitton had her intellectual roots in early twentieth-century charity and child rescue work, had been a mothers' allowance administrator and remained a staunch defender of nineteenth-century liberalism, as symbolized by her laudatory postwar biography of the Victorian man of letters, Goldwin Smith. Certainly the King Liberals used the language and iconography of children's rights as emotive symbols by which to propagandize on the benefits of family allowances.[6] However, such language must not be equated with the government's real intentions.

A close investigation of the minds of the policymaking élite – those individuals and groups who actually formulated government policy – together with a study of the economic and social imperatives driving the federal government's policies, yields a very different interpretation. Far from being a humanitarian social policy aimed at eliminating poverty,[7] family allowances were conceived and introduced by the King government primarily as a means to foster postwar consumption, which in turn would ensure full employment, economic equilibrium, and social stability.[8] The Family Allowances Act of 1944 was the offspring of young Keynesian activists in the government such as Principal F. Cyril James, who headed the Committee on Reconstruction, his research advisor, Leonard Marsh, and experts within the powerful Economic Advisory Council. While many social commentators endorsed family allowances in the belief that they were the proper nucleus for a comprehensive postwar social security package, their hopes for more generous unemployment benefits, health insurance, and old age pensions were foiled by the ingenuity of Mackenzie King and his government. The fact that the Liberal government introduced *only* family allowances, and no other security measures, well demonstrated (as contemporary observers noted[9]) the degree to which policymakers conceived of children's allowances as wholly severed from social imperatives and humanitarian concerns. The major promoters within government of these family bonuses envisioned them as a fiscal measure alone, and saw in family allowances the ultimate safeguard of traditional values. Family allowances would protect the commitment to a small state by obviating the need for more extensive programs such as unemployment insurance; not only that, but they would also shore up the concept of lesser eligibility. In addition, such cash payments would uphold the belief, widespread during wartime, in the individual's freedom to choose and spend. Most importantly, by creating jobs for men, they would strongly reinforce the time-honoured verities of the family wage, the responsibilities of the male breadwinner, and family self-sufficiency. In the final analysis, family allowances, far from forming a radical new departure – as Sir William Beveridge and Leonard Marsh so often proclaimed – were a distinctly conservative government intiative that preserved and indeed amplified the gendered welfare state.

World War and the Yearning for a 'Sense of Security'[10]

On the eve of the Second World War, the Ex-Servicemen's Widows Association, together with the Canadian Soldiers' Non-pensioned Widows' Association, lobbied the federal government for an independent right for women to a war service pension on the basis that they had allowed their husbands to fight in the Great War and that they had contributed equally to the defence of the nation both by nursing their husbands and by raising a new generation of healthy and fit citizens.[11] As the response of the Minister of Pensions and National Health, the Hon. C.G. Power, made abundantly clear, the responsibility of the government to provide aid in cases of demonstrable need stopped abruptly with the death of the soldier husband. In other words, these women had no statutory rights apart from their husband's ability to work and provide for them while they were alive. The debate that ensued revolved around whether the fact of widowhood alone or actual disability of the soldier formed the criterion for state welfare support. To recognize women's independent claims for government assistance would establish new parameters of governmental obligation; more disturbingly, it would also transgress the pre-eminence of male welfare rights that had been so studiously defended through new federal welfare programs such as unemployment insurance.

The claims of the 10,000 surviving First World War widows that they had served the State just as much as their husbands by protecting their families were quickly dismissed by government officials. 'In war, public service may be required from every citizen,' asserted Brigadier General H.F. MacDonald, chairman of the Canadian Pension Committee, 'and to recognize that service as a future basis of compensation from the State, would be to abandon the principles of proper citizenship as well as the principle that [a] pension is compensation for actual disability or handicap suffered through service.'[12] Mothers' allowances were first instituted during the Great War as a pension analogous to compensation for soldiers.[13] However, by 1939, welfare policies had been retooled so that they no longer emphasized family reproduction as the cornerstone of national regeneration, but instead emphasized waged labour as the fundamental criterion for welfare entitlements. As a result, motherhood no longer constituted an independent claim on the State. Like all other unemployable women, needy and aged war widows were perceived to be a 'social problem' and so eligible only for municipal relief.[14] Any rights women did have for federal government aid, they derived solely through their role as wives. And while the Second World War would see a great expansion in popular support for more comprehensive social security measures, this did not alter the gendered logic of the modern welfare state; rather, gendered notions of work and welfare were *reinforced* through the incubus of war.

This limited vision of state responsibility asserted by C.G. 'Chubby' Power in 1939, which was based on the belief that women had no welfare rights independent of their husbands, was entirely accepted by the federal government with respect to its policies for assisting military families during the war. As soon as mobilization for war began in the fall of 1939, the federal government established the Dependents' Allowance Board, which provided a system of supplementary allowances to help offset the low rates of pay for common soldiers and junior officers. That the government did not envision this board as a significant new foray extending government powers was made clear by the emphasis that officials placed on the fact that the primary responsibility for the welfare of military families remained with the male breadwinner, who was himself to assign a great deal of his pay before any government supplements might be awarded to his dependants. During the First World War the federal government had departed significantly from established practice by creating a government agency to assume total responsibility for maintaining soldiers' families. Now, on the eve of the Second World War, officials from the Department of National Defence were taking pains to emphasize that their new powers did not commit them to any new welfare initiatives. Expenditures from the Dependents' Allowance Board, they maintained, were not 'paid of right.' As A.B. Brown, the acting chairman of the Dependents' Allowance Board, and a veteran of the First World War, declared:

Allowances made to soldiers are not paid as remuneration for services rendered but are purely grants made to encourage recruiting and to maintain the morale of the individual soldier and the army as a whole. In general, dependents' allowances are granted for the same purpose, that is to say, to encourage recruiting and to relieve the soldier from anxiety as to the financial welfare of his dependents. I do not believe that it is the proper thing to do that the enlistment of a man in the defence forces during war-time places himself in the same category as a wage earner drawing salary or wages in a civil occupation.[15]

To underscore the official perception that a man and a wife formed one marriage unit, wives who 'in the nature of things' were dependent domestically on their husbands because they were 'non-worker type dependants' were automatically entitled, once the soldier assigned his pay and thus officially denoted her role as a dependant.[16] In contrast to British military practice in 1939, whereby all soldiers' dependants were means tested,[17] Canadian wives received their allowances automatically by virtue of their marital relationship. Wives of British soldiers, however, were granted government assistance only when they had children. In Britain, motherhood still formed the foundation stone for wartime state entitlements for women.[18] In contrast, common law wives in Canada who had lived with the soldier for at least two years previous to enlistment were fully entitled to both his assigned pay and a dependants' allowance, even if they were childless. The Canadian dependants' allowances were not de jure a statutory right; however, in practice a wife's 'pay'[19] was wholly conditioned by her husband's war service, and as such seen to be an extension of the husband's work for the nation and his citizenship rights.

The privileges of wives were distinctly superior to those of mothers of soldiers, who had to prove, through extensive investigation, that their sons had fully supported them prior to enlistment – an often difficult feat, given that a large proportion of soldiers under the age of twenty-one had never worked and had themselves been maintained by government relief.[20] And even mothers who could demonstrate both dependency and need were eligible for a mere five days' assigned pay – a meagre $6.50 per month – if their sons had married prior to embarking for overseas service.[21] These rulings created considerable hardship for mothers of soldiers who were widowed; they also created tremendous resentment among mothers, who believed that the contributions of older children belonged to them by right. As the Secretary of the Child Welfare Board of Manitoba, Gertrude Childs, remarked, widows believed that they were fully 'entitled' to federal government benefits for their 'services rendered' as mothers, particularly 'where families would be self-supporting from the earnings of these older children who enlist and would also apply to families where the enlistment of the son makes the family dependant, who had otherwise been self-supporting.'[22]

However, by the Second World War a decisive cultural shift had occurred. In the wake of the Depression, during which there was heightened urgency surrounding the problems of youth unemployment and inadequate technical training, which together gave rise to the increased problem of late marriages (and, it followed, increased sexual impropriety among Canadian youth), government officials and social workers began to campaign against older government policies that compelled older children to contribute their wages to the household.[23] In part also, this was a government response to the problem that working-class young people were refusing to contribute to the family unit.[24] As a result, the Dependents' Allowance Board's policies had built into them strategies that allowed older children to pursue higher levels of education and demanded only that working children pay the mother for their room and board. They were thus no longer obligated to forgo their own personal savings, which government policymakers preferred to see invested in postwar marriage and the creation of stable family life.[25] In lieu of enforcing employment among 'teenagers' – a term first used in Canada in wartime – the Department of National Defence advocated a better system of children's military allowances, paid on a sliding scale to take into account the special needs of older children.[26]

That a woman's capacity as a mother was no longer deemed the foundation of her right to public assistance during the Second World War was demonstrated by the fact that a wife was automatically granted $35.00 per month even if she did not have any children; whereas during the Great War the Canadian Patriotic Fund penalized childless women by severely restricting their benefits. The Depression-era emphasis on the male family wage had so permeated welfare ideology that even during wartime, policymakers continued to regard married women as unemployables. Despite the increasing need for female labour, the Department of National Defence (DND) was reluctant to make deductions from wives – even if they had no children and were

thus able to work – out of the conviction that her government cash provision was an extension of husbands' citizenship rights to full government support while they were 'in the service of His Majesty.'[27]
Denying wives their rights meant breaking with a military convention
'which treat of a married allowance as one of right and not subject to
deduction as to outside income nor subject to be fixed upon the basis
of pre-enlistment support.'[28] And even though the DND allowed
wives to earn an unlimited wage, these women were never viewed as
economically independent individuals, separate from their husbands;
their earnings were valued only because they would create a stable
home environment for the returned soldier. In other words, because
her pay was never deducted from her government assistance, her
wages, however large, were never seen as impinging on the rights of
the male soldier to function as the primary family breadwinner.[29] Similarly, the male breadwinner ideal was promoted by federal employment policies which held that women, even should they undertake
industrial work regularly covered by unemployment insurance, were
not eligible for these benefits after the war if they had an able-bodied
husband to support them. Wartime policies, therefore, reaffirmed the
principles of welfare entitlements, laid down during the Depression,
that permitted female access to such state protection only under the
auspices of the male breadwinner.[30]

Wartime government reinforced the state entitlements of male breadwinners. In addition, the system of dependants' allowances established
a clear wage policy, one that would later undergird the civil Family
Allowances Act. The family wage supplied entirely by the male breadwinner was pegged by wartime military authorities at a level that
would maintain the soldier and three dependants: either a wife and
two children, or any other familial dependants, such as a mother, sister,
or father. In effect, the government was granting a bonus to each soldier over and above the assigned pay he allocated to his wife, sufficient
to support a family of two children. Early in the war, there had been little commitment to a system of children's or family allowances that
would end the anomaly between the breadwinner's wage and family
need, because the military wished to discourage married men with
families from enlisting.[31] During the First World War the wage rate or
combined pay and separation allowances had been established at a
level that would support only the soldier and his wife, so in this respect
soldier families in the Second World War fared somewhat better. However, large families were better maintained during the Great War

because the semi-independent CPF was able to establish its own family policy, which provided grants to an unlimited number of children for families in need. During the Second World War, large families suffered greatly, as there was no CPF to supply this deficiency. Families with more than two children were forced to petition local charitable societies, which had been dragooned by the federal government into acting as the administrators and investigators for the Dependents' Allowance Board. Each local social agency was paid $1.00 per report – a system that continued under the Family Allowances Act of 1944.[32]

Thus state assistance was not allowed to exceed the government definition of what constituted a minimum living wage. This had cataclysmic effects both for families and for social agencies, which were immediately besieged by new military clients. The Protestant and maternal-feminist ideal of a small, intimate family was enshrined in wartime federal policies; according to military authorities, it was the duty of private agencies to supplement 'the men's wages [which] did not cover the needs of a large family.'[33] Most families had only three or four children, but even these suffered greatly once their breadwinners enlisted; in Montreal alone, fully 80 per cent of applicants for supplementary aid had no savings and needed extra funds for mere subsistence needs.[34] So burdensome were the military caseloads that social agencies in Montreal – the Montreal Council of Social Agencies, the Fédération des Oeuvres de Charité Canadienne Française, the Federation of Catholic Charities, the Federation of Jewish Philanthropies, and the Soldiers' Wives League, all of which represented the needs of working-class families – got together to form the Directional Service for the Families of Enlisted Men. Fully 49.7 per cent of their caseloads involved impecunious French-Canadian families; 70 per cent of all new applications were related to either sickness or evictions. Significantly, however, no cases were related to the mismanagement of funds.[35] These family agencies protested strongly that because military families were not indigent, they were not 'legitimate charges on charity.'[36] The social agencies, many of which had seen a 93 per cent increase in their workloads since the war began,[37] were thus the most strenuous advocates for greater government intervention. Even stalwart defenders of family responsibility such as Charlotte Whitton agreed that the country could no longer depend on voluntary effort for welfare services.[38] As a result of this pressure from private family welfare agencies, in 1942 the federal government established the Dependents' Board of Trustees (DBT), which would be responsible for investigating families in need of further supplements to the soldier's wage: for emergencies such as funerals and house fires; for unforeseen medical expenditures; and, if the family had more than two children, for reasons 'owing to no fault of their own.'[39]

The DBT was intended to replace the privately funded CPF. However, its outlook was vastly different from that of its predecessor, even though it was instructed to means test all applicants. Its first chairman, G.M. Weir, British Columbia's former Minister of Health and Welfare and the architect of that province's path-breaking health insurance legislation, strenuously challenged traditional notions of welfare management and quickly established a new set of principles – that would later infuse popular wartime notions of social security. Although all families applying to the DBT were investigated, the moral judgments so characteristic of earlier welfare supervision were almost wholly absent during wartime. In one astounding instance, an enlistee training to fly abducted his young girl and set her up with his 'housekeeper' mistress in Brandon. The social worker observed of the mistress that despite a number of 'unfortunate affairs,' this '[did] not necessarily mean that her character is not what it should be.'[40] In Manitoba, the pejorative attitudes of the social worker Miss Roe, a former visitor with the provincial mothers' allowances board, were overturned by a member of the DBT, who wrote, regarding the home of a Mrs B., a recent immigrant from Britain and an infrequent churchgoer: 'The place is not too clean and I must say that the children are rather dirty looking, but I think they have plenty to eat and they have also enough clothing ... Altogether, this is what we may call a rough place, where cursing is heard more often than prayers, I would not like to have little Marie brought up in that home, but at the same time, I don't think there is ground for supervision, as suggested in your letter.'[41]

The new social attitudes occasioned by wartime exigencies were especially evident in how separated, deserted, and common law wives of soldiers were treated by military authorities. According to military procedure, women who were without a formal separation agreement and who could not demonstrate dependency on the estranged soldier-husband, as well as women who arbitrarily refused to live with the husband (in other words, women who had transgressed the marriage bond), were in effect disentitling themselves to the husband's financial support. A soldier's wife was only entitled to government benefits 'as a matter of right' if she was performing a wife's proper function.[42] Women who deserted the marital home were cast adrift and ordered to 'depend on direct relief for subsistence.'[43] While wartime military assistance was not intended to support people 'who would otherwise be in receipt of public assistance,' the official regulations were interpreted with the greatest of latitude for these 'dependent women' especially when children were involved.[44] In practice, a woman who left her husband who was serving overseas was not disentitled, especially when the case involved cruelty and drinking, such as that of the wife of Michael Miguel. On this occasion, federal authorities directly flouted their own regulations and compelled the recalcitrant husband to assign his pay and allowances to his wife and child.[45] Similarly, John Fleuelling's wife left him in 1941 after he repeatedly abused her when she was pregnant, drank, and (before his enlistment) failed to keep a steady job as a common labourer with Massey Harris in Woodstock. Military officials decided that only her children were entitled to his pay and allowances – though not because of any moral opprobrium directed toward the wife, but rather because she was already working. Nevertheless, the government cheques were still addressed to the wife and mother, though she had deserted her husband.[46]

However much government officials affirmed that wives of soldiers were not entitled by right to government payments, the overriding need to keep up the morale of citizen-soldiers led to the waiving of long-standing preoccupations with the moral, Christian family unit. The degree to which wartime exigencies expunged traditional moral categories is best illustrated by the fact that common law wives were declared equally entitled as legal spouses of soldiers, as long as they had lived with the soldier for at least two years, were known in the community as his wife, and were financially dependent on him. There was also a clause stating that she must not be 'commonly regarded as a loose character.' By March 1940 the term 'unmarried' wife had been abolished, thus eradicating any stigma attached to the absence of a Christian marriage.[47] While protests were registered within the government, especially over the practice of financially maintaining both a legal and a common law wife (which D.M. Ormond claimed was an endorsement of concubinage and contrary to the ideals of a Christian nation), moral irregularities were not treated as a basis for disqualifying women from welfare assistance.[48] If there was a moral tincture to the government's family policy during wartime, it was that the male breadwinner had a 'moral obligation'[49] to maintain his family, whether it was sanctioned by Christianity or legality. The question of soldiers' morale was paramount in determining government decisions. As Captain S.A. Sutton attested: 'It should be recognized that our whole social order depends upon the willingness of men in the Armed Forces to eventually return to their homes and resume their responsibilities as husbands and parents. It would therefore be dangerous as well as impractical in a citizen army to adopt the attitude that men should, even if they could, forget their concern over their dependants.'[50]

Government policy regarding military families was thus perceived as an extension of the breadwinner ideal; in this light, the responsibility of the federal government was a variant on the soldier's personal sense of responsibility toward his dependants. This is why the federal government quickly went to the aid of Mary Oleschuk of Montreal, the common law wife of Sapper Dymtro Panezyszyn, even while his legal wife was sequestered in the Verdun Protestant Hospital for the Insane. Even though investigators discovered that Mary had illegitimate children and was believed to be of 'low' mentality, government administrators provided her with full benefits because the soldier, whose morale was in question, had so requested.[51] The common law wife of gunner Anthony Bouthillier had been forced to work as a waitress after negligent investigators disentitled her because of her illegitimate child. The lawyer of this soldier commented regarding the bungling of investigators who handled this case: 'You have not kept faith with the men who enlisted with the idea that he was leaving his loved ones secured.' Investigators had been attempting to force 'Mrs. Bouthillier' to work. It was finally resolved by the military hierarchy that 'women represented as wives' and as such should be classified 'virtually as wives,' and as such entitled to full state benefits.[52] Women were not disenfranchised because of moral indiscretions even when they had deserted their husbands to begin relationships with enlisted men, despite the protests of civilians and of their own soldier-husbands.[53] One of the few accepted reasons for disentitling a common law wife was that she already had a legitimate husband. In such cases the government believed that the responsibility for support devolved to the legal husband rather than to the government and, by implication, to the soldier with whom she lived.[54] In the name of the breadwinner ideal, government policymakers were fully willing to countenance what some castigated as the subsidization of 'philandering'[55] and illicit sexual relationships. The government's view was that by endorsing government dependants' allowances to both 'immoral' wives and common law wives, they were compelling soldiers to financially maintain their families.

The government's supposed largesse during wartime was thus simply another means for promoting family self-sufficiency after the war ended. The case of airman Irwin Kennedy illustrates the degree to which the military's family policies during wartime were designed to sustain traditional conventions regarding the wage-earning husband and his dependent wife. Kennedy's common law wife had left her abusive 'legal' husband, and had cohabited with Kennedy since 1930. She was refused government military allowances on the legal technicality that she was not dependent on his earnings because she had been compelled to work during the Depression while Kennedy was receiving relief.[56] Thus, although common law and other 'irregular' wives were entitled to government assistance on a 'discretionary' basis,[57] in practice such assistance evolved into rights-based welfare entitlements by virtue of the government's overwhelming compulsion during wartime to artificially uphold the breadwinner's responsibility to maintain his dependants. A woman's status as a dependant, rather than her moral character, was what conferred access to government benefits in time of war.

Likewise, the DBT's grants, although ostensibly based on need, were reinterpreted by the board's chairman, G.M. Weir, as a means to protect family savings so that a threshold of minimum postwar standards of living would be created well above traditional charitable subsistence levels. Weir warned social work administrators against managing recipients' funds, declaring that it was natural for all families to have difficulty in making ends meet. He also eschewed punitive relief philosophies and generously permitted the purchasing of washing machines, chesterfields, and radios as legitimate and normal family expenditures.[58] Federal policymakers saw these supplementary grants as a way to uphold the living standards of white-collar and skilled workers' families, whose standards of living had declined because of the wartime absence of the male breadwinner[59]; in practice, however, these grants were used to elevate the living standards of hundreds of families who had been on relief for several years. In this way, the work of the DBT broke with traditional welfare practices – which sought to punish unskilled and seasonal labourers, who were believed to lack a proper work ethic – by allowing women the luxury of establishing their own budgets.[60] One woman in Selkirk, Manitoba, whose husband had been on relief prior to enlistment, was awarded a substantial grant that allowed her to buy a stove and wallpaper her whole house; another Selkirk soldier's wife was allowed extra funds to send her children for music lessons.[61]

A few women flagrantly misspent their husband's pay (such as one Winnipeg women who married her husband ten days before he enlisted and was reported as having frequent 'booze' parties instead of paying her rent[62]), and were chastised by visiting social investigators. That being said, the watchword of wartime social investigation was *saving* – not simply to build character through thrift, but for the purpose of purchasing a home and its accoutrements after the war. The notion of saving for the purposes of deferred *spending* was for the first time viewed in positive terms, and would later be encapsulated in the famous Beveridge Report, which would contend that means testing destroyed incentives among the working classes.[63] This outlook was informed both by a popular Keynesianism that related national wealth to spending, and by a newfound belief that the hope fostered by economic security was the great bastion of a revivified postwar democracy. As B.K. Sandwell, the editor of *Saturday Night*, remarked in 1943, it was now 'socially undesirable that any citizen should have to go without certain goods or services or a certain income.'[64] It was no longer the duty of the working classes to save against social risk; rather, the new wartime ideology of abundance celebrated purchasing power, which had come to symbolize the very attributes of citizenship: initiative, ambition, and the ability to maintain one's dependants.

In the hundreds of case files of women who applied to the DBT in Manitoba, very few applicants were accused of improvidence. Rather, most were praised for careful household management, despite their obvious overspending. A Ukrainian woman in Winnipeg, whose husband had been on relief for ten years prior to his enlistment, had previously been granted medical assistance from the Ukrainian Sick Benefit Club, and had then run up extensive debts. Even so, investigators granted her requests for more money, arguing that she was trying hard to manage on her funds. This, even though both the woman in question and her husband had previously been convicted of theft.[65] More remarkable was the case of a young Métis woman in Manitoba. Officially, the DND recommended that the funds of all native and Métis wives of soldiers be administered, in the belief that they were by nature improvident. Indeed, based on the reports of various Indian agents, native women were not granted the full amount of their husband's assigned pay and separation allowance unless they agreed to buy War Savings Bonds.[66] In practice, however, Métis women, such as Mrs L. whose husband had absconded with all her war savings to buy drink, were treated more leniently and were in many cases not penalized for the husband's lack of thrift. Mrs L., who at first had been forced to return to her husband, despite her adamant refusal for fear of another pregnancy, was later granted an extra $70.00 per month once it was discovered that her husband had repeatedly failed in his family responsibilities.[67]

This more relaxed wartime attitude toward working-class women infected even such bastions of traditional poor law ideology as the children's aid societies. In Brockville, CAS caseworkers blithely ignored the fact that a soldier's wife had openly formed a sexual liaison with another man, accepting without question her statement that she was her lover's father's nurse. Moreover, even though they had been instructed by the soldier-husband to administer his wife's funds, they claimed that they were allowing the wife 'almost complete latitude in the spending of the allowances and are really doing little more than paying the bills.'[68] For the most part, wives of soldiers were allowed complete discretion in the use of their funds, and were granted munificent supplementary allowances even when their income surpassed their needs, largely because the priority of wartime family policy was to ensure sufficient means by which to 'maintain their homes' while awaiting the breadwinner's return.[69] Thus a soldier's wife in the working class suburb of Charleswood, outside Winnipeg, was awarded an extra government grant, even though she had only one child and lived with her parents, on the basis that she was saving 'in order that the soldier may be able to buy a farm after the war.'[70] Preserving family stability and encouraging of postwar spending power were the underlying goals of the DTB. While seeming to break with the past by allowing a much larger sphere of discretionary spending for women on the homefront, the government's family policy nevertheless affirmed traditional breadwinner norms by stimulating wartime savings so that military families would remain self-sufficient once the breadwinner returned. It was logical, therefore, that Mrs Nellie G. McLearn of Upper Kennectcook, Nova Scotia, was permitted to own a large farm, a nice house, and a new electric washer and stove, as well as an expensive sewing machine, all because she swore that her sons' assigned pay and allowances were being saved so that they could marry and establish their own homes once the conflict ended.[71]

Despite the relative generosity of financial assistance to soldiers' dependants, protests began in 1941 once prices for food and housing began to soar. In response, the federal government granted a cost of living bonus, as it had to civilians employed in war industries, and extended children's allowances up to four children in November 1941.[72] The cost of living bonus did little to dampen agitation among military families, and failed to bridge the gap between wages and family need. Government officials tried hard to avoid paying allowances to large families, arguing that soldiers with more than three dependants should not have enlisted. By the end of 1940 the implementation of home service conscription, together with the escalation of the war in Europe, had rendered this argument obsolete. The federal government now realized that if it failed to extend financial support to large families, enlistment would continue to slacken. As the chairman of the Dependents' Allowance Board informed Maj.-Gen. B.W. Browne, while 'it may be well argued that the Government should not have enlisted men with more than three dependents, unless prepared to provide adequately for all their defendents,' state policymakers could no longer avoid the fact that 'once a man is enlisted, public sentiment places the responsibility for support of the soldier's dependents on the Government.'[73] Indeed, military authorities greatly feared popular agitation, especially in the highly politicized national veterans' organizations, which their spy, Walter S. Woods, reported were even more 'leftward' than in the previous war.[74] In the final months of 1941, dozens of women's and church organizations were lobbying the federal government to follow the lead of Australia, New Zealand, and the United States by granting children's allowances to an unlimited number of dependants.[75] By the fall of 1942, persistent new evidence had been marshalled to show a dramatic, 15 per cent increase in the cost of living, food prices having jumped 26.2 per cent and clothing 19.9 per cent.[76] By 1942 it was no longer possible in political terms to force military dependants to accept Depression-era standards of living. In an effort to avoid paying further cost of living increases – which were in effect indirect pay increases for soldiers – in keeping with their overall federal government policy of national wage restraints, and 'to forestall agitation,' the Minister of National Defence, J.L. Ralston, instituted an across-the-board increase to all soldiers' dependants and increased the allowable number of child dependants to eight, when it was revealed that a mere 8 per cent of military families had over five children.[77]

'The Dominion Government may be said to have entered the welfare field with the present war,' declared George Davidson, the future administrator of family allowances in the Department of National Health and Welfare. 'Some of its welfare responsibilities are older, but the expansion in wartime has been striking. It has entered the fields of housing, of public assistance, of child care, and of community organization, each on a large scale.'[78] Whether the wartime military welfare system directly inspired the later civil movement for social security is difficult to ascertain. On the one hand, some contemporary observers, including Davidson and Margaret Strong, a prominent social worker, who believed that the work of the Dependents' Allowance Board led directly to later achievements in social security.[79] Certainly the DND was pressuring policymakers in the Department of Pensions and Health to have medical benefits, retraining programs, and children's allowances accorded military families extended to the whole civilian population once hostilities ended.[80] On the other hand, there was no direct administrative connection between the work of the Dependents' Allowance Board and the civilian machinery of government; nor does it appear that Leonard Marsh's blueprint for postwar planning was greatly influenced by the activities of this military board.

Payments to children under the Dependents' Allowance Board may not have provided a direct model for the King government's family allowance scheme, even though Leonard Marsh alluded to the fact that 'soldiers, sailors and airmen and their dependants really have a microcosm of social security already.'[81] However, assistance to military families was crucial in defining the broader contours of later family welfare policies in three important respects: it established a downward sliding scale of benefits past the fourth child – a feature directly incorporated into the Family Allowances Act of 1944 and into Marsh's report on social security; it established that the granting of family allowances was unrelated to the mother's unpaid work of raising children but was a concomitant of the male breadwinner's citizenship entitlement; and lastly, it emphasized the notion, among local board administrators, that families must be paid well in order to stimulate postwar consumer spending – a notion that became the cornerstone of the economic and social philosophy of the reconstruction era. In many respects the modern social security state, and especially family allowances, were perceived as a payment to men for their wartime suffering. It was in this context that J.W. Knight, the secretary of the Unemployed Ex-Service Men's Association of the Calgary Labor Temple, explained that generous family allowances were but a public acknowledgment of his sacrifice: 'The Father is doing his bit to kill Hitlerism and those with four or even five children are right up against it.'[82]

The responsibilities of the Dependents' Allowance Board and the Dependents' Board of Trustees were similar to those of the CPF. The principle that allowances were to be based on family need was not embedded in legislative codes at the conclusion of the First World War. So why was such a principle immediately translated into a universal civilian program of family allowances in 1944? One important difference during the Second World War was that military welfare intiatives were entirely funded by the federal government; this was an important distinction in that it helped demonstrate clearly that civilian welfare expenditures were not beyond the competence of the modern State. Harry Cassidy remarked to the Social Planning Council of Winnipeg in 1942: 'People were saying everywhere, that the government is finding billions for war and that it can find money to provide self-respecting standards of living in peace.'[83] But equally decisive was the conception that the Second World War was a *total* war, one in which previous boundaries between military and civilian life had been erased. R.S. Lambert's statement that the 'modern soldier is not, as formerly, a mere fighting machine; the distinction between soldier and civilian is being broken down; both are mixed up together in the modern fighting line,'[84] was a commonplace of wartime social commentary. Accordingly, civilian welfare was perceived to be commensurate with military aims, and was thus believed to have universal implications. In the estimation of policymakers and the local administrators of wartime military welfare assistance, their programs foreshadowed a new era of 'full-orbed public service' as 'there was a philosophy engendered in the war years that might easily be taken as a yardstick in dealing with our peactime problems, in which assistance on the basis of need should be the right of all the citizens of our community.'[85] This, wrote Ernest Majury, the Superintendent of the Nipissing Children's Aid Society, which administered the wartime local DTB, was the legacy of wartime family allowances.

Wartime family policies were thus a reflection of the seismic shift in cultural attitudes and values that occurred between 1940 and 1945. During the final years of the Depression, many social workers rejected the negative work incentives implicit in public relief policies and came to recognize that 'generous help' did much more to foster the work ethic, which depended on faith, courage, and self-respect – character traits that many now believed had been weakened by fears of economic insecurity.[86] In part, this attitude was fuelled by the emergence of a popular Keynesianism that saw poverty as debilitating of general prosperity. In this new cultural climate, saving in and of itself was considered antisocial. Thus, even conservative economists such as J.R.

Beattie, who later became Deputy Governor of the Bank of Canada, concluded that 'under modern conditions where few can meet their basic needs with their own hands, it may be that a certain minimum security of income will encourage people to face the changes and take the risks that are necessary for rapid economic progress.' It was now widely accepted that social security might function as the principal guarantor of full employment. This view brought together business and organized labour[87]; both groups saw social security programs as a public recognition that 'all culture is the result of social labour, and to every worker belongs a share in that culture.'[88]

This perspective on the economic or materialistic basis of the national polity was in keeping with the Depression-era emphasis on *work as culture*. But during wartime, when the nation was sharply divided along religious and ethnic lines, the prospect of a 'common sharing of material welfare'[89] took on heightened meaning to become the modern signifier of national purpose. According to wartime commentators, a society was cohesive not because of ethnic or religious identity; rather it was based on a culture of abundance; and democracy itself was the culmination of the sum of individuals' common sense of economic security. History no longer furnished direct pathways for developing 'a strong national feeling'; rather, a unified identity could be created only by exploring the fundamentals of a democratic society, that is, the process by which individual citizens came to form allegiances with the State.[90] The links thus forged between the modern social security state and national unity were a feature of wartime ideology, and they were shaped and nurtured by succeeding Liberal governments. This new wartime nationalism was interpreted as a celebration of a mass movement that represented the will of the 'common people.'[91] For the first time in Canada, the nation and the apparatus of the State were seen as one and the same entity, in which an individual's 'personality'[92] or identity was conditioned by his or her sense of social security. A variation on this theme was the commonly held view that state welfare protected the sanctity of individual life and that the State itself was the creation of and servant to its citizens: 'Apart from them [the people], the State is nothing and has nothing.'[93]

It was this relationship between individual will and the State that reconciled postwar planning, led by an élite cadre of experts, with democracy; and it was this individualistic definition of collectivism that produced a loose consensus between left and right. That notion that postwar planning was a populist movement was reinforced by advertisements in mass circulation magazines. In 1945, an ad in the *Canadian Home Journal* selling floors showed a husband and wife drawing up house plans. Its caption was 'Are You A Post-War Planner?'[94] The Brave New World of postwar state planning was not to be feared. As David Bowman of Winnipeg confidently informed one of the principal architects of postwar government reconstruction, F. Cyril James, 'We have long ago past the stage where we feared the oppression of the state for we long ago learned that we were the state.' Thus, social security was valued not as a radical new form of government intervention or as the harbinger of a new era of socialist collectivism. Rather, the modern social security state was represented as the actual *fulfilment* of democracy, individualism, and the liberal creed. As Paul Martin, one of the rising stars in King's Liberal cabinet, wrote in his 1945 pamphlet, *Labour's Post-War World*, social security planning and the establishment of a minimum cash income for all fulfilled the fundamental aims of democracy by fostering a notion of economic security around which all labouring male citizens could agree. In the same vein, comprehensive social security was viewed as the realization of true liberalism, for in Martin's estimation it ensured 'less government and more liberty for all.' However, this realization of 'man's personality' through government provision of economic security entailed a peculiarly gendered conception of the modern democratic state.[95] As a particularly revealing advertisement for lipstick made clear, the war's ultimate aim of defending our 'democratic way of life' was intimately connected to the preservation of traditional gendered norms regarding workplace and home, and regarding the male breadwinner's ability to maintain a family. It stated that men were fighting overseas so that women could keep their 'femininity even though [they were] doing a man's job.'[96] Even conservative social Catholics such as Père Emile Bouvier justified postwar planning on the basis that it did not represent 'state paternalism' because its vision of social security was synonymous with the tradition of protecting the working man's 'right of a living wage.'[97]

The emphasis on social security as the central pillar or 'social dynamic' of national prosperity, class harmony, and the maintenance of gender boundaries was reinforced by the wartime preoccupation with revitalizing democracy in the face of the threat of totalitarianism. In their pamphlet *Dynamic Democracy*, Philip Child and John Holmes argued that if Western governments hoped to free democracy from the bondage of the 'economic anomalies of the depression' and reinstitute conditions for economic efficiency, growth, and trade cooperation among nations, working Canadians – both the working class and the middle classes – must be shown 'the life of a better world.' The ideal of universal social security gained ascendence in wartime precisely *because* it was seen as directly linked to international security and peace. The connections between economic, political, and international security were reaffirmed when in 1941 the allied nations proclaimed the Atlantic Charter, which declared that freedom from want was the main precondition of world peace.[98] Thus social security came to be seen as a central aim of the war, and one that would also preserve war morale. This psychological aspect of social policy was equally prominent in the movement for postwar planning: 'Above all,' wrote Beverly Baxter, 'it satisfies the human conscience which rightly looks upon poverty and slums and unemployment as forms of blasphemy.'[99]

Discussion of social security was thus conducted around the confluence of two important psychological currents: the economic fears engendered in the Depression, and the maintenance of wartime morale. Together, these powerfully shaped a public consensus – one that crossed all party lines – around the ideal of a cradle-to-grave welfare state. Large political constituencies on both the right and the left came to advocate generous government cash assistance, such as children's allowances, on a universal and non-contributory basis, in the belief that direct financial assistance would maximize human efficiency – namely, the productivity of workers.[100] It was perceived that universal welfare benefits would serve very conservative economic and social purposes; even the most left-leaning member of King's cabinet, Ian Mackenzie, stated that generous government allowances were intended to bolster the contributions of individuals to the national wealth by helping keep Canadians healthy and working. Family allowances, by indirectly contributing to 'the national and social importance of maintaining the family income,'[101] would obviate the need for broader social insurance programs.

Postwar reconstruction was to be a 'common man's crusade,'[102] yet at the same time social security was largely a psychological measure whose practical implementation was somewhat beside the point. Many social commentators and politicians considered the *idea* of freedom from want to be more important than concrete government action. For example, Leonard Marsh informed the House of Commons Special Committee on Social Security in June 1943 that he envisioned his report as mainly a psychological weapon – as a spur for morale that would allow Canadians to better prosecute the war in Europe.[103] It is somewhat unclear whether Marsh and other advisers on postwar reconstruction ever believed that his recommendations would ever need to be implemented. Marsh constantly rejected the assumption that his was a blueprint for postwar planning. As he confided to his mentor, Sir William Beveridge: 'The only danger is that it will be too easily assumed that all that is set out herein is going to be immediately implemented! What is nearer the truth is that it must serve as an instrument of education for some time.'[104] In the view of government policymakers, allegiance to the State was to be founded on the belief instilled in ordinary Canadians that governments had taken on a new, positive function in protecting the welfare of all Canadians – a cultural ideal that in fact absolved the King government from ever having to act on its wartime pledges. Family allowances, with their limited protection of the family economy, served no purpose except to assuage the psychological need for security among the masses. The Brave New World[105] of postwar social security was thus a labyrinth of politicial obfuscation and propaganda that deftly exploited the hope of the masses that true social and economic democracy would be realized; yet at the same time it functioned as an effective tonic for rejuvenating the work ethic. The CCF member for York South, J.W. Noseworthy, fresh from his victory over the arch-reactionary Arthur Meighen, pointed out that the mass of working Canadians now expected a better postwar society. This was in a letter to the Minister of Pensions and Health, Ian Mackenzie, in which he confidentially stated that the government should increase welfare benefits 'so that they *appear* sincere.'[106] The concepts of 'security for all' and postwar reconstruction were thus but other means of avoiding the threat of economic depression and 'social conflict and confusion,'[107] and were aimed at undermining the power of what had come to be seen as an 'unreasonable and rapacious labour aristocracy.'[108]

'Drowned ... in a butt of Beveridge Beer'[109]

Within federal government circles, soon after the war began, eyes turned to the problem of postwar reconstruction, primarily because there existed a primal fear of an immediate postwar recession. For this reason the Advisory Committee on Reconstruction was struck in the spring of 1941 to develop 'a comprehensive policy for reconstruction as well as specific machinery to carry it out. This body was headed by the principal of McGill University, F. Cyril James, an Englishman and a graduate of the London School of Economics, who had earlier taught at the prestigious Wharton School of Economics at the University of Pennsylvania. His conservative credentials were impeccable, in that he had served as the economist for the First National Bank of Chicago in 1937–38 before assuming his position as Professor of Political Economy at McGill in 1939.[110] Although this committee, which reported directly to the prime minister, appeared to have a sweeping mandate, its main purpose was to develop economic policies in close conjunction with the goals of the powerful Economic Advisory Council, which had been established in 1939. James personally appointed Leonard Marsh as his research director in May 1941, without cabinet approval, because of Marsh's strong interest in employment policies.[111] That James's committee was chiefly interested in shoring up free enterprise is evidenced by its personnel: J.S. McLean, the food adviser, was a former president of Canada Packers; Edouard Montpetit, the director of the School of Social, Economic, and Political Science at the University of Montreal, was a leading social Catholic and economist; W.A. Mackintosh, a Queen's University economics professor, would serve as the liaison with the Economic Advisory Committee; and Tom Moore, the president of the Trades and Labour Congress, had formerly been a director of the Canadian National Railway.[112]

The essential philosophy of the Advisory Committee on Reconstruction was articulated at the outset by James himself, who was personally committed to Keynesian-inspired economic principles and to modernizing the monetary and fiscal policies of the federal government. James's economic views epitomized what has come to be known as the Keynesian 'middle way' of the mixed and managed economy.[113] James concurred with those Keynesians who argued that 'national economic planning' must form 'an integral feature of national policy ... With the increasing complexity of social and economic life, it is doubtful that private initiative alone can be depended upon to carry us through both good times and bad.'[114] In James's estimation, the central challenge of postwar planning was to reconcile the free market economy with collectivism and labour goals. In short, reconstruction policies must revivify capitalism by working out 'a new equilibrium between private interest and public welfare.' The solution to all of this was the Keynesian one of using indirect monetary and fiscal incentives to foster full employment. This was a species of planned capitalism in keeping with the thinking of Beveridge and the PEP in Britain.[115] It had as its ultimate goal the preservation of the free market, individual liberty, and democratic institutions. All of the above depended on a healthy business climate.

Like Keynes, James was cautious about any policies that might lead to the expansion of the State. As an economic analyst concerned mainly with reviving Canada's international trade,[116] James was a decidedly conservative voice in the Liberal administration, but he was listened to closely, for he sanctioned state intervention only to the extent that it would stimulate free enterprise so that it might ultimately be freed from government restraint. James thus assigned a high priority to government policies that would ensure full employment; in his view and that of organized labour, the individual's strongest protection against social risk was work. 'The central problem of postwar reconstruction,' stated James in 1941, 'is the finding of adequate *employment opportunities* for the returning soldiers and the men who are no longer required in munition factories.' James's definition of full employment, however, was decidedly gendered, for it did not include the paid labour of married women; rather, his conception of political economy defended the verities of the breadwinner ideal, which saw a gainfully employed male as the chief guarantor of postwar family security. Thus, like his businessmen associates, James championed the protection of 'the whole manhood' of Canada first and foremost, and saw full employment rather than social welfare programs as the best prophylactic against poverty.

While James recognized that the government would have to make new commitments in the field of welfare policy in order to salve the mass desire for 'security' after the war, he conceived of social insurance measures as a faint second line of defence, to be deployed only in the event that national employment policies faltered. Thus he concluded: 'It is also desirable, although of secondary importance, that the general standard of living of all people in the community should be raised.'[117] However, postwar standards of living were to be raised by private means – by the sweat and toil of the male breadwinner rather than through government paternalism.[118] Because the intent of James's ideal of expert planning was to achieve national efficiency and to preserve equanimity between capital and labour 'without unnecessary interference by the state,'[119] his interest in social security programs was marginal. It can be argued that James saw no practical reason to implement national social security measures, which he saw mainly as propaganda devices for forging a 'common climate of opinion' that need not outlast the war.[120] On other occasions, James focused narrowly on those social insurance policies that could function as monetary mechanisms to stimulate consumer spending and stabilize the business cycle – an idea borrowed directly from the American Keynesian, Alvin Hansen.[121] Social security programs were thought to be wholly dependent on the achievement of full employment. According to James, social security measures were to be only temporary – a limited fiscal provision for sustaining full employment in the first few critical years following the War's end. 'I feel very strongly,' wrote James to his business associate P.C. Armstrong of the CPR, 'that we shall need a comprehensive social security plan for several years after the war. If the need for it diminishes with growing prosperity, it will not be hard either to increase the benefits or reduce the contributions proportionately.'[122] Social welfare programs were to help even out the business cycle; but even more significantly from the perspective of James and the other Keynesians in the Liberal administration, such programs were to be tied to the employment level and were to expand and contract with its fluctuations. Thus, social security commitments were merely an expendable subset of national income policies and wholly unrelated to the problem of income maintenance among the very poor. In the final analysis, James's prescriptions for postwar reconstruction greatly appealed to traditional business and political interests, for they were premised on the notion of small government; and were meant to utilize a limited range of government monetary mechanisms for the specific purpose of reinvigorating business, which had chafed under wartime regulations; and celebrated individual liberty in terms of the male breadwinner's freedom to earn and save for his dependants.

James's attitude to social security programs was essentially negative. He likened them to an irrigation ditch: they moved money around but they did little to spur national income development.[123] This was a source of great frustration among the progressives in the federal government. Among James's critics was the Minister of Pensions and Health, Ian Mackenzie, a former leader of the Great War Veterans' Association and a poor Scottish crofter's son, who protested throughout 1941 that there still existed little 'interest in governmental circles on problems of social security.'[124] On 9 December 1942, Mackenzie wrote to the prime minister that 'with the wave now sweeping over the world in regard to social security, your Government should take some definite action before very long.'[125] So perturbed was Mackenzie about King's reluctance to forge ahead with new welfare initiatives that in late 1942, as a further prod to the somnolent King administration, he erected his own social security committee to study health insurance.[126] Given the prime minister's well-demonstrated lack of interest in social security, and given the conservatism of his principal economic advisers, what then ignited the Liberal government to pursue a markedly different course? And what prompted Mackenzie King to personally intervene on 17 February 1943 to have Leonard Marsh's research findings on social insurance published rather than the long-awaited economic recommendations of James's committee?[127]

Probably the catalyst was the publication of the Beveridge Report in Britain in December 1942. It immediately sent a jolt through conservative–liberal regimes on both sides of the Atlantic, for here was a document that like no other showed the citizens of the allied nations what they were fighting for. On its release, Vincent Massey, the Canadian High Commissioner, quickly recognized the international signficance of the report. 'The B.B.C. have made extensive use of the Beveridge Report in their foreign propaganda as evidence of the continuing vitality of the British people who, in the midst of so stern a struggle are able to envisage such a step forward in social conditions,' Massey relayed to James. 'One cannot but feel that this intelligent and courageous attack on the problems of economic insecurity may prove a milestone in the social history of the British people.' As Massey made clear, the Beveridge Report was important because it created a popular consensus around the goal of social security and effectively squelched the ideological conflict that threatened to explode beneath the surface of politicial life in Britain and Canada.[128]

In Canada, the political right and left raced to see who would be the first to drink of the Beveridge beer. Charles E. Campbell confided to Ian Mackenzie that King must quickly forge a program of social security, because it had the potential to revive Liberalism as nothing else. B.K. Sandwell of *Saturday Night*, representing the political centre, thought a comparable Canadian document would be the best means for capitalism to scoop the socialist agenda. The *Canadian Forum* contended that the Beveridge Report had at last awakened Canadians to the benefits of centralized government planning.[129] Harry Cassidy, a former member of the League for Social Reconstruction, hailed the Beveridge Report as an antidote to the Nazis, socialists, and communists, and saw it as a signifier that liberal capitalism still possessed the ability to restore popular faith in democracy.[130]

Many Liberals, including Walter S. Woods, hoped that their party would appear like pioneers in the field by issuing its own package of postwar social legislation. Unfortunately for them, the Progressive Conservatives had beaten them to the punch by making public their party platform, which included health insurance, extensive veterans' benefits, contributory widows' pensions, and better unemployment insurance coverage, in the very same month that the Beveridge Report was released. Liberals like Ian Mackenzie, who had long been prodding King in this very direction, rushed to the breach, telling fellow Liberals that they must stress the Meighen-dominated Winnipeg platform of the Conservatives and portray them as nothing more than advocates of a 'narrow protected nationalism.' Above all he argued that the best strategy of the Liberals would be to revive the 'socialist menace' of the CCF.[131]

However, the threat from the left did not need to be manufactured. In December 1942, fears of postwar labour agitation were escalating both within and outside government and adding considerable steam to the Beveridge juggernaut, as were the increasingly feverish protests from disgruntled soldiers' families over the rising cost of living.[132] Robert England alerted Ian Mackenzie to the potential for political unrest among the working classes, whose sense of social injustice was growing exponentially with their resentment over government wage constraints, which were making it impossible for them to save money to buy homes after the war.[133] To a degree unprecedented since 1919, government policymakers found themselves confronted with the spectre of social catalysm. Conservative businessmen like Sir Joseph Flavelle trumpeted the warning, and so did spokesmen for organized labour like Tom Moore and Eugene Forsey, who made veiled threats against the government. 'Without social security,' Forsey stated, 'there is simply no chance of orderly social reconstruction: we face, at the least, a resumption in more acute form of the social struggles of the 1930s, with the ever-present possibility that these conflicts will lead to violence.'[134] At the conclusion of 1942, organized labour's disenchantment with wartime wage policies coalesced with the publication of the Beveridge Report to radically alter expectations of postwar society.[135] Colonial obeisance to British precedents,[136] compounded with the political need to co-opt labour back into the war, dramatically raised interest in social welfare issues within the King cabinet which finally bowed to the pressure from Ian Mackenzie and issued a Canadian version of the Beveridge Report.

At first Mackenzie and James felt vindicated by this upsurge of government interest in their strategies for postwar reconstruction. James was one of the first in King's government to recognize the explosive potential the Beveridge Report had to transform government priorities after the war. James was a longtime disciple of Beveridge and appreciated that the underlying purpose of the Beveridge plan was to redistribute national wealth to such an extent that male working-class breadwinners would be able to support their families without the need for additional state social services. But in the popular press in both Britain and Canada, the document was heralded as a blueprint for a far-reaching welfare state, and its author's call for full employment was shunted aside. James bemoaned this turn of events in a letter to R.A. Butler, the foremost British Conservative Keynesian advocate of the mixed economy and close ally of Harold Macmillan, in which he noted despondently that the Beveridge Report had received so much attention in the press that popular thinking was now focused entirely on social legislation.[137] It is clear that even as the Marsh report was being written, James feared he would be eclipsed by his rogue protégé. Ironically, even though James had been corresponding regularly with Beveridge concerning the British economist's policies for maintaining industrial efficiency, high employment, and free enterprise,[138] he was eventually forced to publicly criticize the perception among the public that the Beveridge scheme amounted to government protection 'from cradle to grave.'[139] This was an effort to corral those who wished to emphasize the more statist implications of the report.

By January 1943 it had become doubly apparent that public debate had to be shifted back to government policies for full employment, and away from social welfare policies unconnected with economic considerations; for by that time Leonard Marsh had closeted himself in his suite of rooms in the Chateau Laurier to pen a homegrown version of comprehensive government planning for the postwar utopia. James thus undertook a speaking tour in which he stressed the need for government capital investment, for the creation of a federal universal minimum wage policy, and for social legislation to stabilize consumer spending.[140] This was all in an effort to combat the hijacking of the Beveridge plan by left-leaning Liberals and to stage-manage a harmonious interweaving of the James and Marsh reports, which he still believed would be published simultaneously later that year by the King government. On 18 March 1943, F.R. Scott wrote to his friend Marsh: 'Congratulations on your elevation to the position of Canada's

Beveridge.'[141] The competition to receive this accolade had been fierce, and many in Ottawa were clearly surprised that it had gone to Marsh. James's ambition, like that of the federal Minister of Pensions and Health, Ian Mackenzie, had been to shape federal postwar reconstruction policies. But his efforts to do so were shouldered aside by Marsh, who exploited the international popularity of the Beveridge Report by producing an almost exact replica of it for Canadian consumption. In March 1943, Marsh trumped the James report on employment and Mackenzie's initiatives on health insurance – projects that had been germinating for close to two years – by releasing his *Report on Social Security for Canada* to the House of Commons Committee on Reconstruction one week before Mackenzie released his own scheme.[142] James had appointed Marsh as his research adviser, and he had earlier championed Marsh's social security research in the expectation that, given the enormous popularity of social security issues, this preliminary report on social security would do much to publicize James's own, more comprehensive statement on reconstruction and full employment.[143] Indeed, before Beveridge had been so wildly adulated, Marsh had been interested mainly in delineating new initiatives for social policy at the provincial level, in the tracks of the division of constitutional powers laid down by the Rowell–Sirois Report. James, clearly, had been oblivious to Marsh's personal ambitions,[144] and he retaliated by refusing to publicly endorse Marsh's report. Mackenzie, meanwhile, fumed to the president of the *Montreal Star* that the Marsh Report had been prematurely released. He also predicted it would die quickly, noting disparagingly that it was only 'a survey of possibilities' – an official viewpoint to which the Finance Minister, J.L. Ilsley, lent further credence when he stated that it was not regarded by the King cabinet as a blueprint for legislative action.[145]

What rankled was that it was clear to all that Marsh had won the prize cheaply. As Harry Cassidy, another commentator on postwar social security who was scooped by Marsh, ruefully commented, Marsh's reputation was conveniently sealed once King realized that his government would have to make some concessions to popular demands after the worldwide publication of the Beveridge Report.[146] Marsh was thus hastily commissioned to write a Canadian companion volume in January 1943. With help from social workers Bessie Touzel of the Toronto Welfare Council, Stuart Jaffray of the University of Toronto, the Deputy Minister of Labour, Allon Peebles, and George Davidson – who actually penned the long sections on old age assistance and pensions, mothers' allowances, and social insurance – Marsh completed his task in just six short weeks.[147]

Fully thirty years later, in his introduction to the re-release of his *Report on Social Security for Canada*, Marsh would still be trying to duck the criticism that his hurried report was merely a diluted version of Beveridge's. (It is clear that by 1975, in the wake of Lester Pearson's achievement of a more or less comprehensive social security state, Marsh wished to be seen as the first visionary of our modern welfare edifice.[148]) In 1943, Beveridge's prestige was both useful and impossible to ignore, and Marsh cast his achievements in more modest terms. He emphasized his intellectual debt to Beveridge, stressing on a number of public occasions that he was a protégé of Beveridge, even though his PhD had been granted by McGill University.[149] Beveridge himself pointed out the close affinities between the two reports when he spoke to the House of Commons Special Committee on Social Security on 25 May 1943 – a performance that did much to elevate Marsh's profile in the government. For the sake of squelching potential criticism, Marsh was not averse to wearing the armour of Beveridge's prestige, explaining in a letter to Harry Cassidy in 1943 that the sections on widows' and orphans' pensions, maternity benefits, marriage grants, and bonuses to women as wage earners 'as a special matter of consideration' had been deliberately adapted 'à la Beveridge.'[150] Significantly, this focus on the problems of women would be downplayed in the final version of his report. Otherwise, the greater part of Marsh's recommendations tracked the Beveridge Report closely and directly: he focused on social insurance, postulated a conception of the husband and wife as one unit, and promoted family allowances as the cornerstone of his social security package, arguing not only that these would rectify anomalies both between individual wages and family need, but also that they would preserve the concept of lesser eligibility by obviating the need to build dependants' allowances into social insurance programs like unemployment insurance. Echoing Beveridge, Marsh portrayed family allowances as the 'key to consistency' in his overall plan. He also described them as a fundamental departure in Canadian social welfare even though the principle of children's allowances had long been part of public debate and had been incorporated into the relief policies of the 1930s. And like Beveridge, Marsh negated the individual contribution of the unpaid labour of married women, folding their welfare entitlements into the individual personality of the husband, in order to ensure that the wage standard for men would be preserved.[151]

The modern social security state was thus intended to reinforce a trend already evident in government policy during the Depression: the notion that the family was not an interdependency of separate contributing individuals, but rather was coextensive with the individual personality of the male breadwinner. Marsh's plan sought to extend the right of the male breadwinner to be his family's sole provider by establishing a system of social insurance that would tabulate welfare benefits on the basis of the male wage and not according to the needs of dependants. Family allowances thus preserved a *lower* standard of wages, in that they established the wage unit as a man and his wife.[152] Eva Hubback and D.H. Stepler saw in family allowances a public recognition of the married woman's contribution to the national common weal through her work in the home; Marsh's conception of social security was male gendered and saw family allowances as a means to reaffirm the right of men of all classes to a 'minimum wage'[153] – that is, a wage supplemented by family allowances, sufficient for a man to support himself and his family. Marsh's conceptualization of the modern welfare state was generally geared to a vision of a classless society, one in which the nineteenth-century liberal creed of 'eliminating unequal opportunity'[154] was fulfilled, but one constructed around carefully drawn gender boundaries between home and work. The modern social security state did not represent a radical departure in family policy; rather, it reflected a network of attitudes toward work and family that upheld the right of men to work and to be the sole provider – a concept laid down during the Depression.

If Marsh's plan established 'social minimum standards,' these were not related to the problem of poverty per se; rather, they were designed for those male workers already in the workforce. Indeed, he recommended that family allowances be granted only to those skilled workers who paid into the existing unemployment insurance scheme. In only two respects did Marsh's plan diverge from that of Beveridge. Following the model of military family welfare policy, Marsh recommended a graduated scale of allowances[155] – a strategy in keeping with unemployment insurance benefits, which aimed to preserve distinctions between unskilled and skilled workers. Ironically, given that King's 1944 Family Allowances Act would be castigated as a sop to Quebec, this sliding scale of allowances was meant to uphold the Protestant ideal of the small family and was actually prejudicial to large families. Had Marsh and King been attempting to redress the problem of poverty in large families, they would have made payments applicable to families with three children or more, as Father Lebel had proposed in 1929. This seemingly small detail reveals the lack of real interest in the problem of family poverty, despite widespread public concern about indebtedness among large families.[156] For Marsh and the Liberal government, family allowances were not a means of relieving poverty; rather, they were a wage policy – a fact well appreciated by organized labour – and a mechanism for stimulating postwar spending and ensuring jobs for returning soldiers.

Beveridge had made family allowances the cornerstone of British social security; it can be argued that full employment was the keystone of Marsh's welfare design. In this, Marsh's scheme had affinities with the vision of Cyril James, who posited a causal relationship between employment and social security. Marsh would later repudiate his own wartime preoccupation with full employment, but in 1943, he expressed his present outlook to James in a memo concerning his report: 'It is designed to emphasize the important point that social security legislation in a postwar context has no firm foundation without special employment measures for the transition period.'[157] In a confidential memorandum to the Advisory Committee on Reconstruction, Marsh likewise placed great emphasis on employment policies, government public works programs, and postwar training schemes; and dismissed social insurance and even unemployment insurance as decidedly secondary matters in postwar planning.[158] Though he later denied it, Marsh saw a strong emphasis on full employment as vital to the achievement of social security; his corollory was that social security measures – most especially family allowances – were meant to stimulate public spending and thus to act as the main engines in the drive toward full employment. In all of this he owed much to the research of Alvin Hansen, the American Keynesian.[159] The idea that social welfare benefits could function as monetary tools on par with government public works was alien to Beveridge in 1942, but he later embraced it after he became a convert to Keynesianism in 1945.[160] From the start, however, this Keynesian interpretation of family allowances formed the fulcrum of Marsh's plan. James had less to fear from the Marsh plan than he had from Beveridge, for Marsh's philosophy of social planning was more closely related to the business goals of plans like that of the Lever Brothers, which he commended just before issuing his report as the 'best pamphlet on postwar reconstruction.'[161] Social security thus came to be one and the same as national economic efficiency, just as 'social minimum standards' implied the breadwinner's quest for a living wage, not government handouts.[162] That Marsh in 1943 emphasized work and wages for men was not surprising, given that he had once penned an election pamphlet for Lloyd George titled *Work for All*, and that during the 1930s had written extensively on the need for governments to create jobs.[163] It might well be argued that the success of the Marsh Report lay in its very traditionalism. It preserved, in the words of Marsh, 'family stability,' by shoring up the work expectations of married men so that they might make 'individual provision'[164] to their dependants; it also held out the promise of protecting that male individual as head of the family, and thus was also seen as an affirmation of 'personality' and the fulfilment of individualism. Social security was the hope for democracy because it renewed the identification of male citizens with the State. Individualism had come to pervade the assumptions underlying postwar ideals of social security. Nowhere was this more evident than in Quebec, a society in which Catholics had long upheld the family as the firmament of society. Yet even there, by 1944, the modern, individualist conception of the family had infused Catholic thought. Thus the University of Montreal professor François-Albert Angers, a member of the business school, hailed Marsh's full employment policies as a bulwark against state authority and the primary means by which the individual could be preserved.[165] Marsh received widespread support not because he was confirming a new, positivist vision of government responsibility for the family, but because of the convergence that social security – or what President H.J. Cody of the University of Toronto termed 'socialized individualism' – brought about between the 'social principle of individual liberty,' 'the moral principle of respect for personality,' and the 'domestic principle of the sanctity and solidarity of the family, which is the natural development of the [male] individual.'[166] Seen from this perspective, Marsh's plan was simply a reprise with modern instruments of the *leitmotif* of family self-sufficiency. In short, Marsh's report was a manly brew with a froth of socialist foam.

If, as James maintained, the Marsh Report was intended largely to 'provoke public discussion' – or as Harry Cassidy termed it, 'a flier to sound out public opinion'[167] – the decision of Mackenzie King to publish it had just that effect. Unlike the Beveridge Report, which was treated in the Canadian press as a utopian vision and as a powerful tool for boosting war morale, the Marsh Report was viewed more directly as a blueprint for postwar government legislation. Its reception was therefore more mixed. As Allon Peebles, Deputy Minister of

Labour and chief executive officer of the Unemployment Commission, informed Cassidy in April 1943: 'The Marsh Report had wide publicity but the aftermath editorials were inclined to be critical of the comprehensiveness of his proposals and of course the financial papers raised the question of Canada's ability to finance such a programme.'[168] However, Marsh's harshest critics were his fellow social science colleagues, each of whom was fighting for a piece of the social security research pie. Thus, it may well be argued that the public discourse on postwar reconstruction was determined as much by professional ambition as by a commitment to a particular social philosophy.

This helps explain the position of Harry Cassidy, a left-leaning Liberal who in other circumstances would have been one of Marsh's champions. Cassidy, fearing that Marsh intended to scoop his next book as well, threw in his lot with Charlotte Whitton, and in doing so helped shift the public debate over social security toward the right. Cassidy joined another former member of the League for Social Reconstruction, Dal Grauer, in impugning Marsh's technical research, writing petulantly that Marsh's wartime social security plan looked like a new edition of *Social Planning for Canada*. Cassidy at first celebrated the left-leaning aspects of Marsh's comprehensive package of social welfare measures, gently chiding him that they might be too 'far-reaching'[169] for public consumption at that time; but soon enough he began exerting his own influence over government policy through a barrage of criticism in the press – a campaign that proved instrumental in reducing public acceptance for centralized government planning.[170] Marsh's Achilles' heel was his refusal to use actuaries to undertake his social security statistics[171] – a glaring oversight much exploited by both Cassidy and Whitton. When Cassidy learned that Marsh was again writing on his turf,[172] he began to cultivate Whitton, noting in a letter to her how Marsh had 'a bad economy bug about research. That's too bad. How about ganging up on him a bit?'[173] Stinging from his inability to land either a Canadian university job or a prized government research position like Marsh's, Cassidy urged Whitton on, praising her for her 'trenchant criticism of the Marsh report and the ingenious ideal that you have worked out yourself.' And in a postscript, he added: 'Poor Leonard! You do catch him with his pants down all over the place.'[174]

As I argued in the previous chapter, Cassidy's philosophy regarding centralized government planning and the social and economic goals of social welfare policies had been slowly coalescing around a conservative *telos* throughout the 1930s. In 1937, in a revealing letter to Dal Grauer, Cassidy defended decentralized and limited government intervention, arguing that in the name of more efficient administration (by which he meant controlling the state's tax bills) 'progressives in the social field' must seek out common ground with businessmen.[175] Although Cassidy had earlier campaigned for social insurance, by the time the war began he was advocating (much like Charlotte Whitton) the building up of social assistance so that the 'old distinctions between social insurance and social assistance' could be eradicated in the interests of 'salvaging human wreckage.'[176] Thus by the Second World War Cassidy's long drift toward support for corporatist social engineering had reached its full conclusion. Like many of his contemporaries, Cassidy considered the *expectation* of social security to be more important than actual government legislation to implement it. In his view, social security measures had the limited purpose of avoiding postwar 'chaos on the social front.'[177] His perspective on family allowances was particularly revealing of the intellectual alliance he had made with business interests. In 1943, just after the release of the Marsh Report, he commented to his former student, S. Eckler, a frequent contributor to *Saturday Night*, that he 'wanted to make clear also that it [family allowances] was not of necessity a levelling device whereby the rich were to be dispossessed of their wealth and income for the benefit of the poor.'[178] Even after the release of the Marsh Report, in which family allowances appeared front and centre, Cassidy continued to advocate wage increases, even though he was later to criticize Whitton, after family allowances were an accomplished fact, for her foolhardiness in believing that an adequate living wage could be achieved for working-class wage earners 'under the present state of capitalism.'

In many respects, Cassidy supported family allowances only insofar as he believed that they would promote marriage and procreation. This was a complete inversion of the feminist argument for family limitation – which Cassidy condemned as undermining war morale.[179] In a 1947 lecture, Cassidy outlined the conservative gender implications of family allowances. He maintained that they aimed to uphold the work ethic by preserving the tenets of lesser eligibility in social insurance programs; he also maintained that they would contribute to family stability and would thereby help contain the modern problem of neuroticism among women and children.[180] The best illustration of Cassidy's temperament is that he believed in a contributory system administered at the local level rather than in a universal plan. The plan he proposed would include only those breadwinners who were already in the workforce – thus making family allowances a payment for hard work and thrift – and would reinforce the underlying aim of defining women's entitlements in terms of the rights of their husbands.[181] Cassidy's views were not that dissimilar from Whitton's, or from those who advocated social utilities such as school meals, free milk, and free medical care.[182] As late as 1944, Cassidy wasn't sure whether family allowances should be paid in cash or in kind.[183]

Cassidy's professional competition with Marsh added fuel to his criticisms of the *Report on Social Security* and did much to bring about what Bessie Touzel most feared: 'splits in public opinion in its expressed demand for broad social security programs.'[184] Cassidy's 'political' defection to Whitton was all the more damaging given that the social work fraternity, which was now headed by Touzel's faction, had succeeded in dethroning Whitton from her power base as the director of the Canadian Welfare Council. Those social workers who had witnessed for too long vivid tragedies of family poverty saw Whitton's removal as ridding their ranks of the last roadblock to achieving comprehensive program of postwar social security. While some old-fashioned child welfare advocates such as Robert Mills of the Toronto Children's Aid Society continued to defend the tradition of family casework and counselling, most social workers endorsed the principle of family allowances as long as they were enacted at the same time as a minimum wage policy.[185] Many of the more 'progressive' social workers, including Bessie Touzel, supported family allowances in the belief that they would help remedy problems such as family instability, child neglect, and delinquency; that being said, what set these professionals apart from traditionalists was that they no longer believed that 'dependency' was only a working-class problem. Rather, for the first time, they saw family moral and economic problems as a 'universal' problem that crossed class boundaries, and for that reason they eschewed both counselling and means testing in favour of rights-based welfare programs.[186]

That the official endorsement of family allowances by social workers represented both older and newer trends in social thinking was best demonstrated by the appointment of George Davidson in the spring of 1942 to replace Whitton as director of the Canadian Welfare Council.[187] A graduate in modern languages from the University of British Columbia and in classics from Harvard University, Davidson's career was firmly rooted in the older, child welfare and charity approach to social salvaging. Under British Columbia's Provincial Secretary, George Weir, Davidson, a Maritimer by birth, became the Superintendent of Welfare and of Neglected Children, and in that capacity oversaw the Mothers' Allowances Commission. He later succeeded J.H.T. Falk as the executive director of the Vancouver Council of Social Agencies, and in 1939 he took the post of Director of Social Welfare, recently vacated by Harry Cassidy.[188] While Davidson recognized that by the Second World War it had become generally unpopular to recommend counselling dependent families,[189] he did not entirely abandon his view that there would always be some families who needed to be both investigated and educated. He wanted a high level of private welfare services preserved to function alongside a national system of family allowances; he also advocated that a series of pamphlets be included with the monthly family allowance cheques so that all families could be indirectly and impersonally trained to conform to middle-class ideals.[190] At the same time, he was one of the foremost advocates of centralized government planning for rights-based welfare initiatives. Indeed, he was adamant about excluding orphanages and other child protection institutions from the family allowance program because he believed that family allowances would help redistribute funds between families and, in addition, would reinforce federal control of the tax burden so that the poorer provinces might be helped. More ominously, he refused to reverse his policy on orphanages. He intended to use federal government welfare strategies to break the hold of the Catholic church over welfare policies in Quebec by forcing the Duplessis government to institute 'modern' welfare measures such as compulsory education, stricter child labour laws, and a system of foster homes.[191]

Moreover, Davidson was a keen supporter of the two-tier welfare state – that is, of augmenting federal, universal, rights-based programs with provincially run, means tested social assistance relief. He believed that family allowances would reinforce such a system by putting an end to provincial mothers' allowance programs.[192] Family allowances thus became a means to sustain the gendered aspects of the welfare state, in that Davidson envisioned them as an extension of the breadwinner's ability to maintain his family.[193] By abolishing specialized forms of relief for women at the provincial level, Davidson's wartime initiatives helped undermine later efforts – most notably those of Harry Cassidy in 1947 – to establish rights-based entitlements for

women founded on a federally funded system of contributory widows' pensions.[194] Family allowances were thus consciously designed
to function as an entering wedge by which the federal government
could usurp control over provincial welfare services and override the
constitutional balance established by the Rowell–Sirois Report. Constitutional divisions were thus symbolic of gender divisions. In this light,
the campaigns against family allowances launched by Maurice Duplessis and George Drew were astute responses to a real and formidable
federal flank attack, rather than atavistic excrescences of the political
right.[195] Davidson was made the new director of the Canadian Welfare
Council precisely *because* he could sponsor family allowances in such a
way as to defuse the power of the traditionalists within the social work
network, who remained tied to the notion of provincial control of
social welfare. The inner cabinet of the King government had gravitated to family allowances rather than to other social security measures
such as health insurance, because their popular appeal in relieving
poverty and stimulating postwar abundance was the perfect disguise
for the federal government's drive to preserve its wartime taxing powers. For his propaganda efforts, Davidson was later granted one of two
prized deputy minister posts within the newly created Department of
Health and Welfare, from which he oversaw the implementation of the
1944 Family Allowances Act.

Davidson may have succeeded in squelching criticism of the Marsh
plan, but he had not calculated on the vigour of Whitton's challenge.
Like Bessie Touzel and Harry Cassidy, Whitton well understood the
power of public opinion during the Second World War and used it to
great effectiveness. On the publication of the Marsh Report, Whitton
launched a barrage of articles denouncing it for emphasizing social
insurance and family allowances rather than the already established
network of social services (in which she included medical insurance),
because of her long-standing commitment to protecting maternal and
natal health.[196] Here, Whitton gained the support of a large number of
women's groups and social workers – whose power lay in the fact that
they managed such services at local and provincial levels – especially
after she deftly appealed to wartime nationalist sensibilities by por-
traying Marsh's report as a pale shadow of the better-known Beveridge Report and as an invasive import that was antagonistic to the
Canadian way of life.[197] However, on other occasions, for all her frequent railing against the 'sacrosanctity of the Beveridge and Marsh
Reports.'[198] Whitton manipulated the emphasis that Beveridge himself

placed on social assistance measures to argue for preserving the principles of need and investigation in Canadian welfare policies.[199]

Whitton was always a feisty public debater, and her diatribes against Leonard Marsh became even more strident after he made the strategic error of attempting to co-opt her by making her one of his research assistants. In response, Whitton tartly replied that she had her own book on social security, that she was accustomed to proper remuneration, and that she intended to critique his blueprint for reconstruction to the parliamentary committee.[200] Yet despite the increasing acerbity of Whitton's articles, during 1943 she still commanded a wide hearing. The Whitton whom historians know best is the Whitton of 1945. That was the year when, out of frustration at the Conservative leader John Bracken's betrayal on the question of family allowances, and at his subsequent rejection of her political candidacy in Renfrew, she shifted her position firmly toward the antediluvian right and her shrill denunciations of Catholicism and Quebec made her a figure ripe for caricature. The review by Ronald Hambleton of *The Dawn of an Ampler Life*, the volume commissioned by the Progressive Party, reflected the public's perception of the Whitton of 1945. In his review, Hambleton fulminated against her poor law ideology, terming her program a 'lugubrious hymn of fears' and emphasizing the anti-humanitarian stridency of her eugenicist attacks on Quebec society.[201] Indeed, when Whitton and her co-conspirator, Rev. Edwin Silcox, the author of the famous pamphlet *The Revenge of the Cradles*[202] drew a link between birthrates and national standards of living, most Canadians, who wished to approach the postwar era with hope and optimism, saw it as a needlessly cynical and partisan exercise. By 1945, Whitton's views were clearly out of step with majority opinion, and she was thus a very easy target for Harry Cassidy, who after family allowances were an accomplished fact joined ranks with Margaret Gould, who launched a rather personal attack on Whitton.[203] Whitton *was* in fact fair game, for the question of family allowances had by 1944 become sharply politicized, provoking Whitton to quip: 'It's an election baby – we're calling it Einstein, but – William Lyon, for short.'[204] While Whitton continued to spar from the sidelines, calling the 1944 Speech from the Throne 'a disgrace to honest thought'[205] and pillorying John Bracken for entering 'the bribery competition'[206] when he finally voted for family allowances, her star had clearly fallen. Her accusations that family allowances would ensure 'social sinking by senseless subsidy,' together with her obsession with large French-Canadian families and race suicide, won few plaudits.[207] Whitton frankly recognized that she had lost the fight to sway public opinion. In a letter to the president of Confederation Life, V.R. Smith, on the eve of the federal election, she expressed her disgust and frustration: 'Ever since the Beveridge Report, immature social and political "experts" in this country have been outbidding in clamour every half developed, emotional conception – I wish I could say immaculate – of this and that Tom, Dick, and Harriet who choose to don the garment of welfare. You are either reactionary or political if you ask for sound consideration when as a matter of fact the person who does so is the real servitor to progress in such protection.'[208]

In 1943, when political events were still fluid, Whitton's criticisms of Marsh were accepted as 'sound consideration' and occupied an important place in the mainstream of public debate. Indeed, George Davidson, Lothar Richter at Dalhousie, and Lorne Pierce, editor of the influential Ryerson Press, all recognized the gravity of her criticisms and were also well aware that her objections would lead to some 'real sandpapering' of the Marsh Report.[209] Of course, it was true, as Bessie Touzel observed, that Whitton's opposition to family allowances – indeed, to all government social insurance programs – meant, in its logical conclusion, a perpetuation of poor law principles.[210] Whitton herself characterized family allowances and the concept of universality as simply a dole that would render everybody 'wards of the State.'[211] It was also true that Whitton was a champion of the middle classes, whom she correctly contended were being misled into thinking they were increasing their net income when, in fact, family allowances were being excessively taxed. This particular criticism resonated in many quarters and was very difficult to counteract; even that valiant proponent of family allowances, George Davidson, found it difficult to fix the numbers to show how the comfortable middle- and working-classes would benefit.[212] For a society already fearful of excessive post-war taxation, the notion that family allowances were merely a psychological tease was difficult to dispel after Whitton went to work on Marsh's fallible statistics.[213]

Whitton's antagonism to the direct cash principle of family allowances must not be automatically characterized as a bogey merely of the right. Dal Grauer, a former member of the League for Social Reconstruction, was also an adamant opponent of cash family allowances. Like Whitton, he believed that social services would better address the problem of poverty.[214] Moreover, Whitton did not entirely oppose Marsh's idea of a national minimum;[215] rather, she preferred plans such as the one propounded in Britain by the Liberal, Lady Rhys-Williams, who suggested a simple tax on all citizens and allowances for all dependants, including women, children, and the aged – a plan that correlated with Beveridge's but that also had the signal advantage of addressing the demands of the existing tax structure.[216] It might well be argued that such a tax plan was even more universal than Marsh's concept of a national minimum and had the advantage of not needing separate contributions from beneficiaries of the welfare state, as did unemployment insurance. While we must not downplay Whitton's dedication to poor law principles, or forget her vociferous campaigns against the 'social gospel of welfare,'[217] we must also recognize that (as she wrote to Cassidy in 1943) she was not against redistribution of national resources. Even more importantly, her antagonism to the character of Canadian social insurance programs sprang from her feminism. As she explained to Cassidy, she objected to social insurance programs that only recognized male heads of the family: 'And *most important*, it is not only *male* adult and dependents but *income earning head* – in case of a *female!'*[218]

The most unassailable aspect of Whitton's critique of the Marsh Report related to the problem of how to achieve a 'living wage.' In her 1943 Behind the Headlines pamphlet, *Security for Canadians*, Whitton argued that the 'first social commandment in the modern industrial state' is for governments to intercede directly to manage the economy in such a way that production is maximized.[219] This was simply a restatement of Marsh's mantra of full employment. It is remarkable, given Whitton's bad press, that she was one of the first during wartime to distinctly call for a government policy of full employment combined with a guarantee of a living wage[220] – a proposal that effectively stymied both Marsh and Cassidy, especially when Whitton won the favour of labour leaders in Canada, who likewise perceived that family allowances were in effect a wage subsidy subversive of their wartime campaign for collective bargaining.[221] Cassidy in his rejoinder claimed that a living wage was untenable within capitalism – a charge that laid bare the contradictions of his own position on family allowances, which he supported because they would stimulate spending and thus help revitalize capitalism. It could be said of Cassidy, Marsh, and Whitton, therefore, that they were all capitalist planners now.

Despite later caricatures of Whitton as an ossified exemplar of fundamentalist Toryism, in 1943 her allegations that a comprehensive program of postwar social security would be too expensive, would

overtax Canadians, would leave working-class families little disposable income, and might undermine the responsibility of the male
breadwinner to maintain his family, did much to shape the public
debate on government planning. Both Whitton and Cassidy, by publicly exposing deficiencies in Marsh's conclusions, directly influenced
the inner circle of the King government, for by the fall of 1943, inertia
had swept through the King cabinet. So effective had Whitton's campaign been in galvanizing conservative opinion behind the issue of fiscal probity that by the following year King had even taken to lecturing
the most conservative members of his cabinet, T.A. Crerar and C.D.
Howe, on the necessity of 'economy.' As Grant Dexter observed on
22 September 1944: 'King is cock-a-hoop. He has suddenly become
quite Conservative ... Spoke slightingly of family allowances and said
that those things had to be paid for and what about taxpayers and
what not.'[222] The deft manipulation of public sentiment by those on
both the right and the left after the publication of the Marsh plan in
1943 deflated public expectations and directly led to a truncated postwar welfare program in which there would be no comprehensive protection of the individual from cradle to grave. Whitton and Cassidy
had thus contributed in no small way to diluting the robust Beveridge
stout. It is indeed ironic, given the fierceness of Whitton's objections,
that when the King government finally decided to implement a single
aspect of Marsh's blueprint for reconstruction, it turned out to be family allowances. Why King chose family allowances rather than the
enormously popular proposal for national health insurance is the
theme of the next section.

'The "Virtue of Economic Independence"'[223]

In November 1942, Stuart Jaffray, a professor from the University of
Toronto and one of Marsh's collaborators, pessimistically observed of
James's Reconstruction Committee: 'It has expansive terms of reference, as you know, including social security, but has never had more
than token support, either spiritual or financial, from the Cabinet.
[The] Beveridge Report created some interest, but not enough to spur
Mr. King to action.'[224] King's lack of interest was confirmed by others,[225] and is best exemplified by a story (most likely apocryphal) told
years later by the journalist Bruce Hutchinson. In the story, King met
the son of a soldier who had perished in the First World War. Supposedly, in this moment of 'intuition,' when King realized that this tal-

ented young man might have succeeded had he been able to have his education funded, he became an instant convert to a system of government allowances. While this 'sentimental moment' of King's may have been sheer fantasy,[226] Hutchinson's tale does reinforce the general view that King was largely disinterested in the problem of social security. How, then, did King come to embrace Marsh's plan, especially his recommendation for family allowances? What social and economic principles underlay this path-breaking welfare measure? And did it actually expand the administrative structures of the federal government and thus fundamentally alter the scope of the State?

In December 1942 the chairman of the Advisory Committee on Reconstruction, Cyril James, had been misled into thinking that since his committee reported to King, the prime minister intended to interest himself personally in a comprehensive scheme of postwar social security measures.[227] But as James was to discover in the first months of 1943, the inner wheels of Cabinet were already shifting the issue of social security away from its social policy moorings toward the fiscal policy perspectives of the Economic Advisory Council, which had taken control of the Marsh plan.[228] Grant Dexter likewise observed that the Liberal government was 'not too enthusiastic on social security' and so had moved the James Committee away from Ian Mackenzie's Department of Pensions and Health because 'as things got hotter, the brain trust insisted on taking it away from Ian and James, and so it was transferred in January to Willie, thus letting Clark, Towers et al. in on the ground floor.'[229] That this represented a new conservatism within Liberalism was noted by George Davidson, who at first commended the ability of W.A. Mackintosh and the Economic Advisory Committee to tame the Marsh Report,[230] but later bemoaned the fact that social security had been hijacked by the financial experts. As he confided to Cassidy in March 1943: 'They are pretty obviously the boys who are going to write the postwar ticket, and once again we have an imposing line-up of money economists with hardly a drop of humanitarian blood in the lot of them.'[231] By March 1943, just as family allowances were surfacing as the priority of the King government, the financial experts were attempting to prevent James's report from being made public so that the fiscal and wage control facets of the Liberal social security strategem would be well obscured within the web of government bureaucracy.[232] Even progressives in the Cabinet like Ian Mackenzie feared the reformist temper of popular opinion, and confidentially reported to King that the social security research of Marsh, that 'advanced Liberal,' had been quietly moved to the Economic Advisory Committee, 'where no publicity attends his work.'[233]

Even though James had made the Marsh Report public in March with the specific goal of pressuring the Liberals, King was able to stall on the issue of social security because of the mixed reception accorded the Beveridge plan by the British government.[234] As Whitton reported to Cassidy in her usual inimitable way, Marsh's book 'is being left pretty much the little bastard by the powers that be.'[235] In May, with Beveridge's visit to Ottawa, there was a renewed but brief flurry of public interest in social security,[236] but it was apparent that even the creation of House of Commons and Senate committees on social security was little more than window dressing. Harry Cassidy observed ruefully that the pervasive ignorance demonstrated in these committees confirmed the government's lack of interest in the Marsh plan. As he quipped to Marsh in September: 'You must find it amusing as one of the main architects of "Social Security Planning for Canada" to see the consternation of your liberal masters about the trend from the left. Is it possible that concern for their political future will lead them very soon to the preparation of detailed provisions for social security?'[237]

Cassidy's observation was particularly prescient, for later that year the Liberals began to recognize the rising power of the CCF, which coincided with increased agitation from soldiers' families for better welfare measures. Janet Carmichael, a longtime Liberal supporter, explained to the still somnolent King that unless his government offered some tangible evidence that it was committed to postwar social security, the CCF and the Tories, whose appeals were directed to the common man and the common soldier in the field, would win the next election. 'The Government has the advantage,' she added, 'in that, as in the matter of Family Allowances and such, the ball can be set rolling and the reform presented as an accomplished fact, not as in the case of the others as election promises.'[238] Finally, in December 1943, as a result of the growing popularity of the CCF, the Liberals decided to hold back on James's recommendations concerning full employment, so that this more conservative vision of postwar reconstruction might be used as election ammunition. James saw his hopes for a permanent government research organization thus dashed, and recounted in a mournful letter to William Beveridge that the King Liberals had left his report 'in escrow' and thereby transformed the issue of reconstruction from a policy of 'general agreement' into 'a matter of political controversy.'[239]

By the end of 1943, King did not seem any more personally committed to social welfare legislation than he had been prior to the war. Not only had the prime minister not acquainted himself with either Marsh's or James's recommendations, but he was considering making C.D. Howe – an avowed opponent of family allowances and a conservative voice in Cabinet – the first minister of the proposed Ministry of Reconstruction.[240] If family allowances did not find favour in King's cabinet, how then did they rise to become the Liberals' flagship social welfare measure? Since early 1941 the issue of health insurance had been a top government priority, one that garnered the widespread support of organized labour, the business community, social workers, and ordinary Canadians, and thus inspired the Department of Finance to develop its own scheme.[241] At the same time, Ian Mackenzie appointed Dr Heagerty to outline a legislative plan in consultation with Canadian doctors. Opinion polls showed that three-quarters of Canadians ranked health insurance ahead of family allowances as their preferred social security measure, and many both within and outside official circles believed that health insurance was so firmly entrenched as part of the Liberal reconstruction agenda that it 'can't be shoved off.'[242] However, by 1944 the proposed assessed contribution rate of $26.00 per year per male breadwinner had alienated both labour and the farming constituencies, although it is doubtful that this alone explains why the health insurance bill was hastily withdrawn and replaced by family allowances on 13 April 1944.[243]

If the Liberals reckoned that they could satisfy popular expectations by passing only one welfare recommendation in the Marsh plan, why did they choose family allowances? Intractable constitutional problems would have posed a real threat in the case of health insurance. However, Marsh's argument that social security had become 'shackled by the reactionaries'[244] was probably much closer to the truth and is borne out by contemporary evidence. That Mackenzie King remained uninvolved in directing the course of social security legislation, and that the Economic Advisory Committee was the chief engine propelling the government toward practical commitments on those issues, was abundantly demonstrated in the spring of 1943, as the financial experts plotted in the background, slowly building a case for family allowances. Government acceptance of the principle of family allowances had already been confirmed when in May of that year the DND instituted a sliding scale of children's allowances for up to six children.[245] While the military model may have foreshadowed the civilian family allowances system, government interest in family allowances was further accelerated in the late summer of 1943 with the release of the McTague Report, which directly linked them to the government's wartime wage control policy. In his report, Justice C.P. McTague tried to elaborate strategies for dissipating upward pressure on wages. Moreover, after Canada had been forced by wartime exigencies to accept the presence of large numbers of women in the workforce, McTague and his fellow commissioners also sought ways to uphold the principle – so strongly defended by organized labour – of the concept of equal pay for equal work. But McTague's support of the idea of equal pay for equal work was not meant to further feminist aspirations. Rather, it was intended to uphold the rights of men to a living wage not depressed by the competition of women in the industrial workplace. Family allowances were geared specifically to protect the wage standard of male unionized labour. Interestingly, it was this dimension of the male breadwinner's right and responsibility to maintain his family that garnered the support of big business. As Donald Gordon wrote to the Minister of Finance, J.L. Ilsley: 'Existing wage rates represent the result of a long period of adjustment and frequently of struggle and it is regarded as undesirable to break down the structure by a reduction in labour costs at the present time.' Gordon feared the inflationary effects of wage increases; more importantly, he also objected to women entering the workplace and countenanced equal pay only for those female workers who directly replaced men. Women had no intrinsic right to paid work apart from the anomalous wartime situation, whereby they nominally became men by substituting for them in the workplace.

In this context, family allowances offered the perfect solution. They appealed both to conservative business interests, who wished to contain wage inflation, and to organized labour, who wished to defend the status of the male breadwinner. Moreover, there was solid support among ordinary Canadians for wage and price controls, as was demonstrated in a Gallup poll in December 1941.[246] As McTague observed, family allowances would add to the family wage, and thus discourage the present growth of double-income households and uphold the rights of 'the wage-earner who is the sole support of his family.'[247] In this same vein, McTague also recommended strongly that children's allowances be paid to the father; by doing so he was reinforcing the notion that such allowances were an extension of his pay packet. For years, Canadian governments had been indirectly implementing a family wage policy that was based on maintaining a man, a wife, and one child. Family allowances would uphold the government's conventional living wage policy; not only that, but by paying benefits to all children, they would actually contribute to a scaling back of this official conception of a family wage, now defined as one that would support just a man and his wife. From the perspective of the War Labour Board, family allowances were a means for continuing repressive wartime wage and price controls into peacetime.

By the end of 1943, the temper of the cabinet had shifted dramatically to the right. Progressive Liberals, such as Ian Mackenzie, exhorted King to implement family allowances immediately in concert with the policies of the financial brains trust led by W.C. Clark, which had by October of that year switched its attention away from price controls toward the question of wages.[248] George Davidson related to his confidant, Harry Cassidy, that the Cabinet's support for family allowances was consciously intended to reinforce the recommendations of the National War Labor Board: 'You will be surprised to learn 'that children's allowances are very much to the fore in Canada at the present time, and the Government is giving pretty serious consideration to them right now as a means of easing the pressure on the wage ceiling without blowing the price ceiling wide open.'[249] That family allowances were a ploy by the federal government to avoid implementing across-the-board wage increases was immediately apparent to organized labour. Here is a clear case where the modern welfare state was forged not by the demands of labour,[250] but rather by business interests. Both the Trades and Labour Congress and the Canadian Congress of Labour adamantly protested this government system of wage supplements, viewing them as a direct challenge to their campaign for collective bargaining.[251]

The policy of wage controls through family allowances could not have been timed more poorly by the federal government. As Laurel Sefton McDowall has argued, industrial unrest reached a peak in 1943 in part because of labour's long-standing concerns over not being consulted by the federal government.[252] N.A. McLarty, the Minister of State and former Minister of Labour, was one of the few members of King's cabinet to oppose family allowances on the grounds that they were a wage control policy; he warned King in November that family allowances would not 'allay the agitation for higher wages.'[253] Members of the TLC saw family allowances as a system of embarrassing doles intended to allow the government to circumvent their plea for a national policy of minimum subsistence wages.[254] Other labour representatives perceived them as akin to the 'grudging, stingy, niggardly reward' wartime cost-of-living bonuses. More disturbing still, because family allowances were to be paid to *all* children, they directly flouted labour's agitation for a proper family or living wage, for they were based on the wage rate that could maintain only a man and his wife. In Australia, family allowances were perceived by Labour to be much less provocative, for they were paid after the first child and were accompanied by a government minimum wage policy.[255] Canadian labour officials, such as Percy Bengough, had been hoping that with adequate postwar government employment policies, a man's wage might be high enough to maintain a family of three to four children.[256] It was from this perspective that labour perceived family allowances as so destructive to its policy of collective bargaining.[257]

Organized labour was not, however, unified on the question of family allowances. At their 30 August 1943 convention, the more moderate TLC made no mention of family allowances; however, the CCL vociferously opposed their adoption until the federal government granted them collective bargaining.[258] As they argued, they would officially endorse family allowances only if they were not introduced as a supplement to adequate wages.[259] Moreover, several locals of the TLC happily endorsed a national system of family allowances.[260] Organized labour did not automatically oppose the principle of family allowances, for throughout 1942 and 1943 the TLC had pressed for more generous military children's allowances, in part to forestall women from entering the workforce and thereby undermining the wage scale of male workers.[261] Rather, organized labour had strategically protested against family allowances in order to obtain collective bargaining; after collective bargaining became an established fact, both the TLC and the CCL endorsed family allowances, in October 1944.[262]

The federal government's family allowance policy was not simply aimed at suppressing wartime wage escalation; rather, it was intended to buttress its postwar full employment policies by reducing business costs. Whitton's stinging partisan comment that family allowances were 'a political and fiscal rather than a social measure' and that as such they were merely 'masquerading' as a 'first instalment of social security' was, however, in the main correct. It was obvious to many that the 'Baby Bonus' was a 'humanitarian sprat thrown out to catch the whole of another term in office,'[263] and in fact federal cabinet members were by 1944 being very explicit about the employment and fiscal rather than the social security objectives of the Liberal government. This strategy was aimed principally at forestalling labour dissent. While government propaganda stressed that family allowances were 'an instalment in social security,' Brooke Claxton, the first Minister of Health and Welfare, stated categorically in myriad speeches, broadcasts, and articles that 'family allowances represent a method of creating employment which is just as effective as public investment expenditure' and thus the most 'powerful weapon with which to ward off general economic depression.'[264] In a radio broadcast, Claxton merely parrotted the mantra of the Keynesian mandarins when he stated: 'Social security cannot be achieved without economic security.'[265] There is no better illustration of the fact that increased consumer spending was the main goal of family allowances than the apoplectic reaction of Brooke Claxton when he discovered that Eaton's was advertising savings accounts for children where they could deposit their monthly family allowance cheques.[266] Family allowances were the quickest way 'of funnelling out purchasing power into the hands of consumer groups,'[267] and this had obvious appeal to business interests, who wanted the government to stimulate the economy without maintaining wartime controls. Thus, family allowances provided the perfect balance between priming the economic pump and preserving the maximum amount of free play for market forces.[268]

In July 1944, even while actively refurbishing his image as a great humanitarian committed first and foremost to the relief of poverty, King in fact believed that poverty should be relieved mainly through the fulfilling of familial responsibilities by the able-bodied male breadwinner. King's ideology of government intervention had developed little since he wrote *Industry and Humanity*, in which he conceived of government as an impartial umpire. He countenanced only an imperceptible increase in state responsibility: the role of government was to create economic conditions that were ripe for capital growth and personal savings; from this would flow the traditional liberal verity of equal opportunity. In short, family allowances were intended to 'maintain' a national minimum standard of living by traditional means – by creating jobs for men.[269] King saw family allowances as the best protection for individual effort and family independence, because they would create so much employment as to obviate the need for both postwar taxation and government paternalism.[270] In family allowances the wily King had discovered an issue that was truly consensual and that provided the ideological glue for the cause of national unity, in that it bridged left and right, labour and business, women and men, and French and English Canada in a way that no other contemporary issue could. 'We shall have a Canadian nation,' wrote Dorothy Stepler, 'only when we can feel that pretty generally a Canadian child is entitled to certain economic advantages, whether he is French, or Scotch, or Ukrainian, by origin, whether he is in Quebec or Alberta, whether he is the son of a Roman Catholic or Presbyterian or Lutheran, or even a Marxian Communist.'[271] Social security became the metaphor for wartime nationalism – a modern ideology that soon displaced traditional ethnic, religious, and linguistic definitions of nation. The provenance of our modern conception of Canada thus lies with King Liberalism.

The avowed Communist Stanley B. Ryerson called the Liberals the 'artisans of a finer, more richly democratic and progressive Canada' because their social security policy 'combined [the] forces of liberalism and labor'[272] into a new spirit of unity. While his remarks may seem hopelessly utopian, in pragmatic terms King's policies had just such a result; by wedding family allowances – a policy that was anathema to organized labour – to full employment, King was able to defuse labour's objections, because the central plank in the platform of unionized labour and the federal CCF was federally sponsored job creation policies. As the labour representative on James's Advisory Committee on Reconstruction, Percy Bengough had championed government economic management of the economy as well as measures to increase individual spending, arguing that Canadian workers had 'a right to expect useful creative employment with a decent standard of living in balance with our times and productive ability.'[273] Similarly, A.R. Mosher and Pat Conroy of the CCL, in their submission to the House of Commons Committee on Reconstruction and Re-establishment, demanded greater government economic controls aimed at reviving capitalism and international trade as well as stimulating full employment.[274] Perhaps the best barometer of labour's attitude was an observation by J.L. Cohen: 'Social security without jobs is much like the biblical sentence "bricks without straw."'[275]

The Family Allowances Act of 1944 was a strategic *tour de force* on the part of the King Liberals. It satisfied rural constituencies – especially those in Western Canada, which were tilting toward the Progressive Conservatives under the prairie farmer, John Bracken.[276] Not only that, but by promoting family allowances as a fiscal rather than a social service measure, the federal Liberals were able to circumvent the troublesome shoals of constitutional conflict. By solidifying its taxation and fiscal powers, the federal government was shifting powers to the centre so that it would be able to control the peacetime economy in such a way as to override the opposition of organized labour.[277]

In addition, family allowances divided the left and in doing so disabled the election appeal of the CCF.[278] Unfortunately for the CCF, in the same year that its members had voted at their convention to endorse the social security program of Sir William Beveridge, in which family allowances featured prominently, it had forged closer links with the CCL, the labour organization most strongly opposed to family allowances.[279] This laid bare the fragility of the CCF/CCL alliance. The CCF had difficulty shaking off its long-term association with the policy of family allowances especially considering that its first leader, J.S. Woodsworth, was the foremost sponsor of them in 1928. The most formidable problem facing the CCF, however, was that it had not moved away from its roots as a protest movement,[280] and had issued no new platform since the Regina Manifesto of 1933. The election agenda of the CCF thus seemed woefully antiquated during wartime, as did its organization, which had not seen fit to hire a social security expert, even in the wake of the Beveridge Report. Just prior to the forecast 1944 election, the CCF had to depend for its research on either Liberal party publications or the talents of Liberal sympathizers such as George Davidson and Harry Cassidy.[281] Indeed, the Keynesian notion of the 'mixed economy,' which so animated the work of James and Marsh, formed the basic intellectual sustenance of Major Coldwell, Woodsworth's successor.[282] That the CCF was split between the new Keynesianism and pre-Depression British Socialist ideology was evident from the comments of one of its former fellow-travellers, Harry Cassidy. Writing to L.R. Shaw, the erstwhile Director of Research for the CCF, Cassidy exhorted the party of Woodsworth to modernize its views of social security:

> For some comments on the Beveridge Report and the comparative lack of interest in social security which was displayed by some C.C.F. people with whom I talked last summer gave me the impression that this point of view is not uncommon. I think that the essential point to make is that while social security programs do not solve or pretend to solve all social issues, they are nevertheless inseparable parts of a total policy to guarantee decent living standards and reasonable freedom for the bulk of the population.[283]

In eschewing social security as a mere palliative that fell far short of socialism, the CCF had failed to respond to the demands of the masses. In the absence of any comprehensive blueprint for social insurance, the CCF's reconstruction platform revolved essentially around the quest for full employment through centralized government planning – a platform indistinguishable from that of the King Liberals. The CCF's leader, Major Coldwell, could only echo Brooke Claxton when he declared that social security must be based on full employment.[284] The coupling of family allowances with full employment stymied dissent from both the left and the right, for neither group could launch any effective criticism of Liberal social security without appearing merely partisan and at worse antediluvian. Even the Social Credit premier of Alberta, Ernest Manning, championed family allowances as but a Liberal version of his party's economic panacea of the 'national dividend' – even though he well recognized them as a 'diabolically clever' bait for votes.[285] Clearly, the extreme political fractiousness that characterized 1945 was founded paradoxically on the highest level of ideological agreement in Canadian political history. Cassidy presciently observed: 'In principal, both capitalists and socialists are committed to the idea that every child should have a fair chance; and with that as a major premise, there is much the same premise for social security planning. Hence, it need not be a field in which there are broad disagreements of policies between the major political groups.'[286] In sum, through rigorous propaganda King and his party had ensured that Canadians were indeed all liberals now.

'Keeping the home inviolate'[287]

If, as I have argued, family allowances merely extended male citizenship rights established by government welfare and social insurance programs during the Depression, how then did women react in wartime to federal government recommendations concerning family allowances? Did women challenge the gender divisions upheld by Canadian welfare policies? Did they envision family allowances as a means to establish women's economic independence either in the home or in the workplace? Or were they merely complicit in protecting the stature of the male breadwinner?

For the most part, Canadian women's organizations only mildly supported the principle of family allowances and played only a small role in refashioning the ideology undergirding the idea of cash supplements to the male wage. Many Canadian women would have preferred that postwar reconstruction policies had coalesced around the question of better maternal health and child welfare services, especially since most of the women's organizations were politically powerful at the provincial level.[288] As Mrs Mary Kendell, a working-class housewife from Victoria, British Columbia, informed Prime Minister Mackenzie King, although family allowances were welcomed, health insurance, improved day nurseries, well-baby clinics, and reduced rates for services to mothers would have been better sources of security for women like her.[289] Women's organizations endorsed family allowances only because they helped preserve gender boundaries between the home and the workplace. The one demonstrable kernel of opposition from women to family allowances centred on whether they should be payable to the husband or the wife, and even this revolved around the issue of how best to stabilize family life. The agitation to have family allowances paid to mothers was not a new, radical feminist departure; rather, this movement represented the conventional maternal-feminist evocation of the spiritual, maternal-dominated home. What these women were agitating against was the post-Depression idea that the family was the total reflection of the personality of the father. These women wished to reassert a conception of the maternalist family whereby the children remained firmly under the aegis of the mother's spiritual and affectional tutelage. Far from constituting an attack on traditional gender norms, the campaign to pay allowances to women was meant to 'recognize the high place of the mother in a home in relation to her children and to the community in which they live.'[290] Indeed, Hilda Ridley advocated a combined scheme of voluntary and state family allowances as a reassertion of 'spiritual motherhood,' which she believed held an uncertain tenure in contemporary Canadian culture.[291] The 1944–45 campaign by Canadian women to have family allowances paid to mothers was thus simply a reaffirmation of the concept of separate spheres, in which the mother commanded the affectional ties within the home while the breadwinner provided economic security. Even the fiercest defenders of making payments to the mother, like Mrs Cora T. Casselman, the Liberal MP from Edmonton, conceded that these allowances remained in essence a component of the male wage, since they were applied to his tax bill.[292] From her point of view, therefore, payments to mothers were largely symbolic, for as she herself contended, the male breadwinner 'by right of his being a

Canadian citizen and a father of a family' still held the paramount right to these allowances.[293]

Indeed, the Report of the Advisory Committee on Reconstruction's Sub-Committee on Post-War Problems of Women, chaired by Mrs Margaret McWilliams, the head of the Canadian Association of Social Workers and a long-time organizer of Winnipeg private relief agencies, was predicated on the idea that reconstruction must begin with full employment for returned soldiers. McWilliams and her female colleagues were determined to show that postwar policies could not be conceived apart from the problems of women; but they did little to disturb the disposition of the federal government that family allowances 'upholds the family and the home as the foundation of family life.'[294] Thus, they may have countenanced the presence of single women in the workforce after the cessation of wartime hostilities; but they offered 'warm support of the principle of the two-person unit' within marriage, whereby the wife's welfare entitlements were derived solely from the status of the male breadwinner; and they promoted family allowances principally because they would, by shoring up the family income, encourage married women to return to their natural sphere, the home. Like mothers' allowances a generation before, family allowances were to signal public recognition for the unpaid labour of married women in the home: 'This group makes a tremendous contribution to the welfare of the country if they keep their husbands and children healthy, happy and efficient. The work is vital, though unpaid.'[295] What is particularly striking about McWilliams's conclusions is that neither she nor any other Canadian women perceived family allowances as a means of providing women in the home with economic independence; nor did they arrive at the notion that by removing the variable of family need in determining the wage standard, family allowances would help affirm the principle of equal pay for equal work for women who did wish to enter the labour market. Canadian feminists were much more concerned that home life be preserved, that child delinquency be combatted, and that the trend toward higher divorce rates be nullified through the erection of policies reaffirming the status of the male breadwinner. In this regard, McWilliams and her committee endorsed those economic policies which would confirm the male breadwinner's sole right to maintain his family, and they urged that married women retreat from the workplace so that they would not depress men's wages. All of this, even though they upheld the democratic ideal that women should have the right to choose either work or the home.[296] Working-class women also shared the view of these policymakers. As Miriam Chapin, a working-class housewife, commented: 'But unless the government goes in for children's allowances on a big scale, it is the women with the little ones who want the work most, and they will go.'[297] The only dissenting voice concerning postwar gender relations was that of Harriet Roberts Forsey, a member of the CCF and a vociferous critic of Margaret McWilliams, who advised men to take over many of the 'social and organic functions' of women, 'without feeling loss of manhood,' so that women could indeed become full-fledged citizens and independent individuals in a renewed democracy by engaging in full-time paid employment.[298] Thus, while Gail Cuthbert Brandt's conclusion that the McWilliams committee was marginalized is in the main correct, in the larger scheme of things this committee added little in the way of feminist dissent from the dominant male-directed discourse of full employment for men.[299]

By endorsing the concept of family allowances, Mrs McWilliams and her female colleagues were adhering to a principle that pervaded the Beveridge and Marsh Reports – that wives 'are insured in virtue of their husbands.'[300] As a long-time administrator in local relief and charitable agencies, Mrs McWilliams supported government programs that would uphold the work ethic and family self-sufficiency. She thus supported family allowances because of the role they would play in creating employment for men and in preserving lesser eligibility. Both these results had become central goals of Canadian welfare. During the Depression, many social workers had noted the dangerous anomalies created in large families where cash relief for child dependants provided a family income higher than the standard wage of unskilled labourers.[301] One of the most important though least publicized goals of the government promoters of family allowances was to exclude dependants' benefits from social insurance programs, thereby reducing the potential for financial strain on the federal treasury. This was a key part of the government's overall strategy, which was to use family policy to uphold the work ethic among men. This strategy was first enunciated by the National Employment Commission in 1938, when it insisted that unemployment aid not be used as an alternative to decent wages and work.[302] If the aim of full employment was to create an efficient workforce, it was equally crucial to compel even those on the lowest economic rungs – unskilled and seasonal workers – to wean themselves from government assistance. From this perspective, family allowances did not signify the beginning of a new era of positive government; rather, they served to *contain* government growth by reducing the 'units of social security' benefits to what would sustain a man and his wife.[303] In using family allowances to lower the scale of social insurance benefits, Marsh and the Liberals showed themselves to differ little in their outlook from Charlotte Whitton.[304] Thus, as George Davidson commented, family allowances protected the federal taxing power without creating any new contractual rights between the government and its male citizenry.[305]

As a consequence of the drive toward full employment at the end of the war, women were encouraged to leave paid employment. However, in the wake of Keynesian economics, which saw spending as creating national economic wealth, the pressure for women to return to the ambit of the home and family was decidedly weaker than it had been in the First World War. Indeed, even Gilbert Jackson, the conservative economist who wrote the reports for the James Committee on industrial conversion, which focused on the demobilization of women from the workforce, accepted a wide degree of latitude regarding postwar female employment, largely because he believed that if more women worked there would be even higher levels of disposable income, which would contribute exponentially to priming the Canadian economic pump. Moreover, it was conventional wisdom among reconstruction planners that because of the higher mortality rates among men during the war, a large number of women would remain single and thus demand paid labour at high wages. Lastly, government policymakers had reluctantly accepted that the war had changed attitudes regarding the gendered complexion of the workplace, and were basing their postwar family policies to a large degree on the notion that many women would refuse to give their pay packets and the independence these offered.[306] It is noteworthy that in the midst of the war, even big business interests generally accepted that 'Winnie the war worker' was firmly 'wedded' to her job and might well refuse to rely on her husband's money after the war. In part this was because businessmen shared the dominant wartime ideal of postwar abundance, whereby one's status would be directly linked to one's ability to purchase consumer goods. Interestingly, businessmen were at the forefront in changing attitudes toward women's ability to perform in the industrial workplace; in contrast to the First World War, they greatly praised the abilities of women and indeed restructured their modern industrial training methods in response to the reality of the 'post-war women-power problem.' What is particularly striking is that for the first time, businessmen were asserting a decided preference for the married female worker.[307]

These attitudes toward married women's work in the postwar era must, however, be evaluated in the context of the pattern of women's employment between 1939 and 1945. On the basis that numerous women entered the workplace during wartime, Ruth Roach Pierson has highlighted the precipitousness in the decline in women's work after 1945.[308] These aggregate employment statistics for women must be analyzed in terms of the marital status of female workers. Contemporary statistics well demonstrated that the vast majority of women working in war industries were single. By 1942, women made up one-third of the Canadian workforce, but as James's researchers discovered, this was coincident with the number of single women available for work.[309] Mrs Rex Eaton, the head of the women's section of the National Selective Service, found that only 10 per cent of working women were married; as she stated, 'women's instinctual natural preference is for home and family.'[310] Admittedly, this tendency was encouraged by the paucity of government day nurseries; even so, the wartime tax structure did encourage married women to work.[311] Since government policies thus cancelled one another out, it is evident that married women with small children did not desire paid employment outside the home, and these women took on full-time work only after their children reached school age. But even among this constituency of married women workers, only 50 per cent chose to work full-time.[312] The pattern of women's war work was also determined strongly by region. At the peak of wartime industrial production, fully 47 per cent of the workforce in Ontario was composed of women; in Quebec this number was only 30 per cent, and in the rest of Canada only 12 per cent.[313] Thus, outside the manufacturing heartland, the proportion of women in the workforce had not risen above the prewar average of 13 per cent – the lowest proportion of women in the workforce in the Western industrialized world.[314] By 1944 the supply of single women's labour had been depleted. Only 26.9 per cent of the female workers were married, and as Mrs Rex Eaton informed the National Selective Service Advisory Board, 'a large number were already showing signs of desire to return to their homes.' More striking still, when the demand for trained nurses was at its peak, fully half stated that they were housewives and preferred only part-time or emergency work.[315] Thus, if married women sought war work, they did so largely because of economic pressures created by the dramatic upsurge in the cost of living in 1944, which forced many soldiers' wives, who had previously lived adequately on their government military allowances, to take up paid work.[316] Married women entered the workplace with some reluctance, and envisioned their capacity to earn as a temporary one, and perceived their work largely as a form of war service. Well before the war ended, women were voluntarily drifting out of the workplace. The result was a constant and often crippling shortage of female labour after the fall of 1944.[317]

In contrast to demobilization during the First World War, the impetus for relegating women back to the domestic sphere did not emanate chiefly from men. At the conclusion of the Second World War, government, business, and organized labour were strangely silent on this question because they could discern from wartime employment statistics that there would be no great disjuncture in the traditional pattern whereby married women abjured permanent paid work outside the home. The issue of whether married women would jettison the home for the workplace was largely a preoccupation of women, and the divided discourse in women's journals over this question reveals much about the character of wartime feminism. For every article like that by Rica McLean Farquharson in the *Canadian Home Journal*, which insisted that the majority of Canadian women relished 'the thrill of a pay envelope,' there were just as many which upheld the view that women wished to return home because they are 'women in the full sense.'[318] It appears from these articles that many of the women who were determined to stay in the workforce were unmarried and had worked prior to the war. For example, Dorothy Norwich in her article 'Women in a Man's World' reported the case of a woman who had always worked as a domestic but who hoped after the war to buy a farm for herself and her girlfriend.[319] Of the relatively small proportion of married women doing war work, many polls and surveys consistently showed that half of them intended to return to the home at the end of the war.[320]

The Canadian Association for Adult Education maintained in 'Equal Pay for Equal Work: Are Women Getting a Fair Deal?' – an article endorsed by the Canadian Congress of Labour – that the prevailing prejudice that the husband must be the sole provider was rapidly being worn away.[321] Similarly, Walter S. Woods, one of Cyril James's advisers on his reconstruction committee, supported the likely expansion in postwar married women's work on the grounds that this would raise consumer demand and thus obviate the need for expensive new government social security measures.[322] However, most articles written by women refused to directly challenge the exclusive right of the husband to be the primary breadwinner. Postwar Canadian feminists had shifted their ideological perspective away from maternal feminism, insofar as they championed the right of women to choose between work and home; even so, they never launched a full-scale critique of the long-standing ideal of separate spheres. Mme H. Vautelet, the author of *Post-War Problems and Employment of Women in the Province of Quebec*, encouraged women to bring the spirit of 'economic independence' into their homelife, largely as a means to shore up the vision of the democratic family, in which the husband and wife cooperated in managing the family finances and raised the children in peaceful partnership. Like many contemporary feminists, Mme Vautelet preserved the bifurcation between social security for women and work for men. Thus, even though she recommended liberalizing the Unemployment Insurance Act, she did so only to help promote the field of domestic service for women. She thereby failed to delineate any new initiatives for women's employment and likewise never openly challenged the breadwinner ideal; rather, she exhorted women to reconcile marriage and economic independence by seeking only part-time work outside the home. However, Mme Vautelet echoed the sentiments of earlier maternal feminists when she evoked the image of the Madonna in the home defending the nation through her reproductive capacity.[323]

For the majority of female commentators during the war, employment for women meant part-time work only. While it might be argued that by articulating a harmonization between home and work, wartime feminism was taking tentative steps toward a more modern feminist perspective, it must be underscored that these feeble first steps toward defending the economic rights of women in the marketplace would not gain any real force for another two decades, and that even amidst the liberalizing demands of the wartime economy, Canadian women consistently subordinated women's right to choose between work and home to their defence of the man's right to be the sole and exclusive breadwinner. Women were thus cast in their traditional role as part-time earners of pin money by which to supplement the family wage[324] – all in the name of consumerism, the ideal of postwar abundance, and full employment. If women's citizenship rights were being transformed in this era, it was through the creation of hundreds of local

Women's Schools of Citizenship, which focused on extending already established political and social rights of women.[325]

In 1943, Charlotte Whitton encapsulated the cultural and economic aims that sustained the Liberal government's social security program: 'The family is regarded as the essential unity in an economically and socially stable state ... and as a corollory, that the individual's responsibility for maintaining himself and those dependent upon him is primary to the community's responsibility.'[326] Here was the ideological template that was invoked in the Family Allowances Act of 1944. This legislation marked no new significant or radical departure from the past, nor did it create any new welfare entitlements. Rather, it was a strongly conservative economic measure, a temporary 'gift' rather than a new universal welfare right, and it had been wrapped quite deliberately by the King Liberals in the Christmas tinsel of 'Santa Claus' state protection from cradle to grave. The hope held out to Canadians by the prospect of government largesse and the implications of this legislation for wartime morale and optimism were in many respects more important than its substantive qualities. The Liberals' family policies were wartime psychological weapons launched by a government that had little commitment to ever implementing the comprehensive social security package outlined by Leonard Marsh in his now famous report. Family allowances represented the politically acceptable minimum that would both secure the essence of the individualistic Canadian character and respond to the newly created popular demand for 'collective security.'[327] It was an inspired gambit, in the sense that it became a touchstone for every conceivable wartime concern. Many saw it as a remedy for wartime family instability, and its promise of full employment eased lingering fears of depression in both business and labour circles. At the same time, its privileging of the individual appealed to a wide cross-section of the Canadian community, which saw in it both a bulwark against totalitarianism and a symbol of renewed democracy. For fiscal conservatives in the King cabinet, it promised lower insurance benefits and a reduction in the basic family wage. Yet at the same time, for those of progressive sympathies, it was the harbinger of a much larger, interventionist, and beneficent welfare state. As a friend of Harry Cassidy's wife Bea optimistically exclaimed in 1944, when family allowances were announced: 'Canada is on the move and moving to the left [and the King government] will have to go far, very far, in the field of social legislation.'[328] Finally, family allowances appealed to King and his Cabinet, ever occupied by the issue of Canadian unity, because social security in this idealized formulation forged a new equation between Liberalism and nationalism.[329] Family allowances became the vehicle by which King warded off the fate of the British Liberal party during the First World War, which found itself destroyed between the Scylla of militant Toryism and the Charybdis of the emerging Labour Party. King had thus deftly turned the political tables on Sir Robert Borden, who had once (prophetically) sent him as a gift his own personal copy of George Dangerfield's *The Strange Death of Liberal England*.[330]

However much family allowances were utilized to create a broad public consensus and thereby enforce popular allegiance to the State, or as a partisan tool to win elections, they nevertheless were designed to defend particular principles and traditions. Though firmly swathed in the language of universal rights and the panacea of social security, family allowances were anchored in the conservative Keynesian promise of full employment. Far from launching a new era of government expansion, family allowances in 1944 represented the end of a period in welfare history in which social policies had as their ultimate goal the preservation of the right of men to work and of their responsibility to maintain their female and child dependants. If ordinary Canadians like Mrs Annie Cresswell, the harried wife of a war veteran, complained that her family allowance cheque was insufficient to meet family needs and relieve the threat of poverty,[331] this was as the federal government had intended. From the Liberals' point of view, family allowances were but a temporary cash bonus. While they promised access to postwar abundance, they were in fact yet another defence of the old Victorian work ethic.

Conclusion:
'The Endangered Family'[1]

This book has preceded on the premise that there is a dynamic relationship between public thought and government policies, and that the development of the Canadian welfare state cannot be explained solely in terms of the activities of government legislators but rather, must be studied from the vantage point of the public arena of ideological discussion and conflict and seen as the reflection of broadly based ideological concerns. In *Engendering the State* I have argued that welfare entitlements were directly determined by changing ideas of what constituted the national interest. As the definition of national prosperity was gradually severed from the question of population growth, and as the notion of social purpose came to be identified with economic efficiency and full employment as opposed to the educative characters of the domestic sphere, the maternalist vision of social citizenship waned and the rights of wage-earning men were moved to the fore. Except for a brief period immediately following the First World War, when the death or incapacity of thousands of men galvanized public sentiment around the issue of female dependency, welfare policies in Canada were rarely constructed to address the problem of social distress and poverty; rather, government welfare policies fulfilled the imperatives of national economic efficiency. As a result, the welfare strategies that emerged in Canada in the first four decades of the twentieth century were decidedly conservative in their aims and were implemented to affirm the laws of the marketplace, or to contain social instability, or most importantly to defend the family and the gender roles on which it was founded.

In their origin and development, Canadian welfare policies were unique in the industrialized world because of their talismanic identification with family stability and independence. In other countries, welfare architects developed measures in response to the politicization of the labouring classes or the demands of businessmen, or to address problems of urban poverty and widespread social dependency; in Canada, in contrast, welfare reformers saw social forces as but a reflection of familial relationships, and issues relating to urban decay, social dependency, economic instability, and political conflict were inevitably drawn into the vortex of the national preoccupation with stabilizing the family and the gendered roles on which it was founded. Because social chaos was perceived as synonymous with gender disorder, Canada's welfare policies had as their goal to protect the self-reliant family by enforcing the breadwinner ideal. The watchword of welfare advocates was 'personal responsibility' of the male head of the household, whose exclusive duty it was to defend the polity against the threat of social dependency by securing his own family's economic self-sufficiency. That the development of Canadian welfare policies was mediated at all times by the breadwinner ideal and its evocation of family independence explains the central paradox of state building in Canada – namely, that it developed not as a linear process from individualism toward collectivism, but that government welfare policies developed in such a way as to reinforce the family. While the perceived crisis in the breadwinner ideal may have resulted in increasing government policing and intervention into the private, domestic sphere, it produced no real revolution in government, nor did it result in a redrawing of the boundaries between private and public. Whatever the rhetoric of the King government, which declared in 1944 that the Canadian national identity was commensurate with governmental security measures, the growth of the state bureaucracy involved no fundamental antithesis between state welfare and individual liberty. Rather, the welfare entitlements that were created between 1900 and 1945 took a form that only confirmed the verities of the limited state enshrined in nineteenth-century liberalism; they upheld and indeed strengthened the forms of civil society that revolved principally around the private family. Government expansion was thus a means of rehabilitating individual freedom, the ideal of masculine self-reliance, and family independence – all hallmarks of liberal democracy. Twentieth-century state building in Canada was thus a *conserving* process that had as its goal the containment of social ferment and the tempering of gender anomalies.

Because social solidarity and economic progress were believed to flow from an ideal of family cohesion based on specific gender roles,

Canadian welfare reform did not focus on correcting economic structures or on reforming the changing social environment; rather, it
emphasized regenerating the individual – more specifically, rectifying
and disciplining male behaviour. The expression 'no fault of their
own,' first articulated immediately following the First World War, was
a rhetorical injunction applied to both women and men to exonerate
individuals from the strictures of poor law ideology. Its frequent use
represented a widespread acknowledgment among reformers, social
workers, and welfare administrators that social dependency had deep,
environmental causes. But, however much social investigators attributed an individual's economic distress to forces beyond his or her control (e.g., illness, death, unemployment) the solution to welfare
problems was believed to lie with regenerating individuals. State policies emphasized educating, reforming, and disciplining husbands who
were not measuring up to the breadwinner ideal, whether they had
abandoned their families or were simply unemployed. A central theme
of *Engendering the State* has been to show how an increasing emphasis
on the ideal of the individual male breadwinner resulted in women
being expunged from the welfare landscape in such a way that
'femaleness' became synonymous with dependency. This was inevitable in the decades when the family was being reoriented so that it was
no longer an essentially spiritual, maternal-centred entity but rather
primarily an economic unit dominated by the male wage earner. The
Canadian welfare state emerged hand in hand with a strengthening of
male citizenship rights; this eradicated the ideology of separate
spheres according to which female and male functions were complementary. By the end of the Second World War, the male breadwinner
was the centre of the family – a cultural dynamic hastened, reinforced,
and made rigid by the creation of exclusively male welfare entitlements during the 1930s.

Public interest groups and government policymakers placed an
overwhelming priority on the family as the core of all social relationships, and their preoccupation with strengthening gender conventions
arrested the development of structural and environmental explana-
tions for poverty and dependency. This prolonged the life of an individualist cultural outlook. One effect of this was to truncate a native
tradition of social investigation; thus, analyses of wages, unemployment patterns, and family living standards were still in an embryonic
state at the end of the Second World War. In the mid-1920s, various
groups began marshalling statistical evidence to illustrate the often

yawning gap between the male wage and family need – an issue first brought to public attention by J.S. Woodsworth and Léon Lebel, who agitated for government family allowances in 1928–29. Even so, a thorough investigation of wages, nutrition, and the causes of unemployment was still largely absent from the field of family social policy well into the 1940s. That social research remained underdeveloped throughout this period can be explained also by the fact that it was undertaken by private family welfare agencies and organizations like the Canadian Council on Child Welfare, which concerned itself almost exclusively with female dependency and maternal health – issues that never would be perceived as fundamental social crises, given the conventions militating against the presence of women in the workplace, and given the dominance of the breadwinner ideal. Only in the 1930s did social scientists begin in any consistent way to apply scientific knowledge to the field of public policy. And as I have shown with regard to the work of Leonard Marsh, this research focused on male unemployment and so only reaffirmed the economic goals of welfare policy and in doing so actually drew public attention *away* from the problem of social dependency, which had come to be defined as an exclusively female problem. And the research that was carried out had little impact on actual policy formation, as the fate of the Marsh Report makes clear. Policy continued to be created within a conservative bureaucracy and was ultimately determined by a coterie of old-line Liberals – a network stubbornly resistant to the new scientific vision of government planning.

Between 1900 and 1945, the Canadian welfare state evolved in such a way as to enshrine the breadwinner ideal in culture and society. Indeed, the breadwinner ideal was constantly refined so that it remained the locus of public discussion even while the language of welfare entitlements changed. The period between 1900 and 1945 witnessed a transformation from the maternal-centred, needs-based welfare structure of the pre-Depression era to a rights-based conception of citizenship that gave clear precedence to waged labourers; and by 1945 the ancient poor law philosophy (i.e., that fear of starvation was the most efficient goad for compelling men to work) had been replaced by a more optimistic outlook which insisted that hope was the best elixir for ambition and productive labour. Yet despite all this, the notion that the best family security was a husband with a job remained the one, constant fixture underlying the myriad debates and cross-class, cross-gender contestations over the means to accomplish this consensual goal. The breadwinner ideology was never static, nor was it ever an irrefutable axiom. As I argued in this book, prior to 1900 the breadwinner ideal was merely implicit in Canadian society, and remained an unstated cultural convention until it was threatened repeatedly by the various world crises of the early twentieth century. As the family, and the breadwinner norm in particular, came under assault through the growth in child abandonment, family desertion, unemployment, military service, and illegitimacy, all of which revolved around the inability of men to financially provide for their families, traditional gender ideologies could no longer simply be assumed; rather, they had to be made explicit and defended by public authority. Thus, as men began failing to fulfil their masculine duties, new mechanisms of social control, in the form of government welfare measures, were devised to uphold gender boundaries.

But as *Engendering the State* contends, the deviants from these social norms were invariably *men*, not women. This study thus takes issue with the canonical historical interpretation, inspired by feminists' modern-day preoccupation with workplace rights for women, that women were active agents in dismantling traditional gender norms. The pattern of married women's work in Canada between 1900 and 1945 profoundly challenges this assumption, for even during periods of great economic upheaval, such as the Depression and the two world wars, when the demand for female labour escalated as men served abroad, married women did not enter the workforce in large enough numbers to contest gender norms, and those women who did engage in waged labour saw their work as temporary and aberrant, and their wages as mere supplements to the primary male wage. It would take two more decades before the 'masculine wife' would enter the workforce in substantial numbers and for the 'double wage'[2] family to be considered a 'normal' feature of Canadian society.

Dependent women, the majority of whom were married to working-class men, adamantly supported the breadwinner ideal. Even after the male head of the household died, or deserted, or became incapacitated, or lost his job, or went off to war, these women preferred to receive government welfare assistance rather than to seek work for wages and thereby transgress on the breadwinner's role. Indeed, class and gender conflicts between the two world wars revolved mainly around the meaning and implications of the breadwinner ideal. Except during wartime, when working-class men invited the state to substitute for them as household heads, skilled workingmen eschewed the growth of the interventionist state. Because organized labour identified the dignity of labour with male self-reliance, and because the notion of independence from governmental authority was the *leitmotif* of workplace politics, labour leaders opposed welfare, and favoured an adequate living wage, and endorsed only those government policies which did not interfere with the fundamental right of male workers to protect the economic security of their families. Thus, they supported unemployment insurance and mothers' pensions to the extent that they were prophylactics against women entering the workforce. During the 1930s, the belief among labour leaders that capitalism should yield men a living wage coalesced with their belief which they shared with social scientists and legislators that work was central to men's individual identity and also to the collective identity; at this juncture, organized labour became more closely allied to the mainstream architects of the small state, such as Charlotte Whitton and Leonard Marsh, who likewise championed the privileging of male work over welfare handouts. Working-class women had a different understanding of the breadwinner norm. In their view, once the husband abdicated his obligations he also renounced his citizenship rights, which they believed should be conferred on deserving women like themselves, who, unlike the delinquent men, were keeping their families together. In the belief that state welfare assistance should replace the absent or delinquent breadwinner's wage, working-class and dependent women consistently demanded greater rather than lesser state control of families. They disdained both the narrowing and the engendering of welfare citizenship rights largely because this forced women to transgress gender norms by entering the arena of male work. However much working-class women may have contested the mainstream interpretation of the breadwinner ideal and its rationalization for limiting state protection of women, their individual pleas for greater female entitlements that would allow them the freedom and independence to fulfil their responsibilities as mothers went largely unheeded except in wartime, when their commitment to preserving the family happened to intersect with the national interest.

Although there were brief flurries of concern over married women's work, the temporary overstepping of gender boundaries by women was never conceived by welfare reformers to be of such magnitude as to precipitate a social crisis. More important to them was the increasing reality that men were failing to fulfil their responsibilities as breadwinning household heads. Delinquent male behaviour was thus the central concern when the modern welfare state was being established. The debate about welfare between 1900 and 1945 was pervaded by a preoccupation with the deficiencies and aberrant behaviour of delinquent husbands and fathers, and all welfare measures instituted between 1900 and 1945 sought to remedy this breeching of the breadwinner norm by using government regulations to compel men to work and maintain their dependants within a stable family unit. If women were at times 'morally regulated' by intrusive government administrators, men – especially working-class men – were constantly being compelled to fulfil their obligations to their families and to society. The means applied to this end was a web of deeply held cultural assumptions, along with formal governmental controls. Worth noting here is that the church-dominated evocation of the maternal-centred family had developed as a reaction against the perceived deficiencies of male religious and moral behaviour; and that the early child welfare movement, mothers' allowance legislation, and the work of the Canadian Patriotic Fund all focused on the disfunctional female-headed family in which the male wage earner was absent through death, or desertion, or military service. The hallmark mothers' allowance legislation, which was enacted in five provinces between the First World War and the early 1920s, reflected a subtle cultural shift away from maternal concerns, for while these allowances were ostensibly established to protect the domestic sphere by keeping women at home, in practice they were employed to uphold the male work ethic by forcing widows to work for wages and thus take over the breadwinner's traditional role, so that the allowances paid by the State would not be seen as interfering with the deeply rooted belief in family self-sufficiency on which the breadwinner ideal was based. This breadwinner ideal was even more overtly articulated, by government legislators and social scientists alike, during the Depression, when federal relief and later the Unemployment Insurance Act of 1940 directly moulded welfare policies around the exclusive right of men to obtain work and wages. The 1930s was a pivotal decade in which welfare citizenship was decisively redefined in economic terms, and the family in materialist terms. This final refutation of the spiritual and affectional sanctity of the domestic sphere established the conditions under which the Family Allowances Act of 1944 was implemented. Far from championing the rights of children within the female-centred home, family allowances were an extension of the male wage. The public widely perceived this legislation as an effort to shore up to the breadwinner's ability to economically support his family – that is, as a purely fiscal policy that, by lowering wages and encouraging spending, would ensure full employment for returned soldiers and usher in a period of consumer abundance. Family allowances reconceived the home as a direct extension of the marketplace; the traditional Madonna, shorn of her reproductive labour, had been transformed into a female consumer automaton. And like previous welfare legislation, family allowances were endorsed by the public because, by creating employment opportunities, they were the most efficacious means to encourage returning soldiers to mend their broken homes.

The Family Allowances Act of 1944 thus reinforced what had been a central tenet of all social welfare legislation since just prior to the First World War – namely, that the only kind of family social security that would be publicly countenanced was that provided by the wages of the male breadwinner. Family allowances as instituted by the King Liberals encouraged the work ethic, preserved the principle of lesser eligibility, upheld individual freedom, appeased organized labour and the political left by stimulating full employment, prevented social unrest, and created loyalty to the State by fostering a sense of social security. But most important, because the allowances were intended as supplements to the male wage, they did not interfere with a husband's responsibility to maintain his family, and thus they helped in a very significant way to uphold the liberal ideal of the small, non-interventionist welfare state. Male conformity to gender norms was enforced more stringently than policies designed to discourage married women's participation in the workforce for the simple reason that the ability of the responsible male breadwinner to work for adequate wages was the guarantee of family self-sufficiency and thus the greatest bulwark protecting the inviolability of the principle of limited government intervention in the private sphere of the family. Because the development of the modern welfare state remained ideologically tethered to the notion that male citizens rather than government were responsible for family security, the appearance of expanding social welfare entitlements in reality was intended to promote the eventual withering away of the State. All governments were reluctant to enter the field of family welfare policy, and when they did so, the intention was never to build a permanent and expanding State; rather, even under the rubric of the new social security state, social welfare assistance was conditional on and subservient to a sound economy. Indeed, the dominant theme uniting public discussion of welfare legislation was a suspicion of government growth – a suspicion shared by businessmen, organized labour, the intellectual left, and feminists alike. The belief that welfare assistance was socially beneficial as long as it did not encroach on the rights and responsibilities of the male breadwinner contributed enormously to shackling popular agitation among ordinary Canadians for an expanded welfare structure. The voices of working-class and dependent women were the only discordant note in the paean of praise for limited state intervention in the domestic sphere. Although various social constituencies critiqued poor law ideology, the wage structure, and capitalism's ability to provide sufficient jobs, none ever challenged the male breadwinner ideal. Neither the right nor the left in Canada strayed from the keystone idea of liberalism – that state welfare was essentially an anomaly, a temporary corrective to periods of disruption in the economy, which was presumed to provide, when at equilibrium, work and wages sufficient to meet family needs. Despite the increasing evidence that widespread poverty and economic distress existed in Canada, welfare advocates never fully subscribed to the view that poverty and economic dislocation were endemic features of modern industrial society. Indeed, this credo of the liberal state reached its apogee in 1945, when all three major political parties championed the notion that free market capitalism could be rejuvenated through government planning and the indirect mechanisms of fiscal management and welfare spending, and that the achievement of full employment would again confirm that Canada was still an emerging and prospering industrial nation.

The imperatives of state welfare policies were thus confined to stimulating economic progress and national wealth – goals that served likewise to reaffirm both the work ethic and the ability of the male breadwinner to fulfil his natural role as the head of his household. The Canadian welfare state neglected to provide at any time in the first four decades of the twentieth century either adequate cash benefits or a national minimum standard of living. At the same time, it consciously evaded popular appeals for more generous financial assistance on the basis that by so doing it would be infringing on the rights of the male breadwinner and relieving him of his family responsibilities. The absence of an adequate welfare net was neither the result of the ideas of particular individuals nor the product of bureaucratic parsimony; rather, it was a reflection of a general, conservative cultural consensus that transcended both class and gender boundaries and cohered around the cultural ideal of family independence and the liberty of individual men to pursue their goals untrammelled in the marketplace – ideals predicated on the maintenance of discreet gendered spheres between the home and the workplace. This seamless convergence between family stability, the breadwinner ideal, and free market liberalism fulfilled the doctrine of the limited state articulated by Mackenzie King in 1918 in his book *Industry and Humanity* – a doctrine that was maintained intact by his government's Family Allowances Act, which despite its language of universalism, far from presaging the modern social security state actually *conserved* the tenets of Victorian liberalism, in which the poles of state activity were confined to creating economic conditions ripe for the work ethic and thus confirming the adage that economic security began at home. And because the fear that the family was constantly in danger due to the increasing failure of breadwinners to fulfil their masculine roles formed the principle wellspring engendering the welfare state, the development of the Canadian welfare state was ineluctably a gendered process, one that progressively rendered the concept of female citizenship irrelevant to the collective national identity.

Notes

Introduction: The Cultural Context of the Canadian Welfare State

1 Susan Pedersen, *Family, Dependence, and the Origins of the Welfare State: Britain and France, 1914–1945* (Cambridge: Cambridge University Press, 1993); and Gisela Bock and Pat Thane, eds., *Maternity and Gender Policies: Women and the Rise of the European Welfare States, 1880s to 1950s* (London: Routledge, 1991).

2 The argument that the welfare state was part of a state effort at class conciliation was a later development in Canada. See Bryan Palmer, *Working-Class Experience* (Toronto: Butterworth, 1983), 269.

3 Pat Thane, *The Foundations of the Welfare State* (London: Longman, 1982); Francis Castles, *The Working Class and Welfare: Reflections on the Political Development of the Welfare State in Australia and New Zealand, 1880–1980* (London: Allen and Unwin, 1985); Ann Shola Orloff and Theda Skocpol, 'Why Not Equal Protection? Explaining the Politics of Public Social Spending in Britain, 1900–1911, and the United States, 1880s-1920,' *American Sociological Review*, 49 (Dec. 1984); Colin Gordon, *New Deals: Business, Labor, and Politics in America, 1920–1935* (Cambridge: Cambridge University Press, 1994); Jose Harris, 'Society and State in Twentieth-Century Britain,' in F.M.L. Thompson, ed., *The Cambridge Social History of Britain, 1750–1950*, vol. 3, *Social Agencies and Institutions* (Cambridge: Cambridge University Press, 1990); Dennis Guest, *The Emergence of Social Security in Canada* (Vancouver: University of British Columbia Press, 1980); Kenneth Bryden, *Old-Age Pensions and Policy-Making in Canada* (Montreal: McGill-Queen's Press, 1974); Patricia Rooke, *Discarding the Asylum: From Child Rescue to the Welfare State in English Canada* (Lanham, Maryland: University Press of America, 1983); James G. Snell, *The Citizen's Wage: The State and the Elderly in Canada,*

1900–1951 (Toronto: University of Toronto Press, 1996); and James Struthers, *The Limits of Affluence: Welfare in Ontario, 1920–1970* (Toronto: University of Toronto Press, 1994).

4 For the state as umpire, see Paul Craven, *'An Impartial Umpire': Industrial Relations and the Canadian State, 1900–11* (Toronto: University of Toronto Press, 1979); James Struthers, *'No Fault of Their Own': Unemployment and the Canadian Welfare State, 1914–1941* (Toronto: University of Toronto Press, 1983); and Allan Greer and Ian Radforth, eds., *Colonial Leviathan: Aspects of State Formation in Nineteenth-Century Canada* (Toronto: University of Toronto Press, 1992).

5 Leonore Davidoff, *Worlds Between: Historical Essays on Gender and Class* (New York: Routledge, 1995), 263; Barbara Leslie Epstein, *The Politics of Domesticity: Women, Evangelism, and Temperance in Nineteenth-Century America* (Middletown: Wesleyan University Press, 1981); Mary P. Ryan, *Women in Public: Between Banners and the Ballots, 1825–1880* (Baltimore: University of Maryland Press, 1990); Judith Walkowitz, *City of Dreadful Delight: Narratives of Sexual Danger in Late-Victorian London* (Chicago: University of Chicago Press, 1992); and Carolyn Strange, *Toronto's Girl Problem: The Perils and Pleasures of the City, 1880–1930* (Toronto: University of Toronto Press, 1995).

6 National Archives of Canada [NAC], Canadian Council of Social Development, MG28 I10, 77:564, 'Some Notes on an Address by Professor Richard M. Titmuss on Home and Work in Industrial Britain,' 9 May 1957, 1. This synopsis was written by Marion V. Royce, the Director of the Women's Bureau, Department of Labour, Ontario. See, ibid., Margery Pewtress to Royce, 27 Nov. 1956, in which the writer falls into the same gender trap as Titmuss by arguing that the only real contribution to the country is through paid labour and not that which women undertake in the home. For a similar fallacy, see James Struthers, *'No Fault of Their Own': Unemployment and the Canadian Welfare State, 1914–1941* (Toronto: University of Toronto Press, 1983).

7 Stuart K. Jaffary, 'Social Security: The Beveridge and Marsh Reports,' *Canadian Journal of Economics and Political Science* 10 (1944): 591.

8 For a discussion of how to combine these two approaches, see Joy Parr, *The Gender of Breadwinners* (Toronto: University of Toronto Press, 1991); and Anna Clark, *The Struggle for the Breeches: Gender and the Making of the British Working Class* (Berkeley: University of California Press, 1995), 2–4. For the privileging of 'materialist-feminist' over discourse analyses, see Joan Sangster, *Earning Respect: The Lives of Working Women in Small-Town Ontario, 1920–1960* (Toronto: University of Toronto Press, 1995), 9–10.

9 Bettina Bradbury, *Working Families: Age, Gender and Daily Survival in Industrializing Montreal* (Toronto: McClelland and Stewart, 1993).

10 The Gramscian thesis of cultural hegemony has been revised heavily in recent British scholarship of class and culture. See Dror Wahrman, *Imagining the Middle Class: The Political Representation of Class in Britain, c. 1780–1840* (Cambridge: Cambridge University Press, 1995); Patrick Curry, 'Towards a Post-Marxist Social History: Thompson, Clark and Beyond,' in Adrian Wilson, ed., *Rethinking Social History: English Society, 1570–1920 and Its Interpretation* (Manchester: Manchester University Press, 1993); Patrick Joyce, *Visions of the People: Industrial England and the Question of Class, 1848–1914* (Cambridge: Cambridge University Press, 1991); Eugenio Biagini and Alastair J. Reed, eds., *Currents of Radicalism: Popular Radicalism, Organized Labour and Party Politics in Britain, 1850–1914* (Cambridge: Cambridge University Press, 1991), 'Introduction'; and Patrick Joyce, 'The End of Social History? A Brief Reply to Eley and Nield,' *Social History* 21, no. 1 (Jan. 1996): 96–8.

11 See, for example, Mimi Abramovitz, *Regulating the Lives of Women: Social Welfare Policy from Colonial Times to the Present* (Boston: South End Press, 1989); and Jane Ursel, *Private Lives, Public Policy: One Hundred Years of State Intervention in the Family* (Toronto: Women's Press, 1992).

12 Provincial Archives of Manitoba [PAM], Edith Rogers Papers, Deserted Wives Case Files, P190, file 2. For a similar line of interpretation, see Linda Gordon, ed., *Women, the State and Welfare* (Madison: University of Wisconsin Press, 1990), especially her article 'Family Violence, Feminism and Social Control.'

13 Dorothy Stepler, *Family Allowances in Canada* (Behind the Headlines, 1942), 6.

14 Denyse Baillargeon, *Ménagères au Temps de la Crise* (Montreal: Editions du Remue-Menage, 1991); Baillargeon, '"If You Had No Money, You Had No Trouble, Did You?": Montreal Working-Class Housewives During the Great Depression,' in Wendy Mitchinson, et al., *Canadian History: A Reader* (Toronto: Harcourt Brace, 1996), 251–68; Baillargeon, 'Fréquenter les Gouttes de Lait: L'Expérience des Mères Montréalaises 1910–1965,' *Revue d'Histoire de l'Amérique Française* 50, no. 1 (Été 1996): 29–68; Dominique Marshall, *Aux Origines Sociales de l'État-Providence: Familles Québécoises, Obligation Scolaire et Allocations Familiales* (Montréal: Les Presses de l'Université de Montréal, 1997); and Andrée Levesque, *Making and Breaking the Rules: Quebec Women, 1919–1939* (Toronto: McClelland and Stewart, 1994).

15 Maternal feminism evolved much later in Quebec, and reached its apex in the 1930s and 1940s. Archives Nationales de Québec à Montréal, P120, Fonds Fédération Nationale de St-Jean Baptiste, P120/48–12, 'Sauvegar-

dons l'Enfance,' 14 Jan. 1944; and ibid., P120/48–11, 'En Marge de Projet de Loi Pour la Protection de l'Enfance.' See also Marie Lavigne, Yolande Pinard, and Jennifer Stoddart, 'The *Fédération nationale Saint-Jean-Baptiste* and the Women's Movement in Quebec,' in Linda Kealey, ed., *A Not Unreasonable Claim: Women and Reform in Canada 1880s–1920s* (Toronto: Canadian Women's Educational Press, 1979), 71–88. On the importance of the Catholic Action Movements to this development, see Michael Gauvreau, 'The Emergence of Personalist Feminism: Catholicism and the Marriage Preparation Movement in Quebec, 1940–1966,' in Nancy Christie, ed., *Households of Faith: Family, Religion and Social Change in Canada* (forthcoming).

16 Here I use the definition of feminism offered by Linda Gordon, *Pitied but Not Entitled: Single Mothers and the History of Welfare* (New York: The Free Press, 1994), 8.

17 Nancy Christie and Michael Gauvreau, '*A Full-Orbed Christianity': The Protestant Churches and Social Welfare, 1900–1940* (Montreal and Kingston: McGill-Queen's University Press, 1996).

18 See James Struthers, 'A Profession in Crisis: Charlotte Whitton and Canadian Social Work in the 1930s,' *Canadian Historical Review* 62, no. 2 (June 1981). On Whitton, see also P.T. Rooke and R.L. Schnell, *No Bleeding Heart: Charlotte Whitton, a Feminist on the Right* (Vancouver: University of British Columbia Press, 1987).

19 My conclusions reaffirm those of Denyse Baillargeon, *Ménagères au temps de la crise* (Montreal: Editions du Remue-Menage, 1991), 87.

20 A similar argument to that which I present has recently been advanced in the United States by Joanne L. Goodwin, *Gender and the Politics of Welfare Reform: Mothers' Pensions in Chicago, 1911–1929* (Chicago: University of Chicago Press, 1997).

21 For an argument that pays signal attention to the fact that some recipients of welfare are more closely monitored than others, see Barbara Nelson, 'The Origins of the Two-Channel Welfare State: Workmen's Compensation and Mothers' Aid,' in Linda Gordon, ed., *Women, the State and Welfare* (Madison: University of Wisconsin Press, 1990), 123–51.

1: The State and the Redefinition of the Patriarchal Family

1 Donna T. Andrew, *Philanthropy and Police: London Charity in the Eighteenth Century* (Princeton: Princeton University Press, 1918), 42, 187.

2 Reverend J. Nicol, 'The Influence of the Home on the Nation,' *Canadian Home Monthly*, Sept. 1911, 40. For nineteenth-century evangelical definitions of proper patriarchal relations within families, see Marguerite Van Die, '"A

Woman's Awakening": Evangelical Belief and Female Spirituality in Mid-Nineteenth-Century Canada,' in Wendy Mitchinson et al., *Canadian Women: A Reader* (Toronto: Harcourt Brace, 1996), 53; and Cecilia Morgan, *Public Men and Virtuous Women: The Gendered Languages of Religion and Politics in Upper Canada, 1791–1850* (Toronto: University of Toronto Press, 1996), 27, 126–7.

3 For the close connections between evangelicalism, the emergence of middle-class values, and ideals of domesticity, see Leonore Davidoff and Catherine Hall, *Family Fortunes: Men and Women of the English Middle-Class, 1780–1850* (Chicago: University of Chicago Press, 1987); Mary P. Ryan, *Cradle of the Middle Class: The Family in Oneida County, New York, 1790–1865* (Cambridge: Cambridge University Press, 1981); Barbara Leslie Epstein, *The Politics of Domesticity: Women, Evangelism, and Temperance in Nineteenth-Century America* (Middletown: Wesleyan University Press, 1981); and Kathryn Kish Sklar, *Catherine Beecher: A Study in American Domesticity* (New Haven and London: Yale University Press, 1973). For Canada, see Marguerite Van Die, *An Evangelical Mind: Nathanael Burwash and the Methodist Tradition in Canada, 1839–1918* (Montreal and Kingston: McGill-Queen's University Press, 1989); and Sharon Anne Cook, *'Through Sunshine and Shadow': The Woman's Christian Temperance Union, Evangelicalism, and Reform in Ontario, 1874–1930* (Montreal and Kingston: McGill-Queen's University Press, 1995).

4 For feminist interpretations of domesticity that view this ideology as both conservative and confining for women, see Linda Kealey, ed., *A Not Unreasonable Claim: Women and Reform in Canada 1880's to 1920's* (Toronto: The Women's Educational Press, 1979); Ramsay Cook and Wendy Mitchinson, eds, *The Proper Sphere: Women's Place in Canadian Society* (Toronto: Oxford University Press, 1976); and Janet Guildford and Suzanne Morton, eds., *Separate Spheres: Women's Worlds in the 19th Century Maritimes* (Fredericton: Acadiensis Press, 1994). For a useful critique of the concept of separate spheres, see Linda K. Kerber, 'Separate Spheres, Female Worlds, Woman's Place: The Rhetoric of Women's History,' *The Journal of American History* 75, no. 1 (June 1988): 9–39. In considering nineteenth-century France, Judith Coffin has argued that there was no single 'bourgeois ideal' of domesticity. See Coffin, *The Politics of Women's Work, 1750–1915* (Princeton: Princeton University Press, 1996), 12.

5 Hannah Lane, '"Wife, Mother, Sister, Friend": Methodist Women in St. Stephen, New Brunswick, 1861–1881,' in Janet Guildford and Suzanne Morton, eds., *Separate Spheres: Women's Worlds in the Nineteenth-Century Maritimes* (Fredericton: Acadiensis Press, 1994), 93–117.

6 On the nineteenth century, see Lynne Marks, *Revivals and Roller Rinks:*

Religion, Leisure, and Identity in Late-Nineteenth-Century Small-Town Ontario (Toronto: University of Toronto Press, 1996). On the importance of women to the emergence of social Christianity in the twentieth century, see Nancy Christie and Michael Gauvreau, *'A Full-Orbed Christianity': The Protestant Churches and Social Welfare in Canada, 1900–1940* (Montreal and Kingston: McGill-Queen's University Press, 1996).

7 See Davidoff and Hall, *Family Fortunes*; and Epstein, *The Politics of Domesticity*; and Ryan, *The Cradle of the Middle Class*.

8 John Webster Grant, *A Profusion of Spires: Religion in Nineteenth-Century Ontario* (Toronto: University of Toronto Press, 1988).

9 Marks, *Revivals and Roller Rinks*.

10 A. Margaret Evans, *Sir Oliver Mowat* (Toronto: University of Toronto Press, 1992), 192, 286–7. For a discussion of the conjunction of retrenchment in government and evangelical thought, see Boyd Hilton, *The Age of Atonement: The Influence of Evangelicalism on Social and Economic Thought 1785–1865* (Oxford: Oxford University Press, 1988).

11 Christie and Gauvreau, *'A Full-Orbed Christianity,'* especially chapter 3.

12 Marjorie Cohen, *Women's Work, Markets and Economic Development in Nineteenth-Century Ontario* (Toronto: University of Toronto Press, 1988), 24; Craig Heron, 'Factory Workers,' in Paul Craven, ed., *Labouring Lives: Work and Workers in Nineteenth-Century Ontario* (Toronto: University of Toronto Press, 1995), 495–500.

13 Ryan, *Cradle of the Middle Class*, xi.

14 'Ontario Women's Institutes,' *Canadian Home Journal*, July 1911, 30, which stated that the economic work of women in the home is 'distinctly related to the production of wealth.'

15 Morgan, *Public Men and Virtuous Women*, 150.

16 United Church Archives, Reverend Robert Wallace Papers, Vol. I, file 8, Lecture 'Homes and How to Make them Happy,' March 1881, delivered at West Church, Toronto. In '"A Woman's Awakening,"' Marguerite Van Die has demonstrated that mid-nineteenth-century prescriptive evangelical literature focused on the spiritual role of women within the family. Wallace's lecture is an important departure insofar as he is demarcating the larger economic implications of domesticity.

17 See Cook and Mitchinson, *The Proper Sphere*, 6; Susan E. Houston, 'Victorian Origins of Juvenile Delinquency: A Canadian Experience,' in M. Katz & P. Mattingly, eds., *Education and Social Change: Themes from Ontario's Past* (New York: New York University Press 1975); and Terrence Morrison, 'The Child and Urban Social Reform in Late Nineteenth Century Ontario, 1875–1900,' PhD thesis, University of Toronto, 1971.

18 NAC, J.J. Kelso Papers, MG 30 C 97 [hereafter cited as NAC, KP], 5: 'Ontario's Welfare System,' extract from 1897 report; ibid., 1: Autobiographical files, 'A Plea for the City Waif,' n.d.

19 NAC, KP, 1: correspondence 1915–34, G.A. Macdonald to Kelso, 28 June 1911.

20 NAC, KP, 1: correspondence 1915–34, Macdonald to Kelso, 28 June 1911; ibid., 3: 'Adoptions 1925,' untitled excerpt; ibid., 1: correspondence 1915–34, Kelso to Charles J. Hastings, 28 Jan. 1913; Kelso, 'The Problem of Charity,' *Canadian Municipal Journal* (Sept. 1916); and Mrs H.M. Moswell, 'The Home Versus the Institutions,' *Woman's Century* 3, no. 2 (August 1915).

21 Rev. Dr. Ryerson, *The New Canadian Dominion: Dangers and Duties of the People* (n.p., 1867), 4, 9.

22 Ibid., 20.

23 Ibid., 20, 24, 27.

24 Kelso, 'Have Faith in the Child,' *Woman's Century* 4, no. 4 (October 1916): 4.

25 John Millar, 'Education for the Twentieth-Century,' *Methodist Magazine and Review,* January 1901, 26–8, 31; and Kelso, *Can Slums Be Abolished or Must We Continue to Pay the Penalty?* (n.p., n.d.), 18.

26 Nicholas Flood Davin, *The British Empire* (n.p., 1897). See also Joseph Krauskopf, 'As the Twig is Bent,' *Everywoman's World*, Nov. 1914, 36.

27 James L. Hughes, 'The National Economic Association,' *Methodist Magazine and Review,* June 1901, 59; James L. Hughes, 'The Training of Queen Victoria's Family,' *Methodist Magazine and Review,* Dec. 1901, 494; John Millar, *The Place of Religion in the Public School* (n.p., n.d.), 3; NAC, KP, 8: 'Notebook,' n.d.; 'Public School Teachers Versus Mothers,' *Canadian Home Journal*, Oct. 1911, 6; and Miss Una Saunders, 'Christian Citizenship for Girls,' *Woman's Century* 3, no. 4 (Oct. 1915): 27.

28 Alison Prentice, *The School Promoters* (Toronto: McClelland & Stewart, 1977), 170.

29 Kelso, *Revival of the Curfew Law* (n.p., 1896), 13; and NAC, KP, 4: file 'Charity and Charity Organizations,' 'Cultivate Self-Respect.' For a critique of state incursions into families see, ibid., 1: Autobiographical files, untitled clipping, *Toronto Globe*, 11 April 1893. Stefan Collini has demonstrated that not all arguments for the expansion of the state rested upon 'collectivist' reasoning. See *Liberalism and Sociology: L.T. Hobhouse and Political Argument in England, 1880–1914* (Cambridge: Cambridge University Press, 1979), 17–18. See also Pat Thane, 'Labour and Local Politics: radicalism, democracy and social reform, 1880–1914,' in Eugenio F. Biagini and Alastair J. Reid, eds., *Currents of Radicalism: Popular Radicalism, Organized Labour and Party Politics in Britain, 1850–1914* (Cambridge: Cambridge University Press, 1991).

30 J.L. Cohen, *Mother's Allowance Legislation in Canada* (Toronto: Macmillan, 1927); and John Macdonald, *Business Success* (n.p, 1972). For British working-class support for the limited state, see Eugenio Biagini, *Liberty, Retrenchment and Reform* (Cambridge: Cambridge University Press, 1992).

31 'The Responsibility of Motherhood,' *Everywoman's World*, July 1914, 7.

32 Kelso, *Thoughts on Child-Saving* (n.p., 1898), 14.

33 NAC, KP, 4: 'Family Preservation,' 'Preserve the Home.'

34 Christie and Gauvreau, *A Full-Orbed Christianity*, 3–5.

35 NAC, KP, 4: file 'Charity and Charity Organization,' untitled extract.

36 NAC, KP, 8, untitled extract; ibid., 1: file 'Speech Notes,' untitled extract from speech in Lindsay, 21 Jan. 1912; ibid., 8: 'Notebook 1897–31,' in which he wrote: 'Social service without the power and inspiration of a living Christ behind it must always be weak and ineffective.'

37 Rev. T.E. Shore, 'Methodism and City Mission Work,' *Methodist Magazine and Review*, July 1901, 51.

38 Christie and Gauvreau, '*A Full-Orbed Christianity*,' especially chapters 3 and 6.

39 Archives of Ontario [AO], RG 8–5, Provincial Secretary Correspondence [Ont. Prov. Sec.], Box 45, Kelso to McPherson, 22 July 1919; ibid., Box 43, J.C. Robertson to McPherson, 31 May 1918; and NAC, KP, 1: file 'Correspondence 1915–34,' Mrs Beall, Whitby, to Kelso, 21 December 1910.

40 For Kelso's links with local church élites, see NAC, KP, 3: 'Daily Journal,' 31 Jan. 1894, 2 Feb. 1894, 22 Feb. 1894, 29 Sept. 1894, 30 Sept. 1894, 13 Oct. 1894.

41 NAC, KP, 1: 'Correspondence 1915–34,' B.M. Heise to Kelso, 30 May 1933.

42 Van Die, *An Evangelical Mind*, 33, 191; Neil Semple, '"The Nurture and Admonition of the Lord": Nineteenth-Century Canadian Methodism's Response to Childhood,' *Histoire Sociale/Social History* 14 (1981): 157–75.

43 NAC, KP, 8: 'Notebook,' n.d.

44 Kelso, *Homes Wanted for Boys and Girls of All Ages* (pamphlet, n.d.), 6.

45 NAC, KP, 2: 'Diary,' 7 Sept. (year unknown).

46 Kelso, *Reforming Delinquent Children* (pamphlet, 1903), 1.

47 NAC, KP, 1: 'Correspondence 1915–34,' W.K. Richardson to Kelso, 14 Mar. 1912; ibid., Richardson to Kelso, 14 Oct. 1915.

48 NAC, KP, 5: 'Ontario's Welfare System,' 'Widows and their Children,' extract 1913; ibid., 1: 'Autobiographical Files,' untitled typescript in which Kelso described child-saving as creating in his charges an 'unwavering obedience to the inner voice and calm reliance on Him.' *A Work of Faith and Labor of Love* (pamphlet, 1903), 2.

49 University of Waterloo, Special Collections, Elizabeth Smith Shortt Papers, 20, no.809, Elizabeth Smith to Adam Shortt, 15 Aug. 1883.

50 Thomas Bengough, 'Hon. Dr. Cody, Ontario's New Minister of Education, Outlines his Plans,' *Canadian Home Journal*, July 1918; N. Burwash, 'The Lessons of Life, W.E.H. Massey,' *Methodist Magazine and Review*, Jan. 1902, 16–17; and Rev. W.A. Mackay, 'My Mother,' ibid., Nov. 1904, 402.

51 'A New Evangelism,' *Methodist Magazine and Review*, June 1905, 566.

52 NAC, KP, 1 'Autobiographical Files,' Kelso 'Juvenile Offenders,' n.d.

53 Mrs Donald Shaw, 'Women Who Work for Women,' *Everywoman's World*, June 1914, 23; Mrs Donald Shaw, 'Bringing up Mothers.' Ibid., May 1914, 28–30; 'Around the Hearth,' *Canadian Home Journal*, Sept. 1911, 18; Constance Lynd, 'Alberta,' *Woman's Century* 7, no. 7 (July 1920): 11; 'The Need for a Women's Court,' *Woman's Century* 2, no. 11 (April 1915).

54 Krauskopf, 'The Ascendancy of Womanhood,' *Everywoman's World*, Feb. 1914, 25.

55 Dr. Laura S. Hamilton, 'Teaching Truths Concerning the Beginnings of Life,' *Canadian Home Journal*, Aug. 1918, 12.

56 This analysis is a synthesis of the argument presented in *A Full-Orbed Christianity: The Protestant Churches and Social Welfare in Canada, 1900–1940* (Montreal: McGill-Queen's University Press, 1996). For a superb interpretation of the influence of evangelicalism upon political and social thought, see Boyd Hilton, *The Age of Atonement: The Influence of Evangelicalism on Social and Economic Thought, 1785–1865* (Oxford: Clarendon Press, 1988); and Marguerite Van Die, *An Evangelical Mind: Nathanael Burwash and the Methodist Tradition in Canada, 1839–1918* (Montreal: McGill-Queen's University Press, 1989).

57 Albert Roberts, 'The Changing World,' *Woman's Century* 7, no. 10 (Oct. 1920): 36; and Krauskopf, 'The Responsibility of Motherhood,' *Everywoman's World*, July 1914, 7.

58 Roberts, 'The Changing World,' 36.

59 Lynne Marks, *Revivals and Roller Rinks*; and Hannah M. Lane, '"Wife, Mother, Sister, Friend": Methodist Women in St. Stephen, New Brunswick, 1861–1881,' in Guildford and Morton, eds., *Separate Spheres*.

60 Christie and Gauvreau, *'A Full-Orbed Christianity,'* chapter 3.

61 Cook, *'Through Sunshine and Shadow.'*

62 NAC, KP, 4 'Child Placement', 'Non-Supporting Fathers'; ibid., 4 'Charity and Charity Organizations,' untitled extract; ibid., 8: 'Notebook 1897–1931,' undated extract; and ibid., 4: 'Family Preservation,' untitled extract.

63 NAC, KP, 5: 'Ontario's Welfare System,' 'Mother's Allowance Act' (n.d.).

64 For the argument that reform of the family emerged out of a conservative desire to protect the home rather than as a derivative of individualistic women's rights, see Philip Girard and Rebecca Veinott, 'Married Women's Property Law in Nova Scotia, 1850–1910,' and Judith Fingard, 'The Preven-

tion of Cruelty, Marriage Breakdown, and the Rights of Wives in Nova Scotia, 1880–1900,' in Guildford and Morton, eds., *Separate Spheres*.

65 W.R. McIntosh, *Canadian Problems* (pamphlet, 1910), 62–3. The use of maternalism as a social critique was widespread in this period. See, for example, Constance Lynd, 'The Passing of the Servant in the Home,' *Woman's Century* 5, no. 9 (Sept. 1918): 37; NAC, KP, 4: 'Child Welfare Organizations,' clipping *Montreal Star*, 22 Mar. 1909; ibid., 1 'Speech Notes,' 'Woman's Work,' n.d.; and ibid., 8: 'Notebook 1897–1931,' undated extract. On the relationship between private and public in the nineteenth century, see Davidoff and Hall, *Family Fortunes*, 13.

66 A.A. Perry, 'Helen Gregory MacGill, M.A., M.B.,' *Woman's Century* 6, no. 11 (Nov. 1918): 38.

67 While critical of the 'state patriarchy' school of thought, Gordon nevertheless asserts that Carole Pateman has recognized that dependence on the state was often preferable to reliance on individual men. See Linda Gordon, 'The New Feminist Scholarship on the Welfare State,' in Linda Gordon, ed., *Women, the State and Welfare* (Madison: University of Wisconsin Press, 1990), 22–3.

68 Gordon, 'The New Feminist Scholarship on the Welfare State,' 20. For the later advancement of the concept of the democratic family in the United States, see Sonja Michel, 'American Women and the Discourse of the Family in World War II,' in Margaret Randolph Higonnet, Jane Jenson, Sonja Michel, and Margaret Collins Weitz, eds., *Behind the Lines: Gender and the World Wars* (New Haven and London: Yale University Press, 1987), 155.

69 For these various provincial campaigns, see 'The National Council,' *Woman's Century* 5, no. 3 (Mar. 1918): 7; ibid. 7, no. 2 (Feb. 1920): 10; and ibid. 7, no. 4 (April 1920): 7.

70 'The National Council,' *Woman's Century* 7, no. 1 (Jan. 1920): 12.

71 Clara Brett Martin, 'Legal Status of Women in the Provinces of the Dominion of Canada (except the Province of Quebec), in *Women in Canada, Their Life and Work* (1900), quoted in Cook and Mitchison, eds., *The Proper Sphere*, 94. Women reformers claimed that this struggle began with the nineteenth-century crusade for the revision of the Married Women's Property law.

72 NAC, KP, 4: 'Family Preservation,' 'Ill-Treated Wives'; ibid., 'Notebook, 1897–1931,' undated extract describing how woman must realize her individual value by attaining equal rights with the man within the family.

73 N. Burwash, 'The Lessons of Life, W.E.H. Massey,' *Methodist Magazine and Review,* Jan. 1902, 19.

74 For the religious clauses of the Child Protection Act, see AO, Ont. Prov. Sec., Vol. 45, 'Illegitimate Children Suggested Amendment,' n.d.; ibid., Vol.

45, Kelso to McPherson, 21 Aug. 1917. For the shifting role that gender has played in the development of welfare policies, see Linda Gordon, 'Social Insurance and Public Assistance: The Influence of Gender in Welfare Thought in the United States, 1890–1935,' *American Historical Review* 97, no. 1 (Feb. 1992): 19–54. For the influence of religion on child welfare policies, see Edward Ross Dickinson, *The Politics of German Child Welfare from the Empire to the Federal Republic* (Cambridge: Harvard University Press, 1996), 15.

75 NAC, W.L. Scott Papers, MG 30 C27 [hereafter NAC, Scott Papers], 5 'Association of Children's Aid Societies,' Scott to E.C. Hall, 14 May 1915.

76 AO, RG 29 (Department of Public Welfare) 19: Kelso files, 'Rev. J.E. Starr, Children's Judge,' clipping, Nov. 1911; ibid., 'Special Judge for Children,' clipping, n.d.; ibid., 'Editorial in Brief,' n.d.; 'Poverty and Criminals,' *Morning World*, 2 June 1899; and ibid., *Presbyterian Review*, July 1910.

77 AO, RG29, 19: Kelso files, 'She Sent me to Steal,' clipping, n.d.; and 'The Children's Aid Societies,' *New Freeman* (St. John, N.B.), 30 Mar. 1918.

78 R.S. Pennefather, 'The Orange Order and the United Farmers of Ontario 1919–23,' *Ontario History* 61, no. 3 (Sept. 1977): 178. Kelso supported E.F. Clarke, the Orangeman, for mayor of Toronto in 1888. See NAC, KP, 2: 'Diary,' 8 Jan. 1888.

79 Mark McGowan, 'Toronto's English-Speaking Catholics, Immigration, and the Making of a Canadian Catholic Identity, 1900–30,' in Terrence Murphy and Gerald Stortz, eds., *Creed and Culture: The Place of English-speaking Catholics in Canadian Society, 1750–1930* (Montreal and Kingston: McGill-Queen's University Press, 1993), 205, 208, 213.

80 NAC, KP, 1: 'Correspondence 1915–34,' Kelso to Hon. H.C. Nixon, Provincial Secretary, Ontario, 22 Nov. 1922.

81 For one particular case, see NAC, KP, 1 'Adoption Files,' copy of marriage consent between Nathaniel John Dunn and Mary Ann Sherbot, 19 Jan. 1917, in which Dunn agrees to bring up the children in the Roman Catholic religion 'even if Mary Anne Sherbot should happen to be taken by death.'

82 NAC, KP, 1: 'Adoption Cases 1927–34,' 'Memo re Adoption of Reginald Badgerow,' 2 Nov. 1933.

83 AO, Ont. Prov. Sec., 44, Kelso to H.C. Nixon, 9 July 1921.

84 W.J. Hanna to Kelso, 12 April 1913; Kelso to Hanna, 15 April 1913. If Kelso could locate any relatives who were Protestant, he willingly used this as a basis for arguing against the increasingly vocal demands of the Roman Catholic CAS agents and inspectors.

85 AO, Ont. Prov. Sec., 44, Kelso to McPherson, 23 April 1919.

86 AO, Ont. Prov. Sec., 45, Kelso to McPherson, 21 Aug. 1917.

87 NAC, Scott Papers, 5: 'Association of Children's Aid Societies,' E.C. Hall to Scott, 15 May 1915; and ibid., Hall to Scott 13 May 1915.

88 AO, Ont. Prov. Sec., 44, Kelso to McPherson, 10 Sept 1918.

89 NAC, KP, 1: 'Adoptions Files,' 'Memo re. Jewel Folkard, 14 Nov. 1927.'

90 AO, Ont. Prov. Sec., 46, William O'Connor to McPherson, 25 July 1917.

91 NAC, Scott Papers, 11: 'Greek Catholics,' Scott to T.W. McGarry, 3 April 1919.

92 AO, Ont. Prov. Sec., 44, Kelso, 'Memorandum to Children's Aid Society Agents,' 19 Nov. 1914; and ibid., 44, 'Memorandum regarding Greek Catholics,' 28 Oct. 1918, in which members of the government claimed that Kelso had nothing to do with issuing the controversial 1914 circular and that it had the agreement of the Roman Catholic inspector for the CAS, Mr O'Connor.

93 AO, Ont. Prov. Sec., 44, Bishop Scollard to McPherson, 26 July 1917; ibid., 44, William O'Connor to J.R. Cartwright, Deputy Attorney General, 4 Dec. 1914; ibid., 44, 'An Act to Incorporate the Ruthenian Greek Catholic Episcopal Corporation of Canada,' affidavit of Right Rev Nicetas Budka, n.d. 1913; ibid., 44, W.L. Scott to Kelso, 29 Nov. 1917; and ibid., 44, W.L. Scott, *Eastern Christian Churches* (pamphlet, n.d.), 25.

94 AO, Ont. Prov. Sec., 44, Kelso to Hanna, 22 Oct. 1914; and ibid., Judge E.W. Boyd to McPherson, 9 Nov. 1918.

95 Ibid., 44, Bishop Scollard to McPherson, 26 July 1917.

96 AO, Ont. Prov. Sec., 44, Scott to Kelso, 16 July 1917, 17 July 1917, 12 May 1917.

97 AO, Ont. Prov. Sec., 44, Kelso to Frank Blain, CAS agent, Fort William, 3 March 1917.

98 AO, Ont. Prov. Sec., 44, Scollard to Hanna, 14 Aug. 1916, Scollard to Kelso, 3 April 1917, Kelso to Scollard, 22 March 1917, J.P. Reed to Kelso, 8 Dec. 1915.

99 AO, Ont. Prov. Sec., 44, Rev J.A. Klesnikoff to Kelso, 25 June 1917.

100 AO, Ont. Prov. Sec., Judge E.W. Boyd to James Ballantyne, 9 Nov. 1919. Although it was the law, Boyd believed that the inability of the courts to place Greek Catholic children in Protestant homes was an 'outrage.'

101 On the ways in which working-class families utilized state welfare legislation to defend their own interests, see Linda Gordon, 'Family Violence, Feminism and Social Control,' in Linda Gordon, ed., *Women, the State and Welfare*, 186–93.

102 AO, Ont. Prov. Sec., 46, 'In the Supreme Court of Ontario, 2 July 1918.'

103 NAC, Scott Papers, 5: 'Association of Children's Aid Societies,' T. Louis Monahan, barrister to Scott, 17 May 1915.

104 NAC, Scott Papers, 5: 'Children's Aid Cases, 1916–19,' Kelso to Scott, 28 Dec. 1916.

105 For details of this case, see NAC, Scott Papers, 5:16A35l, 'In the Supreme Court of Ontario,' 28 Sept. 1923, 13 Oct. 1923; and Scott to Col. B.T. Irwin, 16 Oct. 1924; Scott to Kelso, 30 Jan. 1924; Scott to Kelso, 11 Dec. 1923, Scott to editor, *Catholic Record*, 24 Dec. 1923; and Kelso to Scott, 13 Dec. 1923.

106 Judge Boyd, for one, worked hand in hand with the Orange Order and McPherson to ensure the Protestant affiliation of many Greek Catholic children. See AO, Ont. Prov. Sec., 44, H.V. McIntyre, County Orange Lodge, Toronto, to McPherson, 30 Jan. 1918; ibid., Scott to McPherson, 26 Sept. 1918; Scott to Kelso, 24 Oct. 1917, 20 July 1917; Judge Boyd to Kelso, 5 Sept. 1918; Boyd to McPherson, 6 Sept. 1918; and Kelso 'Memorandum,' 23 July 1918, stating that Judge Boyd must move fast to determine the religious status of a Greek Catholic child before the Catholic Church got wind of the case.

107 NAC, Scott Papers, 5:16A351, Charles Gautier to Scott, 15 Oct. 1923.

108 Brian Clarke, 'The Parish and the Heath: Women's Confronternities and the Devotional Revolution Among the Irish Catholics of Toronto, 1850–85,' in Murphy and Stortz, *Creed and Culture*.

109 NAC, Scott Papers, 11: 'Child Protection Act 1914–24,' 'An Outline of Suggestions Bearing on Ideas, Which the Workers of Children's Aid Societies throughout this Province Would Like to See Incorporated in the Child Protection Act,' n.d., 1–2; and ibid., 5:16, Scott to Father Foley, 7 Jan. 1914. Scott enlisted other religious minority groups in his campaign to amend the Child Protection Act, especially Jewish constituencies. See ibid., 11: 'Child Protection Act 1914–24,' Scott to S.W. Jacobs, 29 April 1919.

110 Ibid., 11: 'Child Protection Act 1914–24,' Scott to G. Howard Ferguson, 9 June 1920.

111 Ibid., 11: 'Child Protection Act 1914–24,' Scott to Manning Doherty, 22 Dec. 1920.

112 Ibid, 11: 'Greek Roman Catholics,' T. Louis Monahan to Scott, 21 Dec. 1918, Scott to Monahan, 24 Dec. 1918.

113 Ibid, 11: 'Child Protection Act 1914–24,' Scott to Hon. Manning Doherty, 17 Jan. 1921.

114 AO, Ont. Prov. Sec., 44, 'Memorandum of Interview between Mr W.L. Scott, Ottawa, and Rev Mr Quartermaine, Regarding Proposed Amendments of the Child Protection Act,' 31 Oct. 1917; NAC, Scott Papers, 11: 'Child Protection Act 1914–24,' T.L. Monahan to Scott, 25 May 1916; and ibid., 5: 'Association of Children's Aid Societies,' Scott to Rev E.C. Hall, n.d.

115 *Report Upon the Sweating System in Canada* (Ottawa: Queen's Printer: 1896), 17.

2: Gender and Social Policy, 1914–1918

1 Queen's University Archives [QUA], Frontenac County Records, Canadian Patriotic Fund [CPF], 39 'Correspondence 1916–17,' J.J. Kerr to Our Friend Mr Rankin, 27 March 1917. The chapter title is taken from NAC, Sir Robert Borden Papers, 81, 'The Soldiers' Wives League,' *The Whizz-Bang*, 22 July 1916.
2 Paul Kellogg, *The Patriotic Fund of Canada* (pamphlet, 1917), 39.
3 Ibid., 39.
4 Robert Craig Brown, *Robert Laird Borden: A Biography*, vol. 2, *1914–1937* (Toronto: Macmillan of Canada, 1980), 19; QUA, Frontenac County Records, CPF, 40: 'Correspondence 1920,' Louisa Laferme, application to Manitoba Patriotic Fund; ibid., 39: 'Correspondence 1916,' Ronald McAnna to Dear Sir, n.d.; and McCord Museum, Canadian Patriotic Fund, Montreal Branch [CPFMB], 1: 'Minutes of Meeting,' 26 Aug. 1916.
5 Kellogg, *The Patriotic Fund of Canada*, 32–3, 39.
6 NAC, RG 36 series 18, The Dependent's Allowance Board, 29: Mother's Allowance Files, Mr A.G. McNamara, chairman, to A.G. MacLachlan, secretary to the Minister of National Defence, 5 June 1940, who observed that in 'the last war ... the Federal Treasury should carry the cost of the grant of one dependent; other dependents were taken care of through the Canadian Patriotic Fund ...'
7 Ibid., 29: 'Complaints File,' 'Decision Soon on Allowances for Dependents,' news clipping, 1941; and ibid., 1: 'Set-Up File,' 'The Canadian Patriotic Fund.'
8 Ibid., 'The Canadian Patriotic Fund.'
9 Sir Herbert Ames, 'Fight or Pay: Canada's Solution,' *North American Review*, June 1917, 860. Helen Reid was one of the foremost pioneer social workers in Montreal. She was in the first McGill University class to include women, graduating in modern languages. After attending the University of Geneva, she was a charter member of the Charity Organisation Society when it was founded in Montreal in 1902. Before 1914 she headed the Relief Committee of the Victorian Order of Nurses during the typhoid epidemic, and helped establish kitchens in factory neighbourhoods, and was one of the principal founders of the McGill University Settlement. For Reid, see Kellogg, *The Patriotic Fund of Canada*, 16; and 'In Memoriam,' *Canadian Welfare* 17, no. 2 (July 1941): 18. On the role of the war in strengthening family life in

England and Germany and Austria, see J.M. Winter, 'Some Paradoxes of the First World War,' Richard Wall, 'English and German Families in the First World War, 1914–18,' and Reinhard F. Seider, 'Behind the Lines: Working-Class Family Life in Wartime Vienna,' in Richard Wall and J. Winter, eds., *The Upheaval of War: Family, Work, and Welfare in Europe, 1914–1918* (Cambridge: Cambridge University Press, 1988).

10 This song was written in Britain with the specific aim of encouraging public subscription to the Patriotic Fund, see NAC, Borden Papers, 267, 'CPF Bulletin,' Feb. 1916, 2.

11 McCord Museum, CPFMB, 1, 'Minutes,' 30 Jan. 1900. On the Patriotic Fund, see, Robert Craig Brown and Ramsay Cook, *Canada 1896–1921: A Nation Transformed* (Toronto: McClelland & Stewart, 1974), 222–3; Margaret McCallum, 'Assistance to Veterans and their Dependants: Steps on the Way to the Administrative State, 1914–1929,' in W. Wesley Pue and Barry Wright, eds., *Canadian Perspectives on Law and Society: Issues in Legal History* (Ottawa: Carleton University Press, 1988), 157–77; and Barbara M. Wilson, ed., *Ontario and the First World War, 1914–1918* (Toronto: University of Toronto Press, 1977), 9–16.

12 NAC, Canadian Patriotic Association, 'Executive Minutes,' 19 April 1917.

13 Kellogg, *The Patriotic Fund of Canada*, 25.

14 Ibid., 5.

15 Brown and Cook, *Canada 1896–1921*, 222.

16 NAC, Canadian Patriotic Association, 'Circular No. 2,' n.d.; and Kellogg, *The Patriotic Fund of Canada*, 5; and McCord Museum, CPFMB, 2, 'Executive Meeting,' 8 Oct. 1915.

17 Kellogg, *The Patriotic Fund of Canada*, 5.

18 NAC, MG 28 I 5, The Canadian Patriotic Association, 'Minutes of Executive Meeting,' 20 Feb. 1917.

19 NAC, RG 9 III, Department of Militia, file 10-13-15, 'Comparative Statement of Disbursements by Head Office and Branches during the Month Ending May 1919.'

20 NAC, Canadian Patriotic Association, 'Minutes of the Meeting Held in the Premier's Office,' 18 Aug. 1914; and Brown, *Borden, Vol. II*, 11.

21 McCord Museum, CPFMB, 1: 'Minutes,' 6 Nov. 1914.

22 McGill University, Department of Rare Books and Special Collections, CH 370.S330, Canadian Patriotic Fund, Florence Minden Cole, head of the Soldiers Wives' League to Mayor, St. John, Quebec, 7 Nov. 1914; Cole to Herbert Ames, 5 Nov. 1914; and Herbert Stewart, Gourock Ropeworks to Florence Cole, 17 Nov. 1914.

23 Ibid., Cole to secretary treasurers of Canadian Pacific Railway and Grand

Trunk Railway, 30 Sept. 1914; memorandum Rufus Smith, n.d.; and Carrie Derick to Ames, 10 Aug. 1914.

24 'Words of the Patriotic Fund,' *Montreal Herald*, 3 Feb. 1917; 'Work of Caring for Families of Soldiers,' *Montreal Evening News*, 20 Jan. 1917; McCord Museum, CPFMB, 2: 'Minutes of Executive Meeting,' Nov. 1915; and ibid., 2: 'Correspondence July–Aug. 1920,' Executive Secretary to Ross, 22 July 1920.

25 McCord Museum, CPFMB, 1: 'Minutes,' 11 Aug. 1914. On the impact of the war in changing social attitudes toward women in society, see Brown and Cook, *Canada 1896–1921*, 223.

26 NAC, Borden Papers, 267, Sam Hughes to Borden, 30 Oct. 1915; ibid., 'Patriotic Fund Bulletin,' Oct. 1915; ibid., 269, Sgt G.S. Hayes to Hon J.D. Hazen, Minister of Marine and Fisheries, 16 Dec. 1915. The transmutation of the CPF into a tool of recruitment was perceived by Sir Sam Hughes to be an infringement on his personal control of the military side of the war effort and caused much friction between him and Sir Herbert Ames: see Borden Papers, 269, Ames to Borden, 23 Nov. 1915, in which he states that Hughes gave 'a most irrelevant and undignified reply' to Ames' initiatives regarding the fund and recruitment.

27 McCord Museum, CPFMB, 1: 'Minutes,' 10 Sept., 4 Sept. 1914.

28 QUA, Frontenac County Records, CPF, 41: 'Printed Material,' Herbert Ames, 'Untitled Circular,' 8 Sept. 1914.

29 NAC, Borden Papers, 331, *Canadian Patriotic Fund Annual Report, Aug. 1914–Aug. 1915*, 38.

30 NAC, Borden Papers, 30391–3, M.C. Lewis to Borden, 18 June 1916, quoted in Brown and Cook, *Canada 1896–1921*, 222.

31 'Patriotic Fund Will Be Raised,' *Montreal Gazette*, 12 Aug. 1914. On the connection between the Canadian Patriotic Fund and recruiting, see NAC, Borden Papers, 267, *Speaker's Patriotic League: Report of Executive Committee* (pamphlet, 1916), 5–7.

32 AO, Premier W.H. Hearst Papers, 03-03-0-090, 'Toronto and York County Patriotic Association,' n.d.

33 'Duke Will Fire First Shot Today,' *Montreal Gazette*, 9 Feb. 1917.

34 In 1914, 36,000 men had enlisted; by Oct. 1915, 165,000, by 1916, 180,000; and by June 1917, 410,000. See Ames, '"Fight or Pay,"' 853; and Craig Brown and Donald Loveridge, '"Unrequited Faith": Recruiting the C.E.F. 1914–1918,' *Revue Internationale d'histoire militaire* 51 (1982). In 1917, monthly recruiting rates fell drastically; see A.M. Willms, 'Conscription 1917: A Brief for the Defence,' in Carl Berger, ed., *Conscription 1917* (Toronto: University of Toronto Press, [1969?]), 12–13. The connection between the work of the CPF and recruitment has been absent from recent historical scholarship. See Paul

Maroney, 'The Great Adventure: The Context and Ideology of Recruiting in Ontario, 1914–17,' *Canadian Historical Review* 77, no. 1 (March 1996): 67–71; and Jeffrey A. Keshen, *Propaganda and Censorship During Canada's Great War* (Edmonton: University of Alberta Press, 1996).

35 NAC, Canadian Patriotic Association, 'Executive Meeting,' 13 Jan. 1915; McCord Museum, CPFMB, 1: 'Minutes,' 15 Jan. 1915; NAC, Borden Papers, 267, Clarence F. Smith to Philip Morris, 29 Oct. 1915; ibid., 331, *Canadian Patriotic Fund Annual Report, Aug. 1914–Aug. 1915*, 39; QUA, Frontenac County Records, CPF, 39: 'Correspondence 1916–17,' Philip Morris to J.W. Bradshaw, 19 March 1917; ibid., 39: 'Correspondence 1918,' Philip Morris to Bradshaw, 18 Jan. 1918; McCord Museum, CPFMB, 1: 'Minutes,' 18 Dec. 1914; NAC, Canadian Patriotic Association, 'Executive Meeting,' 10 Feb., 9 Dec. 1915, 9 June 1916; NAC, Department of Militia, 10-13-15, 'CPF Bulletin,' April 1918, 33; and ibid., 10-13-2, W.R. Ward to Deputy Minister, 5 Feb. 1917.

36 For the importance of the First World War in embedding conceptions of a male breadwinner and dependent wife into social policy, see Pedersen's excellent comparative study, *Family, Dependence, and the Origins of the Welfare State*, 79–130.

37 Kellogg, *The Patriotic Fund of Canada*, 27–8.

38 '"Fight or Pay": Canada's Solution,' *North American Review*, June 1917, 860.

39 QUA, Frontenac County Records, CPF, 41: 'Printed Material,' 'CPF Bulletin,' 23, March 1917, 2; ibid., 39: 'Correspondence 1916,' Philip Morris to Bradshaw, 9 Nov. 1915; AO, Hearst Papers, 03-03-0-089, 'CPF Bulletin,' 2 Jan. 1915; NAC, Borden Papers, 267, Borden to Ames, 10 Feb. 1917; and McCord Museum, CPFMB, 1: 'Minutes,' 14 August 1914.

40 NAC, Borden Papers, 267, 'Minutes of Meeting of Executive Committee of CPF,' 6 Oct. 1915.

41 NAC, Canadian Patriotic Association, 'Executive Minutes,' 13 Oct. 1914.

42 QUA, Frontenac County Records, CPF, 39: 'Correspondence 1917,' J.W. Bradshaw to Militia Headquarters, 2 Aug. 1917; ibid., 41: 'Printed Material,' *The Canadian Patriotic Fund: Its Objects, Methods and Policy*, n.d., 7–8. Although unmarried wives were eligible, they were often discriminated against. For example, May Commodore from Frontenac County was in the end denied assistance, despite her obvious need and claim.

43 NAC, Borden Papers, 267, A.E. Ross, administrator of the federal emergency appropriation fund, to Mr Calder, 22 Jan. 1920; and ibid., Col. John Thompson to H.P.O. Savary, 22 Dec. 1919.

44 NAC, Department of Militia, 10-13-15, 'CPF Bulletin,' 41, Nov. 1918.

45 NAC, Borden Papers, 331, *Canadian Patriotic Fund Annual Report*, 1915, 10.

See also McCord Museum, CPFMB, 1: 'Minutes' 9 Oct. 1914; and Kellogg, *Patriotic Fund of Canada*, 36.

46 McCord Museum, CPFMB, 1: 'Minutes,' 4 Sept. 1914; NAC, Canadian Patriotic Association, 'Circular No. 2,' n.d. The monthly amount paid by the Canadian government was slightly more than the 15 shillings per week paid by the Imperial Army. In Britain, separation allowances were paid according to the number of children in the family; in Canada they were paid on a flat rate, and the Patriotic Fund was the body that paid separate children's allowances.

47 McCord Museum, CPFMB, 1: 'Scrapbooks,' 'Duke Starts Big Fund Campaign for $2,500,000,' *Montreal Evening News*, n.d.

48 QUA, Frontenac County Records, Canadian Patriotic Fund, 41: 'Printed Material,' Philip Morris to Bradshaw, 10 Aug. 1915.

49 QUA, Frontenac Country Records, CPF, 41: 'Printed Material,' 'CPF Bulletin,' 20, Jan. 1917.

50 *The Second Year of the War, What It Means to the Canadian Patriotic Fund* (pamphlet, Sept. 1915), 8.

51 Pat Thane, 'Government and Society in England and Wales, 1750–1914,' and Jose Harris, 'Society and State in Twentieth-Century Britain,' in F.M.L. Thompson, ed., *The Cambridge Social History of Britain, 1750–1950, Vol. 3* (Cambridge: Cambridge University Press, 1990).

52 McCord Museum, CPFMB, 1: 'Minutes,' 6 Nov. 1914, 'Minutes,' 14 Aug., 10 Sept., 25 Sept., 9 Oct. 1914.

53 NAC, Borden Papers, 312, J.H. McVety, President of the British Columbia Federation of Labour to H.H. Stevens, 15 April, 18 Dec. 1916; ibid., Blanche Pook to Borden, 12 Dec. 1916, F.A. Acland to Blanche Pook, 16 Nov. 1916; and NAC, Canadian Patriotic Association, 'Executive Minutes,' 19 April 1917.

54 NAC, Dept. of Militia, 10-13-15, 'The Separation Allowance Board and Its Policy,' 'CPF Bulletin,' 35, May 1918; QUA, Frontenac County Records, CPF, 39: 'Correspondence 1918,' 'Grounds for Refusal of Separation Allowance,' n.d. Mothers had to prove that before the war their sons had been their *sole* support – a difficult procedure, given that many sons gave relatively little to their mothers, a situation exacerbated by the widespread pattern of seasonal employment in Canada.

55 Susan Pedersen, 'Gender, Welfare, and Citizenship in Britain during the Great War,' *American Historical Review* 95, no. 4 (Oct. 1990); and 'The Failure of Feminism in the Making of the Welfare State,' *Radical History Review* 43 (1989).

56 Ames, '"Fight or Pay,"' 852.

57 Kellogg, *The Patriotic Fund of Canada*; QUA, Frontenac County Records, CPF, 41: 'Printed Material,' 'CPF Bulletin' 43, Feb. 1919, 1.

58 NAC, Dept of Militia, 10-13-15, L.J. Brock to dear sir, 12 Oct. 1918.

59 NAC, Borden Papers, 267, Ames to Borden, 13 Jan. 1916; ibid., W.H.S. Grange, South Prince Albert Patriotic Fund to Borden, 21 Feb. 1916; and Ames to Borden, 31 May, 13 Oct. 1916.

60 *Montreal Mail*, 28 Jan. 1916.

61 McCord Museum, CPFMB, 1: 'Montreal Patriotic Campaign 1917,' 'Volunteer Workers at Headquarters'; ibid., Box 2, 'Executive Committee Minutes,' 3 Sept. 1915; Ames '"Fight or Pay,"' 858; 'Indians Giving to Patriotic Fund,' *Montreal Daily Star*, 8 Feb. 1917; 'Forms French Teams to Work for Fund,' *Montreal Gazette*, 9 Feb. 1917; and NAC, Borden Papers, 267, 'CPF Bulletin,' Feb. 1916, 1.

62 NAC, Borden Papers, 267, 'CPF Bulletin,' Feb. 1916; and McCord Museum, CPFMB, 1: 'Scrapbooks,' undated newspaper clipping, 'Tax for Patriotic Fund.'

63 'Opinions No Bar to Aiding Funds,' *Montreal Gazette*, 15 Feb. 1917; QUA, Frontenac County Records, CPF, 41: 'Printed Material,' 'CPF Bulletin' 20, Jan. 1917, 2; and NAC, Borden Papers, 267,: 'CPF Bulletin,' Feb. 1916, 1.

64 'Financial Houses Give Generously Today,' *Montreal Daily Star*, 13 Feb. 1917; Kellogg, *Patriotic Fund of Canada*, 56.

65 QUA, Frontenac Country Records, CPF, 39: 'Correspondence 1916–17,' 'Private and Confidential, Untitled Memorandum from Head Office,' 6.

66 NAC, Borden Papers, 267, 'Mass Meeting of Citizens of Edmonton,' 19 Nov. 1916; and NAC, Dept. of Militia, 10-13-15, 'CPF Bulletin,' 32, Feb. 1918.

67 QUA, Frontenac County Records, CPF, 39: 'Correspondence 1914–20,' K.W. McKay, County Clerk, Elgin County to Bradshaw, 2 Oct. 1916; McCord Museum, CPFMB, 2: 'Minutes of Executive Meeting,' 23 Dec. 1915; and NAC, Borden Papers, 267, I.E.A. Haw to Borden, 6 Nov, 1915, Ames to T.C. Casgrain, 13 Jan. 1916, James Elliott, Pakenham, Ontario to Borden, 27 Nov. 1916.

68 NAC, Borden Papers, 2493, 'Memorandum: Proposal for Obtaining Additional Farm Labour,' n.d.

69 NAC, Borden Papers, 267, W.A. Blair, Vancouver Board of Trade to Borden, 24 Aug. 1918, W.J. Abraham, Mayor of Huntsville to Borden, 7 Feb. 1916, J.B. Wallace, Saskatoon Trades and Labour Council to Borden, 10 Feb. 1916; and ibid., R.S.L. Series, 1589, C.J. Brown, City Clerk, Winnipeg to Borden, 26 June 1917.

70 NAC, Borden Papers, 2281, W.A. Janes to Borden, n.d.

71 NAC, Borden Papers, 267, F.M. Kidd to Borden, 28 Oct. 1916.

72 NAC, Borden Papers, 1793, T.W. Crothers to Hugh Clark, 13 Sept. 1917.

73 Ibid., 267, 'Minutes of Executive of CPF,' 14 June 1917.

74 Kellogg, *The Patriotic Fund of Canada*, 37; Ames '"Fight or Pay,"' 858. In the
    Boer War it was the Soldiers' Wives Leagues that lobbied for greater relief
    measures for wives and families. See McCord Museum, CPFMB, 1: 'Minute
    Book, Canadian Patriotic Fund, Montreal Branch, 1899–1915,' 7 Nov. 1899.

75 QUA, Frontenac County Records, CPF, 40: 'Correspondence 1919,' Brad-
    shaw, 'Memo to Investigate Sapper J.A. Murray, 166th Battalion,' 10 Sept.
    1919. On the desire of women to have the state intervene to reinforce male
    obligations within the family, see Fingard, 'The Prevention of Cruelty, Mar-
    riage Breakdown and the Rights of Wives in Nova Scotia, 1880–1900,' in
    Separate Spheres, 185–210. On the obligations of men and women in work-
    ing-class Britain, see Ellen Ross, '"Fierce Questions and Taunts": Married
    Life in Working-Class London, 1870–1914,' *Feminist Studies* 8 no. 3 (1982):
    575–605.

76 'Told of Canada's Patriotic Fund,' *Montreal Gazette*, 9 Feb. 1917.

77 McCord Museum, CPFMB, 1: 'Minutes,' 18 Dec. 1914.

78 NAC, Canadian Patriotic Association, 'Minutes of Executive Meeting,'
    9 Sept. 1915, 13 Oct. 1914, 11 Nov. 1914; ibid., 'Circular No. 2 Separation
    Allowances and Assigned Pay,' n.d.; and McCord Museum, CPFMB, 1:
    'Minutes,' 14 Aug., 24 Aug., 26 Aug., 4 Dec., 18 Dec. 1914.

79 QUA, Frontenac County Records, CPF, 41: 'Printed Material,' Philip Morris
    to Bradshaw, 20 May 1915; ibid., 'CPF Bulletin,' 20, Jan. 1917, 2; AO, Hearst
    Papers, 03-03-0-089, 'CPF Bulletin,' July 1915; NAC, Canadian Patriotic
    Association, 'Minutes of Executive Meeting,' 31 March 1915, 6 Oct. 1915. On
    the relationship between working-class women and the family budget in
    the United States, see Martha May, 'The Good Managers: Married Working
    Class Women and Family Budget Studies, 1895–1915,' *Labor History* (Sum-
    mer 1984); and Daniel Horowitz, *The Morality of Spending: Attitudes Towards
    the Consumer Society in America, 1875–1940* (Baltimore: Johns Hopkins Uni-
    versity Press, 1985).

80 QUA, Frontenac County Records, CPF, 41: 'Printed Material,' Philip Morris
    to Bradshaw, 20 May 1915.

81 QUA, Frontenac County Records, CPF, 39: 'Correspondence 1915,' Mrs J.W.
    Carey, Sharbot Lake, to Bradshaw, 9 April 1917.

82 NAC, Dept. of Militia, 10-13-15, 'CPF Bulletin,' 41, Nov. 1918; and QUA,
    Frontenac County Records, CPF, 41: 'Printed Material,' Philip Morris to
    Bradshaw, 10 Aug. 1915.

83 Ibid., 41: 'Printed Material,' Philip Morris to Bradshaw, 10 Aug. 1915.

84 See Bernard Waites, *A Class Society at War: England 1914–1918* (Hamburg

and New York: Berg Leamington Spa, 1987); J.M Winter, *The Great War and the British People* (Cambridge: Harvard University Press, 1986); Arthur Marwick, *The Deluge* (London: Bodley Head, 1965); and Wall and Winter, eds., *The Upheaval of War*.

85 Marwick, *The Deluge*; Waites, *A Class Society at War*.

86 Canadian Reconstruction Association, *Industrial Relations* (pamphlet, 1918), 4.

87 AO, Hearst Papers, 03-03-0-089, 'CPF Bulletin' 1, June 1915.

88 *The Patriotic Fund of Canada*, 26.

89 Ibid., 26; Bettina Bradbury, 'The Home as Workplace,' in Paul Craven, ed., *Labouring Lives: Work and Workers in Nineteenth-Century Ontario* (Toronto: University of Toronto Press, 1995). For Britain, Ellen Ross has well described the degree to which a major part of the weekly pay packet was used for the feeding and clothing of husbands and working sons to the exclusion of women and younger children. See Ellen Ross, *Love and Toil: Motherhood in Outcast London, 1870–1918* (New York and Oxford: Oxford University Press, 1993), 22.

90 Helen R.Y. Reid, *A Social Study along Health Lines of the First Thousand Children Examined in the Health Clinic of the Canadian Patriotic Fund, Montreal Branch* (pamphlet, 1920), 34.

91 QUA, Frontenac County Records, CPF, 41: 'Visitors' Record Cards,' 'Pearl Carey,' n.d.

92 Ibid., Box 40: 'Correspondence 1919,' Mrs Louisa Laferme, Parham, Ontario, to Bradshaw, 16 April 1918. On the cross-class tradition of French women owning sewing machines for home work, see Judith G. Coffin, *The Politics of Women's Work, 1750–1915* (Princeton: Princeton University Press, 1996), 14.

93 QUA, Frontenac County Records, CPF, 41: 'Visitors' Record Cards,' 'Ida Copp,' n.d. On the dearth of lodgers during the war, see NAC, MG 30 A 16, Sir Joseph Flavelle Papers, 22: 'Sir Sam Hughes 1915–19,' W.T.G. Brown, Sherbourne Methodist Church to Flavelle, 27 Jan. 1916.

94 QUA, Frontenac County Records, CPF, 41: 'Visitors' Record Cards,' 'Cecilia Doyle,' n.d.

95 For the proportions of enlistment among various categories of workers, see NAC, Borden Papers, 493, 'Proposals for Future Development of the Work' (CPF), n.d., 162.

96 QUA, Frontenac County Records, CPF, 41: 'Visitors' Record Cards,' 'Ellen Gillings,' n.d.

97 Ibid., 41: 'Visitors' Record Cards,' 'Almeda Cassell,' n.d.; 39: 'Correspondence 1918,' Rev Kirkpatrick, secretary Soldiers' Aid Commission to Bradshaw, 20 Sept. 1918.

98 On the rejection of the Speenhamland poor law system in the 1830s in the wake of Malthusian influence on political economy, see Raymond G. Cowherd, *Political Economists and the English Poor Laws: A Historical Study of the Influence of Classical Economics on the Formation of Social Welfare Policy* (Athens, Ohio: Ohio State University Press, 1977), 15–16. On the New Poor Law and its critique of wage supplements that were believed to stimulate overpopulation and hence improvidence, see Peter Dunkley, 'Whigs and Paupers: The Reform of the English Poor Laws, 1830–1834,' *Journal of British Studies* 20 (1981): 124–49. On the general cultural debate on poverty and charity in nineteenth-century Britain, see Hilton, *The Age of Atonement*; on its eighteenth-century precursors, see Donna Andrew, *Philanthropy and Police*. In Britain, the New Poor Law survived unscathed until the advent of the Labour government in 1945. See Pat Thane, *The Foundations of the Welfare State* (London and New York: Longman, 1982), 140–2.

99 QUA, Frontenac County Records, CPF, 41: 'Visitors' Record Cards,' 'Elizabeth Cox,' n.d.; ibid., 39: 'Correspondence 1915, Visitors' Record Cards,' 'Grace Hawke,' n.d.; ibid., 41: 'Paylists 1915–16,' 'Paylist,' 1 Dec. 1916, cases of Mary McVeigh, Nettie Kellar, Zilpah Silver, and Sarah Struthers, who attained varying levels of income largely determined by each woman's number of children.

100 Ibid., 41: 'Visitors' Record Cards,' cases of Vallinnia Davey and Margaret Jane Courtenay, and Margaret Evans, Mrs Freeman.

101 'Worlds of the Patriotic Fund,' *Montreal Herald*, 3 Feb. 1917.

102 McCord Museum, CPFMB, 1: 'Scrapbooks,' 'Patriotic Kindness Shown by a Complaint,' newspaper clipping, n.d.

103 NAC, Borden Papers, 81, 'Your Mother,' *The Maple Leaf* 11, no. 6 (Dec. 1916): 66.

104 In such cases women had to rely on the fact that local authorities could vouch for them. For example, see QUA, Frontenac County Records, CPF, 39: 'Correspondence 1915,' 'Visitors' Cards,' 'Mrs Jeannette Walker'; and 41: 'Visitors' Record Cards,' 'Rachel Hayes.'

105 QUA, Frontenac County, CPF, 41: 'Printed Material,' Philip Morris to Bradshaw, 10 Aug. 1915; and 39: 'Correspondence 1918,' Bradshaw to Dept. of Militia, 30 Jan. 1918.

106 NAC, Borden Papers, 267, Cobourg Patriotic Fund to Philip Morris, 4 Feb. 1916.

107 QUA, Frontenac County Records, CPF, 41: 'Printed Material,' Philip Morris to Bradshaw, 10 Aug. 1915.

108 Ibid., 39: 'Correspondence 1918,' A.C. Bradley to J.W. Bradshaw, 29 June 1918.

109 Ibid., 39: 'Correspondence 1919,' Bradshaw to Dept. of Militia, 8 Jan. 1919; 'Correspondence 1918,' Bradshaw to Dept. of Militia, 24 Oct. 1918; and 41: 'Visitors' Record Cards,' 'Mrs James Campbell.'

110 NAC, Borden Papers, 267, Loring Christie to Fred J. Alger, Bromptonville, Quebec, 14 June 1918. It was indeed an understatement to call Mrs W.H. Langsford 'deserving of aid,' for she had no less than six sons fighting, a husband with tuberculosis who was 'absolutely not able to work,' and eight other children still at home. See QUA, Frontenac County Records, CPF, 39: 'Correspondence 1916–17,' Rev W.F. Fitzgerald, Rector of St Paul's church to Bradshaw, 17 Oct. 1916.

111 AO, Premier E.C. Drury Papers, 03-04-0-019, A. Jones to Drury, 6 Feb. 1920; NAC, Borden Papers, 267, Loring Christie to Mrs Isabella Black, Hespeler, Ontario, 13 June 1917; and ibid., Mrs Margaret Collinson to Borden, 12 Aug. 1916.

112 'The Patriotic Fund,' *Montreal Daily Star*, 12 Feb. 1917.

113 'Thousands Need Assistance of Patriotic Fund,' *Montreal Herald*, 6 Feb. 1917.

114 McCord Museum, CPFMB, 'Scrapbooks,' Clarence F. Smith, 'To The Proud Wives and Mothers of the Men at the Front' (leaflet), Aug. 1915.

115 Ibid.

116 NAC, Borden Papers, 267, 'CPF Bulletin,' Oct. 1915, 2.

117 Valverde, *The Age of Light, Soap and Water*.

118 On the vastness of the investigation networks within Montreal alone, see Kellogg, *The Patriotic Fund of Canada*, 11–13. In rural areas, like Frontenac County, there was a paucity of investigators, and so most women were exempted from such minute inspection of their behaviour and circumstances.

119 QUA, Frontenac County Records, CPF, 39: 'Correspondence 1916–17,' undated press clipping.

120 'Wards of the Patriotic Fund,' *Montreal Herald*, 3 Feb. 1917; and Kellogg, *The Patriotic Fund of Canada*, 12–13.

121 On the coercive attitudes of the fund, see NAC, Borden Papers, 267, 'CPF Bulletin,' Oct. 1915; and NAC, Dept. of Milita, 10-13-15, 'CPF Bulletin' 31, Feb. 1918. The fund did offer some benefits to wives; see, for example, AO, E.C. Drury Papers, 03-04-0-041, 'York and Toronto Patriotic Fund, Address of the President Sir William Mulock'; NAC, Borden Papers, 331, 'CPF Annual Report, 1914–15,' 42–3; Kellogg, *The Patriotic Fund of Canada*, 22; QUA, Frontenac County Records, CPF, 41: 'Printed Material,' 'CPF Bulletin,' 45, April–May 1919, 1.

122 NAC, Canadian Patriotic Association, 'Minutes of Executive Committee,' 14 June 1917.

123 Kellogg, *The Patriotic Fund of Canada*, 31–4; NAC, Borden Papers, 267, George Yates to Philip Morris, 16 Jan. 1919, Yates to J.J. Kelso, 16 Jan. 1919; and QUA, Frontenac County Records, CPF, 41: 'Visitors' Record Cards,' 'May Commodore.'

124 QUA, Frontenac County Records, CPF, 39: 'Correspondence 1916–17,' 'CPF Application for Margaret Lothian,' n.d.; 'Correspondence 1918,' Mrs Jessie James to Bradshaw, 15 May 1918; and NAC, Borden Papers, 267, 'CPF Bulletin,' Sept. 1915, 1.

125 NAC, Borden Papers, Loring Christie to Ames, 8 April 1918; ibid., Business Manager, Toronto and York CPF, to Borden, 15 Oct. 1918; Kellogg, *The Patriotic Fund of Canada*, 32–3; and QUA, Frontenac County Records, CPF, 39: 'Correspondence 1916,' Bradshaw to Dept. of Militia, 22 Dec. 1916.

126 Kellogg, *The Patriotic Fund of Canada*, 22; and QUA, Frontenac County Records, CPF, 39: 'Correspondence 1919,' E.J. Whiltett, accountant, Canadian Pacific Railway, to Bradshaw, 21 March 1919. This appears to have been the only discovered case of fraud in the Frontenac Country CPF case files.

127 QUA, Frontenac County Records, CPF, 40: 'Correspondence 1919,' Bradshaw to Mrs Annie Flint, 3 April 1919; and ibid., W. Douglas, director of Separation Allowances and Assigned Pay, to secretary, Soldiers' Aid Commission, Sydenham, Ontario, 27 March 1919.

128 Ibid., 39: 'Correspondence 1917,' Bradshaw to T.J. Munro, Reeve, Sharbot Lake, n.d.

129 Pedersen, *Family Dependence and the Origins of the Welfare State*, 113.

130 QUA, Frontenac County Records, CPF, 39: 'Correspondence 1914,' Mrs Sidney Charlton to Bradshaw, 28 Oct., 20 Oct. 1914.

131 NAC, Canadian Patriotic Association, 'Minutes of Executive,' 20 Feb. 1917.

132 QUA, Frontenac County Records, 39: 'Correspondence 1919,' Bradshaw to Mrs Helen Rea, 7 July 1919; 40: Mrs Helen Rea to Bradshaw, 23 July 1919, 6 Aug. 1919, Bradshaw to Philip Morris, 24 July 1919; L.A. Copping, Dept. of Militia, to Bradshaw, 26 July 1919; Bradshaw to Copping, 31 July 1919; R.A. Reaton, Dept. of Militia, to Bradshaw, 13 Aug. 1919; Bradshaw to Mrs Rea, 11 Sept. 1919; and Mrs Rea to Bradshaw, 22 Sept. 1919.

133 Ibid., 40: 'Correspondence 1919,' 'Report of Investigation of Case of Mrs Sarah Jane Kish.'

134 Ibid., 39: 'Correspondence 1918,' 'Memorandum for Committee re Mrs Prudence Hancock (Manning), 303 Seaton,' 2 June 1916; Toronto and York Country Patriotic Fund Association to Bradshaw, 14 Jan. 1915; and Bradshaw to Lieut. Col. C.W. Ingall, 4 Feb. 1918.

135 Ibid., 39: 'Correspondence 1915,' Mrs Daniel Riddell to Bradshaw, Sept.

1915, C. Turner, Paymaster to Bradshaw, 20 Sept. 1915, Mrs Riddell to Bradshaw, 20 Dec. 1915.

136 Ibid., 39: 'Correspondence 1916–17,' Bradshaw to Militia Headquarters, 3 Aug. 1917, Bradshaw to Philip Morris, 6 Aug. 1917; and 40: 'Correspondence 1919,' Mrs James Ward, Plevna, Ontario to Bradshaw, 25 March 1919.

137 Ibid., 39: 'Correspondence 1916,' J.W. Borden, Paymaster General to Bradshaw, 26 Aug. 1916, Bradshaw to Borden, 29 Aug. 1916, G.A.M. Carter to Mrs Emma Madigan, 7 Aug. 1916.

138 Ibid., 39: 'Correspondence 1918,' Mrs Bertha Kirk to Bradshaw, 9 May 1918, Mrs W.H. Turnham to Bradshaw, 8 May 1918, Mrs Mildred Brewer to Bradshaw, 25 Nov. 1917.

139 Ibid., 39, Philip Morris to dear sir, 29 Nov. 1917.

140 NAC, Borden Papers, 267, Henry Tucker to Borden, n.d. 1918, Tucker to Borden, 27 Feb. 1918, 1 March 1918.

141 NAC, Borden Papers, 267, 'CPF Bulletin,' Oct. 1915, 1.

142 QUA, Frontenac County Records, CPF, 39: 'Correspondence 1918,' Mrs Albert James to Bradshaw, 27 Jan. 1916, J.C. Crawford to Bradshaw, 19 Nov. 1917, Mrs Charles Wood to Bradshaw, 24 May. 1918.

143 QUA, Frontenac County Records, 'Correspondence 1915,' Mrs J.W. Carey to Bradshaw, 9 April 1917.

144 McGill University Archives [MUA], MG 4003, Women's War Registry Papers [WWR], 'Notice Sent to Papers,' 7 Sept. 1916.

145 'The Feminine Side of the War,' *The Weekly Tattler*, 17 June 1916, n.p.

146 See, for example, Ceta Ramkhalawansingh, 'Women during the Great War,' in Janice Acton et al., eds., *Women at Work: Ontario, 1850–1930* (Toronto: Canadian Women's Educational Press, 1974). That gender relations were not altered by the war, see Alison Prentice et al., *Canadian Women: A History* (Toronto: Harcourt Brace Canada, 1996, 2nd ed.), 144–6.

147 NAC, Flavelle Papers 9: 96, Flavelle to C.W. Gordon, 9 Aug. 1918; and Flavelle to W.F. Nickle, 15 Oct. 1918.

148 MUA, WWR, 'Women with Experience in Factories,' n.d.; 'Volunteer Workers,' n.d.; 'Minutes of Meeting,' 22 July 1916; 'Women's War Register: Wives and Mothers of Soldiers,' n.d.; and 'Montreal Women's War Register,' n.d.

149 NAC, Borden Papers, 10147, H.K.S. Hemming to Borden, 21 Aug. 1916.

150 Ibid., James Brierley to Mrs Hurlbatt, 10 July 1916.

151 'Many Women Make Munitions in the Toronto Plants,' 13 July 1916, *Montreal Daily Mail*. For Montreal statistics, see MUA, WWR, D.L. Derrom, Munitions Dept., Canada Cement Co. to Hurlbatt, 21 Sept. 1916, J. Stewart,

Canada Cement Co. to Gordon, 18 Dec. 1916, which only had 24 married applicants and 60 single female applicants. The greatest expansion of female work was in the banks; see ibid., Albert J. Brown to Hurlbatt, 22 June 1916, in which he states that the Bank of Canada had just hired 1,200 women. This pattern in Canada was replicated in France, Germany, and Britain, where fewer than estimated women worked and most of these entered particular areas of the workforce. See Jean-Louis Robert, 'Women and work in France during the First World War'; Ute Daniel, 'Women's work in industry and family: Germany 1914–18; and Deborah Thom, 'Women and work in wartime Britain,' in Wall and Winter, eds., *The Upheaval of War.*

152 James Naylor, *The New Democracy: Challenging the Social Order in Industrial Canada, 1914–25* (Toronto: University of Toronto Press, 1991), 35.

153 NAC, Borden Papers, 1047, H.K.S. Hemming to Borden, 21 Aug. 1916.

154 MUA, WWR, M. Chase Goring to Hurlbatt, 16 Sept. 1916.

155 H.K.S. Hemming, 'Recruiting and Registration,' *Montreal Star,* 19 Aug. 1916.

156 MUA, WWR, A.O. Dawson to Mrs Hurlbatt, 30 Aug. 1916; and NAC, Canadian Patriotic Association, 'Minutes of Executive,' 14 Sept. 1916.

157 Kellogg, *The Patriotic Fund of Canada,* 27. In Britain, government day nurseries encouraged married women's work. No such system was established in Canada, ostensibly because the federal government preferred the policy of the CPF, which aimed to keep women at home. See NAC, Borden Papers, 267, G. Fowler, treasurer War Day Nursery, London, to Borden, 28 July 1917.

158 For the policing of married women's work, see NAC, Canadian Patriotic Association, 'Minutes of Executive Committee,' 19 April 1917; Kellogg, *The Patriotic Fund of Canada,* 29; 'Soldiers' Wives Encouraged to Support Selves,' *Montreal Gazette,* 31 Jan. 1917; NAC, Borden Papers, 267, Thoburn Allan, Secretary Calgary Patriotic Fund, to Ames, 20 Nov. 1915, protesting the removal of Mrs Collinson from the fund because of her work as a waitress; and ibid., Philip Morris to Borden, 18 July 1916, which describes the investigation of Mrs Lewis, who worked for the R.R. Co. in Saskatoon. On the tight control asserted by the Montreal Patriotic Fund over the Women's War Registry, see MUA, WWR, Helen Reid to Miss Gordon, 5 Dec. 1916, Reid to Secretary W.W.R, 5 Jan. 1917.

159 NAC, Borden Papers, 1047, Flavelle to Col. Ogilvie, 13 May 1916. For a study of Flavelle's career, see Michael Bliss, *A Canadian Millionaire: The Life and Business Times of Sir Joseph Wesley Flavelle, Bart.* (Toronto: Macmillan, 1978).

160 NAC, Borden Papers, 1419, Trades and Labour Congress, 'Pronouncement of Organized Labour in Canada on War Problems,' n.d. On organized labour and the First World War, see Naylor, *The New Democracy,* chapter 1.

161 On the use of internment camp labour, see NAC, Borden Papers, 1052, D.H. McDougall, General Manager Dominion Steel Company, to Mark Workman, 2 Sept. 1916.

162 Heron, 'Factory Workers,' in Craven, ed., *Labouring Lives,* 479–590.

163 NAC, Flavelle Papers, 9, no. 94, 'Alien Labour in Munitions Plants,' n.d.; ibid., 22: 'Borden 1915–16,' W.W. Davidson, Mayor of Moose Jaw to Borden, 22 Jan. 1916; ibid., 38: Irish 'Report of Labour Conditions in the City of Winnipeg,' 7 March 1917. Social workers also believed in hiring men first, because they saw at first hand the degree to which unemployment remained a factor despite the avowed 'shortage of labour.' See ibid., 35, Miss Helen Grange, Social Service Commission, Toronto, to Flavelle, 17 Jan. 1916.

164 NAC, Flavelle Papers, 38, Irish to Contractors, IMB, 23 April 1918; ibid., Irish to Flavelle, 16 Feb. 1917; MUA, WWR, 'Women Workers Commended by Munitions Board,' 14 Jan. 1916. To publicize the benefits of women's labour, the IMB made a series of films depicting women successfully undertaking munitions work, which in 1917 were circulated in Nova Scotia and New Brunswick.

165 MUA, WWR, 'Minutes of Meeting,' 20 Dec. 1916; 'Y.W.C.A. Asked to Find Housing for War Workers,' n.d.; H.M. Jaguays, Steel Company of Canada, to Miss Hurlbatt, 8 Sept. 1916; James Riley to Miss Hurlbatt, 5 Sept. 1916; and NAC, Flavelle Papers, 38, Mark Irish to Flavelle, 15 March 1917.

166 NAC, Flavelle Papers, 11:104, Irish to Flavelle, 21 Jan. 1918.

167 NAC, Flavelle Papers, 38, Irish to N.W. Rowell, 3 May 1918.

168 MUA, WWR, G.A. Morris, Ogilvie Flour Mills Ltd., to Miss Hurlbatt, 1 Sept. 1916; President, B.J. Coghlan Ltd. to Miss Hurlbatt, 30 Aug. 1916; J.H. Sherrard to Miss Hurlbatt, 9 Dec. 1916; and NAC, Borden Papers, 709, Algoma Steel Corp. to Borden, 16 March 1916.

169 NAC, Borden Papers, 1052, 'Munitions – Circular,' n.d.; ibid., 1047, Flavelle to Mr A. Boyer, President of Canadian Inspection and Testing Laboratories, 23 March 1917; and MUA, WWR, 'Conference on Recruiting in Canada Report,' undated newspaper clipping.

170 MUA, WWR, Mrs Marjorie Dapp to Hurlbatt, 17 Jan. 1916.

171 NAC, Flavelle Papers, 38: Irish to N.W. Rowell, President of the War Council, 3 May 1918, in which he explictly pointed out how dilution of labour would serve the government's recruitment aims.

172 NAC, Borden Papers, 1052, T.W. Crothers, 'Memorandum on the Alleged

Shortage of Labour,' 15 Sept. 1916. On the new category of women as 'unemployed,' see ibid., 1052, H.R. Morgan, Imperial Munitions Board, 'Memorandum to Sir Robert Borden,' 26 Oct. 1916.

173 NAC, Flavelle Papers, 38, Irish to Flavelle, Oct. 1916.
174 NAC, Flavelle Papers, 38, Irish to Flavelle, 18 Oct. 1916; Irish to Flavelle, 14 Feb. 1917, Flavelle to Irish, 5 March 1917, Flavelle to dear Gentlemen, May 1917. Bennett clearly defended the rights of male labour; see ibid., 22: Bennett to Flavelle, 10 Jan., 22 May 1917. There was later division within the union government over the issue of dilution of labour. For example, N.W. Rowell believed that the Department of National Service must follow Britain's example by securing the utilization of women's labour. See NAC, Borden Papers, 496, Rowell to Borden, Sept. 1918, 'Strictly Private and Confidential'; and ibid., 491, Hon. R.D. Robertson, Chairman, Canada Registration Board, 'Memorandum Showing Plan of Organization and Progress Made by the Canada Registration Board,' n.d., in which he endorsed the dilution of labour.
175 Pedersen, *Family, Dependence and the Origins of the Welfare State*, 83.
176 NAC, Borden Papers, 505, Workman to Borden, 30 March 1918.
177 NAC, Borden Papers, 312, H.H. Stevens to Borden, 20 Dec. 1916, 22 Dec. 1916.
178 NAC, Borden Papers, 312, *The British Columbia Federationist*, 22 Dec. 1916; and NAC, Flavelle Papers, 22, 'FA Acland 1916–18,' TLC, 'Pronouncement of Organized Labour in Canada on War Problems,' 11 June 1917.
179 MUA, WWR, Mrs R.W. Peardon to Hurlbatt, 23 Nov. (year unknown).
180 NAC, Flavelle Papers, 22, 'Sir Robert Borden 1915–16,' W.L. Hichens, London, to Borden, 4 Jan. 1916; and ibid., 38, Irish to Flavelle, 21 May 1918.
181 NAC, Flavelle Papers, 38, Irish to Flavelle, 15 Nov. 1918, in which he describes circulating a memorandum regarding the continued employment of women to all munitions contractors, Irish to Flavelle, 17 April 1917; and NAC, Borden Papers, 267, 'Resolution No. 22' (TLC), n.d. Writing from a very different perspective, Ida Fairbairn, the Honourary Secretary of the Women's Emergency Corps, Military Division No. 2, was concerned about the fate of women after the war. See MUA, WWR, Fairbairn to Miss C.A. Steen, 27 April 1916.
182 NAC, Flavelle Papers, 9, no. 94, Dominion Treasurer of GWVA to Flavelle, 31 Aug. 1917; and Flavelle to Irish, 26 March 1918, Irish to Flavelle, 28 March 1918.
183 'Women in Industry,' *Journal of Commerce*, 21 May 1916, n.p.
184 'Women Will Work to Let Men Enlist,' *Montreal Gazette*, 4 June 1916.
185 MUA, WWR, Mark Irish to Ethel Hurlbatt, 11 Sept. 1916.

186 MUA, WWR, Montreal Trades and Labour Congress, 'Memorandum,' n.d.

187 'Women Will Work to Let Men Enlist,' *Montreal Gazette*, 4 June 1916. Emphasis is mine.

188 On the changing class nature of the Women's War Registry, see MUA, WWR, unsigned copy of letter to Captain Ware, Sept. 1916; Hurlbatt to J.H. Sherrard, office of Director of National Service, 4 December 1916; Miss C. Edgar of Miss Edgar and Miss Cramp's School, to Hurlbatt, 30 Dec. 1916; Mrs E.A. LaRue to Hurlbatt, 25 Sept. 1916; and Hurlbatt to Brierley, 22 June 1916.

189 MUA, WWR, Hurlbatt to Mrs E.C. Hutchinson, 21 June 1916.

190 NAC, Borden Papers, 709, Dr A.H. Abbott, 'The Women's Emergency Corps,' 1 Sept. 1916.

191 MUA, WWR, Helen Reid to Miss Gordon, 9 Nov. 1916.

192 NAC, Borden Papers, 267, 'Minutes of Executive, CPF,' 12 Sept. 1917, in which they had to relent and allow women to work, given the high rates of inflation.

193 MUA, WWR, Helen Reid to Ethel Hurlbatt, 13 June, 30 Oct. 1916; 'Keeping Soldiers' Homes Together,' *Montreal Gazette*, 2 March 1917. For the financial constraints on the CPF, see QUA, Frontenac Country Records, CPF, 39: 'Correspondence 1914–20,' J.W. Bradshaw, 'Minutes,' 16–19 Nov. 1918; NAC, Borden Papers, 1047, T.S. Griffiths, President, Canadian Inspection and Testing Laboratories, to Flavelle, 1 June 1916; and 'False Ideas as to War Register Very Prevalent,' *Montreal Star*, 15 June 1916.

194 'Booklet Shows Share of Women in Shell Work,' *Montreal Star*, 2 Dec. 1916; Janet Brooks, 'Women Have Chance to Secure Great Reform,' *Montreal Daily Mail*, 7 April 1916, who feared that war work for women would overturn prewar labour legislation designed to protect women; and NAC, Flavelle Papers, 38, Irish to Flavelle, 7 Aug. 1917, recounting the protests of the mayor of Toronto concerning long hours for women in factories.

195 NAC, Borden Papers, 491, 'Supplementary Report – Sub-Committee on Labor of the Agricultural Interests,' 31 Jan. 1918; and ibid., 312, 'War Committee of the Cabinet – Labour Conference,' Jan. 1918.

196 QUA, Frontenac County Records, CPF, 41: 'Printed Material,' 'CPF Bulletin,' 23, April 1917, 3. See also 'First Luncheon at Windsor Today,' *Montreal Gazette*, 12 Feb. 1917, which outlined the need to preserve the wages of the 'good mechanic.'

197 'Patriotic Fund Will Increase Grants to Homes,' *Montreal Herald*, 24 Feb. 1917.

198 NAC, Borden Papers, 323, 'The Soldier's Return: A Little Chat with Pri-

vate Pat,' n.d. This item concludes with the instruction that soldiers must not 'sponge on other people.'

199 NAC, Borden Papers, 2457, W.P. Purney, President, Dominion Command, GWVA, to Borden, 9 June 1919; ibid., 1546, N.F.R. Knight, GWVA to Borden, 14 June 1917; and 'Battle Veterans Guests at Great Patriotic Rally,' *Montreal Daily Star*, 14 Feb. 1917.

200 On new conceptions of dependency, see McCord Museum, CPFMB, 2: 'Correspondence April–May 1920,' Major L. Gauvreau, 'Memorandum No. 2,' 7 April 1920.

201 NAC, Borden Papers, 2457, Alberta Returned Soldiers Commission to Borden, 11 Oct. 1918; ibid., RSL series, 1589, Donald Solandt, Secretary Manitoba Patriotic Fund to Borden, 30 June 1917; and Canadian Reconstruction Association, *Women and Reconstruction* (pamphlet, 1918), in which they describe the family as a unit, 3. The work of the CPF revealed extensive poverty among larger families; see Helen R.Y. Reid, *A Social Study along Health Lines of the First Thousand Children Examined in the Health Clinic of the Canadian Patriotic Fund* (pamphlet, 1920), in which she declared her opposition to pensions for soldiers. See also NAC, Borden Papers, 2266, Miss R.M. Leives, secretary, Commission, Political Survey, Saskatchewan Unit to Borden, 8 March 1920, in which she studied national morality and poverty among soldiers' families.

202 McCord Museum, CPFMB, 2: 'Correspondence 1920,' 'Canadian Patriotic Fund – Federal Emergency Appropriation Dept., Montreal Branch, Order-in-Council,' 9 Dec. 1919. Support for large families also came from the GWVA; see NAC, Borden Papers, 2457, N.F.R. Knight to Borden, 21 Feb. 1918.

203 QUA, Frontenac Country Records, CPF, 41: 'Printed Material,' 'CPF Bulletin,' 37, July 1918, 2; McCord Museum, CPFMB, Box 2, Ames to Miss E.L. Martin, general secretary, Montreal Soldiers' Wives League, 5 June 1919; and ibid., Mrs Elliott Busteed J.W. Ross, 12 June 1919, who disliked that their program of aid to dependents was being marginalized by the emergency fund.

204 W.J. Roche, *Women's Work in Canada: Duties, Wages, Conditions and Opportunities for Domestics in the Dominion* (pamphlet, 1915), 3.

205 McCord Museum, CPFMB, Box 2, 'Correspondence 1920,' Major L. Gauvreau, 'Memorandum,' 19 March 1920; ibid., Gauvreau, 'Report of Operations,' 24 Dec. 1919. For the animosity demonstrated for single unemployed soldiers, who were vigorously investigated, see ibid., Gauvreau, 'Report of Opertions,' 11; QUA, Frontenac Country Records, CPF, 39: 'Correspondence 1919,' Philip Morris to Bradshaw, 23 Feb. 1920,

in which he declared that no help should be given single men; and 40: 'Correspondence 1920,' A.E. Ross, Administrator Federal Emergency Appropriation, to J.W. Bradshaw, 4 Feb. 1920. Returned soldiers themselves tried to undermine the rights of single men. See NAC, Flavelle Papers, 9, no. 94, Brenton B. Harris to Borden, 27 July 1917, in which he stated: 'I need the position and am more entitled to the position than the single man.'

206 AO, Drury Papers, 03-04-0-041, W.A. Riddell to Mr Rollo, Minister of Labour, 13 Jan. 1920.

207 AO, Hearst Papers, 03-03-0-044, Minister of Labour, 'Extract from Report of Departmental Committee on Demobilization,' 7 May 1917.

208 On federal government labour policy and the creation of postwar provincial employment bureaux, see Struthers, *No Fault of Their Own*, chapter 1.

209 Pedersen, *Family, Dependence and the Origins of the Welfare State*, 115.

210 QUA, Frontenac County Records, CPF, 40: 'Correspondence 1919,' Secretary-treasurer, Frontenac Branch, to Bradshaw, 10 Sept. 1919; and 39: 'Correspondence 1916–17,' 'Untitled Memorandum of Patriotic Fund,' n.d.

211 NAC, Borden Papers, 2504, F.N. Knight, GWVA to Borden, 27 March 1918.

212 NAC, RG 38, Department of Veterans' Affairs, 168, House of Commons Commitee, 27 May 1921, Major Hume Cronyn, 'Third and Final Report'; NAC, Borden Papers, 1722, D.G. Campbell, Calgary Board of Trade to Borden, 31 Oct. 1918; and 1648, Janet C. Kemp, President, War Widows' Association, to Borden, 31 March 1920. Widows were paid on average $55.00 per month and $6.00 for each child, a living wage commensurate with that paid unskilled labour during the war. See Borden Papers, 2366, E. King to Mrs Florence Cournsell, 5 Oct. 1917; and 2513, Austin Taylor, Director IMB, Dept. of Aeronautical Supplies, to Mr Fitzgerald, n.d. On World War I government pension policies in Canada, see Desmond Morton and Glenn Wright, *Winning the Second Battle: Canadian Veterans and the Return to Civilian Life, 1915–1930* (Toronto: University of Toronto Press, 1987).

213 NAC, Borden Papers, 2457, J.C. Kemp to Borden, 3 March 1920; Kemp to Borden, 6 March 1920; and 1648, Kemp to Sir George Foster, 16 April 1920. There was a parallel Mother's Association that lobbied for pensions for mothers of dead soldiers on a basis equal to that of widows. See NAC, Borden Papers, 1648, 'Resolution of the United Farmers of Manitoba at their Convention in Brandon,' March 1920; and Harriet Dick, Winnipeg, to Sir George Foster, 10 May 1920. See also ibid., RSL series, 1589, President, Canadian Association of Mothers and Wives of Soldiers and Sailors of Greater Vancouver and Burnaby, to Borden, 15 June 1917.

214 NAC, Borden Papers, RSL series, 1589, R.A. Rigg to Borden, 12 June 1917;

2457, 'Undated Memorandum Submitted by the Dominion Executive Committee, G.W.V.A.,' n.d.

215 NAC, Borden Papers, 1699, Florence E. Carpenter, Medicine Hat to Borden, 27 Sept. 1917.

216 McCord Museum, CPFMB, 2: 'Correspondence Jan.–June 1923,' 'Soldiers' Families Relief Cease,' newspaper clipping, *Montreal Gazette*, n.d.

217 NAC, Borden Papers, 2534, N.W. Rowell to Borden, re 'Women's War Conference,' n.d., 1918; and 491, J.C. Watters and Tom Moore, 'To Organized Labour in Canada,' n.d. who referred to the need to keep women at home in order to protect 'the mothers of our future citizens.'

3: Maternalism, National Efficiency, and Mothers' Allowances

1 The title 'a peaceful evolution of industrial citizenship' is derived from NAC, Kelso Papers, Vol. 1, Autobiographical Files, undated clipping, 'The Juvenile Court.' The epigraphs are taken from AO, Premiers' Papers, 03-03-0-049, Rev. Peter Bryce, 'Pensions for Widowed Mothers,' n.d., and W.A. Riddell, superintendent of Trades and Labor, Government of Ontario, 'Memorandum on Mothers' Pensions,' 15 Feb. 1917.

2 The path-breaking work on mothers' pensions in Canada is James Struthers, *The Limits of Affluence: Welfare in Ontario 1920–1970* (Toronto: University of Toronto Press, 1995), chapter 1. See also Margaret Little, 'The Blurring of Boundaries: Private and Public Welfare for Single Mothers in Ontario,' *Studies in Political Economy* 47 (Summer 1995), and '"Claiming a Unique Place": The Introduction of Mothers' Pensions in British Columbia,' *B.C. Studies* (Spring–Summer 1995). In the American context, the most important studies of mothers' pensions are Theda Skocpol, *Protecting Soldiers and Mothers: The Political Origins of Social Policy in the United States* (Cambridge: Harvard University Press, 1992); Linda Gordon, *Pitied but Not Entitled: Single Mothers and the History of Welfare* (New York: Macmillan, 1994); Molly Ladd-Taylor, *Mother-work: Women, Child Welfare, and the State, 1890–1930* (Urbana and Chicago: University of Illinois Press, 1994); and Gwendolyn Mind, *The Wages of Motherhood: Inequality in the Welfare State, 1917–42* (Ithaca: Cornell University Press, 1995). For a comparative study of the United States and Britain, see Miriam Cohen and Michael Hanagan, 'The Politics of Gender and the Making of the Welfare State, 1900–1940: A Comparative Perspective,' *Journal of Social History* 24, no. 3 (Spring 1991).

3 *The Limits of Affluence*, 19–49.

4 Susan Pedersen, *Family Dependence and the Origins of the Welfare State*, 138–77.

5 AO, Provincial Secretary's correspondence [Ont. Prov. Sec.], Vol. 45, J.H.T. Falk to J.J. Kelso, 23 April 1918. See also 'Mothers' Pensions,' *Toronto Globe*, 6 May 1918, in which the Bishop of Huron called the relief of poverty-stricken widows the 'business of motherhood.' On the convergence of social welfare and economic concerns as the benchmark of New Liberalism, see Roger Davidson, 'The State and Social Investigation in Britain, 1880–1914,' in Michael J. Lacey and Mary O. Furner, eds., *The State and Social Investigation in Britain and the United States* (Cambridge: Cambridge University Press, 1993), 247. This paradigm of the links between economic principles and social welfare was at the core of the theories of John Maynard Keynes. See Jose Harris, 'Economic Knowledge and British Social Policy,' in Mary O. Furner and Barry Supple, eds., *The State and Economic Knowledge: The American and British Experiences* (Cambridge: Cambridge University Press, 1990), 379–400.

6 Helen R.Y. Reid, *A Social Study along Health Lines of the First Thousand Children Examined in the Health Clinic of the Canadian Patriotic Fund, Montreal Branch* (pamphlet, 1920), 36–9.

7 Ibid., 5.

8 Hon. J.W. Longley, *The Future of Canada* (pamphlet 1892).

9 AO, Premiers' Papers, 03-03-0-049, J.J. Kelso, 'Aiding Destitute Mothers,' *The Canadian Municipal Journal*, n.d., quoted in W.A. Riddell, *Report on Mothers' Allowances*. See also Otto McFeely, 'Mothers' Pensions in America,' *Woman's Century*, 5, 2 (Feb. 1918): 17. On Kelso's opposition to creches, see NAC, Kelso Papers, Vol. 5, 'Ontario Welfare System,' 'The Creche a Compromise.' There were only a few prominent supporters of the creche. See AO, RG 29, Kelso Scrapbooks, John Ross Robertson, 'School System is Too Complex,' clipping 1899; and Nellie McClung, 'Listen – Ladies – in which the Writer Urges Many Necessary Reforms,' *Everywoman's World*, June 1919.

10 AO, Premiers' Papers, 03-03-0-049, W.A. Riddell, *Memorandum on Mothers' Pensions*, 1917, 31. The movement against the institutional care of children was, however, crucial to clearing the way for outdoor relief for widows, for in Quebec, where the Catholic church – dominated orphanages held sway, the movement for mothers' pensions remained stalled until the 1930s and remained within the circle of private family welfare organizations. See *Canadian Child Welfare News* 11, no. 2 (15 May 1926): 27; and NAC, Canadian Council on Social Development, vol. 62, file 497, 'Memo. for the Files,' 20 May 1937, regarding the experimental system of private mothers' allowances in Quebec City established by Mlle Cecile Joncas in 1935.

11 NAC, Kelso Papers, Vol. 1, 'Autobiographical Files,' undated clipping, 'Commitee on Child Labour.' Kelso's idea of narrowly Christian citizenship

was transformed following World War I. For Kelso's conception of citizenship, see ibid., 'Thoughts for Workers,' n.d.

12 AO, Ont. Prov. Sec., Vol. 45, Kelso to W.D. McPherson, 18 May 1918.

13 J.J. Kelso, 'A Pension for Widowed Mothers,' *Social Service*, Nov. 1904. The campaign for delinquency alone did not galvanize government support for mothers' allowances. Similar arguments were proferred in Quebec in the 1920s with little effect. See 'Mothers and Children Kept Together by the Family Welfare Association of Montreal,' *Canadian Child Welfare News* 11, no. 2 (15 May 1926).

14 NAC, Kelso Papers, vol. 1, 'Autobiographical Files,' excerpt from 1896 report.

15 AO, Premiers' Papers, 03-03-0-049, J.J. Kelso, 'Aiding Destitute Mothers,' in Riddell, *Report on Mothers' Allowances*.

16 NAC, Montreal Council of Women, MG 28 I 164, Minute Book, April 1908– May 1913, 'Minutes,' 17 Feb. 1915, 13 Oct. 1915, 21 May 1919. In Quebec, women had also to fight against the pauperization concerns of the Charity Organization Society, which held views similar to those of the Ontario CAS regarding relief. See ibid., 15 Feb. 1922. Efforts to bolster the CAS system were especially pressing in 1918, when they feared that their principles of child saving were being encroached on by the federal pension system. See NAC, Scott Papers, Vol. 11, 'Soldier's Children 1917–18,' Scott to Stanley B. Coristine, secretary Board of Pension Commissions, 28 March 1918, 19 March 1918, J.J. Kelso to Scott, 25 May 1917.

17 NAC, Scott Papers, Vol. 11, 'Children's Protection Act 1914–24,' Hugh Ferguson to Scott, 11 March 1921.

18 Frank N. Stapleford, 'The Canadian Conference of Charities and Corrections,' *Christian Guardian*, 3 Oct. 1917, 8.

19 C.E.H. 'The Canadian Woman,' *Woman's Century* 7, no. 8 (Aug. 1920): 24.

20 NAC, Scott Papers, Vol. 11, 'An Explanation of the Need for the Dominion Act Dealing with Juvenile Delinquency,' 1908.

21 'The Society for the Protection of Women and Children,' *Canadian Child Welfare News* 1, no. 2 (May–July 1924): 52, 57.

22 AO, RG 29, Kelso clippings, 'Progressive Legislation: Mothers' Allowances in Alberta,' n.d.

23 Ernest Blois, *Ninth Annual Report of the Mothers' Allowance Commission for Nova Scotia*, 1938, 15.

24 Frank Stapleford, 'A Mothers' Allowance Act for Ontario,' *Christian Guardian*, 26 March 1919, 7. On the connection between motherhood and national well-being in Britain, see Ellen Ross, 'Good and Bad Mothers: Lady Philanthropists and London Housewives before World War I,' in Dorothy O.

Helly and Susan M. Reverby, eds., *Gendered Domains: Rethinking Public and Private in Women's History* (Ithaca: Cornell University Press, 1992), 201.

25 Sir Robert Borden, *Canada at War* (pamphlet, 1916), 6.

26 Sir Robert Borden, *The War and Its Causes and Its Messages* (pamphlet, 1914), 9, 17.

27 Jose Harris, 'Society and State in Twentieth-Century Britain,' in F.M.L. Thompson, ed. *The Cambridge Social History of Britain, 1750–1950*, vol. 3, *Social Agencies and Institutions* (Cambridge, Cambridge University Press, 1990), 64–71; James T. Kloppenberg, *Uncertain Victory: Social Democracy and Progressivism in European and American Thought 1870–1920* (New York and Oxford: Oxford University Press, 1986), 176, 395–6; and Eugenio F. Biagini, ed., *Citizenship and Community: Liberals, Radicals and Collective Identities in the British Isles, 1865–1931* (Cambridge: Cambridge University Press, 1995, 1.

28 Frank Stapleford, 'Social Changes during the War,' *Christian Guardian*, 28 Feb. 1917, 7.

29 Mrs S.R. Russell, 'The Aim and Policy of the Y.W.C.A.,' *Woman's Century* 7, no. 1 (Jan. 1920): 30.

30 Stapleford, 'Social Changes during the War,' 7. Doug Owram has argued that there was a backlash among academic commentators immediately following the war against State intervention. See *The Government Generation: Canadian Intellectuals and the State, 1900–1945* (Toronto: University of Toronto Press, 1986), chapter 4.

31 AO, RG 29, Kelso clippings, 'Child Welfare Institute,' n.d. For the coalition between clergymen, women's organizations, and labour leaders created around the issue of child welfare, see Nancy J. Christie and Michael Gauvreau, *'A Full-Orbed Christianity': The Protestant Churches and Social Welfare in Canada, 1900–1940* (Montreal and Kingston: McGill-Queen's University Press, 1996), chapter 3.

32 Canadian Reconstruction Association, *Women and Reconstruction* (pamphlet, 1918), 3. See also AO, RG 29, Kelso clippings, 'Excellent Pictorial Address by S.M. Thomson,' 18 February 1909. In 1915 Kelso noted that 'both the country and the child are bound to materially prosper,' in Kelso, 'Conservation of Child Life,' *Woman's Century* 2, no. 11 (April 1915): 6. On the movement for national efficiency in Britain, see Geoffrey Searle, *The Quest for National Efficiency: A Study in British Politics and Political Thought, 1899–1914* (Oxford: Basil Blackwell, 1971). In periods when labour is viewed as the key to national wealth, population is deemed beneficial and so welfare policy favours mothers. On this point in the eighteenth century, see Donna T. Andrew, *Philanthopy and Police* (Princeton: Princeton Univer-

sity Press, 1989), 23–4. For the nineteenth century, see Edward Ross Dickinson, *The Politics of German Child Welfare from the Empire to the Federal Republic* (Cambridge: Harvard University Press, 1996), 29.

33 NAC, J.S. Willison Papers, MG 30 D 29, Vol. 26, file 19096, A.B. Macallum to Willison, 28 Aug. 1918. See also Professor J.C. Fields, *Science and Industry* (pamphlet, 1918); and Frank Jewett, *Industrial Research* (pamphlet, 1919); *Research and the Problems of Unemployment, Business Depression and National Finance in Canada* (pamphlet, 1922).

34 'W.C.T.U. Convention,' *Woman's Century* 4, no. 3 (Sept. 1916): 19.

35 Mrs Wilson, 'Made-in-Canada,' *Woman's Century* 2, no. 10 (March 1915): 10.

36 NAC, Kelso papers, Vol. 5, 'Ontario Welfare System,' 'Thoughts on Social Welfare,' May 1912, 3.

37 NAC, Willison Papers, Vol. 22, 16192, Professor Gilbert Jackson to Willison, 26 Jan. 1915.

38 Ontario Legislative Assembly, *Report of the Committee on Child Labor* (pamphlet, n.d.), 3; and J.J. Kelso, *Homes Wanted for Boys and Girls of All Ages* (pamphlet, n.d.), 4.

39 See J.J. Kelso, 'The Child as a Wage-Earner,' *Canadian Municipal Journal* (April 1916).

40 *Old Age Annuities – Speeches Delivered in the Senate of Canada during the Third Session of the Tenth Parliament* (pamphlet, 1907), 24.

41 Ibid., 32.

42 NAC, Kelso Papers, Vol. 4, 'Charity and Charity Organizations,' 'Wages and Hours of Labor,' n.d.

43 Herbert Ames, *Canadian Political History* (pamphlet, 1894), 55–7.

44 C.V. Corless, *Educational Reform: Its Relations to a Solution of the Industrial Deadlock, Transactions of the Royal Canadian Institute* (pamphlet, 1919), 41–3, 59.

45 Kelso, 'The Child as a Wage-Earner,' *Canadian Municipal Journal* (April 1916).

46 NAC, Kelso Papers, Vol. 8, 'Notebook 1897–31,' untitled extract.

47 E.A. Bott, *Studies in Industrial Psychology,* Vol. IV, University of Toronto Studies, Psychological Series, 1920, 5–6, 11, 48.

48 AO, RG 29, Kelso clippings, 'Training of Youth,' quoting Mr T.H. Preston, MPP for South Brant; and ibid., 'The Child Offender,' undated clipping, quoting W.L. Scott on the need for labour. Mothers' allowances were viewed as an adjunct to the development of technical education. On technical education, see S. Morley Wickett, 'Canada and Technical Education,' *Transactions of the Royal Canadian Institute,* April 1908.

49 AO, RG 29, Kelso clippings, 'Child Welfare in War Time: A Selected Bibliography.'

50 AO, Premiers' Papers, 03-03-0-049, Riddell, *Report on Mothers' Allowances,* 10. Born near Glasgow into a working-class Scottish family in 1869, Peter Bryce later became a Methodist clergyman after immigrating to Canada in 1903. For most of his career he ministered to the skilled working-class community living around the the railway neighbourhood of Earlscourt in Toronto. He was one of the founding members of the Toronto Neighbourhood Workers' Association, and as its president between 1916 and 1919 he lobbied for mothers' pensions. On Bryce, see University of Toronto, Thomas Fisher Rare Books, Stuart Jaffray Papers, MS 113, 1: 'Peter Bryce.'

51 *Report of the Committee on Child Labour,* n.d.

52 'Should Get Home Training,' *Toronto Globe,* 12 Jan. 1919, quoting speech by the Rev Peter Bryce at the Oddfellows' Hall. See also Ontario Mothers' Allowance Commission, *Fourth Annual Report 1923–24,* 15.

53 AO, Premiers' Papers, 03-04-0-366, 'Reports Indicating the Value and Services Rendered by the Investigators of the Mothers' Allowance Commission,' to the Hon. E.C. Drury, 23 March 1923.

54 Ontario Mothers' Allowances Commission, *Fifth Annual Report 1925–26,* 15.

55 NAC, Kelso Papers, Vol. 5, 'Humane Society of Toronto,' 'Pensions for Widows,' 31 May 1918.

56 Peter H. Bryce, *National Social Efficiency* (pamphlet, 1917), 9.

57 *Report of the Committee on Child Labor,* n.d., 7.

58 AO, Ont. Prov. Sec., Vol. 43, Rev S.D. Chown, 'Sagiasto – Sagiasto,' 1917, 4–5.

59 This is a contrast with the experience in the United States, where desertion became central to public debates regarding single women during the 1890s. See Gordon, *Pitied but Not Entitled,* 25.

60 NAC, Society for the Protection of Women and Children, MG 28 I 129, Vol. 1, G.B. Clarke, 'Rehabilitation in Family Desertion,' 1925, 4.

61 NAC, Society for the Protection of Women and Children, Vol. 1, 'Minutes,' 15 Jan. 1930, 21 Jan. 1925, 16 Jan. 1929; ibid., G.B. Clarke, 'Domestic Relations and Problems of Child Dependency: A Study of Broken Homes,' n.d., 1–2; and *Canadian Child Welfare News* 2, no. 3 (August 1926): 32.

62 NAC, CCSD, Vol. 22, file 99, George H. Corbett, executive secretary, Society for the Protection of Women and Children, to Helen Reid, 26 Feb. 1925. It was generally recognized that the incidence of desertion had escalated particularly among soldier's families. As a result, reformers lobbied the federal government to pass a law similar to the Imperial Maintenance Act of 1911. See Corbett to Reid, 2 Feb. 1925.

63 AO, Premiers' Papers, 03-03-0-049, Riddell, 'Report on Mothers' Allowances,' testimony of Frank Stapleford, 17–18.

64 NAC, Kelso Papers, Vol. 4, 'Family Desertion,' untitled extract, which juxtaposes the 'sensitive mother' against 'the recalcitrant husband.'

65 NAC, Society for the Prevention of Cruelty to Women and Children, Corbett to Reid, 26 Feb. 1925.

66 AO, Premiers' Papers, 03-03-0-049, W.A. Riddell, 'Memorandum on Mothers' Pensions,' 1917, 29.

67 It also had a distinctly racial complexion. See AO RG 29, Kelso clippings, 'What Makes Criminals,' 1908, in which a Miss Cook claimed that there was more family desertion among Jews than any other group in Toronto.

68 AO, RG 7-12-0-21, Ministry of Labor, 'Mothers' Pensions,' 17.

69 For this movement, see NAC, Scott Papers, Vol. 5, 'CAS Cases 1916–19,' 'Memorandum of Action Decided on at a Meeting Held Wed., 13th Day of November, 1918'; NAC, Kelso Papers, Vol. 1, 'Autobiographical and Reform Cause,' untitled clipping, *St. Thomas Journal*, 12 July 1918; and ibid., 'Family Desertion,' n.d.

70 AO, Premiers' Papers, 03-03-0-049, Riddell, 'Memo on Mothers' Pensions,' 1917, 6.

71 NAC, Kelso Papers, Vol. 4, 'Family Desertion,' untitled extract, n.d.

72 AO, RG 7-12-0-21 'Mothers' Pensions,' 10–11.

73 Ibid., 11.

74 'Mothers' Pensions,' *Toronto Mail*, 7 Nov. 1919.

75 AO, Ont. Prov. Sec., Vol. 45, J.J. Kelso, *Small Newsboys* (pamphlet, 1911).

76 NAC, Kelso Papers, Vol. 1, 'Speeches,' untitled address to New Jersey Conference of Social Workers, n.d., 2.

77 AO, RG 7-12-0-21, 'Mothers' Pensions,' 2–6.

78 AO, RG 29, Kelso clippings, 'After the War.'

79 Ibid.

80 PAM, Edith Rogers Papers, P 189–90, Deserted Wives' Case Files. Ontario and British Columbia did provide for women who had been deserted for seven (later, five) years.

81 On the outlook of ninteenth-century poor relief in England, see Robert Humphreys, *Sin, Organized Charity and the Poor Law in Victorian England* (London and Hampshire: St. Martin's Press, 1995), 112.

82 J.J. Kelso, *Can Slums Be Abolished or Must We Continue to Pay the Penalty?* (pamphlet, 1910), 19; Kelso, 'Aiding Destitute Mothers,' *Canadian Municipal Journal*, n.d., quoted in AO, Premiers' Papers, 03-03-0-049, Riddell, 'Report on Mothers' Allowances'; and AO, Premiers' Papers, 03-04-0-366, K. Powell, Hamilton Kiwanis Club to Miss E. Storms, 9 Feb. 1923.

83 J.J. Kelso, *Can Slums Be Abolished or Must We Continue to Pay the Penalty?* (pamphlet, 1910), 18; and NAC, Kelso Papers, Vol. 1, 'Speeches,' 'Methods of Reforming Children,' n.d., 2.

84 Canadian Reconstruction Association, *Bolshevism: The Lesson for Canada* (pamphlet, 1919), 1.

85 In British Columbia the law regarding mothers' pensions was more liberal in scope and less stigmatizing. See Guest, *The Emergence of Social Security in Canada*, 54–5; and Little, '"Claiming a Unique Place": The Introduction of Mothers' Pensions in British Columbia.'

86 'The Cradle and the Nation,' *Woman's Century* 4, no. 4 (Oct. 1916): 20.

87 Anne Anderson Perry, 'Helen Gregory MacGill,' *Woman's Century* 6, no. 11 (Nov. 1918): 38.

88 Anne Anderson Perry, 'Woman, Where are You Going?' *Woman's Century* 5, no. 9 (Sept. 1918): 133.

89 L.W. Claxton, 'Who is Stealing our People?' *Everywoman's World*, Oct. 1920, 7; and George Birmingham, 'What Are We Agitating For?' *Everywoman's World*, Dec. 1920, 2. The idea that women were to become chiefly mothers of the future race was not a concept imposed upon women by men. Rather, women wrote extensively on the problem of the falling birthrate and championed natalist policies as a frontline defence of women's rights. See, for example, Mary Gray, 'The Canadian Child,' *Woman's Century* 7, no. 8 (Aug. 1920): 30; Charlotte Carson Talcott, 'Home and Abroad,' *Woman's Century* 3, no. 4 (Oct. 1915): 25.

90 McMurchy was quoted in Mary Gray, 'The Canadian Child,' *Woman's Century* 7, no. 10 (Oct. 1919): 48. Replenishing the race was a constant theme of articles in women's magazines immediately following the war. Although in some instances race specifically referred to the birthrate of Anglo-Saxon stock, in many cases the term corresponded to the concept of 'nation.' For specific references to 'foreigners' and motherhood, see NAC, Kelso papers, Vol. 1, 'Autobiographical files,' 'Started without Funds,' n.d.; and ibid., 'Social Progress,' n.d. On the racial configuration of maternal feminism, see Carol Bacchi, *Liberation Deferred* (Toronto: University of Toronto Press, 1983); Marilyn Lake, 'A Revolution in the Family: The Challenges and Contradictions of Maternal Citizenship in Australia,' in Seth Koven and Sonya Michel, eds., *Mothers of a New World: Maternalist Politics and the Origins of Welfare States* (New York and London: Routledge, 1993), 379–88; Gwendolyn Mink, *The Wages of Motherhood: Inequality and the Welfare State* (Ithaca: Cornell Univesity Press, 1995); and Mink, 'The Lady and the Tramp: Gender, Race and the Origins of the American Welfare State,' in Linda Gordon, ed., *Women, the State and Welfare*, 109–10. On the racial-

ist aspects of reform thought in the early twentieth century, see Mariana Valverde, '"When the Mother of the Race Is Free": Race, Reproduction, and Sexuality in First-Wave Feminism,' in Franca Iacovetta and Mariana Valverde, eds., *Gender Conflicts: New Essays in Women's History* (Toronto: University of Toronto Press, 1992), 3–26. In *The Limits of Affluence*, Struthers has argued that racial attitudes were embedded in social legislation, 46. From my reading of case files in both Ontario and Manitoba, the notion that race constituted a barrier to receiving benefits remains less clear. In Ontario the number of non–Anglo-Saxon recipients of mothers' allowances was in direct proportion to their numerical relationship to the general population. See, for example, Ontario, *Third Annual Report of the Mothers' Allowances Commission for the Year 1922–23*, 11. In Manitoba, the first years' tabulation of application shows no discrimination by ethnic origin; indeed, by proportion, more widows of European origin were provided with state entitlement than British immigrant women. Moreover, in Manitoba each ethnic group had a visitor from their own ethnic community. For example, Miss Ostry, a Jewish visitor, served the Jewish community of North Winnipeg. PAM, RG5 G4, Health and Welfare, Child Welfare Division, 'Widows with Children Schedule, Case History Agendas, 1918–19.' The issue of race and welfare policy deserves greater exploration.

91 Kathleen Bowker, 'The Woman and the Nation,' *Woman's Century* 5, no. 5 (Nov. 1917): 7.

92 Helen Reid, *Report of the Women's War Conference Held at the Invitation of the War Committee of the Cabinet, February 23–March 2 1918* (pamphlet, 1918), 32. On the connections between women and public health initiatives, see 'An Ontario Experiment in Mothers' Pensions,' *Woman's Century* 7, no. 12 (Dec. 1920); and Edith M. Cuppage, 'British Columbia,' *Woman's Century* 7, no. 2 (Feb. 1920), in which women defended mothers' allowances and state social insurance as a public health issue. On the overwhelming priority given to physical fitness at the conclusion of war, see 'Your Real Success in Life is Your Baby,' *Canadian Home Monthly*, Sept. 1918, 3. For an argument that stresses the patriarchal aspects of the infant health movement, see Cynthia R. Comacchio, *Nations Are Built of Babies: Saving Ontario's Mothers and Children, 1900–1940* (Montreal and Kingston: McGill-Queen's University Press, 1993), 4. It was essentially women who lobbied for a Division of Child Welfare within a Dominion Department of Health; see *Report of the Women's War Conference*, 19.

93 'The National Council,' *Woman's Century* 7, no. 11 (Nov. 1920): 12; and 'The Cradle and the Nation,' *Woman's Century* 4, no. 4 (Oct. 1916): 20.

94 Agnes Maule Machar, 'The Citizenship of Women,' *Woman's Century* 3, no. 9 (March 1916): 9.

95 Ibid., 9.

96 Ibid., 9; *Ninth Annual Report of the Mothers' Allowances Commission* (Nova Scotia), 17. For the important role women played in redefining welfare rights, see Koven and Michel, eds., *Mothers of a New World*; Virginia Shapiro, 'The Gender Bias of American Social Policy,' in Gordon, ed., *Women, the State and Welfare*, 36; and Leonore Davidoff, 'Some "Old Husbands" Tales: Public and Private in Feminist History,' in Leonore Davidoff, *World Between: Historical Essays on Gender and Class* (New York: Routledge, 1995), 257. For a critique of how welfare historians have ignored female constructions of citizenship by positing the typical citizen as the male householder whose paid work entitles him to unemployment insurance, see Ann S. Orloff, 'Gender and Social Rights of Citizenship: The Comparative Analysis of State Policies and Gender Relations,' *American Sociological Review* 58, no. 3 (June 1993): 308.

97 For the alliance between women's organizations and the Protestant churches during the 1920s, see Christie and Gauvreau, 'A Full-Orbed Christianity,' chapter 3.

98 Adelaide Hoodless, 'Ontario Women's Institutes,' *Canadian Home Journal*, Nov. 1909, 26.

99 See, for example, Dr Egerton Ryerson, *The New Canadian Dominion: Dangers and Duties of the People* (pamphlet, 1867), 3–4; and Goldwin Smith, *Loyalty, Aristocracy and Jingoism* (pamphlet, 1891), 62.

100 Smith, *Loyalty, Aristocracy and Jingoism*, 62; Rev Principal Grant, *Advantages of Imperial Federation* (pamphlet, 1891), 5, 13, 19; and George Grant, 'Our National Objects and Aims,' in *Maple Leaves* (pamphlet, 1891), 10, 12, 20. For other, older views of political nationalism, see Hon. J.W. Longley, *The Future of Canada* (pamphlet, 1892); and Professor William Clark, *Imperialism* (pamphlet, 1903).

101 George Wrong, 'The Growth of Nationalism in the British Empire,' *American Historical Review* 22, no. 1 (Oct. 1916): 50–1, 57. On modern nationalism in Canada, see Carl Berger, *The Sense of Power* (Toronto: University of Toronto Press, 1970), 136–8. On biological definitions of nationalism, see Nancy J. Christie, '"Prophecy and the Principles of Social Life" (Sydney University, unpublished PhD thesis, 1987).

102 On this novel idea that the development of character constituted a separate and prior entity to political liberty, see Stefan Collini, *Public Moralists: Political Thought and Intellectual Life in Britain, 1850–1930* (Oxford: Oxford University Press, 1991), 92, 98.

103 Mrs Warwick Chipman, *A Few Thoughts on the Subject of Loyalty* (pamphlet, 1896), 13. See also James Gibson Hume, *Political Economy and Ethics* (pamphlet, 1898), 11, 31–2; Corless, *Educational Reform*, 44.

104 For a critical discussion of the terms 'social' and 'maternal' feminism in the United States, see Linda Gordon and Theda Skocpol, 'Gender, State and Society: A Debate,' *Contention* 2, no. 3 (Spring 1993): 139–89; 'Maternalism as a Paradigm: Symposium,' *Journal of Women's History* 5, no. 2 (Fall 1993): 95–131; and Karen Offen, 'Defining Feminism: A Comparative Historical Approach,' *Signs* 14 (Autumn 1988), 119–57.

105 AO, RG 29, Kelso clippings, 'The Big Legislative Issues,' 1919. See also 'The Cradle and the Nation,' *Woman's Century* 4, no. 4 (Oct. 1916): 20.

106 AO, RG 29, Kelso clippings, address by Rabbi I. Leucht, 'New Orleans Conference, National Conference of Charities and Corrections,' 1897.

107 'What Twelve Canadian Women Hope to See as the Outcome of the War,' *Everywoman's World*, April 1915, 7.

108 Jane Lewis, *The Voluntary Sector, the State and Social Work in Britain: The Charity Organisation Society/Family Welfare Association Since 1869* (Aldershot: Edward Elgar Press, 1995), 10, 27; and Jill Roe, 'The End Is Where We Start From: Women and Welfare Since 1901,' in Cora N. Baldock and Bettina Cass, eds., *Women, Social Welfare and the State in Australia* (Sydney: Allen and Unwin, 1983), 2.

109 Bettina Bradbury, *Working Families: Age, Gender and Daily Survival in Industrializing Montreal* (Toronto: McClelland & Stewart, 1993), 209–12; Gordon, *Pitied But Not Entitled*, 6–7; and Humphreys, *Sin, Organized Charity and the Poor Law in Victorian England*, 34–5.

110 Agnes Maule Machar, 'Outdoor Relief in Canada,' *The Charities Review* 6, nos. 5–6 (July–Aug. 1897): 457–65.

111 'Charitable Problems,' *Guelph Mercury*, 10 June 1899. On J.J. Kelso's earlier moral analysis of poverty, see NAC, Kelso Papers, Vol. 8, 'Notebook 1887,' in which he favourably quotes Thomas Chalmers, the British clergyman and poor law reformer, on the need to change the moral habits of the poor in order to attain social progress.

112 Frank Stapleford, 'Causes of Poverty,' *Christian Guardian*, 16 April 1919, 9–10. For a similar dissection of poverty, see Rev. Peter Bryce, 'Earlscourt in Time of War,' *Christian Guardian* 10, 17 Nov. 1915, 19; and NAC, Kelso Papers, Vol. 8, 'Notebook 1909–14,' in which he notes that poverty is a massive social problem not an individual one.

113 Constance Lynd, 'Race Suicide,' *Woman's Century* 7, no. 2 (Feb. 1920): 51.

114 NAC, Kelso Papers, Vol. 1, 'Speeches,' 'Social Work as Affected by War,' Address to Probation Officers, Binghampton, N.Y., Nov. 1917, 245.

115 AO, Premiers' Papers, 03-04-0-019, 'Memorandum to Premier Drury,' 7 April 1919.

116 Otto McFeely, 'Mothers' Pensions in America,' *Woman's Century* 5, no. 2 (Feb. 1918): 17.

117 Ibid.

118 NAC, Kelso Papers, Vol. 4, 'Charity and Charity Organizations,' untitled extract, n.d.

119 'Mr Kelso Gives Some Good Advice,' *Regina Morning Leader*, 4 Feb. 1909.

120 Male unemployment was adamantly rejected as a means to state welfare benefits. See AO, Premiers' Papers, 03-03-0-049, Riddell, 'Memorandum on Mothers' Pensions,' 1917, 24. On mothers' pensions as a significant welfare accomplishment that established new principles of state intervention, see Gordon, *'Pitied but Not Entitled,'* 38; and Kathryn Kish Sklar, 'The Historical Foundations of Women's Power in the Creation of the American Welfare State, 1830–1930,' in Koven and Michel, eds., *Mothers of a New World*, 46–7, 50.

121 'Why the Delay?' *Woman's Century* 7, no. 2 (Feb. 1920): 9; Kathleen Bowker, 'The Woman and the Nation,' ibid., 5, no. 4 (April 1918): 11; and Mrs Rose Henderson, 'The Foundation of Democracy,' ibid., 5, no. 8 (Aug. 1918): 10.

122 'Mothers' Pensions in Ontario,' *Ottawa Journal*, 14 Aug. 1920. For the argument that British women were at the forefront in Britain in redefining the tenets of liberalism, see Martin Pugh, 'The Limits of Liberalism: Liberals and Women's Suffrage, 1867–1914,' in *Liberals, Radicals and Liberal Identities*, 63.

123 AO, Ont. Prov. Sec., Vol. 41, Minnie Campbell, 'A Brief in Favour of the Establishment of a Canadian Child Welfare Bureau,' March 1918, 4–5; Mrs Campbell to Sir Robert Borden, 4 March 1918; Borden to Mrs Campbell, 12 March 1918, in which he stated that he was circulating her pamphlet, *Canada's Greatest Asset*, to members of Parliament. Concerns for falling middle-class standards of living were a feature of postwar articles in women's magazines. See, for example, Mary Walden, 'How I Earn Money at Home and In This Way Make Up for Henry's Shrinking Salary,' *Everywoman's World*, Jan. 1921, 3.

124 AO, Ont. Prov. Sec., Vol. 41, Mrs C to McPherson, 11, 18 May 1918; McPherson to Mrs C., 14 May 1918; and Rev R.P. Bowles, Victoria College, to McPherson, 29 April 1918.

125 AO, RG 29, 36, 2.5, 19 Jan. 1937; AO, RG 7-12-0-18, F.G. McDairmid, Minister of Public Works, 'Investigation of Union,' n.d.; AO, Premiers' Papers, 03-06-0-1184, Mrs Ernest Monck to Ferguson, 29 March 1926; ibid., 03-06-0-1471, George Grant to Mr Jamieson, 5 June 1929; AO, Ont. Prov. Sec., Vol.

44, Kelso to McPherson, 10 Sept. 1918; and 'Mother Robbed of Children,' *Jack Canuck*, Oct. 1919.

126 *Report of the Accomplishments of the Department of Labor and Health* (pamphlet, 1923), 6.

127 'W.C.T.U.,' *Woman's Century* 2, no. 10 (March 1915): 9; AO, Ont. Prov. Sec., Vol. 44, Belleville, CAS to Kelso, 1 Feb. 1918; and AO, RG 7-12-0-2, 'Mothers' Allowances,' 41, testimony of Mrs Urquhart, CAS.

128 NAC, Kelso Papers, Vol. 4, 'Child Welfare Organizations,' extract of speech to women's club, Montreal, 22 March 1909; and 'Pensions for Widowed Mothers,' *Toronto Globe*, 25 Nov. 1919.

129 AO, Premiers' Papers, 03-03-0-049, W.A Riddell, 'Memorandum on Mothers' Pensions,' 15 Feb. 1917.

130 'Protecting the Home,' *Winnipeg Free Press*, 2 May 1919; Alison Craig, 'Pedestals and Pillories,' ibid., 5 Jan. 1918; and 'Women to Launch Food Campaign,' ibid., 9 Jan. 1918; and 'Women's Work of Vast Importance,' ibid., 11 Jan. 1918.

131 Aunt Adelaide, 'Mainly About Women,' *The Statesman* 1, no. 18 (23 Nov. 1918): 11. On the more radical aspects of Eleanor Rathbone's campaign for the endowment of motherhood in Britain, see Pedersen, *Family Dependence and the Origins of the Welfare State*, 143–5; and Jane Lewis, 'Models of Equality for Women: The Case of State Support for Children in Twentieth-Century Britain,' Gisela Bock and Pat Thane, eds., *Maternity and Gender Policies*, 74. Arguments for state protection of women in Canada had closer affinities with the social Catholic discussions of French women. See Susan Pedersen, 'Catholicism, Feminism and the Politics of the Family During the Late Third Republic,' in Koven and Michel, eds., *Mothers of a New World*, 246–76; and Karen Offen, 'Body Politics: Women, Work and the Politics of Motherhood in France, 1920–50,' in Bock and Thane, *Maternity and Gender Policies*, 140. For the affinities between French minimum wage laws and Canada, see 'Women in Mass Meeting Seek Many Changes in Laws,' *Winnipeg Free Press*, 22 Jan. 1918.

132 See, for example, 'Johnson Explains Minimum Wage,' *Winnipeg Free Press*, 19 April 1919.

133 See, for example, S.F. Wise, 'Upper Canada and the Conservative Tradition,' in Edith G. Firth, ed., *Profiles of a Province* (Toronto: Government of Ontario, 1967); 'Liberal Consensus or Ideological Battleground: Some Reflections on the Hartz Thesis,' Canadian Historical Association, *Historical Papers*, 1974, 1–14; Carl Berger, *The Sense of Power*; and Louis Hartz, *The Founding of New Societies*. For the British context, see Eugenio Biagini, *Liberty, Retrenchment and Reform* (Cambridge: Cambridge University Press,

1993), in which he stresses the aspect of community within British liberal traditions.

134 Alison Craig, 'Amendments to the Laws,' *Winnipeg Free Press*, 2 Feb. 1918; and 'Declares Church Must Eliminate Its "Dead Heads,"' ibid., 13 April 1918. Later, leaders of the Winnipeg General Strike, including F.G. Tipping, R.B. Russell, and F.J. Dixo, also defended protective legislation for women on the basis of motherhood. See 'Ten Dollars Urged as Woman's Wage,' ibid., 8 Feb. 1918; and 'Labor Hall Notes,' ibid., 1 May, in which R.B. Russell talks to women's home economics classes.

135 'Strong Plea for Minimum Wage,' *Winnipeg Free Press*, 8 Feb. 1918. On Macmillan's contributions to minimum wage policies in Manitoba, see 'Ministers Endorse a Minimum Wage,' ibid., 5 Feb. 1918.

136 AO, RG 7-7-111-0-6, 'Married Women in Industry,' n.d., 3–4.

137 *Report of Women's War Conference*, 20.

138 'Growing Unrest and Discontent among Farmers,' *Winnipeg Free Press*, 6 May 1919.

139 AO, Premiers' Papers, 03-04-0-012, National Council of Women, 'Resolution from the Provincial Council of the National Council of Women,' in which they approve of mothers' allowances and minimum wage boards, both as alternatives to schemes of social insurance; 'Interim Report on the Women's Platform of the National Council of Women,' *Woman's Century* 7, no. 1 (Jan. 1920): 55; and 'Canadian Women's Societies "Give Work,"' *Everywoman's World*, April 1915.

140 Alison Craig, 'Over the Tea Cups,' *Winnipeg Free Press*, 2 Nov. 1918. See also 'Women Continue Study of Problems,' ibid., 1 March 1918, which compares the women's conference with the men's labour conference.

141 'Poverty and Social Conditions,' *Woman's Century* 3, no. 4 (Oct. 1915): 4. Contrast this with, AO, RG 7-12-0-118, 'Summary Minimum Wage Board,' Sept. 1922, in which goverment policy on women's wages was declared to be based 'upon the cost of living of an independent, self-supporting working woman' without regard for her dependents. For an analysis of the Ontario minimum wage legislation, see Margaret McCallum, 'Keeping Women in their Place: The Minimum Wage in Canada, 1910–25,' *Labour/Le travail* 17 (Spring 1986): 21–39.

142 Quoted in Frances Fenwick Williams, 'The Social Welfare Congress in Montreal,' *Woman's Century* 7, no. 2 (Feb. 1920): 33; 'Montreal Water Strike,' ibid., 7, no. 3 (March 1920): 58; and Mary Murphy, 'When Is It Good Not to Economize?' *Everywoman's World*, Nov. 1920, 1. The plight of the skilled worker also suffused government and organized labour. See 'Industrial Councils Would Help to Remove Present Dominion-Wide

Unrest,' *Winnipeg Free Press*, 2 July 1919; AO, RG 7-12-0-18, 'Not a Charity Bureau,' n.d.; ibid., RG 7-12-0-20, 'Minimum Wages,' 27 Feb. 1919; and ibid., RG 7-111-0-7, A.J. Cooper, 'Memorandum,' 8 Nov. 1922, on the priority given to married over single men by government relief policies.

143 AO, RG 7-12-0-21, 'Mothers' Allowances,' 58. Women campaigned in the United States for mothers' pensions in order to reinforce the male wage; see Linda Gordon, 'The New Feminist Scholarship on the Welfare State,' in Gordon, ed., *Women, the State and Welfare*, 21.

144 Pamphlet, 1923.

145 Frances Fenwick Williams, 'The Social Welfare Congress of Montreal,' *Woman's Century* 7, no. 2 (Feb. 1920): 37; and Ontario Mothers' Allowances Commission, *First Annual Report, 1920–21*, 29.

146 University of Waterloo Library, Department of Special Collections [UWL], Elizabeth Smith Shortt Papers, file 2216, 'Mrs. Shortt Chosen on Pensions Board,' n.d.

147 'The Cradle and the Nation,' *Woman's Century* 4, no. 7 (Jan. 1917): 6.

148 See, for example, 'Child Welfare and Canadian Labor,' *Canadian Child Welfare News* 11, no. 1 (Sept. 1926): 17; and NAC, Canadian Council on Social Development [henceforth cited CCSD], Vol. 14, file 68, 'Federal Department of Labor file,' C. Whitton to Gerald H. Brown, Deputy Minister of Labor, 11 Jan. 1927, in which she stresses her alliance with labour organizations.

149 'Munition Workers Came in on Last Night's Train,' *Winnipeg Free Press*, 10 May 1919.

150 'Dixon Says Strike Grows in Strength,' *Winnipeg Free Press*, 1 June 1919.

151 Union Government Publicity Bureau, *Women's War Talks to Women* (pamphlet, 1917); *Report of the Women's War Conference*, 9; and Canadian Reconstruction Association, *Buy Canadian Products* (pamphlet, 1921), 16.

152 Canadian Reconstruction Association, *Work or Unemployment* (pamphlet, 1920), 1.

153 AO, RG 7-12-0-11, 'To Women Workers – Are You Working for Love or Money,' n.d.; see also ibid., 'Women – Work and Soldiers,' n.d.; and 'To the Woman Worker Who Does Not Need to Work outside Her Home,' n.d., which concluded: 'Of course you will go back to your home in order that the man may have a job.' For similar campaigns to rid the workplace of unskilled child labour, see ibid., RG 7-12-0-23, 'Industrial Department Report,' Dec. 1918, RG 7-12-0-41, Margaret Strong, Director, Women's Department, to H.D. Hudson, 17 Jan. 1918. Single female workers also wanted married women out of the workplace. See RG 7-111-0-2, untitled clipping from *Toronto Telegram*, n.d., in which single working girls stated:

'It isn't fair for women with homes to come down and compete with us. So often, too, they work for less money.'

154 Jean Thomson Scott, *The Conditions of Female Labour in Ontario.* University of Toronto Series in Political Economy, W.J. Ashley, editor (pamphlet, 1892), 29. For an examination of how it was the fear, rather than the reality, of married women entering industry that served as the basis for complaints regarding the shortage of male work, see Miriam Glucksman, *Women Assemble: Women, Workers and the New Industries in Inter-War Britain* (London: Routledge, 1990), 216–25.

155 'Minimum Wage Everyone's Right,' *Winnipeg Free Press*, 14 Jan. 1918. On the trades unions' ongoing campaign, since the 1880s, to limit child labour, see John Bullen, 'Hidden Workers: Child Labour and the Family Economy in Late Nineteeth-Century Urban Ontario,' in Laurel Sefton MacDowell and Ian Radforth, eds., *Canadian Working Class History: Selected Readings* (Toronto: Canadian Scholars' Press, 1992), 269–87.

156 Review of R.M. MacIver, *Labor in the Changing World, Woman's Century* 7, no. 1 (Jan. 1920): 57.

157 For Tom Moore's ideology, see 'Preface,' in J.L. Cohen, *Mothers' Allowance Legislation in Canada* (Toronto: Macmillan, 1927), 5–10. Tom Moore was one of the key witnesses at hearings preceding the enactment of Ontario's Mothers' Allowance legislation. See AO, Premiers' Papers, 03-03-0-049, Riddell, 'Report on Mothers' Allowances,' 19–25. See also ibid., 03-06-0-947, 'Canadian Labour Party Resolutions,' James Simpson to Ferguson, 14 April 1926, which wanted to extend both mothers' allowances and minimum wages for women.

158 *Report upon the Sweating System of Canada* (pamphlet, 1896), 51. The best work on women in the sweated trades in Canada is Ruth A Frager, *Sweatshop Strife: Class, Ethnicity and Gender in the Jewish Labour Movement of Toronto, 1910–1939* (Toronto: University of Toronto Press, 1992).

159 'The Soldiers' Wives,' *Woman's Century* 4, no. 2 (Aug. 1916): 8.

160 For the best discussion of the role of women in creating this organization for household service, see Saskatchewan Archives Board [SAB], Violet McNaughton Papers, A1, file E28, 'Canadian Council for the Immigration of Women for Household Service,' Janet Wood to McNaughton, 11 May 1919, Jean Robson to McNaughton, 16 May 1919, Mrs Olson to McNaughton, 2 Nov. 1919, Helen Reid to McNaughton, 1 Nov. 1919; and ibid., Grain Growers' Association, B2, 'Women's Section, Minutes 1914–25,' 'Minutes of Executive Meeting,' 28 July 1916. On the movement among Ontario farm women, see AO, Premiers' Papers, 030-04-0-009, file Immigration – Housing of Women, 'Report of the Privy Council,' 27 Oct. 1919. This

movement included the IODE, the National Council of Women, the WCTU, the YWCA, and the Interprovincial Council of Farm Women. On domestic service in Canada, see Magda Fahrni, '"Ruffled" Mistresses and "Discontented" Maids: Respectability and the Case of Domestic Service, 1880–1914,' in *Labour/Le travail* 39 (Spring 1997): 69–97. On the ongoing problem of securing a supply of female domestics, see 'Household Service,' *Winnipeg Free Press*, 15 Feb. 1918; 'Conference of Women with War Committee,' ibid., 3 March 1918; 'Why British Women Hesitate to Come,' ibid., 8 May 1919; 'Repatriation Board Does Splendid Work,' ibid., 2 July 1919; and 'Strike in East Grows; Garment Workers Quit,' ibid., 3 July 1919, which describes the attempt to form a Domestic Workers' Union in Toronto, which stated it would 'down mops, brooms or the new china set' if certain demands were not met.

161 On the connections between mothers' allowances and the domestic servant problem, see 'National Council Favours Mothers' Pensions,' *Toronto Globe*, 26 Oct. 1915; and UWL, Elizabeth Smith Shortt Papers, 2214, 'Anticipate Trouble at Mothers' Meeting,' clipping, *Toronto Star*, 1927.

162 SAB, McNaughton Papers, E28, McNaughton to Jean Robson, 15 Oct. 1919.

4: Mothers' Allowances and the Family Economy

1 PAM, RG5 G2, Health and Welfare Supervision Board, 8:100, A.P. Paget, 'Memorandum' to Hon. Edward Brown, Provincial Treasurer, n.d. For the epigraphs, see ibid., Paget to Brown, n.d.; and NAC, CCSD, 63: Mother's Allowance 1936–51,' Whitton to Ernest Blois, 27 Feb. 1936. By 1936, Blois and other child welfare administrators were questioning the regulation that forced children to work.

2 PAM, Health and Welfare Supervision Board, 8:100, British Columbia, 'Sixth Annual Report made under the Mothers' Pensions Act for the Year Ending September 30, 1928,' 3–4.

3 'Canadian Women Help the Empire,' *Everywoman's World*, July 1914, 8; and NAC, Kelso Papers, Vol. 1, 'Correspondence,' G.A. Macdonald to Kelso, 11 Feb. 1916.

4 AO, Premiers' Papers, 03-03-0-049, Riddell, 'Memorandum on Mothers' Pensions,' 1917, 13.

5 AO, RG 7-12-0-21, 'Mothers' Allowances,' n.d., testimony of Mr Campbell, Mrs Bellanchy, and Mr A. Griffiths, Independent Labour Party, who continued to liken such assistance to soldiers' pensions, 7, 44, 47–9; and AO, Premiers' Papers, 03-04-0-366, Peter Bryce to Mr Horace Wallace, 18 April 1923.

On this two-tier system in Australia, see Lorraine Wheeler, 'War, Women and Welfare,' in Richard Kennedy, ed., *Australian Welfare: Historical Sociology* (Sydney and Melbourne: Macmillan, 1989), 180–92. On the greater benefits for soldiers' families, see 'Soldiers' Pensions,' *Woman's Century* 5, no. 8 (Aug. 1918): 7, where a family with a widow and five children received $82.00 per month. See also AO, RG 29, Kelso clippings, 'Increase Pensions for Children,' *Monetary Times*, n.d., in which families with three children received $60.00 per month.

6 Ibid., 3.

7 Ibid., 4–5.

8 Ibid., 24–5. For the influence of the women's lobby on mothers' allowances in Ontario, see Struthers, *The Limits of Affluence*, chapter 1.

9 'The National Council,' *Woman's Century* 7, no. 1 (Jan. 1920): 13.

10 Support for these classes of women was widespread among women's groups; see Mary Gray, 'The Canadian Child,' ibid., 7, no. 1 (Jan. 1920): 46; Edith Lang, 'The Legal Status of the Child of Unmarried Mothers,' ibid., no. 4 (April 1920): 13; Constance Lynd, 'Alberta,' ibid., 7, no. 7 (July 1920): 11; and 'Canadian Women's Institutes,' *Canadian Home Monthly,* May 1920, 56.

11 NAC, CCSD, Vol. 4, 'Child Welfare Nova Scotia,' Whitton to Ernest Blois, 10 Jan. 1929, regarding the survey by Dr. Hincks of illegitimacy in Nova Scotia, and that in Montreal, which analysed 1,100 cases of unmarried motherhood for their causal factors.

12 Magistrate Emily Murphy, 'The Family Tree and Its Graftings,' *Woman's Century* 7, no. 8 (Aug. 1920): 11.

13 'Hammer and Tongs: The Unmarried Mothers and the Laws of France Concerning Her,' *Woman's Century* 7, no. 7 (July 1920): 50.

14 NAC, CCSD, Vol. 49, file 147, Whitton to Hon. E.W. Montgomery, Minister of Health and Public Welfare, Manitoba, 12 Jan. 1929.

15 AO, RG 7-12-0-21, 'Mothers' Allowances,' 25–9; AO, RG 29, Kelso clippings, 'A House For the Children of Soldiers,' n.d.

16 AO, Premiers' Papers, 03-03-0-049, *Report of the Committee on Mothers' Allowances* (pamphlet, 1918).

17 AO, Premiers' Papers, 03-06-0-1405, Ferguson to Dr David Jamieson, chair, Mothers' Allowances Commission, 24 Sept. 1927. On desertion, unmarried motherhood, and individual responsibility, see NAC, CCSD, Vol. 49, file 147, Whitton to Mr Robert Mills, Toronto CAS, 14 June 1928; and AO, Ont. Prov. Sec., Vol. 45, Howard Falk to Kelso, 23 April 1918, who wrote that under no circumstances would he include deserted women as 'there is such a thing as desertion in collusion' and that desertion was largely due to 'the inability of the wife to make a happy home.'

18 AO, Premiers' Papers, 03-04-0-366, W.C. Nelson to Drury, 8 Feb. 1923, Drury to Nelson, 16 Feb. 1923, Bryce to Drury, 21 Feb. 1923.

19 For the 1919 campaign, see NAC, Kelso Papers, Vol. 1, 'Correspondence,' Rev Peter Bryce to Kelso, 20 Aug. 1919; UWL, Elizabeth Smith Papers, 2216, 'New Pensions Board Starts upon Big Task,' undated newspaper clipping.

20 UWL, Smith Papers, 2216, 'New Pensions Board Starts Upon Big Task.'

21 Ibid., 2214, 'Urge Mothers' Allowances in Best Interests of Community,' n.d.

22 Ibid., 2214, 'Widows Bless Allowance Act,' *Montreal Star*, 27 Dec. 1922; and ibid., untitled newspaper clipping, *Ottawa Journal*, 15 Oct. 1920. For similar views on the relationship between feeble-mindedness and unmarried motherhood, see NAC, Montreal Council of Women Papers, MG 28 I 164, Vol. 7, Carrie Derick, 'The Social Menace of Feeble-Mindedness,' May 1919, 8.

23 UWL, Elizabeth Smith Shortt Papers, file 1795, 'Mothers' Allowances,' address to the Victorian Order of Nurses, 1 Dec. 1921, 21. This article also appeared in *The Farmers' Advocate*.

24 Ibid., file 1795, 'Mothers' Allowances,' n.d.

25 Ibid., Box 21, file 850, Elizabeth Shortt to Adam Shortt, undated letter 1908; ibid., Box 22, file 855, Elizabeth Shortt to Adam Shortt, 18 August 1920. Shortt was closely associated with W.F. Nickle, the reform-minded Conservative MPP from Kingston, and worked closely with him during the transition of the CPF to Mothers' Allowances.

26 Ibid., 'Takes Long, Long Time to Catch up with Work,' address, 1929.

27 Ibid., 'Pensions Help Is Given Many under the Ontario Act,' *Ottawa Citizen*, 27 July 1922.

28 Ibid., 1814, 'Mothers' Pensions,' n.d.

29 Ontario Mothers' Allowances Commission, *First Annual Report*, 23; and AO, Premiers' Papers, 03-03-0-049, 'Brief for the Mothers' Allowances Act,' 4.

30 AO, Premiers' Papers, 03-0-30-049, Riddell, 'Report on Mothers' Allowances,' 4.

31 *First Annual Report*, 23; AO, Premiers' Papers, 03-03-0-049, Riddell, 'Report on Mothers' Allowances,' 5; and AO, RG 7-12-0-21, Riddell, 'Mothers' Allowances,' 14.

32 Alice C. Gray, 'Humane Education as a Character Builder,' *Woman's Century* 7, no. 6 (June 1920): 10. See Kloppenberg, *Uncertain Victory*, 274, 282, 289. In the United States, feminists were united on this question of the need for investigation. See Gordon, *Pitied but Not Entitled*, 60.

33 Jose Harris, *William Beveridge: A Biography* (Oxford: Oxford University Press, 1977), 355.

34 AO, Ont. Prov. Sec., Vol. 45, Mrs L. to Mr Mageau, 3 Oct. 1920; and NAC, R.B. Bennett Papers, file 336263, Mr H. Pearce to Bennett, n.d.

35 PAM, Health and Welfare, Child Division, 10: Mothers' Allowance Case Files, Case of Mrs G. See also the conflict over children working of Mrs B. an Icelandic woman, and Mrs C., an Austrian born widow.

36 AO, RG 29, file 36 Mothers' Allowance Case Files, cases 1.9, 1.8, 1.10, 1.11. Policymakers explicitly stated that benefits were tied to previous standards of living. See RG 29, Kelso clippings, 'Four Years of Experience in Mothers' Aid,' 1919.

37 AO, Premiers' Papers, 03-06-0-1405, Dr. Jamieson to Premier Ferguson, n.d.; ibid., 03-06-0-1471, Jamieson to Ferguson, 7 Feb. 1929.

38 AO, RG 29, 36, 1.2.

39 Ibid.

40 PAM, Health and Welfare, child division, 9: Mothers' Allowance Case Files, 1916–54, case of Mrs A.

41 For the argument that the central priority of mothers' allowance policymakers was the moral and sexual regulation of women, see Struthers, *Limits of Affluence*, chapter 1; and Little, 'The Blurring of Boundaries,' 97. There were only a few advocates of mothers' pensions as a remedy for prostitution. See 'Social Service Congress,' *Woman's Century* 4, no. 8 (Feb. 1917): 13; and Mrs Blanche Read Johnston, 'Methods of Mitigating the White Slave Trade,' ibid., 5, no. 4 (Oct. 1917): 21.

42 Nova Scotia, *Ninth Annual Report on Mothers' Allowance for 1938*, 13–14.

43 *Canadian Child Welfare News* 5, no. 3 (15 Aug. 1929): 29–31; and Ontario Mothers' Allowances Commission, *Ninth Annual Report for 1928–29*, 5.

44 University of Toronto Archives [UTA], Harry Cassidy Papers, B72-0022, Vol. 57, file 3, W.J. Patterson, Premier of Saskatchewan, to Cassidy, 17 Dec. 1942.

45 On this point, see Linda Gordon, 'Family Violence, Feminism and Social Control,' in Gordon, ed., *Women, the State, and Welfare*, 180. On the way the poor used charities to strengthen parental authority, see Christine Stansell, *City of Women: Sex and Class in New York, 1789–1860* (Urbana and Chicago: University of Illinois Press, 1987), 54.

46 AO, Premiers' Papers, 03-06-0-1471, Mrs H. Huntley to Ferguson, 1929.

47 AO, Premiers' Papers, 03-06-0-1184, Mrs McKie, Paris, Ontario, to Ferguson, Jan. 1926.

48 Ibid., Mrs McKie to Ferguson, 27 Jan. 1926.

49 AO, RG 29, 36, 1.13; and AO, Premiers' Papers, 03-04-0-366, John Fraser, Barrister, Wallaceburg, Ontario, to Premier Drury, 10 March 1923.

50 AO, RG 29, 36, 3.12.

51 Struthers, *The Limits of Affluence*, 33.
52 NAC, CCSD, Vol. 6, file 28, Helen Reid to Whitton, 17 June 1925. For the need among American women for basic advice regarding birth and child rearing, see Molly Ladd-Taylor, *Raising a Baby the Government Way: Mothers' Letters to the Children's Bureau, 1915–32* (New Brunswick and London: Rutgers University Press, 1986).
53 Ontario Mothers' Allowances Commission, *First Annual Report, 1920–21*, 17.
54 AO, RG 29, 36, 2.14.
55 PAM, Health and Welfare, Child Division, 10: Mothers' Allowance Case Files, Case of Mrs C.; ibid., 9: Mothers' Allowance Case Files, Case of Mrs A. R.B. Russell. The secretary of the One Big Union intervened over the question of Mrs A.'s access to her insurance money.
56 UWL, Elizabeth Smith Shortt Papers, Box 2, file 75, copy of letter from Mrs Hannah Campbell to Mrs Genin-Preston, investigator for Mothers's Allowances Commission, 7 March 1922.
57 Bradbury, *Working Families*, 170–1; Sharon Myers, '"Not To Be Ranked As Women": Female Industrial Workers in Turn-of-the-Century Halifax,' in Guildford and Morton, eds., *Separate Spheres*, 167. On the importance of women's contribution to the family economy through their household work, see Marjorie Cohen, *Women's Work, Markets, and Economic Development in Nineteenth-Century Ontario* (Toronto: University of Toronto Press, 1988).
58 PAM, RG 5 G4, Health and Welfare, Child Welfare Division, 'Widows with Children Schedule, Case History Agendas, 1918–19.'
59 Ontario Mothers' Allowances Commission, *Second Annual Report 1921–22*, 13.
60 Marjorie Cohen, *Women's Work, Markets, and Economic Development in Nineteenth-Century Ontario* (Toronto: University of Toronto Press, 1988), 119, 134, 140.
61 On boarders, see Bettina Bradbury, 'The Home as Workplace,' in Paul Craven, ed., *Labouring Lives*, 453; Bradbury, 'Widowhood and Canadian Family History,' in Margaret Conrad, ed., *Intimate Relations: Family and Community in Planter Nova Scotia, 1759–1800* (Fredericton: Acadiensis Press, 1995), 25. On the occupations of mothers' allowance beneficiaries in Nova Scotia, see NAC, CCSD, Vol. 4, 'Child Welfare in Nova Scotia 1931,' Ernest Blois to Whitton, 28 Dec. 1931.
62 Bott, *Studies in Industrial Psychology*, 65; and Hon. W.J. Roche, Minister of Interior, *Women's Work in Canada: Duties, Wages, Conditions and Opportunies for Domestics in the Dominion* (pamphlet, 1915), 19.
63 *Report of the Accomplishment of the Department of Labour and Health* (pam-

phlet, 1923), 11–12; Kathleen Bowker, 'The Woman and the Nation,' *Woman's Century* 5, no. 5 (Nov. 1917): 9.

64 NAC, CCSD, Vol. 49, file 147, Mrs Mina White, 270 Furby St, Winnipeg, to Whitton, 24 Sept. 1928.

65 UWL, Elizabeth Smith Shortt Papers, Box 2, file 79, Mrs Eva Carriere to Rev Peter Bryce, n.d.; ibid., file 61, Mary Brown, Hamilton, Ontario, to Shortt, 28 July 1921; and AO, RG 29, 36, 1.6.

66 AO, Premiers' Papers, 03-06-0-1471, Mrs W. Waddell to Ferguson, 23 Oct. 1929; and AO, RG 29, 36, 2.10.

67 NAC, CCSD, Vol. 49, file 147, 'Mothers' Allowance Questionnaire,' 1928.

68 UWL, Elizabeth Smith Papers, 2214, 'Says Merson's Statement Not Based On Facts,' *Toronto Star*, n.d.

69 I am here dissenting from the notion of regulation set forth by Mariana Valverde, *The Age of Light, Soap and Water*; Margaret Little, '"No Car, No Radio, No Liquor Permit": The Moral Regulation of Single Mothers in Ontario, 1920–1993,' PhD dissertation, York University, 1994. In *Limits of Affluence*, 49, Struthers conflates the regulation of sexual behaviour, housekeeping, character, thrift, and industry; whereas I argue for the need to draw a finer distinction between government priorities in this regard. For a similar argument, see Goodwin, *Gender and the Politics of Welfare Reform*.

70 *Canadian Child Welfare News* 5, no. 3 (15 Aug. 1929): 29.

71 Struthers, *The Limits of Affluence*, 38.

72 *First Annual Report for 1920–21*, 24–6.

73 AO, RG 29, 36, 2.2.

74 NAC, CCSD, Vol. 49, file 147, G.B. Clarke to Whitton, 12 May 1928.

75 *Second Annual Report*, 28.

76 In Ontario, deserted wives were required to wait five years before applying for mothers' allowance. An Order-in-Council issued later in the 1920s permitted them to apply to the commission for benefits after three years.

77 AO, RG 29, 36, 1.3.

78 In *The Politics of Women's Work, 1750–1915* (Princeton: Princeton University Press, 1996), Judith Coffin has argued that French women saw economic autonomy in terms of their ability to combine waged and unwaged work. They also preferred home work over factory work to avoid the stigma of a working-class identity. (152–7)

79 NAC, CCSD, Vol. 49, file 147, Clarke to Whitton, 12 May 1928.

80 NAC, CCSD, Vol. 5, file 'Mothers' Allowances 1927,' A.P. Paget to Miss Agnes McNab, Mothers' Pension Board, Vancouver, 12 March 1927.

81 AO, Premiers' Papers, 03-06-0-1471, Jamieson to Mrs Isabella Curtiss, 26 Nov. 1929; and AO, ibid., 03-04-0-366, Peter Bryce to Drury, 23 March 1923.

82 Ontario Mothers' Allowances Commission, *Third Annual Report 1922–23*, 21–2.
83 Ontario Mothers' Allowances Commission, *Second Annual Report*, 35; and AO, RG 29, 36, 2.8.
84 AO, RG 29, 36, 2.8.
85 AO, RG 29, 36, 2.1.
86 Ibid. On the imperative of having male sons support widowed mothers, see AO, Premiers' Papers, 03-06-0-1184, Mrs Shortt to George Grant, 3 Nov. 1926.
87 For a similar argument to the one I have advanced, see the recent publication, Goodwin, *Gender and the Politics of Welfare Reform*. See especially her fine introduction, which critiques previous historians who in her view de-emphasized the regulation of work.
88 AO, RG 29, 36, 1.2.
89 AO, RG 29, 36, 3.5.
90 AO, RG 29, 36, 1.13.
91 See, for example, Ontario, *Seventh Annual Report of the Mothers' Allowances Commission for the Years 1925–26*, 27.
92 Ibid., 3.9.
93 Ibid, 1.16.
94 *Second Annual Report*, 30.
95 *Fourth Annual Report 1923–24*, 17.

5: Labour, Social Work, and Social Catholicism Debate Family Policy

1 James Naylor, *The New Democracy*, has argued that the power of the ILP declined during the 1920s in terms of labour organization; however, in terms of national political power the ILP achieved dramatic success at the federal level out of proportion to its numerical strength in the House of Commons, largely because Mackenzie King's minority Liberal government needed to court Progressive and ILP members. As a consequence, Woodsworth was able to lobby effectively for otherwise unattainable measures such as old age pensions and a national system of family allowances. Because of this peculiar political conjuncture, family allowances had a better hearing in government circles in Canada than they did in Britain, where the question of family allowances, though debated within the ILP, never succeeded in breaking through into official government corridors. See Kenneth McNaught, *A Prophet in Politics: A Biography of J.S. Woodsworth* (Toronto: University of Toronto Press, 1959), 218–19; and Pedersen, *Family, Dependence and the Origins of the Welfare State*, 179–81. Whitton also had

much influence within King's government, since at this time she was the secretary to the Minister of Trade and Commerce, the Hon. T.A. Low. See Rooke and Schnell, *No Bleeding Heart*, 63.

2 NAC, MG 28 I 10, Canadian Council on Social Development [CCSD], 43:206, 'Memorandum for Quebec Commission on Social Insurance, 1931.' The epigraphs are from CCSD, Vol. 5, file: Mothers' Allowances 1927, A.P. Paget to Miss Agnes McNab, 12 March 1927; and Leon Lebel, *Family Allowances* (pamphlet, 1929), 11.

3 Journals of the House of Assembly, Nova Scotia. *Eighth Annual Report of the Mothers' Allowances Act* (1938), 8.

4 'Mothers' Allowances in Nova Scotia,' *Child Welfare News* 9, no. 2 (July 1933): 20.

5 NAC, CCSD, 10:52, Mrs Agnes McNabb, Mothers' Pension Board, British Columbia to Whitton, 26 Sept. 1928, Whitton to McNabb, 8 Oct. 1928; and 'Memorandum re: Mothers' Allowances, Nova Scotia, Dec. 1929.'

6 Ibid., 26:133 Whitton, 'Memorandum re: Certain Child Welfare Problems in the Province of Saskatchewan,' 20 Jan. 1930.

7 Ibid., 10:45, A.P. Paget to Miss Agnes McNabb, 12 March 1927; and ibid., 10:42, 'Memorandum re. Mothers' Allowances, Nova Scotia, Dec. 1929.'

8 On Ivens's demands, see NAC, CCSD, 29:147, A.P. Paget to Whitton, 30 March 1928.

9 NAC, 29:146, case reader, Social Service Commission, Winnipeg, to Whitton, 21 Aug. 1928; and Whitton to Ivens, 28 Aug. 1928.

10 NAC, CCSD, 29:146, A.P. Paget to Whitton, 19 Feb. 1928.

11 Ibid., Manitoba Department of Public Welfare, Child Welfare Division, untitled memorandum, 10 Feb. 1928. In Ontario an edict distributed in 1929 stressed that 'all wage earning children must work.' See ibid., 10:52, Harry Bentley, chief investigator, Mothers' Allowances Commission, Ontario, 'Advice to Beneficiaries,' Oct. 1929.

12 *Canadian Child Welfare News* 5, no. 3 (15 Aug. 1929): 33.

13 J.L. Cohen, *Mother's Allowance Legislation in Canada* (Toronto: Macmillan, 1927), 32. The agitation to reform mothers' allowance legislation was largely initiated by organized labour, but was also supported by women's organizations and family welfare agencies, such as the Women's Directory of Montreal, which cared for children born out of wedlock. On the labour perspective, see 'The Mother's Allowance Controversy,' *Child Welfare News* 3, no. 1 (15 Feb. 1927): 30; University of Toronto Archives [UTA], B72-0022, Harry Cassidy Papers, 29:2, 'Labour Resolutions at Liberal Convention, Toronto,' Dec. 1920; ibid., 22:2, 'Outline of Permanent Program for Reducing Unemployment and Relieving the Unemployed,' May 1931, resolution

of Toronto local of the International Brotherhood of Electrical Workers; and NAC, Mackenzie King Papers, MG 26 Jl, Vol. 320, A.M. Whitelaw, TLC to King, 19 July 1941. On the role of women, see NAC, CCSD, 43:206, Jane Wisdom, the Women's Directory, Montreal, to Whitton, 29 April 1931; ibid., 43:280, Elizabeth King to Whitton, 14 Feb. 1933; and ibid., 10:45, Arma McLaws, Local Council of Winnipeg to Whitton, 9 Aug. 1930.

14 Cohen, *Mother's Allowance Legislation*, 32.

15 Ibid., 12, 34, 107.

16 NAC, CCSD, 29:147, Elizabeth King to Whitton, 23 Aug. 1928.

17 *Canadian Child Welfare News* 5, no. 3 (15 Aug. 1929): 22–9; and NAC, CCSD, 29:147, Whitton to Dr. E.W. Montgomery, Minister of Health and Public Welfare, Manitoba, 9 May 1928.

18 NAC, CCSD, 29:147, E.W. Montgomery to Whitton, 15 Jan. 1929, 24 Jan. 1929, 20 Aug. 1929.

19 Ibid., Whitton to Howard Falk, 27 Dec. 1928, Mabel Finch to Whitton, 16 Feb. 1929, Whitton to Dr Jamieson, 4 Oct. 1928.

20 Ibid., Whitton to C.W. Montgomery, 28 Jan. 1929.

21 Ibid., Montgomery to Whitton, 20 Aug. 1929. D.B. Harkness and the new director of child welfare, the Methodist Minister J. Mutchmor, continued to fight to have unmarried and deserted women supported by mother's allowances. See NAC, CCSD, W.A. Weston, general secretary, Children's Aid Society, Winnipeg to Whitton, 11 Jan. 1929.

22 NAC, CCSD, 10:52, Bentley to Elizabeth King, n.d.

23 Ibid., 1:4, Whitton to Ernest Blois, 19 Dec. 1933.

24 Ibid., 1:4, Harold Putman to Whitton, 9 June 1925.

25 UTA, Cassidy Papers, 32:2, Whitton, 'London Bridge Is Falling Down,' n.d., 2.

26 NAC, CCSD, 43:208, Whitton to Mrs D.G. MacPhail, 31 Nov. 1931, Whitton to the Hon. S.L. Howe, 19 Nov. 1931; and ibid., 'Memorandum re: Mothers' Pensions in British Columbia for the Honourable Provincial Secretary,' n.d.

27 Ibid., 43:208, P. Walker, deputy provincial secretary, British Columbia, to Whitton, 2 Dec. 1931.

28 Ibid., 43:208, 'Memorandum re: Mother's Pensions'; and ibid., Minister of Finance, British Columbia, to Whitton, 22 Oct. 1931.

29 Ibid., 43:208, 'Memorandum re. Mother's Pensions'; and ibid., Minister of Finance, British Columbia to Whitton, 22 Oct. 1931.

30 Ibid., 43:208, Whitton to William Manson, Superintendant of Welfare, British Columbia, 3 Dec. 1931, Whitton to Adam Bell, Deputy Minister of Labour, British Columbia, 13 Nov. 1931.

31 The evolution from rights-based pensions to needs-based general assis-

tance was not a linear one, for between Whitton's report in 1931 and the final distilling of mothers' pensions into a system of mere relief at the end of the 1930s, Harry Cassidy, the director of public welfare, attempted to once again expand and broaden the Mothers' Pensions Act in 1936. See UTA, Cassidy Papers, 17:02, Cassidy to Agnes, 22 April 1936; ibid., 58:4, Cassidy, 'The Effect of Tuberculosis and the Venereal Diseases upon Mother's Pension Costs,' 2 April 1937; and NAC, CCSD, 62:497, Whitton to Robert Mills, 9 Nov. 1927. For popular reactions to Whitton's cuts in British Columbia, see NAC, CCSD, 43:208, P. Mather, Deputy Provincial Secretary to Whitton, 18 April 1933, Portia to Whitton, Jan. 1932, who protested that the government had been spending like 'drunken sailors' and helping mothers who were 'shiftless and lazy.'

32 NAC, CCSD, 10:52, Whitton to Dr Jamieson, chairman, Mother's Allowance Commission, Ontario, 12 June 1928, Whitton to Ernest Blois, 5 Sept. 1934. In 1928 the period a deserted woman had to wait before applying was shortened from five to three years. See ibid., 10:52, John McCullogh, secretary Mothers' Allowances Commission, to Whitton, 20 Aug. 1928.

33 NAC, CCSD, 43:206, 'Memorandum for the Quebec Commission on Social Insurance 1931.'

34 NAC, CCSD, 62:497, 'Memo. for the Files,' 20 May 1937.

35 NAC, CCSD, 10:52, 'Underlying Principles of Mother's Allowances,' 1930.

36 NAC, CCSD, 10:52, 'Some Problems New Brunswick Must Face in Introducing Mothers' Allowances,' 1930.

37 NAC, CCSD, 1:4, Whitton to Blois, 11 April 1930, Blois to Whitton, 8 April 1930; and ibid., Whitton, 'Memorandum re: Proposed Mothers' Allowance Legislation, Nova Scotia,' n.d.

38 NAC, CCSD, 1:4, Blois to Whitton, 28 March, 5 April, 13 February 1930. There was a similar movement in Saskatchewan. Ibid., 26:133, 'Saskatchewan – Report of the Bureau of Child Protection, Fiscal Year 1930–31,' n.p. Not all aspects of Whitton's prescriptions for child welfare policies were fulfilled in Nova Scotia – for example, namely the provision that rigorous family casework be instituted. Investigations both for mother's allowances and old age pensions were lax in Nova Scotia, where most families were investigated every two to three years. See UTA, Cassidy Papers, George Davidson to Cassidy, 18 Nov. 1943.

39 NAC, CCSD, 1:4, Blois to Whitton, 3 April 1929.

40 NAC, CCSD, 14:68, Miss H.R. Ogden, Halifax Welfare Bureau, to Whitton 19 Aug. 1930; and ibid., 1:4, Blois to Whitton, 18 May 1932. The premier reviewed the legislation in 1932 with the aim of extending the classes of beneficiaries.

41 NAC, CCSD, 1:4, Blois to Whitton, 5 April 1930.
42 'Executive Director's Thirteenth Annual Report to the Council,' *Child Welfare News* 9, no. 1 (May 1933): 16.
43 Ibid., 15; NAC, CCSD, 10:52, 'Memorandum re: Administrative Costs and General Expenses in Mothers' Allowances,' Nov. 1932; and ibid., 10:52, Blois to Elizabeth King, 10 June 1932.
44 NAC, CCSD, 29:147, Elsie Lawson, 'Report on the Community and Social Services in the City of Brandon,' 12 Oct.–12 Dec. 1932; and House of Assembly, Nova Scotia, Journals. *Seventh Annual Report of the Director* (1937), 10.
45 NAC, CCSD, 16:68, Whitton, 'The Challenge of Relief Control,' 1934; and ibid., 10:52, Whitton to Mr A. MacNamara, Assistant Deputy Minister of Public Works, 2 March 1934. The best discussion of Whitton's relief policies is James Struthers, *No Fault of Their Own*.
46 NAC, CCSD, 45, file 'Institutions and Immigrant Homes,' Dorothy King, Supervisor, Montreal Family Welfare Association, 'Social Welfare Conditions in the City of Saskatoon.'
47 NAC, CCSD, 14:68, Gertrude Childs to Whitton, 18 Aug. 1930; ibid., 62:497, M.G. Sorsoleil, Deputy Minister of Welfare for Ontario to Miss Muriel Tucker, Canadian Welfare Council, 11 March 1936; ibid., 14:68, J.W. McKee, Deputy Minister of Pensions to Whitton, 18 Feb. 1933; and ibid., J.P. Oliver, Greater Winnipeg Advisory Relief Commission to Mr Jacobs, n.d.
48 Sara Burke, *Seeking the Highest Good: Social Service and Gender at the University of Toronto, 1888–1937* (Toronto: University of Toronto Press, 1996), has argued that there was a clear gender division within the practice of social work, between the women who advocated technical skills and the men who adhered to a conception of social work founded upon moral ideals (7). Charlotte Whitton was both an advocate of technical skills and moral reform, and her example and that of many other female social workers, such as Jane Wisdom, Elizabeth King, and Dorothy King, to name a few, call into question this supposed gender bifurcation. A division between practical social work and the technocratic vision of economists like Harry and Cassidy did emerge throughout the 1930s, a theme pursued in the next chapter. For a different interpretation of the intersection of empiricism and religion within social work, see Christie and Gauvreau, *A Full-Orbed Christianity*, chapter 4.
49 NAC, CCSD, 1:4, Blois to Whitton, 14 Dec. 1932. For the more traditional perspective on maintaining Canadian standards of family life, see ibid., 45, 'Institutions and Immigrant Homes,' Dorothy King, 'Social Welfare Conditions in the City of Saskatoon'; ibid., 62:497, 'Memorandum on Mother's Allowances in Saskatchewan,' n.d.

50 NAC, CCSD, 1:4, Blois to Whitton, 14 Dec. 1932.

51 NAC, CCSD, 62:497, 'Aid to Dependent Mothers and Children in Canada,' 1939. If the psychological effects of the Depression on the family were studied, these analyses focused almost exclusively on the morale of the male breadwinner. This point will be developed at length in the next chapter. See, for example, ibid., 14:68, 'Proposed Memorandum re Reference to Social Agencies,' 1930.

52 NAC, CCSD, 10:52, Blois to Whitton, 10 Sept. 1934; ibid., 1:4, Whitton to Blois, 28 Dec. 1931. See also, ibid., 62:497, 'Memorandum re: Mother's Allowance Analysis,' n.d.; ibid., 14:68, 'The Problem of Relief for Children over the Age of Pension Legislation,' n.d.

53 AO, RG7-12-0-16-7, 'Committee IV, Sub-Committee C – Related Problems in Child Care.'

54 NAC, CCSD, 62:497, Whitton to John Appleton, secretary-treasurer, The Canadian Life Insurance Officers' Association, 18 April 1935. Whitton concluded this diatribe against mother's allowance beneficiaries with the following boast: 'You know that I would yield a first place to no one in advocacy of social security for any of those in need of it.'

55 NAC, CCSD, 43:290, Whitton to P. Walker, 27 May 1931; and ibid., 1:4, Whitton to Blois, 24 Feb. 1930, 24 March 1930, Blois to Whitton, 31 Jan. 1930.

56 NAC, CCSD, 45, 'Institutions and Immigrant Homes,' Dorothy King, 'Social Welfare Conditions in the City of Saskatoon'; ibid., 26:133, 'Excerpt from Saskatoon Welfare Bureau Report,' 1932.

57 AO, RG29-74-1-71, E.A. Horton, Deputy Minister of Public Welfare, to provincial relief administrators, 24 Nov. 1938.

58 'Mother's Pensions in British Columbia,' *Child Welfare News* 9, no. 6 (March 1934): 31; NAC, CCSD, 43:206, Whitton to Edouard Montpetit, chairman, Quebec Commission on Social Insurance, 18 March 1931; and UTA, Cassidy Papers, 27:4, 'Problems of Unemployment,' 1933.

59 UTA, Cassidy Papers, 55:1, Cassidy to Laura Holland, Department of the Provincial Secretary, British Columbia, 3 Jan. 1944; and ibid., 61:5, Cassidy, 'The Economic Burden of Social Services in Newfoundland,' 19 Aug. 1951, in which he advocated that mothers' allowance beneficiaries be granted 'temporary social assistance' so that they could 'work out their affairs independently.' See also ibid., 31:3, Whitton to Cassidy, 3 Jan. 1941.

60 NAC, CCSD, 62:497, J.H. Creighton, Superintendent of Welfare, British Columbia, to Whitton, 8 Aug. 1940; ibid., 'Aid to Dependent Mothers and Children in Canada,' n.d; ibid., 'Mother's Allowance Material,' n.d.; and UTA, Cassidy Papers, 13:5, Whitton, 'Whither Canada?' n.d. The constitutional aspect of these debates will be discussed at greater length in the next chapter.

61 NAC, CCSD, 62:497, 'Mother's Allowance Material,' undated.

62 'Veterans and Pensioners in Receipt of Public Aid,' *The Canadian Welfare Summary* 14, no. 5 (Jan. 1939): 20–1.

63 Leon Lebel, *Family Allowances* (pamphlet, second edition, 1929), 1; and NAC, MG 26 J1, Mackenzie King Papers, 183, Leon Lebel to King, 14 May 1928.

64 NAC, Society for the Protection of Women and Children, Montreal Council of Social Agencies, 'Committee on Cost of Living and Wages in Montreal, 1926.' A series of family budgets were published in the *Labour Gazette* in 1927; see Lebel, *Family Allowances*, 26. On economic conditions during the 1920s, see Struthers, *No Fault of Their Own*, 42.

65 NAC, Society for the Protection of Women and Children, Montreal Council of Social Agencies, 'Committee on Cost of Living and Wages – 1926.'

66 Georges Pelletier, 'La budget familial,' dans *La Famille: Semaines Sociales de Canada* (Montreal: École Sociale Populaire, IVe session, 1923), 94–6. Similar arguments were offered on behalf of family allowances by the labour movement in Norway. See Ida Blom, 'Voluntary Motherhood 1900–1930: Theories and Politics of a Norwegian Feminist in an International Perspective,' in Gisela Bock and Pat Thane, eds., *Maternity and Gender Politics*, 34–6.

67 Parliament of Canada. 'House of Commons Debates, 1926–27,' 14 Dec. 1926, 68.

68 Ibid., 69.

69 AO, RG7-12-0-90.2, 'Proceedings of the Fourth Annual Conference of Ontario Office Superintendents, Employment Service of Canada,' 13–15 May 1926, especially the arguments of R.A. Rigg.

70 Pedersen, *Family, Dependence, and the Origins of the Welfare State*, 179–81.

71 Jose Harris, *William Beveridge: A Biography* (Oxford: Oxford University Press, 1977), 98; and Jane Lewis, 'Models of Equality for Women: The Case of State Support for Children in Twentieth-Century Britain,' in Gisela Bock and Pat Thane, eds., *Maternity and Gender Politics*, 74–85.

72 On the racial aspects of family allowances in Britain, see John Macnicol, *The Movement for Family Allowances, 1918–45: A Study in Social Policy Development* (London: Heineman, 1980), 81–2.

73 Eleanor Rathbone, *The Disinherited Family* (London: Allen and Unwin, 1949, 3rd. ed., first published 1924), 122.

74 Pedersen, *Family, Dependence and the Origins of the Welfare State*, 189–222.

75 Bettina Cass, 'Redistribution to Children and to Mothers: A History of Child Endowment and Family Allowances,' in Cora V. Baldock and Bettina Cass, eds., *Women, Social Welfare, and the State in Australia* (Sydney: Allen and Unwin, 1983), 74. See also Jill Roe, 'The End Is Where We Start From:

Women and Welfare since 1901,' in Baldock and Cass, 7–9. Despite the *Harvester* judgment in 1907, which formally established the idea of the family wage, family allowances were used to depress wages.

76 Pedersen, *Family, Dependence, and the Origins of the Welfare State*, 224–88.

77 Select Standing Committee on Industrial and International Relations, 3.

78 Leon Lebel, 'Should Family Allowances Be Given to the Parents or to the Children?' *Relations*, July 1944.

79 For the growing tension between traditional liberalism and ideas of Catholic corporatism in Quebec, see Pierre Trepanier, 'Quel corporatisme? (1820–1965),' *Cahiers des Dix*, 1994, 159–212.

80 Standing Committee on Industrial and International Relations, 29; and Lebel, *Family Allowances*, 52.

81 Lebel, *Family Allowances*, 23.

82 On the success of the natalist lobby in France, see Miriam Cohen and Michael Hanagan, 'The Politics of Gender and the Making of the Welfare State, 1900–1940: A Comparative Perspective,' *Journal of Social History* 24, no. 3 (Spring 1991): 476. Quebec had previously instituted other natalist policies. For example, in 1890 the government gave a cash gratuity or land to fathers with twelve or more children. By 1905, when it was repealed, this legislation had aided 5,413 families. See W.L. Scott, 'Ballots and Bassinets,' *Canadian Child Welfare News* 6, no. 7 (May 1934): 12.

83 On Macphail's views on women's rights in the workplace, see Terry Crowley, *Agnes Macphail and the Politics of Equality* (Toronto: James Lorimer, 1990), 153.

84 Lebel, *Family Allowances*, 17.

85 Select Standing Committee on Industrial and International Relations, 112.

86 See Georges Pelletier, 'Le budget familial,' dans *La Famille: Semaines Sociales du Canada* (Montreal: École Sociale Populaire, IVe Session, 1923), 94.

87 House of Commons Debates, 14 Dec. 1926, 71.

88 Lebel, *Family Allowances*, 3, 13.

89 Lebel, *Family Allowances*, 17.

90 Lebel, *Family Allowances*, 1, 4–5, 47.

91 Select Committee on Industrial and International Relations, 53.

92 On businessmen's hostility to social legislation during the 1920s, see Alvin Finkel, 'Origins of the Welfare State in Canada,' in Blake and Keshen, *Social Welfare Policy in Canada*, 235.

93 Harris, *William Beveridge*, 343; and see also Pedersen, *Family, Dependence, and the Origins of the Welfare State*, 184–6.

94 Select Standing Committee on Industrial and International Relations, 68.

95 Pat Thane, 'Women, Liberalism and Citizenship, 1918–1930,' in Eugenio F.

Biagini, ed., *Citizenship and Community* (Cambridge: Cambridge University Press, 1995), 84; and Hilary Land, 'Eleanor Rathbone and the Economy of the Family,' in Harold Smith, *British Feminism in the Twentieth Century* (Amherst: University of Massachusetts Press, 1990), 117–18.

96 In Britain, there was a strong alliance between the eugenics movement and that for family allowances. See Macnicol, *The Movement for Family Allowances*, 144.

97 Select Committee on Industrial and International Relations, 1, 69, 71.

98 Ibid., 113.

99 The primary source for discussions concerning family policy in Quebec during the Depression is the Reports of the Quebec Social Insurance Commission, 1933. For Whitton's testimony, see NAC, CCSD, 43:206, 'Memorandum re: Child and Family Welfare in the Province of Quebec Prepared at the Request of the Quebec Commission on Social Insurance,' 1931. Her arguments are essentially those presented to the 1928 Select Committee on Industrial and International Relations. Family allowances were included in the 1934 platform of the Action Liberale Nationale. See B.L. Vigod, 'The Quebec Government and Social Legislation During the 1930s: A Study in Political Self-Destruction,' in Blake and Keshen, *Social Welfare Policy in Canada*, 153–4. For the attitudes of Edouard Montpetit, see, for example, NAC, CCSD, 'First Bilingual Conference on Child Welfare,' Quebec City, 23–5 Feb. 1931. Montpetit spoke on 'The Protection of the Child – the Protection of the Nation.' His ideas regarding national efficiency closely parallel those in Ontario on behalf of mothers' allowances during the 1920s.

6: The Great Depression and the Subversion of the Maternalist State

1 Province of Quebec, *Report of the Commission on Social Insurance*, 1933, 43–4, testimony of Charlotte Whitton.

2 NAC, MG 28 I 129, Society for the Protection of Women and Children, Paul A. Douglas, 'The Changing Basis of Family Support and Expenditure,' 4.

3 Leonard Marsh, *Employment Research* (Oxford: Oxford University Press, 1935), 55.

4 See NAC, Society for the Protection of Women and Children, Douglas, 'The Changing Basis of Family Support and Expenditure,' from *Family Life To-Day*, n.d., 2–4.

5 See, for example, Allan Irving, 'Canadian Fabians: The Work and Thought of Harry Cassidy and Leonard Marsh, 1930–1945,' in Raymond B. Blake and Jeff Keshen, eds., *Social Welfare Policy in Canada: Historical Readings* (Toronto: Copp Clark, 1995), 201–20; Marlene Shore, *The Science of Social*

Redemption: McGill, the Chicago School, and the Origins of Social Research in Canada (Toronto: University of Toronto Press, 1987); and Doug Owram, *The Government Generation: Canadian Intellectuals and the State, 1900–1945* (Toronto: University of Toronto Press, 1986).

6 Ruth Roach Pierson, 'Gender and Unemployment Debates in Canada, 1934–40,' *Labour/Le Travail* 25 (Spring 1990); Margaret Hobbs, 'Equality and Difference: Feminism and Defence of Women Workers during the Great Depression,' *Labour/Le Travail* 32 (Fall 1993).

7 American historians argue that the two-tier welfare system originated during the Progressive Era. See Barbara J. Nelson, 'The Origins of Two-Channel Welfare State: Workman's Compensation and Mothers' Aid,' in Linda Gordon, ed., *Women, the State and Welfare*, 124.

8 R.S. Hoskins, 'The Family Court,' *Child Welfare News* 8, no. 3 (Sept. 1932): 35; NAC, CCSD, 11:53, 'Report of the Executive Director.'

9 Adelaide M. Plumptre, *Canada's Child Immigrants* (pamphlet, 1925), n.p.

10 James Struthers, *'No Fault of Their Own: Unemployment and the Canadian Welfare State 1914–1941* (Toronto: University of Toronto Press, 1983).

11 Linda Gordon has traced a similar transition in the United States in 'Social Insurance and Public Assistance: The Influence of Gender in Welfare Thought in the United States, 1890–1935,' *American Historical Review* 97, no. 1 (Feb. 1992): 19–54.

12 Leonard Marsh, *Employment Research: An Introduction to the McGill Programme of Research in the Social Sciences* (Oxford: Oxford University Press, 1935), 21–2.

13 Ibid., 2.

14 Ibid., 5.

15 Ibid., 14.

16 Leonard Marsh, *Canadians In and Out of Work* (Oxford: Oxford University Press, 1940), 403. Marsh particularly castigated the work of Innis, by claiming that the solution to horizontal mobility was no longer the 'unbounded' exploitation of natural resources. On Innis' economic thought, see Carl Berger, *The Writing of Canadian History: Aspects of English-Canadian Historical Writing: 1900 to 1970* (Toronto: Oxford University Press, 1976), 102–3.

17 See Shore, *The Science of Social Redemption*, especially chapter 6. For Marsh's outline of his research project, and its gendered approach, see McGill University Archives [MUA], RG2, 60:1047, 'Executive Committee Meeting,' 19 Dec. 1930, 11 Oct., 22 Nov. 1932; and Michiel Horn, *The League for Social Reconstruction: Intellectual Origins of the Democratic Left in Canada, 1930–1942* (Toronto: University of Toronto Press, 1980), 10, 67. For an exception, see Richard C. Helmes-Hayes and Dennis Wilcox-McGill, 'A Neglected Classic:

Leonard Marsh's *Canadians In and Out of Work,' Canadian Review of Sociology and Anthropology* 30, no. 1 (Feb. 1993): 83–109.

18 Marsh, *Canadians In and Out of Work,* 1.

19 Ibid., 167.

20 Ibid., 1.

21 Ibid., 4.

22 Ibid., 28.

23 Ibid., 189.

24 Ibid., 217 (author's emphasis).

25 Ibid., 390.

26 Ibid., 32–3.

27 Ibid., 173.

28 Ibid., 28.

29 Ibid., 32–3.

30 Ibid., 29.

31 L. Richter, 'Nature and Extent of Unemployment,' in L. Richter, ed., *Canada's Unemployment Problem* (Toronto: Macmillan, 1939), 12, 33, 35.

32 G.V. Hawthorne, *Land and Labour: A Social Survey of Agriculture and the Farm Labour Market in Central Canada* (Oxford: Oxford University Press, 1941), 196, 221, 552.

33 H.M. Cassidy and F.R. Scott, *Labour Conditions in the Men's Clothing Industry* (Toronto: Thomas Nelson and Sons Ltd., 1935), 22; Cassidy, *Unemployment and Relief in Ontario* (Toronto: J.M. Dent, 1932), 51, 179, 183. Cassidy's was one of the few voices in academic circles to call for more extensive studies of transient women and their families. See H.M. Cassidy, 'Social Services for Transients,' in L. Richter, *Canada's Unemployment Problem*, 187.

34 AO, RG7-12-0-156, Cassidy, 'Unemployment Relief,' 19 April 1932, in which he quotes Gould's belief that governments should consult social workers rather than economists on the problem of the family economy; and UTA, Cassidy Papers, 27:2, Gould to Cassidy, 8 April 1932.

35 See, for example, AO, RG7-12-0-204, unsigned letter from Puslinch, Ontario, to Leopold McCauley, 10 June 1934, defending the rights of married men with 'large families.' There were also constant complaints about hiring single rather than married men. See AO, RG7-12-0-172, H. Desjardins, Superintendent, North Bay Zone, to H.C. Hudson, General Superintendent, Ontario Employment Offices, 3 Jan. 1933. On this point, see Margaret Hobbs, 'Gendering Work and Welfare: Women's Relationship to Wage-Work and Social Policy in Canada During the Great Depression,' PhD dissertation, University of Toronto, 1995, chapter 1; and Veronica Strong-Boag, *The New Day Recalled: The Lives of Girls and*

Women in English-Canada, 1919–1939 (Toronto: Copp Clark Pitman, 1988), 44–7.

36 AO, RG7-12-0-320, Miss Lavyne Bast to Premier Hepburn, 8 May 1935; ibid., RG7-12-0-229, J.R. Prain, Inspector, to J.F. Marsh, Deputy Minister of Labour, 24 Sept. 1934. Much of the protest was on behalf of single women workers. See AO, RG7-12-0-72.1, 'The Trades and Labour Congress of Canada and Its Policies on Employment, Unemployment and Underemployment, 1883–1931,' memorandum, 1931, 13; and ibid., RG7-12-0-204, unnamed widow, Brantford, Ontario, to Minister of Labour, 27 April 1934. On the feminists arguments on women's right to work, see Margaret Hobbs, 'Equality and Difference: Feminism and the Defence of Women Workers During the Great Depression,' in Wendy Mitchinson et al., eds., *Canadian Women: A Reader* (Toronto: Harcourt Brace, 1996), 212–33.

37 AO, RG7-12-0-82, undated newsclipping, 'C.L.D.L. Urged Tim Buck Be Freed at Once.'

38 AO, RG7-12-0-383.1, Miss Asselin, Renfrew, to Hon. David Croll, Minister of Labour, 7 Jan. 1936.

39 NAC, CCSD, 47:564, A. Tixier, Assistant Director, International Labor Office, to dear sir, 2 Dec. 1937. This letter was forwarded by Whitton to the Minister of Labour, Norman McLeod Rogers. See also ibid., Winifred Langfield, Catholic Women's League, to Whitton, n.d. For an excellent discussion of the equal rights arguments of feminists during this period, see Hobbs, 'Equality and Difference.'

40 On this climate of opinion, see Hobbs, 'Gendering Work and Welfare,' chapter 1.

41 UTA, Cassidy Papers, 41:2, Robert Jacob, Chairman, Greater Winnipeg Unemployment Advisory Board, to W.R. Clubb, Minister of Public Works and Labour, Manitoba, 25 Nov. 1932. Women were, however, only allowed to earn $10 without penalty.

42 See AO, RG7-12-0-71, H.C. Hudson to A.W. Crawford, Deputy Minister of Labour, 12 May 1931.

43 Denyse Baillargeon, '"If You Had No Money, You Had No Trouble, Did You?": Montreal Working-Class Housewives during the Great Depression,' in Mitchinson et al., *Canadian Women: A Reader*, 257.

44 Pedersen, *Family, Dependence and the Origins of the Welfare State*, 311.

45 Margaret Gould, 'The Day Nursery in the Programme of Child Care,' *Child Welfare News* 9, no. 2 (July 1933): 7–10. Gould believed that day nurseries should be expanded so that more women could work. For Whitton, see 'In Home and Office: In Factory and Shop,' ibid., 13, no. 4 (Nov. 1937): 10. While Gould insisted that women worked because of need, Helen Hart

argued that women should work by choice. See Hart, 'Day Nurseries in a Changing World,' ibid., 9, no. 2 (July 1933).

46 Whitton, 'The Gainful Occupation of Women,' *Child and Family Welfare* 13, no. 5 (Jan. 1938): 16–17.

47 Whitton, 'In Home and Office,' 3–4. She estimated that in Canada there were 1.5 million unmarried women, of which 663,000 were 'gainfully employed' as family care-givers, while 67,000 worked for pay. Of these, 15,000 were employable female heads of families, and 4,500 were unemployable heads of families, 8–10.

48 UTA, Cassidy Papers, 31:3, Charlotte Whitton, *This Weary Pilgrimage: The Dependency Outlook, Canada 1939* (pamphlet, 1939), 6. This was even after the introduction of a system of needy mothers' allowances.

49 UTA, Cassidy Papers, 57:3, 'Interview Notes for Saskatchewan,' n.d.

50 'Relief Problems in Western Cities: Foreigners, Single Men, Single Women and Graduating Students,' quoted in Michiel Horn, ed., *The Dirty Thirties: Canadians in the Great Depression* (Toronto: Copp Clark, 1972), 265.

51 See 'A Mountie Reports the Social Effects of Unemployment Relief,' quoted in Horn, *The Dirty Thirties*, 268.

52 NAC, Society for the Protection of Women and Children, Vol. 1, 'Secretary's Report,' 1933. There was a debate over whether the Depression increased desertion by causing increased family discord or whether it in fact helped contribute to its *decrease* because men could get relief only if they were maintaining families. See NAC, CCSD, 14:68, Jean McTaggart, Central Bureau of Family Welfare, Hamilton, to Whitton, 16 Aug. 1930.

53 'The Effects of Unemployment on Children and Young People,' *Child Welfare News* 10, no. 3 (Sept. 1934): 30.

54 See Marsh, *Employment Research*, 130; and Cassidy, *Unemployment and Relief in Ontario*, 239.

55 For an excellent discussion of the notion of separate spheres, see Leonore Davidoff, 'Regarding Some "Old Husband's Tales": Public and Private in Feminist Theory,' in Davidoff, *Worlds Between*. She has also called for the need to examine how these categories were enmeshed with the development of welfare states.

56 Marsh, *Employment Research*, 11.

57 NAC, MG30 E256, Charlotte Whitton Papers, Vol. 21, file 'Some Considerations of Unemployment Insurance 1932,' 8.

58 Provincial Archives of Manitoba [PAM], RG5 G2, Health and Welfare Supervision Board, 1:14, Rev J. Phillips to J.R. Mutchmor, 31 May 1933.

59 PAM, MG10 B20, Social Planning Council of Winnipeg, P660, file 8, 'School of Social Work Lectures,' 9 Nov. 1934.

60 Ramsay Cook, ed., *Politics of Discontent* (Toronto: University of Toronto Press, 1967), vii–x.

61 See H. Blair Neatby, *The Politics of Discontent: Canada in the Thirties* (Toronto: Macmillan, 1972); and J.H. Thompson and Allen Seager, *Decades of Discord: Canada 1922–39* (Toronto: McClelland & Stewart, 1986). For an important exception, see Hobbs, 'Gendering Work and Welfare.'

62 'The Effects of Unemployment on Children and Young People,' *Child Welfare News* 10, no. 3 (Sept. 1934): 25; and AO, RG7-12-0-169, 'Unemployment Relief in Canada,' 15 March 1933, 6.

63 'Unemployment and the Social Agencies,' *Child Welfare News* 6, no. 7 (March 1931): 43–4.

64 George McCullagh, *Marching on to What?* (pamphlet, 1939). For the ideology of the Leadership League, see Brian Young, 'C. George McCullagh and the Leadership League,' in Ramsay Cook, ed., *Politics of Discontent* (Toronto: University of Toronto Press, 1967), 76–102. Significantly, Young notes that in 1938, McCullagh launched his campaign for a spiritual revival with a series of five '"intimate man-to-man broadcasts"' (85).

65 Quoted in Struthers, *No Fault of Their Own*, 71.

66 AO, RG7-12-0-379, W.A. Case, 'Financing of Public Works,' 1936, 8 (author's emphasis).

67 For a discussion of this paper, see 'Mental Hygiene and Unemployment,' *Child Welfare News* 9, no. 2 (July 1933): 34. See also *Twelfth Annual Report of the Social Service Commission of Winnipeg* (pamphlet, 1934), 6.

68 A.P. Kappelle, Welfare Commissioner, 'City of Hamilton Set-Up,' *Child Welfare News* 6, no. 7 (May 1934): 52.

69 AO, RG7-12-0-169, 'Unemployment Relief in Canada,' 15 March 1933, 6.

70 NAC, RG 27, Vol. 2067, file: Minister of Labour, 1931, John Verhooven, Chapleau Avenue, Montreal, to Minister of Labour, 23 Oct. 1931; and AO, RG29-74-1-86, J.S. Band, memorandum to Hon. George S. Henry, 28 July 1932. See also AO RG7-12-0-153, Ernie Jeffrey to Dear Cap and Mac, Camp 1-F06, Kenora, Ont.: 'Gee Cap if you could only realize what a relief it is to get away from accepting charity, to working for a living again ... Gone is the worry and the haunted looks that appear on the faces of the down and out, and in its place is the look of contentment that appears with the knowledge of a day's work well done.' This was a piece of government propaganda.

71 So paradigmatic has this modern evaluation of work become that is now informs the conceptual framework accepted by historians of the workplace. Work is equated with culture. See, for example, Bryan Palmer, *A Culture in Conflict* (Montreal and Kingston: McGill-Queen's University Press, 1978); and Joy Parr, *The Gender of Breadwinners* (Toronto: University of Toronto

Press, 1990), who defines women's experience wholly in terms of their work for pay. Moreover, studies of the family that stress the economic rather than the cultural relations of family life are likewise influenced by this conception of work. See Bettina Bradbury, *Working Families*, and Bettina Bradbury, ed., *Canadian Family History: Selected Readings* (Toronto: Copp Clark Pitman, 1992).

72 Whitton, 'In Home and Office; In Factory and Shop,' *Child Welfare News* 13, no. 4 (Nov. 1937): 11.

73 Ibid., 17.

74 UTA, Cassidy Papers, 41:2, 'Report of Unemployment Relief, City of Winnipeg, 1930–31,' 5. This study was undertaken by Mrs Edith Rogers, a local MLA and the Assistant Deputy Minister of Public Works, A. McNamara. Of the 434 single women who were unemployed, 17.6 per cent were widows and 27.1 per cent had separated from their husbands; 49 per cent had previously worked as domestics, 22 per cent were waitresses, and only 13 per cent worked in factories. Interestingly, a full 49 per cent had been unemployed for a long time prior to 1931. The problem of unemployment among women in Ontario was also officially acknowledged in 1931. See AO RG7-12-0-103, H.D. Hudson, undated memorandum. By 1936, female employment status was recognized, but was still based on the idea that most women were 'unemployable' because of their home duties. See AO RG7-12-0-375, 'Analysis of Unplaced Applicants,' 1 Oct. 1936.

75 NAC, CCSD, 14:68, 'Report of Committee for Unemployed Women and Wives of Unemployed Men,' 1931.

76 W.R. Bone, 'The Vancouver Set-Up,' *Child Welfare News* 6, no. 7 (May 1934).

77 NAC, RG27, 3349:5, 'Twelfth Report of the Social Service Commission of Winnipeg, 1929–34,' 6–7; and 'Social Work in Winnipeg,' *Child Welfare News* 9, no. 14 (Nov. 4 1933): 57. The one consistent theme was that it was primarily the father's responsibility to support his family.

78 'Canada's Oldest Family Agency,' *Child and Family Welfare* 13, no. 6 (March 1938): 55–8.

79 NAC, RG27, 3349:28, Mary Sutherland to Mrs Crawford, 'Crawfordale Farm,' Quebec, 10 March 1937; and AO RG7-12-0-84, Norman Lett, City Clerk of Ottawa to the Hon. George S. Henry, 17 Nov. 1931.

80 Dorothy King, 'Unemployment Aid (Direct Relief),' in Richter, *Canada's Unemployment Problem*, 83. See also NAC, CCSD, 11:53, M.A. Proulx to Whitton, 1 Oct. 1929.

81 AO, RG29-74-1-3, Wallace R. Campbell, 'Report on Provincial Policy on Administrative Methods in the Matter of Direct Relief in Ontario,' 1932, 10.

82 Ibid., 14.

83 PAC, CCSD, 14:68, Harry Hereford, Director of the Distribution of Relief, Ontario, to Whitton, 31 Oct. 1930.

84 For the increasing conflict both between government relief organizations and voluntary groups, see PAM, RG5 G2, Health and Welfare Supervision Board, 1:14, Whitton to J.R. Mutchmor, 27 Oct. 1931; and ibid., 12:149, Rev Hugh Dobson to Mutchmor, 20 July 1933. By 1933 there were obvious rifts definite between 'professional' social workers like Whitton and church-based welfare workers.

85 NAC, CCSD, 16:68A, Miss H.R. Hogden, General Secretary, Halifax Welfare Bureau to Whitton, 8 May 1931.

86 NAC, RG27, 3355, National Employment Commission, J.E. Walsh, Executive Director, Federation of Catholic Charities, Montreal, to H. Spencer Ralph, 22 Sept. 1937; and ibid., Walter J. Bossy, Montreal, to A.B. Purvis, National Employment Commissioner, 15 Sept. 1937. On the independence of these religious-based agencies, see Malca Freidman, 'Family Welfare and Related Problems,' *Child Welfare News* 6, no. 7 (May 1934): 27. Jewish welfare organizations continued to supplement relief throughout the Depression because they wished to ensure that Jewish religious traditions could be preserved, especially regarding food.

87 NAC, CCSD, 16:68A, Miss H.R. Hogden to Whitton, 8 May 1931.

88 'Unemployment and the Social Agencies,' *Child Welfare News* 6, no. 4 (Sept. 1930): 11.

89 'The Montreal Council of Social Agencies,' *Child Welfare News* 8, no. 1 (May 1932): 19.

90 Marjorie Bradford, Assistant Secretary, Montreal Council of Social Agencies, 'Handling Unemployment in Montreal,' *Child Welfare News* 6, no. 6 (Jan. 1931): 14–15. She also commented on the divisiveness in welfare administration arising from religious denominationalism, 46.

91 'The Montreal Council of Social Agencies,' *Child Welfare News* 8, no. 1 (May 1932): 18–19.

92 'The Family Welfare Association of Montreal,' *Child Welfare News* 9, no. 6 (March 1934): 30.

93 NAC, CCSD, 11:53A, Whitton to Edith Appleton, Director Women's Department, Ontario Employment Office, 1 April 1933.

94 *Child Welfare News* 7, no. 4 (Nov. 1931): 13, 42.

95 'Unemployment and the Social Agencies,' *Child Welfare News* 6, no. 7 (March 1931): 37–42.

96 'The Saint John Welfare Bureau,' *Child Welfare News* 7, no. 4 (Nov. 1931): 50.

97 NAC, RG27, 3349:24, 'Women Befriend Women,' *Daily Colonist*, n.d.

98 PAM, RG5G2, Health and Welfare Supervision Board, 2:22, Violet Fillmore,

President, Canadian Women's Hostels, to S. Hardyment, Institutions and Relief Department, 20 Nov. 1935. Mrs McWilliams, who headed the Social Service Commission, led this initiative. On the career of McWilliams, see Mary Kinnear, *Margaret McWilliams: Inter-War Feminist* (Winnipeg: Manitoba University Press, 1994).

99 NAC, RG 27, 3349:32, Mary Sutherland, National Employment Commission to Miss Hazeltine S. Bishop, Secretary, Montreal Council of Social Agencies, 30 Dec. 1936.

100 On the workcamps and male hostels as a means to fight Communism, see PAM, RG5 G2, Health and Welfare Supervision Board, 13:156, Frank Dawson Adams, *The Day Shelter for Unemployed Men in Montreal*, n.d., 23. For the workcamps, see James Struthers, *No Fault of Their Own*.

101 NAC, RG27, Department of Labour, 3349:21.

102 Ibid.

103 NAC, CCSD, 43:208, Whitton to Mr Adam Bell, Deputy Minister of Labour, British Columbia, 13 Nov. 1931.

104 AO, RG7-12-0-179, L.O.R. Kennedy, 'The Relationship between the Depression and the Employment of Women,' 43.

105 AO, RG7-12-0-304, 'The Domestic Employment Situation in Toronto as at June 24 1935,' 2. In Toronto alone, 4,527 women, many of whom were skilled workers, were placed in domestic service occupations. On women's wages, see UTA, Cassidy Papers, 27:5, Miss I.M. Lunn, 'Report on Minimum Wage Law Violations,' Feb. 1934, who reported widespread wage reductions for women in restaurants, laundries, and the clothing and paper box industries.

106 AO, RG7-12-0-375, Crawford, memorandum to Hon. Dr J.D. Monteith, 12 Sept. 1933.

107 AO, RG7-12-0-112, 'Summary – Minimum Wage Board,' Sept.–Oct., 1932; AO RG7-12-0-236, 'Evidence Given by Miss Winifred Hutchison before the Price Spreads Commission on January 23–24 re: Conditions in the Needle Trades'; and UTA, Cassidy Papers, 27:5, Lunn, 'Report on Minimum Wage Violations.' On the threat of a strike among garment workers, see AO, RG7-12-0-375, A.W. Crawford, memorandum to Hon. Dr J.D. Monteith, Minister of Labour, 12 Sept. 1933, R.B. Bennett, telegraph to Hon. G.S. Henry, 5 Sept. 1933, Crawford to Monteith, 6 Oct., 16 Oct. 1933.

108 NAC, CCSD, 16:68A, Whitton to G.B. Clarke, General Secretary, Family Welfare Association, Montreal, 21 March 1933; AO RG29, MS 728, reel 1, G.R. Hodgson to Eric Cross, 13 June 1939; AO RG7-12-0-113, Bernard Shane, Superintendent of Joint Board of the Cloak, Suit, and Dressmaker's Union, to J.D. Monteith, 5 Feb. 1931, regarding the impending strike; and

ibid., A.O. Dobbs to H.C. Hudson, Superintendent of Ontario Employment Offices, 22 May 1931.

109 For a discussion of the On-To-Ottawa Trek, see Struthers, *No Fault of Their Own*; and Ronald Liversedge, *Recollections of the On-To-Ottawa Trek*, with related documents edited by Victor Hoare (Toronto: McClelland & Stewart, 1973).

110 NAC, CCSD, 26:133, 'Memorandum Hamilton,' n.d., 3.

111 NAC, RG27, Dept. of Labour, 3349:32, 'Memorandum on Domestic Work,' n.d.

112 AO, RG7-12-0-173, 'Report of Placements,' 1933.

113 Ibid.; and NAC, RG 27, 3356:16, F.R. Clarke to Mary Sutherland, n.d. Enclosed was his 'Report on Women's Section, Protestant Employment Bureau,' 1 Oct. 1936. On the reluctance of women to take jobs as domestics because the hours were usually from 7 a.m. to 11 p.m., with average wages of $15.00 per month, see AO RG7-12-0-299, L.O.R. Kennedy to H.C. Hudson, General Superintendent of Employment Services, 25 April 1935.

114 NAC, RG 27, 3349:30, letter from unidentified woman to Unemployed Women's Protective Association, 16 Dec. 1936.

115 AO, RG7-12-0-95, L.O.R. Kennedy to H.C. Hudson, 28 June 1932.

116 NAC, RG27, 3356:8, Whitton memorandum to relief service, Hull, 20 Nov. 1936.

117 AO, RG7-12-0-95, copy of anonymous letter from a member of The Canadian Daughter's League to Miss Kennedy, 12 Oct. 1930. On Miss Kennedy's attitudes to older female workers with spunk, see AO RG7-12-0-09.2, 'Proceedings of the Tenth Annual Conference of Ontario Office Superintendants, Employment Service of Canada, 6–8 May, 1931,' 8.

118 AO, RG7-12-0-95, Kennedy to Hudson, 15 Oct. 1930.

119 AO, RG7-12-0-371, Hudson to Kennedy, 5 May 1936.

120 AO, RG29-74-1-96, Harkness to all municipal clerks, 26 July 1935. As Harry Cassidy was to observe, poor relief was never mandatory in Ontario, where there was no official Poor Law Act. In contrast, in Nova Scotia and New Brunswick relief was never deemed to be discretionary, though it meant committal to a local workhouse. See AO, RG29-74-1-4, H.M. Cassidy, 'Unemployment and Relief in Ontario,' n.d., 5, 25. Traditionally, single persons were only inegligible for relief if they lived with their parents. See AO, RG29-74-1-6, 'Principles in Giving Relief to Families of the Unemployed,' July 1935.

121 AO, RG7-12-0-322, James F. Marsh, Deputy Minister of Public Welfare, to D.A. Croll, Minister of Public Welfare, 13 Dec. 1935.

122 Marsh, *Canadians In and Out of Work*, 289.

123 See *Final Report, National Employment Commission* (pamphlet, 1938), 85. Domestic service was an explicit work category that fell outside the Unemployment Insurance Act of 1940. On the gendered complexion of this act, see Pierson, 'Gender and Unemployment Debates in Canada, 1935–40,' 99.

124 Struthers, *No Fault of Their Own*. For an example of local mass protests on behalf of single men on relief, see AO, RG29-74, MS 728, reel 1, C. Cook to Eric Cross, 10 June 1938.

125 Margaret Hobbs is the exception. See 'Equality and Difference.'

126 'Survey Ordered on Relief for Single Women,' *Regina Leader Post*, 29 Sept. 1937; AO, RG7-12-0-179, Miss Appleton, Director of Women's Division, Ottawa, 'Women's Employment Work'; NAC, CCSD, 16:68A, Margaret E. Anstey, CAS, Saint John, New Brunswick, to Whitton, 18 April 1933; NAC, RG7, 3350:17, Mary Cahill, President, The Catholic Women's League of Canada, to Mrs T.W. Sutherland, 16 Nov. 1936; ibid., 3349:30, Evelyn Grey, Unemployed Women's Association to dear sir, 2 Feb. 1937; and ibid., 3349:21, Gladys Church to Hon. George S. Pearson, 7 Dec. 1936.

127 AO, RG7-12-0-84, G.S. Ford to J.D. Monteith, 23 Nov. 1932.

128 AO, RG7-12-0-179, L.O.R. Kennedy, 'The Relationship between the Depression and the Employment of Women,' n.d., 44.

129 AO, RG7-12-0-179, Kennedy, 'The Relationship between the Depression and the Employment of Women,' 46.

130 NAC, RG27, 3349:32, Hazeltine Bishop to Mary Sutherland, Chairman, Women's Employment Committee, 12 Dec. 1936.

131 NAC, RG27, 3349:32, 'Memorandum to the Women's Employment Committee of the National Employment Commission, Endorsed and Presented by the Montreal Council of Social Agencies,' 12 Dec. 1936. This report was written under the auspices of the YWCA, the Family Welfare Association, the Big Sisters Association, the Protestant Employment Bureau, and the Business and Professional Women's Club.

132 NAC, RG27, 3356, file Protestant Children's Home, Kathleen Gorrie to National Employment Commission, 22 Oct. 1936.

133 Ibid.

134 This committee was made up of Mrs Walter Lindal (Winnipeg), a lawyer on the executive of the Central Council of Social Agencies; Mme Maurice Cormier (Montreal); Mrs A.J. Currie (Govan, Saskatchewan); Mrs L.G. Ferguson (Westville, Nova Scotia); and Miss Ruth Low (Kitchener, Ontario). Miss Low was a graduate of McGill University and Emmanuel College, the Methodist theological school at the University of Toronto. She was a social worker with the YWCA in Toronto, where she headed the Foreign

Born Department. Her specialty was unemployment among immigrant women. Although there was a distinct rural presence on this committee, most of the input came from the two urban members, Mrs Lindal and Miss Low.

135 NAC, RG27, 3348, Women's Advisory Committee, J.L. Lindal to Mary Sutherland, 20 Jan. 1937; ibid., 2067, 'The Unemployed Women,' *Stanstead Journal*, 5 Nov. 1936; and 'Training for Domestic Help,' *Woodstock Sentinel*, 20 Nov. 1936.

136 Ibid., 3349:20, Sutherland to J.T. Mutrie and Son, Vernon, British Columbia; and ibid., 3348, Women's Advisory Committee, Lindal to Sutherland, 2 Dec. 1936, 13 Jan. 1937.

137 NAC, RG27, 3349:17, Sutherland to D.M. Allan, private secretary to the Minister of Agriculture, Ottawa, 10 April 1937. James Struthers has rightly criticized Sutherland's rural outlook. See *No Fault of Their Own*, 167.

138 Ibid., Sutherland to Winifred Hutchinson, Department of Economics, YWCA, 27 Nov. 1936, Sutherland to Mutrie, 6 April 1937. The committee's animus against government intervention was not simply the product of a rural disposition. See Ruth Low to Mary Sutherland, 16 Jan. 1937.

139 NAC, RG27, 3348, Women's Advisory Committe, Lindal to Sutherland, 1 Dec., 2 Dec. 1936. This aspect of the committee's work was criticized, especially in Manitoba, by organized labour and R.D. Mackenzie, the former Minister of Agriculture.

140 NAC, RG27, 3349:30, Evelyn Cahill to Dear Sir, 2 Feb. 1937; AO, RG7-12-0-167, 'The Care of the Destitute Single Woman,' n.d.; and NAC, CCSD, 26:133, 'Memorandum Hamilton,' 5. An exception to this rule was Mary Cahill, the president of the Catholic Women's League of Canada, who heartily protested against the lack of work and poor wages for women. See Mary L. Cahill, *Unemployment Conditions throughout Canada as Affecting the Single Woman* (pamphlet, 1934). One notable exception was Mary Burnham, Supervisor, Women's Branch, Department of Immigration, Ottawa. See NAC, CCSD, 16:68A, M.V. Burnham to Whitton, 21 April 1933, in which she wrote: 'According to our records in these times of unemployment there is very little money in prostitution and over a period of three years of unemployment our problems in connection with the immigrant girls have not been aggravated by that trouble. The "alternative occupation" as prostitution is sometimes known has no money in it.' She did, however, concede that immoral living was on the rise.

141 AO, RG7-12-0-167, 'The Care of the Destitute Single Woman.'

142 Ruth Low, Executive Secretary, Social Service Department, YWCA, 'The Unattached Woman,' *Child Welfare News* 11, no. 5 (1936): 19.

143 AO, RG7-12-0173, A.W. Crawford, Deputy Minister of labour, 'Memorandum re: Miss Margaret Lade,' 17 Nov. 1933.

144 AO, RG7-12-0-173, Margaret Lade, Memorandum, to the Committee on Unemployment amongst Single Women in Toronto, 27 Sept. 1933.

145 AO, RG7-12-0-173, A.W. Crawford to Hon. Dr J.D. Monteith, 18 Oct. 1933; ibid., 'Memorandum re. Miss Margaret Lade'; and ibid., A.W. Crawford to Miss M. Lade, 23 Nov. 1933.

146 AO, RG7-12-0-173, 'Memorandum re. Miss Margaret Lade.'

147 AO, RG7-12-0-179, 'The Woman out of Work,' 50.

148 AO, RG7-12-0-173, Miss Lade to A.W. Crawford, 10 Oct. 1933.

149 AO, RG7-12-0-173, Miss Lade, The League of Community Workers, to Mr A.W. Crawford, 6 June 1933, H.C. Hudson to L.O.R. Kennedy, 30 May 1933.

150 AO, RG7-12-0-179, Miss M. Lade, 'The Woman Out of Work,' 49.

151 AO, RG7-12-0-167, 'The Care of the Destitute Single Woman.'

152 AO, RG7-12-0-173, Lade to the Committee on Unemployment amongst Single Women, 27 Sept. 1933; and ibid., Lade to Crawford, 6 June 1933.

153 AO, RG-12-0-84, A.W. Crawford, Memorandum, 21 Nov. 1932; and RG7-12-0-225, H.C. Hudson to J.F. Marsh, 29 Nov. 1934. For an opposite view, see RG7-12-0-173, Margaret Lade, 'Suggestions re. Organizations of Unemployed Women.'

154 AO, RG7-12-0-167, Committee V, 'Report of Committee on Employment, Occupational and Recreational Projects,' which was composed of Tom Moore, H.M. Cassidy, and A.W. Crawford. Interestingly, one of Moore's recommendations was to settle families on the land to help settle the 'adolescent' problem.

155 AO, RG7-12-0-84, A.W. Crawford to Hon. Dr Forbes Godfrey, Minister of Health and Labour, Ottawa, 29 April 1930. Rigg wanted the government employment service restricted to true unemployment cases, and thus objected to 'Le Foyer,' a charitable institution, overlapping its efforts with the employment centres. A similar position was adopted by the Deputy Minister of Labour in Ontario. See AO, RG7-12-0-173, Crawford to Miss Lade, 23 Nov. 1933.

156 See H.M. Cassidy, *Unemployment and Relief in Ontario*, 43; NAC, Society for the Protection of Women and Children, G.B. Clarke, 'Domestic Relations and Problems of Chjild Dependency: A Study of Broken Homes,' 1–2.

157 UTA, Cassidy Papers, 28:1, 'Report of a Committee Convened by the Montreal Council of Social Agencies to Consider, Report and Recommend on the Attitude to Be Adopted in the Matter of Unemployment Insurance,' Dec. 1932, 15, 23, 29.

158 Marsh, *Canadians In and Out of Work*, 341. Harry Cassidy held a similar view, and is frequently quoted by Marsh. See ibid., 368, on Cassidy's distinctions between unemployment relief and other 'types of assistance.'

159 NAC, CCSD, 39:167, Whitton, 'The Relation between Social Work and Fraternal Organizations,' address to Canadian Fraternal Organization, 22 May 1933.

160 NAC, CCSD, 16:68IV, Marsh to Whitton, 13 Feb. 1934. Even opponents of unemployment insurance, like the Ontario Deputy Minister of Labour, James F. Marsh, believed that seasonal workers should be entitled to benefits. See AO, RG7-12-0-363, Marsh to D.A. Croll, 26 Nov. 1936. For one of the few commentators on unemployment insurance policies in Canada who did not believe that they should encourage self-help among workmen, see J.L. Cohen, *The Canadian Unemployment Insurance Act – Its Relation to Social Security* (Toronto: Thomas Nelson & Sons, 1935), 157. Cohen not only wanted the program to be entirely state-funded, but he also wished to include unskilled and seasonal workers.

161 Irving, 'Canadian Fabians'; and Michiel Horn, *The League for Social Reconstruction: Intellectual Origins of the Democratic Left in Canada 1930–1942* (Toronto: University of Toronto Press, 1980).

162 Marsh, *Canadians In and Out of Work*, 402. On the generalized fear that work skills and wage levels were being eroded with the proliferation of unskilled work in the 1930s, see 'Public Welfare Services,' *Canadian Welfare Summary* 14, no. 4 (Nov. 1938); and AO, RG7-74-1-6, Mrs A. Ethel Parker, 'An Allowance for Household Extras,' memorandum to D.B. Harkness, Supervisor, Unemployment Relief Branch, 8 April 1935. On the vulnerability of unskilled workers during the Depression, see Struthers, *No Fault of Their Own*, 4. Forty per cent of unskilled workers were unemployed compared with 12 per cent of skilled workers.

163 Daniel Ritschel, *The Politics of Planning: The Debate on Economic Planning in Britain in the 1930's* (Oxford: Oxford University Press, 1997). For the Canadian variant of this whiggish point of view, see Horn, *The League for Social Reconstruction*; and Doug Owram, *The Government Generation*. Owram identifies a constituency of conservative planners in Canada; nevertheless, he still attributes the 'progressive' nature of their planning philosophy to the achievement of Keynesianism.

164 Ibid., 50.

165 Ibid., 113.

166 Ibid., 50, 145–230, 324.

167 UTA, Cassidy Papers, 8, no. 3 (28 June 1930). For Cassidy's biographical information, see ibid., 16, no. 4 (26 Dec. 1939).

168 See Struthers, *No Fault of Their Own*, 64.
169 UTA, Cassidy Papers, 55:1, Cassidy to Carlton McNaught, 27 April 1943; and ibid., 58:1, H.M. Cassidy, 'Reorganization of British Columbia's Health and Welfare Services: A Report with Recommendations,' 2–4. This report was most likely written in 1938, the final year of Cassidy's tenure as Director of Public Welfare in British Columbia.
170 UTA, Cassidy Papers, 55:1, Cassidy to Carlton McNaught, 27 April 1943. Cassidy later ran for the Liberal Party in Ontario, but during the 1930s he worked for the Liberal government in British Columbia, under Premier T. Dufferin Pattullo. On Pattullo, see Margaret A. Ormsby, 'T. Dufferin Pattullo and the Little New Deal,' in Cook, ed., *Politics of Discontent* (Toronto: University of Toronto Press, 1967), 28–48.
171 UTA, B72-0025, Harold Adams Innis Papers, 19/29, 'For the People,' *University of Toronto Quarterly* 5, no. 2 (Jan. 1936): 280.
172 James Struthers, 'A Profession in Crisis: Charlotte Whitton and Canadian Social Work in the 1930s,' in Allan Moscovitch and Jim Albert, eds., *The Benevolent State* (Toronto: Garamond Press, 1987). My assessment of the 1930s as the crucial decade in the transition from a social work to an economic perspective informing welfare policies follows Struthers's general argument.
173 NAC, CCSD, 16:68IV, Moore to Whitton, 1 Feb. 1934.
174 Ibid., Whitton, 'The Essentials of a Relief Programme for Canada.'
175 Ibid., Marsh to Whitton, 13 Feb. 1934, Cassidy to Whitton, 26 Jan. 1934.
176 NAC, CCSD, 16:68IV, 'The Essentials of a Relief Programme for Canada 1934–35.' In recommending compulsory widows' and orphans' insurance, Whitton was following guidelines established by the International Labour Conference in Geneva. See AO-RG29-74-1-6, 'Memoranda of Information to Various Social Services in Canada – Federal and Provincial,' 1935, 32. For the most part, those who continued to stress 'hazards of the present social and industrial system' which fell outside unemployment, were family welfare workers. See, for example, AO, RG7-12-0-167, 'Report of Committee Meeting – Sub-Committee D,' with comments of Dorothy King on the need for minimum standards for families. This was part of the Round Table Conference of 1933.
177 See Struthers, *No Fault of Their Own*, for this statement by Whitton, 78.
178 'Welfare Services for the Canadian People,' *The Canadian Welfare Summary* 14, no. 2 (July 1938): 11.
179 UTA, Cassidy Papers, 41:3, 'The Essentials of a Relief Programme for Canada 1934–5.'

180 Whitton, 'What of the Future?' in Richter, *Canada's Unemployment Problems*, 390–1.
181 AO, RG7-12-0-338, H.C. Hudson to A.W. Crawford, 3 Nov. 1933.
182 AO, RG7-12-0-338, R.K. Finlayson, 'Summary of Talk on Unemployment Insurance Delivered Before the Study Club of Ottawa,' 8 Feb. 1935. Bennett's unemployment insurance scheme provided for separate contributions from men and women, and allowed benefits at $2.70 per adult dependents and $.90 per child per week. Compared to King's 1940 Unemployment Insurance Act, Bennett's legislation was much less male-biased.
183 UTA, Cassidy Papers, 31:4, L.C. Marsh, 'Unemployment and the Sirois Plan: Administrative Implications, Preliminary Memorandum,' n.d.
184 UTA, Cassidy Papers, 28:1, D.V. Varley, 'Dependents' Allowances in Unemployment Insurance,' *Social Security*, Jan.–Feb. 1943, 3–4; and ibid., 'Montreal Social Agencies on Unemployment Insurance,' 1932, 37–42, whose memoranda were written by Marsh. This is the earliest rejection of family allowances within unemployment insurance that I have seen in Canada. The disaggregation of the family economic unit and the individualization of work was suggested from many sources. See, for example, NAC, RG27, 3356:16, F.C. Clarke, Protestant Employment Bureau, Montreal, 'Report to the Youth Employment Committee of the National Employment Commission,' n.d.
185 UTA, Cassidy Papers, 16:2, Bryce Stewart, Director of Research, Industrial Relations Councillors, to Cassidy, 19 June 1931.
186 UTA, Cassidy Papers, 31:4, L.C. Marsh, 'Unemployment and the Sirois Plan,' 5. Cassidy supported benefits for dependants in welfare legislation such as health insurance when these were not seen to immediately conflict with the wage system. See 'British Columbia's New Health Insurance Act,' *Child Welfare News* 12, no. 1 (May 1936): 4.
187 *Child Welfare News* 7, no. 4 (Nov. 1931): 43, in which it was stated that there is 'no firm demarcation between private and public' welfare management.
188 NAC, CCSD, 26. Oct. 1934.
189 UTA, Cassidy Papers, 31:4, H.M. Cassidy, 'Comments on Memorandum on "Public Assistance and Unemployment Relief," prepared for the Royal Commission on Dominion–Provincial Relations by A.E. Grauer,' 12 Nov. 1938; and ibid., 31:2, Cassidy to Whitton, 29 Oct. 1938.
190 NAC, MG26 J1, Prime Minister Mackenzie King Papers, Vol. 297, G.F. Towers to King, 15 Aug. 1940. The Ontario Deputy Minister of Labour, Mr McNamara, also endorsed a federal program of unemployment assistance. See UTA, Cassidy Papers, 31:3, Whitton to Cassidy, 16 Dec. 1940.

191 Cassidy, 'Public Reorganization in Canada,' *Public Affairs* 5, no. 2 (Winter 1941): 88.

192 NAC, CCSD, 16:68VI, Whitton to Dr Frank Sanderson, Department of Insurance, Ontario, 21 March 1934.

193 Ibid.; UTA, Cassidy Papers, 15:3, Arthur Purvis to Cassidy, 20 March 1939; and ibid., 14:4, Marsh to Cassidy, 9 June 1943.

194 UTA, Cassidy Papers, 31:2, Cassidy to Whitton, 4 Jan. 1941. 'You may hesitate also about my suggestion that logically the administration of old age assistance and mother's allowances should be returned to the municipal agencies, if they are to handle general relief.' See also ibid., 57:4, Cassidy, 'Interim Notes – Ontario,' 25 July 1942. F.R. Scott wanted mother's allowances to be administered federally, but as he told Cassidy, it was not worth the constitutional fight because it did not involve issues of wages and hours. See ibid., 71:1, F.R. Scott, 'Comments on a Labour Code,' n.d.

195 UTA, Cassidy Papers, 17:4, Cassidy to Purvis, n.d., April 1939; ibid., 18:1, Cassidy to Marsh, 18 June 1943; ibid., 31:3, Whitton to Cassidy, 16 Dec. 1940; and ibid., 11:4, Cassidy to Whitton, 6 April 1943, stating that 'I am a little pessimistic that not one of the three major political parties will be very receptive to the administrative ideas which I think you and I share.' See also ibid., 17:1, Cassidy to Norman Rogers, 4 July 1935. Whitton, however, disliked Cassidy's grant-in-aid recommendations. See ibid., 31:2, Cassidy to Whitton, 12 Dec. 1940.

196 UTA, 13:5, Cassidy to Dal Grauer, n.d. Cassidy believed that his recommendations regarding administrative efficiency greatly appealed to businessmen.

197 UTA, Cassidy Papers, 13:5, Cassidy to Dal Grauer, 16 Oct. 1937. 'A large part of the failure of the social workers to sell themselves derives from the fact that they constantly give the impression that they are expensive luxuries rather than people who, in salvaging human wreckage, will help to keep under control the enormous bills of the state.' See also ibid., 72:1, Cassidy to Paul Martin, 28 July 1947.

198 UTA, Cassidy Papers, 17:4, Cassidy to Miss Martha Chickering, Associate Professor of Social Economics, University of California at Berkeley, 28 Sept. 1938. See also ibid., 31:3, Whitton to Cassidy, 3 Jan. 1941; and ibid., 13:4, H.A. Corry, School of Commerce and Administration, Queen's University to Cassidy, 29 Nov. 1943.

199 UTA, Cassidy Papers, 61:5, 'Dominion–Provincial Relations and Social Security,' 29 Nov. 1945, 17. He opposed means testing, but still advanced general assistance 'to respond to the actual needs of the family group,' family here denoting women and children.

200 UTA, Cassidy Papers, 31:4, Cassidy, 'Comments on "Memorandum on Social Insurance by A.E. Grauer,"' 5 Nov. 1938.

201 UTA, Cassidy Papers, 18:1, Cassidy to Professor E.F. Beach, Director, School of Commerce, McGill Univerity, 18 March 1943. He also defended his segregation of relief to provincial and municipal jurisdictions, claiming that policy experts like himself were not architects who could build from scratch, but that the welfare edifice was powerfully determined by pre-existing materials. See ibid., 17:3, Cassidy, 'Comments on Mr Ernst's Papers,' 31 May 1938.

202 UTA, Cassidy Papers, 71:1, Frank Pedley, Executive Director, Financial Federation of the Montreal Council of Social Agencies, to memorandum to Cassidy, n.d., 16.

203 UTA, Cassidy Papers, 54:5, Amy Leigh, Assistant Superintendent of Relief, British Columbia, to Cassidy, 8 Jan. 1944; and ibid., 58:4, Amy Leigh, 'The Tide of Public Welfare,' 10 July 1942. Municipalities had to pay entirely for unemployables. On this problem, see also AO, RG7-12-0-167, 'The Care of the Destitute Single Woman,' which warned against confusing the truly unemployed with the chronically destitute, aged, and incapacitated.

204 *Final Report, National Employment Commission*, 47; and Marsh, *Canadians In and Out of Work*, 351.

205 Ibid., 372.

206 Marsh, *Employment Research*, 130; NAC, RG27, 3356:8, Whitton to Harry Baldwin, Superintendent of the Relief Division, 22 July 1936.

207 NAC, RG27, 2067, file Minister of Labour 1937, 'Memorandum for the Minister re Legislation to Succeed the Unemployment Relief and Assistance Act, 1936,' 19 Dec. 1936.

208 NAC, RG27, 3067, file 'Material Aid – General,' 'Memorandum, Department of Labour,' 6 Feb. 1939; and Marsh, *Canadians In and Out of Work*, 351.

209 Ibid. A few women attempted to validate women's status as employables. See ibid., 3348, 'Women's Advisory Committee,' submission by Cecile Bouchard, Quebec's provincial inspector for minimum wages for women.

210 AO, RG29-74-1-16, 'Preliminary Remarks Relating to Dominion-Provincial Proposals August 1945.'

211 *Interim Report of the National Employment Commission* (Ottawa: King's Printer, 1937), XII.

212 NAC, RG27, 3349:5, Baldwin to Mary Sutherland, 25 Aug. 1936; and ibid., 3355, Catholic Welfare Bureau 1937, Frank G. Pedley, Executive Director, Montreal Council of Social Agencies, to H. Spencer Ralph, 20 Sept. 1937.

213 NAC, RG27, 3349:5, A.W. Barbour to Baldwin, 25 Aug. 1936.

214 *Interim Report of the National Employment Commission*, X–XI.
215 H.A. Weir, 'Unemployed Youth,' in Richter, *Canada's Unemployment Problem*, 120.
216 NAC, RG27, 3349:25, H.M. Cassidy to Baldwin, 14 Sept. 1936.
217 Ibid., S. McNamara to Baldwin, 25 Aug. 1936.
218 NAC, RG27, 3349:5, Michel Guimot, Department of Municipal Affairs, Trade and Commerce, Quebec, to Baldwin, 24 Aug. 1936. Guimot estimated that there were 6,269 employable female heads of families and only 296 truly unemployable female workers in Quebec.
219 Ibid., Baldwin to R.H. McKay, Supervisor of Relief, Department of Labour, Nova Scotia, 21 Aug. 1936.
220 'The Relief of Unemployment,' *Child Welfare News* 12, no. 1 (May 1936).
221 For such labelling of women, see AO, RG29-74-1-12, George S. Tattle, Deputy Minister of Public Welfare, 17 Nov. 1941; UTA, Cassidy Papers, 57:4, E.H. Horton, Director, Unemployment Relief, Ontario, to Municipal Clerks, 24 March 1941; and AO, RG29-74-1-11, F.C. Jackson, Department of Public Welfare, 'The Question of "The Tough and Permanent Core of Relief,"' 14 Sept. 1939.
222 UTA, 17:4, Cassidy to C.E. Silcox, Christian Social Council of Canada, 13 Sept 1939. Cassidy placed unemployables, the large majority of whom were women, among the 'unfit' categories of the aged and sick who made up British Columbia's public assistance rolls.
223 H.M. Cassidy, 'Canada's Public Welfare Bill,' *The Canadian Welfare Summary* 15, no. 1 (April–May 1939): 7.
224 UTA, Cassidy Papers, 40:5, Bryce Stewart, 'Federal and State Unemployment Insurance,' paper delivered to the New York Academy of Political Science, 1935, 92.
225 AO, RG29, Ms728, reel 1, 'Some Questions and Answers Relating to Direct Relief,' 27 June 1944.
226 *Interim Report of the National Employment Commission* (Ottawa: King's Printer, 1937), 7–8.
227 UTA, Cassidy Papers, 31:3, Whitton, 'Controlling the Public Welfare Bill,' 18; and NAC, RG27, 3349:32, Montreal Council of Social Agencies 'Memorandum to the Women's Unemployment Committee of the National Employment Commission,' n.d. On the changing definition of 'dependency,' see Nancy Fraser and Linda Gordon, 'A Genealogy of *Dependency*: Tracing a Keyword of the U.S. Welfare State,' *Signs* 19, no. 2 (Winter 1994): 309–36; Fraser and Gordon, 'Civil Citizenship against Social Citizenship? On the Ideology of Contract-versus-Charity,' in Bart van Steenbergen, ed., *The Quality of Citizenship* (London: Sage, 1994), 90–107.

228 'Minutes of Forty-Ninth Annual Meeting,' 15 Jan. 1930, 5. This perspective was also reinforced by family caseworkers, who saw in the marginalization of female welfare entitlements to the provincial sphere a means to reassert the authority of private welfare agencies. See Dorothy King, 'Unemployment Aid,' in Richter, *Canada's Unemployment Problem*, 96–7. King was the Director of the Montreal School of Social Work.

229 AO, RG29-74-1-88, J.S Band to Provincial Inspectors and Administrators, 9 July 1940; ibid., E.A. Horton to Municipal Clerks, 12 May 1941; and UTA, Cassidy Papers, 31:3, Cassidy, 'Public Welfare Re-Organization for Canada.'

230 AO, RG29-74-1-15, 'Summary of Major Findings and Recommendations re. the Administration of Welfare Services in the Province of Ontario, 1944.' The term *dependency* applied only to women, except among the aged. Significantly, government tables analysed relief cases in terms of sex in 1945. It was found that women formed the majority of relief cases for the first time since the Depression. See AO, RG29-74-1-126, J.S. Band, 'Case-Load and Sex of Persons in Receipt of Relief – Month of July 1945.' Women made up 63.8 per cent of relief cases in Ontario.

7: Family Allowances and the Politics of Postwar Abundance

1 For this interpretation, see Michael Bliss, 'Preface' to Leonard Marsh, *Report on Social Security for Canada* (second edition: Toronto, University of Toronto Press, 1975; first edition, Ottawa, King's Printer, 1943), ix. For a synthesis of the secondary literature, see James Struthers, 'Family Allowances, Old Age Security, and the Construction of Entitlement in the Canadian Welfare State, 1943–1951,' in Peter Neary and J.L. Granatstein, eds., *The Veterans Charter and Post–World War II Canada* (Montreal: McGill-Queen's University Press, 179–204). The epigraphs are Brooke Claxton, 'What's Wrong with Parliament?' *Maclean's Magazine*, 1 March 1943, 13; NAC, CCSD, 77:568, Harry Cassidy to Nora Lea, 24 Feb. 1945; and Hope Stoddard, 'No Women Being Hired,' *Canadian Forum* (June 1946): 58.

2 Margaret Gould, *Family Allowances in Canada: Facts versus Fiction* (Toronto: Ryerson Press, 1945), 14–15.

3 Ibid., 15.

4 NAC, CCSD, 59:490, Elizabeth Wallace, Executive Secretary, Canadian Association of Social Workers, to Editor, *Ottawa Citizen*, 8 July 1944.

5 'Family Allowance Fund,' *Canadian Forum* 24, no. 284 (Sept. 1944): 1.

6 Dominique Marshall, 'The Language of Children's Rights, the Formation of the Welfare State and the Democratic Experience of Poor Families in Quebec, 1940–55,' *Canadian Historical Review* 78, no. 3 (Sept. 1997): 409–41.

7 Dominique Jean, 'Family Allowances and Family Autonomy, Quebec Families Encounter the Welfare State, 1945–1955,' in Bettina Bradbury, ed., *Canadian Family History: Selected Readings* (Toronto: Copp Clark Pitman, 1992), 402–5; and Raymond B. Blake, 'Mackenzie King and the Genesis of Family Allowances in Canada, 1939–44,' in J.L. Granatstein and Peter Neary, eds., *The Good Fight: Canadians and World War II* (Toronto: Copp Clark, 1995), 320–33. Many contemporary observers were well aware that the relief of poverty was not uppermost in the minds of government policymakers. See, for example, the observation of Dr Bryce Stewart, in 'The Beveridge Plan,' *Canadian Business*, Feb. 1943, 29, and the comments of Premier Garson of Manitoba, in 'Purchasing Power First,' *Edmonton Journal*, 26 Aug. 1944.

8 For a similar argument, see Brigitte Kitchen, 'The Marsh Report Revisited,' *Journal of Canadian Studies* 21, no. 2 (Summer 1986): 38–48.

9 NAC, CCSD, 59:490, Philip S. Fisher to J.G. Turgeon, chairman of the House of Commons Select Committee on Rehabilitation and Reconstruction, 29 Dec. 1943.

10 NAC, Dependent's Allowance Board [DAB], RG 36, series 18, Vol. 3, Dependents' Board of Trustees, 'Minutes of Second Annual Meeting,' 27 May 1942.

11 NAC, Department of Veterans' Affairs, RG 31, Vol. 178, 'Non-Pensioned Widows,' Anne Coiner, Winnipeg to Hon. C.G. Power, Minister of Pensions and National Health, 13 Sept. 1939; W.H. Jacobs to Power, 15 June 1939; C.E. Silcox, Social Service Council of Canada to Power, 9 March 1938; NAC, Ian Mackenzie Papers, MG 27 III B5, Vol. 35:B-87, 'Widow's Pensions,' 18-6-43; and ibid., R. Hale, 'Pensions for Widows,' *The Legionary*, Sept. 1942.

12 NAC, Department of Veterans' Affairs, RG 31, Vol. 179, 'Non-Pensioned War Widows,' Brig. Gen. H.F. MacDonald to C.G. Power, 20 Feb. 1939; Charles G. Power to Miss Agnes Macphail, 28 June 1939; and J.L. Melville, 'A New Appeal for Pensions,' 7 March 1938.

13 NAC, CCSD, 62:497, 'Aid to Dependent Mothers and Children in Canada,' 1939, 3–4.

14 NAC, Ian Mackenzie Papers, Vol. 35:B-87C, Memo. 2, 'The Claim for Pensions for Widows of War Veterans,' quoting Hon. C.G. Power in Hansard, 25 Feb. 1938.

15 NAC, DAB, Vol. 29, 'Mothers' Allowance files,' A.B. Brown to Arthur MacNamara, 15 April 1940; AO, RG29, microfilm 728, reel 2, 'Directory of Canadian Community Agencies Servicing Dependents of the Forces, revised to Feb. 1942, supersedes "The Folk at Home," directory April 1941,' 1–2.

16 NAC, Department of Labour, Vol. 2067, file 'Material Aid General,' memorandum 6 Feb. 1939.

17 NAC, DAB, Vol. 1, 'Set-Up file,' 'Improved Arrangements for Making Provision for Families of Members of H.M. Forces during the Present War,' 1941; and ibid., Vincent Massey to R.O.G. Bennett, 22 Nov. 1941.

18 NAC, DAB, Vol. 1 'Set-Up file,' 'Improved Arrangements for Making Provision for Families.'

19 NAC, DAB, Vol. 29, 'Complaints,' Mrs Sarah McLaughlin, Tracadie, N.B., to R.O.G. Bennett, chairman, DAB, 12 June 1944. Many women such as Mrs McLaughlin may have viewed this as their 'pay,' but it was granted by virtue of their husband's service.

20 NAC, DAB, Vol. 29, 'Complaints,' R.O.G. Bennett to Private Secretary, Minister of National Defence, 10 Jan. 1944; and ibid., 'Mother's Allowance files,' A. McNamara to Miss Durham, Office of Minister of National Defence, 13 August 1940. Because so many soldier-sons had been on relief before enlisting, the rules which required that the son be the sole support of his mother were relaxed in January 1940. That the rights of wives took clear precedence over those of mothers often created a high degree of familial and ethnic conflict. See, for example, the case of a Ukrainian soldier who just prior to embarkation quickly married a Canadian girl. Angered by their precipitous fall in income, the soldier's mother pressured the young bride to endorse her cheques over to her. This occasioned the remark from the local social worker that 'in this case, there is the clash between the people of the Old World and the New, and question of a war marriage, where the boy thought his wife could live with his family and help them, and this has not worked out.' See PAM, Family Services of Winnipeg, Board of Director's Meetings, Thirty-fifth meeting, n.d.

21 NAC, DAB, Vol. 4, Dependent's Board of Trustees, Minutes of Executive Committee, 2 Feb. 1942. Mrs Mary LeClair was granted a mere $6.50 because her son had abruptly married before embarking overseas. She was instructed to apply to local social agencies.

22 NAC, DAB, Vol. 29, 'Mother's Allowance files,' Gertrude Childs to R.O.G. Bennett, 19 March 1942.

23 H.A. Weir, 'Unemployed Youth,' in Richter, Canada's Unemployment Problem, 129, 143–4, 161.

24 NAC, CCSD, 58:489, Charlotte Whitton to C.W. Griffith, Administrator, Unemployment Relief Branch, Victoria, B.C., 9 Dec. 1941; and PAM, Family Services of Winnipeg, Board of Directors' Meetings, Forty-third Meeting, n.d. Many working-class families agitated for increased children's allowances so that their older children could attend high school. However, there were some who still preserved the older tradition of insisting that their children contribute to the family economy. During the war, military officials

resisted such conventions. See, for example, PAM, Department of Health and Welfare, RG 3731, Military Dependents' Allowance Commission Files [MDAC], Box 24, file Ha–Hi. In this case, the male breadwinner refused to contribute to his family and wanted his older children to support his wife, from whom he was estranged. The DAC objected to his failure to maintain his family and instituted compulsory assigned pay.

25 NAC, DAB, Vol. 4, Dependents' Board of Trustees, Minutes of Executive Committee, 9 March 1942; ibid., Vol. 5, Executive Meeting, 2 June 1942; and ibid., Vol. 1, file 2–3, 'Children in High Schools and Other Courses of Instruction Approved by the Board,' 8 Aug. 1945. From 1 Jan. 1943, children of soldiers were allowed to get a government allowance up to the age of nineteen if they were attending high school or taking higher education courses. Hair dressing, part-time and evening courses, religious instruction, and apprenticeship were excluded.

26 NAC, DAB, Vol. 4, Dependents' Board of Trustees, Minutes of Executive Committee, 16 March 1942.

27 NAC, DAB, Vol. 36, 'Petitions for Unmarried Applicants,' K.M. Macdonald, memorandum, 'Article 98,' 3 Feb. 1943. This breadwinner ideal was also championed by the common soldier, who saw this form of government assistance as a right rather than charity. See DAB, Vol. 29, 'Complaints,' C.E. Noel to DAB, n.d. 'I have never received a penny of welfare or help from anybody and have brought up my family alone without any help.' He claimed government protection as a right on the basis that 'I am at their service.'

28 NAC, DAB, Vol. 29, 'Mother's Allowance files,' A. McNamara to Norman McLeod Rogers, Minister of National Defence, 10 June 1940. Interestingly, this letter was written the day France fell to the Germans. The obvious need for more voluntary recruitment was a further spur to generously supporting wives of soldiers.

29 NAC, DAB, Vol. 29, 'Complaints,' R.O.G. Bennett to Mrs C.M. Wright, Consumer Branch, Wartime Prices and Trade Board, 7 Oct. 1943. Despite increasing demand for female labour after 1942 government officials never fully countenanced women's right to work.

30 Mothers of soldiers were, by contrast, encouraged to become economically independent, as they were allowed initially to earn only $20.00 a month before deductions were made from their dependant's allowance. Only under pressure for more wartime female labour were mothers allowed to later earn up to $40.00 a month. Mothers were also encouraged to depend on provincial mothers' allowances for their maintenance. To spur them in this direction, no deductions were made from their mothers' allowance

once their son assigned his pay and dependant's allowance. This was to reinforce the son's initiative to support his mother after the war. Unfortunately, mothers who were without a dependant's allowance were later denied a soldier's pension. NAC, DAB, Vol. 29, 'Complaints,' R.O.G. Bennett to A.E. McMaster, Assistant Co-ordinator of Controls, Department of Munitions and Supply, 7 Dec. 1944; ibid., D. McIvor, M.P. Fort William to Bennett, 29 Feb. 1944; ibid., Vol. 29, 'Mother's Allowance files,' Ernest Blois to Bennett, 19 Nov. 1943; ibid., Bennett to C.W. Lundy, Superintendent of Welfare, Victoria, B.C., 14 March 1945; ibid., Vol. 29, 'Complaints,' R. Taylor, chairman, DAB, Port Colborne, to Bennett, 18 Oct. 1944; and ibid., C.R. Avery, Industrial Relations Officer, General Engineering Company Ltd., Toronto, to A.E. McMaster, 22 Nov. 1944. Fathers were also eligible for DAB although they too were rigorously investigated. See ibid., Theodore Dumont, Ville Trois Pistole, P.Q., to Bennett, 17 July 1944. Most mothers of soldiers were also ineligible for a mother's allowance and were consigned to local relief. See AO, RG 29, MG 728, Reel 2, Mrs Bender, Mountain Grove, Ont., to Eric Cross, 15 April 1940.

31 AO, RG 29, MG 728, Reel 2, 'Directory of Canadian Community Agencies Serving Dependents of the Forces,' 2; and ibid., Eric Cross to Mrs Baxter, 9 Oct. 1940.

32 UTA, Cassidy Papers, 57:7, 'Interview Notes Ontario 25 July 1942'; PAM, MDAC, Vol. 27, file 'Information,' memorandum re: investigation, 30 Oct. 1939; NAC, Whitton Papers, MG 30 E256, Vol. 5, Gwyneth Howell to Whitton, 9 June 1945; and NAC, DAB, Vol. 28, 'Montreal Welfare Department files,' Eleanor Barnstead, Montreal War Services, to Bennett, 26 June 1944.

33 NAC, DAB, Vol. 28, 'Montreal Welfare Department files,' ROG Bennett to Mr Charles E. Geoffrion, president, Bureau d'Assistance Sociale aux Familles, 31 July 1944.

34 Ibid., memorandum to Mr Bennett, 6 May. 1944; and Bennett to Mrs Elinor Barnstead, 21 July 1944.

35 Ibid., Miss M. Geldard-Brown, Executive Secretary, Directional Service, to Col. J.G. Raymond, DAB, 5 Aug. 1941.

36 NAC, DAB, Vol. 28, 'Montreal Welfare Department,' 'Memo. on Difficulties Experienced by Social Agencies in Financing Families,' n.d.

37 UTA, Cassidy Papers, 55:1, George Davidson, 'Canadian Welfare Services,' Aug. 1943, 7. Davidson later became one of the foremost advocates of family allowances and as Deputy Minister of National Health and Welfare oversaw the implementation and administration of the new Family Allowances Act.

38 NAC, Whitton Papers, Vol. 19, 'Social Services in a State of War,' n.d. Speech to the Vancouver Council of Social Agencies.

39 NAC, DAB, Vol. 29, 'Complaints,' Bennett to secretary, Army Consulting Committee of the Inventions Board, Department of National Defence, 15 March 1945; and ibid., Vol. 3, 'Dependents' Board of Trustees file,' 'The Dependent's Board of Trustees, Its Origin and Development,' Jan. 1942. The chairman of this body was G.M. Weir who was the former Minister of Health and Welfare in Premier Pattullo's Liberal government in British Columbia.

40 PAM, MDAC, Box 22, file B. This case was finally adjudicated in Ottawa, where the chairman of the DAB, R.O.G. Bennett, personally intervened to ensure that the child was returned to its rightful mother.

41 PAM, MDAC, Box 22, file B, A. Roulin to Miss Roe, 22 Feb. 1944.

42 NAC, DAB, Vol. 49, 'Procedures,' A.H. Brown, 'Procedure and Ruling No. 32,' 17 Feb. 1941.

43 NAC, DAB, Vol. 49:28, 'Procedure'; ibid., Vol. 49:39, 'Procedure: Separated Wives, Wives Living Apart and Deserted Wives'; and AO, RG 29-74-1-10, James S. Band, memorandum Dependents' Separation Allowance, 4 Dec. 1939.

44 AO, RG 29-74-1-72, S.C. Legge to E.A. Horton, Director of Unemployment Relief, n.d. 1939.

45 NAC, DAB, Vol. 6, 'Executive Meetings,' 'Minutes,' 13 Dec. 1943.

46 Ibid., 'Minutes,' 7 April 1943.

47 NAC, DAB, Vol. 36, file 'Petitions of Unmarried Applicants,' Bennett to J.L. Ralston, 8 Aug. 1942; ibid., Vol. 1:2–3, 'DAB Rulings and Procedure No. 22,' 15 June 1943; ibid., Vol. 36, 'Petitions of Unmarried Applicants,' D.M. Ormond, 'Memorandum,' 26 Nov. 1942; and PAC, Department of Labour, Vol. 620, 'DAB – Procedure and Rulings,' 2 April 1940. While soldiers who left their wives for another woman were not penalized, women who deserted their husbands for another man were declared 'morally unworthy,' largely because this subverted morale in the armed forces.

48 NAC, DAB, Vol 1:2–3, 'DAB Rulings and Procedure No. 22,' 15 June 1943; and ibid., Vol. 36, 'Petitions of Unmarried Applicants,' D.M. Ormond, 'Memorandum,' 26 Nov. 1942.

49 NAC, DAB, Vol. 36, 'Petitions of Unmarried Applicants,' Arthur Leighton, barrister, Nanaimo, B.C., to R.W. Mayhew, MP, 30 July 1942.

50 NAC, DAB, Vol. 2, 'Conference Chairman file,' Capt. S.A. Sutton, 'The Moral Implications of Person and Family Problems – the Canadian Army,' n.d., 5.

51 NAC, DAB, Vol. 5, 'Executive Meetings,' 'Minutes,' 17 March, 1943.

52 NAC, DAB, Vol. 36, 'Petitions of Unmarried Applications,' Weir and Weir, Barrister and Solicitors, to Bennett, 23 Oct. 1942; Deputy Minister of National Defence to Bennett, 27 Nov. 1942; and G.S. Currie to Bennett, 27 Nov. 1942.

53 NAC, DAB, Vol. 29, 'Complaints,' anonymous letter to DAB, 14 Oct. 1944.

54 NAC, DAB, Vol. 36, 'Petitions by Unmarried Applicants,' 15 Jan. 1940.

55 Ibid., Vol. 36, 'Petitions of Unmarried Applicants,' D.M. Ormond, 'Memorandum,' 26 Nov. 1942. He referred to government funding of legal and common-law wives as 'synchronous polygamy.'

56 NAC, DAB, Vol. 5, 'Executive Meetings,' 'Minutes,' 20 Jan. 1943.

57 NAC, DAB, Vol. 36, 'Petitions of Unmarried Applicants,' Bennett to Director of Administration, Department of National Defence, 8 March 1943. In practice, the breadwinner's obligation to maintain took priority over other variables. Ibid., H.E. Whiffin, memo to DAB, 1 Dec. 1942; ibid., Vol. 6, 'Executive Meetings,' 'Minutes,' 13 Dec. 1943; and ibid., Vol. 1:2–3, Bennett to Mr R.J. Rogers, Department of National Defence, 21 July 1942. Suspensions of wives' allowances for 'improper conduct' were only acted on after vigorous investigation, and in many cases the women were still awarded support if they had children. Ibid., Vol. 50, 'Procedure 40'; and Ruth Robertson to Bennett, F.N. Stapleford to Joseph Laycock, CWC, 24 June 1941. Although a traditional social worker, Stapleford advocated granting aid to immoral wives and their illegitimate children. One of the reasons that many soldiers' claims against their wives were ignored, is that government administrators feared that they were seeking quick divorces so that they might marry their English loves. Ibid., Vol. 6, 'Executive Meetings,' 'Minutes,' 13 Dec. 1943.

58 NAC, DAB, Vol. 3, 'The Dependents' Board of Trustees, Its Origin and Development,' 14. In her article, 'Welfare,' *Canadian Forum*, March 1943, Eleanor Godfrey argued that social work was now unconnected with charity and that social workers broadly interpreted government policies, 354–5.

59 NAC, DAB, Vol. 4, 'Dependents' Board of Trustees,' Minutes of First General Meeting, 12–13 Jan. 1942.

60 UTA, Cassidy Papers, 55:1, 'Canadian Trip 1942,' interview with Miss E.J. Lawson, chief examiner, Dependents' Board of Trustees.

61 PAM, MDAC, Box 22, file A, 4 case files.

62 PAM, MDAC, Box 22, file B, 'Investigator's Report,' 22 Oct. 1943.

63 Harris, *William Beveridge*, 97.

64 B.K. Sandwell, 'The Theory behind the Marsh Report,' *Saturday Night*, 27 March 1943, 6. There was decided conflict within the social work community over whether cash payments would create pauperization or stimulate the work ethic. By the late war, old-style social workers such as Robert

Mills – who together with Whitton had extinguished the family allowance campaign of 1929 – were clearly in the minority. NAC, CCSD, 59:490, Robert Mills, CAS, Toronto, to George Davidson, director, Canadian Welfare Council, 19 Dec. 1944. Davidson succeeded Whitton in this position.

65 PAM, MDAC, Box 22, file A, E.B. Francis to Mrs J. Edmison, 12 Feb. 1944.

66 NAC, DAB, Vol. 49, 'North American Indians file,' Bennett to J.L. Ralston, Minister of National Defence, 2 May 1942; Bennett to Ralson, 6 April 1942; and J.P.B. Ostrander, Indian Agent, Battleford, Sask., to Bennett, 8 Jan. 1942. Native women had their defenders, such as M. Christianson, Superintendent of Indian Agencies; see his note to Bennett, 11 March 1942. Christianson believed that Indian wives 'should be treated the same as white women.' The federal government also didn't pay the full amount due to Indian wives whose children were in residential schools. See also NAC, Department of Labour, Vol. 620, 'Procedure Regarding Payment of Dependents' Allowance and Assigned Pay in the Cases Where Indians Enlist,' 10 Sept. 1940, which noted that large sums of money would demoralize women and cause jealousy. There was also a fear that native women would become accustomed to a higher standard of living, which the returned soldier would not be able to supply, and that this would cause dissension and divorce in native communities. See Ostrander to Bennett, 8 Jan. 1942.

67 PAM, MDAC, Box 24, file Mc, 'Report of E.J. Lawson,' 22 Aug. 1944; and Gertrude Childs to Miss E.J. Lawson, 24 Aug. 1939.

68 NAC, DAB, 6, 'Executive Meetings,' 'Minutes,' 13 Dec. 1943.

69 NAC, DAB, Vol. 2, 'Conference of Chairmen,' 'First Conference of Chairmen of Dependents' Advisory Committees,' 29 June 1943, 13.

70 PAM, MDAC, Box 22, file C. In another case a woman from Charleswood was granted supplementary aid, even though her war pay was well above her budget, because she planned to save to buy a home.

71 NAC, DAB, Vol. 5, 'Executive Committee Meetings,' 'Minutes,' 2 June 1943.

72 NAC, DAB, Vol. 29, 'Complaints,' Bennett to Miss O.J. Waters, private secretary, Minister of National Defence, 3 Dec. 1943.

73 Ibid., Chairman, DAB, to Maj.-Gen. B.W. Browne, 13 Dec. 1940.

74 NAC, DAB, Vol. 14, 'Vancouver file,' C.N. Senior, private secretary to Walter S. Woods, Director of Veterans' Welfare Division, 24 Jan. 1941.

75 NAC, DAB, Vol. 29, 'Complaints,' Bessie Touzel, Welfare Council of Toronto, to J.T. Thorson, Minister of National War Services, 6 Oct. 1941. See also petitions from Vancouver Council of Jewish Women, Vancouver South Christian Temperance Union, Women's Association First United Church, Vancouver, Vancouver Local Council of Women, Women's Auxiliary to Military Units, the League of Women Voters, the Family Bureau of Winnipeg,

and the Catholic Women's League. There were also delegations from municipalities across Canada and the Canadian Legion, which had a private audience with Mackenzie King.

76 NAC, DAB, Vol. 29, 'Complaints,' Alex Walker, Dominion President, Canadian Legion, to Mackenzie King, 3 Sept. 1942, O.T.G. Williamson, Canadian Corps Association to King, 14 Oct. 1942, Gwendolyn Shand, Executive Secretary, Halifax Council of Social Agencies, to A.H. Brown, Acting Chairman, DAB, 18 Sept. 1941. The Canadian Council of Nutrition in Halifax hired Professor E.G. Young of Dalhousie University to undertake a cost of living analysis, which showed that the majority of military families occupied the lowest income groups.

77 NAC, DAB, Vol. 29, 'Complaints,' Bennett to Hon. J.L. Ralston, confidential, 10 Sept. 1942; ibid., Vol. 6, 'Dependents' Board of Trustees – Correspondence,' Jack Pembroke to Col. G.S. Currie, 6 Oct. 1942; and NAC, Ian Mackenzie Papers, 72:G-25, 'Memorandum on Social Security,' 1943. As of August 1942, a mother and one child received $67.00 per month, a woman and two children $79.00, a woman and three children $88.00, four children $94.00, and those with five to eight children received a flat rate of $6.00 per child. This downward sliding scale became the template for the Family Allowances Act of 1944. See ibid., 'Minutes of the Meeting Attended by the Chairman of the Dependents' Allowance Board and the Interservice Committee,' 3 Aug. 1942.

At the same time, benefits for mothers of soldiers were raised, and wives were allowed to make up to $40.00 per month working before deductions were made. Military benefits had a direct impact on the raising of wartime mothers' allowance levels; but more interestingly, federal military family policy altered the principles underlying mothers' allowances insofar as it deemed one part of her income as her own income – a decisive departure from the ideology of children's benefits, and one that was in keeping with the general wartime emphasis on the fact that government aid to women was allocated on the basis of their being wives and was thus derived from a man's citizenship rights. NAC, DAB, 'Mother's Allowance files,' C.W. Lundy, Superintendent of Welfare, B.C., to Bennett, 26 July 1943, Dr F.W. Jackson, Deputy Minister of Health and Welfare, MB, to A. MacNamara, 5 April 1940, Bennett to Miss R. Robertson, 25 Jan. 1944; AO, RG 29, MG728, reel 1, 'Brief to Hon. R.O Vivian, Minister of Health and Public Welfare,' 29 Sept. 1943; and NAC, CCSD, 63: Mother's Allowances 1941–43, Bessie Touzel to Harold J. Kirby, Minister of Health and Welfare, Ont., 31 March 1943.

78 MUA, Principal James Papers, RG2, 192:6603, George Davidson, 'Welfare Activities, Governmental and Private,' n.d.

79 Margaret Strong, 'Welfare Services – Canada,' *Canadian Welfare* 3, no. 2 (Oct. 1942): 11–13.

80 NAC, Ian Mackenzie Papers, 52:519–36(3), Alex Ross, memorandum to C.N. Senior, Department of Pensions and Health, 11 May 1944.

81 House of Commons, Special Committee on Social Security, *Minutes and Proceedings of Evidence*, testimony of Leonard Marsh, 9 June 1943, 92.

82 NAC, DAB, Vol. 29, 'Complaints,' J.W. Knight to Department of National Defence, 3 Dec. 1940.

83 PAM, Social Planning Council of Winnipeg, P642, file 12, 'Minutes of Council Meeting,' 22 June 1942; and S. Eckler, 'A Programme for Employment Security,' *Saturday Night*, 26 Sept. 1942, 8.

84 R.S. Lambert, 'Learning – and What Next?' *Food for Thought*, Feb. 1941, 10. See also Lambert, 'Our Other War Aim,' ibid., April 1941, 4.

85 NAC, Vol. 2, 'Letters of Appreciation file,' Ernest Majury to DAB, 18 April 1947; ibid., Vol. 4, 'Dependents' Board of Trustees,' 'The Report of the Retiring Chair, Dr G.M. Weir,' 27 May 1942, 3. It might also be argued that the impetus toward a national health insurance program also emerged from the work of the DBT.

86 NAC, CCSD, 29:147, 'Evidence of Good-Will,' *Winnipeg Tribune*, n.d.

87 NAC, Canadian Congress of Labour Papers [CCL], Vol. 342, 'Full Employment file,' J.R. Beattie, 'Some Aspects of the Problem of Full Employment,' *Canadian Journal of Economics and Political Science* 10, no. 3 (Aug. 1944): 339. Charlotte Whitton also accepted the link between social security and prosperity. NAC, Whitton Papers, 5: Correspondence June 1945, Whitton to W.H. Williamson, Federal Security Agency, Washington, 13 June 1945.

88 Violet Anderson, ed., *Canada and the World Tomorrow* (Toronto: Ryerson Press, 1944), vii; and NAC, Ian Mackenzie Papers, 40:G-25, 'Social Security Consultation on Income Maintenance and Medical Care,' n.d.

89 B.S. Keirstead, 'National Policy,' in Alexander Brady and F.R. Scott, eds., *Canada After the War: Studies in Political, Social and Economic Policies for Post-War Canada* (Toronto: Macmillan, 1943), 17.

90 UTA, Harold Innis Papers, B72/0025, 004/02, J.J. Talman, 'To Members of the Provincial History Centre Committee,' n.d.; and Max W. Ball, President, Abasand Oils Ltd., Edmonton, *The Essential Freedom* (pamphlet), 20 Nov. 1941, n.p. For the older tradition of historical writing that gave priority to culture over the institutions of the political state, see Christie, '"Prophecy and the Principles of Social Life."'

91 MUA, Cyril James Personal Papers, Vol. 5, Mrs E.M. Mellor to James, 21 July 1941, describing the tidal wave of the common man as the engine of the social security movement.

92 Sir Robert Falconer, 'Forward,' in Philip Child and J.W. Holmes, *Dynamic Democracy* (Behind the Headlines, 9 May 1941), 2.

93 'State Spends What People Earn,' *Globe and Mail*, 19 March 1943; and 'Welfare in a Democracy,' *Canadian Welfare* 16, no. 2 (April–May 1942): 3.

94 *Canadian Home Journal*, Sept. 1945, 69; 'Planning for Post-War Canada,' *Canadian Forum* 23, no. 268 (May 1943): 40; Stanley McConnell, 'The Menace of Collectivism,' *Saturday Night*, 19 Sept. 1942, 35; and MUA, Cyril James Personal Papers, Vol. 5, 'People Must Dictate Peace – Mackenzie Says,' news clipping, n.d.

95 Paul Martin, *Labour's Post-War World* (Behind the Headlines, 5:1, 1945), 3, 7–8, 12–13. See also Francis Flaherty, 'A Conservative Philosophy,' *Saturday Night*, 19 Sept. 1942.

96 *Canadian Home Journal*, Oct. 1943, 25.

97 MUA, Principal James Papers, 188:6585, Père Emile Bouvier, L'Ecole Service Sociale, University of Montreal, 'Memorandum,' 1942, 8–9.

98 Philip Child and J.W. Holmes, *Dynamic Democracy* (Behind the Headlines, No. 9, May 1941), 24; Gwendolyn M. Carter, *Consider the Record* (Behind the Headlines, 2:6, 1942), 6–7; Ronald Oliver MacFarlane, *Canada and the Post-War World* (Behind the Headlines, 2:5, 1942), 20; MUA, Principal James Papers, 188:6515, P. Ackerman, Electrical Engineer, to James, 2 Aug. 1943, James to Ackerman, 6 July 1943; S. Eckler, 'The War for Social Security,' *Saturday Night*, 15 Aug. 1942, 12; and UTA, Cassidy Papers, 54:6, Donald Leslie, 'Is Canada Ready for the Peace?' *Calgary Herald*, 29 May 1943.

99 Beverly Baxter, 'Charter of the Future,' *Maclean's Magazine*, 1 Jan. 1943, 32. Baxter was a Canadian politician who was elected as a Conservative MP in Britain during the war.

100 'The Psychological Importance of Children's Allowances,' *Toronto Star*, 19 July 1944; B.K. Sandwell, 'The Theory Behind the Marsh Report,' *Saturday Night*, 27 March 1943, 6–7.

101 NAC, Ian Mackenzie Papers, 40:G-25, 'Social Security Consultation on Income Maintenance and Medical Care,' n.d.

102 S. Eckler, 'The War for Social Security,' *Saturday Night*, 15 Aug. 1942, 12.

103 House of Commons Special Committee on Social Security, *Minutes and Proceedings of Evidence*, 9 June 1943, testimony of Leonard Marsh, 71.

104 University of British Columbia Library, Department of Special Collections, Leonard Marsh Papers, Marsh to Beveridge, 1 July 1944.

105 MUA, Cyril F. James Personal Papers, MG1017, Box 4, C.W. Peterson, editor, *Farm and Ranch Review*, Calgary, to James, 28 July 1941.

106 NAC, Ian Mackenzie Papers, 72:544–29, Noseworthy to Mackenzie, 21 May 1942 (Author's emphasis).

107 NAC, Ian Mackenzie Papers, 45:M-2, 'Report on Post-War Reconstruction Policies,' 1944.
108 MUA, James Personal Papers, Box 4, C.W. Peterson to James, 28 July 1941.
109 NAC, Whitton Papers, 5: 'Correspondence June 1945,' Whitton to V.R. Smith, President Confederation Life Association, 13 June 1945.
110 MUA, Principal James Papers, 189:6542, James to Dr Robert Warren, Institute of Advanced Studies, Princeton, N.J., 24 March 1941; ibid., 192:6603, 'Reconstruction Planning Organization in Canada,' Sept. 1941; and 'Social Security Plan Giving Voice to People's Aspirations,' *Toronto Star*, 17 March 1943.
111 NAC, Ian Mackenzie Papers, Vol. 95, 'Reconstruction Committee,' Robert England to Mackenzie, 7 May 1941.
112 MUA, Principal James Papers, 192:6603, 'Reconstruction Planning Organization'; and ibid., 192:660, 'Reconstitution of Postwar Reconstruction Advisory Bodies.' A large number of Canadian economists, geographers, sociologists, and political scientists served in research capacities. See UTA, Innis Papers, 01/05, Burton S. Keirstead to Innis, 22 Aug. 1940, H.R. Kemp to Innis, 25 Feb. 1941; and ibid., 01/06 Marsh to Innis, 30 May 1942. Marsh, like James, wanted to use the committee as a model for a permanent research department within the federal government. This did not happen. See MUA, F. Cyril James Personal Papers, Vol. 5, 'Report on the Present Governmental Organization and Policy in the United Kingdom,' 6 April 1942.
113 MUA, Principal James Papers, 189:6607, James to Dr W.H. Coates, Imperial Chemical Industries Ltd., 24 July 1944. The first real impact of Keynesian thought occurred in government circles during the Second World War. For an alternative view see Doug Owram, *The Government Generation: Canadian Intellectuals and the State, 1900–1945* (Toronto: University of Toronto Press, 1986), 200–1. This early genesis of Keynesian ideas in Canada is highly untenable, given that neither Britain nor the United States instituted Keynesian-inspired budgets until 1945. See George C. Peden, 'Old Dogs and New Tricks: The British Treasury and Keynesian Economics in the 1940s and 1950s,' and William J. Barber, 'Government as a Laboratory for Economic Learning in the Years of the Democratic Roosevelt,' in Mary O. Furner and Barry Supple, eds., *The State and Economic Knowledge: The American and British Experiences* (Cambridge: Cambridge University Press, 1990). For the best revisionist assessment of Keynesian planning, see Ritschel, *The Politics of Planning*.
114 MUA, F. Cyril James Personal Papers, Vol. 4, Robert Newton, 'The Wise

Utilisation of Our Resources,' 21 May 1941. For a revisionist perspective on Keynesianism, see Ritschel, *The Politics of Planning*, 313.

115 NAC, Whitton Papers, 28: 'Correspondence 1943–45,' W.R. Williamson, 'Review of the Dawn of an Ampler Life,' 9 Jan. 1945. On the influence of PEP on Beveridge, see Harris, *William Beveridge*, 380.

116 NAC, Ian Mackenzie Papers, 46:CNS-2, 'Reconstruction Committee,' James to Mackenzie, 17 June 1941; MUA, Principal James Papers, 188:6515, P.C. Armstrong, CPR, to James, 18 Oct. 1943; ibid., 189:6545, E.A. Brownell to James, 19 Dec. 1944; and 'Why Some Support Family Allowances,' *Financial Post*, 29 July 1944.

117 MUA, Principal James Papers, 188:6533, 'Committee on Reconstruction Memorandum,' 27 March 1941; ibid., 188:6515, P. Ackermann to James, 2 Aug. 1943; and MUA, F. Cyril James Personal Papers, Vol. 7, 'Committee on Reconstruction Memorandum,' n.d., 3.

118 MUA, Principal James Papers, 189:6523, 'Advisory Committee on Reconstruction Report,' 24 Sept. 1943, 81.

119 MUA, F. Cyril James Personal Papers, Vol. 6, 'Social Insurance,' P.C. Armstrong, 'The Theory of Social Insurance,' n.d., 12.

120 MUA, Cyrial James Personal Papers, Box 5, 'Report on the Present Governmental Organization of Policy,' 6 April 1943, 32.

121 A. Brady, 'Reconstruction in Canada: A Note on Policies and Plans,' *Canadian Journal of Economics and Political Science* 8 (1942): 465–8.

122 MUA, Principal James Papers, 188:6515, James to P.C. Armstrong, 9 Feb. 1943; and ibid., 187:6613, James to Lord McGowan, 4 Jan. 1942. Alvin Hansen was invited by James to address the Canadian government in 1942. See ibid., 189:6616, James to Dr Lionel Robbins, Cabinet Secretariat, England, 3 Nov. 1942; and NAC, William Lyon Mackenzie King Papers, MG 26 J1, Vol. 342, John J. Kinley, Lunenberg, N.S., to King, 22 Dec. 1943, on the uses of family allowances to serve the needs of capitalism.

123 House of Commons, Special Committee on Reconstruction and Re-Establishment, *Minutes of Proceedings and Evidence*, testimony of Principal James, 9–11 March 1943, 18.

124 UTA, Cassidy Papers, 55:1, Cassidy to Ian Mackenzie, 31 Jan. 1944.

125 NAC, King Papers, Vol. 328, Mackenzie to King, 9 Dec. 1942.

126 NAC, Mackenzie Papers, Vol. 79:562–27 (2), Mackenzie to deputy minister, 12 Jan. 1942.

127 MUA, Principal James Papers, 192:6603, James to Marsh, 17 Feb. 1943, Marsh to James, 17 Feb. 1943. The Marsh report had been initiated by James as a subsection of his own report in Jan. 1943, following on the heels of the release of the famous Beveridge Report. It must be noted that

Leonard Marsh personally believed that social security had no integrity
apart from policies of full employment; see above, Marsh to James, 17 Feb.
1943. Marsh had worked hard within the James committee to transform its
agenda toward his interests. See UTA, Cassidy Papers, 31:3, Marsh to
Cassidy, 8 July 1941.

128 MUA, F. Cyril James Personal Papers, Vol. 6, 'Social Insurance,' Vincent
Massey to James, 10 Dec. 1942. On the public impact of the Beveridge
Report, see Harris, *William Beveridge*, 381.

129 NAC, Ian Mackenzie Papers, 79:562–27 (2), Charles E. Campbell to Mac-
kenzie, 11 Dec. 1941; and B.K. Sandwell, 'From Malthus and Brougham to
Beveridge,' *Saturday Night*, 9 Jan. 1943; and CMAG, review of 'A Plan for
Britain,' *Canadian Forum* 21, no. 244 (May 1941). There was very little press
criticism of the Beveridge Report. See 'Beveridge Scheme in a Nutshell,'
Industrial Canada 43, no. 9 (Jan. 1943); 'Beveridge Plan is Made Public,'
Montreal Star, 1 Dec. 1942; and MUA, Principal James Papers, 189:6545,
'Canada Seen Needing a Beveridge Plan,' *Christian Science Monitor*, clip-
ping, n.d.

130 UTA, Cassidy Papers, 32:5, 'The Beveridge Report,' paper presented to
Berkeley Club, 1943; and Martin Bell, 'A Cabinet Minister on Post-War
Reconstruction,' *Canadian Forum* 21, no. 262 (Nov. 1942): 235.

131 NAC, Ian Mackenzie Papers, 79:562–27 (2), Mackenzie memorandum,
'Progressive Conservative Platform,' Dec. 1942; and ibid., Walter S. Woods
to Mackenzie, 18 Dec. 1942.

132 NAC, King Papers, Vol. 320, G.M. Weir to King, 3 Sept. 1941; NAC, DAB,
Vol. 4, 'Dependents' Board of Trustees,' 'Minutes of Executive Committee,'
29 April 1942; and ibid., Vol. 7, 'Cost of Living file,' 'Canadian Institute of
Public Opinion News Service Release,' 25 Nov. 1942.

133 NAC, Ian Mackenzie Papers, 46:CNS2, 'Reconstruction Committee,' Robert England to Mackenzie, 23 Oct. 1941; and NAC, King Papers, Vol. 301,
Joseph Caine to King, 24 Dec. 1940.

134 Eugene Forsey, 'Review of Harry Cassidy, *Social Security and Reconstruction
in Canada*,' *Canadian Unionist*, April 1943, 269; Tom Moore, 'Organized
Labour and the War Economy,' in J.F. Parkinson, ed., *Canadian War Economics* (Toronto: University of Toronto Press, 1941), 170; NAC, King
Papers, Vol. 324, Flavelle to King, 8 Jan. 1942; ibid., Vol. 272, Ian Mackenzie
to King, 30 Oct. 1939; and ibid., 302, Hughes Cleaver, MP, Burlington to
King, 9 Oct. 1941.

135 NAC, King Papers, Vol. 328, H.B. McKinnon to King, 19 Dec. 1942; and
MUA, Principal James Papers, 189:6577, Rev J.C. Beaudoin to James, 11 Dec.
1942, who voiced the concerns of the Catholic trade unions in Quebec.

136 UBC, Special Collections, Marsh Papers, 29–30, Albert Duncan to Marsh, 17 March 1945, stating that Canada only passes welfare legislation when Britain does.

137 MUA, Principal James Papers, 189:6606, James to R.A. Butler, President, Board of Education, Jan. 1943; and James to Ernest Bevin, Minister of Labour, 18 Feb. 1943. On R.A. Butler, see Ritschel, *The Politics of Planning*, 343. Bevin and James were in accord insofar as they both opposed the idea of placing social security measures ahead of government creation of jobs. On Bevin, see Pedersen, *Family, Dependence and the Origins of the Welfare State*, 344.

138 Ibid., 189:6545, Beveridge to James, 4 Nov. 1942.

139 MUA, Cyril James Personal Papers, Vol. 7, 'Reconstruction,' 'Comments on Glenday's Report,' 13 March 1943.

140 MUA, Cyril James Personal Papers, Vol. 7, 'Basic Memoranda,' James, 'The Beveridge Report: Some Implications for Canada,' speech to the Canadian Club of Montreal, 18 Jan. 1943; and MUA, Principal James Papers, 189:6613, James to Lord McGowan, Imperial Chemical Industries, 4 Jan. 1943. Lord Harry McGowan was a British sponsor of capitalist planning and, like James, endorsed business leadership in postwar reconstruction. See Ritschel, *The Politics of Planning*, 215. James promoted the Lever Brothers concept of monetary and industrial planning in which government would foster capital investment and stable employment. 'The Problem of Unemployment,' *Industrial Canada*, April 1943, 61; and 'We Interview the Lever Plan,' *Canadian Business*, April 1943. These were clear responses to the Marsh and Beveridge Reports.

141 UBC, Special Collections, Marsh Papers, Scott to Marsh, 18 March 1943.

142 'Ottawa Press Releases Not According to Plan,' *Globe and Mail*, 18 March 1943; and UTA, Cassidy Papers, 59:5, Marsh to Cassidy, 18 Feb. 1943.

143 MUA, Principal James Papers, 192:6603, James to Marsh, 17 Feb. 1943.

144 That Marsh had long been hatching a plan to wrest control away from James was noted by Whitton. See UTA, Cassidy Papers, 31:3, Whitton to Cassidy, 28 July 1941.

145 UTA, Cassidy Papers, 55:1, Cassidy to Marsh, 27 March 1944. Marsh was thus forced to concede that his report only reflected his 'personal views.' Ibid., 59:3, Mackenzie to Cassidy, 5 Jan. 1944; NAC, Mackenzie Papers, 79:562–27 (4), Mackenzie to J.W. McConnell, 17 March 1943; and ibid., Ilsley to Mackenzie, 17 March 1943.

146 UTA, Cassidy Papers, 18:1, Cassidy to Marsh, 18 June 1943, with his enclosed review of Marsh for the *American Historical Review*; ibid., 32:1,

Cassidy to Kay, 18 April 1943; and ibid., 54:5, Cassidy to Marsh, 20 Nov, 1942.

147 UTA, Cassidy Papers, 59:4, Davidson to Cassidy, 12 March 1943; and NAC, Whitton Papers, 4: 'Correspondence Jan.–Aug. 1943,' Marsh to Whitton, 27 Jan. 1943. Marsh had tried to entice Whitton and Cassidy on board as collaborators in order to squelch criticism. See MUA, Principal James Papers, 192:6603, Marsh to James, 13 Jan. 1943. Stuart Jaffray was a graduate of the University of Alberta, where he studied labour economics and the rise of the One Big Union. He obtained his doctorate from the School of Social Service Administration at the University of Chicago, with a specialization in prison reform. See University of Toronto, Thomas Fisher Rare Books, Jaffray Papers, 1: 'Correspondence 1936–41,' Jaffray to Cassidy, 19 July 1938, Jaffray to Miss Edith Abbott, 17 Nov. 1937.

148 Marsh, 'Introduction,' *Report on Social Security for Canada*, xiii.

149 NAC, Ian Mackenzie Papers, 95:652-27 (8), 'Biographical File – Leonard Marsh.' Marsh had graduated in 1928 from the London School of Economics, where for a brief time he had done research for Beveridge in the New Survey of London Life and Labour (1929–30). In 1931 he moved to McGill, where he completed his PhD.

150 UTA, Cassidy Papers, 59:5, Marsh to Cassidy, 15 Jan. 1943.

151 On a more feminist conception of social security, see Eva M. Hubback, 'Family Allowances in Great Britain,' *Public Affairs*, Dec. 1940, 83; and D.H. Stepler, *Family Allowances for Canada?* (Behind the Headlines, 3:2, 1942), 23. As these two publications make clear, Marsh was not the first to publicize family allowances in Canada during wartime. For a gender analysis of the Beveridge Report, see Pedersen, *Family, Dependence and the Origins of the Welfare State*, 337–40.

152 Marsh, *Report on Social Security for Canada*, 210–13; 'Social Security,' *The Labour Gazette*, April 1943, 2; and UTA, Cassidy Papers, 18:01, Cassidy to Marsh, 18 June 1943, on the fact that Marsh conceived of social insurance need based on a husband, a wife, and one child. On the continuing emphasis upon the preeminance of the male 'family' wage, see MUA, Cyril James Personal Papers, 6: 'Nutrition file,' 'Family Income and Expenditure in Canada, 1937–38 (A Study of Wage-Earning Families, Including Data on Physical Attributes),' (Ottawa: King's Printer, 1941), 10–11. It showed that in English-Canadian families only a mere 2 per cent of family income was supplied by those other than the 'family head.'

153 UTA, Cassidy Papers, 71:1, Marsh to Cassidy, 28 July 1933.

154 Marsh, *Canadians In and Out of Work*, 446.

155 These sliding scales, which reduced payments to large families, were

finally amended in 1954. See NAC, CCSD, 58:490, Peter Stanne, Secretary, Family and Child Welfare Division, CWC, to Miss Margaret Conliffe, Cornwall Family Welfare Bureau, 2 Dec. 1954.

156 See, for example, H.F. Greenway and D.L. Ralston, 'Household Budgets of Wage-Earners in Canadian Cities,' *Public Affairs*, Aug. 1940, 10.

157 MUA, Principal James Papers, 192:6603, Marsh to James, 17 Feb. 1943.

158 MUA, Cyril James Personal Papers, 6: 'Social Insurance,' 'Committee on Reconstruction, Interim Report on Social Security in Canada,' confidential, n.d., 3; and UTA, Cassidy Papers, 59:5, Marsh to Cassidy, 15 Jan. 1943.

159 MUA, Principal James Papers, 192:6603, Marsh to K.M. Cameron, Department of Public Works, 9 July 1942.

160 Harris, *William Beveridge*, 430–4.

161 MUA, Principal James Papers, 192:6603, Marsh to James, 22 March 1943.

162 MUA, Principal James Papers, 192:6603, Marsh to James, 17 Feb. 1943.

163 'Marsh – the Man and his Plan,' *The Standard Magazine*, 27 March 1943; and Anne Fomer, 'Social Security in Canada,' *Saturday Night*, 20 March 1943, 6.

164 House of Commons Special Committee on Social Security, *Minutes and Proceedings of Evidence*, testimony of Leonard Marsh, 9 June 1943, 72.

165 François-Albert Angers, 'French Canada and Social Security,' *Canadian Journal of Economics and Political Science* 10 (1944): 355–64.

166 H.J. Cody, 'Recapitulation and the Ideals of Reconstruction,' in C.A. Ashley, ed., *Reconstruction in Canada: Lectures Given in the University of Toronto* (Toronto: University of Toronto Press, 1943), 138–40. The Beveridge plan was more socialist in its bias than Marsh's. See House of Commons Special Committee on Social Security, *Minutes and Proceedings of Evidence*, testimony of Beveridge, 25 May 1943, 369.

167 MUA, Principal James Papers, 189:6545, James to Mr Bing-Shuey Lee, First Secretary, Legation of the Republic of China, 12 April 1943; and Cassidy, 'Review of Leonard Marsh, *Report on Social Security for Canada*,' *American Historical Review* 33, no. 3 (Sept. 1943): 709.

168 UTA, Cassidy Papers, 15:1, 5 April 1943.

169 UTA): Cassidy Papers, 18:1, Cassidy to Marsh, 4 March 1943.

170 Cassidy mailed a copy of his 'Three Social Security Plans for Canada,' *Public Affairs* (Winter 1944), a comparison of Marsh, Cassidy, and Whitton, to all and sundry, including the Prime Minister himself. UTA, Cassidy Papers, 54:5, Mackenzie King to Cassidy, 20 Dec. 1943; and ibid., 55:1, Cassidy to King, 10 Dec. 1943.

171 MUA, Principal James Papers, 192:6603, Marsh to James, 7 July 1943.

172 UTA, Cassidy Papers, 18:1, Cassidy to Davidson, 16 June 1943.

173 NAC, Whitton Papers, 4: 'Correspondence Jan.–June 1944,' Cassidy to Whitton, 6 Jan. 1944. Although George Davidson publicly supported Marsh, he worked behind the scenes to undermine Marsh, as did Marsh's former League for Social Reconstruction colleague, Dal Grauer. See UTA, Cassidy Papers, 55:1, Cassidy to Davidson, 4 April 1944; and ibid., 54:5, Dal to Harry, 2 May 1943.

174 NAC, Whitton Papers, 4: 'Correspondence Sept.–Dec. 1943,' Cassidy to Whitton, 18 Nov. 1943.

175 UTA, Cassidy Papers, 13:5, Cassidy to Grauer, 16 Oct. 1937.

176 Ibid.; and UTA, Cassidy Papers, 55:1, Cassidy to George Davidson, 3 April 1944.

177 UTA, Cassidy Papers, 63:1, Cassidy, 'Public Reorganization in Canada I,' *Public Affairs* 5, no. 2 (Winter 1941): 86.

178 UTA, Cassidy Papers, 18:1, Cassidy to S. Eckler, 12 April 1943. In 1942, Cassidy was somewhat circumspect about family allowances. See ibid., Cassidy to John W. Holmes, Canadian Institute of International Affairs, 26 Oct. 1942, Holmes to Cassidy, 6 Oct. 1942; and ibid., Cassidy to R.W. McBurney, Canadian Institute of International Affairs, 26 Aug. 1942.

179 UTA, Cassidy Papers, 62:1, Cassidy, 'Government Aid to Marriage and Parenthood among Service Men'; and NAC, Whitton Papers, 4: 'Correspondence,' 15 Feb. 1944. Pronatalism was a decidedly minority voice among the supporters of family allowances. For an example of this reasoning, see Steven Cartwright, *Population Canada's Problem* (Toronto: Ryerson Press, 1941).

180 UTA, Cassidy Papers, 62:1, Cassidy, 'Family Allowances – the Keystone of Social Security,' 16 June 1947, 8–10.

181 MUA, Cyril James Personal Papers, 6: 'Social Insurance,' Cassidy, 'A Social Security Programme for Canada,' 15 July 1942, 6. In this regard, Cassidy's outlook owed much to the Beveridge scheme. See UTA, Cassidy Papers, 32:5, Cassidy, 'Review of *Social Insurance and Allied Services* by Sir William Beveridge,' *San Francisco Chronicle*, Dec. 1942, 5.

182 Whitton was not the only advocate of these. See CCSD, 58:490, E.J. Lawson, Department of National Defence, DAB, to Davidson, 28 July 1944, Gwendolyn Shand, Halifax Council of Social Agencies, to Davidson, 8 Feb. 1944; and ibid., 77:568, Miss Caroline McInnes, Halifax, to Nora Lea, 26 Dec. 1945. On Whitton's concept of social utilities, see Struthers, *The Limits of Affluence*, 129–31.

183 Cassidy, 'Three Social Security Plans for Canada,' 71.

184 UTA, Cassidy Papers, 57:4, Bessie Touzel to Cassidy, 16 Dec. 1943.

185 AO, RG29–01–2085, file 'Social Workers 1938–70,' 'Brief by the Canadian

Association of Social Workers on the Marsh Report,' 2; NAC, CCSD, 77:568, Nora Lea to Cassidy, 26 April 1945; UTA, Cassidy Papers, 57:3, Toronto Welfare Council, 'Council Comments,' VI:4, April 1943; and 'Approved Cash Allowances,' *Montreal Gazette*, 22 July 1944. The Montreal branch of the CASW endorsed family allowances, but also social utilities.

186 AO RG29-01-2085, 'Brief by the Canadian Association of Social Workers,' 3. For the traditional concern with family stability, see UTA, Cassidy Papers, 58:2, 'New Notes,' 3 Dec. 1943, noting regional social work addresses entitled 'The Effect of the War upon Children,' 'Case Work Services for Unmarried Mothers,' and 'The Impact of War upon Family Life'; ibid., 58:3, 'Child Labor Scored by Social Agencies'; ibid., 55:1, Cassidy to Touzel, 28 Dec. 1943, noting her memo to Toronto City Council on delinquency; and NAC, King Papers, 385, Nora Lea, acting executive director, CWC, to King, 22 June 1945, on the problem of broken homes and juvenile delinquency.

187 UTA, Cassidy Papers, 16:4, Whitton to Cassidy, 4 Feb. 1942; and ibid., 18:1, Cassidy to Davidson. With political astuteness, Cassidy announced to Davidson his pleasure that Whitton's 'exhortation and admonition' had been removed from the CWC.

188 'Dr. George F. Davidson,' *Canadian Welfare* 17, no. 8 (Feb. 1942): 4–5; 'Two Canadian Welfare Executives Receive New Appointments,' *The Canadian Welfare Summary* 14, no. 5 (Jan. 1939): 34.

189 NAC, CCSD, 58:490, 'Notes on Some of the Effects of Family Allowances on Child Care Organizations,' n.d.

190 NAC, CCSD, 58:490, Davidson to Robert Mills, 1 Aug. 1944, Davidson to J.J. Vaughan, President United Welfare Chest, Toronto, 27 July 1944, Davidson to F.N. Stapleford, 23 March 1944. These pamphlets addressed themes such as food management, child training, and sex instruction. See CCSD, 58:490, E.R. McEwan to Mrs McLellan, 3 Jan, 1949, Mrs D.B. Sinclair to Bessie Touzel, 21 Dec. 1948.

191 NAC, CCSD, 58:490, 'Impact of the Federal Government Program on Local Agencies,' confidential, n.d., George Davidson memorandum to Minister, 22 May 1946, 1–2.

192 UTA, Cassidy Papers, 59:4, Davidson to Cassidy, 12 March 1943; Frances Weekes, 'Draft Outline and Summary, Report on Provincial Welfare Services,' 29 June 1943; and Davidson, 'The Future Development in the Social Services,' n.d., 12–16. Marsh also believed in abolishing provincial mothers' allowances. See ibid., 41:2, Cassidy, 'The Marsh Report,' *Canadian Affairs*, 15 Nov. 1943.

193 See the interesting exchange between Davidson and Mills on defending

family independence and the breadwinner ideal, in which Davidson posits that government aid will not undermine traditional gender relations. NAC, CCSD, 58:490, Davidson to Mills, 16 Aug. 1944.

194 UTA, Cassidy Papers, 72:1, 'Conference on Social Security Plan,' 4 Oct. 1947; Cassidy, 'Notes on Interview with Skelton, Beattie, Coyne, and Howes of the Bank of Canada,' n.d., 4; ibid., 61:1, Cassidy, 'Summary and Conclusions to a Canadian Program of Social Security,' report to Paul Martin, 16 Dec. 1947; and ibid., 18:1, Cassidy to Davidson, 23 June 1943.

195 For Drew's response, see NAC, George Drew Papers, 20:176, F.W. Bryce to H.A. Bruce, 1 Aug. 1944; ibid., 54:473a, Howard Ryan to Drew, 10 Aug. 1944; and ibid., 131:1329, Drew to Rev C.E. Silcox, 6 Nov. 1945. Doug Owram in *The Government Generation*, 322, has characterized these provincial responses as mere partisanship and obstructionism.

196 UTA, Cassidy Papers, 31:3, Whitton to Cassidy, 25 Oct. 1937, in which she related health insurance to the work of the Division of Maternal and Child Welfare within the Department of Pensions and Health.

197 'Charlotte Whitton Answers,' *Ottawa Citizen*, 14 and 18 July 1944.

198 NAC, Whitton Papers, 4: 'Correspondence Jan.–June 1944,' George Grant to Whitton, 10 Jan. 1944, with Whitton's pencilled reply.

199 Whitton, 'British Baby Bonus,' *Ottawa Citizen*, 27 Dec. 1944; and NAC, Whitton Papers, 4: 'Correspondence Jan.–June 1944,' George Davidson to Whitton, 31 Jan. 1944, Whitton to Davidson, 17 Feb. 194, Davidson to Whitton, 28 Feb. 1944. Davidson argued that Whitton's program emphasized 'replacement of income' rather than protection against hazards.

200 NAC, Whitton Papers, 4: 'Correspondence Jan.–Aug. 1943,' Whitton to Marsh, 6 Feb. 1943.

201 NAC, Whitton Papers, 4: 'Correspondence April 1945,' Ronald Hambleton, 'Book for the Times,' 13 March 1945. For Bracken's political slipperiness, see NAC, Drew Papers, 20:176, Dr James Glendinning to H.A. Bruce, 5 Aug. 1944.

202 Before family allowances became an obvious political weapon, Silcox had mildly endorsed them and the fiscal policies that underlay them. See 'Monetary Policy and Reconstruction: Review of Alvin H. Hansen's "Fiscal Policy and Business Cycles,"' *Food for Thought* 11, no. 9 (May 1942): 9–10.

203 NAC, Whitton Papers, 5: 'Correspondence Nov. 1945,' Whitton to Frank Flemington, The Ryerson Press, 20 Nov. 1945, Lorne Pierce to Whitton, 26 Nov. 1945; ibid., 'Correspondence Aug. 1945,' Silcox to Whitton, 8 Aug. 1945. That Pierce agreed to publish Gould's pamphlet, which he knew had

been ghost-written by Cassidy, indicates clearly how marginal Whitton's perspective had become.

204 Whitton, 'Baby Bonus Puzzles Ottawa,' *Public Opinion*, July 1944, 7; and Whitton, 'We're Calling the Baby Einstein,' *Ottawa Citizen*, n.d., in which she criticizes the 'brains trust' in Ottawa. By 1945 Whitton was firmly aligned with Premier George Drew. See NAC, Whitton Papers, 5: 'Correspondence June 1945,' Whitton to Drew, 26 June 1945.

205 NAC, Whitton Papers, 4: 'Correspondence Jan.–June 1944,' Whitton to Cassidy, 3 Feb. 1944.

206 Ibid., 'Correspondence May 1945,' C.W. Tobey, Orillia to Whitton. Whitton had less kind things to say of Bracken in private. See ibid., 'Correspondence June 1945,' Whitton to Senator A.C. Hardy, 29 June 1945: 'John Bracken takes as long as your letter to make his mind up and then keeps his "make-up" box handy in case he wants to put on a different face.'

207 Ibid. For Whitton's anti-Quebec comments, see John Kendle, *John Bracken: A Political Biography* (Toronto: University of Toronto Press, 1979).

208 NAC, Whitton Papers, 5: 'Correspondence June 1945,' Whitton to V.R. Smith, 13 June 1945, Cassidy to Whitton, 18 June 1945, Rev J. Mutchmor to Whitton, 12 June 1945; and ibid., 'Correspondence Jan.–June 1944,' Whitton to Dr E.A. Corbett, Adult Education Association, 5 Jan. 1944.

209 UTA, Cassidy Papers, 59:3, Davidson to Cassidy, 28 April 1943; ibid., 15:3, Richter to Cassidy, 6 Nov. 1943; and ibid., 55:1, Pierce to Cassidy, 29 April 1943.

210 UTA, Cassidy Papers, 57:4, Touzel to Cassidy, 4 Jan. 1943; NAC, CCSD, 59:490, Mrs K. Jackson, exec. sec., to Miss Mae Flemming, Family Allowance Division, Department of Health and Welfare, 3 May 1946; 'Social Workers and Family Allowances,' *Toronto Star*, 11 March 1944; and 'State Family Allowances,' *Evening Citizen*, 4 July 1944.

211 'Family Allowances: The Dole,' *Ottawa Journal*, 27 June 1944; and 'Dr. Charlotte Whitton's Alternatives,' *Peterborough Examiner*, 3 Nov. 1943.

212 NAC, Whitton Papers, 4: 'Correspondence July–Dec. 1944,' Davidson to Whitton, 12 July 1944; and ibid., 'Correspondence April 1945,' F.G. Ivory to Whitton, 7 April 1945. Davidson used the bogey of allowing families the choice of spending their allowances as they wished on either Borden milk or Molson beer to make his argument.

213 NAC, Whitton Papers, 5: 'Correspondence June 1945,' Senator A.C. Hardy to Whitton, 15 June 1945, Silcox to Whitton, 8 Aug. 1945.

214 UTA, 54:6, Grauer, 'Review of Harry Cassidy, *Social Security and Reconstruction, Canadian Welfare Council Bulletin*, n.d.; and ibid., 59:5, Davidson to Cassidy, 7 Oct. 1943.

215 UTA, Cassidy Papers, 57:4, L. Richter to Cassidy, 9 Dec. 1943, who claimed she opposed the idea of a national minimum on the basis that Whitton saw community life as extending beyond material needs.

216 NAC, Whitton Papers, 4: 'Correspondence Jan.–June 1944,' L.O. Shudde to W.R. Williamson, 29 Aug. 1944.

217 NAC, Whitton Papers, 5: 'Correspondence Oct. 1945,' W.R. Williamson to Whitton, 23 Oct. 1945.

218 NAC, Whitton Papers, 4: 'Correspondence Sept.–Dec. 1943,' Whitton to Cassidy, 9 Dec. 1943; and ibid., 'Correspondence Jan.–June 1944,' Whitton to Davidson, 26 Jan. 1944, in which she championed Swedish models of welfare in which women had entitlements independent of their spouses, and highly commended Mrs Myrdal's 'The Nation and the Family.' In Sweden, family allowances were used for distinctly feminist ends.

219 Charlotte Whitton, *Security for Canadians* (Behind the Headlines, 3:6, 1943), 8.

220 UTA, Cassidy Papers, 59:3, Whitton to Cassidy, 9 Dec. 1943; ibid., 18:3, Cassidy to Whitton, 15 Feb. 1944; and Harry Cassidy, 'Another Plan for Social Security,' *C.C.F. News Comment*, Nov. 1943, 2.

221 UTA, Cassidy Papers, 31:5, Whitton, 'Human Relief Vultures,' *The Financial Post*, 5 Sept. 1936, in which she charged that relief functioned as a wage subsidy.

222 Grant Dexter, memorandum, 22 Sept. 1944, quoted in Frederick Gibson and Barbara Robertson, eds., *Ottawa at War: The Grant Dexter Memoranda, 1939–1945* (Winnipeg: Manitoba Record Society, 1994), 446, 482; NAC, Brooke Claxton Papers, MG 32 B5, Vol. 167, 'Bracken Critical of Family Bonus,' newsclipping, n.d.

223 Dorothy King, 'Unemployment and Direct Relief,' in Richter, *Canada's Unemployment Problems*, 109.

224 UTA, Cassidy Papers, 14:2, Jaffray to Cassidy, 25 Nov. 1942.

225 UTA, Cassidy Papers, 31:3, Whitton to Cassidy, 20 Jan. 1941; Grant Dexter memorandum, 21 March 1943, quoted in *Ottawa at War*, 405; and MUA, Principal James Papers, 189:6523, James to King, 24 Sept. 1943, who advised King to undertake further study on economic and social reconstruction, in part to prolong his own influence in Ottawa when he was being elbowed aside by the Economic Advisory Committee.

226 Bruce Hutchinson, *The Incredible Canadian* (Toronto: Longman's Canada, 1952), 327–8.

227 MUA, Principal James Papers, 189:6606, James to Lord Barnby, 31 Dec. 1942.

228 Ibid., 192:6624, 'Minutes of Meetings of Committee on Reconstruction,' 8–10 Jan. 1943.

229 Dexter memorandum, 21 March 1943, quoted in *Ottawa at War*, 405.

230 UTA, Cassidy Papers, 2 Feb. 1943 in which he hoped the economists would not take Marsh's glib and superficial conclusions at 'face value.' On the trend toward conservatism, see 'Canada: The New Conservatism,' *Round Table*, 1943, 171. Symbolically, Mackintosh seconded Marsh to the Economic Advisory Council in March 1943. See MUA, Principal James Papers, 189:6493, Mackintosh to James, 30 March 1943; and ibid., 189:6543, James to H.G.T. Percy, Chairman, Bureau of Post-War Rehabilitation and Reconstruction, B.C., 10 June 1944.

231 UTA, Cassidy Papers, 59:4, Davidson to Cassidy, 12 March 1943.

232 MUA, Principal James Papers, 192:6603, Marsh to James, 8 Nov. 1943; and NAC, King Papers, 310, Mackenzie to King, 23 July 1945, Mackenzie to King, 8 Oct. 1943.

233 NAC, King Papers, Mackenzie to King, 8 Oct. 1943.

234 UTA, Cassidy Papers, Davidson to Cassidy, 12 March 1943.

235 UTA, Cassidy Papers, 59:5, Whitton to Cassidy, 5 May 1943, Davidson to Cassidy, 19 Aug. 1943.

236 UTA, Cassidy Papers, 18:1, Cassidy to King Gordon, 29 June 1943, Cassidy to Marsh, 20 Aug. 1943. On Beveridge's visit, see Harris, *William Beveridge*, 428, who spoke before the House of Commons on the issue of social security. See also MUA, Principal James Papers, 192: 6577, James to Dr Weir; ibid., 192:6603, Marsh to James, 18 May 1943, concerning Beveridge's meeting with Brooke Claxton; and NAC, King Papers, 349, N.A. Robertson to King, 13 May 1943, on Beveridge meeting with the Economic Advisory Council. Beveridge was especially concerned to have parity of social security measures in Britain, Australia, and Canada to promote postwar unity throughout the Commonwealth and to ease immigration. See 'Social Security Plan for Britain,' *Montreal Gazette*, 26 Sept. 1944.

237 UTA, Cassidy Papers, 55:1, Cassidy to Marsh, 20 Sept. 1943; and ibid., 18:1, Cassidy to Davidson, 20 Sept. 1943.

238 NAC, King Papers, 338, Janet Carmichael to King, 4 Nov. 1943, 7 Sept. 1943; and ibid., 340, H. Farley Faulkner to King, 8 March 1943, on the soldier's demands for welfare legislation.

239 MUA, Principal James Papers, 189:6545, James to Beveridge, 3 Jan. 1944; ibid., 189:6606, James to Lady Beveridge, 18 Feb. 1944; ibid., 189:6613, James to Lord McGowan, 30 Dec. 1943; and ibid., 192:6603, James to Marsh, 21 Dec. 1943.

240 MUA, Principal James Papers, 192:6603, Marsh to James, Dec. 1943, James

to Marsh, 15 Nov. 1943; and NAC, King Papers, 342, Howe to King, 17 Nov. 1943. Howe did support 'full employment for men in their active years.'

241 NAC, Ian Mackenzie Papers, 79:567–27, Ilsley to Mackenzie, 1 Nov. 1941.

242 UTA, Cassidy Papers, 32:1, Cassidy to Davidson, 18 April 1943; NAC, Mackenzie Papers, 79:562–27 (2), Mackenzie to R. Wodehouse, 10 March 1942; and UTA, Cassidy Papers, 15:3, Richter to Cassidy, 2 June 1943. Business also endorsed health insurance. See J.A. Hannah, 'The Problems Facing Industry and the Medical Profession in Relation to Health Insurance,' *Industrial Canada* 43, no. 11 (March 1943): 68.

243 UTA, Cassidy Papers, 14:3, Mackenzie to Cassidy, 14 May 1943; ibid., 54:5, Mackenzie to Cassidy, 12 Feb. 1944, the health insurance plan was sent to the financial experts; ibid., 59:5, Davidson to Cassidy, 7 Oct. 1943; NAC, Mackenzie Papers, 41:G-25E, Mackenzie, 'Statement on Revised Health Bill 1944 Session,' 23 July 1944; and AO RG29-01-1666, memorandum 13 April 1944. Marsh had been fully confident that health insurance was to be legislated in the spring of 1944. See UTA, Cassidy Papers, 59:3, Marsh to Cassidy, 4 March 1944.

244 UTA, Cassidy Papers, 59:3, Marsh to Cassidy, 3 April 1944.

245 NAC, DAB, 2: 'Conference of Chairmen,' 'First Conference of Chairmen,' 29 June 1943, in which Judge Eugene DesRivières noted that government policymakers were closely watching their work. See also MUA, Principal James Papers, 192:6624, 'Minutes,' 27 Feb. 1943. That in some respects at least, military allowances foreshadowed the Family Allowances Act of 1944, is demonstrated by the fact that R.B. Curry, a leader within the Canadian Legion and an administrator with the DAB, became the head of the Family Allowances Division within the Department of Health and Welfare.

246 NAC, MG30 A94, J.L. Cohen Papers, 34: National War Labour Board Correspondence 1943, 'Problems of the Wartime Wages Control Policy,' 24 April 1943.

247 University of Toronto Library, Thomas Fisher Rare Book Room, Gilbert Jackson Papers, ms. 178, 6:1, C.P. McTague Report, 19 Aug. 1943, 17, 23, 18. The minority report was written by J.L. Cohen, who adamantly opposed family allowances. See also ibid., 6:2, Donald Gordon to Ilsley, 21 Jan. 1943. J.L. Granastein states that family allowances were first officially mooted in Feb. 1943 as a result of the McTague Report; however, it was not released until Aug. 1943. See J.L. Granatstein, *The Politics of Survival: The Conservative Party in Canada 1939–45* (Toronto: University of Toronto Press, 1967). In 'Family Allowances, Old Age Security and the Construction of

Entitlement in the Canadian Welfare State, 1943–1951,' in Peter Neary and
J.L. Granatstein, eds., *The Veterans Charter and Post–World War II Canada*
(Montreal and Kingston: McGill-Queen's University Press, 1998), James
Struthers has argued that family allowances erected new social rights of
citizenship, 179. I have argued that they were a continuation of male rights
accorded during the 1930s.

248 NAC, King Papers, 347, Humphrey Mitchell to King, 25 Oct. 1943; and
ibid., 338, W.C. Clark to Mr Turnbull, secretary to King, 11 Nov. 1943; ibid.,
345, Mackenzie to King, 17 Oct. 1943.

249 UTA, Cassidy Papers, 59:5, Davidson to Cassidy, 7 Oct. 1943; and ibid.,
55:1, Cassidy to Mr F.E. Andrews, Russell Sage Foundation, 20 Sept. 1943,
in which he states that family allowances would be used to stave off a general wage increase. See also ibid., 59:3, 'Payment by Government of Family
Allowances Possible,' news clipping, 19 Sept. 1943; Dexter memorandum
17 Sept. 1943, 6 Oct. 1943, in *Ottawa at War*, 432, 444; and NAC, Brooke
Claxton Papers, Vol. 138, 'Committee on Unemployment file,' 'Dominion-
Provincial Conference: Report of the Committee on Unemployment Assistance,' 29, in which the government asserted its intention to keep wage
controls after the war.

250 For this line of argument, see Allan Moscovitch and Jim Alberts, eds.,
The Benevolent State: The Growth of Welfare in Canada (Toronto: Garamond
Press, 1987), 'Introduction,' 27; and Struthers, *The Limits of Affluence*,
conclusion.

251 NAC, Cohen Papers, 34: National War Labour Board Correspondence
1943, W.M. Martin, Court of Appeal, Saskatchewan, to Cohen, 26 June
1943; and ibid., Cohen to McTague, 19 Aug. 1943. Labour also protested
the reluctance of the federal government to declare on the issue of labour
legislation. Ibid., Tom Parkin to Cohen, 20 Aug. 1943; and ibid., Percy
Bengough, J.B. Ward, and A.R. McMaster, memoranda to King, 7 Sept.
1943, 9 Sept. 1943.

252 McDowall, 'The Formation of the Canadian Industrial Relations System
during World War II,' in Granatstein and Neary, eds., *The Good Fight*, 301.
See also Bora Laskin, 'Collective Bargaining in Canada,' *Food for Thought*
11, no. 3 (Nov. 1941); Andrew Brewin, *Labour and the War* (Behind the
Headlines, Jan. 1941); and David Malcolm Young, *The Unarmed Forces*
(Behind the Headlines, 3:7, 1943).

253 NAC, King Papers, 345, N.A. McLarty to King, 19 Nov. 1943; and MUA,
Cyril James Personal Papers, 7, 'Bonus in Force at New Levels on November 15,' *Montreal Gazette*, undated clipping. McLarty had argued that the
act of freezing wages in wartime effectively suspended collective bargain-

ing. See also MUA, Principal James Papers, 188:6524, Percy Bengough, TLC, to James, 29 July 1943.

254 'The Unions and Children's Allowances,' *Toronto Daily Star*, 5 Oct. 1943. The Ontario government sided with labour because it opposed family allowances on constitutional grounds. See. AO, RG29-01-1665, 'Family Allowances.'

255 This was the policy championed by the CCL's lawyer, J.L. Cohen. See NAC, Canadian Congress of Labour Papers, MG28 I103, 210:19, J.L. Cohen, Canadian Labour Research Bureau, to W.T. Burford, secretary, All Congress of Labour, 21 June 1928.

256 NAC, CCSD, 89:490, 'Family Allowances'; 'Family and Wages,' *The Ottawa Citizen*, 26 July 1944; NAC, Whitton Papers, 4: 'Correspondence Feb. 1945,' Premier Drew to Whitton, 12 Feb. 1945, approved of the Russian system of paying allowances after the third child. The CCL and Charlotte Whitton also formed a loose alliance over the question of family allowances. See ibid., 4: 'Correspondence 1944,' Whitton to Forsey, 22 Feb. 1944, Forsey to Whitton, 16 Nov. 1943. Forsey praised Whitton's *The Dawn of an Ampler Life* perhaps to make her an ally of labour: 'It is really a masterpiece. Every page merits the most serious study.'

257 AO RG29-01-1670, 'National Health and Welfare file,' 'Cash Family Allowances'; J.W.A. Nicholson, 'Maritime Labour Irritation,' *Canadian Forum* 21, no. 247 (Aug. 1941): 145; and NAC, Claxton Papers, 167, 'Family Allowances,' *Canadian Unionist*, n.d.

258 'Family Allowances,' *Labour Gazette*, Oct. 1943; and Edward E. Schwartz, 'Some Observations of the Canadian Family Allowance Programs,' *Social Service Review* SS, no. 4 (Dec. 1946): 20.

259 NAC, CCL Papers, 334: file 'Canadian Congress of Labour,' *Political Action* (pamphlet, 1943), 4. The policies of the CCL were endorsed by the United Church of Canada. See ibid., Vol. 310, 'Report of the Secretaries of the Board of Evangelicalism and Social Service of the United Church of Canada,' 1947, 6; J.R. Mutchmor, 'What is the Church Doing for the Working Man,' *United Church Observer* 3, no. 18 (Nov. 1941): 25, in which he argues for a higher family wage; L.S. Paisley, Simcoe United Church 'Resolution,' 12 Feb. 1942, calling for federal recognition of collective bargaining; and Norman S. Dowd, executive secretary of CCL, 'Labour's Rights and Duties,' sermon, Parkdale United Church, 6 Sept. 1942. It is interesting to note that the radical CCL's Hamilton convention in 1943 opened with prayers by the evangelist E. Crossley Hunter. See ibid., 240:10, J.R. Mutchmore to Dowd, 12 July 1943. The United Church and the CCL also shared a common interest in removing women from the workplace. See ibid.,

240:3, 'Minutes of Thirty-third Meeting,' 17 May 1946. See also NAC, King Papers, 356, John Coburn, United Church, to King, 24 July 1944, Alfred Charpentier to Humphrey Mitchell, 31 July 1944. The United Church wanted allowances paid after the second child, and the Catholic Confederation of Labour after the fourth child.

260 NAC, King Papers, 352, Moose Jaw TLC, to King, 28 Sept. 1943; ibid., 357, International Brotherhood of Boiler Makers, Montreal Lodge 134, to King, 8 July 1944; ibid., 360, Oshawa TLC to King, 9 Aug. 1944; and ibid., 368, Vancouver Aeronautical Mechanics to King, 3 Aug. 1944.

261 NAC, DAB, 29: 'Complaints,' H.R.L. Henry, private secretary to King, to T. Parkin, International Association of Machinists, 19 Oct. 1944; 'Halifax TLC Resolution,' 31 May 1943; and Touzel to King, 22 Dec. 1942. The Catholic Syndicates in 1933 sponsored family allowances in Quebec. Davidson, 'Should Canada Bonus Babies,' *Financial Post*, 2 Oct. 1943.

262 NAC, CCSD, 58:490, 'Resolution Adopted at Convention of TLC of Canada,' 23–30 Oct. 1944; and ibid., Eugene Forsey, Director of Research, Canadian Congress of Labour to Mrs Close, Survey Graphic, 29 June 1949. Forsey maintained that the CCL passed no resolution on family allowances at its 1944 convention. For a different view, see ibid., 'Fifth Convention,' Canadian Congress of Labour, 16–20 Oct. 1944, where they approved of family allowances. Organized labour roundly supported health insurance and Marsh's template of comprehensive social security. See ibid., B.W. Heise, deputy minister, Department of Public Welfare, Ontario to Davidson, 21 Sept. 1944.

263 NAC, Whitton Papers, 4: 'Correspondence April 1945,' H.J., 'Service or Bonus,' in *The Western Producer*, April 1945, 12.

264 *Family Allowances: A Children's Charter* (pamphlet, 1945), 1; NAC, Claxton Papers, 139, 'Committee on Social Security,' 'Social Security,' 48; and ibid., 167, House of Commmons, 'Debates,' 26 July 1944, draft of speech by Claxton, 3. Anti-Keynesians did not believe that family allowances would stimulate postwar spending. See, for example, Claris Edwin Silcox, 'Are Family Allowances Unconstitutional?' *Saturday Night*, 7 Oct. 1944; 'From Peter to Paul,' *The Ottawa Journal*, 22 March 1945; and UTA, Innis Family Papers, B72–0003, 5:18, Innis to Angus L. Macdonald, Premier of Nova Scotia, 17 Jan. 1946.

265 NAC, Claxton Papers, 167, 'Family Allowances,' radio broadcast, n.d., 5.

266 NAC, Whitton Papers, 5: 'Correspondence Nov. 1945,' N.R Smith, President Confederation Life Assurance Co., to Whitton, 5 Nov. 1945; and NAC, Claxton Papers, 167, 'Family Allowance Letters,' 15 Nov. 1945.

267 NAC, CCSD, 59:490, Davidson to Mrs R.F. McWilliams, 19 April 1943.

268 NAC, CCSD, 59:490, Davidson to Guy S. Cunliffe, associate editor, *Montreal Gazette*, 6 July 1944; Gray Turgeon, 'A Realist Looks at Post-War,' *Canadian Business*, Dec. 1943; R.J. Deachman, 'Family Allowances – Both Sides of the Problem,' *The Financial Times*, 25 Aug. 1944; and D.C. MacGregor, 'The Project of Full Employment and its Implications,' in Brady and Scott, *Canada After the War*, 173–4, 195.

269 NAC, King Papers, 338, W.C. Clark, Finance Department, to Jack Pickersgill, 5 Dec. 1943; ibid., 362, Ilsley to King, 4 Jan. 1944, 8 Jan. 1944; ibid., 380, Claxton to King, 3 Jan. 1945; and 'The Plain Man's Guide to Full Employment,' *Food for Thought* (May 1945): 30. The conflation between war aims and the ideal of postwar spending and abundance was underscored in popular journals. See, for example, the advertisement for Westinghouse appliances titled 'Blueprint for the Future,' picturing FDR and Roosevelt meeting in Casablanca, *Saturday Night*, 2 Oct. 1943, 32.

270 'Premier King Rejoices as MP's Unanimously Back Social Measure,' *Toronto Star*, 29 July 1944. For the view that social security would shore up individualism by encouraging spending, see B.K. Sandwell, 'The Babies of 1943,' *Canadian Home Journal*, March 1943, 31.

271 Quoted in AO RG29-01-1665, 'Family Allowances,' B.W. Heise 'Memorandum,' 5 Oct. 1944.

272 NAC, King Papers, 370, Ryerson to King, 8 June 1944.

273 MUA, Principal James Papers, 188:6524, 'Memorandum,' n.d.; and ibid., Bengough to James, 29 July 1943.

274 NAC, CCL Papers, 356, 'Reconstruction,' 'Memorandum submitted by the CCL to House of Commmons Committee,' 15 July 1943, 11; and ibid., TLC, *Victory: What Then* (pamphlet, 1943), 11.

275 UBC, Special Collections, Marsh Papers, J.L. Cohen to Marsh, 17 March 1943.

276 AO RG29-01-1666, Gordon K. Fraser, M.P., 'Why Do We Need Family Allowances,' n.d., 2; Edward E. Schwarz, 'Some Observations of the Canadian Family Allowance Program,' *The Social Service Review* 20, no. 4 (Dec. 1946): 18–19. Schwarz saw that family allowances would provide farm wives with their own money.

277 'Garson Fears Baby Bonus Effect on Other Benefits to Canadians,' *Montreal Gazette*, 28 Aug. 1944; UTA, Cassidy Papers 33:1, 'Allowance Act Infringes Rights of Provinces,' news clipping, n.d.; and George Davidson, 'Should Canada Bonus Babies,' *Financial Post*, 2 Oct. 1943.

278 NAC, Whitton Papers, 4: 'Correspondence April 1945,' Violet McNaughton to Whitton, 28 April 1945.

279 Davidson, 'Should Canada Bonus Babies'; 'Family Allowances Not Low Wage Substitute,' *New Commonwealth*, 28 Oct. 1943; and McDowell, 'The Formation of the Canadian Industrial Relations System,' 309.

280 Dexter memorandum, 1 March 1943, *Ottawa at War*, 399.

281 UTA, Cassidy Papers, 54:5, Edward Jolliffe, Ontario CCF leader to Cassidy, 2 Dec. 1943; ibid., 59:5, Davidson to Cassidy, 7 Oct. 1943; and George Davidson, untitled article, *News Comment* 3, no. 7 (1 April 1943): 2.

282 UTA, Cassidy Papers, 54:5, Carlton McNaught to Cassidy, 21 April. The CCF had also imbibed the ideas of Alvin Hansen, who was also an expert advisor for Bracken's Progressive Conservatives.

283 UTA, Cassidy Papers, 18:1, Cassidy to L.R. Shaw, 12 March 1943.

284 UTA, Cassidy Papers, 33:1, 'Statement Released by M.J. Coldwell, M.P. on Marsh's Social Security Report,' 18 March 1943; Eugene Forsey, 'Planning from the Bottom – Can It Be Done?' *Canadian Forum* 25, no. 290 (March 1945); ibid., Part II, 25, no. 291 (April 1945); UBC, Special Collections, Marsh Papers, 'The Beveridge Report,' *Canadian Forum* (Jan. 1943); and George A. Graham, 'The Beveridge Plan,' *Canadian Forum* 23, no. 244 (March 1943): 347.

285 NAC, Whitton Papers, 4: 'Correspondence March 1945,' Whitton to Manning, n.d.; and Manning to Whitton, 10 March 1945.

286 UTA, Cassidy Papers, 55:1, Cassidy to Whitton, 28 Dec. 1943; and ibid., 13:5, Davidson to Cassidy, 30 June 1944.

287 Eleanor Dane, 'Looking on Wartime Life,' *Canadian Home Journal*, June 1943, 76.

288 UTA, Cassidy Papers, 57:3, Bessie Oliver, President, Local Council of Women, 'Submission to Saskatchewan Reconstruction Council,' 13 March 1944; ibid., 55:1, Cassidy to Mrs J.C. Oliver; MUA, Principal James Papers, 189:6543, Vancouver Women's School of Citizenship, 'Brief Submitted to the Post-War Rehabilitation Council of British Columbia,' June 1943; NAC, Whitton Papers, 5: 'Correspondence June 1945,' Mrs Anne Perry to Whitton, 18 June 1945; and 'War Babies Dismay Women's Societies,' *Vancouver Sun*, 20 Aug. 1943. It is interesting to note that James originally recommended that family allowances be a provincial program. See MUA, Cyril James Personal Papers, 6: 'Social Insurance,' 'The Beveridge Report,' Jan. 1943, 6.

289 NAC, King Papers, 362, Mary Kendell to King, 1 Aug. 1944.

290 NAC, Montreal Council of Women Papers, 10, 'Local Council Protests Manner of "Baby-Bonus" Payments Here,' *Montreal Gazette*, 19 June 1945; and Hilda M. Ridley, *The Post-War Woman* (Toronto: Ryerson Press, 1941).

291 Ridley, *The Post-War Woman*, 32.

292 NAC, King Papers, 379, Therese F. Casgrain to King, 8 June 1945; ibid., 361, Hilda Hesson, President, Canadian Federation of Business and Professional Women's Clubs, to King, 23 Dec. 1944; ibid., 381, Mrs G.D. Finlayson, National Council of Women, to King, 3 Aug. 1945; ibid., 369, Mrs Irving E. Robertson, President, Canadian Mothercraft Society, to King 2 Aug. 1944; ibid., 356, Mrs Cora Casselman to King, 30 June 1944; and 'Un Appel Aux Femmes du Québec,' *L'Action Catholique*, 2 June 1945.

293 NAC, Mackenzie Papers, 40:G-25, Mrs Cora T. Casselman, 'Untitled Address,' 19 July 1944.

294 NAC, King Papers, 381, King to Premier Duplessis, 3 Feb. 1945; and ibid., 380, W.J. Turnbull, Office of the Prime Minister, to Claxton, 7 Feb. 1945.

295 NAC, CCL Papers, 'The Report of the Advisory Committee on Reconstruction, Sub-Committee on Post-War Problems of Women,' 30 Nov. 1943, 2–3. It is not surprising that organized labour supported this report, as it hastened the movement of married women to the home.

296 MUA, Principal James Papers, 188:6522, 'First Report of the Sub-Committee on Post-War Problems of Women: Social Security Proposals,' 225; ibid., 192:6628, 'Post-War Problems of Women: Final Report,' 7–11, 13; ibid., 192:6628, 'First Meeting on the Post-War Problems of Women,' 2 March 1943, 2–5; ibid., 189:6543, 'Report of Vancouver Women's School for Citizenship,' B.C., June 1943, 2; NAC, Montreal Council of Women Papers, Vol. 7, 'Post-War Opportunities for Women,' Conference YWCA, 27 June 1944, which supported full employment for men, 8; NAC, King Papers, Vol. 385, Gladys W. Kuhring, 'Women in Our Changing Economy,' 27 June 1944; and Hiram McCann, 'Let's Plan Our Private Post-War Worlds,' *Canadian Home Journal*, Aug. 1943, 19–24.

297 NAC, CCSD, 49:448a, 'Day Nurseries Questionnaire 1942–47,' Miriam Chapin to Mrs Parker, 17 March 1942.

298 Harriet Roberts Forsey, 'Will Women Win the Peace?' *Canadian Forum* 24, no. 238 (Aug. 1944): 106–7.

299 Gail Cuthbert Brandt, '"Pigeon-Holed and Forgotten": The Work of the Sub-Committee on the Post-War Problems of Women, 1943,' *Histoire Sociale/Social History* 15 (1982): 239–59. On McWilliams, see Mary Kinnear, *Margaret McWilliams: An Interwar Feminist* (Montreal and Kingston: McGill-Queen's University Press, 1991). McWilliams also advocated very niggardly family allowances and wanted them paid within a health insurance scheme so that women could be better investigated. See NAC, CCSD, 59:490, McWilliams to Davidson, 30 March 1943; and McWilliams, 'More

about the "Hard Core,"' *Canadian Welfare* 16, no. 4 (Aug.–Sept. 1940): 24, on seasonal male unemployment.

300 'Social Security Plans in Great Britain,' *International Labor Review* 47, no. 1 (Jan. 1943): 9.

301 Miss Joan Keagey, Parkdale District Neighbourhood Workers' Association, 'Low Wages and Family Relief,' *Child and Family Welfare* 13, no. 2 (July 1937); and Elizabeth Grubb, Friendly Help Welfare Association of Victoria, 'Looking Backward in a Family Service Agency,' *Child Welfare News* 13, no. 4 (Nov. 1937).

302 National Employment Commission, *Final Report*, 77.

303 NAC, Mackenzie Papers, 41:G-25A, Mackenzie, 'Family or Children's Allowances,' n.d., in which he quotes Leonard Marsh on this issue; and ibid., Vol. 40:G-25, Mackenzie, untitled Vancouver Radio Broadcast, 7 Aug. 1944.

304 NAC, Whitton Papers, 4: 'Correspondence Jan.–June 1944,' W.R. Williamson, actuary, Federal Security Agency, Washington, memorandum, 12 Oct. 1944.

305 UTA, Cassidy Papers, 59:3, Davidson to Cassidy, 16 Aug. 1944; Davidson, 'Should Canada Bonus Babies?' 2; and Stepler, *Family Allowances in Canada*, 18. Marsh was a great advocate of family allowances as a prop for lesser eligibility and for this reason wanted them confined to those workers in contributory schemes. See House of Commons, Special Committee on Social Security, 'Minutes and Proceedings,' testimony of Marsh, 9 June 1943, 92. King retorted that they should be universal in order to increase mass spending.

306 Gilbert Jackson, 'Can We All Get Jobs?' *Maclean's Magazine*, 1 Aug. 1945, 5; MUA, Principal James Papers, 189:6606, James to Vernon, Lord Barnby, 8 July 1943; and ibid., 189:6640, Gilbert Jackson, 'The Population of Canada,' n.d., 4.

307 'Women in Industry,' *Canadian Business*, June 1943, 32–3.

308 Ruth Roach Pierson, *'They're Still Women after All': The Second World War and Canadian Womanhood* (Toronto: McClelland & Stewart, 1986), 22–61. Pierson relies almost exclusively on aggregate statistics. See also Peter Neary and Shaun Brown, 'The Veterans' Charter and Canadian Women Veterans of World War II,' in Granatstein and Neary, *The Good Fight*, 399–404. In relying also on aggregate employment statistics, Doug Owram has overestimated the participation of married women in the workplace during wartime and thus has incorrectly interpreted the movement for domesticity and has ignored the place

of the breadwinner ideal in these debates. See 'Canadian Domesticity in the Postwar Era,' in Neary and Granatstein, *The Veteran's Charter*, 205–23.

309 MUA, Principal James Papers, 192:6628, 'Women in War Work, 1939–1942,' 19.

310 NAC, Whitton Papers, 'Correspondence April 1945,' Alan Randal, untitled article on war industries, 2 April 1945, 1–2.

311 NAC, Whitton Papers, 5: 'Correspondence April 1946,' Whitton to Elizabeth Hammont, *Family Herald* and *Weekly Star*, 10 July 1946. Whitton's feminist ire was raised over this punitive tax system largely because it personally affected her. In her two-woman household, both women were taxed not as a couple but as two single workers. One could argue here that Whitton was an early advocate of same-sex benefits. To discourage married women's work, the tax system was changed after the war. See UTA, Cassidy Papers, 72:3, Dr Albert Rose to Bessie Touzel, 'The Taxation Status of Married Women in Employment, 1946–47.'

312 PAM, Social Planning Council of Winnipeg, P-659:6, surveys of working mothers with children in public school. In all the public schools, 100 mothers worked full-time and 55 part-time. Very few mothers used day nurseries; the majority followed the traditional pattern of leaving children with either older siblings, or neighbours, or relatives.

313 PAM, RG20 B7, Advisory Committee on Co-ordination of Post-War Planning, file 724, 'Sex Distribution of the Persons in Recorded Employment at April 1 1945,' 3.

314 Bernice Coffey, 'Canadian Women at War,' *Maclean's Magazine*, 17 Oct. 1942, 29.

315 University of Toronto Thomas Fisher Rare Book Library, Jackson Papers, 8:8, 'Minutes of National Selective Service Advisory Board,' 26 Jan. 1944, 3 May 1944.

316 NAC, Whitton Papers, 4: 'Correspondence April 1945,' Alan Randal, untitled article on war industries, 2 April 1945, 2. See also NAC, RG38, Department of Veterans' Affairs, 197, 'Department of Veterans' Affairs Training Conferences on Women's Rehabilitation, Feb.–March 1946,' 49–50.

317 University of Toronto Thomas Fisher Rare Book Library, Jackson Papers, 8:9, 'Minutes of National Selective Service Advisory Board,' 11 July 1945.

318 Rica McLean Farquharson, 'Will Women Go Back to the Kitchen,' *Canadian Home Journal*, Jan. 1944; Farquharson, 'As She Goes Back to Civilian Life,' ibid., July 1945, 14–15; and Kathleen McDowell, 'The Post-War Woman,' ibid., July 1945, 16, 30, which stressed the consumer role of women.

319 Dorothy Norwich, 'Women in a Man's World,' *Saturday Night*, 5 Dec. 1942, 28.

320 Janet Tupper, 'Little Woman – What Now?' *Maclean's Magazine*, 1 Nov. 1944, 20, 32.

321 NAC, CCL Papers, 342, 'Equal Pay file,' 'Equal Pay for Equal Work: Are Women Getting a Fair Deal?' n.d.; ibid., 'Report on Equal Pay in Industry in Canada,' *Labour Research Bulletin*, 20 Nov. 1948; and ibid., 362, Anne Francis, 'Why Women Work,' 29 Dec. 1949.

322 MUA, Cyril James Person Papers, 7, Woods, 'Factors of Paramount Importance During the Immediate Post-War Period,' memorandum, n.d., 10.

323 NAC, Montreal Council of Women Papers, 10, Mme H. Vautelet, *Post-War Problems and Employment of Women in the Province of Quebec* (pamphlet, n.d.), 6–8; and ibid., 'Problems of Unemployment Discussed,' news clipping, n.d. For the definition of the postwar democratic family and the problem of family stability, see C.W. Topping, 'The Equalitarian Family as a Fundamental Invention,' *Canadian Journal of Economics and Political Science* 8 (1942); and NAC, CCSD, 62, 'Marriage Counselling 1944–45,' 'The Social Worker Tackles the Problems of Marital Conflict,' n.d.

324 Pauline Shapiro, 'Women in the Post-War World,' *Food for Thought* 3, no. 2 (Nov. 1942): 15; Violet Anderson, 'Part-Time Work for Married Women,' *Canadian Forum* 23, no. 270 (July 1943): 90; and 'Local Council Sponsors Booklet on Post-War Problems of Women,' *Montreal Gazette*, 5 Sept. 1945. This paradigm lasted well into the 1950s. See, for example, NAC, CCSD, 77:564, K. Phyllis Burns to Miss Barbara Fraser, 23 Dec. 1947. For a new emerging consensus around women's rights in the workplace, see Sangster, *Earning Respect*.

325 Carolyn Cox, 'Uneasy Women,' *Canadian Home Journal*, Oct. 1944, 56; NAC, Whitton Papers, 5: 'Correspondence Dec. 1945,' 'War Has Created Better Mothers Says Eaton,' undated news clipping; and MUA, Principal James Papers, 189:6543, Vancouver Women's School for Citizenship, 'Brief Submitted to the Post-War Rehabilitation Council of British Columbia,' June 1943.

326 Whitton, article, in Brady and Scott, *Canada After the War*, 96.

327 NAC, Mackenzie Papers, 45:R-6, Mackenzie, 'Opening Speech at Conference on Reconstruction,' March 1943.

328 UTA, Cassidy Papers, 3:4, Lynn to Bea, n.d. 1944.

329 NAC, Claxton Papers, Vol. 139, 'Social Security,' n.d.

330 Dexter memorandum, 6 Nov. 1944, in *Ottawa at War*, 486.

331 NAC, Department of Labour, 3538, 'Day Nurseries,' Mrs Annie Cresswell to Hon. Humphrey Mitchell, Minister of Labour, 22 May 1946.

Conclusion: 'The Endangered Family'

1 NAC, CCSD, 26:133, 'A Memorandum Explaining the Place and Functions of a Family Welfare Bureau,' n.d.
2 NAC, CCL, Vol. 240:11, 'Report of the Secretaries of the Board of Evangelism and Social Service, United Church of Canada,' 26 Feb.–1 March 1957, 6.

Primary Sources

ARCHIVES AND SPECIAL COLLECTIONS

Archives of Ontario
Department of Labour
Department of Public Welfare
Premier E.C. Drury
Premier Howard Ferguson
Premier W.H. Hearst
Provincial Secretary

Archives Nationales de Québec (Montréal)
Fonds Federation de St. Jean Baptiste

McCord Museum (Montreal)
Canadian Patriotic Fund, Montreal Branch

McGill University Archives
Principal F. Cyril James
F. Cyril James
Montreal Council of Social Agencies
Womens' War Registry

McGill University Library, Department of Rare Books and Special Collections
Herbert Ames Papers

Metropolitan Toronto Reference Library, Baldwin Room
Margaret Gould

National Archives of Canada
R.B. Bennett
Robert L. Borden
John Bracken
Canadian Council of Social Development
Canadian Congress of Labour (CCL)
Canadian Patriotic Association
Canadian Youth Commission
Brooke Claxton
J.L. Cohen
Major Coldwell
Cooperative Commonwealth Federation (CCF)
Arthur Currie
Department of Labour
Department of Militia
Department of Veterans' Affairs
The Dependents' Allowance Board
George Drew
Joseph W. Flavelle
Eugene Forsey
J.J. Kelso
William Lyon Mackenzie King
Ian Mackenzie
Montreal Council of Women
W.L. Scott
Society for the Protection of Women and Children
Charlotte Whitton
John Willison

Provincial Archives of Manitoba
Health and Welfare, Child Welfare
Health and Welfare, Supervision Board
Edith Rogers
Social Planning Council of Winnipeg

Queen's University Archives
Frontenac County Records, Canadian Patriotic Fund

Saskatchewan Archives Board
Violet McNaughton

United Church Archives
Commission on Church, Nation and World Order
Claris Edwin Silcox
Robert Wallace

University of British Columbia Library, Special Collections
Leonard Marsh

University of Toronto, Thomas Fisher Rare Books
Gilbert Jackson
Stuart Jaffray

University of Toronto Archives
Harry Cassidy
Harold Adams Innis

University of Waterloo Library, Department of Special Collections
Elizabeth Smith Shortt

PAMPHLETS

Adams, Frank Dawson. *The Day Shelter for Unemployed Men in Montreal* (n.d.)
Ames, Herbert. *Canadian Political History* (1894)
Bott, E.A. *Studies in Industrial Psychology* (1920)
Borden, Robert. *Canada at War* (1916)
Bryce, Peter H. *National Social Efficiency* (1917)
Cahill, Mary L. *Unemployment Conditions throughout Canada as Affecting the Single Woman* (1934)
Campbell, Mrs M. *Canada's Greatest Asset* (1918)
The Canadian Patriotic Fund: Its Objectives, Methods and Policy (n.d.)
Canadian Reconstruction Association. *Buy Canadian Products* (1921)
– *Industrial Relations* (1918)
– *Women and Reconstruction* (1918)
– *Work and Unemployment* (1920)
Carter, Gwendolyn M. *Consider the Record* (1942)
Child Philip and J.W. Holmes. *Dynamic Democracy* (1941)
Chipman, Mrs Warwick. *A Few Thoughts on the Subject of Loyalty* (1896)
Clark, William. *Imperialism* (1903)
Corless, C.V. *Educational Reform: Its Relations to a Solution of Industrial Deadlock* (1919)
Family Allowances: A Children's Charter (1945)

Fields, J.C. *Science and Industry* (1918)

Gould, Margaret. *Family Allowances in Canada: Facts versus Fiction* (1945)

Hume, James Gibson. *Political Economy and Ethics* (1898)

Grant, Rev. Principal George. *Advantages of Imperial Federation* (1891)

Jewett, Frank. *Industrial Research* (1919)

– *Research and the Problems of Unemployment, Business Depression and National Finance in Canada* (1922)

Kellogg, Paul. *The Patriotic Fund of Canada* (1917)

J.J. Kelso. *A Work of Faith & Labour of Love* (1903)

– *Can Slums Be Abolished or Must We Continue to Pay the Penalty* (n.d.)

– *Homes Wanted for Boys and Girls of All Ages* (n.d.)

– *Reforming the Delinquent Child* (1903)

– *Revival of the Curfew Law* (1896)

– *Small Newsboys* (1911)

– *Thoughts on Child-Saving* (1898)

Lebel, Leon. *Family Allowances* (1929)

Longley, Hon. J.W. *The Future of Canada* (1892)

Martin, Paul. *Labour's Post-War World* (1945)

Macdonald, John. *Business Success* (n.d.)

MacFarland, Ronald Oliver. *Canada and the Post-War World* (1942)

McIntosh, W.R. *Canada's Problems* (1910)

Old-Age Annuities – Speeches Delivered in the Senate of Canada during the Third Session of the Tenth Parliament (1907)

Plumptre, Adelaide M. *Canada's Child Immigrants* (1925)

Reid, Helen R.Y. *A Social Study along Health Lines of the First Thousand Children Examined in the Health Clinic of the Canadian Patriotic Fund, Montreal Branch* (1920)

Report of the Accomplishments of the Department of Labor and Health (1923)

Report of the Women's War Conference (1918)

Ridley, Hilda M. *The Post-War Woman* (1941)

Roche, W.J. *Women's Work in Canada: Duties, Wages, Conditions and Opportunities for Domestics in the Dominion* (1915)

Ryerson, Egerton. *The New Dominion: Dangers and Duties of the People* (1867)

Scott, Jean Thomson. *The Conditions of Female Labour in Ontario* (1892)

Scott, W.L. *Eastern Christian Churches* (n.d.)

The Second Year of the War, What It Means to the Canadian Patriotic Fund (1915)

Silcox, Claris Edwin. *Revenge of the Cradles* (1945)

Smith, Goldwin. *Loyalty, Aristocracy and Jingoism* (1891)

Stepler, D.H. *Family Allowances for Canada?* (1942)

Trades and Labour Congress. *Victory: What Then?* (1943)

Union Government Publicity Bureau. *Women's War Talks to Women* (1917)

Vautelet, Mme H. *Post-War Problems and Employment of Women in the Province of Quebec* (n.d.)

Whitton, Charlotte. *This Weary Pilgrimage: The Dependency Outlook, Canada 1939* (1939)

Young, David Malcolm. *The Unarmed Forces* (1943).

GOVERNMENT PUBLICATIONS

House of Commons, Canada. Special Committee on Reconstruction and Re-Establishment. *Minutes and Proceedings of Evidence* (1943)

– Special Committee on Social Security. *Minutes and Proceedings of Evidence* (1943)

Interim Report of the Unemployment Insurance Commission (1937). *Final Report of the Unemployment Insurance Commission* (1938)

Mothers' Allowances Commission Annual Reports (British Columbia, Manitoba, Nova Scotia, Ontario, Quebec)

Ontario Legislative Assembly. *Report of the Committee on Child Labor.*

Report Upon the Sweating System of Canada (1896)

MISCELLANEOUS PRINTED MATTER

Canadian Patriotic League. *Annual Reports.*

Social Service Council of Winnipeg. *Annual Reports.*

Speaker's Patriotic League. *Annual Reports of Executive Committee.*

Index

gendered view of, 84, 116–17, 120, 223; idealization of 212–14, 267; immigrant women, 145–6; married women's, 49, 72–3, 76, 80, 82, 88, 90, 145–8, 207–10, 227, 255–6, 303–8, 314; in Second World War, 304–7, 431–2 n. 308; and single women, 80–2, 215–17; and skilled, 47, 66–9, 72, 82, 90, 92, 95–7, 102–3, 127, 233, 246, 279; and unskilled, 19, 103, 106, 171, 227, 303; and widows, 132, 145–6, 164–5; and women, 15, 203–5, 207–9, 215, 220–32

work ethic, 4–5, 106, 250, 303; and children, 26; and Depression, 213–14, 233; and mothers' allowances, 132, 148–51; Mrs Shortt on, 136–7; Charlotte Whitton on, 176; and widows, 156–7

working classes: attitudes to state,

34, 40, 51; and breadwinner ideal, 53–4, 150; Canadian Patriotic Fund, 47; and economic independence of women, 121, 157; family ideals of, 50, 62, 75, 77, 82, 84, 137, 146, 148; and family interdependence of, 153–4; gender relations in, 47; generation gap within, 155–6; living standards of, 48, 51–2, 55, 57–8, 65–70, 223, 236, 257, 261, 263–4; men, 76–7; and national efficiency, 104–6; and notions of respectibility, 156; and Protestantism, 18; and relationship to Roman Catholic church, 40–1; and women, 7–8, 47–8, 62–3, 66–80, 315

Young Women's Christian Association (YWCA), 18